DUE DATE	RETURN DATE	DUE DATE	RETURN D

introduction
to communication
disorders

contributing authors

James H. Abbs
University of Wisconsin

Arnold E. Aronson
Mayo Clinic

Daniel R. Boone
University of Arizona

Stanley J. Ewanowski
University of Wisconsin

Theodore J. Glattke
University of Arizona

Thomas J. Hixon
University of Arizona

Rita C. Naremore
Indiana University

William H. Perkins
University of Southern California

Norma S. Rees
City University of New York

John H. Saxman
Syracuse University

Lawrence D. Shriberg
University of Wisconsin

Craig C. Wier
University of Arizona

Terry L. Wiley
University of Wisconsin

EDITED BY

Thomas J. Hixon
University of Arizona

Lawrence D. Shriberg
University of Wisconsin

John H. Saxman
Syracuse University

introduction to communication disorders

Prentice-Hall, Inc., Englewood Cliffs, New Jersey 07632

Library of Congress Cataloging in Publication Data
Main entry under title:

Introduction to communication disorders.

   Includes bibliographies and indexes.
    1. Communicative disorders. 2. Communicative
disorders in children. I. Hixon, Thomas J.
II. Shriberg, Lawrence D. III. Saxman, John H.
RC423.I55   616.8'55   79-4293
ISBN 0-13-480186-5

introduction to communication disorders

EDITED BY
Thomas J. Hixon
Lawrence D. Shriberg
John H. Saxman

© 1980 by Prentice-Hall, Inc., Englewood Cliffs, New Jersey 07632

Printed in the United States of America

10 9 8 7 6 5 4 3 2 1

Editorial/production supervision by Colette Conboy
Interior design by Allyson Everngam and Colette Conboy
Cover design by Allyson Everngam
Cover illustration by Martha Perske
Manufacturing buyer: Harry P. Baisley

PRENTICE-HALL INTERNATIONAL, INC., London
PRENTICE-HALL OF AUSTRALIA PTY. LIMITED, Sydney
PRENTICE-HALL OF CANADA, LTD., Toronto
PRENTICE-HALL OF INDIA PRIVATE LIMITED, New Delhi
PRENTICE-HALL OF JAPAN, INC., Tokyo
PRENTICE-HALL OF SOUTHEAST ASIA PTE. LTD., Singapore
WHITEHALL BOOKS LIMITED, Wellington, New Zealand

To Our Teachers

contents

1   learning to talk and understand   *1*

    Norma S. Rees

signpost *406*

dysarthria 407

Arnold E. Aronson

signpost *448*

disorders of speech flow 449

William H. Perkins

foreword

Certain truths about the field of speech-language pathology and audiology provide an important perspective from which to welcome the appearance of this new introductory text.

One truth is that from its beginnings, the profession of speech-language pathology and audiology has built upon basic physical and social sciences. A review of the thirteen chapters in this book reveals that their content draws heavily from widely distributed bodies of knowledge: general anatomy, anatomy of the head, neck, and torso, and neuroanatomy; physiology, including neurophysiology; general physics; acoustics; electronics; acoustic and physiological phonetics; linguistics, psycholinguistics, and sociolinguistics; neurology; child development; and general, abnormal, and educational psychology. To the degree they believe necessary, the writers provide enlightened guided tours into these related domains. The student and practitioner will find within this text, facts and theory developed within a number of disciplines that contribute to our understanding of the nature and management of people with communication disorders.

Another truth is that what we know came from somewhere. Answers come not by guess but by investigation—by the compiling of information under prescribed conditions, using nonsubjective measurement techniques of demonstrated precision, reliability, and validity; and by expressing the conclusions, whenever possible, in quantitative terms that can be readily understood and communicated. The things we know as a profession, then, have not sprung full-blown from somebody's head; they have emerged from the laboratory or the field, scratched out through systematic observations and experimental studies. This comprehensive book makes clear, through its data presentation and its numerous references, our debt to our predecessors and our contemporaries engaged in developing the knowledge whose implications we sift out and apply in our work.

Lastly, ours is an applied field, a clinical profession. What we know achieves importance not only for itself—as abstract knowledge which the mind is driven always to search for—but additionally because it provides insight into the human condition and specific conditions that impair one's humanity. This book takes us from the laboratory to the patient, who is central. After it delineates for us the nature of communication, it embodies it in people. These are people operating in real-life situations with enormously varied communication demands, endowed with individual capacities, awarenesses, and sensitivities, playing constantly changing roles, coping with malfunction and disease, needing help. And, we, like other helping professionals, are imbued with what Karl Menninger* has designated as "the therapeutic attitude." This is an attitude not of "avoidance, ridicule, scorn, or punitiveness" but of caring, love, and hope. In admirable fashion, this exciting new book shows how the scientist and the clinician together engage in the search for knowledge and in its use for human betterment.

Frederic L. Darley
Mayo Clinic

---

*Menninger, K., *The Crime of Punishment*. New York: Viking Press (1968).

preface

This book is intended as an introduction to communication disorders. The term *communication disorders* encompasses the wide variety of problems that humans may have in language, speech, and hearing. Focus of the book is on the nature of such problems, their causes, their impacts on people, methods for their evaluation, and methods for their management. Our target reader is the undergraduate college student, especially the student with little or no background in communication disorders. The book is written to serve as a textbook for introductory courses on communication disorders and as a comprehensive source book for basic information about such disorders.

One of the realities of the typical introductory course in this area is that course enrollments are usually a mixture of majors and nonmajors. For the former, the book provides the balanced overview needed for beginners embarking on careers in speech-language pathology and audiology. For the latter, care is taken to make the material relevant to allied endeavors. Thus, students from neighboring fields such as physical therapy, occupational therapy, medicine, education, developmental disabilities, special education, nursing, psychology, and linguistics have their disciplines represented in areas where they interface with communication disorders.

Organization of the book is an outgrowth of our own experience in trying to lead beginning students systematically through the broad and complex topics within communication disorders. A variety of organizations are defensible, but the one adopted here has had the greatest appeal to instructors and our students. Each chapter is suitable for a week's reading assignment. In the final assembly of chapters, we sought to achieve a total offering suitable for a single semester's (fifteen week) introductory course.

In the design of the book, we responded specifically to comments from our students over the years about available introductory text-books. We tried to make the level of the material neither too low nor too high, to emphasize what warrants extended coverage, and not to neglect topics that require at least brief coverage. In particular, we attempted to provide solid coverage of information on normal processes so that the disorders may be better understood. Technical jargon is held to a minimum and only critical literature references are included. And, wherever feasible, differences of opinion on topics are resolved by asking authors to take a stand based on what appears to be the most compelling research and clinical evidence.

The contributors to this book were chosen to meet several criteria. Each of our authors is among the foremost persons in his or her specialty. Each is actively engaged in research in the issues discussed and deals daily with people who have communication disorders. Importantly, each author has extensive teaching experience with students at the introductory level.

There are many people to be thanked here. We thank our contributors for sharing their expertise and for their patience with what must have seemed to be our endless editorial "sawing," "sanding," and "polishing" to achieve consistency across chapters. We thank the many students at the University of Arizona, the University of Wisconsin, and Syracuse University who provided telling critique of early versions of chapters. We thank our many colleagues around the country who were kind enough to set aside the time and energy to read and respond critically to near-final versions of the chapters. Finally, we thank Joy Roof for her contribution to the mechanical preparation of the manuscript.

Our hope for the book is that it will ultimately have positive impact on the lives of persons with communications disorders. As disciplines go, ours is a relatively young one. We need advocates for those with communication disorders. We need talented persons to do research, to teach, and to deliver clinical services to the communicatively handicapped wherever needed. Hopefully, readers will take from this book, a feeling for the excitement, challenge, and satisfaction that can be found in helping people with communication disorders.

Thomas J. Hixon
Tucson, Arizona

Lawrence D. Shriberg
Madison, Wisconsin

John H. Saxman
Syracuse, New York

editors' notes for instructors

We are mindful of several problems instructors face when using a new textbook. Seldom does any textbook include coverage of just those materials that an instructor wishes to discuss in class. In part, the instructor must consider the particular interests of students taking the introductory course—education majors, physical therapy majors, communication disorders majors, and so forth. Moreover, few instructors have interests or backgrounds in the range of topics that define a survey course.

Given these student and instructor variables, no one prescriptive study guide for this book will suffice. Rather, we leave it to the instructor to choose from within the book and from within each chapter, just those topics that he or she wishes to have students study. For example, not all instructors will wish to have students be responsible for entire chapters on normal aspects or the sections of the disorders chapters dealing with therapy procedures. In our experience, as long as students understand clearly what terms and concepts they will be responsible for on examinations—perhaps including sample test questions—they will complete weekly reading assignments on time and bring interesting discussion questions to class. Students like teacher-made reading guides, especially as these study guides show concern for students' interests and reflect the instructor's unique areas of professional interests and experiences.

Instructors should consider progressing through this book in one of two ways. One way is to have students read in order Chapters 1 through 13. This route will result in sequential reading of the three chapters on normal processes of language, speech, and hearing (Chapters 1–3), followed by a subset of chapters on language disorders (Chapters 4–6), speech disorders (Chapters 7–11), and hearing disorders (Chapters 12–13). An alternative route is to read each of the normal processes chapters directly *before* reading the corresponding subset of chapters on disorders. Each of these two paths through the territory has various features to recommend it. To allow for maximum flexibility, we have edited the disorders sections of the book so that they may be read in any sequence the instructor deems optimal. Practical issues in course management — arranging for class demonstrations, films, guest speakers, therapy observations, and so forth — generally dictate such matters. Whatever the path of study chosen, brief "signposts" are provided at the head of each chapter. These are statements offering broad perspectives on chapter contents and alerting the reader to key issues addressed by the authors.

about the editors

THOMAS J. HIXON is Professor of Speech Sciences at the University of Arizona. He received his M.A. and Ph.D. degrees in speech pathology from the University of Iowa and did postdoctoral work in physiology at Harvard University. Dr. Hixon is a Fellow of the American Speech-Language-Hearing Association, holds its Certificate of Clinical Competence in Speech-Language Pathology, and is a former Editor of its *Journal of Speech and Hearing Research.* He is also a member of the Acoustical Society of America and the American Association of Phonetic Sciences. Professor Hixon advises many groups, including the National Institutes of Health, the National Science Foundation, the National Technical Institute for the Deaf, and the Veterans Administration. His professional interests center around normal and disordered speech.

LAWRENCE D. SHRIBERG is an Associate Professor of Speech Pathology at the University of Wisconsin. He received his B.S. degree from Syracuse University, an Ed.M. from Boston University, and a Ph.D. from the University of Kansas. Dr. Shriberg holds the Certificate of Clinical Competence in Speech-Language Pathology from the American Speech-Language-Hearing Association and is a member of many professional organizations including the American Psychological Association. His research interests focus on theory, assessment and management of children with severely delayed speech development. Additionally, in collaboration with colleagues at the University of Wisconsin, Professor Shriberg developed a widely used appraisal system that helps students in training become clinically competent.

JOHN H. SAXMAN is Professor and Chairman of Communicative Disorders at Syracuse University. Dr. Saxman completed his Ph.D. degree at Purdue University in Audiology and Speech Sciences and has been actively involved in graduate and undergraduate education in Speech-Language Pathology since 1964. In addition to editorial consultation for major journals, including the *Journal of Speech and Hearing Research* and the *Journal of Speech and Hearing Disorders,* Dr. Saxman served as Vice President of the Association of Speech Pathologists and Audiologists in Mental Hygiene and Chairman of the Professional Advocacy Committee of the National Council of Graduate Programs in Speech-Language Pathology and Audiology. Dr. Saxman's research interests are concerned with isolation of major variables that adversely affect speech and language development in children.

introduction
to communication
disorders

signpost   Chapter 1 gets us started through the territory by considering how normal individuals go about learning to talk and understand. This consideration focuses on the nature of oral-language learning, from its roots in the initial sound-making of infants to the remarkable skill of the mature language user in adapting language to the needs of the listener and the requirements of the situation. Special attention is devoted to various strategies for mastering the knack of language learning and to various factors that play important roles in language acquisition. Solving the mysteries of normal talking and listening is basic to solving the mysteries of normal child development. Although learning to talk and understand have been within the province of child development study for a considerable time, only within the past two decades have they been studied in a systematic and sophisticated fashion within the domain of the communication researcher. It is no exaggeration to say that few areas in all of communication disorders have ever experienced such a major knowledge explosion in such a short period of time. Those concerned with disorders of language must, of course, define, evaluate, and manage disordered language with reference to this expanding normal reference. It is important, therefore, to learn from Chapter 1 how it is that humans acquire and use their unique symbolic code to communicate with one another.

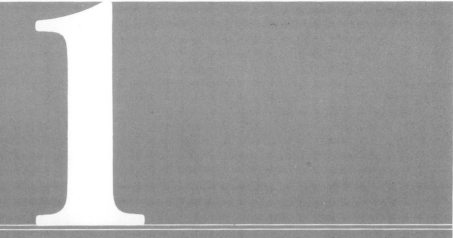

1

Norma S. Rees

learning
to talk
and understand

His mother was in the yard, throwing feed to the chickens. She watched the boy trip and fall and get up and skip again. He came quickly and quietly and stood beside her, then went to the hen nest to look for eggs. He found one. He looked at it a moment, picked it up, brought it to his mother and very carefully handed it to her, by which he meant what no man can guess and no child can remember to tell.*

INTRODUCTION

Unraveling the mysteries of the child's acquisition of that most human of accomplishments, his first language, is no easy task. Even the careful techniques that have been developed for the analysis and recording of exotic languages, a part of the science of linguistic anthropology, are inadequate to the study of the language of children. The major difficulty is that the young child cannot make available to the investigator any of his knowledge about language, except as that knowledge is revealed by his behavior in speaking and listening. In contrast to the adult, the child cannot give the investigator opinions about the grammatical correctness or the acceptability of linguistic utterances. Consequently, the student of child language must find unique methods to gather and interpret data that will yield a full description of the development of language and speech in children. To a remarkable degree such methods have been developed, and the recent scientific study of child language has produced considerable information. It has also produced new questions.

The plan of this chapter is to begin with a discussion of the nature of language and an overview of the study of child language. A

*From W. Saroyan, *The Human Comedy*. New York: Harcourt Brace Jovanovich, 1943. Reprinted by permission.

discussion of the child's development from infant sound-making to early linguistic skills follows. Various approaches to the study of language in the preschool years are then considered within the context of the development of comprehension and production in early childhood. Final sections deal with variables and variants in language learning and the growth of communication skills.

THE NATURE OF LANGUAGE

The study of language development in children is a place where a number of sciences overlap. Psychologists and educators are interested in the acquisition of language as a legitimate part of the study of child development. Linguistics, the scientific study of language, also includes the language of children. Speech-language pathologists and audiologists, while focusing on disorders of human communication, can define and evaluate disordered language only with reference to the normal. The study of child language is therefore a convergence of disciplines, and rests on knowledge and techniques from all these sources. But inasmuch as the study of child language is in some sense the study of language, some basic points about the general subject of language are needed to establish a common framework.

Language and Communication

Although the terms *language* and *communication* are frequently used rather loosely or even interchangeably, it is useful for the purposes of this chapter to distinguish scrupulously between them. We may draw a contrast between the *language code* and the *communication process*. Oral language is a code with structural properties characterized by a set of rules for producing and comprehending spoken utterances. Communication is the process of sharing or giving information, feelings, and attitudes. Language may serve as a tool in the process of communication, possibly the most complex of all tools used for that process. Yet language has uses other than as a tool for communication, while communication uses not only language but other tools as well. Language and communication are therefore not interchangeable constructs. When language is used for communication, the two constructs may be said to overlap. The distinctions between these two constructs, as well as the overlapping, will become more evident in the discussion that follows.

Human communication makes use not only of language, but of other vocal sounds like screams, whines, and coos. Furthermore, these and other vocal qualifiers may accompany a linguistic utterance without having linguistic status in their own right. Every language user is familiar with this distinction, as exemplified in the contrast between two versions of an utterance like *I'll see you at the party.* In one instance the listener may confidently conclude that the speaker fully intends to show up, while in the other he may guess accurately that the speaker will find some excuse to miss the event. The contrasting versions of the utterance may be accounted for not by variation in the sentence structure (which is nonexistent), but by alteration of aspects of voice that are not part of the linguistic structure. Yet these vocal qualifiers have powerful communication value. In addition, speaking rate and other temporal factors impart much nonlinguistic information, as do facial expression, gestures, and other body movements and positions (Birdwhistell, 1970).

Another distinction between the two constructs is that communication, unlike language, is found in all animals. Nonhuman animals, for example, make sounds that indicate their needs and desires to others (Bronowski and Bellugi, 1970). The extensive literature on animal behavior has made it well known that animals at every level of the phylogenetic scale have more or less elaborate systems and rituals of communicating with others (Sebeok, 1968). Yet only humans spontaneously learn to use language to communicate. While the overlapping aspects of language and communication are in practice difficult to separate, for the purposes of this chapter the terms *language* and *communication* will, wherever possible, be distinguished carefully.

Language as Rule-Governed Behavior

We have asserted that the communication systems of nonhuman animals do not qualify as language, with the interesting exceptions of some primates which have successfully been taught elements of human-type languages (Gardner and Gardner, 1969; Premack, 1970). While parrots and some other birds may be taught to imitate stretches of speech with reasonable accuracy, we are not inclined to credit them with the facility for learning language. In contrast, even some very young children ordinarily can demonstrate considerable mastery of language. What is the crucial difference that separates the language of a three-year-old child from both animal communication systems and from the mimicry of "talking" birds? An essential characteristic of human language systems is that they consist of sets of generative rules. The typical three-year-old can produce sentences he has never spoken before and can comprehend utterances he has never heard before. His mastery of language, then, implies the possession of a set of rules for generating novel utterances. Because the potential number of sentences in the language is infinite, a generative grammar must consist of a set of rules that can generate all the utterances that could qualify as legitimate sentences in the language under consideration. Since the influential work of Chomsky (1965) it has become customary to describe the speaker-listener as having internalized the rules necessary to understand and produce grammatical sentences in his language. The process of producing sentences has been called *encoding,* while the process of comprehending the sentences of others has been called *decoding.* Although the language user must be both encoder and decoder, a single set of rules is presumed to underlie both processes. These internalized rules are further presumed to be related to the language structure.

The structure of language may be described as consisting of a number of components, each characterized by its own rules (see Figure 1–1). The *semantic* component is characterized by rules for the meanings of words and word combinations. The meaning of an individual word may be viewed as the set of semantic features appropriate to that word: For example, the meaning of *boy* is the sum total of (at least) the semantic features animate, human, masculine, and young; words like *long* and *short* are alike in that both include semantic features for dimension and length, and differ only in which end of the continuum is referred to. The semantic component of language also includes rules for the meaning of sentences. It includes such notions as the intrasentence semantic relations of actor, action, and object. The language user's knowledge of the rules of the semantic system, then, makes it possible for him to master word meanings as well as to deal with a sentence like *The boy hit the ball* by determining who did the action (actor), what the action was (action), and what was acted upon (object). Semantic knowledge also provides for the language user's ability to know (a) that a sentence is meaningless, like *Gadgets kill passengers from the eyes* and *I came to hear your foot laugh;* (b) that a sentence is semantically ambiguous, like *The house is near the bank;* and (c) that one sentence has the same meaning as another, like *My son gave me a wooden nickel* and *My male offspring gave me a nickel made out of wood.*

At the level of *syntax,* the rules are for how words may be combined into sentences of varying structural types. According to a transformational theory of grammar, any sentence has both a deep and a surface structure. Surface structures, corresponding roughly to the form in which sentences may be spoken, are related to deep structures, corresponding roughly to semantic intent, by a series of operations called transformations. A structurally ambiguous sentence like

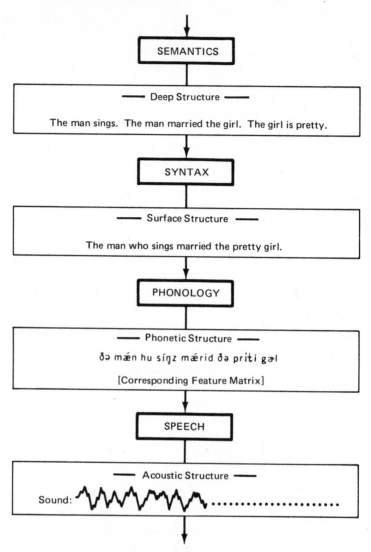

FIGURE 1–1. *Components of language as manifested through the speech mode of language performance. Message flow is through a series of processors that change the form of the message. See text for discussion. (From F. Cooper, How is language conveyed by speech? In J. Kavanagh and I. Mattingly, Eds.,* Language by Ear and by Eye. *Cambridge, Mass.: MIT Press, 1972.)*

Water the plant when thoroughly potted is described as being potentially derived from two different deep structures, one of which specifies that *the plant* is the subject of the verb *potted,* while the other specifies that the subject of the verb is an element like "someone" that does not appear in the surface representation at all. In addition to recognizing

6

such ambiguities, the language user, on the basis of his knowledge of syntax, can also relate sentences of different meanings but similar structures, like *I can't catch you* and *John won't eat fish,* or *Do you have a watch?* and *Did they buy the house?* Furthermore, the language user can judge some sentences to be ungrammatical, like *The burglar robbed themselves.*

The *phonological* component includes rules for the set of sounds or phonemes of the language and for their combination into syllables and words. For example, the initial consonant in the English word *thick* is not found in most other languages; conversely, the German consonant at the end of *buch* is not in the English system. Rules for sound combinations in English permit *t* to be preceded by *s* but not by *sh* at the beginning of a syllable. The consonant at the end of *sing* is fairly common in English, but it never begins an English word.

Finally, the component *speech* in Figure 1–1 refers to the rules relating the phonological system to the acoustic form of spoken utterances. At the level of phonology the sentence may be thought of as an ordered sequence of phonemic units; at the level of speech the conversion to the acoustic signal, via movements of the articulators and vocal tract, is complete (Cooper, 1972). This is the topic of Chapter 2.

Another important insight about the language user is the distinction between *competence* and *performance* (Chomsky, 1965). To speak of the language user as having internalized the generative rules of his language is to credit him with knowledge about language that underlies his ability to decode or encode novel utterances, without commenting on his skill or opportunity to apply the rules. The language user's internalized knowledge of his language makes up his *competence;* by contrast, each act of decoding or encoding is an instance of *performance.* The competence-performance distinction makes it possible to view members of a language community as sharing a common system of linguistic rules, while differing from one another in inclination, experience, habits, and so on in producing and understanding spoken language. Moreover, the competence-performance distinction, as applied to children, leads us from asking only what the child can say and understand to the important question of what the child *knows* about his language.

The terms *language* and *speech* are sometimes used in a confusing way in the literature on child language. In some of the older writings they are even used interchangeably. That approach has the disadvantage of confusing competence and performance, as well as of focusing on the spoken output to the unfortunate neglect of language comprehension. In more current writings, *language* generally refers to the comprehensive system of rules outlined in Figure 1–1. In that case, *speech* is the narrower term, referring to the encoding aspect of language performance, or even more narrowly, to the phonatory-articulatory aspects of the spoken utterance.

THE STUDY OF CHILD LANGUAGE: AN OVERVIEW

Although the development of language in children has always been a subject of interest to parents, writers, and teachers, only fairly recently has this subject acquired respectability as a topic of serious scientific effort (Brown, 1973). The first studies applying rigorous techniques of linguistic analysis were made of the spoken language of very young children in the early 1960s (Braine, 1963; Brown and Fraser, 1964; Miller and Ervin, 1964). Since that time the techniques for careful study of child language have been refined and expanded, and data have accumulated rapidly. The bulk of the earlier studies on child language concerned the acquisition of syntax, with somewhat less attention to developing phonology. Later, interest turned to attempts to describe and account for the child's development of a semantic system. One of the most active themes in the current study of child language is the development of communication in context, or the account of how the child learns to apply his language skills in varying social and interactive roles.

A major assumption in the study of child language is that, like any human language behavior, the language behavior of children is rule-governed. In this fundamental principle the current approach to child language departs from earlier approaches, which tended to view the language of children in terms of its deviations from adult language. In place of describing children's utterances as defective versions of how adults speak, it has become customary to consider each child utterance as reflecting the rules of the child system. In other words, at every stage of development before the child has mastered the adult language, his verbalizations are viewed as having been generated by a set of internalized rules that comprise his language competence at that stage of development. The things children say are seen, then, not in terms of their "errors" with reference to the adult version, but rather as manifestations of their own linguistic rules. The normal development of language in children may thus be regarded as a continuum along which the child progresses on his way to mastering the adult form of the language, each point on the continuum corresponding to an increasing complexity in the linguistic system. Recent efforts in child language study are largely directed at specifying the details of this developmental progression.

PRELANGUAGE

Considerable interest has revolved around the child's first year of life. Investigators have studied the infant's vocal and cognitive behaviors, among others, to find the precursors to later language development. In the next two sections, we consider some of what is known in this regard.

Vocalizations to Verbalizations

The sound-making of infants has been much studied. While the earliest vocalizations are crying sounds, vowel-like sounds may appear in the infant's noncrying vocalizations as early as one month. In the beginning, both crying and noncrying sounds are reflexive rather than intentional on the part of the infant. As the infant matures, his noncrying sound-making becomes more varied. This period is often called babbling and is characteristic of the second six months of life. At the babbling stage infants produce sounds unlike those of the adult language but also sounds that resemble the consonants and vowels of the adult system. In time the infant's sound-making, frequently in the form of repetitive consonant-vowel sequences, becomes more and more speechlike (Ferguson, 1976). Efforts to describe accurately the changing patterns of infant sounds have been hampered by methodological problems. Adult listeners are subject to the perceptual distortions created by their own language habits, and therefore do not always agree on what they hear in the nonlanguage utterances of infants. Techniques for the acoustic analysis of infant vocalizations have been developed only recently.

The changing patterns of prelinguistic sound-making are in large part due to anatomical changes in the maturing vocal tract. The vocal apparatus of the newborn infant (as well as that of the nonhuman primate, to which it is similar) cannot produce the speech sounds of the adult language (Lieberman et al., 1971). It has been suggested frequently that during the first year of life the infant's sounds gradually drift toward the sound pattern of adult speech because of differential reinforcement. The sounds the child accidentally produces that are similar to those in his language environment are reinforced by his own and others' responses to them, while his accidental sounds that differ greatly from the sound system of his language go unreinforced. According to this theory, the reinforced sounds increase in frequency and in their similarity to the model, while the unreinforced sounds gradually drop out (Siegel, 1969). This explanation is used to support the theory that children's first spoken words result from the gradual shaping of random prelinguistic vocalizations.

Oller et al., (1976) also argue for continuity between prelinguistic vocalizations and speech, but from a different standpoint. These authors present data that show "basic phonetic preferences" in the vocalizations of children in the first year of life that are found in adult language systems.

Crystal (1973) regards the infant's early control over intonation and rhythm, occurring well before the first intelligible spoken word, as the beginning of language in the child. Although Crystal's emphasis is not on the individual sounds of the spoken language, he nonetheless traces the onset of language from the earliest stages of infant sound-making.

The Prelinguistic Child's Knowledge about Language

In contrast to the production of vocalizations and speechlike utterances, infants' perception and comprehension of the spoken language of others has been studied relatively little. Parents are often heard to report that their infant "hasn't started talking yet, but she understands everything." While this claim is probably exaggerated, there is considerable evidence that children under one year respond appropriately to much that is said to them (Crystal, 1973). In addition, there is evidence that infants as young as one month can discriminate among speech sounds of the adult system, a remarkable finding which suggests at least that human speech perception utilizes some basic physiological abilities (Eimas et al., 1971). The study of language perception and comprehension in the child's first year has thus far yielded only limited information.

In some research, however, the early development of communication skills is approached more broadly. For example, the gaze behavior of infants between three and four months was studied by Jaffe, Stern, and Peery (1973), who found these infants' looking-at and looking-away patterns to be similar to their vocalizing-pausing patterns. These authors hypothesized that both gazing and vocalization are communication systems showing regular patterns of development beginning in infancy. Crystal (1973) concludes that by the age of one year the child knows a good deal about how language is used to signal the different roles and relationships of persons in his environment. He gives the example of the child who uses consistently different voices in nonlanguage vocalizations while playing with different toy animals. Werner and Kaplan (1963) suggest that children's early sounds which are not yet words may be thought of as "call-sounds," or "ingredients of the straining movements of the child toward objects in the environment which are beyond his immediate reach." The notion of "call-sounds" implies a stage beyond random vocalization that is the start of the communicative use of sound-making. Sugarman (1973) and later Bruner (1975) concluded from their infant studies that the early routines of mother-infant interaction teach the child a good deal about communicative roles and behaviors before language actually begins.

Based upon the preceding discussion, we may conclude that the beginnings of communication are at the beginnings of infancy. Surely, the child has developed considerable knowledge of and control over communication variables well before he has uttered his first intelligible "word."

THE BEGINNING OF LANGUAGE

When does language begin? Traditionally the child has been regarded as having entered on the linguistic scene at the moment he produces his first intelligible utterance, usually a single word that listening adults interpret as meaningful and intentional on his part. Although this notion is a convenient one, it is not without its theoretical risks. As we have seen already, the first word is by no means the only possible evidence that the child has acquired knowledge about language and its functions in communication. It may be more appropriate to equate the onset of language with the beginnings of speech perception and comprehension, or with early communication games between mother and infant. In fact, Crystal (1973) doubts that such a thing as the prelinguistic child exists at all. Furthermore, even if we wish to select the first intelligible spoken utterance as an operational, if arbitrary, definition of the onset of language, there will be instances when observers disagree about whether such an event has actually occurred. When the eleven-month-old utters *dada*, his father may be certain that he heard *Daddy*, while his mother may be just as certain that she heard another of baby's meaningless repetitive vocalizations. In spite of the pitfalls and doubts about what event to label as the beginning of language, we may safely say that in most instances children begin to produce intelligible, intentional single words somewhere between their first and second birthdays. Even this statement is not without its qualifications, for some children reach this stage before the end of the first year while other children, whose language development proceeds along normal lines, do not produce any intelligible words until after the second year. There are occasional reports of children whose earliest utterances are word combinations or "sentences" rather than single words.

The Single-Word Stage

The early single words may be nouns, like *baby, juice,* and *Daddy;* they may be other kinds of words, like *no, hot,* and *allgone.* They may resemble the adult forms of these words only approximately, as in the twelve-month-old who said *kika* for *kitty-cat.* It may be clear that the child is saying a word even when the phonetic form gives no unambiguous clues to the adult version, as in the eighteen-month-old whose vocabulary was limited to one item, *didi,* used to refer to any animal. Typically the child acquires a small number of single words and adds few or no new words for several months, subsequently entering a phase of rapid vocabulary growth while still at the single-word level. Much individual variation occurs in this respect, however.

Precisely what single-word utterances represent has been a matter of much discussion. Many single-word utterances appear to be *holophrastic* — that is, having the force of a complete sentence. For example, when the child utters *car,* he may seem to intend *I see a car,* or *I want to ride in the car,* or *There is a car over there,* or *Give me the car.* Adults who are present are frequently able to make confident judgments about what the child intends by taking into account the nonlinguistic context, as when the child utters *juice* while picking up his empty bottle and carrying it to the refrigerator. The communicative function of such a holophrastic single-word utterance, then, would be expressed in a sentence like *I want juice* in the adult version of the language. Some single-word utterances seem to have no such instrumental function, and are better described as instances of commenting or labeling. Bloom (1970), for example, describes "comments" as speech events that serve to name or point out persons or objects. Certainly children at the stage of rapid vocabulary growth often seem to have a strong interest in the names of things and people and appear to delight in reciting these labels, often to no one in particular. Some of these children are heard to recite strings of label-words and other verbal items before falling asleep at night.

The single-word stage has been of interest to investigators who are concerned with the origins of syntax in the child's mastery of language. One point of view is that children whose utterances are characterized by single words nonetheless know a good deal about the grammatical structure of sentences, and that this knowledge takes the form of underlying grammatical relations that account for the sentencelike meanings the child expresses in his single-word utterances (McNeill, 1970). In contrast, Bloom (1973) denies that children at this stage know much about the grammar of sentences. Bloom views the early period in which single-word utterances predominate as the time when the child learns how to organize his experience and perceptions on a cognitive not a linguistic basis. Single-word utterances therefore express conceptual notions, not grammatical relations. Bloom (1973) distinguishes between two main types of words that occur as single-word utterances: substantive forms, defined as words that refer to classes of objects and events, and function forms, or words that "make reference to aspects of behavior that extend across classes of objects and events." Among the early words Bloom reports in the first group are *chair* and *cookie*, which may indicate the presence of the object named but also may refer to the entire situation or action (usually involving the child) in which the object occurs. The second group, function forms, include examples like *more, no, up, off,* which refer rather to behaviors shared by various objects and events. Of the two types of single words, function forms appear earlier and with greater frequency in the child's output. Bloom concludes that children's single words in the early period represent what they know about people, objects, and events rather than what they know about the grammatical structure of sentences they have not yet learned to produce. The nature of single-word utterances at the beginning of language development has been viewed in still other ways, as will be seen in a later section.

The Growth of Vocabulary and Meanings

The acquisition of new *lexical,* or vocabulary, items is one aspect of language development that is never complete. While the preschool spurt in lexical acquisition is more dramatic than in later years, older children and adults continue to add new items to their lexicons according to their changing needs and experiences. In part this trend matches the historical development of the language itself, for the phonology and syntax of any language change slowly while new words are constantly being added and old words dropping out. Moreover, vocabulary items shift in and out of fashion and alter their meanings. Words like *polyester* and *finalize* are in common use today but were not a generation ago; words like *ecology* and *tranquilizer* were until recently used by only limited groups of speakers; words like *tough* and *waste* have added new meanings. One mother observed a generation gap in vocabulary when she figured out why she often found the ketchup bottle in the freezer: She heard herself telling her nine-year-old son to "put it in the icebox." Similarly, in individual language development, vocabulary knowledge and usage continue to change over time.

It has been recognized for some time that the way young children use the words they know may differ from the adult use of these words. To put it another way, what a given word means may differ in the vocabulary of the child and of the adult. It is not unusual for a two-year-old to call all men *daddy*. One parent took great pains to teach her child the word *cookie* so that he would have something he could ask for; the lesson was successful, but the child subsequently said *cookie* whether he wanted a cookie, a drink of water, or a toy. We may conclude that the meaning of *cookie* to this child at the time was what the adult would encode as *give me*. Incidentally, this anecdote also shows that the earliest words are not exclusively nouns, or the names of objects and people.

The work of Clark (1973b) reveals that when the child first begins to talk, the words he uses only partially reflect their adult meanings. According to Clark, the child's words start out with only a few, or even one, of the semantic features that characterize the adult meanings of those words. For example, *daddy* for the two-year-old may include only the semantic features "male" and "adult," accounting for his application of that word to all grown men. As his semantic system matures, the child may add the feature "father," thus limiting his use of *daddy* to adult men accompanied by small children. In time he adds semantic features that distinguish "his" father from other fathers, restricting the use of *daddy* to the only adult male who holds that kinship relation to himself. Similarly, the twelve-month-old may utter *hot* when referring to a boiling pot, the radiator, or a cigarette; but if he also says *hot* when pointing to his mother's glasses or a sharp knife, we may conclude that a semantic feature something like "don't touch" is the one he is encoding as *hot*, with features relating to temperature or combustion yet to be added.

Sometimes young children's first use of single words seems to mean the very opposite of the meaning those words have for adults. For example, an eighteen-month-old may say *up* when he is clearly trying to get down, as from his highchair to the floor. Actually, the meanings of *up* and *down* are not as disparate as they may seem, for both refer to directions on the vertical dimension. For the child to complete his semantic system for the words *up* and *down*, he need only add the feature specifying the relevant direction along the vertical dimension. When he does so, his use of these words will match their adult uses precisely.

THE DEVELOPMENT OF COMPREHENSION AND PRODUCTION IN EARLY CHILDHOOD

Some time ago a popular magazine carried a cartoon that showed a woman talking to a little child around the age of three. She was saying, "Now that you can talk, shut up." This cartoon reflected the common observation that while the earliest beginnings of language production in children may seem slow and inaccurate, before long the child's language has reached a stage of development that in its sophistication and quantity of output is remarkable and often fatiguing to adult listeners. To describe this process of development more fully, we will examine various approaches to the study of first-language acquisition and consider the ongoing relationship between comprehension and production.

Strategies in Language Learning: Figuring Out How Language Works

Because children acquire only the language or languages spoken around them, it is apparent that language must be learned. Whatever special or even species-specific abilities and propensities the human animal brings to the language-learning task, there remains much to be explained about the process of mastering the knack of language in general and about acquiring a community's language in particular. The strategies children apply to language learning have been approached by examining the sentences they produce, by considering the meanings they are capable of, and—somewhat more recently—by analyzing the uses they can put language to. These approaches may be termed the structural, the cognitive, and the pragmatic.

Structural Approaches.   The syntactic-semantic analysis of children's sentences has been a major topic of linguistic and psycholinguistic study of child language. Based on the assumption that even the earliest sentences are rule-governed, in the 1960s investigators of child language began to examine children's early spontaneous utterances of two words and longer for evidence of their systematic nature (Braine, 1963; Brown and Fraser, 1964; Miller and Ervin, 1964). These early attempts were concerned essentially with syntax, and approached the samples of children's spontaneous productions as if they were utterances in an unfamiliar language presumed to be fully grammatical. The investigators used measures of word frequency and word distribution. For example, in the data for one child the majority of two-word utterances began with *here* or *there*. Many different words appeared in second position, mostly in combination with either *here* or *there* as the first word. *Here* or *there* could combine with any of a large number of words, but never with each other; in other words, the child produced utterances like *here book* and *there cookie*, but never utterances like *here there.* This kind of pattern appearing to account for much of the two-word utterances repertoire in the period under study, the investigators described a simple "pivot" grammar that characterized the earliest productions. Simply put, a "pivot" grammar consists of only two word classes, a small number of "pivot" words that usually appear in the first position in a two-word utterance, and a large (and rapidly growing) "open" class of words that combine with pivot words or with each other. A similar approach was used to write grammatical rules that would generate longer utterances (Brown and Fraser, 1964). To describe how children's sentences grew longer and more complex, this approach classified the words children used into categories or "word classes," and listed the rules that accounted for how, and in what order, the words could be combined.

Although the "grammars" based on distributional criteria soon proved inadequate to the task of describing even early language acquisition, the work they represented had enormous impact on the study of child language. For one thing, it showed that it is indeed possible to discover regularities in children's earliest utterances beyond the single-word stage. Second, it revealed the fruitfulness of studying naturalistic data. Third, it established the technique of examining in depth a large quantity of spontaneous language data for one child at a time. Even so, it was quickly recognized that the technique of syntactic analysis that had driven these studies revealed nothing of the meanings intended by the speakers. The first work that took serious account of meanings in children's two-word utterances was that of Bloom (1970), who showed that the meanings children intend can be understood by relating utterance to context. In her famous example, she pointed out that the utterance *Mommy pigtail* may have a number of meanings, among which its structure does not help the listener to choose. In uttering *Mommy pigtail* the child may mean (1) Mommy has a pigtail, (2) Mommy's pigtail, (3) Mommy, make me a pigtail, or (4) Mommy is making a pigtail. While the utterance itself offers nothing to motivate the selection, Bloom points out that when the child spoke this utterance, neither the mother nor the child had a pigtail, the child had just found a rubber band, the mother had a history of making pigtails, and at that moment the child was pushing her hair up toward her mother. That the child's intended meaning was (3) is entirely obvious, then, when contextual information is used to disambiguate the utterance.

It having been demonstrated that there is a way to retrieve children's utterance meanings, it became possible to consider a more powerful factor than word classes and rules for combining them: the meaning relations that obtain between words in utterances. For example, the utterances *kitty chair* and *Mommy sweater* may superficially (and uninterestingly) be described as Noun + Noun constructions when distributional criteria alone are considered. Using Bloom's (1970) type of analysis, however, *kitty chair* may be described as expressing the relationship between entity, *kitty,* and the location or place where it may be found or is to be placed, *chair.* By contrast, the intended meaning of *Mommy sweater* may be the relationship between possessor, *Mommy,* and possessed, *sweater.* These meaning relations "augment" the meaning provided by the constituent words alone (Bloom, Lightbown, and Hood, 1975), and the meaning potential they provide is the very basis of word combinations in adult as well as child grammar. The types of two-word utterances that predominated in the samples of spontaneous child productions, the so-called "pivot" constructions, were shown to represent several classes of meaning. The utterance *there ball* expresses existence, or refers to the presence of an object; *more car* expresses recurrence, or another instance of the object; and *no cookie* expresses nonexistence, or the absence or disappearance of the object. Even these descriptions may be further refined, as is made clear from a closer look at the *no cookie* example. The intended meaning of *no cookie* might be nonexistence, but it could also be denial (meaning *That's not a cookie*) or rejection (meaning *I don't want a cookie*). [These meaning categories are discussed in Bloom (1973), and Bloom, Hood, and Lightbown (1974).]

A reasonably complete list of the semantic-syntactic relations that account for the bulk of children's utterances while they are at the predominantly two-word stage was compiled by Brown (1973). To arrive at this list, he examined the data on three children whose language development he and his colleagues studied closely and also the data reported by other investigators for children learning English, Swedish, Spanish, Finnish, and Samoan. Brown's list of minimal two-term relations is shown in Table 1–1.

As children mature, the sentences they speak become longer and more complex. At the two-word stage, the child may say *Mommy walk,* but eventually he expresses the same meaning in the form *Mommy's walking,* which reflects his mastery of the auxiliary use of the verb *to be* and the inflectional ending *-ing* for the progressive form of the main verb. Moreover, the child learns to produce sentences with complex grammatical descriptions. For example, his first negative utterances may have taken the form *no cookie,* but eventually he expresses the

Table 1-1. MINIMAL TWO-TERM SEMANTIC-SYNTACTIC RELATIONS IN CHILDREN'S UTTERANCES AT THE PREDOMINANTLY TWO-WORD STAGE.

TWO-TERM RELATIONS	EXAMPLES
Agent and action	Mommy walk; Daddy push
Action and object	hit ball; eat lunch
Agent and object	Mommy pigtail;* Daddy ball**
Action and locative (location)	ride car; sit chair
Entity and locative	kitty chair; baby table
Possessor and possession	baby shoe; Mommy nose
Attribute and entity	pretty dress; more cookie
Demonstrative and entity	this doll; here doggie

*Intended meaning: *Mommy is making a pigtail.*

**Intended meaning: *Daddy is throwing the ball.*

From R. Brown, *A First Language: The Early Stages.* Cambridge, Mass.: Harvard University Press, 1973.

negative meaning in the form *There aren't any more cookies* or *I don't want a cookie.* Obviously, however, the child's primitive sentence forms do not shift suddenly to fully grammatical adult versions, but rather pass through stages of increasing complexity. Klima and Bellugi (1966), reporting on the development of negative sentences, state that the progression may be divided into three stages. In the first stage, corresponding to the point when the child is beginning to string words together, or the earliest phase of syntactic development, he produces negative sentences like *No money, No a boy bed, Not a teddy bear, Wear mitten no.* In the second stage, when the child's utterances average between two and four words in length, the negative sentences include *There is no squirrels, That not "O", I can't catch you, Don't bite me yet.* In the third stage, when the child's mean utterance length is close to four words, among the negative sentences are *I am not a doctor, I didn't see something, You don't want some supper, I didn't caught it, We can't make another broom.* Examination of this progression reveals the child's gradual observance of the syntactic rules for the position of the negative elements *no* and *not* within the sentence, and the use of auxiliary verbs plus negative in constructions like *can't* and *didn't.* It also shows the residual difficulty that the child at stage three has with words like *some* and *any* and the rules of their use in negative sentences as well as other relatively minor deviations from adult-type negatives.

Using the concepts of transformational grammar, Klima and Bellugi (1966) found it possible to analyze the syntactic rules that would generate the children's negative sentences at each stage of development. A similar analysis of *Wh* questions (questions beginning with the words *who, what, where,* etc.) was done by Brown (1968), again revealing stages of development. Early *Wh* questions include *Where my mitten?* and *What the dolly have?;* at a later stage instances with auxiliary verbs like *What he can ride in?* and *Why the kitty can't stand up?* appear. Eventually the child learns to reverse the positions of the subject and auxiliary verb, producing the adultlike construction *What can he ride in?*

As an overview of young children's increasing mastery of the sentence, Brown (1973) outlines five major processes in sentence construction that correspond to five stages of development. Brown's "stages" are defined in terms of mean length of utterance in morphemes,[1] or MLU, of the spontaneous utterances in the samples he collected for three children studied intensively over a period of many, many months. To account for the differences in chronological age at which each of the three children began to combine words, as well as the variation in rate of language development across the three children, Brown and his colleagues compared the children's output only at points of roughly equivalent language development as measured by MLU. The MLUs corresponding to the five stages were these: Stage I, 1.75 morphemes; Stage II, 2.25 morphemes; Stage III, 2.75 morphemes; Stage IV, 3.50 morphemes; and Stage V, 4.00 morphemes.

Although the chronological ages vary at which the children in Brown's and other similar studies reach these stages of mean length of utterance, Brown's work showed that the major process of sentence construction corresponding to each MLU stage is fairly uniform across children. In Stage I the child masters basic semantic roles and syntactic relations within simple sentences; in Stage II he learns to modulate meaning within the simple sentence by appropriate use of some inflectional elements like *-ing* for present progressive, *-s* for plural, *-ed* for past tense, and previously omitted function words like prepositions, conjunctions, etc.; in Stage III he learns to handle other sentence types like questions, imperatives, and negatives; in Stage IV he learns to embed sentences, producing complex constructions like *I hope I don't hurt it* and *Now where's a pencil I can use?;* and in Stage V, the last stage referred to in Brown's (1973) work, the child gains control over more complex relations between simple sentences, permitting constructions like *John bought some gum and a book.*

It is worth reiterating that the analyses of children's sentence development just reviewed were not tied to the children's chronological ages. Children vary greatly in the specific ages at which they enter any given stage of grammatical development and also in their rate of progression through the developmental stages. The effort in the study of

---

[1] A morpheme is defined as the smallest element in the language that has meaning. Some entire words are morphemes, while others may be composed of several morphemes, as in the addition to the word stem of plural markers *-s* or tense markers, *-ing,* *-ed,* etc. The plural *-s;* past tense *-ed,* etc., are morphemes because they convey meaning.

child language has consequently been to outline the order of developmental stages insofar as these have been described for children in general, rather than to specify normal milestones of language development in terms of age in months or years. In any case, there is general agreement that children have mastered the bulk of the basic rules for generating grammatical sentences in their language by school age.

Cognitive Approaches. The relationship between children's language and their evolving cognitive abilities has been another significant area of study. Two major questions have been asked: What meanings are available to children for expression through language? What makes one type of linguistic structure easier for the child to acquire than another?

To address the first of these questions, students of child language in recent years have generally taken the position that language acquisition is dependent on the prior development of a set of cognitive structures—or, to put it another way, that cognition precedes, and is prerequisite for, language. As Sinclair-deZwart (1973) puts it, explicating the view generally ascribed to Piaget, during the first two years of life the child develops cognitive structures "composed of systems of action," from which more sophisticated cognitive structures emerge at a later period. These early cognitive structures form a "universal base" of meanings that may be attached to linguistic utterances. The "systems of action" described by Sinclair-deZwart and others in the Piagetian tradition are sensorimotor schemes in which the child can act upon objects, classifying types of action like pushing or banging and objects that can be pushed or banged. By this stage, the child (around eighteen months) has, in his own cognitive system, become distinct from the objects in his environment and can perform actions upon them. The system thus allows for the mental representation of such meanings as actor, action, and object and meaning relations among them (Sinclair, 1971). The stage is set for the discovery that linguistic utterances express these very meanings (see Figure 1–2).

Sinclair's point of view is consistent with a broader claim by Bloom et al. (1975) that the child learns a grammar "for representing linguistically what he already knows about events in the world." Bloom (1970) had earlier concluded from her study of language development in three children that "the emergence of syntactic structures in their speech depended on the prior development of the cognitive organization of experience that is coded by language." Were this not the case, she argued, the children's early Noun + Noun constructions would express all the possible semantic relations from the start, while the evidence showed, to the contrary, that the meanings the children expressed were limited at first and increased with maturation. In other words, in

FIGURE 1-2. *A little person helping his two friends talk to one another. (Courtesy of the University of Arizona Human Development Preschool.)*

this view, not only is the beginning of language tied to a particular stage of cognitive development (the end of the sensorimotor period, in Piagetian terms; see Ingram, 1976), but the mastery of particular forms is dependent upon the establishment of specific cognitive structures. For example, the child's ability to construct and use sentences about events other than those in the here and now, or to learn the way the language refers to past or future events, will emerge only when the child's cognitive ability permits "decentration," the ability to take a point of view other than his own (Cromer, 1974). Bowerman (1976b), however, reviews a number of studies showing that there is no simple way to match stages of language acquisition with specific cognitive prerequisites. Nonetheless, as Cromer puts it in his explication of the cognition hypothesis, "the evidence is strong that changes in cognition precede the acquisition of new linguistic forms which are normally used by adults to express them." To put it another way, children say only what they know how to mean.

Although the cognition hypothesis may not explain everything we wish to know about the development of language in children, it has had the useful effect of motivating students of child language to pay special attention to meaning. Bowerman (1976a) makes it clear that no account of early language development will amount to much unless it is based on knowledge of the early meanings available to children. The meanings we need to understand, according to Bowerman, are both word meanings and relational meanings, or "concepts involving *relationships* between objects and other objects or events—that underlie children's early rules for word combination."

Where do these meanings come from? With reference to word meanings, Clark (1973a) originally proposed, as noted in an earlier section of this chapter, that children at first acquire only some of the semantic features that make up the full adult meanings of the words they know. According to her explanation, the partial meanings will reflect those semantic features that have the greatest perceptual salience for young children. Her examples suggest movement, shape, size, sound, taste, and texture as the bases for categories of classification. She notes, for example, that very young children reportedly refer to a group of small, round objects by the same name (*apple*), or to a group of objects that make noise by the same name (*choo-choo*). Clark (1973b) described these examples as indications of young children's linguistic hypotheses about word meanings, and went on to offer some nonlinguistic hypotheses as well. The latter group, she claimed, would account for certain biases found in studies of children's comprehension of certain relational terms like *more* and *less* and the prepositions *in, on,* and *under*. Specifically, regardless of instruction to put an object *in, on,* or *under* another object, younger preschool children tended to place the object *in* if the second object were a container, and to place object 1 *on* if object 2 had a surface. In these situations, they never placed object 1 *under* anything. Clark concluded that the young children's response bias was determined by their nonlinguistic strategies to put something *in* whenever possible and to put something *on* if *in* is not possible and *on* is possible. She further theorized that these nonlinguistic strategies determine not only what children think these prepositions mean, but in what order they will fully acquire their meanings. "For example, *in* should be cognitively simpler than either *on* or *under* because it requires minimal adjustment of the child's hypothesis about its meaning."

Bowerman (1976a) goes beyond these theories in pointing out the importance of distinguishing between cognitive and semantic discriminations. For Bowerman, the cognitive discriminations children are capable of do not automatically determine word meanings, but must first become "linked to one or another aspect of language." Until this happens, she argues, cognitive groupings are not yet semantic classifications. The semantic classification could be viewed as a rule for grouping together instances that qualify as a set in the language under consideration—or, to put it another way, as learning to identify the "conditions that must obtain before the word can be used appropriately or correctly." Children derive rules for appropriate uses of words by observing a variety of instances and their associated linguistic symbols. That they operate in this fashion is revealed by their errors as much as their successes: the example of *doggie* for all animals and the examples of overgeneralized application of *daddy, apple,* and *choo-choo* mentioned earlier are to be explained, according to this theory, as wrong inferences rather than as overextensions of labels to a small number of salient attributes. Interestingly, other errors seem to reflect *under*extensions, as in the case for *off* restricted to removal of clothing (Bowerman, 1976a). The story of how children learn to relate concepts to words is a complex one, about which only limited understanding is as yet available.

The other kind of early meaning that must be accounted for is relational meaning, or the meaning that obtains between words and that results from their combination. The kind of meaning referred to was discussed in the section on syntactic-semantic approaches to the study of child utterances, and summarized in Brown's (1973) list of minimal two-term relations on page 18. The sources of relational meanings have also been traced to early cognitive structures, as the earlier comments by Sinclair (1971) reflect. According to Bloom et al. (1975), relational meanings like locative action (*put in box*), possession (*Grandma flower*), and recurrence (*more soap*) are based on children's previously acquired knowledge "about objects, events, and relations in the world." Bowerman (1976a), however, points out that merely presupposing cognitive categories via experimental learning does not explain how children establish the more "abstract relational categories" characteristic of a linguistic system. "Having a practical knowledge that objects can be located in space in a variety of ways, or that the child himself or others are capable of initiating actions which have effects on other objects, or that people have territorial rights over certain objects does not directly translate into having categories like 'location,' 'action,' 'agent,' or 'possessor' upon which rules for generating sentences can operate."

Bowerman also questions whether it is possible to decide just what are the set of relational meanings that best describe the language of young children, pointing out that different investigators find different sets of meaning categories in the data they examine. The relational meanings in the Bloom et al. (1975) study being comparatively broad, it appeared possible to determine a typical order of emergence: according to Bloom et al., the categories of existence, nonexistence, and recurrence appeared before categories that reflected verb relations, while among the verb relations those relations expressing action events appeared before those expressing state events (for example, constructions like *put on chair,* a locative action, appeared earlier than those like *Mommy bathroom,* "Mommy is in the bathroom," a locative state). Other investigators did not necessarily use the same meaning categories or note the same order of development. In the absence of comparable systems or consistent findings, it is virtually impossible to determine in any rigorous way how the conceptual categories of cognitive development match up with the relational meanings in children's word combinations.

Work by Schlesinger (1974) suggests that in fact the progression is not solely from cognitive structures to linguistic expression. Instead, Schlesinger describes an interactive process wherein both practical knowledge and experience with the language combine to produce the relational meanings of early word combinations. For Schlesinger, the relational meanings are not identical with cognitive structures; rather, they are concepts that "make a difference linguistically." Because the child could develop such meanings only by experience with the language (observation about how the language encodes reality), Schlesinger argues that language itself plays a significant role in the child's acquisition of a meaning system.

In the introduction to the section on cognitive approaches to the study of child language, two questions were raised. The second of these questions, what makes one type of linguistic structure easier for the child to acquire than another, will be discussed in the remainder of this section.

Slobin (1971) noted that children learning different languages do not necessarily master a given type of syntactic-semantic construction (for example, negation) at the same time. Why should this be so? To understand Slobin's theory, it is important to recognize that he assumed to start with that certain cognitive prerequisites must be in place in order that the child can grasp the meaning of an utterance, and that these cognitive developments are uniform across all children learning all languages. While cognitive development and hence semantic concepts are invariant ("universals," as they are frequently termed), the linguistic forms that express them vary in complexity from language to language.

A simple way to determine which of two linguistic forms that express the negative is easier for the child to master is to note in which language children acquire the adult form of negation earlier. Using cross-linguistic data based on this theory, Slobin was able to pick out the factors that make linguistic forms easier for children to acquire and summarize these factors into a set of "operating principles" that children apply to linguistic structures they experience in the task of figuring out how the language works. Among these principles are such rules as *pay attention to the ends of words, pay attention to the order of words and morphemes, avoid interruption or rearrangement of linguistic units,* and *avoid exceptions.* Using strategies such as these to work out the organization of a language, Slobin argued, young children will be most successful at mastering structures that conform to their operating principles. To illustrate, a linguistic form that inserts the negative particle into a sentence (as found in English) will be more difficult to learn than one placing the negative particle before or after the sentence (as found in Japanese), because the English form conflicts with the child principle *avoid interruption.*

Slobin's system therefore illuminates a type of cognitive ability different from those reviewed earlier. Whereas the earlier discussion dealt with the relationship between the child's development of a stock of concepts that are precursors to linguistic *meaning,* Slobin adds the point that the child's control of specific linguistic forms also requires a special set of cognitive abilities applied to linguistic *forms.* In a related vein, Bever (1970) offers a number of strategies young children use to process sentences they hear; among them is a basic "segmentation strategy" by which the child isolates and segments those units that correspond to the sequence actor-action-object. This strategy works out well for simple active sentences like *The cow kissed the horse,* but will result in errors when applied to *The horse was kissed by the cow,* the strategy leading the child to conclude that the first noun corresponds to the actor and the last noun to the object of the action. These examples illustrate that children have been regarded as applying cognitive strategies to working out the formal organization of language as well as accumulating a set of concepts that allow them to deal with specific utterance meanings.

Pragmatic Approaches.   In contrast to the concern with syntactic-semantic structures that characterized the early 1960s and the subsequent interest in cognitive prerequisites for language learning, the pragmatic turn has focused on the fact that children do not merely learn language but, from the very start, learn to do things with language. Investigators of child language using pragmatic approaches have sought to understand the processes by which language becomes functional for young children in social situations, and have looked to the social-communicative basis as the very source of language learning (Bruner, 1975; Halliday, 1975; Bates et al., 1977). While earlier investigations sought to account for children's mastery of form and meaning in language, the pragmatic approach introduces an additional goal, that of explaining the child's development of communicative competence.

The pragmatic approach thus engenders a new look at old data. The single-word utterances of the beginnings of language are reexamined, as are both linguistic and nonlinguistic devices children use to communicate with listeners. Naturalistic data and longitudinal samples are scrutinized to reveal the functions of language in young children. Adult-child and child-child linguistic interactions take on a significant role.

At the single-word stage, word meanings are identified with actions rather than with concepts or semantic features. According to investigators like Bruner (1975) and Bates (1976), children's earliest words grow out of the verbalizations associated with actions in ritual play like give-and-take and peek-a-boo games. Vocabulary items that would be classed as nouns in the adult language function differently at the beginnings of language: the meanings of words like *cookie* and *milk* are not the objects they stand for, but rather are embedded in the request function of the child's utterance. Gradually words become separable from the acts the utterances perform and can be used in various combinations to perform other functions. The acts performed through children's single-word utterances are not usually difficult for adult listeners to comprehend. Observation of context and knowledge of the things the child is likely to talk about provide the necessary background for understanding. Thus, if the child says *truck*, the listener generally feels confident in his interpretation that the child is requesting the object, has just seen one, or is indicating that he wants the listener to do something with the object.

Pragmatic factors also govern the specific words children utter at this stage. Children generally talk about the people, objects, and actions associated with their daily lives. What the child perceives in a situation and what he considers worth saying are also matters that appear to affect children's productions. There is some evidence that children select for speaking just those utterances that will be most useful in promoting the listener's understanding. Whether this success is the accidental result of a different factor is hard to say. Greenfield and Smith (1976), for example, conclude from their study that children at the single-word stage select items from their limited repertoire according to a "principle of informativeness." Given that the child may know more than one word that applies to the situation, he will select for encoding that which he perceives as needed to resolve uncertainty. If the child desires a toy cow, he will say *cow* rather than *want* or *gimme;* if he is offered the cow but doesn't want it, he will say *no* rather than *cow.* According to Greenfield and Smith, if the child is able to encode several aspects of the situation, the one he selects will be that significant aspect undergoing change and hence in a state of uncertainty. In another relevant example, if the child is putting toy animals in a bucket, he is more likely to name each animal as he does so than to repeat *in* or *bucket* with each addition. The observations by Greenfield and Smith (1976) and by Bates (1976) suggest that even at the one-word stage children are able to distinguish between "old" or "given" information, which need not be spoken, and "new" information, which must be spoken if the message is to be conveyed.

A particularly significant theme of the pragmatic approach to child language is the interest in children's utterances as *performative* acts. Bates et al. (1977) define the performative as "the act that the speaker intends to carry out with his sentence — declaring, promising, asking questions, and so on." Much of this investigation has been carried on in the framework of speech acts theory, which distinguishes between the speaker's intention and the literal meaning of the sentence uttered. A popular example is *Do you have a match?* which ordinarily the speaker utters as a request for the object, not for information about whether it is in the listener's possession. Speech acts theory is a statement about language in communication, and thus takes as its unit not the sentence but the speech act (Searle, 1969). The importance of the speech act lies in the speaker's intention, which Searle identified with the utterance's illocutionary force and Bates continues to call the performative. According to Bates et al. (1977), at the single-word stage children control at least two performatives: commanding and declaring. Consistent with the example given earlier, then, the child at this stage could say *truck* as a command (or imperative), meaning *Give me that truck,* or as a declarative, meaning *There's a truck out there.* In fact, Bates and her colleagues, as well as other investigators, have presented evidence to show that these early speech acts develop from precursors (action, sounds, and gestures) in the prelinguistic period.

Dore (1976) applied the speech acts analysis to the spontaneous language of three-year-old children, identifying six illocutionary act types: (1) *requests,* which solicit information, actions, or acknowledgements; (2) *responses,* which directly complement preceding utterances; (3) *descriptions,* which represent observable or verifiable aspects of context; (4) *statements,* which express analytic and institutional facts, beliefs, attitudes, emotions, reasons, etc.; (5) *conversational devices,* which regulate contact and conversation; and (6) *performatives,* which accomplish acts by being said (Dore uses this last term more restrictively than Bates does). Other investigators have concentrated on developmental aspects of particular types of illocutionary acts, the so-called indirect directive (*Would you mind getting off my foot?*) having received much attention. Ervin-Tripp (1977) showed that preschool children can handle indirect forms with directive meaning like *We haven't had any candy for a long time* and *That's my truck* (presumably meaning "hands off"). As they grow older, children use more indirect forms like *Do you think you could put your foot right there?* and *My little brother is thirsty*. Ervin-Tripp's data show that oblique hints like *That's where the iron belongs* are the hardest for children to learn.

Attempts to apply the speech acts model to child language share basic difficulties with other efforts to determine the meanings of children's utterances—the decisions about how to classify specific instances seem highly subjective and the systems of classification vary across investigators. Nonetheless, the various approaches to speech acts in child language agree that the goal of language learning is to determine how the language may be used as an instrument of communication. The significant contribution of speech acts theory is that it focuses attention on what children can do with language and the acts they intend their utterances to perform, thus rounding out the picture partially illuminated by the syntactic-semantic and the cognitive analyses of children's utterances.

The Relationship of Comprehension to Production

Most of the studies reviewed in previous sections used children's utterances (productions) as research data, although a few like Clark's (1973b) and Bever's (1970) alluded to children's comprehension strategies. Until fairly recently, the development of comprehension and production were considered to follow parallel paths, with comprehension always in advance of production. Rather simply, it was held that children mastered linguistic forms and their meanings in comprehension before they appeared in production. The experiment of Shipley, Smith, and Gleitman (1969) has often been cited in this connection. Shipley and her colleagues found that children between eighteen and thirty-three months who produced telegraphic utterances in their spontaneous speech nonetheless responded better to well-formed complete sentences than to sentences of the type they produced themselves. For example, Shipley and colleagues' telegraphic speakers responded correctly to instructions like *Throw me the ball* more often than to instructions like *Throw ball*. These findings suggest that children's spontaneous utterances are not as advanced, syntactically, as their comprehension ability.

Some investigators began to note, however, that the data did not always conform to this simple rule. Chapman and Miller (1975) discovered that preschool children produced sentences like *The truck is bumping the dog* correctly more often than they acted out such sentences correctly in an experimental task, leading them to conclude that in some instances grammatical production appeared to precede comprehension. They suggested that these children may apply a semantic strategy to the comprehension task. In other words, in comprehension tasks they interpreted animate nouns as agents of the action encoded by the verb. Chapman and Miller's findings revealed that children might apply different strategies in production and comprehension, and that correct production therefore did not always imply that a similar sentence would be correctly comprehended. In the case of word meaning, once again some findings indicate production in advance of comprehension. Bowerman (1976a) reports that two-year-old children, young enough to make consistent errors on Clark's (1973b) *in, on,* and *under* comprehension tasks, nonetheless use these words correctly in spontaneous production.

There is reason to believe that much of the advantage young children have in comprehension in ordinary situations is more apparent than real. Bloom (1974) points out that the two-year-old child does not need to perform a full syntactic analysis to understand the sentences his mother speaks to him; most often, knowledge of the major constituent words and observation of context is all that is required for his first response to be the expected one. In Bloom's example, the child who hears the sentence *Will is going down the slide* in the playground is more likely to look for Will at the slide than if he hears the same sentence at the dinner table. Furthermore, there are instances where children's spontaneous verbal responses suggest a spurious level of comprehension of questions adults may ask. Ervin-Tripp (1974) studied the patterns of responses to adult's *Wh* questions given by children between one and four years old, revealing among other things that children frequently respond to questions they do not understand with "Because . . ." . Three-year-olds in her data, therefore, answered questions like *How did the man get into the house?* or *When did the sailboat come?* or *Why is the deer eating?* with "Because . . ." responses. Noting only the why-because match in the last example, an observer might mistakenly conclude that the child understands verbal accounts of cause and effect, while the mismatched responses to the *how* and *when* questions illustrate that the child's comprehension has not reached that level of sophistication.

Bloom (1974) concludes that while the complete picture of how comprehension relates to production in child language development is as yet unavailable, the two processes depend on the same source of information, the language itself, but differ with regard to details of performance. Probably the way the processes of comprehension and production relate to one another varies for different elements of the language, in different situations and tasks, and over time in child development.

VARIABLES AND VARIANTS
IN LANGUAGE LEARNING

In this section we will examine a number of factors that have been held to play a role in language acquisition and to produce variation among groups and in individuals. We will briefly consider adult-child interaction, styles of language learning, and imitation.

Adult-Child Interaction

The question of how mothers talk to children is a natural outgrowth of attempts to find support for one or another theory of language learning. If mothers were found to talk no differently to their young children than to older children or adults, theories that emphasize an innate human ability to develop language would acquire some support. If, on the other hand, mothers were found to modify their speech addressed to young children in the direction of simplicity and repetition, theories that emphasize language as learned behavior would be supported. If, finally, mothers or other caretakers responsible for young children typically use special techniques to teach children particular words or structures, these findings would suggest that language is hard to learn without intensive assistance.

Although the controversy among these theories is not as important today as it once seemed, the study of adult-child interaction has, if anything, flourished. The study of adults' language to children has continued, partly because the findings leave some questions unanswered and partly because of the growing interest in the pragmatic considerations of social interaction as a source of language learning and the development of conversational skills in children.

By now it is well known that mothers typically use shorter, simpler, more redundant utterances when addressing young children as contrasted with their talk to other adults (Snow, 1972; Nelson, 1976). The purposes of these modifications are not entirely clear. Nelson (1976) asks: "Why do mothers talk that way? They might do so in order to make themselves understood; consciously to provide an optimal teaching model; or simply as a by-product of the kinds of communication engaged in by mother and child at this time." The several studies that have dealt with this question have not produced any clear-cut finding permitting a decisive choice among these alternative purposes, and Nelson concludes that any or all of them may be in effect at different times. DeVilliers and DeVilliers (1976), who present a comprehensive review of the studies on adult-child speech, find that social factors, pragmatic considerations, and the adult's perception of the child's cognitive and linguistic abilities interact to produce the modifications typical of adult speech to children.

In the context of the pragmatic approach to the study of child language, a somewhat different look at adult-child speech has emerged. In place of considering the effect of the adult's input on what the child learns about the language, the adult and child are viewed as members of a communication event. Communicative interaction not only provides linguistic data for the child to operate on, but even more significantly the earliest communicative interactions are seen as the very source of language learning. In this view, the child's role shifts from that of passive learner about the rules of language to active participant in the communication dyad (Nelson, 1976).

The origins of language in the earliest interactions of mother and infant are described by Bruner (1975), who asserts that the child's primitive language use is to promote shared attention and joint action between child and caretaker. The interactive, give-and-take routines that mothers and infants seem universally to engage in are viewed by Bruner as basic to the development of shared attention and joint reference. The game of *Look!* wherein mother looks at something while uttering that word or some other vocalization, involves the infant as young as four months in looking at the same object as she does. Later mother and infant establish joint routines in which roles can be reversed, which Bruner describes as the origins of discourse and of functional communication. The work of Bruner and others identifies the beginnings of language in the child with the earliest uses to which language can be put, and finds in adult-child interactions the building material for language, communication, and conversation (see Figure 1–3).

Individual Variation: Styles of Language Learning

A characteristic of most studies on child language in the 1960s was the search for universals. Investigators sought to identify those phenomena in early language development that could be regarded as true for all children learning all languages. Those studies that compared data on children from different language communities are particularly good examples of this mode (Slobin, 1971; Brown, 1973; Clark, 1973b). The goal was to isolate those factors of language acquisition that were independent of any particular language or any individual language-learning experience so that broad theories about language development could be established.

Inevitably the researchers noted individual variations in the data they examined. A general picture began to emerge of differing "styles" of children's coping with the language-learning tasks. Nelson

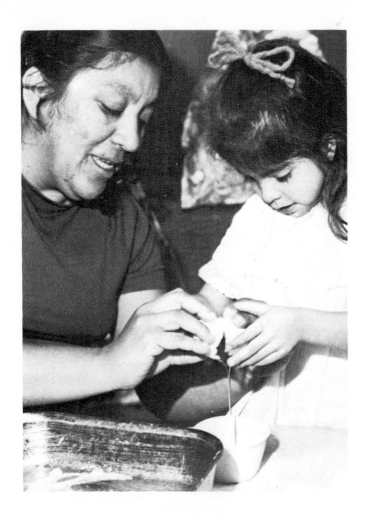

FIGURE 1–3. *Adult and child building a relationship through shared language experiences. (From Joanne Hendrick,* The Whole Child. *St. Louis, 1975, The C. V. Mosby Co., Los Niños Head Start.)*

(1975), who worked with spontaneous language data from children between one and two and a half years, looked at differences in vocabulary acquisition and early word combinations. She concluded that the children fell into two groups, which she called *referential speakers* and *expressive speakers.* The referential speakers began with a higher proportion of nouns, adjectives, and possessives than pronouns, while the expressive speakers began with a balance of nouns to pronouns. The early sentences of the expressive speakers were often strikingly devoid of specific lexical items, with examples like *Do it, I don't know,* and *What do you want?* Nelson concluded that young children adopt different cognitive strategies for language learning, typified in her data by learning names for objects and attributes (referential) or learning relational words and structures filled with "dummy words" like *it* and *that* which may be used to refer to many different items (expressive). Over time, the expressive children acquire more control over vocabulary and the referential children increase their use of pronouns and sentences. Nelson (1975, 1976) related these individual styles to two interdependent factors: the child's original perceptions of the uses to which language may be put, and the child's early language-learning experience.

Other investigators have noted a somewhat similar distinction between language-learning styles in young children (Dore, 1974; Bloom et al., 1975). Dore makes special mention of the relationship between the child's early style of language use and the mother's style, pointing out that in the case of the child in his study who emphasized word acquisition, the mother tended to initiate the verbal interaction, structure it around verbal routines, and frequently named objects for the child to repeat. By contrast, the mother of the child who had greater control over language use was more easily involved in activities initiated by the child and engaged in less direct language-instructional activity. These reports lead to a picture of interaction between the child's cognitive inclinations and the context of early language development producing at least two dominant types of approaches to the task of language learning in the earliest period. Although the incomplete data suggest that some aspects of this variation continue into later childhood (Nelson, 1975, states that referential children tend to have larger vocabularies), on most measures of language acquisition the two groups of children perform similarly. Little is known about how subtle differences in style of language learning and use that derive from individual variation are reflected in older children.

Imitation in Language Learning

Do children learn to talk by imitation? Some rather simple observations reveal that much of language learning cannot be accounted for by imitation alone. For one thing, the child's imitation of utterance he hears could fully explain his learning of only those utterances; imitation is insufficient to explain productivity, the characteristic of being able to produce and comprehend novel utterances. For another, the child's early utterances are likely to include some items produced by no one in his environment, like *I runned, All gone shoe,* and *More no.* These utterances appear to represent original creations on the child's part. The case of *I runned* is particularly interesting, exemplifying as it does not an imitation of a heard pattern, but an overgeneralization of a rule about how to construct verbs in past tense. Another example of a production that could not be an imitation occurred in the data from a three-year-old who consistently sang "Frere Jacques" as follows:

Are you sleeping,
Are you sleeping,
Brother John?
Brother John?
Morning bells is ringing . . .

The child's substitute of *is* for *are* reflects not imitation but a rule that the invariant form of the auxiliary is *is*.

In spite of these observations, it is well known that children do imitate, and various suggestions have been offered about the role of imitation in language learning. One suggestion has been that imitation is a factor in early communicative patterns (Rees, 1975). A number of investigators have shown a common tendency for animals and human infants to imitate the behavior of others in social interaction, and found imitative behavior to mothers' vocalizations especially characteristic of human infants. For children at the early stage of language learning, imitative responses tend to occur more often when the child does not understand what is said to him, suggesting that under these circumstances children tend to resort to imitation when they have no other way to participate in the dialogue. Imitation at least serves as acknowledgment that the respondent was attending to the speaker, and seems to be an early form of conversational response in interaction between young children (Keenan, 1974).

A second approach to the role of imitation in child language was taken by Bloom et al. (1974). While observing considerable variation in the tendencies of children between eighteen and twenty-five months to imitate at all, they noted that, for those children who did imitate, imitation had its use. The imitating children imitated linguistic segments they had developed some control over, but not those that were fully familiar or entirely new. Bloom et al. speculate that the imitation functioned to assist those children in processing difficult material. They concluded that while imitation is not required for language learning, for children who imitate, imitation promotes the acquisition of lexical items and semantic-syntactic relations. Imitation, therefore, while inadequate as a total explanation, appears to play a significant if variable role in the development of communicative and linguistic skills.

THE GROWTH OF COMMUNICATION SKILLS

The early preschool years have been the focus for the greatest portion of studies on child language development. The prelinguistic period of the first year of life has also come in for considerable study, while the language of school-age and older children has had far less attention. It is possible, however, to make some comments about the types of changes that extend beyond the early childhood period.

A broad functional model was outlined by Halliday (1975), who divides the continuum of language learning into three phases beginning at the end of the first year and ending with the adult system. Phase I, in the case of the child Halliday studied intensively, covered the period from about ten to eighteen months. Halliday describes Phase I as consisting of six functions which the child's utterances perform:

1. The *instrumental,* or the "I want" function. This is the function of language to get for the child objects and services that satisfy his needs.
2. The *regulatory,* or the "do as I tell you" function. This is the function of language to get someone to do something, and is different from the instrumental function in focusing on the agent rather than on the object.
3. The *interactional,* or the "me and you" function. In this function the child uses language to interact with the important others of his environment.
4. The *personal,* or the "here I come" function. This is language used to express the self and to intrude the speaker into the speech event.
5. The *heuristic,* or the "tell my why" function. This is language used to explore the environment and to learn, and is represented in its earliest appearances by the request for names of objects.
6. The *imaginative,* or the "let's pretend" function. This is using language to create a make-believe environment, ranging from sound-play to storytelling and eventually the uses of language as an art form.

It is noteworthy that the utterances of Phase I are not made up of words and word combinations, but of sounds, patterns, vocalizations, and wordlike units. Phase I is characterized by the possible functions and, within each, potential meanings. In the case of Halliday's subject, the instrumental function was exemplified by two different utterances with distinct meanings that could be consistently interpreted as *Give me that* and *Give me my toy bird.* The outstanding quality of Phase I is the functional character of the system and the child's utterances.

In Phase II, a transitional period, two functions emerge: the *pragmatic* and the *mathetic.* The pragmatic function is language-as-doing, the mathetic is language-as-learning. Halliday shows how these transitional functions grow out of the Phase I functions, but produce a system that is both more complex and more abstract. The child can now use language in two very different roles, the observer role (mathetic) and the intruder role (pragmatic). One way to identify utterances at this stage is in terms of anticipated response, mathetic utterances seeming to require no response while pragmatic utterances do. The dual system is compatible with observations that children at this stage seem on some occasions to be talking to no one in particular while on others to expect or even demand responses.

The mathetic function is the source of vocabulary, while the pragmatic function is the origin of syntax. In this respect the Phase II system is reminiscent of the types of individual style in approaching the language-learning task discussed by Nelson (1975) and others. During Phase II a seventh specific function, the *informative* or "I've got something to tell you" function, emerges. Halliday claims that this function is late in appearing, depending as it does on the child's experience with the earlier functions and the communicative process itself. For Halliday's subject, Phase II covered the period from eighteen months to the end of the second year.

Phase III begins with the third year and marks the beginning of the adult system. The two basic functions are the *ideational* and the *interpersonal;* a third function, the *textual,* serves the other two. The ideational function arises from the mathetic and may be described as language as a means of talking about the world and events; the interpersonal function arises from the pragmatic, and is language used as an instrument for participation. The textual function is the code, the words and sentences that speakers say and that writers write. The outstanding characteristic of Phase III is that the system of three functions allows adult language users to realize an infinite number of uses of language, in contrast to Phase I, when the child can express only six uses (the six functions of Phase I). The flexibility of the adult system comes from the fact that utterances in this phase are ideational and interpersonal and, of course, textual at the same time. "As soon as the utterance consists of words-in-structure, it has an ideational meaning—a content, in terms of the child's experience; and an interpersonal meaning—an interactional role in the speech situation." As Halliday sees it, having entered into Phase III, the child has mastered a system of "learning how to mean," and from this point on he can use his language to learn about his culture and his role in that culture. To put it another way, "language comes to occupy the central role in the processes of social learning."

In Halliday's terms, then, for older children language is central in the learning. He does not imply, however, that by the start of Phase III the child has learned all he can about the language itself. It is well known that children go on learning about vocabulary and structure of the language well into the school years and possibly beyond. Chomsky (1969), for example, has reported experimental findings showing that comprehension of sentences like *The doll is easy to see* and *John promised Bill to go* may not be mastered by some children until they are nine years old, while sentences like *Ask John what to feed the cat* are imperfectly comprehended by some ten-year-olds.

Learning how to understand and produce sentences in social interaction is not, of course, a matter of mastering words and sentence structures only. Language users must also know when and how to use given forms as appropriate to contextual requirements. Children must develop an awareness of which forms are polite and which are insulting, and a sensitivity to the circumstances that call for each. They must learn variations of how to talk to younger and older children as contrasted with talking to familiar and unfamiliar adults. The details of how children master these subtleties have only recently become the objects of intensive study.

Gleason (1973) points out that adults help children learn how to handle conversational interchange when, in the preschool period, they talk to children in such a manner as to supply the entire conversation. She gives the example of the father picking up his son at nursery school, saying "Where's your lunchbox? I bet it's inside." Gleason's records also show differences in young children's language styles when talking to adults and to other children. Children talking to their peers used more words like *yukk* and more expressive noises, more often sang or entered into dramatic play or pretense, and more often imitated one another's verbalization exactly than did these children when talking to adults. Children talking to younger children tended to switch from the child-to-child style into the parent-to-child style, uttering more warnings and admonitions. Along similar lines, Shatz and Gelman (1973) reported that four-year-old children in their study used shorter sentences and simpler constructions when addressing two-year-olds than when talking to adults. These examples reveal that young children show considerable skill at adapting their language to the needs of the listener and the requirements of the situation. Probably language learning for purposes of social interaction continues far later than the point where control over the structure of his language is achieved, for with increasing maturity the child enters into more and different social situations and takes on new roles requiring continued fine adjustment of the principles of discourse.

CONCLUDING OBSERVATIONS

The study of child language is one of endless fascination. As the review shows, each new development and technique in the science of language and speech is applied to the analysis of language in children, and as partial answers to old questions are being found new questions arise at an even greater pace. For professionals in the area of communication disorders, it is recognized that only the most complete understanding possible of the nature and growth of child language will suffice as basic information with which to approach clinical problems. Normal language development provides not only the base of reference against which to evaluate the communicative functioning of the clinical subject, but also guidelines for assessment and intervention. For example, we have learned that measures of vocabulary and syntax, while important, do not tell us everything we need to know about the individual's language. In the case of intervention, we take into consideration children's language-learning strategies and individual differences when planning therapy programs. Undoubtedly as new knowledge is gained, much of what we do today will be replaced by wiser principles and improved techniques.

REFERENCES

BATES, E., Pragmatics and sociolinguistics in child language. In D. Morehead and A. Morehead (Eds.), *Normal and Deficient Child Language.* Baltimore: University Park Press (1976).

BATES, E., BENIGNI, L., BRETHERTON, I., CAMAIONI, L., and VOLTERRA, V., From gesture to the first word: On cognitive and social prerequisites. In M. Lewis and L. Rosenblum (Eds.), *Interaction, Conversation, and the Development of Language.* New York: Wiley (1977).

BEVER, T., The cognitive basis for linguistic structures. In J. Hayes (Ed.), *Cognition and the Development of Language.* New York: Wiley (1970).

BIRDWHISTELL, R., *Kinesics and Context.* Philadelphia: University of Pennsylvania Press (1970).

BLOOM, L., *Language Development: Form and Function in Emerging Grammars.* Cambridge, Mass.: MIT Press (1970).

BLOOM, L., *One Word at a Time: The Use of Single-Word Utterances Before Syntax.* The Hague: Mouton (1973).

BLOOM, L., Talking, understanding, and thinking. In R. Schiefelbusch and L. Lloyd (Eds.), *Language Perspectives—Acquisition, Retardation, and Intervention.* Baltimore: University Park Press (1974).

BLOOM, L., HOOD, L., and LIGHTBOWN, P., Imitation in language development: If, when, and why. *Cognitive Psychology,* 6, 380–420 (1974).

BLOOM, L., LIGHTBOWN, P., and HOOD, L., Structure and variation in child language. *Monographs of the Society for Research in Child Development,* 40, 1–78 (1975).

BOWERMAN, M., Semantic factors in the acquisition of rules for word use and sentence construction. In D. Morehead and A. Morehead (Eds.), *Normal and Deficient Child Language.* Baltimore: University Park Press (1976a).

BOWERMAN, M., Words and sentences: Uniformity, individual variation, and shifts over time in patterns of acquisition. Paper presented to the Conference on Early Behavioral Assessment of the Communicative and Cognitive Abilities of the Developmentally Disabled, Orcas Island, Washington, May 3–6 (1976b).

BRAINE, M., The ontogeny of English phrase structure: The first phase. *Language,* 39, 1–13 (1963).

BRONOWSKI, J., and BELLUGI, U., Language, name, and concept. *Science,* 168, 669–673 (1970).

BROWN, R., *A First Language: The Early Stages.* Cambridge, Mass.: Harvard University Press (1973).

BROWN, R., The development of Wh-questions. *Journal of Verbal Learning and Verbal Behavior,* 7, 279–290 (1968).

BROWN, R., and FRASER, C., The acquisition of syntax. *Monographs of the Society for Research in Child Development,* 29, 43–79 (1964).

BRUNER, J., The ontogenesis of speech acts. *Journal of Child Language, 2,* 1–19 (1975).

CHAPMAN, R., and MILLER, J., Word order in early two and three word utterances: Does production precede comprehension? *Journal of Speech and Hearing Research,* 18, 355–371 (1975).

CHOMSKY, C., *The Acquisition of Syntax in Children from 5 to 10.* Cambridge, Mass.: MIT Press (1969).

CHOMSKY, N., *Aspects of the Theory of Syntax.* Cambridge, Mass.: MIT Press (1965).

CLARK, E., Non-linguistic strategies and the acquisition of word meanings. *Cognition, 2,* 161–182 (1973a).

CLARK, E., What's in a word? On the child's acquisition of semantics in his first language. In T. Moore (Ed.), *Cognitive Development and the Acquisition of Language.* New York: Academic Press (1973b).

COOPER, F., How is language conveyed by speech? In J. Kavanagh and I. Mattingly (Eds.), *Language by Ear and by Eye.* Cambridge, Mass.: MIT Press (1972).

CROMER, R., The development of language and cognition: The cognition hypothesis. In B. Foss (Ed.), *New Perspectives in Child Development.* Baltimore: Penguin Books (1974).

CRYSTAL, D., Linguistic mythology and the first year of life. *British Journal of Disorders of Communication,* 8, 29–36 (1973).

DeVILLIERS, J., and DeVILLIERS, P., Semantics and syntax in the first two years: The output of form and function of the input. Paper presented to the Conference on Early Behavioral Assessment of the Communicative and Cognitive Abilities of the Developmentally Disabled, Orcas Island, Washington, May 3–6 (1976).

DORE, J., A pragmatic description of early language development. *Journal of Psycholinguistic Research,* 3, 343–350 (1974).

DORE, J., Children's illocutionary acts. In R. Freedle (Ed.), *Discourse Relations: Comprehension and Production.* New York: Lawrence Erlbaum Associates (1976).

EIMAS, P., SIQUELAND, E., JUSCZYK, P., and VIGORITO, J., Speech perception in infants. *Science,* 167, 303–306 (1971).

ERVIN-TRIPP, S., The comprehension and production of requests by children. *Papers and Reports on Child Language Development.* Sixth Child Language Research Forum, Stanford, California (1974).

ERVIN-TRIPP, S., Wait for me, roller-skate. In C. Mitchell-Kernan and S. Ervin-Tripp (Eds.), *Child Discourse.* New York: Academic Press (1977).

FERGUSON, C., Learning to pronounce: The earliest stages of phonological development in the child. Paper presented to the Conference on Early Behavioral Assessment of the Communicative and Cognitive Abilities of the Developmentally Disabled, Orcas Island, Washington, May 3–6 (1976).

GARDNER, B., and GARDNER, R., Teaching sign language to a chimpanzee. *Science,* 165, 664–672 (1969).

GLEASON, J., Code switching in child language. In T. Moore (Ed.), *Cognitive Development and the Acquisition of Language.* New York: Academic Press (1973).

GREENFIELD, P., and SMITH, J., *Communication and the Beginnings of Language: The Development of Semantic Structures in One-Word Speech and Beyond.* New York: Academic Press (1976).

HALLIDAY, M., *Learning How to Mean: Explorations in the Development of Language.* London: Edward Arnold (1975).

INGRAM, D., Sensorimotor intelligence and language development. In A. Lock (Ed.), *Action, Gesture, and Symbol: The Emergence of Language.* New York: Academic Press (1976).

JAFFE, J., STERN, D., and PEERY J., "Conversational" coupling of gaze behavior in prelinguistic human development. *Journal of Psycholinguistic Research,* 2, 321–329 (1973).

KEENAN, E., Conversational competence in children. *Journal of Child Language,* 1, 163–183 (1974).

KLIMA, E., and BELLUGI, U., Syntactic regularities in the speech of children. In J. Lyons and R. Wales (Eds.), *Psycholinguistic Papers.* Edinburgh: University Press (1966).

LIEBERMAN, P., HARRIS, K., WOLFF, P., and RUSSELL, L., Newborn infant cry and nonhuman primate vocalization. *Journal of Speech and Hearing Research,* 4, 718–727 (1971).

McNEILL, D., *The Acquisition of Language.* New York: Harper & Row (1970).

MILLER, W., and ERVIN, S., The development of grammar in child language. In U. Bellugi and R. Brown (Eds.), The acquisition of language. *Monographs of the Society for Research in Child Development,* 29, 9–34 (1964).

NELSON, K., Early speech in its communicative context. Paper presented to the Conference on Early Behavioral Assessment of the Communicative and Cognitive Abilities of the Developmentally Disabled, Orcas Island, Washington, May, 3–6 (1976).

NELSON, K., The nominal shift in semantic-syntactic development. *Cognitive Psychology,* 7, 461–479 (1975).

OLLER, D., WIEMAN, L., DOYLE, W., and ROSS, C., Infant babbling and speech. *Journal of Child Language,* 3, 1–11 (1976).

PREMACK, D., A functional analysis of behavior. *Journal of the Experimental Analysis of Behavior,* 14, 107–125 (1970).

REES, N., Imitation and language development: Issues and clinical implications. *Journal of Speech and Hearing Disorders,* 40, 339–350 (1975).

SAROYAN, W., *The Human Comedy.* New York: Harcourt Brace Jovanovich, Inc. (1943).

SCHLESINGER, I., Relational concepts underlying language. In R. Schiefelbusch and L. Lloyd (Eds.), *Language Perspectives—Acquisition, Retardation, and Intervention.* Baltimore: University Park Press (1974).

SEARLE, J., *Speech Acts.* London: Cambridge University Press (1969).

SEBEOK, T., *Animal Communication.* Bloomington: Indiana University Press (1968).

SHATZ, M., and GELMAN, R., The development of communication skills: Modification in the speech of young children as a function of listener. *Monographs of the Society for Research in Child Development,* 38, 5 (1973).

SHIPLEY, E., SMITH, C., and GLEITMAN, L., A study in the acquisition of language: Free responses to command. *Language,* 45, 322–342 (1969).

SIEGEL, G., Vocal conditioning of infants. *Journal of Speech and Hearing Disorders,* 34, 3–19 (1969).

SINCLAIR, H., Sensorimotor action patterns as a condition for the acquisition of syntax. In R. Huxley and E. Ingram (Eds.), *Language Acquisition: Models and Methods.* New York: Academic Press (1971).

SINCLAIR-DeZWART, H., Language acquisition and cognitive development. In T. Moore (Ed.), *Cognitive Development and the Acquisition of Language.* New York: Academic Press (1973).

SLOBIN, D., Developmental psycholinguistics. In W. Dingwall (Ed.), *A Survey of Linguistic Science.* College Park: University of Maryland (1971).

SNOW, K., Mothers' speech to children learning language. *Child Development*, 43, 549–565 (1972).

SUGARMAN, S., Description of communicative development in the pre-language child. Unpublished master's thesis, Hampshire College, Amherst, Massachusetts (1973).

WERNER, H., and KAPLAN, B., *Symbol Formation.* New York: Wiley (1963).

signpost   Chapter 2 considers the way in which normal speech is produced. The reader needs to proceed only a short distance into the chapter to realize the amazing complexity of the motor act we call speech. The wonder is that anyone at all can generate the sounds of normal speech. Talking requires an extremely intricate coordination of three major functional subdivisions of the speech production mechanism, tens of body parts, more than a hundred muscles, and millions of nerve cells. Chapter 2 examines this complex motor act in several regards: the structures involved, the neuromuscular system's control of these structures, the goal-directed functions of certain groupings of structures, and the physiological coding scheme that man uses to make the nearly four dozen distinctive speech sounds of the English language. The emphasis is on the biophysical events of the speech act—that is, events occurring at the neural, muscular, structural, aeromechanical, and acoustical levels of the speech production process. This coverage of biophysical events provides the reader with a foundation of information to use in other chapters. More specifically, it establishes a framework for understanding later discussions of the causes and symptoms of many of the disorders of speech, and the evaluation and management procedures used to help individuals with impaired communication skills.

2

Thomas J. Hixon & James H. Abbs

normal
speech
production

INTRODUCTION

Speech is our most common mode of performing language and one of the aspects of our behavior that distinguishes us from other primates. Against almost any yardstick, normal speech is a remarkably useful, powerful, effective, and convenient form of communication. We produce speech with equipment we carry with us and that we can call into action at a moment's notice. Unlike other forms of language performance, speech does not require the use of our hands, thus leaving us free to do manual tasks while talking. Speech is a rapid means of communication and one that enables us to transmit large quantities of information in relatively short periods of time. It operates effectively in the dark, around corners, and through various obstacles. The sounds of speech carry information over substantial distances, and because they travel in all directions from the generator, they enable communication with many listeners simultaneously. We could go on and on extolling the virtues of speech and pointing out the integral role it plays in our lives. Certainly, the human capability to produce speech is at or near the top of the list of the most important performance skills we master.

This chapter presents an elementary description of normal speech production. Acquiring knowledge of this topic is an important first step toward understanding many communication problems. With regard to the topics of the present book, the chapter is, perhaps, most significant to an understanding of the speech disorders discussed in Chapters 7, 8, 9, 10, and 11.

There are many points of view from which an elementary description of normal speech can be derived. To the communication engineer, the best description of speech might consider it as a series of sound signals for transmission via telephone lines or radio waves. To the learning theorist, the preferred description might portray speech as both a stimulus and a response, depending upon antecedent conditions and reinforcement contingencies. To the psycholinguist, the most ideal description of speech might be one concerned with its sound patterns in relation to the meanings ascribed to them by language users. Each of these points of view, and many others we could note, has merit and is useful for a particular professional application. For the purposes of this book, normal speech production is best viewed as the biophysical execution of oral language. This view accounts for the fact that speech is generated by biological and physical actions of the human body and that its public existence is dependent upon the generation and transmission of sound waves in air. Importantly, the cause and/or symptoms of many speech disorders are easier to understand when they are examined in terms of biophysical phenomena.

The chapter sections to follow begin with a discussion of the structure of the speech production mechanism. Next is a consideration of how the talker controls his speech production machinery. This is followed by detailed descriptions of how each of the major subdivisions of the speech mechanism contributes to our speech generation ability. Finally, the chapter concludes with a discussion of the essential physiological actions involved in the speech production code.

STRUCTURE OF THE SPEECH PRODUCTION MECHANISM

One of the desirable things about using speech to communicate, as we noted, is that it is produced with equipment that is always at our disposal—namely, different parts of our bodies. Thus, a description of the structure of the speech production mechanism is essentially a description of certain parts of our bodies and how these parts are arranged to form a system that enables us to talk. A useful way to think of the speech production mechanism is that it is a relatively complex biophysical machine. Figure 2–1 presents an artist's rendition of the major elements of this machine. Views depict the speech mechanism at rest. The overall mechanism can be conceptualized as a group of interconnected air-filled tubes whose walls are formed by a variety of stationary and movable structures and fashioned mainly of bone, cartilage, and muscle. These structures are distributed within the upper body, including the trunk, neck, and head.

The machine we call the speech production mechanism is not a system used solely for the generation of speech. Rather, the "speech mechanism" is involved in a sharing relationship for both equipment and operating time with other body mechanisms. It makes use of all of the tubes and structures also considered to be part of the breathing mechanism. The upper portion of the speech mechanism also does a large amount of sharing with other mechanisms used for chewing,

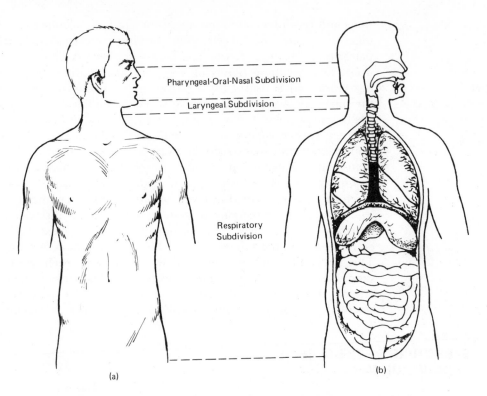

FIGURE 2–1. *An artist's rendition of the major elements of the speech production mechanism. The mechanism is depicted at rest. Panel (a) shows a surface view of the mechanism and panel (b) shows a cut-away view. Respiratory, laryngeal, and pharyngeal-oral-nasal subdivisions of the mechanism are indicated.*

tasting, swallowing, and smelling. There is, then, a great deal of traffic through various parts of the speech mechanism—including air, liquids, solid foods, smoke (unfortunately), and the sound waves of speech about to become public.

For the purposes of this chapter, it is useful to organize the structures of the speech mechanism into three major subdivisions: (1) *respiratory*, (2) *laryngeal*, and (3) *pharyngeal-oral-nasal*. Operating somewhat independently of one another, each of these subdivisions has goal-directed actions that it performs. These subdivisions are discussed in turn in the three succeeding subsections.

Respiratory Subdivision

Structures comprising the respiratory (breathing) subdivision of the speech mechanism are located within the body trunk. These structures form a complex air pump at one end of the speech mechanism.

This pump can be thought of as consisting of two major units, one inside the other. The innermost of these units is the *pulmonary system;* the outermost is the *chest wall* (see Figure 2–2).

The pulmonary system is a large, complex air container made up of two parts, the *lungs* (organs of breathing) and the *respiratory passages* (breathing airways). The lungs can be described as two large elastic sacs (somewhat like balloons) and the respiratory passages as a network of flexible, branching tubes that interconnect different parts of the two sacs. The sole opening to the air-containing pulmonary system is a semi-rigid tube, called the *trachea* or windpipe, located at the upper end.

The chest wall, the second and outermost unit of the respiratory pump, includes all structures within the body trunk except the pulmonary system (Hixon, Goldman, and Mead, 1973). It completely encases the pulmonary system and adheres to the outer surfaces of the lungs in much the same manner that two glass surfaces stick together when a film of water is between them. The chest wall provides a housing for the lungs in the form of a surrounding wall and a floor. The shape of the surrounding wall is determined by the barrel-like *rib cage* and various muscles that fill the spaces between the ribs and cover their inner and outer surfaces. The floor of the housing is made

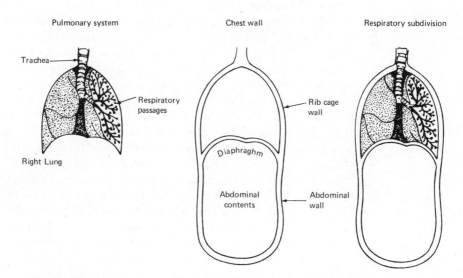

FIGURE 2–2. *Primary structures of the respiratory subdivision of the speech production mechanism. Shown are a mixed, cut-away schematic view of the pulmonary system, a schematic view of the chest wall, and a combined view of the two components as they are normally linked to one another.*

up of a group of structures termed collectively, the *diaphragm-abdomen*. This floor is extremely thick and has as its bulk the abdominal contents. The top of the floor is formed by the muscular *diaphragm* and connective tissue; the bottom is formed by the muscles of the *abdominal wall* (belly) and connective tissue.

Laryngeal Subdivision

The group of structures that forms the laryngeal subdivision is found near the front of the neck (see Figure 2–3a). This subdivision is referred to technically as the *larynx* and commonly as the "voice box." Its location is often given away, especially in adult males, by a prominent bulge at the surface of the neck—the Adam's apple. You can almost (but not quite) encircle more than half your larynx with your thumb and first few fingers of one hand. Structures in the laryngeal area form a moderately rigid tube-valve assembly between the top of the trachea and the *pharynx* (throat). This assembly consists of an intricately fashioned superstructure of bone, cartilage, and connective tissue, and a system of muscles.

The important components of the superstructure of the larynx are illustrated in Figure 2–3b and 2–3c. Together, these components give shape to the walls of the larynx. From bottom to top, the major bone and cartilage elements of the larynx include: (1) the ring-shaped *cricoid cartilage,* which attaches to the top of the trachea—it forms the lower circular wall of the larynx; (2) the pyramid-shaped *arytenoid cartilages,* which perch, one on each side, atop the back of the cricoid cartilage and are connected to it via joints—they form the upper back part of the larynx; (3) the shieldlike *thyroid cartilage,* whose legs straddle the cricoid cartilage and are connected to its sides via joints—it forms most of the sides and front of the larynx; (4) the shoehorn-shaped *epiglottis,* which projects upward from its attachment on the inside of the front of the thyroid cartilage—it forms much of the front wall of the larynx; and, (5) the horseshoe-shaped *hyoid bone,* whose limbs are connected to a pair of horns from the thyroid cartilage—it forms the topmost portion of the front and side walls of the larynx. Sheets and bands of elastic connective tissue serve to attach the bone-cartilage elements of the laryngeal superstructure to one another and to adjacent structures. The laryngeal housing is doubly supported: first, from below through its cricoid-cartilage base, and second, from above through the hyoid bone from which the larynx "hangs" like a net on a basketball hoop.

The muscles of the larynx are partially supported by the laryngeal superstructure and in effect "fill in" the skeletal framework of

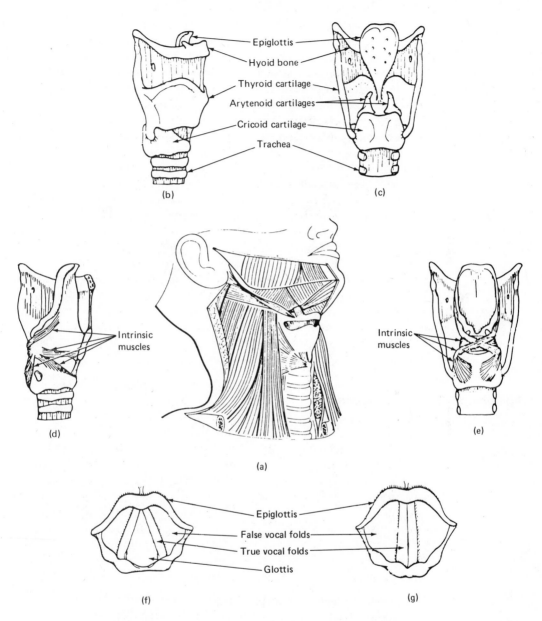

Epiglottis
Hyoid bone
Thyroid cartilage
Arytenoid cartilages
Cricoid cartilage
Trachea

(b)

(c)

Intrinsic muscles

Intrinsic muscles

(d)

(e)

(a)

Epiglottis
False vocal folds
True vocal folds
Glottis

(f)

(g)

FIGURE 2–3. *Principle structures of the laryngeal subdivision of the speech production mechanism. Panel (a) shows the relative positioning of the larynx within the front of the neck. Panels (b) and (c) show right-side and rear-side views of the laryngeal superstructure, respectively. Panels (d) and (e) reveal most of the intrinsic muscles of the larynx (those having both ends inside the housing) in cut-away right-side and rear-side views, respectively. Panels (f) and (g) show views down the larynx from the top, the former with the airway valve open and the latter with the valve closed. See text for further discussion.*

the larynx (see Figures 2–3a, 2–3d, and 2–3e). These muscles run between different bone-cartilage elements of the larynx and to them from other structures located above and below the larynx. Some of the most important muscular tissue forms the bulk of two large flexible shelves, one on each side along the inner walls of the laryngeal tube. Each shelf has a tough, elastic, inner edge formed by a ligament. These shelves — muscular tissue and ligaments together — are termed the *true vocal folds* (sometimes also called cords, bands, or lips). As illustrated in Figure 2–3f, the two folds attach side by side at the front on the inner surface of the thyroid cartilage; at the back of the larynx, each fold attaches to the arytenoid cartilage on its own side. When the larynx is at rest, a triangularly shaped opening is found in the laryngeal tube between the two vocal folds. This opening is termed the *glottis* (see Figure 2–3f). A second set of two flexible shelves is located above the true vocal folds. These shelves are the *false vocal folds*. Each false fold is made up of thick layers of mucous membrane and has a ligament running along its inner edge. A gentle "milking" action of the mucous layers within the false vocal folds provides "lubrication" for the surfaces of the true vocal folds located below. This lubrication is important because, as we will learn later, the true vocal folds frequently collide or rub against one another, sometimes at very high speeds.

Pharyngeal-Oral-Nasal Subdivision

Structures of the pharyngeal-oral-nasal (throat-mouth-nose) subdivision of the speech mechanism are located within the neck and head (see Figures 2–4a and 2–4c). These structures form the walls of an air-filled assembly of tubes and valves. Overall the pharyngeal-oral-nasal system, also referred to as the *upper airway,* is somewhat "F"-shaped (see Figure 2–4b). Its lower end, the pharynx, extends upward from the glottis as a single tube. Its two branches, the oral and nasal segments, extend forward from the pharynx to the outside of the body at the lips and the nostrils, respectively. Each segment of the subdivision's F-shaped assembly deserves further attention.

Pharyngeal Segment. The pharyngeal segment of the upper airway is best described as a flexible muscular tube extending from the larynx to the base of the skull. The back and side walls of the pharynx are formed by connective tissue and muscle. One group of muscles runs from the back toward the front of the tube and attaches to other structures. Still other muscles originate from locations outside the pharynx and attach to its side and back walls. Structures forming the front boundary of the pharynx include the epiglottis, the tongue, and

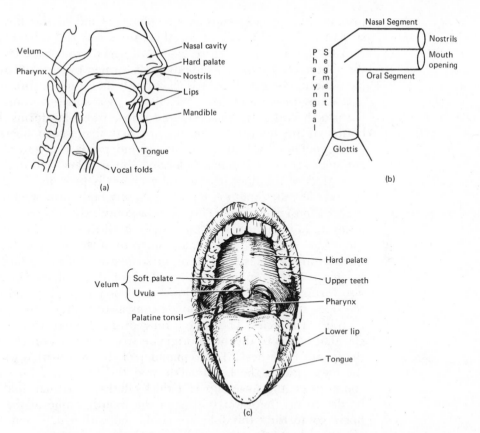

FIGURE 2–4. *Major structures of the pharyngeal-oral-nasal (upper airway) subdivision. Panel (a) depicts the subdivision as viewed from a cut-away right side perspective. Panel (b) shows a simplified F-shaped mechanical analog of the upper airway. In panel (c) the subdivision is seen through the wide-open mouth.*

the *velum* (the fleshy *soft palate* and its tablike ending, the *uvula*), in that order, moving outward along the airway. The epiglottis and tongue are considered elsewhere in this chapter.

The velum can be likened to a thick, hingelike flap. When relaxed, the velum hangs downward from the back of the roof of the mouth. It can be seen easily when the mouth is opened wide. The velum occupies a strategic position within the upper airway because it resides at the juncture where the pharyngeal segment divides into oral and nasal segments. It is composed of connective tissue and a group of muscles that run in several directions within it. Most of the muscles originate from locations above and below the structure and then join together in their attachments to the velum to form its bulk.

Oral Segment. The oral segment of the upper airway is a highly adjustable tube having ends in the pharynx and at the lips. Various structures form the walls of this tube, some soft and others hard. The roof of the tube (see Figure 2–4c) is formed from back to front, by the velum, the *hard palate* (a bony shelf formed by the skull and upper jaw), the upper *gums* (soft tissues around the upper teeth), the upper *teeth* (bony projections from the upper jaw), and the upper *lip*. The last is a thick, fleshy, muscular fold whose free edge forms the upper border of the mouth. The lip is composed of muscular fibers that are partly contained within the structure and partly run into it at different angles from facial muscles located above, below, and to the sides.

Most of the floor of the oral segment is provided by the *tongue*. Structurally, the tongue is a massive, fleshy body fashioned almost entirely of muscular tissue. This tissue is complexly arranged; fibers run in several directions within the tongue itself as well as into it from locations above, below, behind, and in front of the major mass. The base of the tongue is fastened to other structures but its surface has free margins on the top and all sides. Part of the oral segment's floor is also formed by the *mandible* (lower jaw), which borders the tongue at the sides and front. The mandible consists of a large, strong bone and a group of muscles. The bone is hinged to the sides of the skull. Muscles that attach to this bone originate from locations on the skull and the front of the neck. The remainder of the oral floor is provided by the lower gums, the lower teeth, and the lower lip. Like its upper counterpart, the lower lip is a thick, fleshy, muscular fold. Its free border forms the lower border of the mouth. Some of the muscular fibers comprizing this fold are contained within it; others run to it from facial muscles above, below, and to the sides.

Finally, the side walls of the oral segment are formed by the *cheeks* and portions of the upper and lower jaws, gums, teeth, and lips. The cheeks are the fleshy sides of the face below the eyes and include tissue from some muscles of the mandible and the face.

Nasal Segment.   The nasal segment of the pharyngeal-oral-nasal subdivision is a "double-barreled" passage extending from the top of the pharynx forward to the nostrils, the external openings to the nose. Each barrel is a complex, narrow tortuous tube, the roof of which is formed by skull bone and the floor of which is formed by the bones of the hard palate. Side walls of the two passages contain complex shell-like formations, called *conchae,* which are rich with nooks and crannies. The partition that divides the two passages, the *nasal septum,* is made of bone in its rear section and cartilage more toward its front. Several small muscles run around and attach to parts of the rim of each nostril.

CONTROL OF
THE SPEECH PRODUCTION MECHANISM

Now that we are familiar with the structure of the speech mechanism and before we consider the functions of its subdivisions, we need to become familiar with the manner in which the speech mechanism is controlled during voluntary acts.

When we perform any voluntary act, like moving our eyes to read the sentences printed here, or turning the pages of this book, we depend on neuromuscular events to execute our behavior. Voluntary acts of the speech mechanism are no exception. Such acts require that we *will* them, *plan* them with regard to time and space, *program* them with respect to the sequence in which their components occur, *initiate* them through nervous system commands to muscles that will power them, and *stay informed* concerning their performance through feedback (Darley, Aronson, and Brown, 1975). To meet these requirements for even the simplest of voluntary behaviors of the speech mechanism, we must call upon neuromuscular events that are staggering in their number and complexity. In fact, the only man-made device that can perform control tasks with anywhere near the capability of our own neuromuscular control system is the most complex of electronic computers, and even it runs a far distant second.

Our present concern is with the major components of the neuromuscular control system for voluntary behaviors of the speech mechanism and the process whereby this system initiates actions and stays informed concerning their execution. The willing, planning, and programming aspects of such actions are discussed elsewhere in this book (see Chapters 1, 4, and 6). Figure 2–5 is a schematic illustration of the speech mechanism control system. Included within this system are three major components: (1) the *nervous system,* (2) the *muscular effector system,* and (3) the *sensory receptor system.*

The nervous system is the heart of neuromuscular control. It has two structural divisions: the *central nervous system* and the *peripheral nervous system.* The central nervous system consists of the *brain,* a mass of neural tissue within the skull, and the *spinal cord,* a long appendage of the brain that extends downward through the backbone. The peripheral nervous system consists of the *cranial nerves* and the *spinal nerves.* Nerves are cablelike appendages of neural tissue that radiate outward from the central nervous system to different parts of the head, neck, torso, and extremities. Overall, the central and peripheral divisions of the nervous system contain millions and millions of microscopic cells called *neurons.* These are highly excitable and electrically conductive

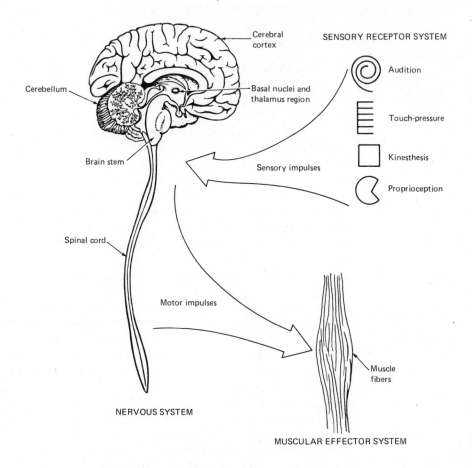

FIGURE 2–5. *Schematic illustration of the speech mechanism control system. Major components of the system include the nervous system, the muscular effector system, and the sensory receptor system. See text for detailed discussion.*

cells that are organized into distinct clusters and interconnecting chains that bind the different portions of the nervous system together into a complex information exchange network (Manter and Gatz, 1961; Gardner, 1968). Most important, for our concern, are the portions of this network that generate and transmit *motor impulses* destined for the muscles of the speech mechanism and the portions that transmit *sensory impulses* coming from receptors within the speech mechanism.

54

Voluntary actions of the speech mechanism have their beginnings in electrical impulses generated by neurons in *motor projection areas* within the *cerebral cortex* (the outer bark of the brain's uppermost convoluted hemispheres). These impulses pass along both *direct* and *indirect* routes that take them toward their destinations, muscles. The direct route carries impulses in neurons with long conducting fibers that lead directly either to the *brain stem* (the stalklike appendage that forms a pedestal between the hemispheres and is continuous with the spinal cord) or to the spinal cord. Impulses traveling the indirect route pass along neurons with relatively short conducting fibers and go through several relays in chains of neurons. These chains course deep within the hemispheres through an important cell body collection, the *basal nuclei,* and then pass on to the brain stem and spinal cord. Taken together, the direct and indirect routes from the cortex to the brain stem and spinal cord are referred to as the *upper motor neuron system.*

From the time electrical impulses are initiated in motor projection areas of the cerebral cortex until the time they exit the central nervous system in route to muscles, their form can be greatly influenced by another portion of the brain called the *cerebellum.* This structure consists of two small convoluted hemispheres of neural tissue positioned behind and astride the brain stem and connected to it. The cerebellum does not itself initiate motor commands, but rather sends impulses to modify the form of commands at the cortex, basal nuclei, brain stem, and spinal cord. We shall return to a discussion of the cerebellum later. For now, it is sufficient to know that the cerebellum receives information concerning the "intention" of the motor commands initiated at the cerebral cortex.

All motor commands reaching the brain stem and spinal cord are relayed to neurons, which transmit them from these two structures directly to the muscles for which they are intended. These last neurons within the motor system are called *lower motor neurons* and the collective system they form is termed the *lower motor neuron system.* Because all normal muscle actions are brought about by motor commands reaching the muscles by way of the lower motor neuron system, the system is also referred to as the *final common pathway* of the motor system. Most of the neural tissue of the lower motor neuron system is contained within the trunks of the cranial nerves and the spinal nerves which interconnect the central nervous system and different parts of the speech mechanism. The link to the muscular effector system, our concern for now, is through the six cranial nerves (V, VII, IX, X, XI, XII) that interconnect the brain stem and the muscles of the larynx and upper airway subdivisions, and through the nineteen spinal nerves (from segments 2 to 7 within the neck, 1 to 12 within the chest, and 1 within the lower back) that interconnect the spinal cord and the muscles of the respiratory subdivision. Each of the many neurons within the lower motor neuron system branches a great many times at the end of its conducting fiber and forms junctions with as many muscle fibers as it has branches. The combination of a motor neuron and the muscle fibers it serves is called a *motor unit.*

The muscular effector system, the second major component of our control system, is the mechanical power source for actions of the speech mechanism. More than one hundred *muscles* may figure into different voluntary actions of the speech mechanism. Each of these muscles consists of a large bundle of tiny fibers that *contract* (shorten) in groups in accordance with the motor units activated. Each contracting fiber acts like a tiny piston and produces a *pulling* force. The combined piston actions of all the fibers in a given muscle are responsible for the overall force generated by that muscle. If a single lower motor neuron is activated, a single *muscle twitch* occurs as a consequence of the contractions of the muscle fibers that neuron serves. When a large number of lower motor neurons are active, many individual twitches, overlapping one another, combine to form a smooth and controlled muscle pull. One way we control the pull of any muscle is by the *number* of lower neurons activated at any moment—that is, the greater the number, the greater the muscle force generated. Another way we control muscle pull is by the *rate* at which we activate individual lower motor neurons. That is, while a single muscle twitch creates a single transient pull, repeated muscle twitches produce a total muscle force that is greater than for individual twitches. When a muscle is contracted maximally, it is presumed that all motor units of that muscle are being activated at their maximal rate. Because the nervous system has enormous numbers of neurons that can be activated in near infinite patterns, we are endowed with a great degree of command flexibility in terms of the patterns of activity we can achieve with the muscular effector system.

We do not send motor command impulses "blindly" through the nervous system to the muscular effector system to generate the movements and positions desired of the speech mechanism. Rather, to insure that appropriate muscle contractions are being carried out and that our intended actions are being achieved, we take advantage of information we have available about the mechanical and acoustical states of events happening within the speech mechanism (Putnam and Ringel, 1979). Such information comes from the *sensory receptor system,* the third of the three major components of our control system. This system provides us with a wide variety of data about *touch-pressure* (sensitivity to mechanical contacts), *kinesthesis* (sensitivity to the rate and direction of body part movement and body part position), *proprioception* (sensitivity to the tension, length, and velocity of length change in muscles), and *audition* (sensitivity to acoustical events).

Sensory information from the speech mechanism has its beginnings in various sensory end-organs that transduce (change the form of energy) physical events into coded electrical impulses. These impulses pass along neurons whose conducting processes are contained within the sensory portions of nineteen spinal nerves (from the same segments discussed earlier for the motor side) and five to seven cranial nerves (V, VIII, IX, X, XI, and possibly VII and XII). Information traveling the spinal nerve routes comes from touch-pressure, kinesthetic, and proprioceptive sensors located within the respiratory subdivision, while information traveling the cranial nerve routes comes from similar sensors within the laryngeal and upper airway subdivisions as well as from the hearing mechanism (see Chapter 3).

Upon reaching the central nervous system, sensory impulses are distributed through a complex of neuron relays that provide information to the spinal cord, brain stem, cerebellum, *thalamus* (an important cell body collection deep within the cerebral hemispheres), and *sensory projection areas* within the cerebral cortex. Only those sensory impulses that convey information to the cerebral cortex are consciously perceived. All other sensory impulses carry information that is below the conscious awareness of the speaker.

Much of the sensory information entering the central nervous system becomes directly accessible to the upper motor neuron system for possible use in modifying its relayed commands. Even more important is the sensory information directed to the cerebellum. Recall that the cerebellum receives information concerning the "intention" of the motor commands initiated at the cerebral cortex. Using this information and the information it gains concerning the "performance" of the different parts of the speech mechanism, the cerebellum is believed to function as an *error controller,* which makes appropriate corrections when it detects that performance does not match intention (Guyton, 1971). The regulatory task performed by the cerebellum is substantial and helps to guide the nervous system in achieving the right force, speed, range, timing, and direction of movements called for by the speech mechanism.

We have made some general statements about the contribution of sensory information to speech mechanism control. It should be recognized, however, that the role of sensory information in control is only partially understood. We do know that many of our everyday speech behaviors rely heavily on some form of sensory information for their execution. For example, take a pencil and hold it between your teeth while you read the next few sentences aloud. As you listen to your speech notice that there is no real loss of your ability to communicate. Even a nonsense word like *pog* will be easily recognized. For your message to survive this mechanical intrusion to your speech mechanism, almost all of the movements and positions of your pharynx, tongue, and lips must be different than usual. That is, by fixing the mandible in one position, as a pipe smoker does, many muscles of the upper airway system must be activated differently. If your experience is like that of most speakers, you will notice that you did not have to think consciously about changing your upper airway behavior to compensate for the pencil's intrusion. Nevertheless, the nervous system somehow had to have been informed of the change in mandible positioning. Otherwise, other upper airway movements and positions would not have been adjusted. A common interpretation of what you experienced in this reorganization of your speech production patterns is that the nervous system monitors the actions of the pharynx, tongue, mandible, and lips, and based upon that information is able to make the necessary adjustments without your conscious intervention. And, because normal speakers do not have to learn to make these adjustments, it has been further suggested that these correction processes are a normal aspect of speech mechanism control (MacNeilage, 1970; Hughes and Abbs, 1976).

The centers of the central nervous system where these compensations originate and the processes involved in them remain somewhat of a mystery (Netsell, Kent, and Abbs, 1978). More than a hint to the solution of some of this mystery may lie in the observation that the areas of the central nervous system that are involved in controlling the speech mechanism are connected with almost equal density to both incoming sensory pathways and outgoing motor command pathways. As the many finely controlled gestures of speech are discussed in the subsequent sections of this chapter, the apparent need for sensory monitoring during speech should become increasingly obvious.

FUNCTION OF
THE SPEECH PRODUCTION MECHANISM

To this juncture we have examined the basic architecture of the speech mechanism and considered how it is controlled during the speech production act. We now discuss the function of the speech mechanism, beginning with its respiratory subdivision and proceeding to the laryngeal and pharyngeal-oral-nasal complexes.

Respiratory Subdivision

The respiratory subdivision, as described earlier, is an air pump located at one end of the speech mechanism. This subdivision's potential as a pump lies in its capacity to act as a reciprocating (to and fro) bellows. Two types of forces enable this bellows to move: inherent forces that are always there and volitional forces that can be supplied when and in the amount desired (Hixon, Mead, and Goldman, 1976). Each type of force warrants brief consideration.

Inherent forces arise from the elasticlike properties of the pump's different parts. These properties cause each of the parts, and the pump as a whole, to behave in manners analogous to coil springs. You can experience these forces for the pump as a whole by taking in a full breath and then relaxing, and by forcing out as much air as possible and then relaxing. In each case, the respiratory pump recoils back toward its resting position; first, like a stretched spring when released and second, like a compressed spring when released. The resting position of the pump, then, is analogous to the resting length of a coil spring and, like such a spring, the further the pump is deformed from its resting position, whether stretched or compressed, the greater the inherent recoil force it generates in attempting to return to rest.

Volitional forces, the second type of force capability of the pump, are vested in the more than two dozen muscles that are a part of the respiratory subdivision's housing. Together with inherent forces, muscular forces serve to power a wide variety of different motions of the wall and floor of the housing. Actions of certain muscles result in increases in the circumference of the wall of the respiratory subdivision, while actions of other muscles bring about decreases in the same wall's circumference. Additional muscles act to cause the floor of the housing to lower and still others cause it to rise. Different combinations of muscular forces applied to the wall and floor of the subdivision result in changes in the size and/or shape of the chest wall and correspondingly, in changes in the size and/or shape of the lungs. To appreciate the range of size possibilities, try to take in and then force out as much air as possible. To appreciate the range of shape possibilities, try to move your abdominal wall out and your rib cage wall in as far as possible and then do the converse. Clearly, the chest wall is capable of an extensive variety of size and shape changes.

The main function of the respiratory bellows is resting breathing. Resting breathing is achieved through alternate increases and decreases in the *volume* (that is, size) of the respiratory bellows. When the volume of the bellows is expanded, air in the lungs is expanded, its pressure is lowered relative to that outside the bellows, and air is sucked into the lungs—we *inspire.* Conversely, volume decreases compress the same air, raise its pressure above that outside the body, and drive air out of the lungs—we *expire.* The inspiration-expiration cycle is repeated twelve or more times each minute in most resting adults and involves about equally long inspirations and expirations. About half a quart of air is exchanged with each breath in and out, while the pressure in the lungs swings back and forth between roughly −1 cm H_2O and +1 cm H_2O, respectively. The inspiratory phase of resting breathing is *active,* in that volitional forces are used to enlarge the respiratory bellows from its resting size. These forces result in circumferential expansion of the subdivision's wall and downward motion of its floor. The expiratory side of the cycle is *passive.* During this phase of resting breathing, the inherent springlike recoil of the subdivision causes the bellows to return to its resting position; no expiratory muscles contribute force to the return. Control of the respiratory bellows is entirely automatic throughout the resting breathing cycle and is something of which most of us are usually unaware.

During speech production, the respiratory bellows takes on a dual role with regard to function: It must continue to adequately ventilate the body yet operate simultaneously as the central power supply for the generation of sounds. The latter is accomplished by using the bellows to provide pressures and flows to act upon and interact with various structures within the laryngeal and pharyngeal-oral-nasal subdivisions. Speech production demands quite different behaviors of the respiratory bellows than those demanded during resting breathing alone. Although we make speech sounds only during expiration, it is necessary to alter the entire breathing cycle to fulfill the needs for speech. Alterations must be made in timing, volume changes, forces, and muscular control (Hixon, 1973).

When the timing characteristics of resting breathing versus speech breathing are compared, it is apparent that we breathe less often during speech and at less regular intervals. Furthermore, we typically use much shorter inspirations and much longer expirations during ongoing conversation than when breathing at rest (see Figure 2–6). Collectively, these adjustments in rate and rhythm enable us to talk in a seemingly continuous fashion, halted occasionally by brief, relatively inconspicuous breaks for breathing refills.

We can speak while at any respiratory volume. Most of the time, however, we make adjustments to speak while at greater lung volumes than those through which we do our resting breathing (Hixon et al., 1973). The typical speaker draws in about twice as deep a breath when refilling his bellows during ongoing conversational speech as he does during resting breathing (see Figure 2–6). Even deeper breaths are drawn when a speaker intends to talk louder than normal during the

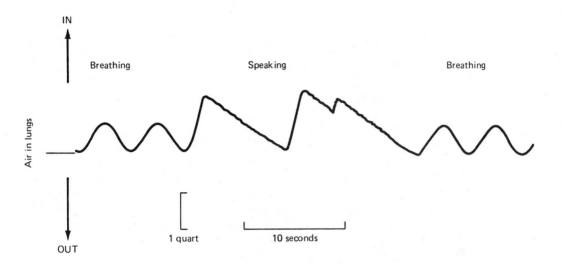

FIGURE 2–6. *Respiratory volume (size) changes characteristic of resting breathing and conversational speech. Volume increases upward and decreases downward on the graph. Utterances occur during the three gently sloping expiratory excursions near the middle of the graph. Note that shorter inspirations and longer expirations are used during speech than during breathing. Note also that speech occurs at greater lung volumes than breathing does.*

next expiration. By breathing somewhat deeper than normal for all our speech, we accomplish two things. First, we can produce long stretches of speech without having to stop for an inspiratory refill. Second, we can take advantage of the greater expiratory recoil force available at higher lung volumes to help drive the respiratory bellows as we talk. The volumes of air exchanged during inspiratory and expiratory efforts in speech are not consistently equal as they usually are in resting breathing. Resting breathing involves a gentle to and fro alternation of lung volume that is dictated by the body's ventilatory demands. Speech, by contrast, involves changes in lung volume that are a slave to the linguistic dictates of the moment, including such things as when a pause is called for or how long an utterance needs to be (Bless and Miller, 1972).

Lung pressures are quite different for speech than the simple -1 cm H_2O to $+1$ cm H_2O pressure swings that characterize resting breathing. Greater subatmospheric pressure is generated during the inspiratory phase to bring about the quicker and deeper inspiratory refills that speech requires. For the expiratory or "speech side" of the breathing cycle the pressure must be raised substantially above its highest resting breathing value in order to be sufficient for normal speech sound production. As portrayed in Figure 2–7, the pressure in our lungs usually hovers around 7·to 8 cm H_2O when we speak in a conversational fashion. Speech that is softer or louder than this requires that the pressure be raised or lowered from this value accordingly. We use a relatively steady background pressure during conversational speech and for activities that involve nearly equal emphasis on each syllable, such as counting or reciting the alphabet aloud (Draper, Ladefoged, and Whitteridge, 1959). Small but lawful fluctuations in pressure do occur from our background pressure. Some of these fluctuations are rather gradual, such as the gentle decrease in pressure at the end of a declarative sentence when the voice trails off to nothing. Others are more rapid than this, especially when we make certain speech segments more prominent (that is, we *stress* them). To achieve such effects, we purposefully increase the pressure in our lungs slightly and quickly to more or less "punch" one segment more than another (Netsell, 1973).

The way in which the chest wall muscles control the respiratory pump is quite different for speech than for our usual breathing. Dur-

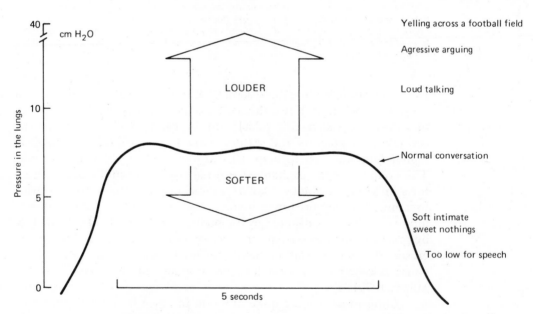

FIGURE 2–7. *Pressure in the lungs during conversational speech production. Zero on the vertical axis is barometric pressure. Pressure is expressed in centimeters of water (cm H_2O). The tracing shown exemplifies pressure during a declarative sentence. Softer speech requires less pressure and louder speech requires more pressure than that indicated by the tracing. Phrases at the right side of the graph indicate roughly the pressure levels that are typical of some familiar speech activities.*

ing the inspiratory phase of speech breathing, more muscular force than usual is needed to inspire rapidly and substantially. Each time we breathe in during conversational speech we interrupt our ongoing communication. To minimize the time spent for such interruptions we keep our chest wall in a special shape that increases the speed with which we can inspire during conversation (Hixon et al., 1976). This shape involves a slight tucking in of the abdomen and a slight elevation of the rib cage (that is, we pull in our waist and stick out our chest slightly). The importance of this shape is that it forces the diaphragm —our major inspiratory muscle—into a highly domed position where its action results in the development of great amounts of inspiratory force very rapidly.

Recall that resting expiration is passive; it results from our springlike recoil alone. This recoil usually provides less pressure than we need to produce speech so that we must supplement our natural recoil with muscular effort in order to speak normally. Our muscular action in this circumstance is analogous to forcing the two ends of a stretched spring together or squeezing the air out of an inflated balloon (Mead, Bouhuys, and Proctor, 1968). How much we supplement depends mostly upon how high the pressure in the lungs must be for the speech we want to produce. Stated simply, the amount of muscular force added must be equal to the difference between the force available from passive recoil and the total force needed. The situation is like that with a sealed, inflated balloon with an internal pressure from its own recoil, but which we can raise more and more by squeezing the balloon harder and harder. Because air comes out of us as we speak, our lung volume decreases and our springlike recoil decreases. To be able to keep the pressure in our lungs steady and at some desired level while our springlike recoil is decreasing, we must gradually increase our muscular effort. This action is analogous to squeezing a balloon harder and harder as it deflates in order to keep its internal pressure at one level. Translating all of our discussion into a "squeezing" action that the chest wall muscles must perform during speech, we can state the following: The louder we wish to speak, the harder we must squeeze ourselves; the smaller we get while squeezing ourselves, the harder still we must squeeze in order to maintain the loudness of speech; and, we must provide the abrupt increases in lung pressure that we need for events like emphasis by quickly squeezing ourselves an additional small amount (Ladefoged, 1968).

In summary, we have seen that the respiratory subdivision performs speech-specific behaviors that differ markedly from those involved in resting ventilation. We have at our disposal a finely regulated power supply that serves to ventilate us and at the same time provides us with a motive force for the generation of speech. The contribution of the respiratory pump is to generate and control the background pressures and flows required for the speech production act. Next, we see how these pressures and flows are modulated and used by the laryngeal subdivision to produce speech sounds.

Laryngeal Subdivision

The muscles of the larynx can put its tube-valve assembly through a number of different adjustments. These include (1) raising or lowering its position within the neck, (2) altering the area and/or shape of the glottis, (3) compressing the true vocal folds (squeezing them together) with varying force, especially in their back one-third, (4) lengthening or shortening the true vocal folds, and (5) increasing or decreasing the tension of the true vocal folds.

The primary importance of the larynx to primates is its function as an adjustable mechanical barrier between the trachea and the pharynx (Negus, 1949). This barrier, mainly in the form of the vocal folds, can be used to close off the airway to prevent unwanted matter from entering the lungs. And, when we need to build up high pressures internally for activities like heavy lifting and different forms of expulsion, the same barrier can be used as a valve to stop the exit of air from the lungs (see Figure 2–3g). In resting breathing, our larynx must offer little hindrance to the movement of air to and from the lungs. This is achieved when the glottis is adjusted to a fairly wide-open position (see Figure 2–3f). A wide-open glottis is also used for the inspiratory refills scattered throughout our conversational speech. It is the actions of the larynx during the speech side of the breathing cycle, however, that are of greater interest here. Adjustments of the larynx during speech are of four types, three of which result in the generation of sound at the larynx. The sounds produced in the latter three types of adjustments result from complex vocal fold actions that disturb the air passing outward through the tube-valve assembly. These disturbances create audible sound waves that, in turn, excite the air contained within the pharyngeal-oral-nasal complex (Broad, 1973).

In the first valving adjustment, the glottis is continuously open and no audible sound is generated at the larynx. The vocal folds are widely separated in this adjustment so that the airstream is permitted relatively free passage through the larynx and into the upper airway. The speech segments produced during this adjustment rely on sound being created elsewhere than in the larynx. The job of the larynx under such circumstances is simply to "stay out of the way" so that the expiratory flow of air may have its full effect in parts of the speech mechanism above the larynx.

A second form of laryngeal valving in speech involves a more constricted airway. If the glottis is narrowed so that the passageway through the larynx is appreciably constricted during expiration, air coursing through the larynx begins to tumble on itself and to flow in counter-currents near the narrowing. This turbulent behavior of the air produces the noisy sound we hear in whispering. A constricted laryngeal airway also is used to produce the hisslike speech sound *h*, as in the word *home*. The *h* is referred to as a *glottal fricative* because it is produced as a consequence of friction between flowing air and the narrowed glottis.

The third type of laryngeal valving for speech includes a sequence of three adjustments: a complete closure of the larynx, a buildup of pressure below the vocal folds, and a sudden release of this pressure by a rapid voluntary opening of the larynx. These events describe the production of a *glottal stop* (so termed because airflow is stopped momentarily at the glottis). The acoustic consequence of the glottal stop adjustment is a *transient* (extremely brief) sound generated at the larynx. This sound is produced as the pent-up air below the closed larynx is suddenly released in a tiny poplike explosion. Perceptually, the glottal stop sounds something like a soft, whispered cough.

Finally, during the fourth type of valving by the larynx in speech, the vocal folds move back and forth across the airway such that the glottis is alternately open and closed (Van den Berg, 1958). Motions of the vocal folds during this type of valving are faster than the eye can follow. The expiratory airflow passing through the larynx is "chopped up" into a series of sharp "air puffs" as a result of the repeated excursions of the vocal folds (Flanagan, 1958). As trains of these puffs disturb the column of air above the larynx, they cause the buzzlike sound we recognize as *voicing* or *phonation*. The nature of voicing, the principal mode of sound generation by the larynx, deserves special emphasis.

The manner in which voicing occurs is similar to another means of producing a buzzlike sound: vibrating your lips with an expiratory flow. Try it! Moisten your lips, close and pucker them gently, and force air through them with a gradually increasing effort until they vibrate easily. (Children are fond of this sound effect for playing "horsy," "motorboat," and such.) Obviously, we do not use muscles to open and close the lips during such an activity. It is impossible to move them voluntarily as fast as we can vibrate them with airflow. Rather, we "set" the lips by closing and puckering them, and then cause them to vibrate by supplying an appropriate expiratory flow. Thus it is with the vibration of the vocal folds in voicing. The vocal buzz is not the result of repeated opening and closing muscular adjustments of the vocal folds, as would be the case with a series of glottal stops. Rather, it is the result of passive vibration of the vocal folds in interaction with an expiratory flow.

The glottal changes that occur during voicing are characterized by a three-phase pattern—*closed, opening, closing*—that is repeated again and again (see Figure 2–8). During the closed phase, the pressure below the larynx builds until it exceeds the force holding the vocal folds together. The vocal folds are then blown apart toward the sides of the airway, permitting a puff of air to escape from the trachea into the pharynx. (With your hand held close to your mouth, vibrate your lips again and feel the series of air puffs.) With the escape of air through the glottis during this opening phase, the pressure below the vocal folds is reduced slightly. Being moved from their "set" position, the relatively elastic vocal folds begin to return toward their original

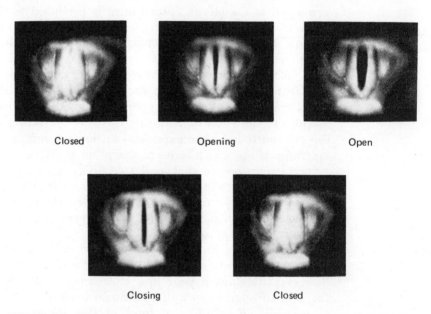

Closed   Opening   Open

Closing   Closed

FIGURE 2–8. *Photographs of the larynx from above that show successive phases in one cycle of glottal vibration. The first and last panels show the larynx closed. In between, the glottis increases in size to a maximum and then decreases in size. Total elapsed time for the one cycle sequence is approximately 8 milliseconds, representing a voice fundamental frequency of approximately 125 Hz. (After J. Flanagan,* Speech Analysis, Synthesis, and Perception. *Berlin: Springer-Verlag, 1972.)*

position (like two parallel rubber bands pulled apart sideways and then released). This return during the closing phase is aided by a sucking force between the edges of the vocal folds caused by the rapid rush of air through the glottis (Broad, 1973). After complete closure of the glottis, the same cycle of events occurs repeatedly as the balance of forces changes alternately back and forth to open and close the glottis. Each repetition of the three-phase pattern of glottal changes is referred to as a *cycle* of glottal vibration.

When producing sound by vibrating your lips, you probably found that you could produce a wide variety of buzzlike sounds — by adjustments in the way you held your lips and in the way you blew air between them. We are able to produce a wide variety of buzzlike sounds at the larynx in much the same way. The three major characteristics of the laryngeal buzz that we can vary are *fundamental frequency, sound pressure level,* and *spectrum.*

The fundamental frequency of phonation is the main factor in our perception of the *pitch* of the voice, pitch being the sensory attribute that refers to location of a tone along the musical scale (Fairbanks, 1960). For voicing, the fundamental frequency bears a one-to-one relationship to the rate at which air puffs are emitted from the larynx. Control of fundamental frequency is vested primarily in adjustments of vocal fold "set" (Hollien and Moore, 1960; Hixon, Klatt, and Mead, 1970). We are able to change the speed with which our lips will vibrate by changing their set within the oral airstream. Similarly, we are able to change the rate at which air puffs are emitted from the larynx by adjusting the set of the vocal folds within the airstream. These set adjustments are of two types and may work singly or in combination: changes in the length of the vocal folds that correspondingly influence their tension and thickness (Hollien and Moore, 1960; Hollien, 1962), and changes in how much of the vocal folds are permitted to participate in the vibratory pattern (Hirano, Ohala, and Vennard, 1969). As a general rule, increases in the length of the vocal folds and/or decreases in the amount of the folds allowed to vibrate will result in the voice having a higher fundamental frequency. The length change part of this rule for the vocal folds is analogous to that of lengthening a vibrating rubber band. That is, when the vocal folds are increased in length by muscular forces that stretch them, their tension increases and their thickness decreases, resulting in a faster rate of vibration. The second type of adjustment, changes in how much of the vocal folds are allowed to vibrate, is analogous to playing notes on any stringed musical instrument. For example, the lower down the neck toward the body of the guitar the player frets a string, the less string available to vibrate, the faster the vibration, and the higher the pitch of the note. Similarly, with vocal fold length, tension, and thickness maintained constant, any action that prevents part of a vocal fold from vibrating will result in an increased rate of vibration in the part that remains free to vibrate. In voice production, this is accomplished by firm compression of the back one-third of the vocal folds so that only the front two-thirds is free to participate in the three-phase action of the laryngeal vibration.

The second major characteristic of the laryngeal buzz that we can vary, its physical magnitude, is directly related to the sharpness and amplitude of the air puffs coming through the larynx during voicing. This magnitude can be expressed in several ways, the most common of which is in terms of the *sound pressure level* of the laryngeal tone. Sound pressure level, the primary factor contributing to our perception of the *loudness* of the voice, is governed mainly by the pressure supplied to the larynx by the respiratory pump. As pressure from the lungs increases, the sound pressure level of the laryngeal buzz also increases (to roughly the third or fourth power of the lung pressure). Were we to double our usual respiratory driving pressure, the equivalent of 9 to 12 decibels would be added to the sound pressure level of our voice (Broad, 1973). It is uncertain whether laryngeal set changes are of major importance in changing the physical magnitude of the laryngeal buzz. Most likely the larynx itself plays a role by increasing its average closing force somewhat to aid in the buildup of the higher pressure in the lungs (Isshiki, 1964; Hixon and Minifie, 1972). Certainly the three-phase pattern of laryngeal vibration changes with increases in the magnitude of the sound being produced in the larynx. The glottis remains closed for a longer period of time, opens faster, and closes faster for phonation that is of successively greater sound pressure levels (Timcke, von Leden, and Moore, 1958). Exactly which of these vibration pattern changes is the result of laryngeal adjustments and which is the result of pressure-flow adjustments remains to be determined.

Finally, the spectrum of the laryngeal tone is the major determinant of our perception of the *quality* or *timbre* of the voice, although voice quality is also conditioned by the passage of the laryngeal tone through the upper airway. The spectrum of a tone specifies the combination of frequencies and amplitudes of which its acoustical pressure wave is comprised (see Chapter 3). For a normal laryngeal buzz, the spectrum consists of a fundamental frequency and successive odd and even harmonics (whole number multiples of the fundamental frequency) that decrease in amplitude. The laryngeal spectrum is determined by vocal fold set and/or respiratory drive, principally the former. In short, any adjustment that influences the vibratory pattern of the vocal folds influences the way in which the expiratory flow of air is "chopped up." Changes in the latter give rise to changes in the acoustic spectrum of the laryngeal buzz. The variety of buzzlike sounds that can be produced at the larynx is seemingly infinite. Consider, for example, the case of *breathy voicing* as one contrast to our usual voicing. Breathiness may result when the firmness of laryngeal closure is insufficient for a given airflow through the larynx or alternately, when the airflow is excessive for a given firmness of laryngeal closure. In either case the result is voicing produced without complete intermittent closure of the larynx (that is, there is no closed phase in each cycle) and with continuous airflow through the larynx. The laryngeal spectrum in breathy voicing differs from "pure" voicing in that the higher harmonics tend to be weaker than those found in pure voicing (Broad, 1973). This results because the air puffs coming through the larynx are not as "sharp" as they are in pure voicing. As a consequence, listeners perceive an overall voicing quality that is softer and less rich than that heard for pure voicing.

In summary, we have learned that the laryngeal subdivision is an intricate valving device that can be adjusted so as to interact with the expiratory airstream in ways that enable the generation of turbulent (hisslike), transient (poplike), and quasi-periodic (buzzlike) sounds. For the latter, we can make fine adjustments in the laryngeal muscles and in the respiratory drive to bring about variations that are perceived as differences in the pitch, loudness, and quality of our voice. We are now ready to examine the function of the third subdivision of our speech machine, the pharyngeal-oral-nasal complex.

Pharyngeal-Oral-Nasal Subdivision

The F-shaped upper airway can be put through a great many adjustments, particularly in its pharyngeal and oral segments. These adjustments are the result of individual actions or combined actions of the pharynx, velum, mandible, tongue, lips, and nostrils.

Adjustments of the pharynx are the result of its own muscular actions and the actions of muscles that move structures bordering the pharyngeal tube. The pharynx can be raised or lowered somewhat within the neck; it can be lengthened or shortened considerably; and its front-to-back and side-to-side diameters can be increased or decreased at different locations along its length.

Velar adjustments, made possible by the actions of different muscles comprising the velum, are considerable. The velar hinge can be swung upward and backward to various degrees, or it can be swung downward and forward to various degrees along the same curved route. Furthermore, the velum can be shortened and it can be tensed and flattened somewhat.

All of the potential adjustments of the mandible are positional, resulting from actions of muscles attached to the structure's bony mass. The hinged mandible can be swung upward and forward to various degrees or it can be swung downward and backward to various degrees through the same gentle arc. It also can be moved from side to side a substantial amount and can be moved forward and backward a significant amount.

The tongue can be adjusted with respect to position and/or shape. Adjustments made possible through actions of the muscular complex forming the tongue are seemingly countless. The tongue's position relative to the roof of the mouth is, of course, partly determined by the position of the mandible on which it rides. The tongue can be raised or lowered substantially, moved forward or backward over a considerable range, and moved from side to side somewhat. Some of the major shapes we can cause our tongue to assume include its being flattened, bunched, thickened, thinned, grooved longitudinally, curled, humped, made convex, and made concave.

The lips are the most mobile parts of the face. Each lip is subject to change in position through the actions of muscles that can raise or lower it substantially, can move it forward or backward considerably, and can move it from side to side a significant amount. The corners formed by the junctures of the lips are also subject to a variety of positional adjustments; they can be moved upward, downward, sideward, and toward the midline. The lips can also be adjusted so as to exert various magnitudes of compressive force against each other and/or against the teeth.

The nasal segment of the upper airway is essentially fixed in size and shape. The most noteworthy exception is that the nostrils can be adjusted through the actions of different muscles of the nose.[1]

Earlier we learned that the F-shaped upper airway is used for many things. Most of the time it is in a configuration for resting breathing. This means that air is passing through the nasal segment of the airway by way of the opening between the resting velum and the pharynx (Proctor, 1964). We breathe through the nasal segment

[1] These adjustments are not of interest here. As discussed in Chapter 9, however, certain speakers with inadequate velopharyngeal function make compensatory constrictions at the nostrils during speech to impede the flow of air and acoustic energy from the nasal passages.

so as to better warm, moisten, and filter the air we inspire. When we take deeper and more rapid than normal inspirations, for an activity like speech, we usually switch from breathing through the nose to breathing through the nose and mouth. The latter requires less work because the overall resistance to airflow is lower when the mouth is open (Peslin, Hixon, and Mead, 1971).

For speech purposes, the structures in the upper airway become astoundingly active during the expiratory side of the breathing cycle. This activity is associated with two important functions that the upper airway fulfills during speech. First, like the laryngeal subdivision, the pharyngeal-oral-nasal subdivision operates as a major generator of speech sounds. Second, it behaves as an acoustical filtering device that modifies all sounds generated within the larynx and within itself. Each of these functions warrants our attention.

Speech Sound Generation. In normal speech of the American English language, two types of sounds are generated in the upper airway: turbulent and transient. Both types are produced exclusively within the oral segment of the upper airway and through intricate interacting adjustments of the oral tube and the expiratory airstream. Nasal segment participation is precluded when the two types of sounds are produced by sealing the entryway into the nasal passages (see Figure 2–9) so that all airflow and sound energy are diverted through the oral

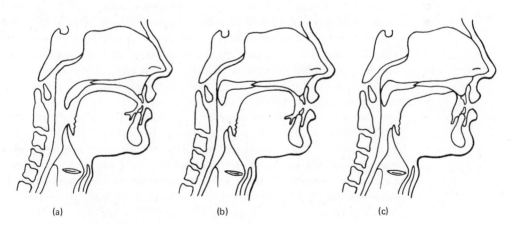

(a)   (b)   (c)

FIGURE 2–9. *Midline configurations for the pharyngeal-oral-nasal subdivision at rest (panel a), during the production of an oral fricative speech sound (panel b), and during the production of an oral stop-plosive speech sound (panel c). In the case of the last, the panel depicts the stop phase of the production. Note that in the cases of the fricative and stop-plosive productions, the velopharynx is closed so that airflow and sound energy are directed through the mouth.*

channel. A seal between the oral and nasal segments is accomplished by pulling the velum up and back and by moving the upper pharyngeal side walls inward—a combined flap-sphincter valving action (Minifie et al., 1970). This important action of the velum and pharynx is termed *velopharyngeal closure*.

With velopharyngeal closure achieved, how then are turbulent sounds produced in the oral segment? Recall that when the glottis is narrowed significantly during expiration, the air in the immediate vicinity becomes turbulent and a hisslike sound results. Hisslike turbulence can be produced similarly in the upper airway by appreciably narrowing the oral channel at different locations along its length while simultaneously forcing an expiratory flow of air through the narrowing (Stevens, 1964). Sounds produced in this fashion are termed *oral fricatives* because they originate in the oral cavity and are a consequence of air-valve friction (see Figure 2–9b). An example of a sound produced in the manner described here is the familiar *sh* that we use to urge silence.

In our earlier discussion of laryngeal valving, we also learned that a transient poplike sound is generated during expiration when the glottis is closed momentarily and then opened rapidly. This sound, the glottal stop, is actually a miniature explosion associated with the release of the air impounded below the vocal folds when they briefly place a barrier across the airway. Poplike transients can be produced in a similar fashion in the upper airway. During expiratory flow, the oral segment can be momentarily closed at different places along its length and then rapidly reopened (Fant, 1960). The transient speech sounds that result are termed *oral stop-plosives* (see Figure 2–9c) because they originate in the oral cavity and are produced by a complete stoppage of airflow followed by an explosive release of pent-up air.[2] An example of an utterance generated by the release of air pent up within the mouth is the speech sound *t*.

Certain essential elements of oral stop and oral fricative sounds are combined under one type of sound generation condition in the upper airway. This condition involves a complete stoppage of expiratory flow, a buildup of pressure within the mouth, and a relatively gradual and smooth release of this pressure in such a fashion that hisslike turbulence is produced for a moderately long period of time. Sounds produced in this way are referred to as *oral affricatives* or *affri-*

[2] In some instances the pent-up air is not released in an explosive burst following the stoppage of airflow and the buildup of pressure in the mouth. Speech elements produced in this fashion are designated as *imploded stops*. Pressure in the mouth for these stops is released by lowering the velum and letting air pass through the nose. Such a release is usually not audible (Minifie, 1973).

cates. Such sounds are generated by occluding the oral channel at a location just to the rear of where *t* is produced and narrowing the channel at the point where *sh* is produced. An example of a speech sound produced as such a combined stop-fricative element is *ch* (as in the word *cheap*).

Speech Sound Modification. In performing its function as an acoustical filtering device, the upper airway importantly "shapes" all of the sounds of speech. We have learned how speech sounds are generated—that is, where the hisslike, poplike, and buzzlike raw material of speech comes from. However, we never actually hear this raw material in its original form. This is because all speech sounds reaching our ears are first acoustically *filtered* by their passage through the upper airway. Filtering is a process whereby energy is selectively extracted from the raw speech wave. This extraction process is somewhat analogous to that performed by an optical filter with which we have all had experience, namely, sunglasses. In the same way that sunglasses allow certain colors (or wavelengths) of the light spectrum to pass through them while impeding or preventing the passage of others, the upper airway permits certain frequencies of the sound spectrum to pass through it while impeding or stopping others (Minifie, 1973).

The basis for filtering or selective sound transmission by the upper airway is its physical action as a resonator. Like all air-filled systems, the upper airway has certain natural frequencies of vibration. Consider, for example, a group of air-filled bottles of different sizes and shapes. Each will have its own characteristic "ring" when struck with a spoon or if its opening is blown across in a certain way. Like these air-filled bottles, the upper airway will also "ring" if the air within it is acoustically excited into vibration. The upper airway, in fact, has many natural frequencies of vibration or frequencies at which it rings. In technical parlance, these natural vibrations are referred to as *resonances* and their frequencies as *resonant frequencies* (Stevens and House, 1961). Resonant frequencies come in sets for the upper airway, their exact values being determined by the size and shape of the system at any moment. Precisely which sound frequencies in the raw material source are allowed to pass freely and which have various amounts of energy extracted from them is determined by the prevailing set of resonances. In other words, the upper airway's acoustical filtration properties are specified by the particular configuration in which the system is placed, each configuration representing a different "tuning" of the filter through which energy from the sound source must pass (Fant, 1960). If the sound energies impinging upon the upper airway include frequencies that are the same as the system's natural frequencies of vibration, then large amounts of energy are transferred from the sound source to the resonator. By contrast, if sound energies from the source include frequencies that are far removed from the natural frequencies of the upper airway, then little or no energy is transferred from the source to the resonator.

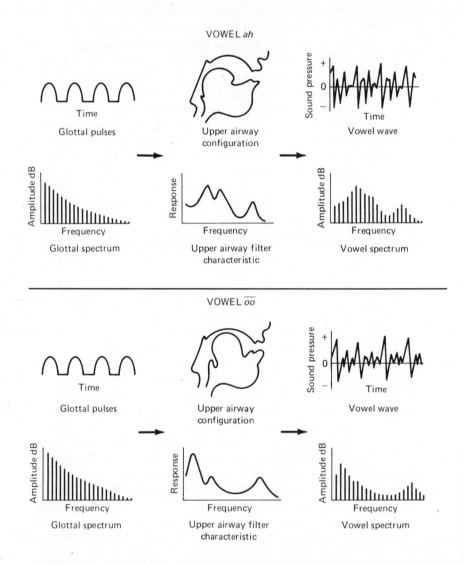

FIGURE 2–10. *A schematic illustration of the speech sound modification process as it applies to the vowels ah and ōō. See text for detailed discussion.* [*After Fig. 2.11 (p. 43) by James F. Curtis in* Processes and Disorders of Human Communication, *Edited by James F. Curtis. Copyright © 1978 by Harper & Row, Publishers, Inc. By permission of the publisher.*]

Figure 2–10 is a schematic illustration of the speech sound modification process as it applies to vowel production. The vowels *ah* and $\overline{oo}$ are shown for contrast. Note in the leftmost panels of the figure that the glottal pulses and their acoustic spectra are identical for the two vowels. That is, the buzzlike sounds produced at the larynx are the same for the vowels. In the middle panels of the figure, however, we see that the upper airway configurations for the two vowels are markedly different. The outlines shown are like those that would be seen in a side-view x-ray photograph of the upper airway. These very different configurations of the upper airway give rise to very different filter characteristics. Note closely the different locations of the resonant frequencies for these two vowels in the panels directly below each upper airway outline. Three resonant peaks of different magnitudes and frequencies occur in each case. Finally, note in the rightmost panels that the resulting acoustic wave and overall vowel acoustic spectrum (see Chapter 3) are distinctly different for the two vowels. Each vowel is given a final unique acoustic signature that is the product of the glottal sound generated and the filtration properties of the upper airway through which that sound passes. Clearly, what is ultimately available for public consumption outside the speaker's mouth is dependent upon the way in which the speaker adjusts his pharyngeal and oral tubes. As we will see in later chapters on speech disorders, some speakers have difficulty making these adjustments.

The principles outlined here for vowels serve for all other speech sounds as well. For example, *s* and *sh* both originate as turbulent sound sources. Yet, these two sounds have final sound patterns that we distinguish readily because each results from differences in the shape and size of the upper airway. Nearly all of the sounds of speech receive their final sound shaping as the result of filtering by the pharyngeal-oral or oral segments of the upper airway. Three of the nearly four dozen sounds of American English, however, acquire their final distinctiveness as a result of their passage through the pharyngeal-nasal segment of the upper airway with the oral segment functioning as a side-branch cul-de-sac. These sounds are *m*, *n*, and *ng*. There is available detailed information about the acoustical characteristics of both the source and filter components of all speech sounds of the English language. Comprehensive accounts are provided by Fant (1960) and Minifie (1973).

THE SPEECH PRODUCTION CODE

It should be clear from previous discussion that the speech mechanism makes nearly continuous adjustments as it generates and modifies the sounds of speech. These adjustments occur in unique clusters for each of the many speech sounds of the English language. Each cluster can be thought of as a *physiological code* with specifications for movements and positions of structures of the speech mechanism. Each cluster (sound), in turn, is an element in the overall sound system code.

Codes take on various forms. Most often they are simply a series of elements, with many elements differing from one another by only a single feature. For example, the printed capital *P* differs from the printed capital *B* by the presence of a single curved line in the latter. The printed capitals *F* and *E* are distinguished from one another by a single straight line. For another example, the *n* and *m* configurations of the hand in the American Manual (fingerspelled) Alphabet differ also by only a single feature: *n* is made by extending two fingers over the thumb, whereas *m* is made by extending three fingers over the thumb (see Figure 13–9). Just as fingerspelling is a code comprised of various clusters of hand movement-position "gestures," so is speech production a code involving sets of speech mechanism gestures. In one sense, an attempt to describe speech production in movement-position coding terms is an attempt to represent each of the conventional speech mechanism valving combinations in an alphabetlike way. For present purposes, we examine speech from the movement-position coding viewpoint under three subsections: *vowels, consonants,* and *the speech stream.*

Vowels

Vowels are types of speech sounds that normally are produced with voicing by the larynx, exclusion of nasal participation by velopharyngeal closure, and sets of other upper airway adjustments (such as tongue, lip, and jaw movements and positions) that leave the pharyngeal-oral tube in relatively unconstricted configurations. The last of these, upper airway adjustments, includes the most important elements of the production coding scheme for vowel sounds. Sixteen vowels comprise the American English vowel system. Production coding of these vowels is dependent upon three major dimensions: *place of major constriction within the pharyngeal-oral tube, degree of major constriction within the same tube,* and *degree of major constriction at the mouth opening* (also referred to as *degree of lip rounding*). Table 2–1 shows how these major dimensions enter into the coding scheme for the sixteen English vowels. Each dimension warrants individual attention.

The place dimension specifies where the airway is maximally constricted along the pharyngeal-oral tube. In American English, three places along this dimension are used; these are designated by the terms

Table 2–1. PRODUCTION CODING SCHEME FOR AMERICAN ENGLISH VOWELS. CODING IS IN TERMS OF PLACE OF MAJOR ORAL CONSTRICTION, DEGREE OF MAJOR ORAL CONSTRICTION, AND DEGREE OF LIP ROUNDING.*

Degree of Major Oral Constriction	Place of Major Oral Constriction			
	FRONT	*CENTRAL*		*BACK*
HIGH	i beat I bit			u fool ʊ full
MID	e bait ɛ bet	ɝ word ʌ above	ɚ onward ə above	o boat ɔ fall
LOW	æ bat a ask			ɒ hot ɑ calm

↑ Increasing Lip-Rounding

*Vowel symbols are those of the International Phonetic Alphabet. A key word example is given below each symbol in the table (Fairbanks, 1960).

front, central, and *back.* Front is the term used for any major constriction formed between the tongue and the upper gum ridge inside the teeth. Central is the term for major constrictions that occur between the tongue and the hard palate or for cases where no obvious point of constriction is to be found. The term back indicates the occurrence of a major constriction between the tongue and the velum or between the tongue and the back wall of the pharynx. Of the sixteen vowels of American English, six are classified within the front place of constriction category, four are within the central category, and six are within the back category. The place of major constriction dimension can be experienced by alternately sustaining the back vowel /ɑ/ and the front vowel /æ/. Notice how the mass of the tongue can be felt to shift from the back of the mouth to the front of the mouth and vice versa as the vowels are alternated. (The effect is enhanced for some speakers when the vowels are whispered. Try it!)

The second dimension of the vowel coding scheme, the degree of major constriction within the pharyngeal-oral tube, describes the cross-sectional size of the constricted airway. Coding elements along this dimension take on one of three designations: *high, mid,* and *low* degrees of constriction. These three cover a range of constrictions that goes from almost complete obstruction of the airway (high), to intermediate size openings (mid), to airway openings that may even exceed those found when the speech mechanism is relaxed (low constriction).[3] Four vowels are classified within the high degree of constriction category, eight belong to the mid category, and four fit within the low category. This overall dimension of vowel coding can be appreciated by sustaining the six vowels of the front vowel series in order of decreasing degree of major oral constriction for their production—/i, I, e, ɛ, æ, a/. In producing these six vowels, note that as you move through them you can feel the tongue drop slightly for each succeeding vowel in the series. This sensation fits with the decreasing degree of constriction that goes through the vowel series. Now, reverse the order and notice how the tongue elevates on succeeding vowels. Finally, try both orders of production while whispering the vowels.

The last of the three dimensions in vowel production coding is degree of lip rounding. This dimension represents a pertinent feature of only the high-constriction and mid-constriction back vowels in American English—/u, U, o, ɔ/. Lip rounding decreases in degree across these four, /u/ being fully rounded and /ɔ/ being only slightly rounded. The lip rounding elements of the production code can be appreciated (especially in front of a mirror) by producing the back vowel series, starting at /a/ and going on through the series to /u/. Note how the lips begin to protrude and round further and further as you proceed higher and higher through the mid- and high-constriction categories. Finally, reverse the sequence and notice how the degree of lip rounding decreases.

Besides the sixteen "pure" vowels of American English (see Table 2–1), there are also five vowel-like speech sounds called *diphthongs* (pronounced diff-thongs) that are produced in a manner closely akin to vowels. Each of these sounds begins as one vowel and then moves through a rapid, continuous transition to end up as another vowel. With respect to production coding, this means that each diphthong starts out with elements from the three coding dimensions for one vowel and then shifts these elements as needed to attain the appropriate combination for the second vowel in the pair. The five

---

[3] The degrees of constriction described by the terms high, mid, and low are often assumed to correspond to the position of the highest point on the tongue relative to the roof of the mouth. That is, when the tongue is high in the mouth, the degree of constriction of the airway is high. When it is in a mid-position, the degree of constriction is mid. And, when it is in a low position, the degree of constriction is low. This notion of congruence between tongue height and degree of constriction, although useful and traditionally ingrained, is not completely satisfactory. For example, for the vowel /o/, the major tube constriction is sometimes between the back of the tongue and the pharynx, quite distant from the location of the highest point on the tongue with respect to the roof of the mouth (Daniloff, 1973).

diphthongs used in English are /eI/, /aI/, /ɔI/, /oU/, and /aU/, as in the words *fail, file, foil, foal,* and *fowl,* respectively. Note that in all of these utterances the first vowel is characterized by a lesser degree of major oral constriction than the second vowel. Three of the five diphthongs combine vowel pairs within the same place of major oral constriction (/eI, aI, oU/), one shifts from front to back (/aU/), and one from back to front (/ɔI/), two involve increasing lip rounding (/oU, aU/), and all terminate in the relatively high front or high back vowels /I/ or /U/. A useful exercise to help in understanding the way in which vowels are combined into diphthongs is to take the diphthong /aI/ (pronounced *I*) and first produce its two vowels separated by a pause (that is, /a— — — — —I/). Next, begin running these two vowels together at increasing speed until *I* results (for example, /a— — — — —I/, /a— — — —I/, /a— — —I/, /a— —I/, /a—I/, /aI/).

Consonants

Unlike vowels and diphthongs, consonant speech sounds are normally produced with a relatively constricted or completely obstructed pharyngeal-oral airway. Moreover, some consonants are made with and some without velopharyngeal closure and some with and some without voicing. Twenty-five unique combinations of valving adjustments are used within the speech production coding scheme for consonants—yielding twenty-five perceptually different classes of sounds. Elements contributing to the consonant production code are listed in Table 2–2. The overall coding scheme includes three dimensions: *manner of production,* with five categories; *place of production,* with seven categories; and *voicing,* with two categories. Of the seventy potentially unique consonants this scheme would permit ($5 \times 7 \times 2$), the American English language uses only twenty-five, roughly a third of the possibilities.

Manner of production refers to the way in which the valves of the larynx and pharyngeal-oral-nasal complex constrict or occlude the airway. Manners of production include *stop-plosive, fricative, affricate, nasal,* and *semivowel.* These five ways of making sounds can be described as follows:

Stop-plosive:[4] occlusion of the oral airway followed by an abrupt opening of the airway and the release of a puff of air.

---

[4] Glottal stops are not included in the listing of Table 2–2. They occur frequently in American English speech but they do not constitute distinctive elements of the production coding scheme. Recall also from footnote 2 that not all stop consonants are released.

Table 2–2. PRODUCTION CODING SCHEME FOR AMERICAN ENGLISH CONSONANTS. CODING IS IN TERMS OF MANNER OF PRODUCTION, PLACE OF PRODUCTION, AND VOICING.*

Place of Production	Manner of Production									
	STOP-PLOSIVE		FRICATIVE		AFFRICATE		NASAL		SEMIVOWEL	
	−	+	−	+	−	+	−	+	−	+
LABIAL (Lips)	p pole	b bowl						m sum	hw what	w watt
LABIODENTAL (Lip–Teeth)			f fat	v vat						
DENTAL (Tongue–Teeth)			θ thigh	ð thy						
ALVEOLAR (Tongue–Gum)	t toll	d dole	s seal	z zeal				n sun		l lot
PALATAL (Tongue–Hard Palate)			ʃ ash	ʒ azure	tʃ choke	dʒ joke				j,r yacht, rot
VELAR (Tongue–Velum)	k coal	g goal						ŋ sung		
GLOTTAL (Vocal Folds)			h hot							

*–For voiceless and+ for voiced. Consonant symbols are those of the International Phonetic Alphabet. Key word examples are from Fairbanks (1960).

Fricative: air forced through a narrowly constricted laryngeal or oral airway.

Affricate: occlusion of the oral airway followed by a gradual opening of the airway and the smooth release of a puff of air.

Nasal: occlusion of the oral airway with an open velopharyngeal valve and sound transmission through the nasal airway.

Semivowel: constriction of the oral airway that is greater than for vowels but less than for other consonants, with sound transmission through the oral segment.

As can be seen in Table 2–2, the fricative manner of production is a coding element used in more consonants than any other manner of production. It figures in the element clusters of nine of the twenty-five consonants we use. By contrast, the affricate manner of production occurs least, being an element in only two cases. The remaining categories, stop-plosive, semivowel, and nasal, contribute to the manner coding of six, five, and three consonants, respectively. The important differences among the various manners of production of consonants can be seen by contrasting production of the syllables /dʌ/, /zʌ/, /dʒʌ/, /nʌ/, and /lʌ/. These five utterances differ in the manner of production of their initial consonants—they include stop-plosive, fricative, affricate, nasal, and semivowel, respectively.

Place of production describes where the consonant constriction or occlusion occurs along the airway. This dimension is partitioned into seven "sites" along the airway in the English language, ranging from the lips to the larynx. These sites are listed down the left side of Table 2–2, moving further into the speech mechanism from the top to the bottom of the listing. Places of production include *labial, labiodental, dental, alveolar, palatal, velar,* and *glottal.* Labial refers to the actions of both the lips and labiodental to the placement of the lower lip against the upper teeth. The terms dental, alveolar, palatal, and velar refer to locations where the tongue either contacts or approaches contacts with other structures. These structures include, respectively, the teeth, the upper gum ridge inside the teeth, the hard palate, and the velum.[5] The term glottal designates that the place of production is at the vocal folds.

Most prominent among the places for making consonants are the alveolar and palatal sites. Each of these places is used for the production of six consonants. The remaining thirteen consonants are divided among the other five categories as follows: labial (five), velar (three), labiodental (two), dental (two), and glottal (one). You can experience most of the range of places of production for English consonants by producing the five fricative speech sounds /f, θ, s, ʃ, h/, sustaining each for several seconds. The place of production of these sounds moves from near the front of the airway to the back. The dimensions of manner of production and voicing do not change across the contrasts. To experience progressively more rearward places of production within the airway for another manner of production category, namely, stop-plosives, try the sounds /p, t, k/, in that order, and notice how the explosion site moves from the lips, to the tongue tip, to the tongue body.

Voicing, the third dimension on which consonant coding relies, is binary in nature. All consonant speech sounds are either *voiced* or *voiceless.* In Table 2–2, this coding aspect is specified for the twenty-five consonants of American English by (−) for voiceless and (+) for voiced above each column of speech sound entries. Sixty percent of the consonants of English are voiced. Nine pairs of consonants are

---

[5] In the case of the narrowing between the tongue and the upper gum ridge behind the teeth, air moving at high velocities may also strike the cutting edges of the teeth and create a secondary source of turbulent disturbance for /s/ and /z/ (Hixon, 1966).

coded in matching manners of production and matching places of production, but differ on the voicing dimension. These nine pairs of consonants are referred to as *cognate pairs,* the difference within each pair being that one of the speech sounds is voiceless and the other is voiced. The preponderance of cognate pairs and individual voiceless consonants are associated with the stop-plosive, fricative, and affricate manners of production. The nasal manner of production is voiced only and the semivowel manner is nearly all voiced. The voiced-voiceless coding distinction occurs across six of the seven place of production sites, the glottal site excepted.

A good way to experience the voiced-voiceless distinction for the voicing dimension is to contrast the production differences between cognate pairs that are sustainable, namely, the four fricative pairs /f–v/, /θ–ð/, /s–z/, and /ʃ–ʒ/. Place your thumb and the fingers of one hand around your larynx and alternately produce the mates in each pair — for example, /s–z–s–z–s/ — without stopping between them. You should easily feel the on-off pattern of vocal fold vibration. Note that for these cognate pairs, as well as for those in other manner categories, the voiceless consonant is made by generating sound at or near an upper airway constriction or occlusion; the voiced consonant of the pair uses the same sound plus an additional sound simultaneously generated at the larynx. Note also that in the consonant coding scheme some consonants have their sound source at the larynx, some in the upper airway, and some a combination of the two.

The Speech Stream

In the two preceding sections, we have used the place-constriction-lip rounding scheme (vowels) and the place-manner-voicing scheme (consonants) to characterize production of speech sounds. While these schemes provide a general notion about the nature of the speech production process, speech sounds do not actually result from highly specific and invariant movement-position patterns. That is, the production patterns we have described for the many speech sounds of English are not like typewriter characters that are produced exactly the same, time after time, when each is called upon to make an appearance.

A more accurate view of the many speech sounds of English is that each vowel and consonant constitutes a category of sound variations. It is these categories that represent the distinctive elements within the speech stream. The members of any category can vary considerably in terms of their physiological and acoustical events. Sets of speech sound variations that have enough common characteristics to be perceived as particular vowel or consonant categories and are different enough from other categories to serve as distinctive elements in the speech stream, are called *phonemes* (Curtis, 1978). Thus, a·spoken word like *Kim* consists of three phonemes: the voiceless, velar, stopplosive consonant /k/, the high, front, unrounded vowel /I/, and the voiced, labial, nasal consonant /m/. Although composed of three phonemes, the word /kIm/ actually consists of many subphonemic sounds that the trained phonetician hears. For example, contrast the *k*-sound in *Kim* with the sound of *k* in the word *skim*. If you say both words loudly and listen closely, you will notice that the two *k*'s are actually quite different. In *Kim*, *k* is followed by an audible puff of air; in *skim* it is not, sounding almost, but not quite, like a *g*. Again, /k/ is a phoneme. It is a category of sounds with many subphonemic members.

It is important to keep in mind that the distinctive phonemes we identify are not executed as separate and independent movement-position patterns sequenced like beads on a string. As has been reviewed in depth by MacNeilage (1970), movement-position patterns for two or more phonemes may take place simultaneously and in such a way that their production gestures will overlap and intermingle. This occurrence of the production characteristics of one phoneme during the time segment we might think is reserved solely for one or more of its neighboring phonemes is called *coarticulation.* Coarticulation has two bases, one within the brain of the speaker and one within the mechanical properties of the speech mechanism. Let us examine how each functions to produce coarticulated speech sounds.

The brain figures into coarticulation by the way it organizes its motor commands to the muscles of the speech mechanism. Organization is such that movement-position patterns for phonemes are prepared for in advance of their place of occurrence in the utterance. An example of this type of anticipatory adjustment is the behavior of the lips during the utterance of a word like *construe*. Produce this word aloud and feel (also watch if you have a mirror) how the lips begin to round and protrude well in advance of the /u/ vowel at the end of the word. High speed x-ray studies of lip motion for this word (Daniloff and Moll, 1968) show that lip rounding actually begins more than four phonemes ahead of the demand for lip rounding on the /u/ vowel, in fact, before the first observable tongue movement toward the /n/ consonant. Next, try producing the words *once true* and notice again that the same type of anticipation of lip rounding for the /u/ occurs even across word boundaries.

CONSTRUE

Lip rounding for /u/ begins   o———————▶

ONCE TRUE

These and many other examples involving different speech structures show clearly that the brain is not operating on a production program that consists of "chunks" of gestures put together on a phoneme-by-phoneme basis. Were we to have to produce each phoneme discretely without anticipatory programming we would need to turn the speech mechanism "on and off" in such a fashion that speech would consist of an interrupted sequence of sounds lacking in smoothness of flow and greatly slowed in its rate of execution. Neurally programmed coarticulation such as we have just described is known by several essentially similar terms: *anticipatory coarticulation, right-to-left coarticulation,* or *forward coarticulation.*

Terms for the second type of coarticulation, by contrast, include: *carryover coarticulation, left-to-right coarticulation,* or *backward coarticulation.* As evidenced by these terms, somewhat the opposite effects from those discussed above occur because of the mechanical properties of the speech mechanism. Due to mechanical-inertial factors, the response of speech structures lags behind the arrival of neural commands to the muscles and responses persist after commands have stopped. The speech mechanism is, of course, a mechanical device whose behavior is subject to universal physical forces that govern the behavior of all mechanical systems. The speed with which the speech mechanism can move is limited and the movements occurring in normally rapid speech are sometimes faster than can be discretely imposed on the mechanism. The result is a blending of movement-position patterns wherein the production characteristics of one phoneme can be observed to some extent during the production of one or more following phonemes. Were we able to freeze the speech mechanism's action for an instant and observe its movement-position characteristics, the residual influence of command instructions for a previous utterance could probably be seen. An example: Consider the mechanically based influence on overlapping speech movements in the rapid utterance of the word *runs.* During this utterance the velum lowers for /n/, and continues to lower and then to rise while the tongue has already reached its position for /z/. Thus, a continuation of "nasalization" occurs within the /z/ (Daniloff, 1973). In this case, the velum simply does not have enough time to achieve air-tight velopharyngeal closure with the pharynx following the /n/. Such carryover coarticulation is an inevitable consequence of the biomechanics of the speech mechanism.

The two bases for coarticulation we have discussed are responsible for much of the sound variation observed within phonemes. Other sources of variation include language-specific constraints (see Chapter 7), and a host of factors associated with the physiological and psychological status of the speaker.

The stream of speech that most of us so effortlessly generate is both complex and yet to be fully understood. As we move on through this book it should become apparent that normal speech is a very precious commodity. Like so many things, it is often not fully appreciated until it is lost.

REFERENCES   BLESS, D., and MILLER, J., Influence of mechanical and linguistic factors on lung volume events during speech. Paper presented to the Annual Convention of the American Speech and Hearing Association, San Francisco (November, 1972).

BROAD, D., Phonation. In F. Minifie, T. Hixon, and F. Williams (Eds.), *Normal Aspects of Speech, Hearing, and Language.* Englewood Cliffs, N.J.: Prentice-Hall (1973).

CURTIS, J., Acoustics, speech production, and the hearing mechanism. In J. Curtis (Ed.), *Processes and Disorders of Human Communication.* New York: Harper & Row (1978).

DANILOFF, R., Normal articulation processes. In F. Minifie, T. Hixon, and F. Williams (Eds.), *Normal Aspects of Speech, Hearing, and Language.* Englewood Cliffs, N.J.: Prentice-Hall (1973).

DANILOFF, R., and MOLL, K., Coarticulation of lip rounding. *Journal of Speech and Hearing Research,* 11, 707–721 (1968).

DARLEY, F., ARONSON, A., and BROWN, J., *Motor Speech Disorders.* Philadelphia: Saunders (1975).

DRAPER, M., LADEFOGED, P., and WHITTERIDGE, D., Respiratory muscles in speech. *Journal of Speech and Hearing Research,* 2, 16–27 (1959).

FAIRBANKS, G., *Voice and Articulation Drillbook.* New York: Harper & Row (1960).

FANT, G., *Acoustic Theory of Speech Production.* The Hague: Mouton (1960).

FLANAGAN, J., Some properties of the glottal sound source. *Journal of Speech and Hearing Research,* 1, 99–116 (1958).

GARDNER, E., *Fundamentals of Neurology,* (5th. Ed.). Philadelphia: Saunders (1968).

GUYTON, A., *Textbook of Medical Physiology,* (4th. Ed.). Philadelphia: Saunders (1971).

HIRANO, M., OHALA, J., and VENNARD, W., The function of laryngeal muscles in regulating fundamental frequency and intensity of phonation. *Journal of Speech and Hearing Research,* 12, 616–628 (1969).

HIXON, T., Respiratory function in speech. In F. Minifie, T. Hixon, and F. Williams (Eds.), *Normal Aspects of Speech, Hearing, and Language*. Englewood Cliffs, N.J.: Prentice-Hall (1973).

HIXON, T., Turbulent noise sources for speech. *Folia Phoniatrica*, 18, 168–182 (1966).

HIXON, T., and MINIFIE, F., Influence of forced transglottal pressure changes on vocal sound pressure level. Paper presented to the Annual Convention of the American Speech and Hearing Association, San Francisco (November, 1972).

HIXON, T., GOLDMAN, M., and MEAD, J., Kinematics of the chest wall during speech production: Volume displacements of the rib cage, abdomen, and lung. *Journal of Speech and Hearing Research*, 16, 78–115 (1973).

HIXON, T., KLATT, D., and MEAD, J., Influence of forced transglottal pressure changes on vocal fundamental frequency. Paper presented to the Acoustical Society of America Meeting, Houston (1970).

HIXON, T., MEAD, J., and GOLDMAN, M., Dynamics of the chest wall during speech production: Function of the thorax, rib cage, diaphragm, and abdomen. *Journal of Speech and Hearing Research*, 19, 297–356 (1976).

HOLLIEN, H., Vocal fold thickness and fundamental frequency of phonation. *Journal of Speech and Hearing Research*, 5, 237–243 (1962).

HOLLIEN, H., and MOORE, P., Measurement of the vocal folds during changes in pitch. *Journal of Speech and Hearing Research*, 3, 157–165 (1960).

HUGHES, O., and ABBS, J., Labial-mandibular coordination in the production of speech: Implications for the operation of motor equivalence. *Phonetica*, 33, 199–221 (1976).

ISSHIKI, N., Regulatory mechanism of voice intensity variation. *Journal of Speech and Hearing Research*, 7, 17–29 (1964).

LADEFOGED, P., Linguistic aspects of respiratory phenomena. *Annals of the New York Academy of Sciences*, 15, 141–151 (1968).

MACNEILAGE, P., Motor control of serial ordering of speech. *Psychological Review*, 77, 182–196 (1970).

MANTER, J., and GATZ, A., *Essentials of Clinical Neuroanatomy and Neurophysiology*, (2nd. Ed.). Philadelphia: F. A. Davis (1961).

MEAD, J., BOUHUYS, A., and PROCTOR, D., Mechanisms generating subglottic pressure. *Annals of the New York Academy of Sciences*, 15, 165–176 (1968).

MINIFIE, F., Speech acoustics. In F. Minifie, T. Hixon, and F. Williams (Eds.), *Normal Aspects of Speech, Hearing, and Language*. Englewood Cliffs, N.J.: Prentice-Hall (1973).

MINIFIE, F., HIXON, T., KELSEY, C., and WOODHOUSE, R., Lateral pharyngeal wall movement during speech production. *Journal of Speech and Hearing Research*, 13, 584–594 (1970).

NEGUS, V., *The Comparative Anatomy and Physiology of the Larynx*. New York: Grune and Stratton (1949).

NETSELL, R., Speech physiology. In F. Minifie, T. Hixon, and F. Williams (Eds.), *Normal Aspects of Speech, Hearing, and Language*. Englewood Cliffs, N.J.: Prentice-Hall (1973).

NETSELL, R., KENT, R., and ABBS, J., Adjustments of the tongue and lips to fixed jaw positions during speech: A preliminary report. Paper presented to the Conference on Speech Motor Control, University of Wisconsin, Madison, Wisconsin (June, 1978).

PESLIN, R., HIXON, T., and MEAD, J., Variations of thoraco-pulmonary resistance during the respiratory cycle as studied by forced oscillations. *Bulletin de Physiopathologie Respiratoire*, 7, 173–188 (1971).

PROCTOR, D., Physiology of the upper airway. In W. Fenn and H. Rahn (Eds.), *Handbook of Physiology, Respiration 1, Sect. 3.* Washington, D.C.: American Physiological Society (1964).

PUTNAM, A., and RINGEL, R., Oral sensation and perception. In W. Williams and D. Goulding (Eds.), *Articulation and Learning,* (2nd. Ed.). Springfield, Ill.: Charles C Thomas (1979).

STEVENS, K., Acoustical aspects of speech production. In W. Fenn and H. Rahn (Eds.), *Handbook of Physiology, Respiration 1, Sect. 3.* Washington, D.C.: American Physiological Society (1964).

STEVENS, K., and HOUSE, A., An acoustical theory of vowel production and some of its implications. *Journal of Speech and Hearing Research,* 4, 303–320 (1961).

TIMCKE, R., VON LEDEN, H., and MOORE, P., Laryngeal vibrations: Measurements of the glottic wave. *Archives of Otolaryngology,* 68, 1–19 (1958).

VAN DEN BERG, J., Myoelastic-aerodynamic theory of voice production. *Journal of Speech and Hearing Research,* 1, 227–244 (1958).

signpost The human ear is a remarkably engineered mechanism for turning sound energy into something we can perceive. This mechanism is the cornerstone of our sensory capabilities: It is important to our safety, to our social development, to our development of speech and language skills, and, indeed, to the very quality and quantity of our contact with the physical environment in general. Chapter 3 is devoted to providing the reader with fundamental knowledge about sound and hearing and how the two serve to link man to events in his outside world. The chapter considers sound with respect to its existence as patterns of molecular motion that are transmitted through various media, especially air. Attention is given to how sound patterns can be quantified and classified and what aspects of them are sensed by the human ear. Also discussed is how different parts of the ear operate on sound signals as they are passed along the chain from the outer ear to the brain. A major section of the chapter deals with our perceptions of the world of sound, including how sensitive our hearing is, how we tell one sound from another, how unwanted sounds interfere with our hearing, how two ears are better than one, and how we perceive speech sounds. The wide-ranging issues covered in Chapter 3 offer the reader an important backdrop of information for subsequent discussions dealing with disordered hearing, its measurement, and its management (see Chapters 12 and 13).

Theodore J. Glattke

sound
and hearing

INTRODUCTION

Hearing is an important and complex link with the outside world. It is exquisitely precise, sensitive, and versatile. We can detect sound which is so faint that the power necessary to light a reading lamp for one second, if converted to sound, could be heard for more than a trillion years. We can locate a mosquito flying about on a dark night and can tolerate the noise from an overhead jet aircraft. If our ability to judge weight were as refined as our sense of hearing, we could estimate the weight of both parsley and watermelons at the produce counter and always be within 10 percent of the exact weight. And, if our body strength were to cover a range like the sensitivity of the ear, we could grasp a butterfly without harming it at one extreme and lift a small aircraft at the other.

The ways in which we are able to use sound energy around us are further cause for marvel. We can attend to one speaker in a group of several and follow a chosen conversation easily, even though many individuals may be speaking simultaneously. We can fall asleep in the presence of noise, music, or conversation and awaken when the sound around us takes a novel turn. In addition to their use in communication, the sounds around us help us to know if all is well or if a dangerous event is about to happen, often long before our visual sense can confirm such things.

The purpose of this chapter is to present fundamental information about sound and hearing. To fulfill this purpose comprehensively, we consider three broad topics: the physical nature of sound energy; the way in which the ear and nervous system react to that energy; and the way in which listeners report their sensations in response to sound.

90

PROPERTIES OF SOUND

Sound is a form of energy that can be heard. The essence of sound is vibration, and *nearly any object that can be set into vibratory motion can generate or transmit sound.* Examples of vibrating objects include the strings of a piano or guitar, the wings of a hummingbird, the leaves on a tree, and the human vocal folds. Sound generated by such sources is normally carried to a listener through air, but other materials such as water, steel, wood, and glass can also be set into vibration and, hence, carry sound energy. In this section of the chapter we are concerned with the essential features of sound in the physical domain. Our discussion encompasses a wide range of topics that are arranged under subdivisions having to do with the analysis of motion, the transmission of sound energy to a listener, and the measurement of the magnitude of sound.

Analysis of Motion

To understand the bases for normal hearing and disorders of hearing, we need first to consider some features of the vibratory motion that produces sound. This is done in the present section by discussing how it is that motion can be captured for study, how its frequency and period are determined, and how it can be categorized into patterns.

Describing Motion. One straightforward description of motion results from taking a series of photographs of a moving object and then using the photographs to make measurements of the object's displacement. Figure 3–1 illustrates how this might be done to describe the motion of either of two children leisurely riding a teeter-totter. To measure the up and down motion of one of the children, we could take photographs at selected time intervals, as shown by the nine illustrations in the figure. After arranging the photographs in a column, all that would be required would be to measure how far either child had moved above or below the starting point. The nine graphs on the righthand side of Figure 3–1 show how the motion would appear if captured at 1/8th-second intervals, as is the case with the illustrations.

If only the child on the left is studied, it will be apparent that she moves in an upward direction, stops, and then reverses direction only to stop again at the bottom of the motion pattern. Finally, she moves upward again and passes through her starting point. The solid "X" in each of the graphs of her motion pattern shows her measured location

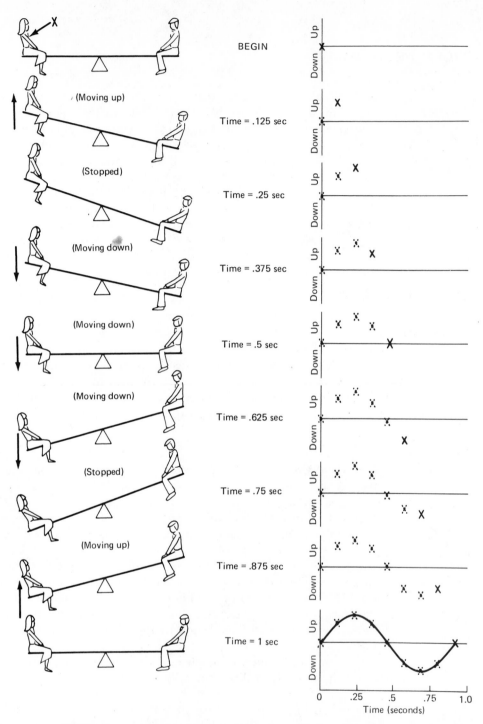

FIGURE 3–1. *A graphic representation of up and down motion of a child on a teeter-totter. See text for explanation.*

above or below the starting point at the instant captured by each illustration. The dashed "Xs" show her previous measured locations. The final (lowermost) graph in the figure was constructed by connecting the individual measures with a solid line. This graph shows the girl's moment-to-moment displacement and can be used to describe the speed, magnitude, and complexity of her motion.

Measures of Frequency and Period. When an object moves to and fro around its resting position, it is said to be going through individual *cycles* of its motion pattern. The girl in Figure 3–1 goes through one complete cycle of motion — from her starting point to maximum upward, then downward displacement, and finally back to her starting point — in one second. Thus, she completes a full swing at a rate of 1 *cycle per second*. The rate, in terms of complete cycles per second, is called the *frequency* of any motion pattern. Slowly moving objects have a low-frequency motion pattern, and rapidly moving objects have a high-frequency pattern. The time required to complete a cycle of motion is called the *period* of that motion. Low-frequency motion has a longer period, or duration, of each cycle, than does high-frequency motion. The frequency of any repetitive motion may be found by dividing 1 second by the time required to complete one cycle of motion. The relationship between frequency (f) and period (T) is:

$$\text{f (frequency)} = \frac{1 \text{ second}}{\text{duration of one cycle}} = \frac{1 \text{ second}}{\text{period (T)}} = \frac{1}{T} \text{ cycles per second.}$$

The units for specifying frequency, cycles per second, are called *Hertz* (to honor an acoustician of that name), and abbreviated as *Hz*. Note that period and frequency are related in such a manner that as one increases the other decreases. For example, changes in frequency from 100 Hz to 200 Hz to 300 Hz to 500 Hz involve corresponding changes in period from 0.010 second to 0.005 second to 0.0033 second to 0.002 second, respectively. Frequency values of interest in the study of hearing and speech include the following:

Lowest frequency perceived as sound by humans	16 Hz (approx)
Typical male voice	120 Hz (approx)
Middle "C" on a piano	256 Hz
Typical female voice	220 Hz (approx)
Important frequencies for understanding speech	500 to 2000 Hz (approx)
Highest frequency perceived as sound by humans	20,000 Hz (approx)

Following abbreviations of the metric scale, frequencies above 999 Hz are designated as *kiloHertz,* abbreviated as *kHz.* For example,

1500 Hz is designated as 1.5 kiloHertz, abbreviated as 1.5 kHz; 2000 Hz is 2 kHz; 20,000 Hz is 20 kHz; and so forth.

Motion Patterns.   All motion patterns, no matter what their nature, can be grouped according to one of two classifications: periodic or nonperiodic. Each classification warrants our attention.

Periodic motion: As its name suggests, *periodic motion* repeats itself regularly as time passes. Examples include the motion of the girl on the teeter-totter in Figure 3–1, the dial tone of a telephone, a sustained musical note, and the "pure" tones used to test hearing.

Periodic motion can be either *simple or complex.* The former is called *simple harmonic motion* or *sinusoidal motion* because of its pattern. Sinusoidal motion has its roots in the pattern of motion of a dot on the edge of a spinning disk, as illustrated in Figure 3–2. Figure 3–2 is similar to Figure 3–1 except that our teeter-totter is replaced by a disk rotating clockwise at a constant speed. Rather than observing the up and down motion of a child, Figure 3–2 considers the up and down motion of a dot on the edge of the disk. We can "freeze" the motion of the disk with photographs at various moments during its rotation, and specify each moment in terms of the number of degrees, of a possible 360°, through which the disk has rotated. The illustrations in Figure 3–2 have captured the motion of the disk at 0° (starting point), 30° (1/12th of one rotation), 45° (1/8th), 60° (1/6th), 90° (1/4th), 180° (1/2), 270° (3/4ths), and 360° (full circle). Graphs to the right of the photographs show the position of the dot (filled circle) above and below its location at the start of rotation. Prior locations are illustrated by open circles. Note that the dot climbs rapidly toward the upper limit of its range of motion, slows, reverses direction at 90°, and then speeds through 180°, only to reverse direction again at 270°.

Location of the dot relative to its starting position can be described with precision by doing the following: First, sketch a line from the dot's starting position to the center of the disk — that is, mark off the radius of the disk. Then, draw a line from each other position of the dot to the center of the disk and determine the *angle* made by the juncture of each new line and the first horizontal line drawn for the starting position. This angle corresponds to the *degrees-of-rotation* of the disk, and once the angle is known, its *sine* can be determined from a table of sine values. Sine values always vary between 0 and 1 or 0 and −1, and the value for any angle can be used to specify how far the dot has moved up or down from its starting position. Exact displacement is found by multiplying the maximum possible displacement by the sine of the angle corresponding with the dot's position. Some exact values are given in Figure 3–3. Because the sine of 30° is 0.5, then the dot has moved through 50 percent of its total up-

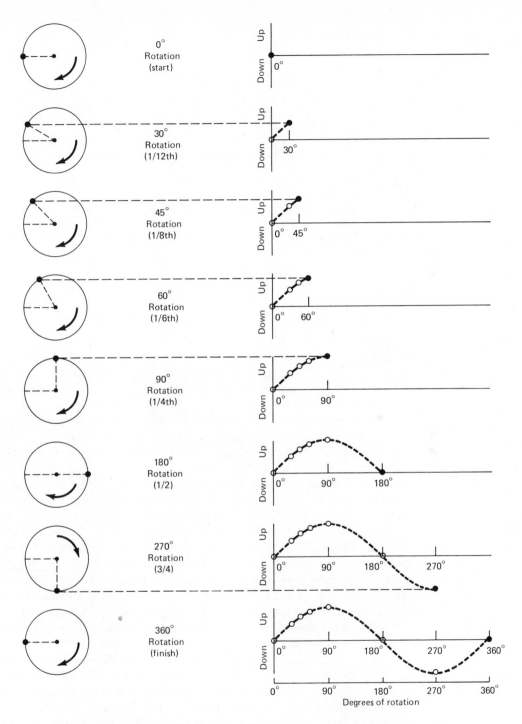

FIGURE 3–2. *A graphic representation of the up and down motion of a dot on the edge of a disk undergoing uniform rotation. See text for explanation.*

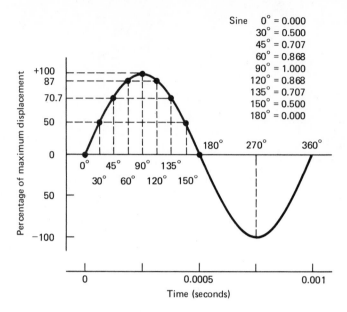

FIGURE 3–3. *An illustration of simple harmonic (sinusoidal) motion.*

ward displacement when the motion pattern is at 30°. The dot reaches approximately 87 percent of its maximum upward displacement at 60°, and reaches the top, or 100 percent of its possible upward displacement at 90°. As the rotation of the disk continues beyond 90°, displacement of the dot continues to change systematically with the sine of the angle, hence the name *sinusoidal.*

Sinusoidal motion is the most elementary form of motion because *every other periodic motion pattern can be shown to be a combination of a series of sinusoidal motions.* Principles underlying the combination of sinusoids into complex periodic patterns were discovered by a mathematician named Fourier, and complex motion patterns can be described precisely when submitted to a *Fourier analysis.* By using Fourier's techniques, it is possible not only to determine exactly *which* individual sinusoidal motions contribute to a complex pattern, but also to determine the *magnitude* of the motions associated with individual frequencies. The graphic representation of individual sinusoidal components of a complex pattern is called the *spectrum* of that pattern.

The spectrum of any complex periodic motion pattern consists of some *fundamental frequency* and other individual frequencies that are exact multiples of the fundamental frequency. These multiples are called *harmonics.* Figure 3–4 provides four examples of spectra associated with different motion patterns. Each of the motion patterns has a period of 1/100th of a second (0.01 second), or a fundamental frequency of 100 Hz. The sinusoidal pattern shown has a spectrum con-

96

sisting of only a single frequency, namely its 100-Hz fundamental. The square pattern contains energy at 100, 300, 500, 700 Hz, and, theoretically, all frequencies that are odd multiples of 100 Hz. The triangular pattern has harmonics at 300, 500, 700 Hz, etc., but these are of much smaller magnitudes than their counterparts in the square wave. The spectrum for the voice pattern contains both odd and even multiples of the fundamental frequency, and the relative amplitudes

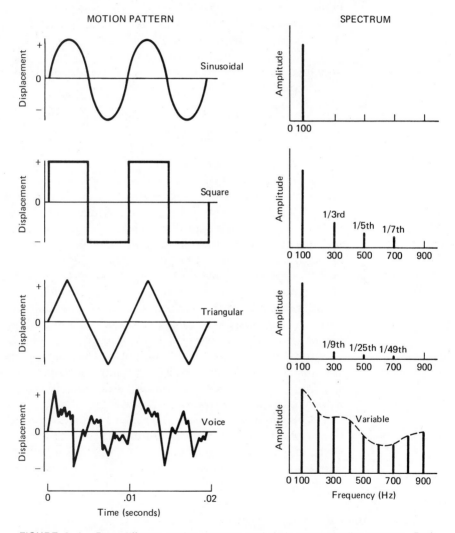

FIGURE 3-4. *Four different motion patterns and their corresponding spectra. Each pattern has a fundamental frequency of 100 Hz. See text for further discussion.*

of the individual harmonics are variable, depending on the particular speech sound produced.

The sounds associated with all of the motion patterns in Figure 3–4 have a common *tonality*. They sound "in tune" with each other in spite of their spectral differences because all have the same fundamental frequency. It is easy to discriminate among the sounds, however, on the basis of the *quality* or *timbre* of each. The sinusoidal pattern produces what is called a "pure tone" and would be distinguished easily from voice or the other patterns considered. Humans are able to detect very small changes in the spectra of sounds, and, hence, *discriminate* among them. For example, differences in spectra enable us to discriminate between two musical instruments playing the same note, two singers joined in a duet, or two individuals reciting the same spoken material.

Nonperiodic motion: We normally think of "noise" as sound that interferes with sound we want to hear. A more technical description of noise is *sound that results from motion that is nonperiodic.* Nonperiodic motion is a form of motion in which a pattern of displacement is not repeated systematically. Thus, knowing the position of the sound generator at one instant does not enable a prediction of its position at any other instant—the motion is random. When energy is spent in such a fashion, the resulting sound is called *white noise.* An example of white noise is the sound produced by a waterfall or the rushing of air through a small vent. The spectrum of white noise consists of *all frequencies.* It is analogous to white light, which contains all colors.

Figure 3–5 illustrates random motion and its spectrum. The graph representing the spectrum shows a single horizontal line. Actually, white noise has a spectrum graph consisting of an infinite number of closely spaced vertical lines, but, for simplification, the single horizontal line connects the "tops" of the lines representing each frequency. This is known as a *continuous* spectrum. By contrast, the spectra of complex periodic sounds, with individual lines for each frequency, are called *discrete* spectra (see Figure 3–4).

Other nonperiodic sounds, which fit our definition of "noise," include sounds of very short duration. Examples are explosions, gunshots, and the sound produced by a toy "cricket" when it is snapped. These *brief, nonperiodic sounds are called transients,* and they, too, possess spectra that extend over a broad range of frequencies.

Transmission of Sound to a Listener

To reach a listener's ear and be perceived as "sound" the *motion* of a vibrating string, a reed in a musical instrument, or the tines of a pi-

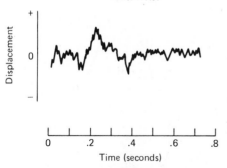

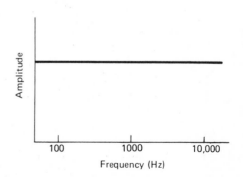

FIGURE 3–5. *An illustration of random-pattern motion and its spectrum.*

ano tuner's "fork" must cause motion patterns in the material that lies between the source and the listener. This material—air, water, earth, etc.—is known as the *medium* through which the energy passes to the listener. In this section of the chapter we are concerned with how sound is transmitted through a medium. Because we usually perceive sound through air, our discussion focuses on the air medium. Topics include sound transmission in air, sound waves, sound shadows, and resonance effects.

Sound Transmission in Air. The molecules comprising air are always in motion, moving about randomly over minute distances and remaining a constant distance from each other, on the average. When a sound generator imposes its motion patterns on an air medium, molecules of the medium are disturbed from their normal activity patterns and undergo patterns of motion that mimic the motion of the generator. It is important to understand that the molecules in air (or any medium) are not pushed all the distance from the source of sound to the receiver. Rather, they move to and fro and force those molecules adjacent to them to move in a to and fro pattern that is dictated by the sound generator.

Figure 3–6 illustrates how a motion pattern might be created and transmitted through air. Drawings on the left side of the figure depict a cylinder containing air and a moving piston. At the right of each drawing a graph shows the displacement of the molecules of air in the cylinder at the instant captured by the cylinder drawing.

Panel (a) shows the cylinder piston at rest and a uniform spacing of the molecules. In panel (b) the piston has moved to the extreme right, pushing molecules ahead of it, and as the graph to the right suggests, causing a *compression* (greater than normal density) of the

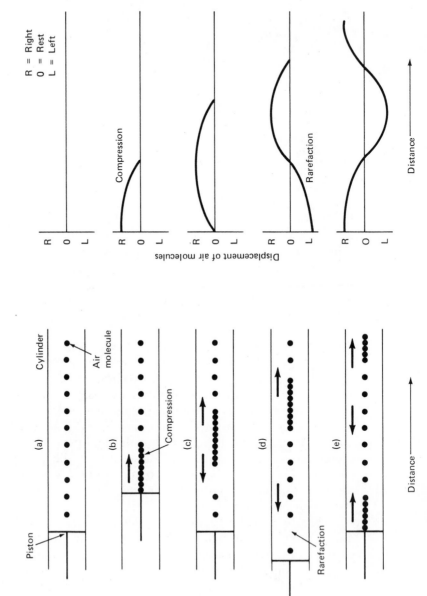

FIGURE 3-6. Schematic (left) and graphic (right) representations of displacement patterns of air molecules caused by sound. See text for detailed explanation. (After L. Beranek, Acoustics. New York: McGraw-Hill, 1954.)

molecules closest to the piston. When the piston moves back toward its starting point, as in panel (c), a few molecules follow and try to regain their original positions. Others, further down the cylinder, also try to expand and, in so doing, disturb their neighbors. In panel (d), the piston has moved to the extreme left of its travel. There are a few molecules close to the piston at this moment, but fewer than would be the case had the piston remained at rest. Thus, a *rarefaction* (less than normal density) region has been formed. The effects of the original compression have, meanwhile, moved further down the cylinder than they were in panel (c). Some molecules now start to recoil from the original compression and move back toward the surface of the piston, as well. Finally, in panel (e), the piston moves back through the starting position again, gathering molecules that were adjacent to it a moment earlier and pushing them back toward the right. The molecules being pushed ahead of the piston are met head-on by others that had been returning to the left, and a new region of compressed molecules is created. Meanwhile, the effects of the original compression/rarefaction disturbance have moved nearly to the open end of the cylinder. Thus, a complete "cycle" has transpired, beginning with and ending with a compression.

Sound Waves. A consequence of disturbing air molecules in compression/rarefaction patterns is the creation of small pressure disturbances in air that mimic the to and fro motion patterns of the generator. These alternating pressure disturbances in the atmosphere form *sound waves.* Sound waves travel through a medium with a velocity determined by the density and stiffness of the medium. For air at sea level and normal room temperature, the velocity of sound is about 1130 feet per second. Most of us are not aware of the time required for sound to travel through air because we are usually quite close to the source of sound. Perhaps you were taught to judge the distance to a bolt of lightning by counting the seconds between seeing it and hearing the thunder. The rationale behind this teaching was that visible energy (the flash) traveled very rapidly (186,000 miles per second), but that sound energy traveled much slower and took longer to reach you.

If we could see the sound progressing from a home music system to a listener, its waves might appear as suggested in Figure 3–7. Pressure disturbances from the compressions and rarefactions would move toward the listener at a rate of about 13.5 inches for each 0.001 second (1/1000th) after they originated at the loudspeaker. For a person sitting about 4.5 feet from the loudspeaker, about 0.004 second would be required before the sound arrived. (These time values may

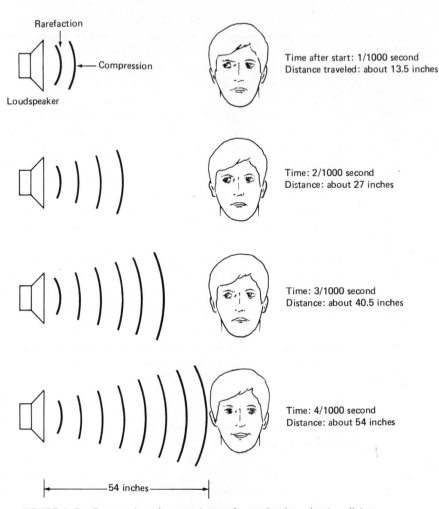

Rarefaction

Compression

Loudspeaker

Time after start: 1/1000 second
Distance traveled: about 13.5 inches

Time: 2/1000 second
Distance: about 27 inches

Time: 3/1000 second
Distance: about 40.5 inches

Time: 4/1000 second
Distance: about 54 inches

|← 54 inches →|

FIGURE 3–7. *Progression of a sound wave from a loudspeaker to a listener.*

seem trivially small, but later we will see how very small differences between the time of arrival of a sound at the two ears can help us locate the source of the sound.)

A fundamental property of sound waves is that the distance between their adjacent regions of compression and rarefaction changes systematically with changes in the frequency of the sound. This distance is called the *wavelength* of the sound wave, and is designated by the Greek lambda (λ). In general, changes in wavelength with changes in frequency mimic the relationship between period and frequency discussed earlier. Formally:

102

$$\lambda(\text{wavelength}) = \frac{\text{velocity of sound (feet per second)}}{\text{frequency of the sound (Hz)}} = \frac{\text{feet}}{\text{cycle}}.$$

Stated otherwise, the wavelength of a sound becomes shorter as its frequency increases, just as the period becomes shorter as the frequency increases. For example, contrasting the two frequencies of 1130 and 2260 Hz, we encounter wavelength values of 1.0 foot and 0.5 foot, respectively.

It is important to realize that the energy imparted to a medium in the form of pressure variations is eventually consumed by the work involved in transmitting the sound. This consumption is the result of minute frictional forces that oppose (resist) motion. The decay of energy associated with a traveling sound wave is quite dramatic. After leaving the source, energy decays at a rate determined by the square of the distance traveled. Thus, sound measured 10 feet from a source will have only about 1/100th of its initial energy remaining. At 20 feet, only about 1/400th of the original energy will exist.

Sound Shadows. *Shadows,* or regions of low energy, may be created for sound waves just as they are for light waves. Place your hand over this page and you will create an area of reduced illumination. This results from a failure of the light waves to "bend" around your hand and fill in the space between your hand and the page. A substantial portion of light energy simply reflects back from the surface of your hand. Similar effects occur for sound energy, as suggested in Figure 3–8. Low-frequency sound waves, having very long wavelengths travel around objects with relatively little disturbance, much in the way that large, slow, ocean waves travel by a piling anchored to the ocean floor. High-frequency sound waves, with shorter wavelengths, may reflect back from a small object, such as a human head, and may fill in the "void" caused by the reflection only after passing a considerable distance beyond the object. Returning to our light analogy, note that there is less and less shadow effect as you raise your hand from the page. The greater illumination is a manifestation of the fact that the light waves are able to fill in the space beneath the hand only after they have traveled some distance beyond it. The analogous sound shadow effect is an important clue we use to locate sounds in space. The ear closest to the source of a sound receives somewhat more energy than the other ear, and the energy difference is due, in part, to a "shadow" created by the head. Large structures such as patio walls also produce substantial shadow effects for sound energy, and they and such objects as office "cubicles" help to provide a measure of privacy for speech communication.

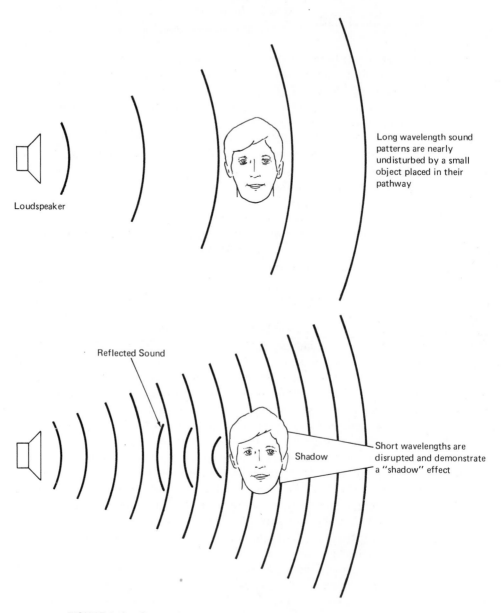

Long wavelength sound patterns are nearly undisturbed by a small object placed in their pathway

Loudspeaker

Reflected Sound

Shadow

Short wavelengths are disrupted and demonstrate a "shadow" effect

FIGURE 3–8. *Sound shadow effects for long and short wavelengths.*

Resonance Effects. When an object within a medium, or the medium itself, is reluctant to respond to sound energy, several things happen. One of these is reflection. We are all aware of sound reflection in the

104

form of echos, such as those that occur when shouting into a large hard-walled canyon. The small motion and pressure changes that comprise a sound wave in air simply "bounce off" very dense or stiff objects in a manner similar to that of light being reflected from a mirror. Reflected energy may sometimes add with energy eminating from a source (called incident energy) to produce an increase in energy at some location. When we look up from a study lamp we can note that some of the illumination provided by the lamp naturally spills over into the room. Were we to use a mirror to capture some of the incident illumination, we could direct it to a "spot" somewhere in the room. This bright "spot" is due in part to the addition of energy that had originally spilled over to that location and the energy reflected from our mirror.

Sound waves cannot be "focused" as precisely as light waves, but they may add together in combinations of incident and reflected energy to produce *selective reinforcement* or strengthening of signals. For example, consider a hollow tube placed in the path of a sound wave and closed at one end, as illustrated in Figure 3–9. When no sound is present, air molecules are free to move about randomly within the tube. As the first compression region of a sound wave enters the open end of the tube, molecules near the entrance are pushed together. The force of the incident energy drives a wave of compression down the tube, just as it would in open air. However, upon reaching the closed end of the tube, the wave of energy is reflected. This produces a compression effect that travels back toward the source of the sound, that is, toward the open end of the tube. If the rarefaction region originating from the source of sound happens to arrive at the open end of the tube at the same moment the reflected compression arrives, the molecules will be driven toward the left with greater energy than could have been supplied by the source. Some of this energy is due to the reflection, and some of it is new incident energy. Once a complete cycle of the sound wave has been treated in this fashion, the molecular motion resulting from reflection complements the incident motion exactly, helping to reinforce the to and fro motion of the molecules.

The closed-tube reinforcement effect is similar to the effect observed when two independent sound generators face each other and work their to and fro motion patterns so that they complement each other exactly, like two persons working on opposite ends of a saw. It should be recognized that the spacing between the two generators would have to be chosen carefully so that the mixture of motion patterns would truly be reinforcing, otherwise they might actually interfere with each other. Closed tubes also have a spacing constraint.

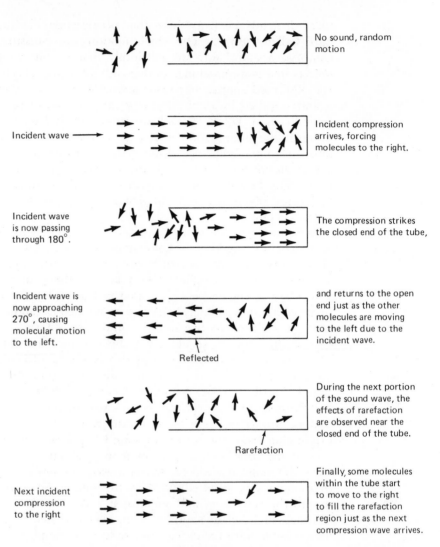

No sound, random motion

Incident wave ⟶

Incident compression arrives, forcing molecules to the right.

Incident wave is now passing through 180°.

The compression strikes the closed end of the tube,

Incident wave is now approaching 270°, causing molecular motion to the left.

Reflected

and returns to the open end just as the other molecules are moving to the left due to the incident wave.

During the next portion of the sound wave, the effects of rarefaction are observed near the closed end of the tube.

Rarefaction

Next incident compression to the right

Finally, some molecules within the tube start to move to the right to fill the rarefaction region just as the next compression wave arrives.

FIGURE 3–9. *Motion patterns within a closed-tube resonator. Arrows show direction of molecular motion. See text for further explanation.*

Their length must be exactly one-fourth the wavelength of a sound wave if they are to provide selective reinforcement for that sound or its harmonics. Because of this constraint, closed tubes are also called "quarter-wave resonators."

In addition to closed tubes, objects such as vibrating strings, tubes that are open at both ends, bars of metal (like the tines of a tuning fork), and crystal glasses all have *resonant properties*. They provide *a preferential response to certain frequencies,* and the preferred frequencies may be predicted after the dimensions of the object and the wavelengths of the vibratory patterns imposed on the object are known.

As discussed in Chapter 2, the airway between the larynx, or source of voice in humans, and the outside air may be considered to be a series of tubes linked together. Dimensions of these tubes are modified during speech production to produce *resonances or energy concentrations.* These resonances help to emphasize selected harmonics of the voice spectrum. Because these resonances can be changed by a speaker over a wide range, humans are naturally able to produce a very wide range of distinguishable speech and speechlike sounds. Parts of the human ear also respond preferentially to certain frequencies in the range between about 1000 and 4000 Hz, a range where much important information regarding speech sounds may be found.

Finally, it should be noted that "resonance" properties may also be built into electronic equipment that is used for hearing testing or home music entertainment systems. The "bass" and "treble" controls on home music systems simply provide for relatively more or less emphasis of low-frequency or high-frequency sounds, adjustments that are accomplished by using electronic components that mimic the effects of density, stiffness, and friction on the electrical replicas of sound waves generated within the system. It is possible to "fine tune" certain electronic equipment so that it behaves like a very narrow-range "filter", which responds only to a restricted range of signal frequencies. Electronic filters are useful in the study of normal hearing and in the testing of hearing-impaired individuals because they allow us to manufacture very complex sounds that can be restricted in terms of the broadness and shape of their spectra. Green (1976) and Durrant and Lovrinic (1977) provide comprehensive reviews of the principles that have been discussed here.

Measurement of the Magnitude of Sound

We have learned that disturbances imposed upon a medium by a sound source ultimately result in minute moment-to-moment changes in pressure within that medium. It is common to measure such pressure events and to use the data obtained as an expression of the magnitude of a sound. Pressure is preferred as the aspect to express magnitude of a sound because it is easier to measure than total energy, and because the ear is a pressure-sensitive receptor.

Pressure is the result of some force acting upon some area. The most commonly used force unit is the *dyne*, a dyne being the amount of force necessary to accelerate one gram at a rate of one centimeter per second, each second. Therefore, a dyne acting on one gram would move it at a rate of 1 cm/sec after one second, 2 cm/sec after two seconds, 3 cm/sec after three seconds, and so on. When pressure is to be measured, the units conventionally used are *dynes per square centimeter*.

The human ear is sensitive to pressure as small as about 0.0002 dyne/cm² and as great as about 200 dynes/cm², or a range of about 1 to 1,000,000! To use our everyday numbering system when working with values covering this range is cumbersome and impractical. Consequently, we use a number scale based on the logarithm of pressure changes rather than on the pressure changes themselves. These log-based measurements form a sort of shorthand.

The unit of measurement in this shorthand is expressed as a *Bel* in honor of the inventor of the telephone. Bels are defined as the logarithm of the ratio of two energies, or:

$$Bel = \log_{10} \frac{E}{E_{reference}}$$

where E may be more or less than the reference.

When the amount of energy used to generate sound changes, the pressure resulting from that change does not vary in a simple one-to-one fashion with the energy change. Rather, pressure increases or decreases with the square root of the change in energy. Expressed formally, the relationship is:

$$\sqrt{\frac{E}{E_{ref}}} = \frac{P}{P_{ref}} \qquad \frac{E}{E_{ref}} = \left(\frac{P}{P_{ref}}\right)^2.$$

This means, for example, that a 2:1 change in energy results in a pressure change of only 1.41:1; or that a 16:1 change in energy results in a pressure change of only 4:1.

When expressed in terms of Bels, one can say that

$$\text{if N Bels} = \log\frac{E}{E_{ref}}, \text{ then N Bels also} = \log\left(\frac{P}{P_{ref}}\right)^2 \text{ or } 2\log\frac{P}{P_{ref}}$$

where the pressure ratio is that which resulted from the indicated energy ratio.

As a shorthand system, the Bel scale is very effective in reducing the size of the numbers with which we must work. For example, a pressure range of 1,000,000 to 1 corresponds to only 12 Bels. (The log of 1,000,000 is 6, and N Bels = 2 × 6 in this case.) When hearing phenomena became the object of precise study, it became apparent that Bel measurements were too large, because the ear is sensitive to small fractions of a Bel. Therefore, it became conventional to use 1/10th of a Bel (*deciBel*) as the unit to express the sound pressure of an acoustic event. Because there are 10 deciBels (*dB*) in each Bel, we can say that:

$$\text{N dB} = 10 \log\frac{E}{E_{\text{ref}}} \text{ or N dB} = 2 \times 10 \log\frac{P}{P_{\text{ref}}} \text{ or N dB} = 20 \log\frac{P}{P_{\text{ref}}}.$$

Table 3–1 shows the relationships between several energy ratios, their logs, and the pressure ratios and logs that result from those energy ratios. The table also shows the dB change corresponding with each of the ratios.

When dealing with dB measurements, it is important to remember that they represent *ratios* of pressure, and that some reference pressure must always be stated or implied when the expression N dB is used. There are three commonly used types of dB measurements

Table 3–1. ENERGY RATIOS AND THEIR LOGS, RESULTING PRESSURE RATIOS AND THEIR LOGS, AND THE dB EQUIVALENT OF THOSE RATIOS.*

A POWER OR ENERGY RATIO THAT IS SHOWN BELOW	HAS A LOG OF	AND THE POWER OR ENERGY RATIO PRODUCES A PRESSURE RATIO OF	WITH A LOG OF	FOR N dB
1:1 (no change)	0	1:1 (no change)	0	0 dB
1.27:1	0.1	1.13:1	0.05	1 dB
1.61:1	0.2	1.27:1	0.10	2 dB
2.00:1	0.3	1.41:1	0.15	3 dB
2.52:1	0.4	1.58:1	0.20	4 dB
3.17:1	0.5	1.78:1	0.25	5 dB
4.00:1	0.6	2.00:1	0.3	6 dB
10:1	1.0	3.17:1	0.5	10 dB
100:1	2.0	10:1	1.0	20 dB
1000:1	3.0	31.65:1	1.5	30 dB
10,000:1	4.0	100:1	2.0	40 dB
100,000:1	5.0	316.5:1	2.5	50 dB
1,000,000:1	6.0	1000:1	3.0	60 dB
10,000,000:1	7.0	3165:1	3.5	70 dB
100,000,000:1	8.0	10,000:1	4.0	80 dB
1,000,000,000:1	9.0	31,650:1	4.5	90 dB
10,000,000,000:1	10.0	100,000:1	5.0	100 dB
100,000,000,000:1	11.0	316,500:1	5.5	110 dB
1,000,000,000,000:1	12.0	1,000,000:1	6.0	120 dB

*The number of dB shown on the right is equal to either 10 times the log of the appropriate energy ratio, or 20 times the log of the resulting pressure ratio. Note that because the square root of the energy ratio equals the pressure ratio, that the log of the pressure ratio is always ½ of the log of the energy ratio. Thus, a 3 dB change in energy produces a 3 dB change in pressure, but the energy ratio corresponding to that change is 2:1, and the resulting pressure ratio is 1.41:1. A 120 dB change corresponds to an energy ratio of one trillion to one, with a resulting pressure change of one million to one.

that have implied reference pressures. They are sound pressure level (SPL), sensation level (SL), and hearing level (HL). The reference pressure for SPL is always 0.0002 dyne/cm². Therefore, an expression such as 20 dB SPL means that the sound pressure is 20 dB above a reference of 0.0002 dyne/cm². (See Small, 1978, for a thorough development of this topic.)

Occasionally, it is more important to study sounds that are maintained at some level above an individual's threshold for those sounds. For example, we may wish to study how well speech signals are understood when they are 40 dB above a listener's threshold for speech signals. In this case, the actual SPL may not be important, but the fact that the signals are 40 dB above someone's threshold is important. When signals are measured in this fashion, they are expressed as dB SL, rather than dB SPL.

Finally, the American National Standards Institute (ANSI) has published "standard" reference pressures for the individual tones that are used to test hearing (ANSI, 1969). As we shall discuss later, humans do not hear all tones with identical sensitivity, and the ANSI standards recognize that normal-hearing individuals require a greater SPL to hear some tones than others. When sound pressures are reported relative to the ANSI standards, they are designated as dB (HL).

STRUCTURE AND FUNCTION OF THE HUMAN EAR

The human ear, illustrated in Figure 3–10, consists of many structures, each of which plays a specific role in the process of sound perception. These structures can be grouped into three major subdivisions: the *outer ear,* the *middle ear,* and the *inner ear.*

The outer ear serves as a sound collector and helps us locate the source of sounds. Structures housed within the middle ear move in response to the motion patterns imposed on the air contained in the outer ear, and help to convey energy to the inner ear in an efficient manner. The inner ear contains the actual sensory apparatus for hearing. Remarkably, its structures not only respond to the complex motion patterns that comprise everyday sounds, but they also analyze those sounds. As a result of the analysis provided by inner ear structures, the nerve connecting the inner ear to the brain is able to carry information about the magnitude and complexity of motion patterns perceived as sound. The sophisticated analysis performed by inner ear structures has yet to be matched by any machine or electronic device that man can conceive, and it is the cornerstone of our wide range of perception. Contributions of each of the subdivisions of the ear to hearing are described in sections that follow.

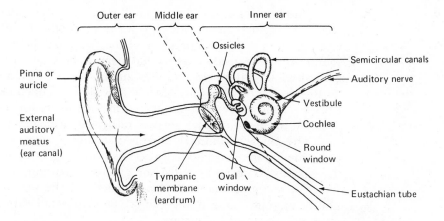

FIGURE 3–10. *Schematic illustration of the human ear showing its outer, middle, and inner sections and their respective structures.*

The Outer Ear

The outer ear consists of a visible portion, the *auricle* or *pinna,* and the *external auditory canal* (ear canal), or *meatus,* which leads from the pinna to the middle ear. The shape of the pinna, like fingerprints, varies considerably from person to person. Its ridges and depressions are formed by small pieces of cartilage that are held together by ligaments and covered with skin. The pinna helps to collect sound energy and direct it into the external auditory meatus. Because of its small size and the immobility of its parts, the pinna makes a relatively small contribution to hearing sensitivity. Its ridges and depressions combine to function somewhat like the resonators described earlier. Because the depressions are small and the distances between ridges are very short, the resonances produced occur only for frequencies having very short wavelengths, namely, those above about 7000 Hz. Pinna resonances do not provide significant assistance for speech communication purposes, but they may help us locate sources of sound that are above or below us, particularly high-frequency sources (Shaw, 1974; Butler, 1975; Zwislocki, 1975).

Near its outer end, the external auditory meatus is formed by a ring of soft cartilage. Like the pinna, the shape of the meatus may vary considerably from person to person. Typically, it is slightly oval, and has a total length of about one inch. The deepest portion of the meatus has a hard, bony foundation. And, at its inner end, it flares outward slightly and provides a firm seat for the *tympanic membrane* (eardrum).

The tympanic membrane combines with the external auditory meatus to form a closed-tube (1/4–wave) resonator. Its effect is to provide a gain in the sound pressure at the tympanic membrane over the sound pressure outside the external meatus. This gain occurs in the region of 2500 to 4000 Hz, and may amount to as much as 10 to 12 dB (3- to 4-fold increase in pressure) (Shaw, 1974). Functionally, this gain provides an improvement in our hearing sensitivity for the frequencies at which the resonance is effective, rather like a small amplifier.

The external auditory meatus also gives protection to the tympanic membrane and middle ear. Hair follicles grow from the floor of the meatus to serve as a barrier against intrusion. A waxlike substance, *cerumen,* is secreted from the floor of the meatus and continuously migrates toward the pinna carrying small dirt particles and other debris out of the meatus.

The Middle Ear

The middle ear is an irregularly-shaped cavity that houses several structures that are free to move. Normally, this cavity is filled with air. Its front wall is perforated by a small passageway called the *Eustachian tube.* This tube runs between the middle-ear space and the nasopharynx (upper throat behind the nose) and is usually closed. The naso-pharyngeal end of the tube is flexible and has muscles attached to it which, when they are active during swallowing, help to open the tube to allow air to pass between the pharynx and the middle ear. This opening adjustment helps keep air pressure in the middle-ear space equal to that outside the space. The Eustachian tube also allows fluid secreted by the thin mucous lining of the middle ear to drain from the space.

The tympanic membrane is a delicate and thin combination of the skin of the external auditory meatus, a supporting fibrous layer, and the thin lining of the middle-ear space. It represents a very tightly stretched barrier between the middle ear and the outside world. As illustrated in Figure 3–11, the tympanic membrane is connected firmly to one of three small bones, or *ossicles,* which move in response to its motion, and which form a connection between it and the inner ear.

The first of the ossicles looks somewhat like a primitive club, and is called the *malleus.* Its long, handlelike portion is attached to the tympanic membrane. The upper portion of the malleus, its head, is attached firmly to the head of the second ossicle, called the *incus.* This ossicle draws its name from the fact that its head is shaped somewhat like a blacksmith's anvil. The handle of the incus is called its "long-process." Because of their firm interconnection, the malleus and incus

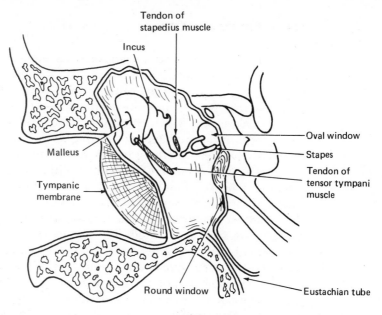

FIGURE 3–11. *Schematic illustration of the middle-ear cavity and its major contents.*

move as a single unit, rather like a wooden-spring clothespin hung upside-down on a washline, and pushed to and fro with pressure on one of its arms.

The third ossicle in the chain of three is shaped like a stirrup, and is called the *stapes.* It attaches to the long process of the incus with a flexible joint that allows it to move in a complex fashion when it is pushed to and fro by the motion of the malleus/incus lever. The stapes is seated in a form-fitting *oval window,* which leads to the inner-ear apparatus.

The middle-ear apparatus functions in a manner that provides for an efficient transfer of sound energy from the outer ear to the inner ear. This transfer involves the passage of energy from an air medium to a liquid medium (the latter in the inner ear). The liquid encased within the inner ear offers a much greater *impedance* to the flow of sound energy than is offered by air. Thus, were airborne sound energy to encounter the inner ear liquid directly, much of this energy would simply be reflected away, just as it would from the surface of a brick wall. The middle-ear apparatus helps to overcome the natural mismatch in impedances between the outside air and the inner-ear liquid. This help is made possible because of certain mechanical features of the tympanic membrane and the ossicles (Zwislocki, 1975; Feldman and Wilber, 1976).

One important feature is that the malleus and incus combine to form a lever. The "leverage" obtained by their combination is due to the fact that they move as a single structure, and that the handle of

113

the malleus is somewhat longer than its equivalent process on the incus. Any force applied to the malleus handle is *increased* at the joint between the incus and stapes due to the length difference. The exact force increase is in proportion to the ratio of the two lengths, about 1.3 to 1 (Wever and Lawrence, 1954; Dallos, 1973). This type of force increase can be appreciated by thinking of the usefulness of a carpenter's claw-hammer. The long handle of that tool provides for a significant mechanical advantage when one is attempting to remove a nail or pry loose a board. This advantage is proportional to the ratio of the length of the handle versus the claw's length.

Another important mechanical feature that enables the middle ear structures to effect an efficient energy transfer from the outer to inner ears is the difference in sizes of the tympanic membrane and stapes bottom, or *footplate*. The useful area of the tympanic membrane is about 18 times that of the footplate of the stapes. Accordingly, the pressure applied (force per unit area) at the stapes is about 18 times as great as that applied to the tympanic membrane (Wever and Lawrence, 1954; Dallos, 1973). The mechanical advantage gained by the area difference between the tympanic membrane and stapes footplate is analogous to that we are all familiar with in nails, tacks, and pins. All of these can be driven or pushed into place more easily because of the relative sizes of their heads and points. Forces delivered to the larger heads are more concentrated when realized at the smaller points.

When the effects of the malleus/incus lever action and the relative area differences of the tympanic membrane and stapes footplate are combined, the resulting increase in pressure at the stapes is about 1.3 (the lever) × 18 (the area ratio), or about 24 times the pressure at the tympanic membrane. This boost in pressure corresponds to approximately 28 dB, a substantial increase and a major contributor to the efficiency of transfer of energy from the outer ear to the inner ear.

The inner ear can be reached through another route that is less efficient than the normal air-conduction route just discussed. Bones comprising the skull can be set into motion either by very intense airborne sound or by applying a mechanical vibrator directly to the skull. When the skull is caused to vibrate, auditory sensation results even though the "normal" route to the inner ear is not used. Hearing sensation that results from skull vibration is called *bone-conduction* hearing. The means by which bone-conduction works are not fully understood (Tonndorf, 1966). It has been suggested that the motion of the skull in response to bone-conducted energy is not in exact synchrony with that of the ossicles, because the ossicles are rather loosely suspended in the middle-ear space and their motion is free to lag behind the skull motion slightly. Although lagging behind the motion of the skull, they move to and fro relative to the liquid in the inner ear, just as if they had been caused to move by sound arriving at the tympanic membrane. Because this form of inner-ear stimulation is believed to depend upon the inertia of the ossicles, the theory that suggests it is called the *inertial* bone-conduction theory.

Another theory regarding bone conduction suggests that the dense bone containing the inner ear undergoes slight compression in response to vibratory energy applied directly to the skull. When compression and subsequent expansion occurs, the cavities comprising the inner-ear space change slightly, effectively "squeezing" the liquid. Because the liquid is not compressible, it is pushed to and fro as toothpaste might be pushed from pressure on a tube containing it. This theory is called the *compressional* bone-conduction theory.

In addition to the middle-ear structures that function to increase our hearing sensitivity, there are two muscles that attach to the ossicles and that selectively reduce motion of the ossicles at times. One of these muscles is the *tensor tympani*. The body of the tensor tympani lies in a small channel that runs parallel to the Eustachian tube. Its tendon crosses from the innermost forward part of the middle-ear cavity to attach to the malleus. The malleus is pulled inward when the tensor tympani contracts, hence, stiffening the tympanic membrane somewhat. The tensor tympani contracts reflexively during such activities as swallowing and talking. It also contracts when the face near the pinna or the pinna are touched, and it contracts in response to sounds that are very intense. A second muscle, the *stapedius*, attaches to the stapes. When it contracts it pulls the stapes outward slightly from its normal position in the oval window. The stapedius is known to contract reflexively in response to sounds that are perceived as having moderate to great loudness. The two middle-ear muscles are said to be *antagonistic*, because they pull in opposite directions. The overall effect of their contraction is to add stiffness to the middle-ear system and reduce its efficiency in transferring energy to the inner ear. Because the muscles contract in response to very loud sounds, they are thought to provide some degree of protection for the inner ear by impairing the efficiency of middle-ear energy transfer for those sounds (Moller, 1974b). They may also help to "tune" the ear for important sounds, because their contraction helps to cut down the transfer of low-frequency energy more than of high-frequency energy (Moller, 1974a).

The Inner Ear

The inner-ear mechanism is located within a series of tortuous channels etched into the dense bone of the skull. As is illustrated in Figure 3–12, this mechanism can be partitioned into three distinct portions:

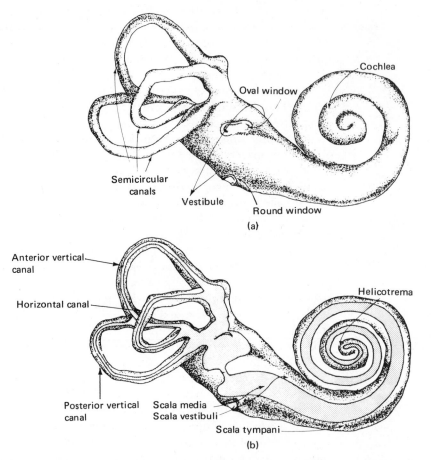

Cochlea

Oval window

Semicircular
canals

Vestibule

Round window

(a)

Anterior vertical
canal

Horizontal canal

Helicotrema

Posterior vertical
canal

Scala media
Scala vestibuli

Scala tympani

(b)

FIGURE 3–12. *Schematic illustration of the (a) bony and (b) membranous labyrinths of the inner ear. (From T. Glattke, Elements of auditory physiology. In F. Minifie, T. Hixon, and F. Williams, Eds.,* Normal Aspects of Speech, Hearing, and Language © 1973, *p. 299. Englewood Cliffs, N.J.: Prentice-Hall, 1973.)*

the *semicircular canals*, the *vestibule*, and the *cochlea*. The semicircular canals are named for their shapes, which conform roughly to a letter "C" as they arise out of the vestibule and then return to it. The vestibule is the "entryway" to the inner-ear labyrinth. The oval window, described previously, is situated so as to face directly into the vestibule. The cochlea is named for its shape, which resembles a coiled conch or snail's shell. A second window, called the *round window* because of its approximately circular shape, opens into the cochlea and is covered with a thin transparent membrane.

Within the bony canals and spaces mentioned, there is a membranous system that contains sensory receptors for each subdivision of

116

the inner ear. This system is surrounded by a clear liquid that is similar to that which surrounds the brain and the spinal cord. Because this liquid lies *outside* the membranous system, it is called *perilymph*. Another type of liquid is encased *within* the membranous labyrinth, and is called *endolymph*. The motion of the liquid perilymph and endolymph within the semicircular canals and vestibule causes different specialized receptor cells to be displaced and stimulated and thereby provides sensory information to visual, proprioceptive, and skeletal-muscle systems. This information is of crucial importance in helping us maintain our balance, perform locomotion, and know our orientation in space. Although our prime concern in this chapter is with hearing, it is important to note that many disorders of the inner ear affect both its hearing portion (to be discussed next) and portions that are involved in the functions just mentioned. One such disorder is Meniere's disease, a condition characterized by episodes of dizziness, spinning sensations, nausea, and hearing loss (see Chapter 12).

Sensory receptors for hearing are found within the cochlea. These important receptors, like those in the semicircular canals and the vestibule, are also sensitive to displacement via liquid motion. Under normal circumstances of hearing by air conduction, the necessary motion is generated by the action of the stapes on the liquids within the cochlea. The basic arrangement of the cochlea and its contents can be understood from Figure 3–13. Ignoring the semicircular canals and the vestibule, we can consider the cochlea to be a hard-walled cavity filled with liquid and having two flexible openings. Part (a) of Figure 3–13 suggests this by portraying the cochlea as a glass cylinder with flexible coverings at each end. In (b), the stapes has been attached to the oval window, and a supporting membrane, called the *basilar membrane,* has been added. This latter addition lies approximately in the center of the hard-walled cavity and divides the cavity into two separate channels, or *scalae*. The upper channel is called the *scala vestibuli* and the lower is designated the *scala tympani*. Part (c) of the figure shows that sensory cells are located on the basilar membrane and that nerve fibers lead from these cells to the brain. In addition, a small passageway between the scala vestibuli and the scala tympani has been added. This passageway is termed the *helicotrema* and it permits liquid to pass from one scala to the other when the stapes is moved slowly, such as when we change altitude or dive under water.

There are about 20,000 receptor cells in each human cochlea, and so the cavity illustrated in Figure 3–13c has been stretched out on one side in (d) to accommodate these cells. The actual length of this extension, from stapes to helicotrema, is approximately 35 millimeters (1 1/2 inches). The cochlea is coiled in life as illustrated in Figure 3–13e. For humans this coil consists of about 2 1/2 turns of successively smaller di-

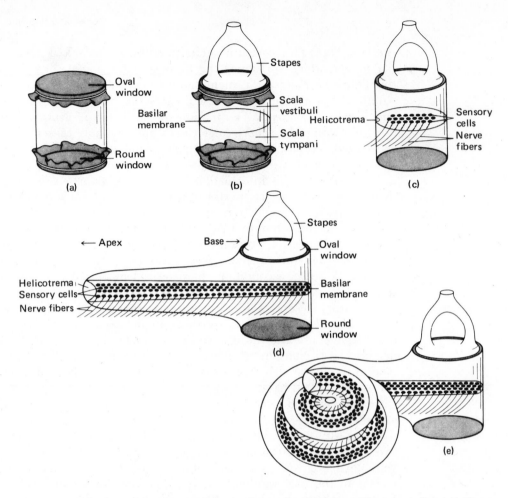

FIGURE 3–13. *The fundamental arrangement of the human inner ear. (From N. Kiang, Stimulus representation in the discharge patterns of auditory neurons. In D. Tower, Ed., The Nervous System, Vol. III, Human Communication and Its Disorders.* New York: Raven Press, 1975.)

ameters. When viewed from the side, the cochlea has a shape that resembles a pyramid, with the widest turn, nearest the stapes, called the *base*, and the smallest turn, nearest the helicotrema, called the *apex*.

More detailed illustrations of the contents of the cochlea are provided in Figure 3–14. Part (a) of the figure is a cross-sectional view that would be obtained were one to slice across the long extension of the cochlea shown in Figure 3–13d. The scala tympani is below the basilar membrane. A third scala, the wedge-shaped scala media, is formed by the basilar membrane on the bottom and *Reissner's membrane* above. The scala vestibuli is the remaining channel. Within the scala media are the sensory cells for hearing. These have many small

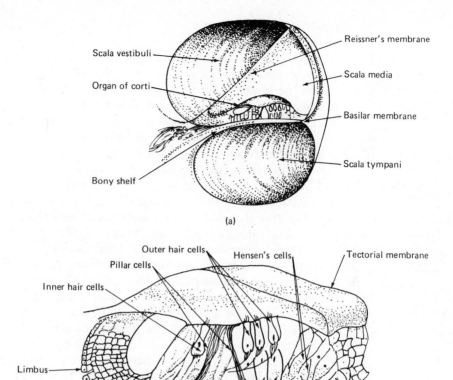

Scala vestibuli

Organ of corti

Bony shelf

Reissner's membrane

Scala media

Basilar membrane

Scala tympani

(a)

Outer hair cells

Pillar cells

Inner hair cells

Hensen's cells

Tectorial membrane

Limbus

Bony shelf

Nerve fibers

Deiters cells

Basilar membrane

Cells of Claudius

(b)

FIGURE 3–14. *Illustrations of (a) an enlargement of a cross-section of a single turn of the cochlea, and (b) an enlargement of the organ of Corti, which is contained within the scala média. (From T. Glattke, Elements of auditory physiology. In F. Minifie, T. Hixon, and F. Williams, Eds.,* Normal Aspects of Speech, Hearing, and Language. *Englewood Cliffs, N.J.: Prentice-Hall, 1973.)*

hairlike projections extending from their upper surface and are called *hair cells* (see Figure 3–14b). Hair cells are grouped together in a single inner row and three outer rows that extend from the base to the apex of the cochlea. The hairlike projections from the sensory cells are in intimate contact with an overlying structure, called the *tectorial membrane*. Additional cells help to support the hair cells and other structures lying within the scala media, and the entire group of cells, together with the tectorial membrane, is called the *organ of Corti*, in honor of the anatomist who first described it. (See Yost and Nielsen, 1977, for a more complete description of the cochlea.)

When the stapes moves in response to acoustic energy, the liquid in the cochlea is displaced in a pattern that corresponds with the motion of the stapes. The organ of Corti reacts to this displacement in a manner dictated by its physical characteristics, particularly those of the basilar membrane. From Figure 3–13c, it should be easy to imagine the basilar membrane being displaced downward by inward movement of the stapes, and upward by outward movement of the stapes. For very low-frequency signals, the in-out motion of the stapes results in up-down displacement of the basilar membrane, as if it were a simple rubber covering placed in the pathway between the oval window and round window. For frequencies above the range of 50–100 Hz, however, the motion of the basilar membrane is *wavelike,* with an up-down displacement pattern that progresses from the basal end toward the apex. As the illustrations in Figure 3–15 suggest, the distance the displacement pattern covers depends upon the frequency of the incoming signal. Displacement patterns for low-frequency signals arise near the base and extend nearly to the apex of the cochlea. As the signal frequency is *raised,* the distance over which the displacement pattern travels is *shortened.* High-frequency signals cause displacement patterns that are confined to the basal end of the scala media, and patterns resulting from mid-range frequencies travel to the middle of the base-apex range (Bekesy, 1960).

As a result of the types of "traveling waves" illustrated in Figure 3–15, hair cells in the basal region of the cochlea receive maximal stimulation from high-frequency signals, and those cells further down the length of the cochlea receive stimulation from progressively lower frequencies. Thus, the organ of Corti provides a *spatially organized* analysis of incoming signals, much akin to the spectral analyses illustrated in Figure 3–4. Each of the cells in the cochlea has a very restricted range of frequencies to which it will respond, and each has a single "best" frequency that is most efficient in producing a response. The "place" versus signal-frequency registration provided by the cochlea is called *tonotopic organization.* This registration of the individual frequencies contained in a signal is also preserved throughout the structures of the brain that respond to sounds. Thus, *place of excitation* within the cochlea and within the brain provides the significant information as to which frequencies are contained in any simple or complex acoustic signal (Brugge, 1975; Evans, 1975; Kiang, 1975).

A second important clue regarding the frequencies arriving at the cochlea is provided by the *rate at which individual auditory nerve fibers respond* to a signal. If a single fiber responds to a low frequency, it is likely to respond at a rate equal to some consistent fraction of the stimulus frequency (Evans, 1975; Kiang, 1975).

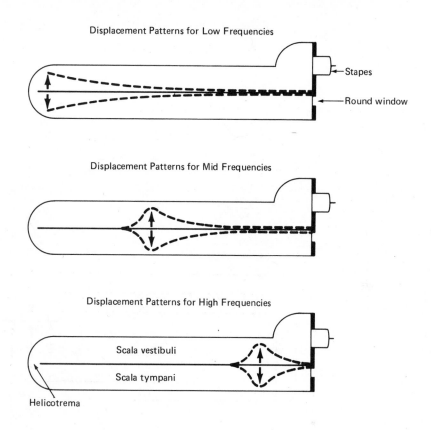

Displacement Patterns for Low Frequencies

Stapes

Round window

Displacement Patterns for Mid Frequencies

Displacement Patterns for High Frequencies

Scala vestibuli

Scala tympani

Helicotrema

FIGURE 3–15. *Examples of traveling-wave displacement patterns for different frequencies. See text for explanation.*

In addition to providing information about which frequencies are present in a signal, the cochlea also gives information about the *magnitude* of each frequency. In general, the magnitude of a signal is manifested in the size of the traveling-wave pattern produced by that signal. Those nerve fibers that respond to a single frequency are likely to show an increase in the number of discharges per stimulus when the stimulus magnitude is increased. In addition, increases in stimulus magnitude are likely to cause *more fibers* to respond to the stimulus (Kiang, 1975).

Connections between the cochlea and brain structures that respond to sound form a very complicated network that passes through several well-defined tracts and structures within the brain stem (Diamond, 1973). A schematic representation of this network is shown in Figure 3–16. The dotted lines in the figure represent the possible pathways that nerve fibers carrying information from the right cochlea

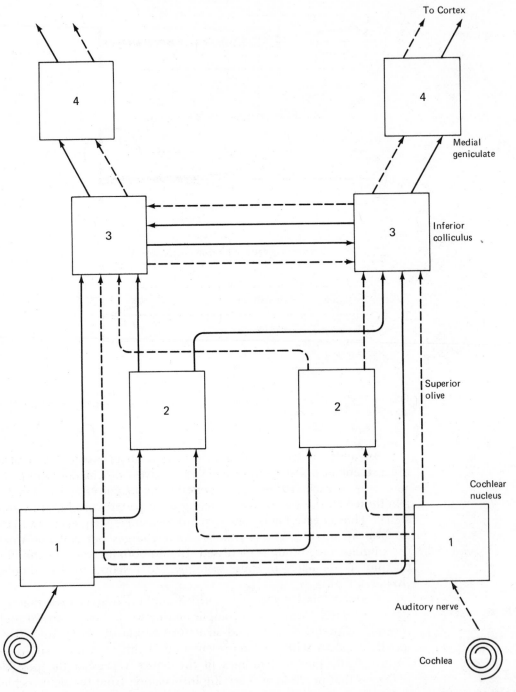

To Cortex

Medial
geniculate

Inferior
colliculus

Superior
olive

Cochlear
nucleus

Auditory nerve

Cochlea

FIGURE 3–16. *Diagram of basic ascending connections within the auditory nervous system. See text for details.*

may follow, and the solid lines show pathways originating in the left cochlea. The individual rectangles represent brain structures where interconnections, or *synapses,* may occur between individual nerve fibers. These structures are the (1) *cochlear nucleus;* (2) *superior olive;* (3) *inferior colliculus;* and (4) *medial geniculate.* All fibers in the auditory nerve (about 25,000) traverse about one inch from the cochlea to the brain stem and then end at the cochlear nucleus. From the cochlear nucleus, fibers may pass up the brain stem on *either side,* or they may pass to *either* superior olive to provide information that is complemented by input from the opposite ear. From the superior olive, fibers may pass with or without crossing the brain stem up to the inferior colliculus. Connections allow for the crossing of information between the right and left inferior colliculi, and information from the inferior colliculi (which by now represents the combined input to the two ears) passes on to the medial geniculate bodies. From the medial geniculate bodies, fibers radiate in a diffuse fashion to the cortical surface. There are many interconnections within the right and left cortices and also between them. The arrangement of the nerve fibers within the brain stem suggests that there is significant opportunity for activity originating in the right cochlea to be compared with that originating in the left cochlea. It is erroneous to think that the "left" brain is wired to the right cochlea and vice versa. Rather, it is appropriate to think of the brain as registering the inputs to the two ears simultaneously, and responding to differences between stimulus frequency, stimulus magnitude, and stimulus time-of-arrival at the two ears (Evans, 1974).

Impressively, the brain not only receives ascending fibers that carry information to it, but it also contains descending, or *efferent,* fibers that carry controlling information back to the ears. The contraction of the middle ear muscles in response to sound is an example of the brain's ability to control the operation of the ear. There are also numerous other efferent connections within the brain stem and cochlea. About 500 nerve fibers originate in the brain stem and terminate either on the hair cells or on the sensory nerve fibers near the hair cells. The role of these fibers is not understood completely, but they seem to function to *regulate* the sensitivity of the cochlea, perhaps to enable us to detect signals under unfavorable conditions.

PERCEPTION OF SOUND

Imagine yourself standing in an open field on a dark, quiet night and unexpectedly you hear someone call your name. You probably could make a number of judgments pertinent to what you had heard. These might include, among others, determinations as to the following: the species of the caller; the sex of the caller; the approximate age of the caller; the approximate physical size of the caller; the approximate direction from which the call came; the approximate distance to the caller; and the identity of the caller, providing you have had prior experience in hearing the caller's voice.

All of the judgments mentioned here would be formed partly on the basis of your experience in listening to human speech, and, of course, on your ability to learn from that experience. Furthermore, to make such judgments, you would have to go through several overlapping steps that included: (1) detection of the sound; (2) discrimination of that sound from others, for example, those produced by animals sharing the field with you; (3) identification of the sound as "speech"; and (4) comprehension of the meaning of the sound. We are quite knowledgeable when it comes to the details of how the ear responds to sound. Yet, we are unable to state exactly how the brain encodes information about sound or how perception results from the reaction of the ear and brain to sound. There is a great leap to be made between observations obtained during experiments with laboratory animals and the understanding of how we are able to perceive tones, speech, music, or other sounds in our environment. The science of *psychophysics* has evolved to assist us in making that leap. In the broadest sense, psychophysics is a discipline concerned with *human perception of the physical attributes of the environment.*

Those using psychophysical methods can ask several types of questions regarding the perception of sound. Some of the most basic of these questions include the following: (1) What is the minimum amount of energy required for an individual to *detect* a signal (tone, noise, speech, etc.)? (2) What types of sounds will *interfere* with an individual's ability to detect a signal? (3) What is the smallest *change* in the frequency or SPL that can be *discriminated* in a signal that has been detected? (4) What can be done to modify a signal to make it easier or more difficult for an individual to *detect, discriminate,* or *identify* it? The sections that follow in this part of the chapter review information pertinent to providing answers to these questions. Although the perception of sound is considered in general in these sections, the focus in intent is to provide the reader with basic information related to how signals as complex as speech sounds can be interpreted and understood by normal-hearing listeners.

Detection of Tones

Human listeners are able to detect acoustic energy over a wide range of frequencies, from about 16 Hz to about 20,000 Hz. However, we do not possess equal sensitivity for all tones in that range. For example, sounds in the range between 500 and 4000 Hz are usually detected at much lower energy levels than the levels needed for the detection of sounds outside that range. Figure 3–17 is a graphic representation of the minimum SPL that a typical young adult listener would require in order to detect tones in the range of frequencies that are audible to humans. The individual data points at 125, 250, and other octave steps up to 8000 Hz correspond with the American National Standards Institute's (ANSI, 1969) recommendations regarding the SPL necessary to reach the threshold of detection of a typical young adult. The dashed lines extending below 125 Hz and above 8000 Hz reveal threshold values outside the range included in the ANSI standards (Davis and Silverman, 1970). The ANSI standard values shown in Figure 3–17 are used as reference points for normal

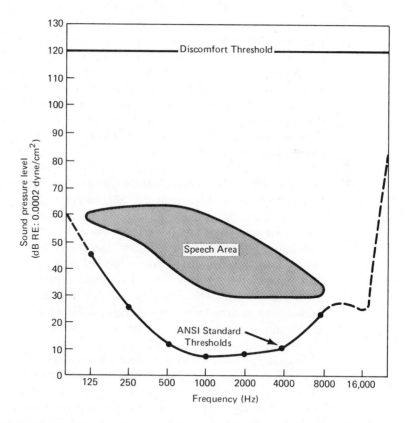

FIGURE 3–17. *American National Standards Institute standard sound pressure levels corresponding to 0 dB HL for audiometers (ANSI, 1969). The shaded area circumscribes the sound pressure levels and frequencies typically contained in conversational speech. (Adapted from* Hearing and Deafness, Third Edition, *edited by Hallowell Davis and S. Richard Silverman. Copyright © 1970, 1960, copyright 1974, by Holt, Rinehart and Winston, Inc. Reprinted by permission of Holt, Rinehart and Winston.)*

hearing and thus represent values against which hearing loss can be measured. The latter use of these standard values is discussed in Chapter 12.

As Figure 3–17 suggests, the hearing sensitivity of a typical listener is about 35 dB poorer at 125 Hz than at 1000 Hz. At 8000 Hz, it is about 15 dB poorer than at 1000 Hz. The relatively poorer sensitivity in the low-frequency region is due to physical characteristics of the middle-ear apparatus. Although the middle ear helps to improve the efficiency of energy transfer from the outer ear to the inner ear, it provides the least assistance in the lower frequencies and the greatest improvement in efficiency in the range between 500 and 4000 Hz (Zwislocki, 1975). The lower sensitivity found in the high-frequency region is not understood completely. It is known that the amount of displacement of the stapes in and out of the oval window is the final critical action associated with transmitting energy to the inner ear, and that the amount of energy required to maintain constant stapes displacement increases for very high frequencies (Moller, 1974a).

The shaded area in the middle of Figure 3–17 shows the approximate frequency and SPL range of everyday conversational speech when measured about three feet from a speaker. The most important frequencies for *understanding* speech fall in the range of 500 through 4000 Hz, the region in which typical hearing sensitivity is best. As is suggested by the shaded area of Figure 3–17, speech in a face-to-face conversation arrives at our ear with an SPL that averages about 45 dB above our thresholds for the critical frequencies between 500 and 4000 Hz. Regardless of the frequency used, audible tones that range up to about 120 dB SPL begin to cause *discomfort,* as indicated by the "discomfort threshold" line in the figure. When tones, speech signals, or noise reach 130 dB SPL or more, they can cause true pain. The range of sensitivity that the typical normal hearer possesses, from detection of a tone to the SPL at which the tone causes pain, thus spans about 120 dB. This is a pressure range of 1,000,000 to 1!

The "typical" threshold values shown in Figure 3–17 are obtained with measurement procedures used routinely in a clinical-testing situation. One aspect of those procedures that is critical is the *duration* of the tonal signal used to obtain a response. In general, tones of long duration are easier to detect than are tones of very brief duration (Watson and Gengel, 1969). Our threshold of detection for a tone only 10 milliseconds in duration may be as much as 20 dB poorer than the threshold for the same tone presented for a duration of 100 to 200 milliseconds. Lengthening a tone beyond about 200 to 400 milliseconds gives no significant further improvement. When thought of from the standpoint of energy summation, it is easy to appreciate that a long signal offers more energy than a signal that is very brief. Thus, the ear is able to "add up" or " integrate" the long signal's energy, an accomplishment that is reflected in an improved threshold measurement for the long signal. Because of our knowledge of the temporal integration properties of the ear, routine clinical testing uses tones that are much longer than 200 milliseconds. This is done to insure that measurements of detection thresholds reflect the patient's best possible performance.

Discrimination among Tones

We are able to detect differences between two tones on the basis of differences in their frequencies, their sound pressure levels, or their durations, among other of their physical properties. In general, humans can detect a difference between two tones that differ by less than 1 percent in frequency. When the tones presented for discrimination are at moderate sound pressure levels, listeners are able to detect the difference between 1000 Hz and 1003 Hz, 2000 and 2006 Hz, and 4000 and 4012 Hz, or a change as small as 0.3 percent (Wier, Jesteadt, and Green, 1977).

When asked to detect whether or not two tones are different on the basis of SPL, human listeners are able to make discriminations of differences of less than 1 dB for moderate to high SPL signals. By contrast, signals that are of relatively low SPL, say near threshold, require that the minimal SPL difference between any two be about 3 dB before the listener detects a difference. In considering discrimination performance at low SPLs, it must be remembered that the actual *pressures* corresponding to a 3 dB change are minute, with discrimination between signals at 0.0006 dyne/cm^2 and 0.0009 dyne/cm^2 being possible (Jesteadt, Wier, and Green, 1977).

Subjective Descriptions of Sound

Many terms are used to describe sounds. Some of the more common of these are "loud," "soft," "high-pitched," "low-pitched," "sharp," "flat," "consonant," and "dissonant." Some of the subjective attributes of sound, especially those related to the pleasure obtained from listening to it, are culturally bound. Anyone who has compared Eastern and Western musical compositions will appreciate this fact. The subjective attributes of complex signals are, themselves, complex and cannot be described adequately here (Geldard, 1972). It should be remembered that waveform (and therefore spectral) differences always accompany perceived differences among sounds. Sounds that are qualitatively different must, therefore, produce different vibratory patterns when they reach a listener's ear. Two aspects of auditory sensation, *loudness* and *pitch* of tonal signals, correspond especially well with physical aspects of signals. In fact, common usage often (incorrectly) results in substitution of the term "loudness" for SPL, and "pitch" for frequency.

The loudness of simple tonal signals is determined *primarily* by the SPL of the tone, but does not grow in a simple fashion with increases in SPL. Impressions of loudness are expressed in terms of *sones*, where one sone is the loudness a listener associates with a 1000-Hz tone presented 40 dB above detection threshold (40 dB Sensation Level [SL]). A change from 40 dB SL to about 50 dB SL is necessary for a listener to decide that the tone has a loudness of two sones. Each doubling of loudness, from one to two to four or more sones, generally corresponds with a new 10 dB increase in the SL of the signal (Stevens, 1975).

The pitch of a tone is expressed in units called *mels*. One thousand mels corresponds with a 1000-Hz tone presented at 40 dB SL, or at one sone on the loudness scale. Pitch rises when frequency increases, and it lowers when frequency decreases, but change in pitch (or number of mels assigned) does not equal the change in frequency. Normal listeners assign a value of about 3000 mels to a 10,000-Hz tone, 2000 mels for about 3000 Hz, and 500 mels for about 350 Hz. Therefore, above 1000 Hz, we need to multiply frequency by about 3 to 1 in order to have a 2 to 1 increase in perceived pitch. Below about 350 Hz nearly 500 mels are covered, so that small changes in frequency are associated with relatively large changes in pitch (Stevens and Volkman, 1940).

Although sound pressure level is the principal determinant of loudness, and frequency is the principal determinant of pitch, *the physical attributes of sound pressure level and frequency are not the sole determinants of perceived loudness and pitch*. If sound pressure level is held constant and frequency is changed, some tones seem louder than others. In general, tones in the mid-frequency range of about 500–4000 Hz require less SPL to seem as loud as other tones outside of that range. It is also possible to cause the pitch of a tone to change simply by changing the SPL at which the tone is presented. In the case of pitch shifts, low-frequency tones seem lower in pitch when their SPL is increased and high-frequency tones seem higher in pitch when the SPL is increased. Tones in the range of about 1000–3000 Hz do not shift as dramatically as those at the frequency extremes (Geldard, 1972). Such shifts in perceived loudness and pitch make one wonder how an orchestra stays "in tune" when ranging from very soft to very loud musical passages.

Interference of One Sound with Another

We all have experienced situations where unwanted background sounds have made it difficult for us to hear a desired sound. Traffic noise, jet aircraft, and loud music are common sources of such interference. When we have difficulty hearing a desired signal, that difficulty is related to an *increase in our threshold* for that signal. When the threshold increase, which is like a hearing loss, is caused by the presence of an interfering noise or tone, we experience *masking* of the intended signal by the interfering source (called a *masker*).

Maskers such as the noises and loud music described above are very disruptive of our ability to hear individual tones or speech signals because they have a great amount of energy spread throughout the audible frequency range. In a laboratory setting where the magnitude and frequency range of a masker can be controlled precisely, the usual finding with normal listeners is that the greatest amount of masking, or change in threshold due to a masker, is confined to a narrow range of frequencies. The narrow range corresponds to those frequencies that are present in the masker itself. The results summarized in Figure 3–18 illustrate this effect (Egan and Hake, 1950). Figure 3–18 displays the amount of masking, or threshold change in dB, due

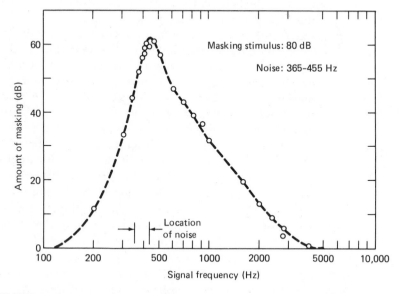

FIGURE 3–18. *Masking of a sinusoid by a narrow band of noise. (After J. Egan and H. Hake, On the masking pattern of simple auditory stimuli.* Journal of the Acoustical Society of America, *22, 622–630, 1950.)*

to the presence of a narrow band of noise between 365 and 455 Hz presented at 80 dB SPL. The amount of masking is shown for several individual tones ranging between about 200 Hz and about 5000 Hz. The greatest amount of masking is observed among frequencies contained in the band of noise with the shift in threshold corresponding to about 50–60 dB. Less and less masking is encountered as signal frequencies move away from the band of noise itself. One can surmize from Figure 3–18 that a rather intense (and loud) band of noise near 400 Hz will have no masking effects for relatively high-frequency signals, such as those above 5000 Hz, or low-frequency signals below about 100 Hz. When Figure 3–18 is examined one may ask why the masking effects of the band of noise spread so far toward the high-frequency region but fall off rather abruptly toward the low frequencies. The answer to this appears to lie in the traveling-wave patterns that were illustrated in Figure 3–15. Any masker arriving at the cochlea develops traveling-wave patterns that are similar to those developed by the individual tones comprising the masker. Those traveling-wave patterns arise from the basal end of the cochlea (the high-frequency end), grow to some maximal size, and then decay abruptly after the maximum has been reached. The abrupt decay occurs on the apex side of the maximum, the low-frequency side. Displacement patterns due to the masker therefore correspond well with the pattern of threshold change caused by the masker, and we may infer from this that a signal will be masked because of the interference of cochlear traveling waves due to the masker with those due to the signal.

The effects of a masker on the threshold of a signal may persist for some time after the masker has been turned off. Seconds, minutes, or even hours may be required for thresholds to return to pre-masking levels (Henderson et al., 1976). The lingering changes in threshold are called *temporary threshold shifts* (TTS), and they are taken as evidence of *auditory fatigue*. Experiments designed to measure the TTS after cessation of a fatiguing stimulus have suggested that the SPL, the duration, and the spectral attributes of the fatiguer can influence the amount of TTS. Furthermore, the amount of TTS present two minutes after cessation of the fatiguer can help us predict just how long a time period will be required for complete recovery. If 10 dB of TTS is present at the two-minute measurement, one can expect about three additional hours of time will be required for complete recovery. A TTS amount in the range of 25 dB may require sixteen or more hours for complete recovery. Our industrial society has contributed to the prevalence of a related phenomenon: noise-induced hearing loss. We are unable to say for certain that permanent loss is an extension of TTS, but available evidence suggests that it is prudent to avoid occupational or recreational situations that leave us with considerable TTS (Henderson et al., 1976). Also, we should not attempt to obtain audiograms for individuals who have experienced recent exposure to intense industrial noise, gunfire, unmuffled snowmobiles, intense music, or other noxious sounds.

Some Effects of Listening with Two Ears

Earlier we learned that the brain stem and cortex centers responsive to auditory stimulation receive a considerable amount of information from both ears. Very small differences in sounds arriving at the two ears may be sufficient to elicit selective responses from the nervous system. Similarly, very small differences in signals arriving at our two ears may influence our perception of those signals. For example, if a 1000-Hz tone is present in our right ear at 60 dB SPL and in our left ear at 50 dB SPL, we may not be aware of the tone on the left. We would miss the left-ear tone were it removed, but our image of the two tones together would favor the right ear only. In this case, the tonal image is said to *lateralize* to the right side. If the SPL of the tone on the left were increased to 52, 54, 56, 58, and, finally, 60 dB, the perceived location of the tones within our head would move from the right side toward the center. If the left tone were further increased, the image would move toward the left ear.

Another effect related to the attributes of signals presented to the two ears is called *release from masking*. If a tone and noise were presented to the right ear, we could set the SPL of the tone so that it was barely audible. Both images, the tone and noise, would, of course, be referred to the right ear. If the noise *alone* were then added to the left ear we would find that (1) the image of the noise would move to the center of the head, (2) the image of the tone would stay on the right, and (3) the tone would be more audible. An increase in the SPL of the masking noise would be required to again make the tone barely audible (Hirsh, 1952; Green, 1976; Yost and Nielsen, 1977).

When different speech signals are provided to the two ears, normal listeners demonstrate a slight favoring of the right ear. For example, if the syllable *ba* is led to the right ear and *pa* is led to the left ear simultaneously and a listener must report which speech sound was heard in which ear, the reports regarding the right ear sound will be somewhat more accurate than those for the left ear. The "right ear advantage" may continue even if signals are made to arrive at the left ear slightly ahead of those arriving at the right (Kimura, 1975).

The most practical aspect of listening with two ears is related to our ability to *locate* sounds in space without visual or other cues as to their whereabouts. There appear to be two major physical cues that are used to pinpoint sounds: (1) time of arrival of the sound at the two ears and (2) the SPL of the sound at one ear as contrasted with its SPL at the other.

Most of us have ears that are spaced some six to eight inches apart, and this small distance dictates that sound arriving on the right side of our heads may require only about 0.5 to 0.7 milliseconds to travel over to the left side. Are we sensitive to such small differences? Decidedly! Normal listeners are not prone to error in judging the location of a sound when it originates directly to their right or left sides, and when there is only a minimal difference between the SPL on the right and the SPL on the left. This type of stimulus, with maximal time differences and minimal SPL differences occurs for low-frequency signals that do not encounter sound shadow effects (see Figure 3–8) when they arrive at the head (Yost and Nielsen, 1977). Another situation in which arrival time, rather than SPL difference, influences our ability to judge the location of sound occurs when sounds are presented directly in front of us. In this situation we might ask how close the sound sources can be together and yet still be discriminated as originating at different points in space. For low frequencies, the minimum angle between two sources that can be discriminated from each other is approximately 2 to 3°. [The actual distance between the two sources may vary, of course, with their distance from the listener (Yost, 1974).]

For high-frequency signals, head shadow effects and resonances due to the outer ear make a significant contribution to our ability to locate the source of a sound. We, of course, favor the side for which the signal has the greatest SPL, and it has been demonstrated that high-frequency sounds (above about 2000 Hz) can lose as much as 15 to 20 dB in passing from a source directly opposite the right ear down to the tympanic membrane on the left side (Shaw, 1974).

Discrimination of Speech

Consideration of our sensitivity to speech stimuli is an important extension of the study of thresholds and other phenomena related to tonal stimuli. In clinical situations a patient's responses to speech stimuli may be very sensitive to disorders of the ear or nervous system, and those responses may provide important clues to the clinician as to how well the patient may function in normal-listening situations.

Some forms of speech are easier to understand than others. An individual hearing a sentence may be able to identify all the words in the sentence. Were each of the same words to be spoken in isolation and in a nonsense order, the same listener might miss recognizing a few of them. This is because normal spoken language has a set of rules regarding syntax and grammar (see Chapter 1) that enable us to fill in gaps if we are unable to understand every word in a sentence.

Because an individual's ability to reproduce sentences might be influenced strongly by language skills, rather than a subtle hearing disorder, the usual materials used to assess the hearing of speech are words spoken in isolation. Even isolated words are not equivalent in their difficulty to be understood. For example, one-syllable words are more difficult than two-syllable words, and both types are used in routine clinical testing. Two basic questions to be asked about a listener's ability to understand speech are: (1) What is the minimum SPL at which he can correctly repeat 50 percent of the individual words presented? (2) What is the maximum percentage score he can obtain when responding to a list of words? (see Small, 1978).

To answer the first of these two questions, two-syllable words called *spondee words* are presented to the listener at various SPLs, and the SPL at which 50 percent of them are repeated correctly is determined. Spondee words are words such as *hotdog* and *airplane* spoken with equal stress on each syllable. Normal listener's responses to spondee words usually conform to the results shown in Figure 3–19.

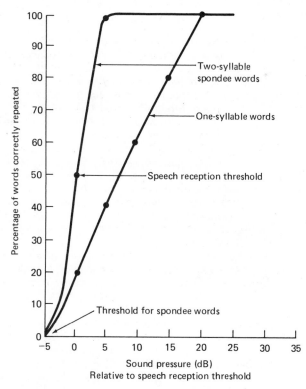

FIGURE 3–19. *Typical responses of a group of normal, adult listeners to two-syllable spondee words and to one-syllable words.*

The words are *detected* at an SPL that is about 5 dB below the SPL required for 50 percent correct responses. Once the 50 percent point is passed, listeners continue to improve so that 100 percent of the words are correctly repeated when an additional 5 dB is added to the signal. The 50 percent point is considered to be the *Speech Reception Threshold* (SRT) for a listener.

Once the SRT has been determined for a listener, monosyllabic words are used to assess how well he can discriminate among the variety of sounds that comprise the language. The relative performance of normal listeners responding to monosyllabic words is also shown in Figure 3–19. Once the SPL of the words has reached a level that is about 20 dB above the SRT, listeners should be able to correctly repeat 100 percent of the words comprising a test list. Failure to reach a high score (for example, greater than 90 percent) for words 30 or 40 dB above the SRT can be an indication of a serious hearing disorder (see Chapter 12).

REFERENCES   American National Standards Institute, *Specifications for Audiometers.* ANSI S3. 6–1969, New York: American National Standards Institute.

BEKESY, G., *Experiments in Hearing.* New York: McGraw-Hill (1960).

BRUGGE, J., Progress in neuroanatomy and neurophysiology of the auditory cortex. In D. Tower (Ed.), *The Nervous System, Vol III, Human Communication and Its Disorders.* New York: Raven Press (1975).

BUTLER, R., The influence of the external and middle ear on auditory discriminations. In W. Keidel and W. Neff (Eds.), *Handbook of Sensory Physiology: Auditory System,* Vol. V/2. Berlin: Springer-Verlag (1975).

DALLOS, P., *The Auditory Periphery.* New York: Academic Press (1973).

DAVIS, H., and SILVERMAN, S., *Hearing and Deafness,* (3rd. Ed.). New York: Holt, Rinehart and Winston (1970).

DIAMOND, I., Neuroanatomy of the auditory system: Report on a workshop. *Archives of Otolaryngology,* 98, 397–413 (1973).

DURRANT, J., and LOVRINIC, J., *Bases of Hearing Science.* Baltimore: Williams and Wilkins (1977).

EGAN, J., and HAKE, H., On the masking pattern of simple auditory stimuli. *Journal of the Acoustical Society of America,* 22, 622–630 (1950).

EVANS, E., Cochlear nerve and cochlear nucleus. In W. Keidel and W. Neff (Eds.), *Handbook of Sensory Physiology: Auditory System,* Vol. V/2. Berlin: Springer-Verlag (1975).

EVANS, E., Neural processes for the detection of acoustic patterns and for sound localization. In F. Schmitt and F. Worden (Eds.), *The Neurosciences Third Study Program.* Cambridge, Mass.: MIT Press (1974).

FELDMAN, A., and WILBER, L., *Acoustic Impedance and Admittance – The Measurement of Middle Ear Function.* Baltimore: Williams and Wilkins (1976).

GELDARD, F., *The Human Senses,* (2nd. Ed.). New York: Wiley (1972).

GREEN, D., *An Introduction to Hearing.* Hillsdale, N.J.: Lawrence Erlbaum Associates, Publishers (1976). (Distributed by Halsted Press Division of John Wiley & Sons of New York.)

HENDERSON, D., HAMERNIK, R., DOSANJH, D., and MILLS, J., *Effects of Noise on Hearing.* New York: Raven Press (1976).

HIRSH, I., *The Measurement of Hearing.* New York: McGraw-Hill (1952).

JESTEADT, W., WIER, C., and GREEN, D., Frequency discrimination as a function of frequency and sensation level. *Journal of the Acoustical Society of America,* 61, 169–177 (1977).

KIANG, N., Stimulus representation in the discharge patterns of auditory neurons. In D. Tower (Ed.), *The Nervous System, Vol. III, Human Communication and Its Disorders.* New York: Raven Press (1975).

KIMURA, D., Cerebral dominance for speech. In D. Tower (Ed.), *The Nervous System, Vol. III, Human Communication and Its Disorders.* New York: Raven Press (1975).

MOLLER, A., Function of the middle ear. In W. Keidel and W. Neff (Eds.), *Handbook of Sensory Physiology: Auditory System,* Vol. V/1. Berlin: Springer-Verlag (1974a).

MOLLER, A., The acoustic middle ear muscle reflex. In W. Keidel and W. Neff (Eds.), *Handbook of Sensory Physiology: Auditory System,* Vol. V/1. Berlin: Springer-Verlag (1974b).

SHAW, E., The external ear. In W. Keidel and W. Neff (Eds.), *Handbook of Sensory Physiology: Auditory System,* Vol. V/1. Berlin: Springer-Verlag (1974).

SMALL, A., *Elements of Hearing Science: A Programmed Text.* New York: Wiley (1978).

SMALL, A., Psychoacoustics. In F. Minifie, T. Hixon, and F. Williams (Eds.), *Normal Aspects of Speech, Hearing, and Language.* Englewood Cliffs, N.J.: Prentice-Hall (1973).

STEVENS, S., *Psychophysics.* New York: Wiley (1975).

STEVENS, S., and VOLKMAN, J., The relation of pitch to frequency: A revised scale. *American Journal of Psychology,* 53, 329–353 (1940).

TONNDORF, J., Bone Conduction Studies in Experimental Animals. *Acta Otolaryngologica Supplement,* 213 (1966).

WATSON, C., and GENGEL, R., Signal duration and signal frequency in relation to auditory sensitivity. *Journal of the Acoustical Society of America,* 46, 989–997 (1969).

WEVER, E., and LAWRENCE, M., *Physiological Acoustics.* Princeton, N.J.: Princeton University Press (1954).

WIER, C., JESTEADT, W., and GREEN, D., Frequency discrimination as a function of frequency and sensation level. *Journal of the Acoustical Society of America,* 61, 178–184 (1977).

YOST, W., Discrimination of interaural phase differences. *Journal of the Acoustical Society of America.* 55, 1299–1303 (1974).

YOST, W., and NIELSEN, D., *Fundamentals of Hearing.* New York: Holt, Rinehart, and Winston (1977).

ZWISLOCKI, J., The role of the external and middle ear in sound transmission. In D. Tower (Ed.), *The Nervous System, Vol. III, Human Communication and Its Disorders.* New York: Raven Press (1975).

signpost

Children with language disorders have become a major concern of the speech-language pathologist in recent years. Witness to this is a newly burgeoning literature on the topic, an increase in clinician caseloads in the area, a changing of one of the American Speech and Hearing Association's certificates of clinical competence from Speech Pathologist to Speech-Language Pathologist, and a renaming of the same Association to the American Speech-Language-Hearing Association. Chapter 4 considers the territory of both developmental and acquired language disorders in children. The relationships of such disorders to cognition, general mental operations, and environment are discussed in detail. Children are considered who do not develop verbal language, who develop qualitatively impaired language, who are delayed in language development, and who are arrested in development after following a normal language course for a time. Methods of assessment of child language disorders are discussed in detail and cautionary statements are offered concerning sole reliance upon available formal tests of language function. Chapter 4 concludes with a concern for management of children with language disorders. The focus is not on correcting the original cause of the child's impairment but on intervention in ways that make language more accessible for the child. The field of communication disorders is continuously re-aligning its educational, research, and service-delivery priorities. Language disorders in children are at or near the top of the list in all three areas. Language disorders have been neglected throughout much of the history of the field of communication disorders and only now are they in their rightful place as a foremost concern of the speech-language pathologist.

4

Rita C. Naremore

language
disorders
in children

INTRODUCTION

When Dietrich Tiedemann's son was six months old, in February of 1782, the father wrote:

> On February 10th he showed the first signs of surprise and approval; so far his only expressions of pain, anger, impatience, and pleasure had been crying, writhing, laughing. Now, when he saw something new and delightful, he greeted it with the exclamation "ach!"—the natural sign of admiration. . . .

He continued his diary description with other entries:

> After all manner of exercise in the production of tones, and after the acquisition of some skill in using the speech-organs variously, he commenced, on the 14th of March, to articulate consciously and to repeat sounds. His mother said to him the syllable "Ma"; he gazed attentively at her mouth, and attempted to imitate the syllable. . . .

> On April 27th . . . when he was asked, where is this or that common and familiar object, he would point it out with his finger. So he had clear conceptions not only of such objects, but also of articulate sounds, and knew furthermore that these sounds designated those objects or images. . . .

> A few words he pronounced clearly on November 27th, and knew also their meanings exactly, these were "Papa" and "Mama," though he did not use them to call persons, but merely by accident, without intending to say anything thereby. . . .

> On the 27th of March . . . if the boy desired anything, he would call it by its name, howbeit this was true of only a very few objects as yet. . . .

> On June 3rd he succeeded in saying short sentences, consisting of a noun and a verb, though without correct grammatical form. . . .*

Friedrich Tiedemann, at the age of twenty-two months, was on his way toward becoming a user of language.

This process, so clearly recorded by a German father in the eighteenth century, is repeated, with individual variations, by normal children everywhere. It has been observed by parents over and over again. Unfortunately, there are children who do not go through this process — children who do not learn language normally and who manifest what are termed *language disorders*. Marge (1972) has estimated that approximately 3 million children between the ages of four and seventeen in this country have language disorders. These disorders result from a variety of causes, and there are many levels of severity involved. The following description given by the mother of three-year-old Billy is not unusual.

> He wasn't like my first baby at all. He cried a lot, a kind of funny cry, and he wouldn't stop even when we picked him up. Then, you know, he doesn't talk at all. Now my first baby, by this age she could talk your head off. But Billy, it's like he can't understand a word you say. I've tried talking to him, and he'll watch my face, but he never tries to talk back.

Billy's mother had been advised by her friends not to worry. As one neighbor told her, "Some children are slow. They start everything late, but they catch up." This statement is quite true. Children are not trains; they do not all run on the same timetable. It is also true, however, that there are some children who do not develop verbal language and some "late starters" who, left to themselves, never catch up. Either they develop language in a disordered, unusual fashion, or their development lags far behind that of their peers. Other children may begin to develop normal language, only to have it interrupted by illness, accident, or other trauma.

This chapter focuses on the problems of children with developmental and acquired language disorders. To enable a better understanding of such disorders, we begin with a discussion of the prerequisites for learning language, centering on what the child must be able to do if he is to use language normally. Following this is a section dealing with the classification of language disorders in which we describe the behavior of various groups of children who do not use lan-

---

*C. Murchison and S. Langer, Tiedemann's observations on the development of the mental faculties of children. *The Pedagogical Seminary and Journal of Genetic Psychology,* 34, 205–230, 1927.

guage normally. Two remaining sections then deal with the assessment and the management of children with language disorders.

At this point, one might ask "Well, what about the causes of language disorders?" The section on the prerequisites for language learning provides some cues as to conditions that can impede the development of normal language. However, specifying causes of language disorders in children is possible only in the broadest terms. Attempts to focus too closely on causes can often restrict understanding of the abilities and disabilities of the individual child, particularly if the focus leads to labeling, with its inherent dangers of stereotyping. Factors such as intellectual impairment, hearing disorder, brain damage, and emotional disturbance may profoundly affect the development of language in children. However, the range of language achievement is great for children within any particular disability group (see Figure 4–1). Appreciating what contributes to the wide range of abilities and individual differences in language performance is easier when general principles that transcend categorical disabilities are understood. More is said about causes of language disorders later in the chapter.

PREREQUISITES FOR LANGUAGE LEARNING

The use of language involves a complex set of behaviors, and so obviously language learning is a complex task. What does being able to learn a language and use it in communication involve? As reviewed in Chapter 1, the best evidence available suggests that, when children learn language, they learn a set of rules, or a grammar, which they employ in constructing their own utterances. The process of language development involves the child's grammar coming to approximate that of the adult. Because no one overtly teaches these rules to young children, it seems apparent that children must somehow figure them out by listening to the language of the environment and abstracting from it the rules that are used to generate it. Many believe that children are able to do this because they are born with some innate predisposition to learn language. As Slobin (1971) describes it:

> The complexity of this task (acquiring the underlying linguistic system) has made it plausible (to some) to postulate that the child's mind is somehow "set" in a predetermined way to process the sorts of structures which characterize human language, arriving at something like a transformational grammar of his native language. This is not to say that the grammatical system itself is given as innate knowledge, but that the child has innate means of processing information and forming internal

FIGURE 4–1. *A child with Down's syndrome using language. The range of language achievement is great for children within any disability group. Labeling presents inherent dangers of stereotyping that are to be avoided. (Courtesy of Shoreline Association, Guilford, Connecticut.)*

structures, and that, when these capacities are applied to the speech he hears, he succeeds in constructing a grammar of his native language.

If children have this inborn ability, then why do they seem to differ in their ability to learn language? What prevents some children from proceeding at a normal rate through the stages of language development? Unfortunately, it is not always possible to say what causes a child to fail to develop language normally (Morehead and Morehead, 1976). Many factors influence development, and their complex interactions often make it very difficult to assign a single reason for a child's difficulty. In addition, as most researchers would be quick to admit, there is much that we do not understand about the process of language acquisition. Lacking a complete picture of what the normal child does, we cannot expect to be able to say exactly what is wrong when a child is not behaving normally. Despite these cautionary statements, it is possible to be more specific about what prerequisites must be met to learn language normally. Three of them are as follows:

1. The child must be able to cognize the physical and social events encoded in language (Slobin, 1973).
2. The child must be able to process, organize, and store linguistic information (Slobin, 1973).
3. The child must be exposed to the referential event and the speech referring to it simultaneously (Ervin-Tripp, 1973).

These preconditions are discussed in the following three sections.

Cognition

When Slobin says that a child must be able to cognize the physical and social events encoded in language, he does not mean simply that children must be able to tell the difference between chairs and airplanes. Children must be able to organize reality in such a way that they can communicate this reality to others through language. It may be difficult for adults to understand what it means to "organize reality." An example may help. One of the easiest ways to see how children's organization of the world is different from that of adults is to observe their early attempts to match words with meanings. Words in a language reflect the categories into which reality has been divided. So, for example, we have a kind of supercategory word *food,* and a subcategory, *fruit,* and a smaller subcategory *citrus fruit,* which has individual members *orange, lemon, lime, grapefruit.* But we do not have a subcategory word for *long skinny fruit* or *round fruit* or *yellow fruit.* Adults simply do not group fruits, in terms of vocabulary, on the basis of shape or color. Children may, however, because they have not learned the proper basis for organizing reality. It is not that children make up words for their inappropriate categories. It is rather that they overgeneralize the words they have. This is common in young children, and persists throughout the early stages of language development. It seems apparent that the language a child uses reflects his perceptual organization of the world about him. The basis for children's early concepts is as yet at issue, though probably a safe assumption would be that the perceptual organization of reality for the child is based not on passive observation but rather on an active process in which he is actively engaged with his environment (Nelson, 1973; Sinclair-deZwart, 1973; Bowerman, 1974).

Although we have referred to the relationship between cognitive and linguistic development in terms of the child's development of word meaning, it is important to keep in mind that the development of the syntax governing word combinations may be rooted in early cognitive development also. Before acquiring language, a child must discover that objects exist as separate entities in the environment, and that they exist permanently, apart from his own ability to see or touch them. Elementary concepts of cause and effect, space, and time must also be acquired. As Morehead and Morehead (1974) have expressed it, "the development of object concept and later of causal relations is an important metric for following the child's differentiation between himself and reality, then between his actions and reality, and finally between objects and events in reality." Once the child can make these distinctions, they can be reflected in language by distinctions between actor and action, or action and acted upon in multiword utterances.

Basic to all of language, of course, is the child's capacity to use symbols to represent reality. Early symbolic behavior can be seen when children pretend; for example, closing the eyes and folding the hands "symbolizes" sleeping. Play activities may also involve representation, as a child pushes a wooden block along the floor making a "motor" sound, thus letting the block represent a truck. This ability to allow one object or behavior to symbolize another object or behavior is a crucial precursor to verbal representation, in which words first symbolize objects or events and later designate concepts. Representation also involves imitation, in which the child moves from immediate repetition of an action in the presence of the model to deferred imitation. The presence of deferred imitation is evidence of the child's ability to represent (literally, re-present) an event or an object that is not immediately present. That is, of course, the essence of symbolic behavior.

As this general discussion indicates, the process of "cognizing" physical and social events is complex, but it is a process inextricably intertwined with language acquisition. This relates it immediately to any consideration of children who are not acquiring language normally. In the past, those concerned with children's language acquisition paid little attention to prelinguistic cognitive development. Only recently have the relationships between cognitive and linguistic development become a focus of attention, and it is likely that this focus will have a significant impact on our descriptions and treatment of children with abnormal language behavior. Consider the case of Larry as an example:

At age three years, seven months, Larry consistently spoke in single-word utterances, and, as nearly as anyone could determine, he used only about 12 different "words," none of which sounded like identifiable words in the adult language. When he was given ordinary children's toys, he stacked the blocks rather clumsily, and carried two small metal cars around in his hand for a short time. When the adult in the room suggested building a bridge to run the cars on, he watched with interest, but did not participate, and refused to give up the cars when the "bridge" was ready. He showed an inconsistent response to the adult's attempts to elicit imitation of such common words as "car" and "ball," sometimes giving an apparently unrelated sound, and sometimes making no response at all. Larry's failure to engage in representational play, and his apparent inability to show even immediate imitation of verbal models, caused the clinician working with him to ask for an assessment of his level of cognitive development, which was found to be quite low. It was decided that, rather than attempting to teach Larry more "words," or to improve his production of the "words" he already had, therapy would focus on improving his prelinguistic cognitive skills, particularly his capacity to handle representation, before addressing his language performance. It is quite possible that, without an understanding of the importance of cognitive development for language acquisition, Larry's clinician might have spent many frustrating hours trying to teach him language forms which he was totally unready to learn.

The important point here is that language development is a part of the child's overall intellectual development, and language cannot be isolated from this general developmental context. A child's language reflects his level of cognitive development, and he will not use a particular linguistic form meaningfully unless he has the cognitive functioning necessary to assign meaning to the form. Thus, most two-year-olds are incapable of using "yesterday" and "tomorrow" correctly because they lack the adult concept of time necessary to understand these terms. If a child who has difficulty acquiring language is ever to become a productive user of language, then language and overall intellectual development must be made to mesh.

Adequate cognitive development is not in and of itself sufficient to ensure normal language development. Although it is probably true that many children who have difficulty learning language also have difficulty in the area of cognitive functioning, many such children also display problems involving the set of general mental operations necessary to process, organize, and store linguistic input.

General Mental Operations

Several writers (Bever, 1970; Clark, 1973; Ervin-Tripp, 1973) take the position that children use a set of general mental operations to structure all sensory input, including auditory input in the form of language. This position has advantages over previous arguments that abilities which enable a child to decode and encode language are specific to language. The most important advantage is that it encourages attention to all aspects of the child's development rather than focusing solely on language. Perhaps the best way to explain how the child uses general mental abilities to organize, process, and store language is through an extended example. Imagine that someone says to you *What is your name?* Your task as a language user is to understand the question and give an appropriate response. For the normal adult, this represents a task of trivial effort. So much so that, as adults, we may be unaware of the complexity involved in decoding and encoding messages and holding them in memory.

Decoding.   Decoding begins with the reception of the auditory input. If hearing is normal, reception is automatic. Physiologically, it involves the transformation of an acoustic signal into a series of neurological events, the brain registering important features. The next stage of decoding includes several mental operations and involves what Studdert-Kennedy (1974) has called "the set of expectations, some learned, some probably innate, by which we can (and without which we could not) perceive the signal as speech, speech as language." At this stage we recognize that the sounds made were speech sounds and we can categorize them according to the sound system of a language. The ability to recognize sounds as "speech" appears to be innate. Even after the acoustic signal is recognized as speech, further conversion is necessary before it is perceived as language. At some point, children must learn which acoustic features are used to discriminate among sounds in their language. No one maintains that the set of phonemic rules used by speakers of a given language is innate—it must be learned as a part of the process of language acquisition.

The final stage of the decoding process is characterized by full comprehension of the acoustic signal as a linguistic event. This comprehension depends on the prior development of symbolic representation, together with a knowledge of syntax, semantics, and the rules for communicative appropriateness. The pattern of speech sounds identified at other stages of the decoding process must be recognized as symbols (words) representing some concept or concepts. The ability to use speech sounds as symbols serves as the basis for all spoken language. If the listener cannot assign meaning to the sounds—that is, if he cannot use speech sounds as symbols—then the decoding process ceases. In addition to assigning meanings to sounds, the listener must also work out the relationships among the various words in the utterance.

Together with a capacity for symbolic representation and a knowledge of semantics and syntax, rules for communicative appropriateness must also be used in the decoding process. The knowledge of the social conventions governing the appropriate use of language in communication situations is a part of what Hymes (1972) has called *communicative competence* and what was discussed in Chapter 1 as pragmatics. A listener's communicative competence allows him to make such judgments as whether an utterance is sarcastic or serious, whether a question is real or rhetorical, and whether the style fits the situation. Very little is known about children's development of such knowledge, although it is assumed to be entirely learned rather than innate.

To summarize the abilities required in this stage of decoding, we can return to the original example, in which a speaker said to you *What is your name?* As a listener, you have *recognized* this utterance as a question, *interpreted* its meaning, and *judged* its appropriateness. All these activities are based on your underlying, tacit knowledge of the conventions governing the use of English.

Memory. If you have comprehended the question *What is your name?* you may be ready to begin the process of encoding a response. Before considering encoding, however, we must consider a mental ability important to both decoding and encoding. This is memory. Memory is involved in language processing in two ways: First, memory limitations to some extent constrain the length of the utterances we are able to process. This is especially true for very young children, whose processing abilities are limited so that they have difficulty storing and retrieving more than two or three items in sequence. To decode complex sentences, one must be able to store the initial items in proper sequence until the entire utterance is heard and then retrieve the entire utterance to examine its meaning or to reflect on it at all. When a child's processing ability is limited, it makes it very difficult for him to deal with a sentence such as *If you had told me before we left, we might have been able to fix it so it wouldn't be bothering you so much now.* (This sentence was addressed by a mother to her two-year-old who was complaining about his broken shoestring.) The transient storage for immediate sentence processing is often referred to as short-term memory, since it has a limited capacity and transient content. Our knowledge of English syntax aids our memory strategies so that as the child's knowledge of language increases, short-term memory becomes a less crucial limitation. To demonstrate this, you can make up a list of fifteen totally unrelated words, call the list out to a friend, and ask your friend to repeat the list, in order. Very few adults can manage this. As Miller (1956) has shown, short-term memory for unrelated words is about seven to nine items for adults. However, if you make up a fifteen-word sentence and read it to your friend, it will be recalled easily. This would seem to indicate that sentences are not stored in or retrieved from short-term memory as lists of independent words, but rather are processed as phrases or clauses. The exact mechanism is unclear. It is clear, however, that for young children there is some memory limitation on sentence processing, both because of a basic inability to recall lengthy material (few young children can recall a list seven items long), and because of the inability to depend on syntactic knowledge to structure material for processing.

The second relation between memory and language processing is more closely tied to meaning and conceptualization. We form categories—of sounds, of events, of objects—on the basis of similarities among their constituent items. Our memory enables us to store past occurrences so that we can relate new phenomena to old ones, and thus categorize the new phenomena. In addition to holding the past in memory, we also hold the system of categories and concepts we are using and the criteria that define them. This function is related to long-term rather than short-term memory, because it requires that the contents be stored for later recall or use over long periods, perhaps a lifetime, and that the capacity for storage be theoretically unlimited.

Encoding. Assume that you have decided to answer the question *What is your name?* You have, then, an intention to communicate. Drawing upon your communicative competence, your syntactic knowledge, and your store of semantic information, you will formulate an answer, such as *My name is Suellen.* We do not know the form in which this statement exists at the beginning of the encoding process. For convenience, we can call it an "intention to say." This intention will be processed through your knowledge of syntax and semantics, and translated into the appropriate phonemes, based on your knowledge of the sound system of English. Then, at the final stage, the brain sends commands to the proper muscles to move, and the "intention to say" becomes an utterance. At each stage, the encoding process is essentially a counterpart of the decoding process described earlier.

It is extremely difficult to discover where or even whether difficulties with the general mental operations involved in decoding and encoding language are responsible for a given child's language problem. Tests can be given to find out about a child's memory abilities, or about his or her ability to match sounds that are the same, for example. The problem with attempting to decide exactly where a child lacks ability is that we are not always sure which specific abilities are related to which aspects of language functioning. As stated earlier, language is complex behavior, and while we may occasionally pull out a piece of the puzzle, we can never be quite sure we have it all. Five-year-old Henry illustrates this point.

> Henry was brought to the clinic by his parents, after being referred by a community social worker. Henry had almost no verbal communication, although he was a lively, physically-normal looking child. He

seemed willing to cooperate in testing situations, but it quickly became apparent that his attention span was short and his tolerance of frustration was low. On visual tasks requiring him to match shapes, or colors, he responded inconsistently, sometimes matching, sometimes seeming to respond randomly, and sometimes refusing to respond at all. Tests involving sequencing of material, both visual and auditory, appeared to be too difficult for Henry. When asked to imitate speech sounds and monosyllabic words, he responded appropriately to almost all isolated sounds, but imitated only two words, "Mom" and "dog" (for which he said "doggie"). For all other words, he said "uh" or "um." Henry seemed to have about a dozen recognizable words in his expressive vocabulary, but most of the sounds he made were unintelligible. The diagnostic team agreed that Henry's overall development, cognitively, socially, physically, and linguistically, was far below what it should be. They also agreed, however, that his defective cognitive functioning was insufficient to explain his lack of expressive language. After much diagnostic work, it was decided that Henry lacked the basic ability to recognize similarity on more than one dimension at a time, and could not recreate a sequence of either visual or auditory material without great difficulty. These general abilities of recognition and organization are a key part of language processing, and without much work devoted to developing these abilities, it is doubtful that Henry will ever develop normal language.

Environment

Because it is often difficult to evaluate the influence of cognitive development or general mental operations on language development, many children's language problems are assigned to "the influence of the environment." This is a trap to be avoided. Every child who develops normal oral language needs a stimulating environment and an opportunity to use language in interaction with other people. Most children are exposed to a variety of language from radio and television, from adults, and from other children. They see, and touch, and smell. They manipulate different materials, and participate in and observe many activities. They are given opportunities to try out their developing language, and in most environments, there is usually somebody who will listen and respond. We know that some children raised in institutions, who lack environmental stimulation (not only auditory, but also visual, tactile, and kinesthetic), and who do not interact with other people, are extremely retarded in language development. In fact, their overall development generally is far below normal. These environments, fortunately, are rare. For the most part, it seems that normal children can learn to talk in the face of seemingly overwhelming odds. Children learn language even though they may be brought up in a one-room slum apartment, with eight people sharing the space, the radio blaring all day and most of the night, and mealtime occurring whenever there happens to be food in the home. While no one would maintain that this is the best environment for a child, neither should anyone maintain that this environment alone is sufficient to interfere with the child's language development. The thing to remember is this: *Information about a child's environment is an important part of the picture of the whole child.* However, it is just that—a part of the picture. In evaluating environmental influences on language development, it is easy to impose one's own cultural biases about what a good environment is, and these biases are as likely to interfere with as they are to facilitate further assessment of the child.

With this caution in mind, it is worth considering what an environment does offer a child that facilitates language learning. Ervin-Tripp (1973) offers a reasoned and succinct statement on this question. She says that a child must be exposed to language that is related to significant events for the child. Language should be associated with reading, dressing, cuddling, and other such child-oriented activities. Children will not necessarily focus on language that occurs as "background noise" in the environment. It would be unlikely, then, that any child could learn to talk just by having a television set turned on for eight hours a day. It is necessary also for the child to hear language in the context of the events or things to which the language refers. Co-occurrence of speech with referential events is crucial. Imagine how it would be to try to learn about the semantic system of a language if you only heard that language spoken in a white-painted room with one table, two chairs, no windows, and a door. Even if you heard a rich vocabulary and perfect syntax, you would find it exceptionally difficult to relate this vocabulary and syntax to anything in reality. Obviously, it is not necessary that there always be an object present for a child to learn what a noun means, or that every verb must be heard in the presence of some overt action. The child's interpretation of reality, and his matching of language to that reality, is more complex than this. Stated simply, children must hear language in conjunction with the total context to which that language refers if they are ever to learn how reality is mapped in the language system.

The co-occurrence of speech with referential events is undoubtedly necessary for language learning, although there are other characteristics of a normal language-learning environment that may or may not be necessary. For example, mothers' speech to young children is generally slower, less complex, and more repetitive than their speech to adults (Broen, 1972; Snow, 1972). Sequences such as the following, addressed to a two-year-old by her mother, are not uncommon:

Put the block in the hole, honey.
That's right, put it right there.
Put it in the hole.

See, the block fits this hole.
Put it right in here, in this hole.

We do not know whether children need to hear this kind of discourse to learn language, or even whether it facilitates language learning. However, it does seem to be a marked feature of some parents' language to children, especially mothers.

We are not sure, beyond a bare minimum, which features of any environment are necessary for language learning to occur normally. Certainly, every child deserves a loving, caring, stimulating home environment, with adult attention and plenty of supervised peer-group interaction. But this does not imply that a child who lacks any of this will lack language or develop deviant language as well.

It seems apparent that the child must be able to cognize the physical and social events encoded in language; process, organize, and store linguistic information; and be exposed to referential events and the speech referring to them simultaneously, all as prerequisites to language learning. The question of concern, then, is what the implications for language learning are of developmental or acquired conditions that interfere with any or all of these assumed prerequisites. It becomes obvious that such factors as sensory deficits, intellectual deficits, restrictive physical limitations, etc., each within the social milieu of the child's language-learning environment, have the potential to disrupt the normal language-development pattern. Disordered language, then, may come about in association with a variety of problems experienced by children. The classification of language disorders is discussed in the next section. A behavioral classification scheme is presented as an alternative to a classification system based upon cause of disorder.

CLASSIFYING LANGUAGE DISORDERS

We are now ready to discuss the problems of children who, for whatever reason, either lack aspects of language-learning prerequisites or have not taken advantage of them to develop language normally. What exactly does it mean to say that a child is not developing language normally? How can we decide, for any individual child, whether language development is progressing as it should? There are no easy answers to these questions. It would seem obvious to say that a child with a language problem is one whose language is underdeveloped for his age. This implies that we know, for any given age, what children are supposed to be able to do with language. Certainly, as pointed out in Chapter 1, we can make some broad general statements about stages of language development, and what children at various stages might be expected to do. These stages are not related precisely to the chronological age of the child, however. The definition above also implies that we could agree on the meaning of "underdeveloped." Clearly, any child over age three who doesn't make sounds at all has an oral-language problem. But that description will encompass only a small proportion of those children who are called "language disordered." It is just as true that there are individual differences among children with language disorders as there are individual differences among normal children. If we wish to establish a scientific base for approaching the problems of children with language disorders, however, we need a framework within which we can organize and generalize our observations of these children's behavior. One way to provide this framework is by a classification system. By choosing relevant dimensions on which to base our classifications, we can derive an approach which is extremely useful for understanding individual differences in behavior, selecting management strategies, and sharing information about children's problems. Of course, one of the major difficulties that we confront in systematizing our approach to children's language disorders is that of choosing the best bases for classification.

The Use of Etiological Labels

The most frequently used method of classification is that based on *etiology*, or supposed cause of the disorder. In such a classification scheme, labels implying neurological damage, such as aphasia, agnosia, apraxia, minimal brain dysfunction, or learning disabled, predominate. Unless these labels, and others like them, are carefully defined every time they are used, they will be essentially useless terms for those working with language-disordered children (Bloom and Lahey, 1978).

Labels can be misleading in a number of ways. As Marge (1972) has pointed out, use of an etiological label implies that there is one single cause for a child's language problem and that eliminating the cause will eliminate the problem. While it is true that there may be some cases in which a single factor is largely responsible for a child's problem with language (as with a hearing-impaired or deaf child), it is more often the case that there are several underlying variables contributing to a language behavior. The frequency with which different diagnoses are made of a single child by different professionals serves to underscore this. Children display complex behavior, and as a consequence the label applied often depends on which aspect of the behavior is under focus. The case of Eva is a good example.

Eva was almost six years old when she was referred for testing. She did not talk in her kindergarten classroom. Her physical development was normal, and her mother reported that she had been babbling and making sounds since infancy. Her first word, "Mom," appeared before she was eighteen months old, but did not always refer to her mother. When Eva was brought for evaluation, she did not respond to her name, and appeared to comprehend almost nothing that was said to her. She did not respond to verbal commands, and did not use any sounds for purposes of communication. She responded quickly and appropriately to visual stimuli and gestures, however. On tests which did not require either verbal comprehension or expression, she performed at a level appropriate for her age. On tests requiring language, she did not respond at all, and appeared not to understand what was required of her. An audiological examination was inconclusive, but her responses were not typical of hearing-impaired children. The clinical diagnosis by some at this point might be "auditory dysgnosia and receptive dysphasia" (see Chapter 6 for a discussion of these labels). According to this diagnosis, Eva could not assign meanings to sounds (auditory dysgnosia) and had difficulty processing auditory symbolic input (receptive dysphasia). In addition, someone might even speculate that she was autistic, because she frequently withdrew from social contact and seemed to have no desire to communicate. Some clinicians might suggest that perhaps Eva had some degree of verbal apraxia or even anarthria because she did not exhibit any ability to make wordlike sounds.

Clearly, whatever Eva's problem was, it involved an inability to understand and produce language. That was known when she entered the clinic for testing, and little more than that would be known after the proposed diagnostic labels were applied. These labels do not provide any new information. The number of labels possible indicates that the disorder was complex, but the precise nature of Eva's behavior was unclear. This is often the case when children with language problems are given diagnostic labels, and it serves to point out a second difficulty with etiological classifications, which is that they encourage attention to cause and discourage attention to behavior. What we need to know about a child like Eva is not only that she may be neurologically impaired, but what her specific strengths and weaknesses are. For example, if she has difficulty with processing auditory-verbal signals, can she handle visual signals? The label "dysphasic" does not provide this information. Has she developed identifiable prelinguistic cognitive behaviors? Does she structure auditory material at all (for example, can she imitate a sequence of sounds correctly)? No label will adequately convey all this information, of course. The problem is not that we have the wrong labels, but rather that they tend to result in a kind of tunnel vision, sometimes causing us to lose sight of the complexity of language behavior.

This does not mean, however, that classifying children's language disorders is impossible or undesirable. It simply means that a different basis for classification is needed. As Hardy (1965) has stated:

> If one expects to be of much help in habilitation or rehabilitation, in education or special education, he must know fairly well which modalities (for having experiences and for learning from them) are working, and which are not; and whether interferences in the central nervous system involve problems of sensory integration, or language comprehension, or formulation, of spontaneous expression, or of imitation. He would like to know, as well, the shape and nature of the constellation of factors working for and working against the individual's possible ability to learn or to relearn language comprehension and use.

Hardy's comments suggest a classification scheme more broadly based than an etiological scheme—that is, one based on behaviors as well as causes. Certainly, where the cause of a child's problem is known, this is valuable information, in particular when the cause may be remediable. If, for example, it were established clearly that a child has a remediable hearing problem, one would want to take all possible steps for remediation of the problem before beginning to work with language. Often, however, we cannot pinpoint *the* cause for a child's language problem, and valuable diagnostic time may be wasted in the attempt—time that might have been better spent getting a close description of the child's language and language-related behaviors. The aim of any management program is to take a child where he is and help him to make as much progress as he can. For this to occur, it is necessary to have a good description of where the child is, and what he can do in terms of language and language-related activities.

A Behavioral Classification

Anyone who works with children who have language problems would agree that it is necessary to look at many kinds and levels of behavior in order to evaluate a child's language ability. For example, given a child with normal hearing who appears unable to match sounds that are alike, one would want to know whether the difficulty resulted from an inability to apply the concepts "same" and "different" in any modality, or whether it was specific to the auditory system. Language development occurs in conjunction with general physical, intellectual, and cognitive development, and it is important to know whether other areas of development are impaired along with language. Useful descriptions of a child's language behavior should be accompanied by descriptions of other behaviors as well.

It is also important to know precisely what kinds of language behavior have been observed in the child. Language behaviors can be classified very generally as imitation, comprehension, or spontaneous production. A child who can imitate the sentence *I see you* may not comprehend it. If one wishes to make any estimate of a child's "capacity" for language, it will be necessary to look at all three kinds of language behavior. This is especially true for children who have language problems, since their performance in one area may exceed that in another. Bearing in mind the fact that language behavior should not be described in isolation from other kinds of behavior, and that all aspects of language behavior (imitation, comprehension, and production) must be considered, we can consider the following an economical and usable scheme for classifying language disorders in terms of language behavior.

Children Who Have Not Developed Any Verbal Language. Any child who, by age three, gives no evidence of either spontaneous production or comprehension of language would fit into this category. Some of these children will be born deaf, and in these cases the specific cause for the failure to acquire language is clear. Occasionally, physical appearance and/or general motor development will suggest global neurological impairment. Many such children will be multiply handicapped, being both deaf and blind, or deaf and severely to profoundly mentally retarded. In other cases, however, the extent of the child's disability cannot be estimated. Many of these children are untestable with formal test instruments because of their inability to attend or respond to tasks in a testing situation, so that evaluations of their overall intellectual or emotional development will be at best gross estimates and be based on informal observational procedures. For some children in this category, the problem appears to be primarily one of processing auditory input. They are physically alert, respond to visual cues, and appear to relate to other people in their environment. For others, the problem will be more general, involving physical and intellectual development as well as language, as with mentally retarded children. In all cases, the key to the classification will be the child's failure to respond to the spoken language of others, and the failure to develop spoken language of his own. A good example of children who fit this category is Michael.

> At age three, Michael had no spoken language at all, although he made a wide variety of noises, most of them very loud. He was extremely aware of his environment—perhaps overly aware. He attended to everything with the same serious concentration: the light switch, the pattern of thumbtacks on the bulletin board, the wastebasket. The slightest sound, such as a pencil rustling on a paper, or the hum of a fluorescent light, caused him to begin to try to locate the source of the noise. In

spite of this awareness, nothing held his attention for long. He moved constantly from one place and one activity to another, and if restrained, he flew into a temper tantrum. When spoken to, he would sometimes look at the speaker, but gave no evidence of comprehending what was said. His physical development appeared grossly normal, although many of his movements were clumsy and awkward. He was not aggressive, but his lack of language and his inability to attend to one activity for any length of time made it difficult for him to interact with other children. Careful evaluation showed that he lacked basic symbolic functioning, and was unable to inhibit his responses to irrelevant stimuli. It was decided to place him in a behavior modification program designed to limit the amount of stimulation to which he was exposed, and to help him begin to focus on speech apart from auditory stimuli. This program proved over time to be successful in aiding Michael's attention to relevant input, and he began to initiate speech sounds and later used some words functionally.

For Michael, as for other children in this category, careful evaluation of prelinguistic cognitive abilities and general mental operations will be necessary to determine the child's capacity for learning and using language. Children who demonstrate no ability to use verbal language present a particularly challenging set of questions, regardless of the cause of their problem.

Children Whose Language Development Is Qualitatively Impaired. A large percentage of children with language problems fit into this category, and the language behaviors exhibited by these children will be extremely varied. Menyuk (1971) studied the production and imitation of language in a group of children with deviant language who had been labeled "infantile," and her findings serve to generally characterize this group. She says:

> Neither the three-year-old nor the six-year-old child in the infantile speech group was using structures which matched those used by a two-year-old normal-speaking child. They had developed a grammar that was more sophisticated in terms of some structures and different in terms of others. Therefore, these children were not simply a little delayed or even substantially delayed in their acquisition of structures. Further, after they had acquired the use of certain structures at age 3, there appeared to be very little change in the structures they used from age 3 to 6.

In terms of their spontaneous production of language, then, the children in Menyuk's study could not be called simply "language delayed." They had all developed some language, but it was not normal language. It would have seemed bizarre, no matter what age child had uttered it. Menyuk (1969) suggests that their language production had been arrested at "some stage" of development. No developmental progress could be observed when the production of a three-year-old language-deviant child was compared with that of a six-year-old language-deviant child.

The kinds of sentences used by children in this category can be seen in the results of an imitation task, in which children were asked to repeat sentences read by an adult. One six-year-old language-impaired child gave the following responses:

> *Boy is break* for *The little boy's dump truck is broken.*
> *Pretty little run* for *The pretty little girl is running fast.*
> *Dump big bed* for *Is the dump truck under the bed?*

These are not the kinds of error responses one would expect from a normally developing child. When given the sentences above to imitate, one normal two-year-old gave the following responses:

> *Dump truck broke* for *The little boy's dump truck is broken.*
> *Little girl running* for *The pretty little girl is running fast.*
> *Dump truck under bed* for *Is the dump truck under the bed?*

Although the two-year-old could not repeat the model sentences accurately, she gave responses that retained some core of the meaning of the model sentence. The language-impaired child, on the other hand, gave no evidence of having accurately processed the meaning of the model utterance, and in one instance even inserted a word that had not appeared in the model. The normal child's imitations also retain basic semantic relations, such as agent-action and location (see Chapter 1), while the language-impaired child failed to retain these basic sentence elements.

Menyuk (1969) reported similar observations in her study of imitation behavior. She found that the language-deviant children in her study did not tend to simplify sentences in terms of their grammars. Rather, they treated a sentence as though it were a string of largely unrelated words, leaving out entire phrases and sometimes repeating only the first or last words. Language-impaired children also did more poorly on the imitation task than they did in production, where in some cases they failed to imitate sentences even less complex than those they could produce spontaneously.

In terms of both imitation and production behaviors, the children in Menyuk's study could be called "atypical." Their behavior was not like that of typical children at *any* age. This is the key characteristic of children in this category. They will not all be like the children Menyuk described. Some will have very little spontaneous production, but they will accurately repeat almost anything said to them. Some demonstrate seemingly adequate language comprehension, with almost no spontaneous production or imitation. Others may produce language in the form of jargon or memorized sequences, but it will not be communicative. One example of a child who would fit this category is Diane.

Diane was four-and-a-half-years-old when her mother first brought her to the clinic for evaluation. She was a clingy, tearful child, and it was difficult to persuade her to take part in any activity. She insisted on holding her mother's hand constantly. She was the only child in the family. When asked a question, Diane generally repeated all or part of it, as though she had not understood. Occasionally she would answer, as when her mother said, "How many fingers do you have?" and she replied "ten." The examiner quickly discovered that this appeared to be a memorized sequence, when Diane made the same reply to "How many eyes do you have?" and "How many mommies do you have?" When prompted by her mother, Diane could repeat accurately several television commercials, but with many misarticulations. The mother reported that Diane was fascinated by the television set, and spent much of her time watching it. She responded appropriately to simple commands such as "Sit down" and "Give me the pencil." Her motor skills were appropriate for her age, and her general physical development seemed normal. It was Diane's spontaneous language production which had caused her mother to worry. Diane seemed to have memorized phrases and sentences from several sources, and she could make some fairly reasonable utterances, such as "The mailman carries the mail" or "Baby duck says quack quack." These sequences were used as she looked through several familiar picture books brought along by her mother. Without these books, or the television commercials, however, Diane's language production consisted of one or two-word utterances, and understanding these was complicated by the difficulty she had in producing speech sounds.

The causes of such language behavior are various and complex. In Diane's case, it is doubtful that much could be gained by speculating about the root of the problem. Instead, it was decided to capitalize on her demonstrated skill in imitating language, and on her attachment to television.

Diane's therapist set up a carefully structured program to introduce her to the stages of sentence formation known to occur in normal children. She was moved to each new stage only after she demonstrated productive use of the stage she was in—and initially, all stimuli were presented to her on videotape, which she was allowed to watch as often as she liked. In addition, Diane was put into a group-therapy situation for work on her articulation and for some peer-group interaction.

After a year in a structured therapy program, Diane had made substantial progress toward spontaneous use of language. Her intelligibility had improved to a point where she was understood readily by most listeners, although her articulation was not error free. Even though Diane was now using language for communication to a much greater extent, she was as yet not close to normative language production for a five-and-a-half-year old.

While therapy for Diane was an individually structured activity, her program did have one thing in common with those of other children in the qualitatively impaired category: She was carefully introduced to and moved through the stages of language development found in normal children. For children whose language behavior is qualitatively different from normal, one must assume that for some reason they are unable to structure language input to formulate linguistic rules that will generate normal sentences. Because these children do not seem to go through normal stages of language development by themselves, it is assumed that they must be taken through these stages as a part of their management program (see Figure 4–2). The assumption about facilitating language learning through following a developmental sequence will be discussed again later in the chapter. For the moment, remember that consideration of developmental stage forms one basis for grouping together children whose language behavior is qualitatively different from normal, regardless of the reason for the difference.

Children Whose Language Development Is Delayed. While the children described in the qualitatively impaired category exhibit language behavior that might be described as "deviant," the children in the delayed development category might accurately be classed as "slowed down." In most instances, their slow rate of development will be reflected in many areas of behavior: motor skills, social adjustment, intellectual ability, and language. They may be labeled "mentally retarded" or "developmentally disabled," although it is important to realize that some children who have been so labeled may easily fit the qualitatively impaired category rather than the delayed category. Many researchers believe that most children with language disorders can be placed in the category of delayed development. It is probably true that the prevalence of language-delayed children is greater than that of totally nonverbal or qualitatively impaired children, although no accurate counts are available. Care should be taken, however, in generalizing from this statement. It sometimes happens that a child will be classified as "language delayed" based on a gross evaluation, when a finer-grained analysis of his language behavior might reveal some behaviors quite different from those of any normal child. The

FIGURE 4–2. *A speech-language pathologist providing individual language therapy to a preschooler. (Courtesy of the University of Arizona Speech and Hearing Clinic.)*

line between "delayed" and "different" language behaviors is at times difficult to draw, but as improved methods of assessment become available, the classifications should become easier to separate.

The language behavior of children who belong predominately in the delayed group would be characterized as normal in all respects, excepting age-appropriateness. The relationships among imitation, comprehension, and production are the same as they are for normal children. The orderly progression from one- and two-word utterances through identifiable stages to sentences using various transformations are observed. The problem with the child's language is that, at any given age, it will be more like the language of a chronologically younger child. A four-year-old language-delayed child may have language that would be perfectly appropriate for a two-year-old. An eight-year-old language-delayed child may sound like a normal five- or six-year-old. These children seem to learn language generally just as typical children do: by formulating rules which they use to generate their own utterances. Although there may be individual instances of bizarre rules, on the whole their grammars will be appropriate for the continued development of normal language (Lackner, 1968). It seems likely, however, that for most children in this category language development will terminate at some stage below what is attained by normal children (Lenneberg, Nichols, and Rosenberger, 1964; Lenneberg, 1967; Naremore and Dever, 1975).

To date, we have very little information about how far a language-delayed child might be expected to progress, especially the child who is developmentally disabled. Children whose language delay is associated with a general delay in intellectual development (mentally retarded children) will obviously continue to use language appropriate to their cognitive level, regardless of their chronological age. A sixteen-year-old with the cognitive level of a ten-year-old will talk like a ten-year-old. Children whose language delay is less easily accounted for by obvious developmental delays in other behavioral spheres represent the more difficult cases. If current theories concerning the relationship between neurological development and language acquisition are correct, however, it seems reasonable to assume that if basic language structures in the first language are not acquired before the onset of puberty, they will be acquired only with great difficulty thereafter.

Jody presents a clear example of a child whose behavior fits the category of language delay.

> At age four, he was small for his age, and seemed "babyish" in many ways. His parents reported that he had walked quite late, that he was a very messy eater, and was still not reliably toilet trained. His first word, "Mama," appeared shortly before his third birthday and almost a year later he had a vocabulary of approximately 80 words and was beginning to make two-word combinations. During a short period in the examining room, he frequently pointed to objects and said "What's that," and he would label things his parents pointed to with such phrases as "Mommy shoe," "Jody shoe," "Daddy nose." At one point, when his father left the room, he said "Daddy go." He seemed to have difficulty concentrating on any activity for very long, although he was not easily distracted as long as his involvement lasted. As his mother phrased it, "It's like he gets tired of things, and he just quits." He was an attractive child, for the most part docile and even-tempered. However, his parents found his inability to "act his age" frustrating.

The progression through normal stages which is observed in children with language delay would tend to suggest that the language processes of decoding and encoding are essentially normal. This is questioned by some researchers (Semmel and Herzog, 1966; Semmel, Lefson, and Sitko, 1966; Jordan, 1967), who believe that the cognitive processing which underlies language may be quite different for these children. While there may be differences at some high levels of cognitive processing, it is not clear whether the differences would affect the goals or methods of language therapy used with language-delayed children.

Children Whose Language Development Is Interrupted. The children described in the first three categories above are those whose language problems appear to be congenital. Children who fit this final category are those who began to develop language, and then the developmental process was interrupted because of illness, accident, or other trauma. Sometimes, such interruptions occur when serious illness such as spinal meningitis or encephalitis results in deafness or brain damage. Brain damage can also result from incidents in childhood such as automobile accidents, falls, or near drownings. If these events happen to a very young infant, the deleterious result may be regarded as congenital so far as language development is concerned. If the disruptive event occurs after the child has begun to comprehend or produce language, however, the resulting arrest in language learning can be said to be an *acquired disorder*. This category describes a feature of the child (having had some language) rather than the state of the child's language as emphasized in the other three categories. It is a category distinct from the others because the presumed course of language learning will be different from that of the others.

Two factors should be considered in assessing acquired language disorders. One is the degree of function lost by the child, and the other is the level of language developed before the interruption occurred. In regard to the relationship between language behavior and degree of diminished function, it is generally the case that extensive cerebral trauma has a higher probability of damaging neural centers that affect language than a more localized trauma. Also, profound hearing loss is usually more debilitating than less severe hearing loss, in which residual hearing can be beneficial in oral-language learning. There are, of course, exceptions to this rule, though some apparent exceptions are probably accounted for by the variability in estimating loss of function in very young children. The case of John is an example of an acquired language disorder in which normal language learning was interrupted.

> According to his mother, when five-year-old John was two years old his speech and language were well within normal developmental milestones. Certainly, his language was as advanced as his older sister's had been at the same age. He was expressing himself in short sentences and was able to write a few nursery rhymes. At the age of two years, three months, John contracted spinal meningitis. His parents' joy and relief at his recovery were short-lived, for, shortly after physical recovery, he was

diagnosed as having a profound bilateral sensorineural hearing loss. Thus was begun a new phase in John's young life, marked so poignantly by his mother, who was heard to comment frequently when reviewing a family photo album ". . . this was before John was deaf . . . this was when Wendy was three . . . this was after John became deaf."

John's mother observed a marked loss of oral skills in him within months of his illness. After almost a year, John's oral language consisted of limited single-word utterances, spoken infrequently and generally unintelligibly. He was seen for therapy at a university speech clinic during that year and little progress in spontaneous language use was noted. He was subsequently enrolled in a preschool deaf program that emphasized a total communication approach.[1] He was given daily speech and language therapy as well as a typical preschool curriculum.

At the conclusion of his first year in the preschool program, John was producing one- and two-sign messages and one-word spoken utterances. One year later, spontaneous language samples indicated use of up to five- and six-sign utterances.

Examples from John's spontaneous language follow:

DATE		MODE
7/11	chipmunk different squirrel	Manual
7/14	different dog	Manual and mouthing (no vocalization)
	see game boat	Manual and mouthing
7/21	what you want eat	Manual and mouthing
	four	Spoken
	yellow	Spoken
	see	Spoken
7/28	what that	Spoken and manual
	Wendy want different candy	Manual

John has limited lip-reading skills and essentially no comprehension of spoken language except in very restricted and highly-structured situations. His comprehension of sign, however, is estimated to be at least at age-level, with his comprehension vocabulary being quite large.

The tie between developmental stage at the time of the interruption and later progress with language is dependent on the nature of the trauma. For children who become deaf, the older they are when deafened, the better, because the older they are, the more exposure to language they will have had. Even though children who are deafened before about age four may have difficulty maintaining and

---

[1] The total communication approach is discussed in Chapter 13. Essentially, it stresses use of all available modalities and means for communication, including use of manual (sign) language and oral language.

further developing their ability to speak intelligibly, their ability to learn through visual and aided auditory channels will be better than that of congenitally deaf children. As Lenneberg (1967) says, "It seems as if even a short exposure to language, a brief moment during which the curtain has been lifted and oral communication established, is sufficient to give a child some foundation on which much later language training may be based." John is a good example of this point. His good comprehension of signs and large comprehension vocabulary are probably attributable to his early experience with a language system—even though it was the spoken language.

For children who suffer brain damage after birth, however, the picture will be reversed. In their case, the younger the child, the better the chance for later language development. As Lenneberg (1967) explains it, there is a critical period for language acquisition which ends around the time of the onset of puberty. After the age of fourteen or so, people who suffer brain damage that affects their language behavior may never regain normal language. Lenneberg explains this by saying that with the onset of puberty, the brain's functions become polarized, with language functions in the left hemisphere. Before this polarization, the brain is relatively plastic and if one area is damaged, its functions may be taken over by some other area. Thus, in very young children, brain damage affecting language may be overcome. However, as the child grows older, the brain is less flexible in this regard, and brain damage is more likely to have a permanent effect on language behavior. The precise nature of the language disability that occurs with brain damage will depend on both the extent and location of the injury (see Chapter 6).

Summary.   The classification scheme used above is based not on the supposed causes for children's language problems, but rather on the language behavior exhibited by various groups of children. The advantage of such a scheme is that it focuses attention on what we wish to change. In an etiologically based classification scheme, labels focus on causes for behavior, which often cannot be eliminated. Medical science simply has not progressed that far. Given, then, that the supposed cause cannot be eliminated, the logical thing to do is treat the symptoms. Unfortunately, labels based on cause do not always give a very clear indication of what to expect in the way of language behavior. These labels are not likely to disappear, however. It is probably reasonable to expect that researchers and clinicians alike will continue to speak of "the hard-of-hearing child" or the child "with minimal brain damage." The assumption made in this chapter, however, is that children grouped on the basis of their language behavior are likely to have more in common when viewed from the perspective of language therapy than children grouped on the basis of some loosely defined label such as "learning disabled." Some support for this assumption will be presented in the section that follows.

ASSESSMENT

After a long day's work in the diagnostic clinic of a local speech, hearing, and language center, an exhausted clinician observed, "You know this wouldn't be so hard if we had one test that took less than 30 minutes to give, was appropriate for children of any age, tested every aspect of language ability, and told you where to start therapy when you finished." Anyone who has ever tried to do a thorough evaluation of a hyperactive three-year-old's language abilities would agree. Unfortunately, there is no test which will fit that description and there probably never will be.

Before discussing the means for assessing children's language, the purposes of assessment should be made clear. These are: First, to obtain a clear picture of what the child can do with language; second, to decide which areas of linguistic or prelinguistic processing are impaired and which are intact; and third, to provide a basis for beginning management. Given such a statement of purpose, we see that assessment has to be comprehensive. Ideally, the assessment should be based on information provided by a developmental history of the child; a thorough physical, including neurological examination; psychological testing; audiological examination; a description of the child's environment provided by a trained social worker; and speech and language testing. It is beyond the scope of this chapter to describe the means for obtaining all this information. Instead, what is presented here is a general scheme for language assessment which is not intended to serve as a guide to specific tests, but rather as a framework into which all available information about the child can be integrated.

A Scheme for Language Assessment

This section presents a scheme for assessment of language and related behaviors that is applicable to the child with a language disorder. We begin by stressing the significance of gathering information about the intactness of the speech production and reception mechanisms, the abilities to process and produce speech stimuli, memory and intellectual abilities, and cognitive functioning. The core of the language assessment is discussed next, organized around the basic language behaviors of imitation, comprehension, and production. Finally, some considerations on the use of language tests are presented.

Before beginning to examine language behavior in detail, it is important to evaluate the basic hearing and speech mechanisms, particularly if there is any reason to question the child's ability to hear or produce sounds. If hearing is impaired, every level of language development may be affected. Because adequate auditory processing is so important for the development of spoken language, careful audiological testing should be a part of every language assessment. On the encoding side, it is important to know what limitations, if any, there are for volitionally controlled movements of the articulators. This would involve information about the physiological integrity of the respiratory system, the larynx, the structures of the oral-pharyngeal cavities, and, of course, the adequacy of the neural signals that initiate and control the movement sequences (see Chapters 8, 9, and 10). The production of speech involves a speed and fineness of muscular movement unequaled by any other activity of the young child, and the inability to make these movements accurately will have obvious effects on the child's spoken language. Physical examination by qualified personnel should always be carried out if there is any question about the child's ability to make the movements necessary for speech. Some gross screening can be accomplished by having the child attempt to imitate various speech and nonspeech movements of the lips and tongue modeled by the examiner.

On a somewhat higher level, the child's ability to recognize, discriminate, and identify speech sounds, together with his ability to reproduce such sounds in imitation, should be assessed. A part of this evaluation can be accomplished by careful observation. Does the child respond differently to speech than to other sounds? What is the nature of his response — does he look for the source of the sound? does he stop whatever he is doing? Beyond simple observation, formal testing will be necessary. One kind of test which is often used involves having a child decide whether a given sound is the same or different from one heard previously. The sounds may be musical notes, pure tones, words, syllables, or sets of syllables. The difficulty of the task depends on the nature of the stimuli and the nature of the response called for. Asking a child to judge sameness of two series of syllables, like *pa-ba-pa* and *ba-pa-pa*, is harder than giving him pictures of a bat and a hat and asking him to point to the picture named twice in the series *bat-hat-hat*. Both tasks may be too complex for very young or severely impaired children, if only because they cannot be made to understand what is expected of them.

Evaluating the child's ability to reproduce speech sounds and sound sequences can be accomplished through a variety of imitation tasks, ranging from repetition of hand-clapping patterns, to syllable sequences such as *pa-ta-ka,* to words and phrases. In both decoding and encoding tasks at this stage, the child's memory is involved. If a child is to judge the likeness of two sounds, he must remember the first until after he has heard the second, and must then compare them in his memory. If he is to imitate a sequence, he must be able to remember the beginning parts until he has heard it all, and he must remember it in order. Separate evaluation of the child's memory is often a useful addition to language assessment at this stage. Rather than analyzing memory capacity, analysis of the recall errors the child makes seems to provide more useful information about function for language. Error patterns reveal the strategies used for memory processing, which in turn give information about the way the child organizes language stimuli.

The ability to respond to stimuli in other modalities is also important to the language assessment. Tests of visual perception and discrimination, for example, can yield valuable insight into the abilities that underlie the child's speech processing, particularly if auditory processing is impaired. Some children may not be able accurately to recall auditory sequences such as *boo-ba-bee,* but may demonstrate a normal ability to recall a visual pattern presented to them. This is important information, because it suggests that at least a part of this general mental ability is intact and can perhaps be exploited to assist in improving recall in the auditory mode. Much of the assessment suggested above can provide insight into the child's general mental abilities. Where it seems warranted, intelligence testing can provide still more information in this area.

Another kind of information basic to the evaluation of a child's language ability is that regarding cognitive functioning. Is the child capable of symbolic representation? If the child does not use words as symbols, it is important to know whether he can see other representational relationships, such as that between pictures and real objects. Earlier in this chapter, and in Chapter 1, other aspects of cognitive development that are related to language acquisition and development were discussed. Some of the types of questions one might ask in evaluating cognitive development are these: Does the child imitate a model not immediately present? Does the child look for hidden objects in the place where he saw them last? Can he make a systematic search for hidden objects? Does the child engage in pretending (such as pretending to sleep or pretending to eat)? Full-scale evaluation of children's cognitive functioning is extremely important information, especially for children who show little or no evidence of having acquired verbal language. As you have undoubtedly concluded from the emphasis of our discussion, a good language-assessment model will include evaluation not only of language, but also of the areas of general mental functioning and cognitive development that are precursors to language acquisition and development. Often, it will be necessary to call on professionals from disciplines other than speech and hearing to conduct this part of the evaluation, but these areas are so important that they must be included in a general evaluation.

Having considered some of the more important general aspects of the language assessment, we turn to the specific evaluation of the child's language behavior in terms of imitation, comprehension, and production.

Imitation. Children's imitations of model sounds or sentences provided by an examiner can yield much information about their ability to comprehend and produce language. If the model presented for imitation exceeds the child's short-term memory, we assume that the child must process the model through his grammatical system if he is to repeat it. Certainly, normal children seem to do this, so that their imitations of model sentences bear a striking resemblance to their own spontaneous productions. A child whose spontaneous production consisted of two- and three-word sentences such as *Baby go out, Where daddy go,* or *Cookie all gone* would be expected to imitate the sentence *Baby's hat is lying on the blue chair* as *Hat on chair* or perhaps as *Baby hat chair.* For children with language disorders, elicited imitation can provide insight into language-processing strategies that cannot be derived by any other means. Thus, if a language-disordered child were given a sentence such as *Daddy is going to work in his office* and imitated it as *Office work,* one would have reason to wonder whether this child was, in fact, handling language input in a normal fashion. (Obviously, imitation of one sentence would not be sufficient evidence.)

Although the use of elicited imitation shows great potential in language assessment, it must be used and interpreted with caution. Stimuli must be carefully constructed to allow the examiner to focus on whichever aspect of language is of interest—phonology, syntax, or semantics. Scoring procedures are often controversial. For example, if one wishes to examine a child's knowledge of locative relationships in sentences, one might present models such as *Billy put the hat in the box.* If a child repeats *hat box,* is that sufficient to show his grasp of how location can be indicated, or must he say *hat in box?* Issues such as this may be resolved through research with normally developing children. In the meantime, the use of elicited imitation in assessing the language of children with abnormal developmental histories remains a valuable tool, when applied intelligently.

Comprehension. In a typical comprehension task, a child is asked to point to a picture or perform some action based on his linguistic knowledge. Usually, sentence pairs with a specific contrast are used, and the child must indicate comprehension of each sentence in the pair. For example, to test for comprehension of pronouns, a child might be presented with two pictures: a girl walking upstairs in one picture and a boy walking upstairs in the other picture. The examiner, without pointing to either picture, might say the two sentences corresponding to the pictures: *He is walking up the stairs. She is walking up the stairs.* The child would then be asked to point to the correct picture as the examiner repeated each sentence. Comprehension tasks also might require the child to manipulate objects to demonstrate understanding of sentences, such as *The bear kisses the elephant* versus *The elephant kisses the bear,* with toy animals being used. Often, tasks using objects are more effective with younger or impaired children who may have difficulty dealing with the two-dimensional space represented in pictures.

Comprehension tasks are not without problems. First, of course, many aspects of language cannot be pictured or acted out easily, and testing a child on comprehension of these is difficult. For example, how would you determine whether a child comprehended the difference between *He came later than I expected* and *He came sooner than I expected?* In addition, it is sometimes impossible to determine whether a child's responses are more a function of guessing than of actual comprehension. Tasks must be carefully constructed and scoring procedures carefully defined to be sure that a task is, in fact, measuring comprehension.

Production.   In assessing a child's language production, two procedures may be used. In one, the production of specific structures is elicited by the examiner. This is often done in a question-answer situation, in which the examiner might hold up two blocks and say *Is this red block taller or shorter than this blue one?* Or a child might be asked, *Tell me how to get to your house from here.* There are occasions when elicited production is the most useful way of assessing a child's ability to use language in specific ways, because the examiner can control the situation in which the language is produced. However, production may be assessed also through the use of spontaneous speech samples collected while the child is engaged in everyday activities. If time is not essential, and if one is interested in general performance rather than in specific kinds of language, spontaneous language samples can provide good evidence of what a child does with language.

Several methods are used to score language samples obtained in elicited or spontaneous production tasks. One might calculate the general mean length of the child's utterances (usually in morphemes), evaluate the developmental complexity of the utterances, or even attempt to write the grammatical rules that would account for the utterances. Most procedures used to evaluate spontaneous language depend on some minimum number of utterances (50 or 100) being obtained. This might be a difficult requirement for some language-impaired children who have very little language. Some researchers have suggested that reliable estimates of a child's language ability can be obtained from fewer utterances, but as yet this is uncertain. A good language sample would include not only the child's utterances, but also those of any other speakers present, as well as any relevant information about the situation. The example below of an interaction between a mother and her language-impaired child shows how such a language sample might look after being transcribed:

Mother: (playing with doll) This is a nice doll. Can you make her eyes close?

           Child: Pull hair

Pull her hair?
You don't want to pull her hair.
Look how her eyes close. (tipping doll's head back and forth)

           (grabs doll and bangs it on the floor) Me see, me see.

You want to see the dolly? Ok, but don't break it.

           (poking finger into doll's face) Hole in there.

Yes, the dolly's mouth has a hole in it. That's to put the bottle in.

           Bottle. Have bottle. (going toward door of room)

No, don't go outside. You don't have a bottle. The dolly has a bottle.

           Have bottle. Outside. Home, Mommy.

Presenting a language sample in such a fashion allows one to see not only what kind of language a child is using, but also how that language relates to the situation and to the language used by others in the environment. Once a sample has been obtained, various scoring procedures can be used to estimate the child's level of language development and to establish a description of baseline behaviors that can be used to build a management program for the child.

Using Language Tests. No attempt will be made here to list or describe specific language tests, but some general considerations will be mentioned. First, anyone who assesses children's language ability should keep in mind the distinction between language performance, or what a child does with language, and language competence, or what underlying knowledge a child has. A complete picture, or even a good partial picture of a child's language competence, would demand far more information than any available test can provide. In one sense, all language tests are tests of language performance, which show what a child can do on a particular set of test items at a particular time. The terms *knowledge* and *ability* are used loosely in test situations, and probably should not be used at all, since no test will enable us to be entirely sure what a child "knows" about syntax or semantics.

Second, a great many of the tests used to assess the child's language-processing abilities are designed to examine only one kind of behavior, usually comprehension. Of those tests which do require that the child encode language, most call for imitation rather than spontaneous production. In using any test which calls for only one kind of language behavior, it is important to remember that for some children who have language disorders, the normal relationships between imitation, comprehension, and production may not exist. Thus, a child's ability to comprehend cannot be taken as evidence that he can imitate, and correct imitation cannot be taken as evidence that the child can comprehend or spontaneously produce a given structure. Ideally, all three kinds of behavior should be assessed.

Third, there are many available language tests, and in deciding which ones to use, the examiner must have a clear idea of what the testing is supposed to accomplish. Sometimes the examiner will want to be able to compare a child's test performance with that of other children, to rank him in comparison with his peer group. To do this, the examiner must use a standardized test, which has group norms. This means that the test has been given to a large number of normal children at different age levels, so that there is information available about what score the average child at a given age made on the test. Standardized test scores are often used to talk about a child's "language age." If a test has not been standardized, and many supposed tests of language have not been, then it can only be used to describe a child's behavior in various areas and to compare one aspect of his behavior with another. It cannot be used to compare his behavior with that of other children. These latter tests can be used very effectively in an integrated assessment of a child's language development, and should not be ignored.

Finally, a good assessment involves some degree of subjective judgment and interpretation. The examiner first must decide which tests are appropriate for an individual child, given his history and his apparent level of performance. Once test results have been obtained, they must be looked at all together. A list of test scores tells very little unless it is accompanied by some explanation of what each score indicates about the strengths and weaknesses in the child's language-processing abilities, and what the total results suggest about the nature of the child's problem and its remediation. The test scores will not define this—it is left to the examiner's interpretation. This means that the examiner must know about language development in normal children, about the general language behavior of various groups of disordered children, and about what language tests can and cannot reveal. It also means that the examiner should proceed with caution, being ready at any time to reconsider a diagnosis when new evidence is available.

These cautions about the use of tests have caused many professionals to rely almost entirely on samples of spontaneous language for evaluating children. A spontaneous language sample is a good technique that often provides more and better information than a formal language test. It is not without pitfalls, however, both in terms of scoring and data collection. Children are not always willing to talk, and even in the best of situations a child may withdraw and refuse to cooperate. Any guide to language assessment would have to include the advice to be calm and patient. Even the most recalcitrant child will eventually have a good day.

Some of the disadvantages in collecting language samples can be diminished if the language samples are tape recorded in the child's home by the mother or another caretaker. The parent must be given precise instructions in how to obtain a natural sample, of course. The potential advantages of having a sample for analysis and evaluation prior to the formal assessment scheduled at the "strange" clinic outweigh the time considerations given to parent training, and samples so obtained are at least equivalent to samples obtained in the clinic (Kramer, James, and Saxman, 1977).

MANAGEMENT

Management for children who have language problems is based on an assumption that may be stated as follows: For some reason, children who do not develop language normally have not been able to derive from the language of their environments sufficient information to formulate normal language of their own. This statement may apply in any number of ways, depending on the individual child's problem. For some children, it may mean that they have not absorbed the connection between words and things, and thus have not developed vocabularies; for others, it may mean that they have not decoded the syntactic rules which govern the combination of words into sentences. For still another group, it may mean that, while some decoding has occurred, impairment of encoding processes prevents the translation of this decoding into spoken language.

The function of language management is not to correct the original cause of the child's impairment. In most instances, this would be an impossible task, because the original cause often is not known, or where it is known, it may not be correctable or may no longer be functionally related to the maintainence of the disorder. Factors that are functionally related to the disorder in a maintainence relationship should be alleviated, if possible. Even in cases where the primary cause of language impairment is known and can be alleviated, as with some hearing-impaired children, some management strategies may still need to be employed. The purpose of language management is to teach language to children who cannot learn it for themselves, regardless of the reasons for their failure to learn. Normal children are not taught to talk any more than they are taught to sit up. They progress from one- to two-word utterances, they start to use grammatical markers such as tense endings and plurals, they phrase questions and negatives, all without being told the rules for any of this. Their mistakes may be corrected and their successes praised, but they are not carefully drilled in the use of grammatical structures. It all seems to occur with little effort by adults in the environment to make it happen. With language-impaired children, this is not the case. They do not develop by themselves; some intervention must occur if they are to learn. This intervention is management.

Because we assume that the child with a language problem is unable to use the language of his environment as a normal child does, the first step in management is to make language more accessible for the child. Where a normal child can presumably structure and organize what he hears for himself, the clinician must structure and organize appropriate language stimuli for the language-impaired child. Language stimuli must be carefully sequenced in terms of normal developmental stages, and each level of response, whether one-word utterances or simple sentences, must be thoroughly practiced before more complex responses are demanded. The child must be given the opportunity to hear and use language appropriate for his abilities in many communicative situations. Techniques for presenting language structures to the child and eliciting language responses from him are varied, and the choice of technique will depend in large part on the nature of the child's problem and his individual learning style.

In this regard, it is important to remember that language is not learned in a vacuum. It is learned in and through a rich environment of varied stimuli and contexts. Children with language problems need such a language-learning environment just as do normal language-learning children. No child can learn effective language in a white-painted cubicle where he spends an hour a day pointing to line drawings in a book as the clinician calls out words. Except for those rare cases in which a child needs to have very limited and controlled stimulation, language therapy should occur in realistic situations, where the child is given someone attentive with whom to talk and something meaningful to talk about. Many children respond well to the companionship and mild competition inherent in group situations, so it is often useful to have three or four children in the situation. Techniques such as interactive-language therapy, in which small groups of children respond in carefully structured ways to stories, or cognitive-based therapy, in which language structures are presented in conjunction with situations designed to make new concepts available to the child, are only two of many therapy styles in current use.

Many clinicians assume that if they present enough language to the child, and if he learns to respond appropriately in the therapy situation, he will be able to continue on his own to become a normal adult language user. In some cases, this may indeed be what happens. We do not have good long-term studies of language development in children who have childhood language problems; we lack information about what happens to these children when they become adults. It does seem unlikely, however, that all language-impaired children, even those who receive professional assistance, will at some magical moment become normal adult speakers. To use language normally, a speaker must have internalized a set of rules—phonologic, syntactic, semantic, and communicative—and must be able to use these rules to generate his own utterances. We cannot teach a child all this. We use many rules of language that we are unaware of, and we are called upon to formulate grammatical, appropriate sentences in many different situations. Teaching all these rules, step by step, to children who cannot learn them alone would be an overwhelming task, one which would not be eased by the fact that we don't understand how normal children learn them to begin with. For the most part, these rules are not taught as such through language management. Rather, the child is presented with structured language stimulation, and it is hoped that if he can be taught to respond appropriately to some basic language, his own processing abilities will begin to function. As Eisenson (1972) says, "What we hope to establish is a large enough basis of what we can teach directly to enable the child to continue on his own to be a creative user of language—to formulate sentences from his lexical inventory and grammar that he has never produced before, with confidence that his formulations will be acceptable according to the verbal habits of his community." This is a great deal to hope for, and it is inevitable that this hope will not be fully realized for every child. This means that whatever language the child is able to learn should be useful language. Naming zoo animals may not be the most useful vocabulary exercise for a language-impaired child; naming eating utensils or articles of clothing may be more appropriate. Regardless of the linguistic form being taught at a given time or the techniques being used to teach the form, the focus in all language management should be on establishing practical language which the child can employ in his everyday surroundings and activities. It is this kind of language that opens up the possibility of real communication with other human beings—a possibility which is the birthright of every person.

REFERENCES   BEVER, T., The cognitive basis for linguistic structures. In J. Hayes (Ed.), *Cognition and the Development of Language.* New York: Wiley (1970).

BLOOM, L., and LAHEY, M., *Language Development and Language Disorders.* New York: Wiley (1978).

BOWERMAN, M., Discussion summary—Development of concepts underlying language. In R. Schiefelbusch and L. Lloyd (Eds.), *Language Perspectives—Acquisition, Retardation, and Intervention.* Baltimore: University Park Press (1974).

BROEN, P., The verbal environment of the language learning child. *American Speech and Hearing Association Monographs, No. 17.* Washington, D.C.: American Speech and Hearing Association (1972).

CLARK, H., Space, time, semantics, and the child. In T. Moore (Ed.), *Cognitive Development and the Acquisition of Language.* New York: Academic Press (1973).

EISENSON, J., *Aphasia in Children.* New York: Harper & Row (1972).

ERVIN-TRIPP, S., Some strategies for the first two years. In T. Moore (Ed.), *Cognitive Development and the Acquisition of Language.* New York: Academic Press (1973).

HARDY, W., On language disorders in young children: A reorganization of thinking. *Journal of Speech and Hearing Disorders,* 30, 3–16 (1965).

HYMES, D., *Towards Communicative Competence.* Philadelphia: University of Pennsylvania Press (1972).

JORDAN, T., Language and mental retardation: A review of the literature. In R. Schiefelbusch, R. Copeland, and J. Smith (Eds.), *Language and Mental Retardation.* New York: Holt, Rinehart and Winston (1967).

KRAMER, C., JAMES, S., and SAXMAN, J., A comparison of language samples elicited at home and in the clinic. Paper presented to the Annual Convention of the American Speech and Hearing Association, Chicago (1977).

LACKNER, J., A developmental study of language behavior in retarded children. *Neuropsychologia,* 6, 301–320 (1968).

LENNEBERG, E., *Biological Foundations of Language.* New York: Wiley (1967).

LENNEBERG, E., NICHOLS, I., and ROSENBERGER, E., Primitive stages of language development in Mongolism. *Proceedings of the Association of Research in Nervous and Mental Disorders,* 421, 119–137 (1964).

MacMILLAN, D., *Mental Retardation in School and Society.* Boston: Little, Brown (1977).

MARGE, M., The general problem of language disabilities in children. In J. Irwin and M. Marge (Eds.), *Principles of Childhood Language Disabilities.* New York: Appleton-Century-Crofts (1972).

MENYUK, P., *Sentences Children Use.* Cambridge, Mass.: MIT Press (1969).

MENYUK, P., *The Acquisition and Development of Language.* Englewood Cliffs, N.J.: Prentice-Hall (1971).

MILLER, G., The magical number seven, plus or minus two: Some limits on your capacity for processing information. *Psychological Review, 63,* 81–97 (1956).

MOREHEAD, D., and MOREHEAD, A., From signal to sign: A Piagetian view of thought and language. In R. Schiefelbusch and L. Lloyd (Eds.), *Language Perspectives—Acquisition, Retardation, and Intervention.* Baltimore: University Park Press (1974).

MOREHEAD, D., and MOREHEAD, A., *Normal and Deficient Child Language.* Baltimore: University Park Press (1976).

MURCHISON, C., and LANGER, S., Tiedemann's observations on the development of the mental faculties of children. *The Pedagogical Seminary and Journal of Genetic Psychology, 34,* 205–230 (1927).

NAREMORE, R., and DEVER, R., A comparison of the language performance of educable mentally retarded and normal children at five age levels. *Journal of Speech and Hearing Research, 18,* 82–95 (1975).

NELSON, C., Structure and strategy in learning to talk. *Monographs for the Society for Research in Child Development, 38* (1973).

SEMMEL, M., and HERZOG, B., The effects of grammatical form class on the recall of Negro and Caucasian educable retarded children. *Studies in Language and Language Behavior, 3,* 1–19 (1966).

SEMMEL, M., LEFSON, M., and SITKO, M., Learning and transfer of paradigmatic word association by educable mentally retarded children: A preliminary report. *Studies in Language and Language Behavior, 5,* 343–363 (1966).

SINCLAIR-DeZWART, H., Language acquisition and cognitive development. In T. Moore (Ed.), *Cognitive Development and the Acquisition of Language.* New York: Academic Press (1973).

SLOBIN, D., Cognitive prerequisites for the development of grammar. In C. Ferguson and D. Slobin (Eds.), *Studies of Child Language Development.* New York: Holt, Rinehart and Winston (1973).

SLOBIN, D., *Psycholinguistics.* Glenview, Ill.: Scott, Foresman (1971).

SNOW, K., Mothers' speech to children learning language. *Child Development, 43,* 549–565 (1972).

STUDDERT-KENNEDY, M., The perception of speech. In T. Sebeok (Ed.), *Current Trends in Linguistics,* Vol. XII. The Hague: Mouton (1974).

signpost   American society is a multicultural scene in which different people speak in different ways. These differences are attributable to many things, some of the most important being geographic environment, ethnic grouping, social class, and educational level. Chapter 5 considers some of the educational and social consequences of these dialectical variations, particularly as they affect certain groups of children entering school. Two socioethnic groups are given particular attention: economically deprived children of the black ghetto and economically deprived children of the Spanish-speaking barrio. These two groups are singled out because of their large numbers, because they show quite different types of dialectical variations, and because they, perhaps more than other groups in American society, are often stigmatized as a result of the language forms they employ. Among the many issues dealt with in regard to this subject is the question of the extent, if any, to which language differences should be changed. In recent years, opposing answers to this question have sparked passionate arguments within many disciplines, communication disorders included. Those responsible for educating children and those speech-language pathologists who must make decisions about possible change in a dialectical variation need to be fully aware of the arguments on both sides of this issue. After reading Chapter 5, the student should be in a relatively good position to decide whether or not a given language difference is one that warrants management clinically.

5

Rita C. Naremore

language
variation
in a
multicultural
society

If by some miraculous intervention all the inhabitants of the world could at four o'clock tomorrow afternoon be made to speak exactly alike, it would not be twenty-four hours before differences would begin to make themselves apparent. Variations in types of character, in daily needs, in attitudes toward life and nature and society would bring about rapid variations in the mode of expression, and unless we are to conceive of the whole world as drowned in sloth or in brotherly love, competition and rivalry would soon give one set of variations precedence over the others, so that after a few generations the lone language would break up into divergent dialects and ultimately into diverging languages. What is true of different races and countries is true also, though in a milder way, of different sections of the same country. There is no nation, so far as I am aware, in which all the citizens or even all the educated citizens use precisely the same speech. (Scott, 1971)

INTRODUCTION

Scott makes an obvious but inescapable point in the statement above: *We don't all sound alike.* A child born and raised in Brooklyn, New York will not speak like a child born and raised in New Orleans, Louisiana. A person born and raised in a wealthy home and educated in the best schools will not speak the same way as a person born and raised in poverty, who dropped out of school at age sixteen, even though both may be from New Orleans. *Just as people in different geographical regions of the country have different ways of speaking, so differences in ethnic grouping, social class, and educational level also lead to differences in speaking.*

Naturally, such variation among adults in a society will also be found among children. Children learn the kind of language spoken in their environment, and if the language use of adults in a given environment reflects various influences, so will the children's. This is usually not a problem until the children enter school, and it may not cause problems even then if their language use is not very different from the kind of language use demanded by the school. There are, however, certain groups of children in American society whose ways of using language do create problems when they enter school. It is with these children and their language use that this chapter is concerned.

The first section of the chapter presents several sociolinguistic terms and concepts. Next we discuss language forms (phonology and syntactic patterns) associated with two socioethnic groups: the economically deprived child of the black ghetto and the economically deprived child of the Spanish-speaking barrio. Our discussion focuses on these particular groups because they involve a large percentage of the population and represent two quite different types of dialectical variations. Moreover, perhaps more than other groups in our society, these children are often socially stigmatized as a result of the language forms they employ. For example, imagine what your own response might be if you were a teacher, and when you asked one of your students why he didn't do his homework, he replied *Teacher, I ain't got no pencil.* Or imagine your response as an employer if a young woman you interviewed for a secretarial job answered your request to "tell me about yourself" by saying, *My name is Rosa Alvarez. I have twenty years of age. I go es-school for learning to type. Is not too hard, this typing.* If these examples sound unfamiliar or "wrong" to you, your response is probably typical of that encountered by economically deprived black or native Spanish-speaking children in the society at large. In the second section of the chapter we discuss the reasons for such responses and the educational and social consequences for the child. Our intention here is not to suggest that these children are the only ones whose language use causes them difficulties in the society; rather, they are the two largest groups in terms of numbers (Jeter, 1977).

The third section of the chapter discusses aspects of language use associated with social class. Differences in language use are differences in how people employ their formal language skills to meet the communication demands of the environment. There are many factors that determine what we say in any given situation. Some are related to our individual personality makeup and some arise out of our knowledge of cultural and social norms for what is appropriate. Just as children learn to use the language forms of their environments (children who hear "ain't" and "he don't" will say "ain't" and "he don't" themselves), so they also learn about appropriate language use from the environment. For example, children who are seldom given approval or affection verbally will have difficulty using language this way themselves.

The final section of the chapter is concerned with the question of changing children's ways of speaking, whether in terms of language form or language use. A philosophical approach to this question is presented, and various pragmatic issues arising from it are discussed.

SOME SOCIOLINGUISTIC TERMS AND CONCEPTS

Before we consider some variations in language form and language use in society, there are a few terms and concepts that we need to discuss. Like all technical terms, the ones that we use may be defined in different ways by different people—so it is important to be clear about definitions and concepts that are basic to this chapter.

Standard English

Most of us carry around in our heads an idea about a variety of English that is "correct" or "proper." *Standard English* is that form of American English that generally appears in textbooks and on radio and television newscasts. It is, in a sense, *an idealized form of the language.* When we describe the rules for "good" grammar and pronunciation, what is being described is this idealized standard. Yet, few people actually speak standard English for it is not identified in any recognizable way with any part of the country, with any particular ethnic background, or with any particular class of people. All of us come from some place, some kind of educational and economic circumstances with some ethnic background. So in order to speak standard English we have to be taught to erase the influences of our backgrounds. For most people, this is difficult and not really worth the effort anyway. So we go around happily or unhappily reflecting our background.

The world would be boring if we all dressed alike or looked alike (see Figure 5–1), and it would be just as boring if we all talked alike. And yet, even while agreeing with this statement, most of us have some sense of limits—some sense that even though language variation is a good thing there are certain ways of speaking that are, in certain situations, wrong. It is when we begin trying to define "wrong" that we begin to disagree about language variation in society.

FIGURE 5–1. *A moment of sharing by some children of our multicultural society. "The world would be boring if we all dressed alike or looked alike . . . and it would be just as boring if we all talked alike." (From* About Me, Volume 14 of Childcraft—The How and Why Library. © 1976 Field Enterprises Educational Corporation.)

Dialect

When we hear a speaker, or a group of speakers, who *systematically deviate from the ideal standard form*, we say they are speaking a *dialect*. The key word here is "systematically." All of us have in our speech occasional "mistakes" or random variations from standard grammar and pronunciation. When these variations become predictable in the speech of certain identifiable groups of people, we have dialects. For example, many speakers may occasionally leave off the *-ing* ending on a word, saying *He's gonna go* instead of *He's going to go*. When this elimination of *-ing* becomes a pattern in a speech of a group of people, so that it occurs almost all the time, as is the case with most southerners, we say that it is a systematic variation, and it is one way of identifying a southern dialect.

Dialects may be associated with speakers from a particular part of the country (Western Pennsylvania, Eastern New England, etc.) or with a particular ethnic or social-class background. Many Jewish comedians, for example, derive much of their humor from their imitation of the dialect of Jewish people with Yiddish-speaking backgrounds. Sometimes regional, ethnic, and class factors influencing a dialect become so intertwined that they are difficult to sort out. But the fact remains that the reason we are able to imitate the speech of certain regions so easily or place certain speakers so readily is that we have identified the systematic variations from standard English which characterize that dialect.

Speaking a dialect is inescapable. The difficulty arises out of the fact that certain dialects in the society are socially valued by some people while others are socially stigmatized. To some listeners, a person who speaks an Appalachian Mountain dialect may be regarded as unsophisticated and of low intelligence, because that dialect suggests such a stereotype. A person speaking an upper-class Boston dialect may, on the other hand, be regarded as sophisticated and intelligent. In reality, of course, the two speakers may be exactly the same in terms of intelligence and sophistication. The good or bad image does not exist in the dialect—it exists in the mind of the listener. If one speaker pronounces *log* to rhyme with *bog* and *fog*, and the other pronounces it as though it were *lawg*, one cannot say that either pronunciation is wrong. Rather, each pronunciation may be socially stigmatized in some parts of the country. In southern Appalachia, saying *lahg* is strange, while in Boston, saying *lawg* is strange. The consequences of speaking a given dialect depend to some extent on where and with whom one speaks it, although it is true that some socioethnic dialects tend to provoke negative responses in many situations outside the socioethnic culture that gives rise to them. We discuss two such dialects in detail later in this chapter.

This leads us to ask why dialects should exist in the first place. To explain why we reflect our backgrounds in our speech, we need to retreat briefly into history. The United States was settled by people who spoke different languages, including people who spoke very different dialects of British English. As groups of settlers populated various parts of the country, their mobility was limited. Except for very rare occasions, they tended to stay within limited areas, generally bounded by such natural barriers as large rivers or mountains. At times and in places where there is little mobility and therefore little contact between different groups of people, there is nothing to cause the various dialects of a language to change in the same way. Under these conditions, the form of language spoken by people who lived in Massachusetts might be expected to vary greatly from the form of language spoken by people in, say, Mississippi. This is not only because the dialects of the settlers in these two regions probably differed to begin with, but also because their isolation from one another and their contacts with different linguistic influences (such as immigrants from elsewhere in Europe into Massachusetts; the slave population in Mississippi; and different resident Indian populations in both areas) tended to cause linguistic change in different directions. Where the boundaries are not so clearly defined (for example, along the Mason-Dixon line), dialect regions have been separated by bands of "in between" speakers, who speak a little like the people on both sides of them. Regional dialects are not nearly so distinct from one another in this country today as they once were, because increased mobility and the influence of radio and television expose most speakers to the leveling influence of "media" English.

However, geographical isolation is not the only kind of isolation. Groups of people can isolate themselves from others, or be isolated by others, for reasons of race or economic status. This type of isolation can result in dialects just as easily as geographical isolation can. Within the southern regional dialect, for example, there are differences between the speech of blacks and whites, and between the speech of the poor and ill-educated and that of the more prosperous and better educated. Such differences exist because until recent times there has been minimum communication between the races and minimum communication between the prosperous and the poor. This isolation of various groups in the society results in different sets of needs and attitudes, and different ways of life. When people don't talk to each other, or talk to each other only in limited ways in well-defined situations, and have very different life styles, there is reason for their language forms and patterns of language use to differ.

Register

Our language is also influenced by factors other than geographic, social-class, and ethnic backgrounds. All of us vary our language to fit the situation in which it is used. Language variations that are due to situational factors are called *registers*. You would probably not talk the same way to a two-year-old child as you would to your father. You would not talk the same way to your best friend in a neighborhood bar as you would to the hostess at a formal reception. In short, you are not limited to one style of language. You vary your language to fit the situation in which it is used. Some of the factors in situations that cause us to vary our language use are: listener characteristics (for example, age, sex, relation to speaker), topic, place (formal or informal setting), and purpose (for example, casual conversation, lecture, persuasive appeal). Importantly, speakers from different backgrounds may change their language in different ways to meet situational demands. That is, one person's most formal register will not necessarily be the same as another person's.

To recapitulate the points made in this section: Language variation in a society is a normal, natural phenomenon. Dialects have arisen because different groups of people have been historically separated from each other, geographically or socially or both. In addition to dialect variation, different styles of speaking due to situational factors can be identified. These situational variations are called registers and all normal speakers use more than one register. We return to a discussion of the social and educational consequences of language variation later in this chapter. We now consider language form and language use in two socioethnic groups.

LANGUAGE FORM

In the years since 1960, a great deal of research has been devoted to the investigation and description of language differences among various groups of children in American society, and much of this research has concentrated on the study of language form. Two quite separate approaches have been taken by researchers. One, labeled the *deficit approach*, holds that any deviation from standard English is to be regarded as an error and is a mark of "substandard" or inferior language use. Based on this point of view, any departure from standard English is a mistake and should be corrected. As previously noted, most of us were taught this in school, and we continue to have difficulty viewing variations from standard English in any other way. The other approach, called a *difference approach*, holds that some deviations may, in fact, result from the systematic application of language rules different from those used in standard English. Certainly it is possible to make errors using language, but it is important to separate random mistakes from systematic rule-governed variation. When a group of people regularly and systematically use a given form, and it can be demonstrated that this form is accounted for by a rule in their grammar, then it is difficult to see why such usage should be called "incorrect."

In this section, as in the chapter as a whole, a *difference approach* is taken. All normal children learn language, and to say that a child who learns to speak a dialect is learning inferior or deficient language makes no more sense than to say that a child who learns to speak French is learning an inferior language. The languages of the world cannot be arranged on a continuum from "best" to "worst" in linguistic terms, and neither can the dialects of any particular language. Baratz and Baratz (1970) submit that there is no reason to assume that any dialect of a language is inherently better than any other. Over time, one dialect in a country may become socially more prestigious than others, and come to be regarded as the standard for the country. But this is not a linguistically based decision—it is rather a sociopolitical decision. There is no reason why any dialect should be regarded as more complex, or more well-structured, or more grammatical than any other.

Modern linguistics has come a long way from the days when anything not found in "the grammar book" was regarded as "substandard." All rule-governed systems of language are grammatical—a grammar is nothing more than a system of rules. All grammars have structure and complexity. With this perspective in mind, we can now examine the formal characteristics of the language spoken by two groups of children most often identified as different in American society and most often studied: economically deprived black children and economically deprived children from Spanish-speaking backgrounds.

The Black-English Vernacular

The form of language spoken by the inner city black child in the large urban centers of this country has been variously called "black English," "Negro nonstandard English," or "black dialect." The term used here, black-English vernacular, has been adopted from Labov (1972) because it is perhaps the most descriptive label available. The discussion in the following pages is organized around three questions: What is the black-English vernacular? Who speaks it? and What are the consequences of being a speaker of black-English vernacular?

The Nature of the Black-English Vernacular. In the words of Labov (1972), the black-English vernacular is "The relatively uniform dialect spoken by the majority of black youth in most parts of the United States today, especially in the inner city areas of New York, Boston, Detroit, Philadelphia, Washington, Cleveland, Chicago, St. Louis, San Francisco, Los Angeles, and other urban centers. It is also spoken in most rural areas and used in the casual, intimate speech of many adults." Black-English vernacular is a definable, consistent language system. It does not result from "poor speech habits" or inadequate environments or cognitive deficiencies. It is governed by a set of identifiable rules, just as is any other language system. For our purposes here, black-English vernacular may be most readily characterized in terms of its principal contrasts with standard English. These are summarized in Table 5–1 and Table 5–2.

It is important that we have some idea of how the list of characteristics presented in Tables 5–1 and 5–2 relates to reality. How does a speaker of black-English vernacular employ these language forms in conversation? It is difficult to convey the sounds of black-English vernacular in writing without using a detailed phonetic transcription. Even then, much of the flavor of the dialect which involves rate of speaking and intonation patterns would be lost. However, consider the following interchange between two ten-year-old boys, Gregory and Michael:

GREGORY: Michael like to play wi' do' girl frien's down nere. Jo Ann Hayes. He like to play wi' dem. He w' play King Kong wi' dem.

MICHAEL: Jo Ann Hayes an' nem not my girl frien'. Cause I took deir ball an' ney ain' get 'n'i' back, until she gimme my back.

GREGORY: You did. An' you took my tennis ba'.

MICHAEL: I slapped her face too.

GREGORY: You took my tennis ba'. An' I got dat back too boy.

MICHAEL: I trew your tennis ball up on ne roof. You got Harry Lee tennis ba'. You do.

GREGORY: So you trow mine's up dere an' keep Harry Lee's.

MICHAEL: So 'pose Harry Lee tell your mother now.

GREGORY: I ma tell my mother dat you trow mine's up dere on ne roof. (Loman, 1967)

The language use in this conversation provides examples of several of the features listed in Tables 5–1 and 5–2. Substitutions of *d* and *t* for voiced and voiceless *th* are in accord with the substitutions listed for fricatives in Table 5–1, as in *trow, dem, dat*. The absence of the third-person singular *-s* on the verb "like" can be seen in Gregory's first utterance, and for "tell" in Michael's question "Pose Harry Lee tell your mother now?" (see Table 5–2 features for "Plural Marker," etc.). The future form, "I ma tell" rather than "I will tell" is seen in Gregory's last utterance. Patterns of negation are interesting in Michael's first utterance. In denying Gregory's statement about Jo

Table 5-1. SOME DIFFERENCES BETWEEN CONSONANT DISTRIBUTIONS IN BLACK-ENGLISH VERNACULAR AND STANDARD ENGLISH.*

BLACK-ENGLISH VERNACULAR	STANDARD ENGLISH
PLOSIVES Voiced plosives tend to be voiceless in final position, thus *rib* may become *rip*, *kid* may become *kit* or *pig* may become *pick*. Weakening of all final plosives may produce words that sound alike such as *boot, book,* and *boo.***	The voice-voiceless distinction (for example, *rib* versus *rip*) is maintained in final position.
NASALS There is a tendency for nasals to be lost in final position; *ng* becomes *n* in medial and final position so that *sing* and *sin* may sound alike.	*m* and *n* occur in all positions; *ng* occurs in medial and final position.
FRICATIVES Voiced *th* becomes *d* in initial position so that *then* and *den* sound alike; medially, voiced *th* becomes *d* or *v* so that *other* and *udder* or *either* and *Eva* sound alike; in final position voiced *th* becomes *v, f,* or *d*.	Voiced *th* as in *the* remains constant in all positions.
Voiceless *th* may become *f* initially so *think* becomes *fink;* it changes to *f, t,* or glottal stop medially making *toothbrush* into *toofbrush;* voiceless *th* changes to *f* or *t* finally, changing *fourth* to *fort*.	Voiceless *th* as in *thin* remains constant in all positions.
LIQUIDS *r* does not occur between two vowels so that *cat* and *carrot* may sound alike. Nor does *r* appear finally or preceding a consonant, thus *bah* and *bar* or *cot* and *cart* may sound alike.	In most standard English varieties, *r* occurs initially, finally, medially between two vowels, and preceding a consonant.
l does not always occur in final position thus *toll* and *toe* may sound alike. *l* may not occur before *t, d,* or *p,* thus *help* and *hep, colt* and *coat,* and *code* may sound alike.	*l* occurs initially, medially, finally, and in final consonant clusters.
INITIAL CONSONANT CLUSTERS *r* tends to disappear after *th, p, b, k,* and *g,* thus *professor* becomes *pofessa* and *brother* becomes *bovva*. *str* may become *skr,* thus *scream* and *stream* may sound alike.	There are 13 clusters that contain *r*.
FINAL CONSONANT CLUSTERS There is a tendency to simplify clusters, thus, *must* becomes *muss* and *bend* becomes *ben*. This tendency to simplify clusters intersects with grammatical categories involving the past (*walk* and *walked* both become *walk*), the plural, and the third-person singular.	Final consonants can be grouped into two categories: 1. Those that occur at the end of a word, for example, *hand*. 2. Those that occur by adding the endings for the possessive, the plural, and the past, for example, *s, z, t,* and *d*.

*The examples given here represent statistically significant differences between standard English and black-English vernacular. However, they may not apply to every individual speaker in every situation.

**Actually, there may be additional rule-bound phonetic cues that allow the speaker and listener to differentiate among these words. This is true of other examples in this table as well.

After R. Fasold and W. Wolfram, Some linguistic features of Negro dialect. In R. Fasold and R. Shuy (Eds.), *Teaching Standard English in the Inner City*. Washington, D.C.: Center for Applied Linguistics, 1970.

Table 5–2. SOME CONTRASTS BETWEEN GRAMMATICAL FORMS IN BLACK-ENGLISH VERNACULAR AND STANDARD ENGLISH.

VARIABLE	BLACK-ENGLISH VERNACULAR	STANDARD ENGLISH
Linking verb	He ⎯⎯ going.*	He *is* going.
Possessive marker	John⎯ cousin.	John*'s* cousin.
Plural marker	I got five cent⎯ .	I have five cents.
Subject expression	John *he* live in New York.	John lives in New York.
Past marker	Yesterday, he ain't had no money for the bus so he walk ⎯ home.	Yesterday he didn't have any money for the bus so he walk*ed* home.
Verb agreement	He run⎯ home.	He run*s* home.
Future form	I*'ma* go home.	I *will* go home.
"If" construction	I ask *did he do it.*	I asked *if he did it.*
Negation	It *ain't no* cat *can't* get in *no* coop *nohow.*	*No man can* get in a coop.
Indefinite article	I want *a* apple	I want *an* apple.
Pronoun form	*Us* got to do it.	*We* have to do it.
Preposition	He over *to* his friend house.	He is over *at* his friend's house.
	He teach ⎯⎯ Francis Pool.	He teaches *at* Francis Pool.
Be	Statement: He *be* here.	Statement: He is here all the time.
Been	He *been* ate the chicken.	He *ate* the chicken a long time ago.
Do	Contradiction: No, he *don't.*	Contradiction: No, he *isn't.*
	He *done been gone.*	He *had left.*
Modals	He *might could* go.	He *might* go.
Wh question	What it is?	What is it?
Verb form	I *drunk* the milk.	I *drank* the milk.

*Linguistic and social contexts will affect the frequency and distribution of the various forms. It is important to remember that this table represents some statistically significant frequency distributions between black-English vernacular and standard English. Some of the forms of black-English vernacular may be shared with other languages, other English dialects, and standard English. It is the sum total (by no means represented here) which constitutes black-English vernacular.

After R. Fasold and W. Wolfram, Some linguistic features of Negro dialect. In R. Fasold and R. Shuy (Eds.), *Teaching Standard English in the Inner City.* Washington, D.C.: Center for Applied Linguistics, 1970.

Ann Hayes, he says "Jo Ann Hayes an' nem not my girl frien'," omitting the linking verb *are.* This is a typical, systematic way of expressing negation, along with patterns involving "ain't," one of which can be seen in Michael's statement "an ney ain' get 'n'i back." The rules governing negative constructions in black-English vernacular are highly complex, but as Labov (1972) has shown they comprise a regular and definable system.

One further example in this dialogue illustrates a complex set of rules for indicating possession. Michael says "You got Harry Lee tennis ba'," leaving off the -'s ending on "Lee." Gregory then says, in his utterance immediately afterward, "Harry Lee's." The difference is that in Michael's statement, the object being possessed followed the name of the possessor, as in *Fred's book."* In black-English vernacular, the possessive ending is omitted in these circumstances because it is redundant. In Gregory's statement, the possessive marker is included because without it, the meaning of the sentence would not be clear.

He did not want to say "Keep Harry Lee," but rather, "Keep Harry Lee's (tennis ball)." This possessive marker is a regular feature of black-English vernacular, and further evidence to support it is seen in Gregory's use (twice) of "mine's" instead of "mine." In his utterances, "mine" is a possessive word appearing without the object of possession being specified right after it (he does not say "my tennis ball"). Therefore, following the rule system of black-English vernacular, he must put the -'s ending on "mine," saying "trow mine's up dere" rather than "trow mine up dere."

The features seen in Michael's and Gregory's language use are not mistakes. They result from the children's use of a set of rules *different* from the set used by speakers of other dialects, and *different* from the rules governing standard English. All dialects result from such systematic, rule-governed usage. If the forms did not appear regularly and systematically, we would not be able to identify a dialect at all—we would, instead, be dealing with a set of random, individual differences, not held in common by large groups of speakers. The language of Michael and Gregory is not a mass of chaotic mistakes. Rather, it reflects the end product of a grammar; and as can be seen in this brief excerpt, black-English vernacular shares many grammatical rules with standard English.

It cannot be overemphasized that it is unlikely that any individual child who speaks black-English vernacular will exhibit all characteristics of the dialect in his language use, or that any given characteristic will appear 100 percent of the time in linguistic environments where it is appropriate. As we discussed earlier, every speaker's language varies from situation to situation, depending on place, topic, listener, or goal. Just as a middle-class, midwestern, white speaker will shift registers when speaking to a child versus an adult, a close friend versus "the boss," or when switching topics from joking about a canoe trip to discussing ecology, so a speaker of black-English vernacular might shift registers in these same situations.

Light (1971) has analyzed the distribution of given black-English vernacular forms in the language used by a group of black children between six and eleven years of age. He wanted to know whether the distribution of plural, possessive, and third-person singular markers, and multiple negatives changed in the children's speech depending on the presence or absence of an adult, the race and sex of the adult, and the age of the child. Light analyzed the percentage of occurrence of the four target forms; that is, given a particular number of times when a child might have pluralized a noun for instance, in how many of those cases did he omit the plural ending? Light summarized his results as follows:

Use of the four nonstandard features considered varied depending upon the following factors:

1. Age of the child, with a higher percentage of nonstandard features being used by the youngest child.
2. Presence or absence of adult interviewers, with absence of an interviewer correlating with a higher percentage of nonstandard features.
3. Sex and racial characteristics of interviewer, with

   a. presence of a white interviewer alone correlating on'the average with a lower percentage of nonstandard features and the presence of a Negro interviewer alone correlating with a higher percentage, and
   b. presence of a single familiar white female correlating with a higher percentage of nonstandard forms than the presence of a white male.

In other words, the nature of the listener affects the nature of the language.

A further observation made by Light is worth noting here, because it serves to point out the fact that children using black-English vernacular may have access to the standard forms. He says:

> The children's productive as well as their receptive control of standard English should not be underestimated. Even with a category such as the third-person singular suffix, which showed an average 84 percent absence for all children, we find in the speech of one child with a 91 percent absence of this suffix, such sentences as:
>
> we wen' on na thing da *go* and den *goes* right back aroun' (121 MJ)
>
> The child is alternating a standard with a nonstandard 'zero' realization of the third singular marker. This alternation is common for other features in these conversations and implies a degree of productive as well as receptive control of standard English.

Light's observation is important: It is not likely that one will encounter a child who speaks black-English vernacular who never uses the standard English equivalent of a given black-English vernacular form.

In line with this discussion, it must be pointed out that there are black speakers who have few, if any, of the features of black-English vernacular, such as we have reviewed, in their speech. It is certainly possible to find black children from many parts of this country whose speech does not differ from that of middle-class white children. For the most part, these tend to be middle-class black children who are either the children of well-educated parents or who are growing up in communities where there are few other black children. It is also possible to find white speakers who live and work in close proximity to black speakers of black-English vernacular whose speech reflects many black-English vernacular features. This sharing of features is found in urban areas and is even more pronounced in the South (recall Labov's definition of black-English vernacular presented on pages 185–186). The distinction between black-English vernacular and the southern regional dialect, however, lies not in the simple presence or absence of given features, but in the pattern of occurrence. For example, white southerners will sometimes omit *is* or *are*, saying *We goin' down to the lake to do some fishin'*. However, this is an occasional usage; *is* and *are* will be more often present than absent. In black-English vernacular, the situation is just the opposite; these verbs are more often deleted than included.

Some Consequences of Speaking Black-English Vernacular.   If pointing out the existence of black-English vernacular is simply an interesting comment on the state of the world, with no real social or educational relevance, then researchers engaged in this activity may be asked why they bother. In fact, this does not appear to be the case. The importance of the dialect for black-English vernacular speakers can be felt in two areas, one educational and one social.

In the classroom, children who speak black-English vernacular may encounter significant *difficulty with reading*. The characteristics of black-English vernacular, some of which were noted earlier in this chapter, are such that many homonyms (words that sound alike) are created. As indicated in Table 5–1, deletion of *r* means that *guard* and *god* sound alike, as will *sore* and *saw*. Deletion of *l* creates problems with *toll-toe, tool-too*. Simplification of final consonant clusters creates *past-pass, cold-code,* and so forth. These phonological variables become particularly important when they interact with the grammatical system. *Passed,* which is pronounced *past* in standard English, is pronounced *pass* in black-English vernacular. If a black-English vernacular speaker says *He pass by me in the hall,* is this a present tense or a past tense statement? Out of context it is impossible to say. This would be problem enough, but Labov (1967) cites evidence indicating that not only do black-English vernacular speakers not pronounce the *-ed* ending on past tense verbs, they may also not recognize its significance when they see it written or printed.

Labov (1967) asked a group of ten- to twelve-year-old boys who spoke black-English vernacular to read the following sentences out loud:

1. Last month I read five books.
2. Tom read all the time.
3. Now I read and write better than Alfred does.
4. When I passed by, I read the posters.

5. When I liked a story, I read every word.
6. I looked for trouble when I read the news.

If a child pronounced *read* to rhyme with *red,* it was taken as indication that he perceived a sentence to be past tense. When a sentence contained adverbs indicating time (1, 2, and 3 above), the black-English-vernacular speakers showed a high level of correct readings of *read.* But when the cue to the pronunciation of *read* depended on the *-ed* ending of another verb (as in 4, 5, and 6 above), the rate of success dropped. The results of the test showed that these boys interpreted *-ed* correctly less than half the time.

This finding raises a fundamental question for teachers. If a black-English-vernacular speaker reads the sentence, *I looked both ways before I crossed* as *I look bof way before I cross,* the teacher's immediate urge may be to say, "No, say I looked both ways before I crossed." This may create several problems. First, the child may not hear any difference between what he said and what the teacher said, and he will be justifiably confused. Second, the child may hear a difference, but may not understand why it matters whether he says *look* or *looked,* in which case the teacher's correction of his pronunciation has not addressed his real problem — understanding what *-ed* means. Finally, the child may hear a difference between what he said and what the teacher said, and may understand the difference between *look* and *looked,* and may resent the teacher's correction as unnecessary. It is obviously crucial that the teacher be able to distinguish among these three problems. This demands more than good will on the teacher's part, and some practical suggestions will be offered in the final section of this chapter.

Beyond this educational difficulty in the classroom, speakers of black-English vernacular encounter a broader *problem in the society at large.* Research into the attitudinal correlates of language (Lambert et al., 1960; Ainsfeld, Bogo, and Lambert, 1962; Guskin, 1970; Naremore, 1971; Williams et al., 1976) suggests that people respond to spoken language in terms of stereotypes. That is, some set of cues in the language you hear from a person triggers a generalized response in you as a listener. This generalized response, or stereotype, may then affect all your other judgments of the speaker. For example, suppose that you have a stereotype of the "disadvantaged child," which includes such characteristics as: slow in school, not well dressed, behavior problem, does not speak standard English. Research indicates that when you hear a child who speaks black-English vernacular, you are likely to respond to that child as being disadvantaged, and that response will include your assuming that he is slow in school, not well dressed, etc. For example, Williams (1970) investigated the responses of a group of black and white teachers to the language of black and white children from both lower- and middle-class backgrounds. The teachers in the study listened to tape recorded samples of children's speech, and indicated their reactions to these samples on a set of scales. The results of Williams' analysis showed that children whose language sounded "ethnic" or "nonstandard" (children who spoke black-English vernacular) were perceived as being "disadvantaged" or "low class" by both the black and the white teachers. Such stereotypic responses are extremely resistant to change, even in the face of many individual exceptions to the stereotype.

The consequence of all this for the black-English-vernacular speaker can be simply stated: to the extent that the dialect is socially unacceptable, to that extent the speaker of that dialect will be categorized negatively. This is the primary reason why many educators, both black and white, urge that speakers of black-English vernacular become "bi-dialectal" (speaking both black-English vernacular and a more standard form of English). A bi-dialectal speaker would be able to use black-English vernacular forms or standard English forms, depending on the situation. The question of whether bi-dialectalism is desirable or possible has profound sociopolitical as well as pedagogical implications. Some of these are discussed in the final section of this chapter.

English of the Spanish-Speaking Child

The English spoken by children of Spanish-speaking backgrounds is in many ways more difficult to describe than that of the black-English-vernacular speaker. In the case of the Latino[1] child, the form of English spoken results from the interference of a second language: Spanish. This interference affects not only the English vocabulary, where Spanish words may often be substituted for English, but also English phonology and syntax, where Spanish sounds and constructions may appear. The nature of the interference will depend, of course, on the variety of Spanish being spoken (Mexican Spanish differs from Puerto-Rican Spanish, and so forth) and on the extent of the child's bilingualism. Some Latino children enter school as monolingual Spanish speakers and must learn English as a second language in the

---

[1] The word "Latino" is used to include residents of the Continental United States who are of Mexican, Puerto Rican, Cuban, or any other Spanish background. It is realized that there are both cultural and linguistic differences among various groups of Latinos, and that much detail will be sacrificed by emphasizing the similarities rather than the differences among them. "Latino" is used as a general term, in place of more specific designations such as "Chicano" or "Mexican-American."

school. Others enter school as monolingual English speakers, with perhaps some Spanish vocabulary or some phonological interference, but without extensive knowledge of Spanish. Many others come to school with some knowledge of both Spanish and English, usually more of one than the other. This section will discuss two aspects of the language of Spanish-English *bilingual* children: the characteristics of their spoken English, and the consequences of their being bilingual.

Characteristics of Spoken Spanish-Influenced English. There have been a number of attempts to classify the "interference points" for the Spanish speaker learning English. These "interference points" are areas where the two languages differ in their representation of a given form. Some interference points are summarized in Table 5–3 and Table 5–4. It must be remembered that the nature of the interference will depend on the particular variety of Spanish available to the speaker, as well as on the variety of English being learned. A New-York-City Puerto-Rican speaker is exposed to different English than a Texas-Mexican speaker, as well as having different Spanish influences. The summaries in Tables 5–3 and 5–4 are therefore very general ones.

The phonological and grammatical interference points as described in Tables 5–3 and 5–4 reflect only some of the problems facing the native-Spanish speaker who learns English as a second language. For example, both languages use several means of indicating the grammatical functions of words and sentences. We can tell whether a word is subject versus object, modifier versus modified, singular versus plural. We know the tense and mood of verbs, and the type of sentence someone has uttered (question, command, statement). These things are conveyed through word order, the use of special word endings, and the use of functional words, such as prepositions. In the English sentence *The boys jumped on the trampoline,* we know by word order that the sentence is a statement, and that *boys* is the subject and *trampoline* is the object of the preposition *on.* We know by the *-ed* ending of the verb that the action occurred in the past, and by the *-s* ending of *boys* that more than one boy jumped. *On* tells us the location of the jumping. Spanish speakers also use the grammatical devices of word endings, function words, and word order, but these are not the same as those used in English. Inspect Table 5–4 for some contrasts.

The degree to which the characteristics given above will appear in the language use of any individual child will, of course, depend on such factors as the length of time the child has been speaking English, the extent of English language use in the child's home, and the re-

Table 5-3. PHONOLOGICAL INTERFERENCE POINTS BETWEEN SPANISH AND ENGLISH.

SPANISH FORM	FORM USED BY NATIVE SPEAKER WHEN SPEAKING ENGLISH
PLOSIVES	
Initial voiceless plosives are not aspirated in Spanish.	The Spanish rule may carry over into English so that *coat* will be pronounced like *goat*.
All final plosives are voiceless.	The Spanish rule may carry over into English so that *web* will be pronounced like *wep* and *pig* will sound like *pick*.
FRICATIVES AND AFFRICATES	
Spanish has neither voiced nor voiceless *th*.	In English, *d* may be substituted for voiced *th*, giving *dis* instead of *this*, and *s* may be substituted for voiceless *th* giving *sing* instead of *thing*.
Spanish does not have a distinction between *b* and *v*.	In English, *b* and *v* may be substituted for one another, or may be replaced by a bilabial fricative sound which is a Spanish phoneme that does not occur in English.
Spanish has the *s* sound, but the *z, zh* (as in plea*s*ure), and *sh* (as in *sh*op) sounds of English are absent. *Ch* (as in *ch*air) occurs in Spanish, but *j* (as in *j*ump) does not.	In English, *s* is frequently substituted for *z*. *Sheep* may become *cheep* and *jump* may become *chump*.
Spanish does not have a sound like the English *h* (a glottal fricative), but does have a velar fricative which resembles *h*, but is more constricted.	In English, *h* may be omitted, or the Spanish velar fricative may be substituted for it.
LIQUIDS	
Spanish *r* and *l* are articulated differently from English *r* and *l*.	Spanish sounds for *r* and *l* may be substituted for English sounds.
VOWELS	
Spanish has no vowel sound like that in *pig* or *fit*.	These words may sound like *peeg* or *feet*.
The English vowel sound that occurs in *fat* and *hat* does not occur in Spanish.	The native Spanish speaker may substitute a Spanish vowel that makes the words sound like *fet* and *het* (rhyming with *set*).
The vowel sound in English *one* and *sun* does not occur in Spanish.	These words may sound as though they rhymed with *John* when pronounced by Spanish speakers.

After F. Williams, H. Cairns, and C. Cairns, *An Analysis of the Variations from Standard English Pronunciation in the Phonetic Performance of Two Groups of Nonstandard-English-Speaking Children.* Center for Communication Research, University of Texas, 1971; J. Sawyer, Social aspects of bilingualism in San Antonio, Texas. In R. Bailey and J. Robinson (Eds.), *Varieties of Present-Day English.* New York: Macmillan, 1973.

gional and social variants of English and Spanish being used. Also, although it may seem an obvious point, it is well to bear in mind the fact that not all children with Spanish surnames come from Spanish-speaking backgrounds. A child named Ana Marie Hernandez may come from a family that has lived in the United States for two generations and never speaks Spanish in the home, or she may come from a family that emigrated from Cuba six months ago in which no one but

Table 5–4. GRAMMATICAL INTERFERENCE POINTS BETWEEN SPANISH AND ENGLISH.

FORM USED BY NATIVE SPANISH SPEAKER WHEN SPEAKING ENGLISH	ENGLISH FORM
WORD ENDINGS	
Comparatives	
He is more big.	He is bigger.
She is most pretty of all the girls.	She is prettiest.
Third-Person Singular Verbs	
He walk__ very fast.	He walk*s* very fast.
Plurals	
The dog__ are gone.	The dog*s* are gone.
Past Tense	
They play__ there yesterday.	They play*ed* there yesterday.
Progressive	
The baby is sleep____.	The baby is sleep*ing*.
Possessive	
This is the car of my father.	This is my father's car.
FUNCTION WORDS	
Negative Commands	
No go there.	Don't go there.
Articles	
Is Mexican child.	Gomez is *a* Mexican child.
Is teacher.	She is *the* teacher.
"Be" Verbs	
I *have* hunger.	I *am* hungry.
He *have* six years.	He *is* six years old.
Prepositions	
It is *in* the table.	It is *on* the table.
"Do" used in Questions	
____you like this?	*Do* you like this?
WORD ORDER	
Pronoun Subjects	
Juan is my brother. Is big.	Juan is my brother. *He* is big.
Negative Sentences	
Marie *no is* here.	Marie *is not* here.
Adjectives	
The grass green is nice.	The green grass is nice.
Questions	
Juan *can go*?	*Can* Juan go?

After A. Davis, English problems of Spanish speakers. Urbana, Ill.: National Council of Teachers of English.

the father speaks English. Between these two extremes there are many variations, and each child must be treated as an individual case.

Technically, Spanish-influenced English reflects language overlap and should not be called a dialect. In this chapter, however, we are using the term *dialect* to mean a language form characterized by systematic variations from standard English and associated with a particular group of people. In that sense, the English of the Latino speaker is a dialect. It should be remembered, though, that this dialect, like others, may vary considerably from speaker to speaker and situation to situation. The interference points described in Tables 5–3 and 5–4 can thus be taken only as a broad outline, not as a picture of any Latino individual.

The Consequences of Spanish-English Bilingualism. Many educated Americans regard the ability to speak more than one language as a valuable skill and a mark of culture and intelligence. Unfortunately, this attitude does not generally carry over when the bilingual speaker happens to be Latino. Instead, children from Spanish-speaking backgrounds are encouraged to become unilingual English speakers in the schools—to such an extent that some children have actually been punished for speaking Spanish.

The blind insistence on this one language—one culture—approach in the schools is exemplified in a practice that was followed in the state of California. For many years, this state had given intelligence tests to all children in English. Consequently, many Latino children whose use of English was not sufficient to allow them to pass these tests were classified as mentally retarded and put into special education classes. As Ortego (1971) reports, "the findings of the special advisory committee to the California State Board of Education . . . (showed that) Mexican-American children, classified as mentally retarded after intelligence tests in English, have done remarkably better with tests in Spanish. . . . After retesting, one Mexican-American student showed an improvement of 28 points while the group's average rose 13 points." Surely this must be the most devastating consequence of being a Latino bilingual: to be classified as intellectually inferior after having been tested in a foreign language!

The low social value ascribed to speaking Spanish is also reflected in the language use of Latino bilinguals. Sawyer (1973) reports that the bilingual adults she observed treat Spanish words in very different ways, depending on whether the listener is Latino or Anglo. For Latino listeners, Spanish words are given Spanish pronunciation, whereas for Anglo listeners even Spanish words in common use, such as *tortilla* or *burro,* are avoided or else their pronunciation is "Americanized." The Americanization of Spanish words sometimes even spreads to the speaker's pronunciation of his own name. For a foreign speaker of Spanish, from Spain or South America, such behavior would be incomprehensible. For this latter speaker, as Sawyer says, "it would be a matter of pride to pronounce (Spanish words) in the true Spanish way and even to correct English speakers who mispronounced them."

To focus once more on education influences, much of this denial of the Spanish language is fostered and perpetuated in our public schools. In most schools, the "English-only" rule is based on the assumption that Latino children will learn English only if they are made to speak it. Hence, much of the language used and demanded of the Latino child in school is truly foreign and incomprehensible. Consider the problems that bilingual children face in having to learn reading and writing and mathematics — all taught in English — at the same time that many of them have to learn English. The difficulties of such a task often go unrecognized. The result is failure, isolation, or both. When his Spanish is denied him, and his accented English is looked down on, it is small wonder that the Latino child is said to be at a disadvantage in the classroom. From the point of view of many Latino parents and educators, the solution must be two part: good bilingual education in the early grades combined with a move toward recognition and acceptance of a multicultural point of view in the larger society.

The differences in language *form* discussed in this section are not the only language differences among children that concern us. Children also differ in the ways that they employ their language skills in communication situations. Differences in language *use* is the topic of the next section of the chapter.

LANGUAGE USE

Jerry, age three, and his mother are playing with his toys:

MOTHER: The horsie is hungry. Why don't you take the horsie to get something to eat?

JERRY: Horsie eat that airplane.

MOTHER: Do you think horses eat airplanes? I don't think horses eat airplanes.

JERRY: Why?

MOTHER: They don't eat airplanes. They eat grass.

JERRY: Grass?

MOTHER: Uh huh. They eat grass.

JERRY: Are they gonna eat the cars?

MOTHER: They don't eat cars.

JERRY: Why?

MOTHER: Cars are too hard. They drink water.

JERRY: Horsie drink water?

MOTHER: Uh huh.

JERRY: Oh.

This pleasant interchange between a black middle-class mother and her three-year-old son is not unusual in middle-class American homes. The mother is serving as both playmate and teacher for her child, providing him with models of adult utterances, answering his questions, and giving him information about the nature of reality. Most middle-class American mothers of any ethnic background do this routinely, without consciously assuming the role of instructor or model. The attitude conveyed by the mother is one of interest in the child's ideas and respect for his questions. While there are undoubtedly times when such a mother would be impatient with her child's questioning, or even angry, her interaction with him generally reflects her assumption of the role of communication model. While many middle-class parents proceed in this way, using language to instruct, to discipline, and to maintain contact with their children, this is not the only kind of environment in which children learn to talk. As Ward (1971) notes, some parents take a very different approach. Ward studied the language and communication development of a group of lower-socioeconomic-class black children living in rural southern Louisiana. In discussing the involvement of parents in these childrens' language learning, she reports: "A child's requests for information are not treated as a demand for knowledge (which adults are expected to supply) or as an attempt to open the lines of communication. Instead, requests are viewed as a behavioral and not as a linguistic manifestation of the child. A child actively engaged in seeking information will be treated as a noisy child, not as an inquiring, curious one. . . ." Ward quotes from an interview with a mother:

MOTHER: Kenneth want to ask the questions. Once he get started on them, boy, asking questions.

INVESTIGATOR: What other questions does he ask?

MOTHER: Oh boy! What this for? What that for? Most of the time he already know. He say, 'What are these things?' I tell him 'a horse.' 'A horse, what that for?' or 'What it do?' or something like that. Anything you say, he want to know what it for, what it do. And once he get started . . . That boy talks so much! I be whip him all the time, all the time.

The reader should be aware that it is doubtful that this mother, or any other normal mother, actually makes a habit of spanking her child for talking. The mother quoted here is simply expressing an attitude, prevalent in her culture, as well as in the culture of other lower-socioeconomic-status groups, that children should talk only if they are asked to or if they have relevant information. Otherwise, they are expected to be as unobtrusive as possible, preferably somewhere other than under the mother's feet. Mothers in such cultures generally feel no obligation to "teach" their children to talk. As Ward says, "After all, her child will learn to talk—all children within her experience have. She is concerned about his overt behavior, not his speaking ability."

The mother-child interactions described above are examples of different approaches to *language use*. Generally, when we talk about language, we talk about language forms, as we did in the previous section of this chapter. It is important to remember, however, that language forms—nouns and verbs, complex sentences, phonological patterns—do not exist in a vacuum. Language is a tool that we use to communicate, and, just as two people given hammers, nails, and boards may create different varieties of bird houses, so two people with access to essentially the same set of language forms may create different varieties of communication. We need to realize that there is more to language than what can be found between the covers of a grammar book. In short, as Hymes (1972) has said, "there is a structure in the use of language that goes beyond the aspect of structure dealt with in grammar. . . . To recognize that language comes organized in terms of use is to recognize that language has more than a single kind of meaning." In the pages that follow, we will explore some of the "kinds of meaning" that arise from language use, with a view to explaining how these relate to the education of certain groups of children in American society.

Language Use and Culture

It might be useful to begin this exploration with just one example of how language use, meaning, and cultural background are tied together. Most readers of this book would probably agree that when someone asks you a direct question, it is rude not to respond. In fact, we often use questions as a means of beginning conversations, particularly with children. Thus, it would not be at all unusual for an adult to approach a child playing with blocks and say, "What have you got there?" or "What are you doing?" with the full expectation that the child would answer. If the child did not answer even after several questions had been tried, the adult would probably assume that (a) the child couldn't hear, (b) the child couldn't speak English, (c) the child was of exceptionally low intelligence, or (d) the child was deliberately rude. Of course, much would depend on what other kinds of behavior, besides silence, the child exhibited. In fact, the true explanation might be that the child and the adult simply did not share the same assumption about what it means when questions are not responded to. Ward (1971) has observed that "comprehension of the intent and grammatical structure of questions addressed to the child does not mean that he feels any social compulsion to answer."

The tendency of children from different cultural backgrounds to respond differently in question-answer communication situations was found in research by Williams and Naremore (1969). They studied the language use of male and female fifth-grade children, black and white, who were from the lower- and middle-social class in Detroit. The children in the study were asked questions on several topics by an adult interviewer. Williams and Naremore noted that all the children in the study met the communication demands imposed by the interviewer. The major difference was that some children went well beyond what was required. The lower-status children tended to give minimal responses to questions. If a question could be answered with one word, they gave one word answers. Middle-status children, on the other hand, tended to take greater advantage of their opportunities to speak, going on to elaborate their own experiences, or to relate more information about the topic. In discussing this finding, Williams and Naremore say:

> Too frequently, in our opinion, social class differences in children's speech are described and explained solely upon the level of distinctions in form — phonological features, vocabulary size, syntactic repertoire, etc. The assumption is that the child's developmental experiences are confined to a certain range of linguistic forms and these serve as the endowment for his growing repertoire. Although this seems patently true, it again overlooks what might be called a child's *communication* development, which would include not only his capabilities in recognizing and creating linguistic forms, but *knowing when and how to use them in a functional sense.* That a child is restricted to hearing only certain forms of language is, in this current era of the mass media, an absurdity. More realistic is the view that children's linguistic development differs mostly in the demands for communication that are placed upon them. Thus it could be argued that the distinctive language behaviors of the lower class child are more a function of the communicative experiences imposed by his social experiences in general, and by his early family life in particular, than they are of linguistic exposure. His language behaviors will most directly reflect what he has learned of language in a functional sense, and that will typically be what his environment has required of him in the role of an active speaker-listener.*

* From F. Williams and R. Naremore, On the functional analysis of social class differences in modes of speech. *Speech Monographs*, 36, 77–102, 1969.

There are many other communication situations, in addition to that of answering direct questions addressed by adults, in which the effects of cultural background on language use could be shown. The point is this: Children who come from very different environments have been exposed to different kinds of communication situations and to different sets of expectations for what is appropriate communication behavior in those situations. To return to the examples given at the very beginning of this section on language use, it might be expected that the child (Jerry) coming out of the environment like the one created by the middle-class mother would have an open, willing approach to communicating with adults. He would expect to be listened to, to have his questions answered, to be treated as an equal in terms of his right to speak and be heard. A child shaped by an environment like the one described by the lower-class mother might be expected to have a very different set of expectations. He might approach communication with adults cautiously, speaking only when necessary, and then minimally. Even though children from these two environments might have access to the same set of language forms, they will employ these forms differently in meeting the demands of communication situations. In other words, the two groups of children might be said to show differences in language use due to different interpretations of what is appropriate communication behavior in a given situation. Such interpretations are derived from one's communication experience, and this experience is, of course, shaped by the environment (see Figure 5–2).

There is no question that we lack insight into the links between environment and communication behavior; however, the existence of communication differences between different groups of children in the society has been demonstrated. Here are two examples from a study by Williams and Naremore (1969). Two children, the first lower-class and the second middle-class, are telling about television programs they watched.

CHILD 1

INTERVIEWER: Could you tell me about one real interesting time when you saw Jesse James?

CHILD: Uh huh.

INTERVIEWER: Well, what happened?

CHILD: See this, that other time they was on, um they was, um, they was on a night camp and some other man came and they was going to whip Jesse with a whip and didn't. Jesse got loose. His brother Frank came out there and helped him. He got loosed and he went on fightin' and killin' them, them other men.

FIGURE 5–2. *Two children and an adult in a communication and learning situation. Language is not learned in isolation. (Courtesy of the University of Arizona Human Development Preschool.)*

CHILD 2

INTERVIEWER: Can you describe one of those programs to me?

CHILD: Well, um the Dating Game, I mean, there was a girl who sits like on one side of the screen or something and then there's three men sitting in these chairs. And then she'll ask 'em questions, and then after she's all through asking them questions, she'll pick one person to like, um to go out on a date with him, a couple nights in a row or something and, then, um, whatever one she picked would go on a date with her and then the other two men, um, the man would tell 'em what their names are. That was about all.*

The main difference between these two samples is that the first child provides no context for the listener to relate to. It is as though the child were assuming that the listener had seen the program with

*From F. Williams and R. Naremore, On the functional analysis of social class differences in modes of speech. *Speech Monographs*, 36, 77–102, 1969.

him. The second child, on the other hand, provides an overall structure for the listener. The two children seem to have interpreted the demands of the situation differently, and are responding accordingly.

Implications of Differences in Language Use

The previous discussion may, in some ways, seem very far removed from the usual concerns of specialists in communication disorders. In fact, it should not be, because the point made is one that we too often lose sight of: Language is not learned in isolation. Both the context of learning and the context of present use will affect what a child brings to bear in a given situation. The child's interpretation of the situation and what is appropriate within that situation may or may not match that of other participants in the situation. When mismatching occurs, communication may not be the only thing to suffer. Consider the following example.

Labov (1970) quotes in its entirety, an interview between a child and a "large, friendly interviewer." The interviewer's task in the situation is to get the child to talk in order to collect a sample of the child's language. The interviewer and the child sit across from one another at a table and the following dialogue takes place:

INTERVIEWER: Tell me everything you can about this.
(12 seconds of silence)
INTERVIEWER: What would you say it looks like?
(8 seconds of silence)
CHILD: A space ship.
INTERVIEWER: Hmmmm.
(13 seconds of silence)
CHILD: Like a je-et.
(12 seconds of silence)
CHILD: Like a plane.
(20 seconds of silence)
INTERVIEWER: What color is it?
CHILD: Orange (2 seconds) An' whi-ite (2 seconds) An' green.
(6 seconds of silence)
INTERVIEWER: An' what could you use it for?
(8 seconds of silence)
CHILD: A je-et.
(6 seconds of silence)
INTERVIEWER: If you had two of them, what would you do with them?
(6 seconds of silence)
CHILD: Give one to somebody.

INTERVIEWER: Hmmmm. Who do you think would like to have it?
(10 seconds of silence)

CHILD: Clarence.

INTERVIEWER: Mm. Where do you think we could get another one of
these?

CHILD: At the store.

INTERVIEWER: Oh Ka-ay!

This is not an unusual example. Interactions like this are repeated every day in classrooms and testing situations involving children from economically deprived backgrounds. It is on the basis of
this kind of communication behavior that many such children are labeled "nonverbal." The judgment made about the child may extend
even further than this, however. Recently, a young language clinician
set out to teach a four-year-old, lower-status child a sorting task—arranging blocks into piles according to color and size. The clinician approached the child and said,

CLINICIAN: Hello, I'm Tom Smith and I've come to play a game with
you and these blocks. Do you like blocks?

CHILD: No answer.

CLINICIAN: (holding up a red block) What color is this block? Can you
tell me?

CHILD: No answer.

The questioning continued for several minutes, with either silence or a
mumbled "I don't know" from the child. Finally, the clinician turned
away and said,

CLINICIAN: I can't teach this child to sort blocks. He doesn't even know
the names of the colors.

In other words, the assumption is that the child is not only "nonverbal," but because he doesn't give answers to questions, he is assumed
not to know the answers. In fact, neither of these conclusions is warranted. Labov (1970) views interviews such as the two preceding examples as situations in which the child is at risk. Anything he says may
be used against him. In fact, the adult is not threatening the child,
does not intend to punish him for his answers, but the child does not
know this. His interpretation of the situation is one demanding minimal response.

Differences between a child's and an adult's interpretations of
the demands of a situation can have marked consequences for communication. Ward (1971), in discussing the communication of some
black children that she observed, assumes that these children were

never expected to "perform" linguistically. They were not normally asked to talk for the sake of talking—and when their mothers tried to get them to talk into Ward's tape recorder, the children's responses were almost nonexistent. Try to imagine what will happen when a child, who has never encountered this use of language, is put into an interview situation with an adult who expects him to "perform." The child's rules governing behavior when questioned might be something like:

1. Adults do not ask questions to which they already know the answers.
2. If they do, it is some kind of trick, and the obvious answer must not be right.
3. If you can't figure out the right answer, keep quiet.

The adult, on the other hand believes that:

1. Children must answer whatever questions you ask.
2. If you want quick answers, ask easy questions.
3. A child who does not answer easy questions is of low intelligence or rude or both.

Looking back at the two preceding interviews, the child's perspective seems well founded. In both instances, the interviewer picks up an object, visible to him and to the child, and asks an obvious question about it: "What color is this?" Any reasonably intelligent child will know that the adult knows the answer to this. So why is he asking? When viewed from this perspective, the child's silence and minimal replies become comprehensible. In such situations, prudence demands that one say as little as possible. The unfortunate fact is, however, that interview situations such as these are used over and over to assess children's verbal capacity. The child's failure to respond is erroneously viewed as a function of inadequate environmental stimulation, inadequate language skill, or cognitive deficiency. It is seldom viewed as a function of what it is: a different interpretation of the demands of the communication situation.

This is not meant to imply, of course, that there are no economically deprived children who have language disorders or problems with cognitive development. There may, in fact, be four-year-old black or white children who do not know the names for colors. The point here is that a tester who is sensitive to differences in language use will not depend on a one-to-one, adult-child, question-and-answer session to find out about these problems. Creativity, imagination, and sensitivity must augment understanding in differentiating real deficiencies (which demand treatment) from differences (which demand respect). This viewpoint will be developed in the final section of the chapter.

ON CHANGING LANGUAGE DIFFERENCES

In 1940, Fries summarized the American educational system's approach to language differences among children as follows:

> The schools . . . have assumed the responsibility of training every boy and girl, no matter what his original social background and native speech, to use this 'standard' English, this particular social or class dialect. . . . Many believe that the schools have thus assumed an impossible task. Certainly the widespread and almost unanimous condemnation of the results of their efforts convinces us that either the schools have not conceived their task adequately or they have chosen the wrong materials and methods to accomplish it.

Although this statement was made approximately four decades ago, it is no less true today. Social-class, ethnic, and regional dialects still exist. There are still many speakers of English whose language does not nearly approximate standard English, even in the most formal speaking situations. To paraphrase Fries: Is the goal of teaching standard English to every child futile? Or have we simply not hit on the proper method?

Teaching Children to Talk "Right"

Before we approach the questions raised above it might be useful to review three concepts presented earlier in this chapter. First, standard English is a form of language that almost no one speaks all the time. Some people have learned to speak it easily in very formal situations. Few people speak it naturally in all situations and those who do are rare individuals. What is written on the pages of most grammar books is an artificial standard that applies more to written than to spoken English for most of us. Second, the regular forms of English used by black-English-vernacular speakers and by children from Spanish-speaking backgrounds should not be regarded as careless mistakes. These dialects are just as much rule-governed systems of language as standard English. Changing dialects is not the same as correcting mistakes. And finally, language forms are closely tied to language use. The language employed by a lower-class child in a given situation may be very different from that employed by a middle-class child, regardless of the race of either child. This is not a matter of dialect differences. It is rather a matter of different language use resulting from differences in how two groups of children interpret the communication demands of the situation. Differences in language use cannot be ignored in any attempt to change children's speaking patterns.

To return to the question: Should children be taught to speak standard English? This question has generated passionate arguments. There are those who say that as long as standard English is the socially valued form of the language, any child who is to participate fully in the society must be able to speak it. "Standard English" is used by these people to mean that form of English associated with the educated, middle-class. Opponents counter with the argument that socioeconomic mobility depends on much more than speaking patterns, and that if every black or Latino child in America suddenly spoke English like Walter Cronkite, these children would still face discrimination. This is an argument that is not likely to be solved by either research evidence or pedagogical theory—it is essentially a sociopolitical argument. In the long run, the question of whether children *should* be taught to speak standard English may be outweighed by the larger question of whether children *want* to be and *can* be taught to speak standard English.

It cannot be emphasized too strongly that children learn to speak the language of their environment—in short, children will sound like those around them sound. Unless a child *wants* to sound some other way, there is very little that can be done to change this situation. We don't usually think about how we sound when we speak, or what sentence forms we want to use. If a speaker is to change his or her *language forms,* these patterns must first become objects of awareness—and it is no easy task to think about what you're saying and *how* you're saying it at the same time. This is particularly true for children. As for changing patterns of *language use,* this may be even more difficult because of the intertwined set of cultural expectations, communication situations, and social roles that give rise to patterns of language use. It may be true, as evidenced by years of unsuccessful classroom correction and drill, that if you want to change the way a child speaks, you must either remove him from the environment which taught him to speak that way or else cause him to want to remove himself from that environment. In the current jargon, you must "motivate him to be upwardly mobile." Children do not aspire to change their social status in response to constant correction of their language by teachers, or because they must participate in pattern practice drills for an hour a day in the classroom.

This does not mean that there is nothing that can or should be done about language differences. First, it is clear that the great majority of children from economically disadvantaged black and Latino backgrounds do not succeed in school. This fact cannot be attributed to their language behavior alone, but language is undoubtedly a part of the complex. It is possible that the form of language spoken by some groups of children may interfere with their reading ability, as was pointed out earlier in this chapter. The answer to this, however, is not to change the child's spoken language, but rather to change the methods and goals of reading instruction. This will demand not only a re-examination of reading pedagogy, but also a clearer understanding of the nature of the linguistic interference that exists. It is also possible that children who have access only or primarily to a context-bound language use will have great difficulty meeting the demands for context-free language use in writing. The teaching of writing skills must take this into account by recognizing that the need to teach clear penmanship, standardized spelling, and explicable paragraphing may be overshadowed by the need to teach the child how to analyze the communication demands of a situation and bring language to bear in meeting these demands. The schools owe these children the entrance to the larger society that reading and writing skills provide.

Beyond the implications for meeting the educational needs of all groups of children in the schools, the existence of language differences in society imposes a further task on the educational system. If variety is not to be abolished, it must be appreciated. We should stop pretending that there is only one way to talk, and learn to value the many options available. James Sledd (1969) put it this way: "Bidialectalism would never have been invented if our society were not divided into the dominant white majority and the exploited minorities. Children should be taught the relations between group differences and speech differences, and the good and bad uses of speech differences by groups and by individuals. The teaching would require a more serious study of grammar, lexicography, dialectology, and linguistic history than our educational system now provides . . .".

Language Differences and the Speech, Language, and Hearing Clinician

It is perfectly reasonable to feel frustrated at this point by the lack of clear-cut, definite answers to the overwhelming questions posed by language differences among children. The fact is, however, that we lack the data on which to base clear-cut answers. This is evident in the questions and issues that clinicians must face when appraising the speech and language of a child who speaks a dialect other than standard English.

1. *How can I tell whether the child has a dialect or a speech and language problem?*

The answer to this question depends primarily on the clinician's understanding of the nature of the dialect. A clinician who does not understand the regularity of the *f* for *th* substitution in the speech of black-English-vernacular speakers may assume that a child who says *mouf* for *mouth* and *toofbrush* for *toothbrush* has an articulation disorder and needs speech management. A clinician who does not understand the regularity of the rules used for forming negatives and questions by children from Spanish-speaking backgrounds may assume that a child who says *No talk! How they make this rule?* is language delayed and needs management. In short, the clinician must have a clear idea of what is to be regarded as "correct" language use for a given child. Any decision made about language training must be based on a clear understanding of the "problem"—a dialect is very different from a disorder.

2. *How can I assess the child's language ability?*

Many clinicians feel that this is the greatest difficulty they encounter. As discussed earlier, an informal question-and-answer session may serve only to silence the child, making it difficult to gather enough spontaneous speech to analyze. In the face of this, many clinicians quite understandably fall back on the use of formal tests, which present another set of problems. First, some tests are culturally biased because they present pictures and/or vocabulary familiar to the middle-class child but outside the range of a lower-class child's experience. It is important to understand that a test is not automatically biased just because lower-status children make lower scores on it than middle-status children. Much depends on what the test is supposed to measure. If a test of some ability distinguishes between two groups in a way that the actual ability does not, then something is wrong with the test. For example, suppose that we administer a test of walking ability to middle- and lower-class four-year-olds, perhaps a measure of the time it takes to walk certain distances. If lower-class children score significantly lower than middle-class children, we should suspect the test. Nothing in reality would support such test results. Lower-class children should have the same proportion of "very good," "average," and "poor" walkers as middle-class children. We expect language ability to be distributed among the population in the same way, with a few being very good, most being average, and a few being very poor. If our tests show that lower-class or minority-group children are clustered at the "very poor" end of the scale, then we need to ask whether the test is really measuring "language ability," or whether it is measuring something else — for example, "knowledge of middle-class vocabulary."

Another difficulty in administering tests involves the influences of extraneous variables on a child's performance. When we give a child a test, we assume that we are getting his best performance. If we are not, then we should disregard his score. We would never knowingly test a child who was sedated so that he could hardly stay awake, or a child who was ill. And yet some people repeatedly test lower-status, minority-group children without taking into account the evidence that their performance may be strongly affected by aspects of the testing situation. These children may be afraid to interact with strangers; they may not be motivated to perform well; they may not understand test instructions; they may be unfamiliar with test format; or they may be overly anxious. Such factors are important to consider when testing any child, but they are particularly important when testing a lower-status, minority-group child. Care should be taken in any testing situation to overcome fear and anxiety, to be absolutely sure that the child understands what he is to do and why, and to give the child plenty of time to accustom himself to the tester and the test.

Finally, there is the problem of test standardization. If the norms used in a given test were obtained on a population that included only white, middle-class children, then the test cannot be used to measure the ability of a lower-class or minority-group child. For example, suppose we administered an intelligence test to a group of lower-status Latino children; the norm group for the test was 2,000 middle-class white children in one Michigan community. Based on the norm group's performance, the testmakers determined that a test score of, say, 75 was equivalent to an IQ of 80. If all of the Latino children tested scored less than 75 on the test, do they all then have IQs of less than 80? Certainly, this would be an unwarranted conclusion. The Latino children's performance on this test may have been affected by any of the variables discussed in the paragraph above, as well as by the interference of Spanish with their English language use. Their performance on the test may thus be a reflection not of their intelligence, but of their response to the testing situation. Because the norm group did not include lower-status or Latino children, the distribution of scores used in standardizing the test did not reflect similar factors.

These are difficult issues to resolve. In fact, it is sometimes necessary to use tests in assessing children's language behavior. Yet even the best available tests may not have norms that are appropriate for a child who speaks a dialect. Faced with this situation, a clinician may have to make subjective decisions about what is a "right" answer for each test item. For example, the score sheet for an imitation task may say that a child must repeat the stimulus exactly in order to receive credit. What can the clinician do if the child repeats items exactly— but in his own dialect? Surely if a child can translate a sentence from standard English into his dialect, it indicates that he understands the standard-English sentence. According to the score sheet, though, his answer must be given no credit—it's "wrong." In this situation, as in countless other testing situations, the clinician must have a clear sense of purpose. What is the clinician trying to find out about the child? Why is this information important? Given this sense of purpose, the only hope is that common sense will prevail until the appropriate tests and test norms are developed.

3. *Should I accept a child for management in order to change features of his dialect?*
Here is the point at which the most difficult clinical decision must be made. Much depends on the specifics of the situation: the age of the child, the motivation of the child and his parents, the nature of the child's language community. For example, is this a twelve-year-old child who has recently moved out of a black-English vernacular-speaking community into a standard-English-speaking community, and who feels sensitive and "different" because of his language? Or is it a six-year-old child from a tightly knit Spanish-speaking family whose parents feel a strong urge to maintain the child's Spanish culture and language along with English, but whose first grade teacher says "I can't understand what he says?" Every situation will have to be judged on its own. There is no rule that can be followed, except possibly this one: *The child who speaks a dialect is a normal speaker in his own community, and changing his language is changing his community and his sense of himself in that community. It should not be undertaken lightly.* Let us conclude with a review of considerations that may cause some to question whether, in fact, it should be undertaken at all.

There are those who maintain that there is nothing in the language use of the black-English-vernacular speaker or of the Spanish-influenced English-speaker that interferes with the communication of meaning. In most instances, the context in which language is used will provide enough cues to prevent misinterpretation, even when a speaker's words are not clearly understood. However, as we have previously discussed in this chapter, what of the educational consequences of a language difference? When a child's language is such that it interferes with his ability to acquire basic reading, writing, and arithmetic skills in the classroom, then something needs to be done. One solution, of course, is to teach "content" in the language the child speaks most readily. For the Latino child whose dominant language is Spanish, this means using Spanish readers and hiring Spanish-speaking teachers. For the child who uses black-English vernacular, it means using readers written in the dialect, and hiring teachers who speak it. On the face of it, this solution sounds obvious.

Nothing is that simple, however. For example, Latino children in this country are not all alike. First of all, they do not all possess the same knowledge of Spanish. Assuming a continuum of language dominance that ranges from monolingual Spanish to monolingual English, where do we draw the line that determines whether a child is put into a Spanish-speaking or an English-speaking classroom? Assessment materials to determine language capabilities are badly needed. Second, not all dominant-Spanish-speakers speak the same kind of Spanish. Children from Cuban, Puerto Rican, and Mexican backgrounds cannot be lumped together and given the same Spanish language readers, anymore than children from rural west Texas, Toronto, Canada, and Nottingham, England could be given the same English language readers. We allow great regional and social class variation among native English-speaking children, and we should be willing to allow equal variation among children learning English as a second language.

The child speaking black-English vernacular faces some problems that are similar to those of the Latino child—and some that are quite different. There is a possibility that his dialect may interfere with learning, especially in reading and spelling. There are different degrees of dialect usage, and there may be regional, class, and age variations among dialect speakers. Few responsible people are proposing, however, that these children need to be taught English as a second language. They are, after all, English speakers—just as children from southern Appalachia who speak a regional dialect are English speakers. In the late 1960s there were a few attempts to write readers in black-English vernacular. These met with poor acceptance from the children's parents, some of whom said, "We didn't send our children to school to learn to read 'ain't'." Even where parents favored the idea, though, the readers were not as useful as many had hoped they would be. As we saw in Tables 5–1 and 5–2, many of the black-English vernacular versus standard-English differences involve *sounds,* and sounds are difficult to convey on the printed page without either using a phonetic alphabet or grossly changing the spelling of English words. The latter would probably cause more problems than it solved.

Society changes slowly, and although we may work toward a more open and tolerant society, we cannot expect it to occur tomorrow. More aware and concerned teachers and more reasonable and flexible classroom practices will do much to alleviate the difficulties faced by children who speak black-English vernacular or Spanish-influenced English. But the problems of social acceptability for these children remain. Until changes in acceptability occur, communication disorders specialists have a responsibility to work with dialect speakers who wish to change their language patterns. In the case of young children, we must depend on the parents' wishes regarding these changes. If the decision is made to accept a dialect speaker for speech or language training, such training should never attempt to eradicate the dialect of the black child or the Spanish of the Latino child. Rather, it should present the child with useful alternatives for certain situations. The focus of training should be the situational use of language rather than formal pattern practice drills. This will demand knowledgeable and careful professionals. That is, after all, what the child has every right to expect.

REFERENCES   AINSFELD, M., BOGO, N., and LAMBERT, W., Evaluational reactions to accented English speech. *Journal of Abnormal and Social Psychology,* 65, 223–231 (1962).

BARATZ, S., and BARATZ, J., Early childhood intervention: The social science base of institutional racism. *Harvard Educational Review,* 40, 29–50 (1970).

DAVIS A., English problems of Spanish speakers. Urbana, Ill.: National Council of Teachers of English.

FASOLD, R., and WOLFRAM, W., Some linguistic features of Negro dialect. In R. Fasold and R. Shuy (Eds.), *Teaching Standard English in the Inner City.* Washington, D.C.: Center for Applied Linguistics (1970).

FRIES, C., *American English Grammar (NCTE Monograph No. 10).* New York: Appleton-Century-Crofts (1940).

GUSKIN, J., The social perception of language variations: Black dialect and expectations of ability. Paper presented to the annual meeting of the American Educational Research Association, Minneapolis (March, 1970).

HYMES, D., Introduction. In C. Cazden, V. John, and D. Hymes (Eds.), *Functions of Language in the Classroom.* New York: Teachers College Press (1972).

JETER, I., Social dialects: Differences versus disorders. Rockville, Md.: *American Speech and Hearing Association* (1977).

LABOV, W., *Language in the Inner City.* Philadelphia: University of Pennsylvania Press (1972).

LABOV, W., Some sources of reading problems for Negro speakers of nonstandard English. In A. Frazier (Ed.), *New Directions in Elementary English.* Champaign, Ill.: National Council of Teachers of English (1967).

LABOV, W., The logic of nonstandard English. In F. Williams (Ed.), *Language and Poverty.* Chicago: Markham (1970).

LAMBERT, W., HODGSON, R., GARDNER, R., and FILLENBAUM, S., Evaluation reactions to spoken language. *Journal of Abnormal and Social Psychology,* 60, 44–51 (1960).

LIGHT, R., Some observations concerning black children's conversations. In R. Jacobson (Ed.), *The English Record,* Special Anthology Issue and Monograph 14, 21, 155–167 (1971).

LOMAN, B., *Conversations in a Negro American Dialect.* Washington, D.C.: Center for Applied Linguistics (1967).

NAREMORE, R., Teachers' judgments of children's speech: A factor analytic study of attitudes. *Speech Monographs, 38,* 17–27 (1971).

ORTEGO, P., Montezuma's children. In R. Octavio (Ed.), *Voices.* Berkeley, Calif.: Quinto Sol Publications (1971).

SAWYER, J., Social aspects of bilingualism in San Antonio, Texas. In R. Bailey and J. Robinson (Eds.), *Varieties of Present-Day English.* New York: Macmillan (1973).

SCOTT, F., The standard of American speech. *The English Journal, 6,* 1–15 (1971).

SLEDD, J., Bi-dialectalism: The linguistics of white supremacy. *The English Journal, 58,* 1307–1315 (1969).

WARD, M., *Them Children.* New York: Holt, Rinehart and Winston (1971).

WILLIAMS, F., Language, attitude, and social change. In F. Williams (Ed.), *Language and Poverty.* Chicago: Markham (1970).

WILLIAMS, F., and NAREMORE, R., On the functional analysis of social class differences in modes of speech. *Speech Monographs, 36,* 77–102 (1969).

WILLIAMS, F., CAIRNS, H., and CAIRNS, C., *An Analysis of the Variations from Standard English Pronunciation in the Phonetic Performance of Two Groups of Nonstandard-English-Speaking Children.* Center for Communication Research, University of Texas (1971).

WILLIAMS, F., HEWITT, N., MILLER, L., NAREMORE, R., and WHITEHEAD, J., *Explorations of the Linguistic Attitudes of Teachers.* Rowley, Mass.: Newbury House Publishers (1976).

signpost   Chapter 6 is concerned with adult language disorders resulting from brain damage. Such disorders come under the label of *dysphasia*. None would doubt that dysphasia is one of the most somber areas in all of communication disorders. Once articulate, intelligent, energetic persons can be rendered grossly impaired in language, thought, and action as consequences of brain damage. Chapter 6 considers the variety of causes of brain dysfunction and how certain symptoms of language disorders are related to the location of damage within the brain. Consideration is given to how language impairment can be distributed along four dimensions: speaking, listening-comprehending, reading, and writing. Included is a discussion of how language-support systems, such as auditory, visual, somatosensory (body sensation), and psychological, may be disturbed by brain damage and also importantly influence communication behaviors. Methods for the assessment of language disorders in adults are given prominent attention, as are methods for their treatment. The latter discussion deals with the often controversial issue of whether or not the speech-language pathologist should work with the patient during the spontaneous recovery period that follows brain damage. The stance taken is that he should. Language disorders in brain-damaged adults are difficult to remediate. The severity of language disability after brain damage and the realistic setting of goals are among the most important variables in the recovery process. Increasing numbers of people are reaching ages where brain-damaging diseases are most prevalent. Thus, this area of communication disorders is ever expanding.

6

Stanley J. Ewanowski

dysphasia
in adults

INTRODUCTION

Communication is a seemingly effortless task for most of us. We go about it in a fashion that appears almost automatic, and rarely, if ever, pause to consider all that is involved. We are able to understand what speakers of our language are saying almost as fast as they say it, and we can read and comprehend printed and written materials with ease. We are similarly facile in deciphering and understanding the variety of body gestures that are in the communication repertoires of users of our language. These skills of comprehending various forms of messages sent by others are paralleled by skills we have for devising and sending messages. The most important and frequently used of these is our ability to pass on information through the use of spoken language. To lesser extents we exercise expression through writing or drawing, as either separate devices or as supplements to what we are attempting to convey through speech. And, finally, most of us use gestures in sending messages to others face-to-face. On occasion we use them as the sole means of communication while at other times we use them to enhance our spoken or written expressions.

The facility we demonstrate with various language behaviors as adults can be lost or impaired to various degrees and in various ways. Some persons will demonstrate a deterioration in language function in association with generalized intellectual impairment and the deterioration of various mental functions with aging (Wertz, 1977). Others may at some time show deviant language function in association with accompanying neurological conditions that lead to confused, irrelevant behaviors (Darley, 1969). Still others, who at some time in their adult life may be labeled schizophrenic, may display language behaviors that are deviant with regard to relevance of responses and that do not fulfill informational communication purposes (DiSimoni, Darley, and Aronson, 1977). And, finally, there are the adults who will suffer brain damage as a result of some disease process or trauma and will manifest impairment in the capacity for interpreting and formulating language symbols to a degree that is disproportionate to impairment in other intellectual functions (Darley, 1969). A disorder of language as manifested by brain-damaged patients is designated as *dysphasia*. Disorders of this latter nature are the topic of the present chapter. We choose to focus on dysphasia in considering language disorders in adults because far more is known about dysphasia than other disorders of language that adults demonstrate. Furthermore, the evaluation and management of dysphasia are more a prime concern of the speech-language pathologist than are the evaluation and management of other adult language problems.

In our effort to understand the perplexing disorder of dysphasia, we begin with a definition. From there we turn to a brief consideration of the neurological bases for communication functioning in normal and damaged brains. Attention is then devoted to various language, speech, and related disturbances that characterize the behavior of the adult whose brain is impaired. The chapter concludes with two sections having to do with the handling of patients with dysphasia; one discusses the procedures used in assessing language capability and the other is concerned with how one goes about treating the deviant communication behavior of the adult with a language disorder related to brain damage.

DYSPHASIA DEFINED

Dysphasia or aphasia[1] is defined as impairment, as a result of brain damage, of the capacity for interpretation and formulation of language symbols; multimodality loss or reduction in efficiency of the ability to decode and encode conventional meaningful linguistic elements (morphemes and larger syntactic units); disproportionate to impairment of other intellectual functions; not attributable to dementia, sensory loss, or motor dysfunction; manifested in reduced availability of vocabulary, reduced efficiency in application of syntactic rules, reduced auditory retention span, and impaired efficiency in input and output channel selection. (Darley, 1969)

[1] The terms dysphasia and aphasia are used interchangeably by many. Traditionally, the prefix *a* is used to indicate a complete loss of functioning, while the prefix *dys* is used to imply less than total loss of functioning. Throughout this chapter we will use the word dysphasia as a generic term to describe all such conditions of loss regardless of the degree.

Key elements in this definition are that *brain damage is known to be the cause of the impaired function* and that the *central feature within the patient's behavior is difficulty in use of the language code* (Wepman, 1976). In one sense, dysphasia can be conceptualized as a negative shift of performance on a language-task continuum (Porch, 1972). This shift can be catastrophic to the individual's social relationships, occupational capabilities, economic security, and ability to interact with other users of his language code in general. Dysphasia is, perhaps, the most somber disorder in all of the field of communication disorders.

The stark reality of a sudden loss of language skills is difficult to appreciate. Consider your dismay if suddenly you were unable to understand what you were reading on this page, or were unable to comprehend what someone had just said to you, or were incapable of deciphering the meaning of a simple gesture made to you. Also consider what it might be like to try to explain your dismay to someone else and all you could say was a single word over and over. Or, think of the frustration you might experience, if in trying to write about your sudden inability to understand or speak, you were only able to scribble down a jumble of nonsense constructions. Finally, think of the anxiety you might experience if, in trying to describe your dilemma through gestures, your actions amounted to meaningless motions of your hands through the air. These examples are but a glimpse of the types of experiences that adults who sustain certain brain damages are faced with as they attempt to do things with language that before seemed to come naturally.

To gain further appreciation of the problem of dysphasia, we close this section with a transcript of an exchange between a clinician and a middle-aged man whose brain was damaged in an automobile accident. As you read the transcript, bear in mind that before the accident the patient was a normal language user with abilities similar to those of the speech-language pathologist testing him. Now he has difficulty comprehending and producing language.

CLINICIAN: What's your name?
PATIENT: Name? Dorg ... Gor ... Jar ... Geor ... George ... George!
CLINICIAN: Can you tell me where you live?
PATIENT: I ... I can tell ... my harm is ... well, oh, it's ... yes.
CLINICIAN: Now I'd like you to count to ten for me.
PATIENT: One, two, three, three, three, three.
CLINICIAN: Tell me about this picture (a man washing his car).
PATIENT: Car ... dirt ... man ... hose ... wash clean.
CLINICIAN: Please write what you just told me about the picture.

PATIENT: (writes)

Cor car ggg diter dik dut

CLINICIAN: Now read what I have written about the picture. (The man is washing his new car.)

PATIENT: (reads) A . . . the . . . man . . . washer . . . her . . . no, no! . . . his now . . . care . . . car.

NEUROLOGICAL BASES FOR COMMUNICATION FUNCTIONING

In this section it is important that we examine how the normal brain processes language and how it is that this processing is affected through disease or injury. We also need to consider the interface between neurology and linguistics, a topic we will discuss in the context of a neurolinguistic model for communication behavior.

Brain Mechanisms Subserving Communication

Figure 6–1 shows several drawings of the human brain. The brain consists of two somewhat similar halves: a *right cerebral hemisphere* and a *left cerebral hemisphere*. There are a number of conventions for designating portions of the brain's two hemispheres. Each hemisphere is comprised of *five lobes: frontal, temporal, parietal, occipital,* and *limbic.* The first four of these are easily visible on the exterior surface of the brain and are labeled accordingly in Figure 6–1a. The fifth, or limbic, lobe is within the brain and cannot be visualized exteriorly. Structures that make up the surface of the hemispheres of the brain are referred to as *cerebral cortex.* Those structures that lie deep within the hemispheres are called *subcortical structures* (see Figure 6–1b).

Those who study the basic functioning of the brain (neuroanatomists and neurophysiologists) are in substantial agreement that all structures within the brain are interconnected and in "communication" (Luria, 1966, 1973). Selected interconnections are portrayed schematically in Figure 6–2. It is apparent from Figure 6–2 that they are extensive and elaborate, a fact that some take as the primary reason that man alone is able to carry out certain forms of communication behavior. This sophisticated neural circuitry for use in communication behavior is often referred to as an innate neurological "prewiring" with which man is endowed at birth and which eventually allows him to execute functions of the complex language code of his species.

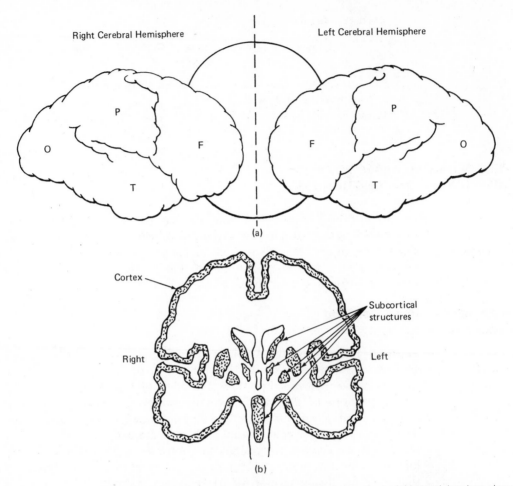

FIGURE 6–1. *Surface and subsurface views of the human brain. (a) Lateral drawings showing major lobes: F=Frontal, T=Temporal, P=Parietal, and O=Occipital. (b) Frontal cut showing the relationship of the cortex to subcortical structures. For explanation see text.*

On gross inspection the right and left cerebral hemispheres appear to be structurally identical. More detailed study shows, however, that the left hemisphere is somewhat larger than the right hemisphere in most adult brains, that it has a greater surface area due to more folding of the cortex (outer surface), and that it has a slightly different blood supply than the right hemisphere (Montcastle, 1961). Some of the most striking structural differences are found in the area subserving auditory function (Geschwind, 1965, 1970).

A substantial body of research has demonstrated that the two cerebral hemispheres also differ importantly in terms of their func-

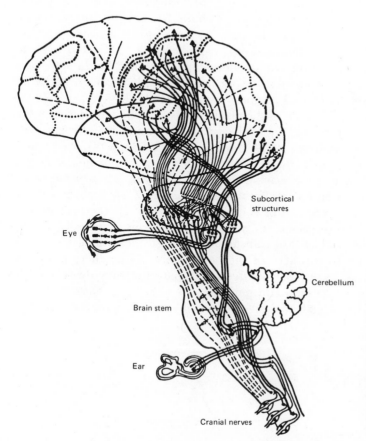

Left Cerebral Hemisphere

Subcortical
structures

Eye

Cerebellum

Brain stem

Ear

Cranial nerves

FIGURE 6–2. *Some major neural interconnections between peripheral, subcortical, and cortical structures of the central nervous system. Note that the spatial relationships among certain of the structures are distorted to make possible more detailed representations of certain pathways. (Modified and reproduced, by permission, from A. Luria,* Higher Cortical Functions in Man. *New York: Basic Books, 1966.)*

tions (Semmes, 1971; Kinsbourne and Smith, 1974). One of the more obvious differences and one of importance to this chapter is the different involvements of the two hemispheres in language behavior. *In most adults the left cerebral hemisphere controls language behavior.* About 90 percent of the general adult population is left-brain dominant (Branch, Milner, and Rasmussen, 1964; Milner, 1971; Krashen, 1972). This same segment of the population is also right-handed for most activities (Davis and Wada, 1978). The remaining 10 percent of the adult population is either right-brain dominant or has mixed-dominance (different hemispheres serve predominantly for different activities) (Moskovitch, 1976). Given these statements about dominance, one might ask whether or not the nondominant hemisphere participates at all in communication functioning. The answer is yes. It is clear that there is some division of labor for communication functioning between the dominant and nondominant hemispheres. The processing and storage of the individual sounds of a language seem clearly to be primarily functions of the left hemisphere. By contrast, the processing of aspects like speech melody patterns seems to be a function of the right hemisphere (Kimura, 1967; Shankweiler, 1971). Further, the formulation and production of speech are controlled by the left hemisphere while the production of nonspeech sounds is controlled by the right hemisphere (McAdam and Whitaker, 1971).

Within the dominant hemisphere (usually the left) different language-related functions are believed to be located in different areas (Penfield and Roberts, 1959; Luria, 1966, 1973, 1974). As is illustrated in Figure 6–3, the *posterior* or back area of the hemisphere is devoted to those tasks having to do mainly with the *recognition* and *comprehension* of language. Because this portion of the hemisphere also deals with the reception of sensory stimuli through the auditory, visual, and somatosensory (body sensation) systems, it is believed that language data, which are transmitted through these same modalities, are processed in this area of the hemisphere. Researchers have concluded that this same part of the hemisphere probably deals with the *storage* of language data and perhaps also with the *formulation* of messages the individual wishes to transmit symbolically (Luria, 1966,

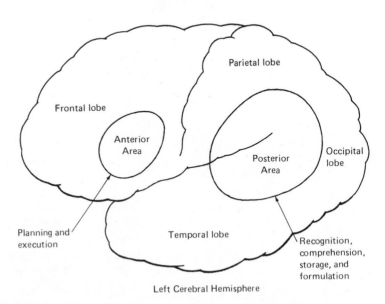

FIGURE 6–3. *Anterior and posterior speech and language areas in the left cerebral hemisphere. The basic function ascribed to each area is indicated. Areas circumscribed are intended only as very gross indications and embody location evidences from electrical stimulation and cortical excision literature as interpreted by the author.*

1973). In contrast to the posterior area, the *anterior* or front area of the hemisphere has to do with the *planning* and *execution* of overt acts such as those that result in speaking, writing, or gesturing (Pribram, 1971). Of course, the posterior and anterior areas of the hemisphere do not operate separately during language functioning.

For normal language production to take place, the posterior and anterior areas of the dominant hemisphere must be in communication. Further, because both cerebral hemispheres participate in communication behavior, it is crucial that there be normal neural interconnections between the dominant and nondominant hemispheres (Kimura, 1973). In addition to the known importance of these various interconnections to normal function, there exist important interconnections between various cortical areas of the hemispheres by way of nerve fibers lying below the surface of the brain (Brown, 1975). Finally, it has been shown that brain areas are also interconnected by nerve fibers that go from the cerebral cortex to subcortical regions and then out to other cortical regions (Brown, 1975). Currently, it is unclear as to which of these latter two modes (that is, cortical area to cortical area or cortical area to subcortical area to cortical area) of interconnections is more crucial to brain functioning for language purposes. There remains much to be learned about brain function and language behavior, including where and how the control and integration of our overall communication behavior takes place (Penfield and Roberts, 1959; Pribram, 1971).

A Neurolinguistic Model for Language Behavior

Although we have much to learn, we already know a great deal about the interface between brain function and language function that it controls. In this section, we consider a simple model that may aid the reader in understanding more about how brain function and language skills relate. We should bear in mind that the ability to communicate through language reflects both the extent to which the nervous system has evolved over the ages and the extent to which it is developed in each language user. Once thought to be a capability unique to man, research has shown that other animals are able to communicate with rudimentary symbol systems. Chimpanzees, for example, can learn to comprehend and produce simple sentences, ask simple questions, and solve simple verbal problems through the use of abstract symbols (Premack, 1971; Rumbaugh et al., 1974).

Whatever model of human language behavior one chooses, it should meet certain criteria. First, it should take into account how the central nervous system is known to function. Second, it should be capable of dealing adequately with the major ways in which language is processed—that is, received, decoded, integrated-stored, encoded, and transmitted. Third, it should be able to account for linguistic theory as it is used to partition language behavior along various aspects such as phonology, syntax, and semantics (Osgood and Miron, 1963; Green, 1970).

Here, we will consider the model proposed by Whitaker (1971). It is a comprehensive model that suits our current purposes and is fairly representative of prominent contemporary thinking on language matters. Briefly, Whitaker's model presents a way of looking at how our knowledge of brain function can be related to our knowledge of linguistic constructs. The model is illustrated in Figure 6–4. Globally, it proposes two basic divisions: a peripheral language system and a central language system. The peripheral system consists of auditory and visual input mechanisms and vocal and graphic output mechanisms. The input mechanisms are responsible for transmission of raw linguistic data from the periphery through the nervous system to the brain, while the output mechanisms have the task of transmission of spoken or written forms of information from the brain through the nervous system to the external world. Hearing and speaking are generally looked upon as the primary means of communication, with reading and writing being secondary in importance. Whitaker accommodates this viewpoint by subdividing the peripheral language system into primary and secondary levels of production and recognition.

Whitaker considers the central language system as composed of those brain structures which act upon the linguistic data that have been received or are being formulated. The linguistic components of this central system include the following: phonological—which deals with the rules relating to the sound system of the language; lexical—which deals with the specific words of the language; syntactical—which deals with the rules used to generate sentences and to transform basic sentences into other forms; and semantic—which deals with the rules that relate to meanings of language units. Related to the central language system's functions are such brain-related behaviors as attention, memory, cognition, problem solving, abstract attitude, etc.

Relating different components of Whitaker's central language system model to specific parts of the brain is speculative but appears to have merit. The author's interpretation of the relationships proposed by Whitaker is illustrated in Figure 6–5. The posterior area of the left cerebral hemisphere is linked to the semantic-syntactic component of language function. Placement of the phonological component of language in relation to specific brain geography is less clear-cut, according to Whitaker. He believes that a segment of this com-

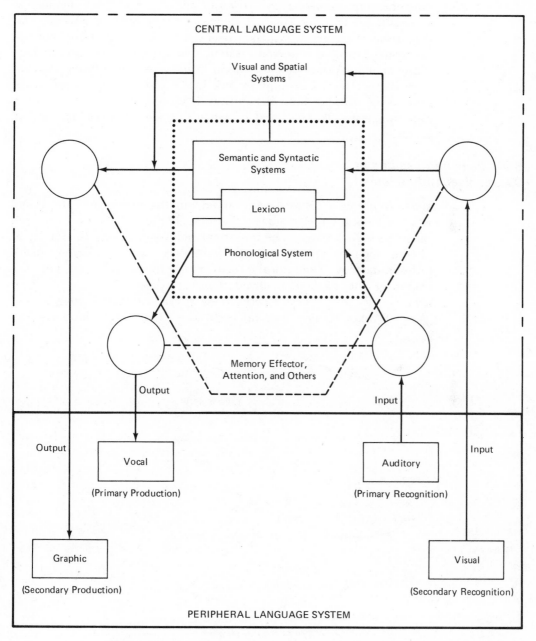

FIGURE 6–4. *A schematized neurolinguistic model of language behavior based on the ideas of Whitaker (1971). Major subdivisions incorporate a central language system and a peripheral language system. For a complete explanation, see text. (After H. Whitaker, On the Representation of Language in the Human Brain. Edmonton, Alberta, Canada: Linguistic Research, 1971.)*

ponent is represented in the posterior area but that the remainder is served by the anterior area together with nerve fibers connecting the two areas. The lexicon, Whitaker believes, is mediated jointly by all of the structures of the nervous system that comprise the central language system. Although some might argue that it is difficult, or perhaps dangerous, to attempt to link brain geography and language skills in the manner done in Figure 6–5, we believe that there exists a clear suggestion from clinical evidence that such linkage has certain validities.

Brain Damage Resulting in Communication Problems

When defining dysphasia, we pointed out that damage to the brain was the basis for the language disorder. There are a wide variety of causes of such damage. The important point is that very similar types of language impairment can be brought about by very different forms of brain damage. The critical information pertains to the location and extent of the damage involved. *Cerebrovascular accidents (CVAs) or strokes are by far the most common cause of brain damage relating to dysphasia.* Strokes result from: (a) occlusions of cerebral blood vessels;

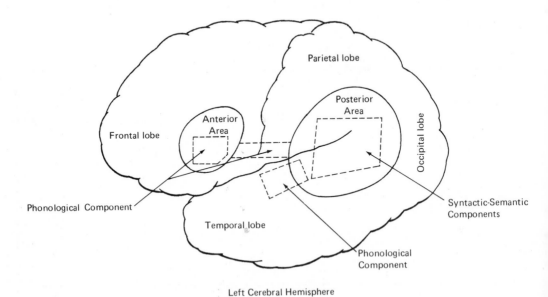

FIGURE 6–5. *Representation of language components in the left cerebral hemisphere of the human brain. The basic components ascribed to each area are indicated. Areas circumscribed are based on the author's interpretations of the notions expressed in the work of Whitaker (1971).*

(b) blockages of arteries through fatty deposits; (c) traveling blood clots; or (d) rupturing of blood vessels due to weaknesses in their walls. Of central importance in all of these stroke-causing agents is the fact that they deprive the cells of the brain of needed oxygen and, as a result, leave them irreparably damaged. Equally grave, although less frequent causes of brain damage in adults, are *tumors,* either malignant or benign, which develop within brain tissue. Dysphasia that results from tumors is typically of more gradual onset than that which would usually be associated with the occurrence of a stroke. An additional cause of brain damage is *direct trauma to brain tissue.* This may occur as a result of various forms of impact skull insults or in the form of surgical results (Smith, 1966). Finally, *infectious diseases, toxic processes,* and various types of *degenerative diseases* can also cause brain damage with subsequent language impairment.

The precise nature of the dysphasia that results when the brain is damaged depends upon which portion or portions of the brain are involved. The underlying neuropathology is the result of conditions that alter the way in which brain tissue normally functions (Schuell, Jenkins, Jimenez-Pabon, 1964; Luria, 1972). Actual alteration in normal functions can come about in several ways. One is through the destruction of nerve cell bodies or their associated processes. Another is through the interruption of interconnecting nerve fibers. Still another is through alterations of brain chemistry within the cell body. Chemical changes within the membrane that surrounds the cell body or at the junction between one nerve fiber and another can also make units nonfunctional. Finally, we should remember that the role played by subcortical structures in language functioning is far from clear. Most of what we know about the agents that cause brain damage pertinent to dysphasia comes primarily from studies of the effects of these agents on the cortex alone.

Given the general localization of various language functions to different parts of the brain, we can expect that damage to different brain structures will differentially affect language behavior. There is agreement that *lesions* (damages) *causing persistent dysphasia are usually found in the left cerebral hemisphere* (Subriana, 1969). In most individuals, damage to the right cerebral hemisphere causes no language impairment, or, at most, very little impairment. Only in patients who are left-handed and right hemisphere dominant would we expect to find persistent dysphasia in relation to right hemisphere damage. Persistent dysphasia may result from lesions in either the posterior or anterior areas of the dominant hemisphere. The severity of dysphasia will be related not only to the site of damage in the dominant hemisphere but also to the size and extent of the lesion. Specific symptoms of language dysfunction are, for the most part, related to the location of the lesion. Generally, *damage in the posterior part of the dominant hemisphere results in problems of comprehension, integration, recognition, storage, and formulation of linguistic behaviors.* By contrast, *damage to the anterior part of the dominant hemisphere results in language production problems involving planning and execution.* Evidence for this differential behavior consequence with different sites of lesions is contained in electrical stimulation studies of the cortex and in patients who have undergone surgery (Penfield and Roberts, 1959). Pertinent evidence in support of these differential effects is also available from clinical patients who have been studied by various means (Luria, 1966). Less well-defined are the problems arising when damage is between the posterior and anterior areas of the brain or when the damage is located in subcortical regions (Geschwind, 1965; Luria, 1977).

LANGUAGE DISORDERS IN DYSPHASIA

Embodied in our definition of dysphasia was the notion that impairment could involve various language modalities. For present purposes we will consider these modalities to include the functions of speaking, listening-comprehending, reading, and writing. Damage to the central nervous system can result in problems for the patient in language behaviors dependent upon any one modality or any combination of these modalities. Such deficits may or may not also be accompanied by other problems related to the patient's brain damage. The next four sections consider some of the language modality disorders that characterize various persons with dysphasia.

Speaking

Many kinds of oral-verbal production problems are manifested by persons with dysphasia. At the *phonological* level, the patient may have difficulty in selecting the appropriate sounds of the language for use in building linguistic units such as words (Blumstein, 1973; Halpern, Keith, and Darley, 1976). Some consequences of disability at this level may be that the patient may generate words that do not exist in the language, called *neologisms,* or he may produce unintelligible utterances, called *jargon.* Further problems for some individuals on this level are that they may produce only a *part of a word* such as a single syllable or repeated syllables. Others with more extreme forms of phonological disorders may only be able to muster *vowel-like grunts* when attempting to generate language. Less extreme, but nevertheless a significant problem for some individuals, is difficulty in applying phonological rules having to do with how to pluralize a word. Following are transcripts of the oral-verbal attempts of two patients with dysphasia. Each of them demonstrates some of the phonological difficulties mentioned here.

> CLINICIAN: I'm going to say some words and I want you to repeat them after me. Say *clock.*
> PATIENT: Swerz.
> CLINICIAN: Say *horse.*
> PATIENT: Swershmrad. I cranazed dref.
>
> CLINICIAN: What did you have for dessert today?
> PATIENT: Peedee . . . Peedee. (accompanied by a gesture indicating eating something with a spoon)
> CLINICIAN: Did you have peaches?
> PATIENT: (nods head yes) Pee . . . Peeee!

Note that when the first patient was asked to repeat the word clock, she used a neologism in her response—*Swerz.* This sequence of sound elements is acceptable within her language, but it does not make up a word. In her second attempt at repeating a word, she offered *Swershmrad* for horse. This is a jargon response containing the sound elements "sh-m-r," an unlikely combination in her language. Finally, the patient in the first transcript ended her response with a neologistic phrase having only one intelligible word in it, "I." The patient in the second transcript came close to giving an appropriate response in answer to the question about what he had eaten for dessert at lunch. His initial two-syllable utterance began with the appropriate initial consonant and following vowel, "Peedee." On his next attempt, he got only the first syllable.

Oral-verbal production problems at the *morphological* (word) level are frequently a part of the complex picture of dysphasia (Buckingham and Kertesz, 1974). At one end of the spectrum is the patient who has only a single utterance available for use as his sole response in every situation. At the other end of the spectrum is the patient whose problem is an inability to express himself adequately all the time because of difficulties in thinking of or using a desired word. Such a selective loss of the ability to evoke specific words is referred to as *dysnomia.* Other types of difficulties present themselves in forms where the patient may be able to do things like count sequentially, recite the days of the week, or name the months of the year, but not be able to use these same words as appropriate responses in other contexts. Some persons with dysphasia can say almost all words in direct imitation of another speaker, but they may be unable to spontaneously produce these same words in different situations.

Other morphological problems observed in dysphasia relate to difficulties in selecting the appropriate word to express a particular idea. Examples include the following: substituting a class noun for a specific name—such as *man* for *John;* using a word that has exactly the opposite meaning to the word intended—such as *fast* for *slow;* and using a word that is related, but which does not mean what is intended—such as *chair* for *sit.* The application of grammatical rules having to do with morphemes is an additional problem faced by many persons with dysphasia. In this case they may have difficulty in appropriately handling such things as plurality, tense, or gender. A patient will sometimes say *man* instead of *men* or *he run* instead of *he ran* or *it came* in place of *she came.*

Syntax is a major problem in oral performance for many persons with dysphasia (Gleason et al., 1975). Some patients are completely incapable of placing words together in grammatically acceptable sequences, while others may show little difficulty with this same task. The patient who has only single words available to him may be trying to produce complete thoughts through his utterances, but by the rules of the language he is not. Other individuals show that they are capable of generating a basic sentence form such as Noun + Verb, or Noun + Verb + Noun, or some other variations on these basic constructions. However, they may be unable to correctly use articles, prepositions, personal pronouns, or auxiliaries. For example, a patient might say *man goes* for *the man goes* or *She's my brother* for *He's my brother* or *I go walk* for *I will go for a walk.* These types of speech behaviors are referred to as *telegraphic* because the patient uses mostly substantive words and only a few of the function words that help to tie a normal sentence together. Additional syntax problems may be heard in the speech of the patient with dysphasia. A limited number of sentence types may be overused. Only fragments of sentences may be generated rather than grammatically complete sentences. Especially difficult may be utterances that contain dependent or relative clauses. And, often, certain types of transformations such as passive, negation, and question will be impossible for the individual to perform (Schuell, Shaw, and Brewer, 1969).

The conveyance of intended meaning is often a major problem for the patient with dysphasia. Thus, speech aspects of the patient's performance frequently reflect difficulty in the handling of *semantic* features (Zurif and Caramazza, 1976). Problems with meaning make it particularly difficult for the patient to engage in conversational speech. Problems may not only be influenced by an inability to handle semantic aspects of communication, but also by oral-verbal difficulties with phonology, morphology, and syntax. Following is a transcribed exchange between a clinician and a patient who has suffered a stroke. In reading the transcript, attend to the difficulties the patient has in expressing his intended meaning. Also, notice how his difficulty with syntax and morphology contribute to his overall oral-verbal semantic disorder.

> CLINICIAN: Who was elected mayor yesterday?
> PATIENT: Oh, he was then . . . the other one that . . . was remember!
> CLINICIAN: Was it Dyke or Soglin?
> PATIENT: Yes. Dyke was one . . . but I are . . . was . . . was the mayor.
> CLINICIAN: Do you mean Dyke won?
> PATIENT: No. He came croze . . . coze . . . close. Lost two thousand.

It is important to stress that deficits in language behavior may be found along the various dimensions discussed and to various degrees. Each patient will show his or her own unique constellation of speech symptoms. Thus, it is often a problem for the clinician to sort out these symptoms and ascribe them to specific aspects of language dysfunction.

Listening-Comprehending

Comprehending spoken messages of others is often a major problem for the patient with dysphasia. In contrast to oral-verbal expressive problems, problems on the listening-comprehending side are more difficult to categorize along individual linguistic dimensions (that is, phonology, semantics, etc.) (Goodglass and Baker, 1976; Boller, 1978). Part of the problem has to do with some patients not being able to adequately discriminate among various sounds of the language following brain damage. Thus, such patients will have trouble comprehending some words because they cannot identify their parts as individual sound elements and therefore cannot decode them. Some patients also have difficulty in deciphering the sequence of phonemes they hear. They may perceive an intended message as a meaningless array of sounds rather than as some linguistic unit. At the single-word level, the individual with dysphasia will sometimes confuse words that may be associated in some way in meaning, for example, *chair-table* or *door-window*. Words associated in categories are particularly vulnerable to such confusions, examples being the names of colors, the days of the week, or numbers. Some patients tend to comprehend common words more easily than words that occur less frequently. Words that have stronger personal significance to the individual are often comprehended more easily than words that are unrelated to the individual's personal interest (Howes, 1964). It is also common to observe that certain parts of speech give certain patients greater difficulty. For example, relatively abstract words are more of a problem for most patients with dysphasia than are relatively concrete words—love versus door.

Problems in dealing with phonology and morphology can compound the attempts of the brain-damaged patient to understand sentences or connected speech. Often the patient with listening-comprehending problems shows more difficulty understanding declarative sentences than questions. He may also have more difficulty with past tense constructions than with present tense constructions. Listening to long sentences that contain dependent or relative clauses will often present substantial problems for those with dysphasia. And, finally, the handling of ambiguous sentences—those that can have multiple meanings—can prove to be a near impossibility for some patients. It should be noted that persons with brain damage frequently have problems in relation to their auditory attention abilities. Such problems can have serious effects on how well the individual can handle incoming oral-verbal messages.

Reading

Many persons who incur brain damage in adult life will exhibit significant problems in understanding materials they attempt to read either silently or aloud (Vinken and Bruyn, 1969). Specific problems can range from failure to recognize that individual letters in certain orders make up the words on the printed page, to being able to read all material but having great difficulty in fully comprehending it. Problems demonstrated by patients we have seen include reading the word *saw* for the word *was*, reading the word *chair* for *table*, and reading the word *over* for *under*. Lexical errors of this nature contribute to the patient's problem in understanding what it was that he just read. Another type of reading problem common to persons with dysphasia is the omission of specific word-forms such as articles, conjunctions, and prepositions. Other problems include difficulties in handling grammatical features such as plurality, possession, and pronominalization in written material. These types of problems are analogous to those involved in the listening-comprehending disorders mentioned earlier. The variety of types of reading difficulties mentioned here may appear in constellation in the patient with brain damage. If coupled with listening-comprehending difficulties, they can render the individual isolated, in varying degrees, from the messages of others.

The majority of patients with dysphasia and oral-verbal expression problems will have problems with written communication that tend to parallel their oral problems (Schuell et al., 1964). At one end of the disability continuum are those patients with difficulty in selecting the proper graphemes or letters required to write a word. The patient may only be able to execute a single letter for each of the other intended letters of a word. Or, he might select the correct number of letters for an intended word but use inappropriate letters to write a jargon construction. At the other end of the continuum is the patient who makes an occasional spelling error or who selects an inappropriate word to write. Many other types of writing problems are found in dysphasia (Keenan and Brassell, 1974). One or several individual words may be all that the patient can put on paper. These words may be appropriately selected and spelled correctly, or they may be spelled correctly but be words that are associated only in meaning to the ones intended. The patient may be able to write and spell long words correctly, but incorrectly spell and use the so-called "small words" of his language. For example, he may correctly write the word *automobile*, but not the word *the*. A common clinical observation is to see a patient who is able to write the first part of a sentence and then is unable to complete it because of difficulty in finding the remaining appropriate words. Still another problem commonly observed is the inability to write meaningful statements.

Following are transcripts that show the efforts at writing tasks of two persons with dysphasia. Many of the writing problems we have just mentioned are found in these transcripts.

CLINICIAN: I want you to write the word *river* for me.
PATIENT: (writes)

CLINICIAN: Let's try another word. Write *run*.
PATIENT: (writes)

CLINICIAN: Can you spell *run* aloud for me?
PATIENT: Okay! r . . . a . . . no! r . . u . . U . . n . . . RUN!
CLINICIAN: Fine. Now write the word *run*.
PATIENT: (writes)

CLINICIAN: Write as much as you can about this picture. Tell me what is happening now, what happened before, and what will happen later. (picture of man painting a house)

PATIENT: (writes)

> this a picture is a man isthore inf isthe
> point of the p house. each is d disgival
> this inf off is think in i would look
> nice i am ech lines. each man fh
> hand gift each man hand ones and
> in holding is a sprayinghandle in
> the each is windows house.

In both examples the patients are responding cursively. For many patients it makes a substantial difference in the quality of their response whether they write cursively or print (Boone and Friedman, 1976). Performance is highly individualized in this regard and the clinician must sample the patient's abilities to determine his preference and the writing style that gives him the most success.

SPEECH DISORDERS ASSOCIATED WITH DYSPHASIA

We have learned that the problem of the person with dysphasia is one of handling the symbolic code of his language. Other problems often accompany dysphasia, as we might expect, because damage to the brain often leads to disturbances in functions other than language. One function frequently disturbed is speech production. The person with dysphasia may not be able to correctly produce the various oral sounds of his language. Impairment may take the form of difficulty in using the speech mechanism as intended, or difficulty in making fine adjustments of the speech structures because of abnormal control over the muscles of speech, or difficulty in generating the variety of speech melody patterns that characterize normal speech. In the three sections to follow, we deal with the problems mentioned: *dyspraxia, dysarthria,* and *dysprosody.*

Dyspraxia

Dyspraxia is a nonlinguistic disturbance (Goldstein, 1948; Vinken and Bruyn, 1969; Brown, 1972). Central to the disorder is a problem for the patient of carrying out the voluntary use of "tools" for their intended purposes. For purposes of communication, the most important

of these "tools" are the hands and the structures of the speech mechanism. Dyspraxia involving the hands will interfere with language function in both writing and gesture. Dyspraxia involving the structures of
the speech mechanism results in problems in producing oral-verbal
language (Dunlop and Marquardt, 1977; Mateer and Kimura, 1977).
The latter is designated as *dyspraxia of speech*. It has been defined by
Darley (1969) as the following:

> An articulatory disorder resulting from impairment, as a result of brain
> damage, of the capacity to program the positioning of speech muscula-
> ture and the sequencing of muscle movements for the volitional pro-
> duction of phonemes. The speech musculature does not show signifi-
> cant weakness, slowness, or incoordination when used for reflex and
> automatic acts. Prosodic alterations may be associated with the arti-
> culatory problem, perhaps in compensation for it.

The following transcript illustrates the speech of a patient with dyspraxia and clearly reflects his difficulties in appropriately selecting the
sounds desired.

CLINICIAN: Say these words for me. *pat*
PATIENT: pat
CLINICIAN: Fine. Now say *play*.
PATIENT: pray ... pay ... play ... play
CLINICIAN: Now say *street*.
PATIENT: steep ... no, no ... streak ... oh, hell ... streep ... streeeet
   ... street

Patients with dyspraxia of speech may show several general characteristics in their utterances. These include: articulation errors that are
highly inconsistent and tend to vary with the degree of complexity of
the sound being produced; more articulation errors on long words
than on short words; and more articulation errors in spontaneous
speech (for example, conversation) than in automatic or repetitive
speech (for example, reciting a memorized poem). The basis for dyspraxia of speech is impairment in the ability to accurately select and
sequence the speech sounds that the speaker wishes to employ (Johns
and Darley, 1970; Trost and Canter, 1974). At times it is difficult to
separate components of dysphasia from those of dyspraxia in the
communication act of the brain-damaged patient. Keep in mind that
dysphasia is a problem in handling symbols while dyspraxia is a problem in assembling the appropriate sequence of movements for speech
production or what might otherwise be thought of as executing the
appropriate serial ordering of sounds for speech.

Dysarthria

Elsewhere in this book an entire chapter is devoted to the topic of dysarthria (see Chapter 10). At this point, it is important that we be aware of the problem of dysarthria for its potential influence on the communication abilities of the patient with dysphasia. *Dysarthria* is not a language disorder but a speech disorder. It can occur in several forms and is the direct result of disturbance in muscular control of the speech mechanism. This problem in control is brought about by damage to the central or peripheral nervous systems and is manifested in slowness, weakness, or incoordination of speech movements. These manifestations may be represented in all subsystems of the speech mechanism: respiratory, laryngeal, and upper airway. When dysarthria accompanies dysphasia, the patient's speech is often characterized by imprecise articulation, disorders of voice, and respiratory inadequacy. Speech may be unintelligible to various degrees, depending upon the severity of the dysarthric involvement. Because the muscles of the speech mechanism are bilaterally innervated (that is, they are innervated by both sides of the brain), unilateral damage to the brain seldom produces a significant dysarthria. However, in bilateral damage to the motor-control portions of the brain, dysarthria is generally the rule (Darley, Aronson, and Brown, 1975).

Dysprosody

Some patients with brain damage have lesions extending to subcortical regions and to the nondominant hemisphere. These patients frequently demonstrate *problems in the control of speech prosody* (Monrad-Krohn, 1947; Darley, 1969). Such patients may show control problems that make them unable to accurately regulate such parameters as vocal pitch and intonation. They also often find it difficult to apply appropriate stress patterning in speech. The effects of difficulties of these types are that the patient's oral-verbal output conveys little or inappropriate affect. One consequence is that the listener may not be able to decipher whether the speaker intended to make a statement or ask a question. Another problem of the patient with dysprosody is that he might be able to speak the words of a song, but not be able to sing the melody. One need only consider the many subtle meanings that normal speakers are able to convey with small changes in vocal pitch, vocal loudness, stress, rhythm, etc. to appreciate the fact that the brain-damaged adult's ability to communicate will be impaired by deficits in his regulation of prosody.

238

OTHER DISORDERS ASSOCIATED WITH DYSPHASIA

There are often disturbances in various language-support systems that add to the problems faced by the brain-damaged patient with dysphasia. In this section we briefly examine some of these disturbances because they sometimes serve to compound the communication problems of the individual with dysphasia and sometimes confound the clinician's understanding of the patient's problems. We divide our consideration into auditory disorders, visual disorders, somatosensory (body sensation) disorders, behavioral disorders, and dysgnosias.

Auditory Disorders

Peripheral hearing impairment is not usually associated with brain damage (see Chapter 12). However, the average age of the population in which strokes usually occur is above fifty years. Thus, we can expect a sizable number of individuals with dysphasia to have decreased hearing sensitivity and reduced auditory discrimination skills that are simply related to the normal aging process. These changes in auditory skills with aging are sometimes significant enough to influence the communication of adults who have not suffered brain damage. Coupled with brain damage and dysphasia, they can contribute to major interferences with the comprehension of oral-verbal language. Other auditory disorders frequently observed in patients with dysphasia include reduced auditory retention span (Darley, 1969) and impairment of auditory recall (Schuell, 1965). Many clinicians working with patients with dysphasia find that their patients' abilities to use auditory feedback to monitor oral-verbal language output seem to be disordered. Deficits of such a nature are extremely important to the patient's language behavior on the output side because the individual may not realize that what he is saying may be inappropriate. If, during utterance, the patient becomes aware of the inappropriateness of his productions, he may make attempts to modify or correct them as he verbally moves along. Such "on-line" correction behavior is especially apparent in patients performing speech spontaneously.

Visual Disorders

Visual disorders are not a frequent occurrence in association with brain damage leading to dysphasia. Thus, the patient with dysphasia would generally be expected to have no more visual difficulty than his peers who do not have brain damage. Such visual disturbances as do occur are most commonly the effect of unilateral brain damage that leads to a *visual field defect* called *hemianopsia*. Patients with hemianopsia have difficulty identifying visual stimuli because part of the normal visual image is either unclear or missing. Whatever the specific nature of the visual field defect the patient with dysphasia may demonstrate, it may have a direct effect on some of the linguistic impairments manifested. For example, one can easily appreciate the increased functional difficulty that might be shown by a patient with a visual field defect who already has linguistic impairments in reading and writing skills. In addition to visual field defects, certain other types of visual impairments are sometimes found to accompany brain damage in patients who demonstrate dysphasia. These include acquired problems in visual discrimination and reduction in patient abilities in visual recognition and visual recall. Again, such problems can greatly influence the linguistic performance of the patient when he is dealing with forms of communication involving either reading or writing.

Somatosensory (Body Sensation) Disorders

A frequent physical correlate to unilateral brain damage, particularly anterior-area damage, is paralysis or weakness of the opposite side of the body. This condition is referred to as *hemiplegia* and is discussed in Chapter 10. Usually the arm or leg opposite to the damaged cerebral hemisphere are most affected, while the face on the side opposite the damaged hemisphere is least affected. Often associated with hemiplegia is a reduction in sensations that come from *tactile* (touch) stimulation to the paralyzed or weak side of the body. Furthermore, there is often a reduction in the amount of sensory information that comes from muscle contractions (*proprioception*) and from the positioning of various joints of the body (*kinesthesia*). The combination of paralysis or weakness and reduced sensory functioning limits the amount of information available regarding movement and touch on the involved side of the body. In the case of arm involvement, this combination may make writing or gesturing difficult, if not impossible. It may also impair the patient's ability to recognize three dimensional objects placed in his hand. This condition is referred to technically as *astereognosis*. Reduced sensitivities in the oral region may also contribute to communication impairment because they contribute to reduced sensory feedback about ongoing speech. Such feedback is believed to be of importance to articulation functions, and its impairment is thought to be a factor contributing to the unintelligible speech of some patients.

Behavioral Disorders

Persons suffering brain damage may present a wide variety of behavioral disorders in addition to the linguistic impairment of dysphasia. These disorders vary from very mild to very severe and differ in constellation from patient to patient. Certain of the behavioral disorders manifested by brain-damaged patients are believed to be new behaviors that are the result of the brain damage, while others are believed to be released behaviors that were present but held under the control of a previously normal brain (Wepman, 1951; Eisenson, 1964). Patients may also exhibit behaviors considered to be natural consequences of their feelings about being ill, about being incapacitated, and about being "less of a person" than he or she was formerly. Given the broad spectrum of problems that may be associated with brain damage, one might conclude that persons with dysphasia would routinely demonstrate behavior problems of considerable magnitude. Fortunately, this is not the case. The majority of persons with dysphasia are emotionally stable, behave rationally, and use good judgment (Schuell et al., 1964).

Generally speaking, those behavior problems found in patients with dysphasia are most likely observed in patients with more severe brain damage accompanied by dysphasic involvement (Schuell et al., 1964; Ludlow and Swisher, 1971). Some of the specific types of dramatic alterations in behavior that have been reported to accompany significant brain damage and to sometimes co-occur with dysphasia include those discussed in the next paragraph.

One behavior often observed in brain-damaged patients is inappropriate or nonemotionally significant laughing or crying. This behavior is referred to as *emotional lability*. It is seemingly unpredictable in many patients and is exceedingly disruptive to communication. Some brain-damaged patients are found to show an abnormal concern for themselves or things going on around them, a condition referred to as *egocentricity*. By contrast, other patients show states of abnormal disconcern for their conditions, or even outward indications of great contentment. Such states are designated clinically as *euphoria*. At times some brain-damaged individuals will demonstrate responses or reactions that are inconsistent, disordered, and highly inappropriate in the face of demands placed upon them. These are designated as *catastrophic reactions* in that they are greatly overreactive to what the situation may call for. Still other persons with brain damage may show some *deficiency in the ability to attend and concentrate* on the task at hand. Patients sometimes also demonstrate a general inability to shift from one task to another, whether the tasks be verbal or nonverbal. This behavior of being "locked" into a task is referred to as *perseveration*. Other types of behavioral problems in patients suffering from brain damage include an *increased degree of dependency on others*, a *generalized impairment in memory processes*, a *lowered tolerance for frustration*, and a *reduced spontaneity of action*. The behavioral problems mentioned here often have a confounding effect on the language deficit existing in patients with dysphasia. They also sometimes interfere significantly with the management-recovery processes involving the patient.

Dysgnosias

One of the most perplexing disorders found to sometimes accompany dysphasia is *agnosia* or *dysgnosia*. Dysgnosia is a nonlinguistic disturbance that affects the ability to recognize or identify incoming stimuli as they are normally received through sensory avenues. Information is transmitted through the different sensory avenues of patients with dysgnosia, but it is not transmitted in an intact manner. For example, the patient may be fully aware that he or she is hearing, seeing, or touching something, but cannot discern what it is or is unable to distinguish it from something else coming in through the same channel. The two most disruptive dysgnosias to communication involve the auditory and visual systems. In the case of auditory dysgnosia, the brain-damaged patient may know that he is hearing sound, but he cannot specify what it is he hears nor tell that it is different from other sounds. Dysgnosia of this variety could, of course, be contributory to oral-verbal communication problems in the patient with dysphasia. In the case of visual dysgnosia, the problem may influence the patient's ability to communicate through written input modes, or even through written expressive modes. When dysgnosia is present in a sensory processing system, it is sometimes very difficult to evaluate the true extent of the patient's linguistic impairment in that channel (Vinken and Bruyn, 1969).

ASSESSMENT OF DYSPHASIA IN ADULTS

There are several reasons to assess the language abilities of the patient who has suffered brain damage. These include describing what the patient's abilities are, determining the severity of the language problem, planning an appropriate rehabilitation program, and predicting the outcome of a rehabilitation program (Kenin and Swisher, 1972).

In this section, we explore the important features of three approaches to assessment of dysphasia in adults: formal testing, linguistic analysis, and informal testing.

Formal Testing

A large number of formal tests and tasks are used by various clinicians to assess communication functioning in patients with brain damage. It is beyond the scope of this discussion to consider all these. Rather, we will capsulize some of the most widely used of the tests to provide the reader with some notion of what the formal testing battery might embody. We will review the *Minnesota Test for the Differential Diagnosis of Aphasia* (Schuell, 1965), the *Language Modalities Test for Aphasia* (Wepman and Jones, 1961), and the *Porch Index of Communicative Ability* (Porch, 1971).

The *Minnesota Test for the Differential Diagnosis of Aphasia* is designed to assess the language behavior of the brain-damaged patient in five major areas: auditory disturbances, visual and reading disturbances, speech and language disturbances, visual motor and writing disturbances, and disturbances of numerical relations. Each of the areas is examined by means of subtests whose items range in difficulty from easy to hard. Listed below are some of the types of behaviors sampled by the subtests in each of the major areas explored.

AUDITORY DISTURBANCES:

Subtests in this area sample the ability to recognize common words, to identify items named serially, to follow directions, to understand sentences and a paragraph, and to repeat digits and sentences.

VISUAL AND READING DISTURBANCES:

These subtests sample the ability to match forms and letters, to match words to pictures and to spoken words, and to determine oral and silent reading comprehension levels.

SPEECH AND LANGUAGE DISTURBANCES:

This area's subtests sample the ability to produce movements of the oral structures, to carry out automatic speech behavior, to use speech to do such things as name and describe pictures, and to define words and re-tell a story.

VISUAL MOTOR AND WRITING DISTURBANCES:

Subtests here sample the ability to copy letters, numbers, and forms, and to write words, sentences, and paragraphs.

DISTURBANCES OF NUMERICAL RELATIONS:

Subtests in this section sample the ability to use numbers and arithmetical skills for such things as making change, setting a clock, and doing number and word problems.

Severity of language impairment is determined on the Minnesota Test by the number of errors made. Based on the pattern of test results, patients are placed into one of five major groups or two minor subgroups. Research has shown that prognosis for patient recovery is different for each of the major groups and minor subgroups (Schuell, 1965).

The *Language Modalities Test for Aphasia* examines the language behavior of the patient from a slightly different perspective than does the Minnesota Test. Wepman and Jones (1961) base their test on a model of language behavior that views language as being composed of three different processes: input, integration, and output. Disorders of input are designated as agnosias, those of integration are referred to as aphasias, and those of output are referred to as apraxias. Agnosias and apraxias are considered to be problems of transmission and not of symbol manipulation (see definitions earlier in this chapter). The *Language Modalities Test for Aphasia* attempts to measure the comprehension of language symbols as well as the ability to imitate such symbols in both speech and writing. This is done through the use of standard visual and auditory stimuli that assess the patient's ability to translate symbols from visual to graphic, visual to oral, aural to oral, and aural to graphic. Opportunity is provided to study the patient's spontaneous language output through a story-telling task. This task provides a measure of the patient's use of syntax and vocabulary. Overall results on the *Language Modalities Test for Aphasia* provide the examiner with a means for determining whether the patient's problem is one of transmission or interpretation of symbols or a combination of these problems. If the person tested is found to have dysphasia, his responses can be analyzed so as to enable classification of the disorder into one or more of the following categories.

PRAGMATIC APHASIA:

This is considered to be a disorder of comprehension in which the patient is unable to interpret what he sees or hears in relation to previously established concepts. Persons fitting within this category convey little meaning in what they say or write.

SEMANTIC APHASIA:

Persons placed in this category show disorders of the formulation of either spoken or written responses in which they are unable to recall or use previously available words. Typically the individual will have most difficulty remembering and using parts of speech such as nouns, verbs, and adjectives. Patients in this category also have difficulty in comprehending material that is long and linguistically complex.

SYNTACTIC APHASIA:

Those falling within this category have difficulty appropriately generating sentences of correct grammatical form. Such patients tend to speak in a telegraphic fashion where they use nouns and verbs but omit such function words as articles, pronouns, and prepositions. Patients in this category often are able to use certain automatic phrases such as *How are you?*, *Let's go,* etc. The receptive abilities of patients in this category are generally impaired.

JARGON APHASIA:

Patients placed in this category are unable to put the individual sounds of the language together in a conventional fashion and as a result produce unintelligible words and sentences. These patients do, however, maintain near-normal speech prosody patterns. Their receptive language abilities are usually seriously impaired.

GLOBAL APHASIA:

Those in this category show both comprehension and formulation problems with language that are so severe that for all intents and purposes their language is nonfunctional. Some patients in this category can occasionally use some automatized syllables, words, or phrases. However, these are generally inappropriate.

The *Porch Index of Communicative Ability* is designed to assess and quantify certain verbal, gestural, and graphic abilities (Porch, 1967, 1971, 1973). Through its use the speech-language pathologist can ascertain general and specific levels of output ability and make inferences concerning input and integrative ability. Patient responses on the test are scored on the basis of a sixteen-point scale, which indicates the accuracy, completeness, promptness, responsiveness, and efficiency of the patient's language reactions. At one end of the scale the patient is scored as exhibiting no awareness of the test item at all, while at the other end, he or she is scored as having given a complex response. The latter would indicate that the patient is capable of accurate, responsive, complex, immediate, and elaborate reaction. By means of a composite score which a patient gets on the *Porch Index,* the speech-language pathologist determines an overall response level for the patient that represents his general level of communication functioning. Separate scores on different parts of the test enable the clinician to determine how well the patient responds gesturally, verbally, and graphically. Language rehabilitation plans can then be structured to take into account the patterns of language behavior elicited through the testing. Figure 6–6 shows a *Porch Index of Communicative Ability Ranked Response Summary* for a patient with dysphasia who has suffered a left hemisphere cerebrovascular accident. This summary shows that this patient has difficulty with language in all communicative modalities and that his language performance is shifted negatively relative to the normal language user. The patient's overall performance is at the 67th percentile.

It should be apparent from this brief review of selected formal tests for dysphasia that all test instruments are not designed from the same perspectives, nor do they label patient behaviors in identical ways. This is in part attributable to the complex problems of categorizing dysphasia symptoms and is in part related to what the test constructor brings to the test in terms of personal convictions about the nature of the disorder.

Linguistic Analysis

A number of investigators have used predominantly linguistic approaches to study the communication problems of patients with dysphasia (Taylor, 1963a; Wepman and Jones, 1966; Whitaker, 1971; Goodglass et al., 1972; Goodglass and Blumstein, 1973; Wagenaar, Snow, and Prins, 1975). These approaches have provided some pertinent new information about specific language problems related to brain injury and disease. This information, coupled with the recent information explosion in the normal language performance area (see Chapter 1), has prompted many speech-language pathologists to do more in-depth linguistic analyses of the behaviors of patients with dysphasia. Although the formal tests discussed in the previous section provide general information about linguistic functioning, none of them were designed to provide a precise determination of dysfunction in specific linguistic parameters. Suitable tests to probe the problems of dysphasia from a linguistic viewpoint are just emerging and remain to be standardized. By whatever means that are available, then, the speech-language pathologist must attempt to sample the patient's abilities along specific linguistic dimensions.

The patient's ability to use the individual sounds of the language should be sampled. It should be determined whether he can discriminate one sound from another. It should also be determined whether he can tell which sound precedes or follows another. Further, determination should be made concerning how the patient can put sounds together in a rule-governed order to make meaningful words. The general question asked is how well does the patient handle the *phonological* aspects of his language.

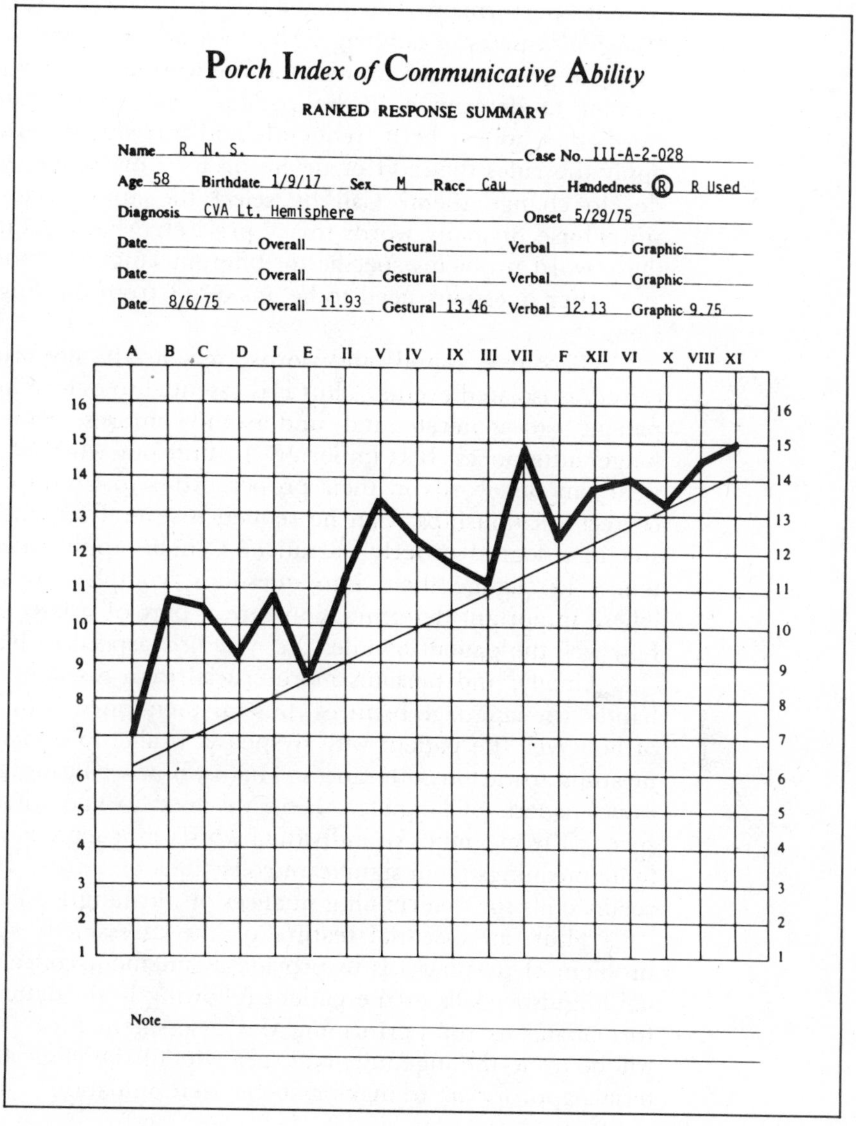

FIGURE 6–6. *PICA Ranked Response Summary for a brain-damaged patient with dysphasia. Overall performance is at the 67th percentile. Gestural, verbal, and graphic scores are given above, as is pertinent information about the patient. (From R. Wertz, Appraisal and diagnosis, in aphasia: Evaluating the effects of treatment. In M. Sullivan and M. Kommers, Eds.,* Rationale for Adult Aphasia Therapy. *Omaha: University of Nebraska Medical Center Publications, 1977.)*

A second general question that can be answered by noting the patient's performance on specific tasks is how well he handles the *morphological* aspects of language. Here we are interested in the patient's ability to generate and understand the words of his language. It is important to determine if the patient can produce and understand words that appear both frequently and infrequently. Does the patient apply the rules that add or delete prefixes or suffixes to words in order to change them? Can he select the appropriate word from a storehouse of many words to say precisely what he wants to say? Are there word problems specific to different language modalities? These and other questions need to be answered from the linguistic point of view.

Of course, sounds and words are not typically produced or perceived as isolated events. Thus it is essential to determine how well the patient can generate and understand phrases, sentences, or even longer utterances. It is important to find out whether or not the patient can put words in their proper order to produce grammatically correct relationships. Can he sequence several sentences that will result in a logical orderly narrative? Can he apply rules to basic sentences to change them into questions, complex constructions, etc.? These important determinations are a part of asking the question of how well the patient handles the *syntactical* aspects of his language.

Finally, and perhaps more crucial than assessing the abilities to handle the language features thus far mentioned is the determination of how well the patient with dysphasia is able to understand and give meaning to various utterances. That is, how well can he handle the *semantic* aspects of language. Here we need to know if the patient can specify the meanings of individual words in a sentence. Can he determine meanings from significant collections of words? Does the patient retain skills for determining nuances of meaning from verbal stimuli?

Thus, an essential feature of the assessment approach to the problem of dysphasia is to provide a statement concerning the residual linguistic skills of the patient following brain damage. Until more formal means for performing this assessment are made available, it will be up to the ingenuity and creativity of the clinician to devise materials appropriate to making such a determination.

Informal Testing

For the speech-language pathologist, formal tests and in-depth linguistic analyses are the methods of choice for assessing the behaviors of patients with dysphasia. However, less structured informal testing methods are also of value and are commonly used. Professionals other than the speech-language pathologist, family, friends, etc. of the brain-damaged patient, are in fact testing his language functioning each time they communicate with him. Running conversation provides a way of determining how well the patient understands what he has heard. Asking questions not only tests understanding, but also tests the patient's skill in producing an appropriate response. Giving the patient something to read and then talking about it with him samples both visual comprehension and speech-language production. Providing an opportunity to write a note or to write an answer to questions assesses still another of the language modalities. Most people would be able to tell whether or not an individual was having language difficulties by means of these informal tests, providing the problem was sufficiently severe. By contrast, however, minor or subtle language disabilities could easily be missed. Thus, informal testing has some major limitations. The structured tests, discussed previously, are designed to deal with both the subtle and the obvious deficits of the brain-damaged patient.

To conclude this section on assessment of dysphasia the point must be made that the assessment of brain-damaged patients is a difficult task. Brain damage results in a wide spectrum of problems beyond those associated with difficulties in handling the symbolic code of language. These other problems frequently make clear-cut statements about the symbolic disorder of the patient difficult to make. As Wertz (1977) has put the problem, one wonders whether the lack of improvement observed in some patients with dysphasia is related to misdiagnosis or the presence of coexisting disorders that were undiagnosed and untreated.

TREATMENT OF DYSPHASIA IN ADULTS

We have learned that there are a multitude of problems that can be associated with brain damage. Here it is not possible to deal with all of them. It is important, however, to realize that many of these problems must be treated simultaneously with the dysphasia problem if the latter is to be successfully managed by the speech-language pathologist (Boone; 1961; Buck, 1968; Stern et al., 1971). The following sections will concentrate primarily on the treatment of dysphasia from the viewpoints of prevention, clinical management, and prognosis.

Prevention

As long as people are going to continue to have diseases that affect the central nervous system and as long as people are going to be involved in situations where the brain can be damaged via trauma, dysphasia and its related problems are going to continue to be with us. With the average human life span increasing year after year, we are also going to see a larger segment of our society reaching ages at which strokes are most prevalent. All other things remaining constant, as the life span of an individual increases, the chances of his becoming dysphasic will also increase.

Medical science has made some significant advances in its strides to prevent brain damage. Early diagnosis of pre-stroke conditions can, through the use of medications or nutritional controls, help prevent strokes from occurring. Prompt and proper use of medical management in infectious diseases and toxic conditions can also prevent the effects of brain damage from being realized. And, while much remains to be done in terms of improvement in the general area of safety control, there have been significant advances made in body restraint and protective headgear devices that reduce the possibilities of sustaining brain damage as a result of trauma from automobile or motorcycle crashes. Thus, the "ideal" way to not be concerned with dysphasia is to prevent it from occurring whenever possible. It is, of course, unrealistic to expect that we could ever completely eliminate conditions causing dysphasia.

Management

In our discussion of assessment we saw how difficult the task was because of the complexities of patient behavior. Management is frought with great complexity also (Longerich and Bordeaux, 1954; Black, 1968; Holland, 1969; Halpern, 1972; Sarno, 1972; Wertz, 1977). What follows in this section is an attempt to provide the reader with some general ideas of how problems of dysphasia might be approached clinically. It is not the purpose here to present a lengthy discussion on all available methods for treating dysphasia. Our discussion is divided to consider the period of spontaneous recovery that the brain-damaged patient typically goes through and how the clinician approaches the problems of the person with dysphasia in a formal manner.

Spontaneous Recovery. Many patients with dysphasia go through a period of partial recovery after brain damage. This recovery may occur in many functions. From the perspective of language performance, the period of spontaneous recovery constitutes a time during which the patient's language skills may gradually return without outside intervention by the speech-language pathologist. Although patients vary in the duration of spontaneous recovery, it is generally thought by most speech-language pathologists that much of spontaneous recovery usually occurs during the first several months following brain damage (Culton, 1969; Darley, 1972; Wertz, 1977). What happens during the period of spontaneous recovery is not exactly known. It is believed by many that brain tissue swelling subsides, that some reorganization of nervous tissue connections is made, and that perhaps portions of the brain that were not formerly used in language behavior may begin to function in a language-processing capacity (Gazzangia and Hillyard, 1971; Kinsbourne, 1971).

Despite our awareness of the period of spontaneous recovery, most speech-language pathologists do not believe that they can justify waiting for several months after the patient has had a stroke to begin language rehabilitation (Eisenson, 1964; Darley, 1972; Smith, 1972). Much can be done during the early post-trauma to facilitate the language rehabilitation process. Perhaps most significant of all during this period is the need to reduce the frustrations of the patient by providing him with some immediate means of communication. It may be that he was unaware that he could write. Or he may be able to gesture, but was not doing so. Just as important as working directly with the patient is the need to work closely with his family and close associates. These individuals need to be shown that there are factors that stimulate and impede language usage (Taylor, 1958; Buck, 1968). Among some of the suggestions that are often given to patients' families to facilitate the communication process are the following: speak slowly; use fewer words to get the message across; be sure there are no competing visual or auditory distractions; gain the patient's attention before attempting to communicate with him; give the patient sufficient time to respond; use a combination of gestural plus verbal communication to give the patient as much information as possible; provide the patient with a good speech-language example to follow rather than correcting his errors.

Formal Language Therapy. Formal language therapy for the brain-damaged individual should be carried out by a speech-language pathologist. Others, of course, will be involved in managing other aspects of the patient's overall disorders, and in certain circumstances the speech-language pathologist will enlist family and allied personnel to aid in language rehabilitation. The program of language therapy should begin as soon as the patient's physical condition is stabilized sufficiently to enable his participation. There is no one universally accepted treatment approach for language impairment in the brain-damaged patient (Wepman, 1972; Brookshire, 1973; Eisenson, 1977). Only recently have systematic attempts been made to analyze what it is that most clinicians attempt to do in dysphasia therapy (Brookshire, 1977). Despite the diversity of dysphasia therapy approaches, there is a common denominator: *to take the patient from his existing level of language functioning and attempt to move him progressively through more complex and difficult levels of functioning.* The ultimate goal is to have the patient return to a level of language functioning that is as near to what it was before brain damage as is possible. There may of course be physical and behavioral variables present that will preclude reaching this goal, and it may in fact be impossible to achieve such a goal because of the severity of the brain damage.

Formal language therapy approaches are highly varied. Here we will review the essential features of the major ones, following the organizational structure suggested by Taylor (1963b). This structure includes the following broad categories: nonspecific stimulation approaches; specific stimulation approaches; and psycholinguistic approaches.

Nonspecific stimulation approaches: Five different approaches comprise the collection of approaches termed nonspecific stimulation approaches. These include environment stimulation, rapport, socialization, psychotherapeutic, and interest approaches. The *environment stimulation approach* uses the combined effects of spontaneous recovery and bombardment with verbal stimulation. This approach does not dictate the kind of verbal stimulation that is necessary, but simply requires that there be a lot of it and that it come through various modalities. Materials and media are very important elements to those who follow this approach to therapy. With the *rapport approach* the crucial element is the establishment of a sincere and warm personal relationship between the clinician and the patient. Here the key is humanistic considerations. Those who use this approach believe that verbal interaction in this kind of a relationship between clinician and patient will be sufficient to enable the recovery of communication skills up to the limit of the patient's potential. The *socialization approach* takes advantage of group dynamics in therapy. It is based upon interactions in which group members do such things as sing, tell stories, participate in verbal games, and carry on conversation. Groups include patients with dysphasia of various degrees and types and at different stages of the recovery process. Closely related to the socialization approach is the *psychotherapeutic approach.* In this approach no direct attempt is made to deal with the patient's language disorder. Rather, the patient is provided opportunity to deal with the psychological-behavioral effect of his problem. Those who ascribe to the psychotherapeutic approach believe that as the patient attempts to talk out his problems, he gains facility in language usage without directly working on language skills. Finally, there is the *interest approach* in which the use of vocational or avocational interests of the patient are the subject matter for language rehabilitation. This approach capitalizes on the patient's developed abilities before brain damage and on things that he most strongly wants to participate in again. The language stimulus materials used in this approach, such as vocabulary, pictures, and reading matter, are based on the patient's interests. (see Figure 6–7).

Many speech-language pathologists choose to use a combination of the five approaches mentioned in this section. The particular combination chosen will, of course, depend upon the specific nature of the patient's language disorder.

Specific stimulation approaches: Three approaches fall into this category of therapy: association, situational, and auditory stimulation. The *association approach* attempts to get the patient to produce words by presenting him with stimuli that might recall other words of the same grammatical class or of similar semantic intent. For example, the patient might be given a category of body parts and then given the word *head* to see if he can associate it with the names of such things as *ears, eyes, nose, mouth,* etc. Or, for another example, if given the word *house,* the patient might be encouraged to assist in various

FIGURE 6–7. *A patient with dysphasia and his speech-language pathologist working with language-stimulus materials that are based on the patient's developed avocational interests. (Courtesy of the University of Arizona Speech and Hearing Clinic.)*

language frames by completing items such as *big house, old house, a big house, live in the house,* etc. By presenting a particular word in a variety of contexts, the hope is to strengthen the patient's association for the word and thereby make it easier for him to recall it at some time in the future. The *situational approach* calls for the development of dialogues that can be used in specific situations that the patient is expected to encounter. Acting out familiar situations is believed to elicit or facilitate the learning of vocabulary or statements that are functionally useful for the patient in that particular situation. The theoretical base of this approach is that language that has some immediate utility will be regained earlier and more easily. Working on job-related situations and social encounter situations are two of the more frequently used aspects in therapies involving the situational approach. The *auditory stimulation approach* incorporates large quantities of controlled auditory stimulation. This stimulation is given in an effort to improve the patient's ability to understand what is said around him with the hope that improved skill along these lines will transfer to other situations and to reading and writing.

Psycholinguistic approaches: Psycholinguistic approaches to language therapy capitalize on our current knowledge of the basic structural patterns of language. Therapeutic efforts are directed specifically toward reestablishing both comprehension and performance skills in the phonological, morphological, syntactical, and semantic aspects of language (Scargill, 1954; Taylor and Anderson, 1968). The amount of time and effort spent on each of these language aspects will depend upon the particular patient. The remainder of this section presents representative examples of the variety of things that might be done.

Persons with dysphasia must be able to produce and sequence the sounds or letters used in language before they can proceed to the stage of reacquiring words and then to the stage of putting them together. Some patients will have retained part of a vocabulary, but it may be limited largely to nouns and verbs. They will need to reacquire other word classes such as prepositions, adjectives, conjunctions, etc. Beyond this, they will have to improve their abilities in dealing with such grammatical constructs as verb tense, possession, number agreement, and pluralization. When only single-word responses are used in speech or writing, the patient will need to reacquire skills for generating phrases and basic sentences.

Of course, there is much more to communicating via speech or writing than merely being able to generate a basic sentence. Applying the rules of syntax, the patient must reacquire how to transform or change basic sentence forms. He may need practice in creating sentences that are complex, that is, have dependent and independent clauses. To develop variety in what he says or writes, the patient may also need practice in rearranging words in a sentence to make it look or sound different while in effect saying the same thing. In asking or writing a question, the patient may need to work on placing *wh*-words, for example, *when* or *where*, in the appropriate position. As the patient regains skill in selecting the elements of the language and in applying the rules for combining them, he will again be able to handle meaning. Not only will he more accurately say what he intends, but he will understand more of what is said to him.

The language recovery process in patients with dysphasia is viewed by many as the recovery of reorganization. The speech-language pathologist's role in helping the patient recover is perhaps best expressed by Eisenson (1977) as follows:

> The role of the clinician is that of a stimulator or *agent provocateur*. The clinician must choose the time, and the opportunity, and must select the materials most appropriate to the interest, needs, intellectual functioning, and linguistic proficiencies of the patient. Assuming that the patient's language competencies are almost always greater than his productions, the clinician must try to help the patient to understand all he is capable of understanding and to produce as nearly as possible on a level related to the competencies. (For details, see Eisenson, 1973.)

Prognosis

One of the tasks facing those who work with patients with dysphasia is trying to predict the extent to which different patients will recover language functioning. Stated another way, the question to be asked is: What factors influence the recovery of communication skills in the person who has suffered significant brain damage? The answer to this question is important to the speech-language pathologist who is planning and carrying out a management program, to the patient himself, and to the patient's family. Many factors influence how well the patient recovers physically from the effects of brain damage (Rubens, 1977) and how well he recovers his ability to communicate again (Kenin and Swisher, 1972). Here we will consider a few of the more important of these factors.

Two important factors related to recovery are the location and extent of damage to the brain. Damage to the posterior part of the dominant hemisphere usually results in more complex and longer-lasting communication problems for the brain-damaged patient. And, generally speaking, the more extensive the injury to the brain, the slower and less complete will be the recovery process. Cause of brain damage will also be an important factor in determining patient recovery. Language recovery is usually better when there has been traumatic injury to the brain than when damage has resulted from cerebrovascular accident or infectious or malignant diseases.

The age of the patient at the time of brain damage will have an effect on overall chances for successful rehabilitation. The younger the individual, the better the chance for language recovery. The learning, relearning, and reorganization that goes on in the recovery process appears to be an easier task for a younger individual. The amount of behavioral, psychological, and emotional overlay present in the overall problem will also influence the rate and extent of recovery by the patient. A patient who is euphoric or emotionally labile or overly dependent tends to make less progress or slower progress in language therapy.

While we know that there is a period of spontaneous recovery following brain damage, it is generally accepted that the earlier language therapy begins, the better is the overall outlook for recovery. Perhaps the best single predictor of the completeness of the pattern of language improvement to be expected in a patient is his overall language disorder severity soon after brain injury (Kenin and Swisher, 1972). That is, patients severely impaired in language skills after brain damage are those who will probably have the greatest difficulty in recovering function with or without language therapy. The longer a patient goes without anyone providing him assistance in reacquiring the skills that he once possessed, the greater chance there is of him developing frustration, depression, and loss of motivation.

The realistic setting of goals is another important variable in the recovery process. Unrealistic goals set either by the patient or by those working with him can lead to either failure in his recovery or less than optimal success. While the long-term goal of the patient might be set as being able to communicate adequately in all social situations or in his former job environment, neither of these may be attainable. Short-range or intermediate goals that are more realistic may have to be accepted.

Setting of goals is related to another factor that is known to correlate with patient recovery—motivation. A patient who is not motivated to want to improve his communication functioning may make little or no progress in therapy. Although we assume that all patients want to resume their ability to communicate, motivation actually differs from individual to individual and from time to time (Hall, 1961; Buck, 1968). For example, while in the hospital, the reason the patient wants to talk is so he can take care of some of his personal needs rather than having to be totally dependent upon nurses, doctors, and others. Later the patient may feel the need to communicate primarily so that he can be with other people again in social situations. Still later he may want to communicate so that he can return to work. Unless the patient is self-motivated or externally motivated, the prognosis will be less than favorable.

Once he leaves the hospital, every patient goes back into some part of society. He returns to family, friends, fellow employees, church, etc. How these individuals or groups respond to the person with brain damage and he responds to them will have an effect on the ultimate recovery process. A helpful and accepting attitude is certainly better than a sympathetic, solicitous one. Too often, well-meaning friends and relatives treat the person with dysphasia as though he were intellectually retarded, emotionally disturbed, or senile. He is typically none of these. He is an individual who has a problem in communication and needs help and understanding from those about him.

REFERENCES   BLACK, J. (Ed.), *Language Retraining for Aphasics.* Proceedings of the Conference Held at the Ohio State University, October (1968).

BLUMSTEIN, S., *A Phonological Investigation of Aphasic Speech.* The Hague: Mouton (1973).

BOLLER, F., Comprehension disorders in aphasia: A historical review. *Brain and Language,* 5, 149–165 (1978).

BOONE, D., Relationship of progress in speech therapy to progress in physical therapy. *Archives of Physical Medicine and Rehabilitation,* 42, 30–32 (1961).

BOONE, D., and FRIEDMAN, H., Writing in aphasia rehabilitation: Cursive vs manuscript. *Journal of Speech and Hearing Disorders,* 41, 523–529 (1976).

BRANCH, C., MILNER, B., and RASMUSSEN, T., Intracarotid sodium amytal for the lateralization of cerebral speech dominance. *Journal of Neurosurgery,* 21, 399–405 (1964).

BROOKSHIRE, R., *An Introduction to Aphasia.* Minneapolis: BRK Publishers (1973).

BROOKSHIRE, R., A system for recording events in patient-clinician interactions during aphasia treatment sessions. In M. Sullivan and M. Kommers (Eds.), *Rationale for Adult Aphasia Therapy.* Lincoln: University of Nebraska Medical Center Publications (1977).

BROWN, J., *Aphasia, Apraxia, and Agnosia.* Springfield, Ill.: Charles C Thomas (1972).

BROWN, J., On the neural organization of language: Thalamic and cortical relationships. *Brain and Language,* 2, 18–30 (1975).

BUCK, M., *Dysphasia: Professional Guidance for Family and Patient.* Englewood Cliffs, N.J.: Prentice-Hall (1968).

BUCKINGHAM, H., and KERTESZ, A., A linguistic analysis of fluent aphasia. *Brain and Language,* 1, 43–62 (1974).

CULTON, G., Spontaneous recovery from aphasia. *Journal of Speech and Hearing Disorders,* 12, 825–832 (1969).

DARLEY, F., Expressive speech and language disorders. Paper presented to the Annual Convention of the American Speech and Hearing Association, Chicago (1969).

DARLEY, F., The efficacy of language rehabilitation in aphasia. *Journal of Speech and Hearing Disorders,* 37, 3–21 (1972).

DARLEY, F., ARONSON, A., and BROWN, J., *Motor Speech Disorders.* Philadelphia: Saunders (1975).

DAVIS, A., and WADA, J., Speech dominance and handedness in the normal human. *Brain and Language,* 5, 42–55 (1978).

DERENZI, E., and VIGNOLO, L., The token test: A sensitive test to detect receptive disturbances in aphasia. *Brain,* 85, 665–678 (1962).

DISIMONI, F., DARLEY, F., and ARONSON, A., Patterns of dysfunction in schizophrenic patients on an aphasia test battery. *Journal of Speech and Hearing Disorders,* 42, 498–513 (1977).

DUNLOP, J., and MARQUARDT, T., Word production in apraxia of speech. *Cortex,* 13, 17–29 (1977).

EISENSON, J., *Adult Aphasia—Assessment and Treatment.* Englewood Cliffs, N.J.: Prentice-Hall (1973).

EISENSON, J., Aphasia: A point of view as to the nature of the disorder and factors that determine prognosis for recovery. *International Journal of Neurology,* 4, 287–295 (1964).

EISENSON, J., Language rehabilitation of aphasic adults: A review of some issues as to the state of the art. In M. Sullivan and M. Kommers (Eds.), *Rationale for Adult Aphasia Therapy.* Lincoln: University of Nebraska Medical Center Publications (1977).

GAZZANGIA, M., and HILLYARD, S., Language and speech capacity of the right hemisphere. *Neuropsychologia,* 9, 273–280 (1971).

GESCHWIND, N., Disconnexion syndromes in animal and man. *Brain,* 88, 237–294 (1965).

GESCHWIND, N., The organization of language and the brain. *Science,* 170, 940–944 (1970).

GLEASON, J., GOODGLASS, H., GREEN, E., ACKERMAN, N., and HYDE, M., The retrieval of syntax in Broca's aphasia. *Brain and Language,* 2, 451–471 (1975).

GOLDSTEIN, K., *Language and Language Disturbances.* New York: Grune and Stratton (1948).

GOODGLASS, H., and BAKER, E., Semantic, naming, and auditory comprehension in aphasia. *Brain and Language,* 3, 359–374 (1976).

GOODGLASS, H., and BLUMSTEIN, S. (Eds.), *Psycholinguistics and Aphasia.* Baltimore: Johns Hopkins University Press (1973).

GOODGLASS, H., GLEASON, J., BERNHOLTZ, N., and HYDE, M., Some linguistic structures in the speech of a Broca's aphasia. *Cortex,* 8, 191–212 (1972).

GREEN, E., On the contribution of studies in aphasia to psycholinguistics. *Cortex,* 6, 216–235 (1970).

HALL, W., A return from silence—A personal experience. *Journal of Speech and Hearing Disorders,* 26, 174–177 (1961).

HALPERN, H., *Adult Aphasia.* Indianapolis: Bobbs-Merrill (1972).

HALPERN, H., KEITH, R., and DARLEY, F., Phonemic behavior of aphasic patients without dysarthria or apraxia of speech. *Cortex,* 12, 365–372 (1976).

HOLLAND, A., Some current trends in aphasia rehabilitation. *Asha,* 11, 3–7 (1969).

HOWES, D., Application of the word frequency concept in aphasia. In A. deReuck and M. O'Connor (Eds.), *Disorders of Language.* London: Churchill, Ltd. (1964).

JOHNS, D., and DARLEY, F., Phonemic variability in apraxia of speech. *Journal of Speech and Hearing Research,* 13, 556–583 (1970).

KEENAN, J., and BRASSELL, E., A study of factors related to prognosis for individual aphasic patients. *Journal of Speech and Hearing Disorders,* 39, 257–269 (1974).

KENIN, M., and SWISHER, L., A study of pattern of recovery in aphasia. *Cortex,* 8, 56–68 (1972).

KIMURA, D., Functional asymmetry of the brain in dichotic listening. *Cortex,* 3, 163–176 (1967).

KIMURA, D., The asymmetry of the human brain. *Science,* 228, 70–78 (1973).

KINSBOURNE, M., The minor cerebral hemisphere. *Archives of Neurology,* 25, 302–306 (1971).

KINSBOURNE, M., and SMITH, W., *Hemispheric Disconnection and Cerebral Function.* Springfield, Ill.: Charles C Thomas (1974).

KRASHEN, S., Language and the left hemisphere. *UCLA Working Papers in Phonetics,* October (1972).

LONGERICH, M., and BORDEAUX, J., *Aphasia Therapeutics.* New York: Macmillan (1954).

LUDLOW, C., and SWISHER, L., The audiometric evaluation of adult aphasics. *Journal of Speech and Hearing Research,* 14, 535–543 (1971).

LURIA, A., Aphasia reconsidered. *Cortex,* 8, 34–40 (1972).

LURIA, A., *Higher Cortical Functions in Man.* New York: Basic Books (1966).

LURIA, A., Language and brain. *Brain and Language,* 1, 1–14 (1974).

LURIA, A., On quasi-aphasic speech disturbances in lesions of the deep structures of the brain. *Brain and Language,* 4, 432–459 (1977).

LURIA, A., *The Working Brain: An Introduction to Neuropsychology.* New York: Basic Books (1973).

MATEER, C., and KIMURA, D., Impairment of nonverbal oral movements in aphasia. *Brain and Language,* 4, 262–276 (1977).

McADAM, D., and WHITAKER, H., Language production: Electroencephalographic localization in the normal brain. *Science,* 172, 499–502 (1971).

MILNER, B., Interhemispheric differences in the localization of psychological processes in man. *British Medical Bulletin,* 3, 272–277 (1971).

MONRAD-KROHN, G., The prosodic quality of speech and its disorders. *Acta Psychiatrica et Neurologica Scandinavia,* 22, 255–269 (1947).

MONTCASTLE, V. (Ed.), *Interhemispheric Relations and Cerebral Dominance.* Baltimore: Johns Hopkins Press (1961).

MOSKOVITCH, M., On the representation of language in the right hemisphere of right-handed people. *Brain and Language,* 3, 47–71 (1976).

OSGOOD, C., and MIRON, M., *Approaches to the Study of Aphasia.* Urbana: University of Illinois Press (1963).

PENFIELD, W., and ROBERTS, L., *Speech and Brain-Mechanisms.* Princeton: Princeton University Press (1959).

PORCH, B., Introduction to the Porch Index of Communicative Ability (PICA). Short course presented to the Annual Convention of the American Speech and Hearing Association, San Francisco (1972).

PORCH, B., *Porch Index of Communicative Ability.* Palo Alto, Calif.: Consulting Psychologists Press (1971).

PORCH, B., *Porch Index of Communicative Ability. Volume I, Theory and Development.* Palo Alto, Calif.: Consulting Psychologists Press (1967).

PORCH, B., *Porch Index of Communicative Ability. Volume 2, Revised Edition. Administration and Scoring.* Palo Alto, Calif.: Consulting Psychologists Press (1973).

PREMACK, D., Language in the chimpanzee? *Science,* 172, 808–822 (1971).

PRIBRAM, K., *Language of the Brain: Experimental Paradoxes and Principles in Neuropsychology.* Englewood Cliffs, N.J.: Prentice-Hall (1971).

RUBENS, A., The role of changes within the central nervous system during recovery from aphasia. In M. Sullivan and M. Kommers (Eds.), *Rationale for Adult Aphasia Therapy.* Lincoln: University of Nebraska Medical Center Publications (1977).

RUMBAUGH, D., GLASERSFELD, V., WARNER, H., PISANI, P., and GILL, T., Lana (chimpanzee) learning language: A progress report. *Brain and Language,* 1, 205–212 (1974).

SARNO, M. (Ed.), *Aphasia: Selected Readings.* New York: Appleton-Century-Crofts (1972).

SCARGILL, M., Modern linguistics and recovery from aphasia. *Journal of Speech and Hearing Disorders,* 19, 507–513 (1954).

SCHUELL, H., *Differential Diagnosis of Aphasia with the Minnesota Test.* Minneapolis: University of Minnesota Press (1965).

SCHUELL, H., JENKINS, J., and JIMENEZ-PABON, E., *Aphasia in Adults.* New York: Harper & Row (1964).

SCHUELL, H., SHAW, R., and BREWER, W., A psycholinguistic approach to the study of language deficit in aphasia. *Journal of Speech and Hearing Research,* 12, 794–806 (1969).

SEMMES, J., Hemispheric specialization: A possible clue to mechanism. *Neuropsychologia,* 6, 11–26 (1971).

SHANKWEILER, D., An analysis of laterality effects in speech perception. In D. Horton and J. Jenkins (Eds.), *The Perception of Language.* Columbus, Ohio: Merrill (1971).

SMITH, A., Speech and other functions after left (dominant) hemispherectomy. *Journal of Neurology, Neurosurgery, and Psychiatry,* 29, 467–471 (1966).

SMITH, A., Diagnosis, Intelligence and Rehabilitation of Chronic Aphasics. Social and Rehabilitation Service Grant No. 14-P-55198/5-01. University of Michigan Department of Physical Medicine and Rehabilitation, July (1972).

STERN, P., McDOWELL, F., MILLER, J., and ROBINSON, M., Factors influencing stroke rehabilitation. *Stroke,* 2, 213–218 (1971).

SUBRIANA, A., Handedness and cerebral dominance. In P. Vinken and G. Bruyn (Eds.), *Handbook of Clinical Neurology,* Vol. 4. New York: Wiley (1969).

TAYLOR, M., *Functional Communication Profile.* New York: New York University Press (1963a).

TAYLOR, M., Language therapy. In H. Burr (Ed.), *The Aphasic Adult: Evaluation and Rehabilitation.* Proceedings of a Short Course, University of Virginia, December (1963b).

TAYLOR, M., *Understanding Aphasia.* New York: Institute of Medicine and Rehabilitation (1958).

TAYLOR, O., and ANDERSON, C., Psycholinguistics and language retraining. In J. Black (Ed.), *Language Retraining for Aphasics.* Proceedings of the Conference Held at the Ohio State University, October (1968).

TROST, J., and CANTER, G., Apraxia of speech in patients with Broca's aphasia: A study of phoneme production accuracy and error patterns. *Brain and Language,* 1, 63–79 (1974).

VINKEN, P., and BRUYN, G. (Eds.), *Disorders of Speech, Perception and Symbolic Behavior.* New York: Wiley (1969).

WAGENAAR, E., SNOW, K., and PRINS, R., Spontaneous speech of aphasic patients: A psycholinguistic analysis. *Brain and Language,* 2, 281–303 (1975).

WEPMAN, J., Aphasia: Language without thought or thought without language? *Asha,* 18, 131–136 (1976).

WEPMAN, J., Aphasia therapy: A new look. *Journal of Speech and Hearing Disorders,* 37, 203–214 (1972).

WEPMAN, J., *Recovery From Aphasia.* New York: Ronald Press (1951).

WEPMAN, J., and JONES, L., *Studies in Aphasia: An Approach to Testing.* Chicago: Education-Industry Service (1961).

WEPMAN, J., and JONES, L., Studies in aphasia: A psycholinguistic method and case study. In E. Carterette (Ed.), *Brain Function, Vol. III, Speech, Language and Communication.* Berkeley: University of California Press (1966).

WERTZ, R., Appraisal and diagnosis in aphasia: Evaluating the effects of treatment. In M. Sullivan and M. Kommers (Eds.), *Rationale for Adult Aphasia Therapy.* Lincoln: University of Nebraska Medical Center Publications (1977).

WHITAKER, H., *On the Representation of Language in the Human Brain.* Champaign, Ill.: Linguistic Research, Inc. (1971).

ZURIF, E., and CARAMAZZA, A., Psycholinguistic structure in aphasia: Studies in syntax and semantics. In H. Whitaker and H. Whitaker (Eds.), *Studies in Neurolinguistics.* New York: Academic Press (1976).

signpost   Chapter 7's portion of the territory includes a discussion of those individuals whose speech is characterized by developmental speech-sound errors. Developmental errors are those attributable to disturbances in the speech-learning process during the normal human developmental period. A decade or so ago such errors were viewed almost entirely from the perspective of articulatory events attendant to the speech production process. Now, however, the modern speech-language pathologist considers such errors within the framework of phonology, a branch of language study concerned with how speech sounds structure and function in communication. Chapter 7 points out the importance of this swing from an articulatory to a phonological view of speech-sound errors and gives the beginning student the information needed to appreciate both perspectives. Discussion is offered relative to the different types of speech-sound errors and various factors associated with their occurrences. Also considered are the important means for assessing delayed phonological development, including determinations of the extent to which such deviancies are handicapping. Issues pertaining to management are handled within the framework of whether the speaker has multiple speech-sound errors or errors on only one or two sounds. Recent years have seen a shift in some school systems across the United States to no longer routinely provide speech therapy services for children with one or two speech-sound errors. Part of Chapter 7 considers the consequences of this general policy and suggests why in some regards it may not be totally wise.

7

Lawrence D. Shriberg

developmental
phonological
disorders

INTRODUCTION

Most of us can remember at least one grade-school classmate who didn't "say his sounds right." The speech teacher called this child out of class once or twice a week for "speech therapy." Not so nowadays. Today, in many schools in this country, children who have only one or two speech-sound errors are not being scheduled for speech therapy. Special education personnel are adopting the view that a consistent error on *r*, for example, is in no way handicapping to a child. Consequently, they reason, the public-school system is not obligated to provide speech services. This view is quite a departure from the clinical thinking of the past fifty years in the field of communication disorders. After sorting through the issues reviewed in this chapter, you should be able to form your own opinion about the consequences of speech-sound misarticulations for children or adults.

We are concerned in this chapter with the millions of children and adults who have *developmental* speech-sound errors. Their errors are not associated with structural defects (Chapter 9) or neuromuscular deficits (Chapter 10). Rather, developmental speech-sound errors are attributed to a disturbance in the learning process during the normal speech development period. In approaching the content of this chapter, we assume that the reader is familiar with the phonetics and speech production concepts presented in Chapter 2, and with information on normal and delayed language development presented in Chapters 1 and 4. We will defer drawing some important distinctions between the terms articulation and phonology until the reader has a clearer picture of the types of articulation errors people make—the topic we turn to first.

NORMAL AND DELAYED PHONOLOGICAL DEVELOPMENT

Types of Articulation Errors

The twenty-five consonants and twenty-one vowels and diphthongs of American English were presented in Chapter 2. Children must learn to articulate each of these sounds correctly in individual syllables and eventually, in swift-moving speech. *Articulation errors* (misarticulations of speech sounds) can take one of three forms—*omissions, substitutions,* or *distortions.*

Omissions. When a speaker does not articulate all the expected sounds in a word the missing sounds are called *omission errors.* The following sentences were said by a child who spoke with sound omissions all the time:

ANDY: 4 YEARS, 9 MONTHS

"we a fi" . . . (We have fish.)
"na tu ee, no" . . . (Not to eat, no.)
"pu i wi hea" . . . (Put it right here.)
"I pu i i a hou" . . . (I put it in the house.)
"I pa dou" . . . (I fall down.)

This transcript from the speech of a child enrolled for speech therapy illustrates two important points about omission errors. First, of the three types of articulation errors—omissions, substitutions, and distortions—children who make omission errors are typically perceived as the most immature or infantile sounding. Studies of misarticulations indicate that omissions are the most severe type of articulation error, both for understanding and for perceived defectiveness. The more omission errors a child makes, the harder it is to understand his or her speech. And children who sound like Andy are likely to be perceived as "babyish." Fortunately, omission errors are seldom observed as residual developmental errors in the speech of older children and adults. They do, however, characterize the speech of people who may have structural or neuromuscular deficits of the speech mechanism.

The second point is that children are apt to omit certain sounds more often than others. Furthermore, omissions tend to occur in certain positions in words. For example, the stop-plosives *t* and *k* are quite often omitted in the speech of very young children. And these two sounds are more likely to be omitted in the final position of a word than in the initial position. For example, Andy says *na tu ee, no* (Not to eat, no.). He omits the *t* in the word-final position (Not, eat) but he says it in word-initial position (to). Some possible explanations for these interesting error patterns will be considered later.

Substitutions. A second type of speech-sound error is the *substitution* of one sound for another. Of the three types of speech errors, substitutions are easiest to simulate. Try saying the following sentence the way that you think a child of about two-and-one-half years might: *He's a pretty little doggie.* Students asked to do this have responded (roughly): "He'da pwetty witto goggie." Notice the substitution errors: a *w* instead of *r* (*pwetty* for *pretty*), *w* and *o* instead of *l* (*witto* for *little*), and a *g* instead of *d* (*goggie* for *doggie*). Children themselves, in fact, use substitutions when they want to affect a more juvenile speech pattern. If one eavesdrops on preschoolers playing "house," the speech of the child designated "baby" will probably contain many simulated consonant substitutions.

The most striking observation about substitutions is that the substituted sound generally sounds somewhat like the one replaced. For example, commonly observed substitutions such as *th/s* (read as "*th* for *s*"), *w/r*, and *s/z*, illustrate this tendency. Because *th* and *s* are both voiceless fricatives, they sound somewhat alike. Likewise, *w* and *r* are both made with gliding movements of the lips and tongue and sound quite similar. And in the case of *s/z*, both are lingua-dental fricatives—they differ in that *s* is voiceless whereas *z* is voiced. This characteristic of articulation errors will be considered in more detail later.

Distortions. A speech-language pathologist uses the term *distortion* (or *approximation*) when production of a phoneme is in the right territory but not quite on target. For some purposes, simply describing an articulatory error as a distortion may be entirely adequate. For example, during a screening test a clinician may make the notation: "Chris distorts the *ch* and *j* sounds." For other purposes, however, the clinician needs to indicate precisely how the distortion differs from customary production of the target sound. To accomplish the latter, clinicians use modifying symbols (*diacritics*) from the International Phonetic Alphabet and other standard sources. We will introduce some of these modifying symbols below as needed.

The term *lisp* shows up in magazines and in child development textbooks to cover all types of distortions. Technically, the term lisp refers only to distortions of the four English *sibilant* sounds, namely *s*, *z*, *sh*, and *zh* (as in azure). Lisps on *s* or *z* are among the most frequently occurring types of articulation errors in children and especially in adults. It is fairly easy to learn to identify and simulate two kinds of lisps; consider first the *dental* lisp:

> To make a dental lisp, place the tip of your tongue just behind but not quite touching the back of your upper front teeth. Say some words that begin with *s* and *z*: "see", "soup", "zebra." The fricative quality of the *s* and *z* should sound almost like a *th*, depending on how close the tip of the tongue is to the teeth. Only a small movement of the tongue tip forward and backward is all that is needed to alternate among the *th* sound (tongue tip between or touching teeth), a dental or dentalized *s* (tongue tip back a little), and a "good *s*" (tongue tip approximately below the line of the gum ridge). The phonetic modifying symbol for dentalized sounds is [ͫ]. The clinician notates a dentalized *s* sound by writing [s̪], or for dentalized *z*, [z̪]. This description provides much more information than simply labeling the error "an *s* distortion."[1]

Another type of lisp, somewhat less frequently occurring than the very common dental lisp, is the *lateral* lisp:

> Lateral lisps can be simulated by trying to make a voiceless *l* sound. First, anchor the tip of your tongue firmly against the gum ridge behind your upper front teeth — at the same place that you would place it to say *l*. Put your hand out in front of your mouth and (keeping your tongue tip firmly anchored) blow gently on your hand. If you have emitted air over the *sides* of the tongue (that is, "laterally"), the sound should be perceptually similar to a lateral *s*. The *s* should sound "slushy." Some people make all their *s* sounds and other sibilants too in this way. Try making lateral *s*'s in the words "sip," "missing," and "Mississippi!" The phonetic modifying symbol for lateralization is [˄], hence [s̬], or [z̬]. This symbol actually resembles the position of the tongue tip in the mouth; that is, the tongue tip touches the top of the mouth allowing air to escape laterally over both sides [˄] (although some people lateralize the air to only one side).

There are several other distortions of *s, z, sh,* and *zh* that occur often enough to warrant brief comment. *Palatal* distortions, indicated as [s̡], [z̡], occur when sounds are made more with the middle part of the tongue than with the tongue tip. A palatalized *s* sounds more *sh-* like, because the air stream becomes turbulent under the middle re-

---

[1] Most clinicians use the term *interdental* lisp for distortions midway between *th* and *s*. It is difficult, however, to use all three classifications reliably (Shriberg and Kent, in preparation). Hence, we use dentalization [ͫ] for all sibilant distortions in which the tongue contacts the alveolar ridge or teeth.

gion of the *palate* rather than under the more forward gum-ridge area. *Retroflex* distortions, indicated as [ʂ], [ʐ], occur when the tongue tip is curled back too far. A retroflex tongue position may produce a slight or even pronounced whistling sound. As you might infer from this limited sample of types of distortions, accurate understanding of exactly how a person misarticulates a sound can be quite important for designing effective clinical management.

Clinical Classification

Speech-language pathologists use a variety of terms for subgrouping children with articulatory errors. For clinical purposes, children may be differentiated by the total number of different sounds in error. Children who have errors on at least three sounds or sound pairs, for example, *s–z, sh–zh*, are referred to as children who have *multiple misarticulations*. Referring to a child as having multiple misarticulations simply describes him as having more speech-sound errors than normal for his age. Another term used to describe the speech of these same children is *delayed speech*. Children may have a "mild," "moderate," or "severe" speech delay—depending on the number of speech sounds in error and the degree to which the child is understandable.

In contrast to the child with delayed speech is the child (or adult) who makes articulation errors on only one or two sounds or sound pairs. We use the term *residual speech errors* to characterize the speech of this subgroup of phonological disorders. Clinically, persons in this subgroup may further be described by the particular sound(s) in error, perhaps including the type of error: for example, a child with a dentalized *s*, a child with a *w/r*, an adult with lateralized sibilants, and so forth. Distortions of *s* and *r* are by far the most common residual speech errors in children and adults.

To conclude this first section on the types of articulation errors, we present transcriptions of the speech of several young clients. Rough spelling notation is used to simulate the phonetic distortions for lateral *s* introduced previously: dentalization [̪] = *ts;* lateralization [̫] = *lsh;* and palatalization [̬] = *sh*. Listening to yourself as you read these transcriptions aloud should give you some feeling for the perceptual impact of the different error types.

SECOND-GRADE CHILD [describing a picture of a fire scene]:

That look*lsh* like ... a *fio*, with a *fiotwuck* and two men climbing up a ladd*ew* ... and *lsh*omone's got a hu*wt* on his head, it look*lsh* like. And the*aw*'s a lot of wate*w* on the *gw*ound and the*w*'s a *fio* hyd*w*ant.

PRE-KINDERGARTEN CHILD [playing with some toys]:

"a wa ge di pipu ow" . . . (I want to get these people out.) "ma da li go aw" . . . (Make the lights go on.) "whey da fafa twuk" . . . (Where's the fire truck?)

FIRST-GRADE CHILD [talking with clinician]:

And we played thi*th* game and *th*ee, yeah . . . she got to go fir*tht*, she, she you know, she wa*th*n't that old becau*th* p*w*etty *th*oon I'm going to be *th*ik*th*. I'm going to be *th*ik*th* on July *th*econd!

None of these children have structural or neuromuscular problems contributing to their speech errors. They have developmental phonological disorders because their speech errors have persisted beyond the normal period of articulatory development.

As we will describe shortly, speech development involves more than just learning how to articulate speech sounds correctly. A review of normal articulatory development is useful at this point. Let's begin with a case example.

Normal Articulatory Development

Four-year-old Kelly was referred to our clinic by her mother because "no one can understand Kelly's speech except her older sister." Testing by a student clinician yielded the following pattern of consonant errors:

Articulation Errors	Position in Word		
	INITIAL	*MEDIAL*	*FINAL*
Omissions	p, b, k, v, r, s	b, t, g, k, d, m, v, s, f, ch, j, th, r, s, zh	t, d, k, g, m, n, f, v, th, sh, ch, j, s, z, l, zh
Substitutions	d/th, t/th, sh/s, ch/s, j/z, w/r, d/g	t/d, d/th, t/s, g/ng	
Distortions	none	s, sh, l	none

How does the clinician decide if Kelly's articulation development is normal for her age? This question presumes two things: that there *is* a normal sequence of speech-sound development across children and that this sequence is age-related.

In point of fact, there does seem to be a roughly ordered sequence to speech-sound development. And, with qualifications, we do have information on the ages at which children apparently "master" each of the vowels and consonants of American English. This information comes from several studies of American children that date back some years (Wellman et al., 1931; Poole, 1934; Templin, 1957) as well as more recent studies (Prather, Hedrick, and Kern, 1975; Arlt and Goodban, 1976). The procedures in these and other studies have been fairly similar. The articulation proficiency of groups of "normal" children has been tested by means of picture-naming tasks in which pictures of familiar objects and animals serve as stimuli for each child to name spontaneously. In each study, the particular set of pictures employed contains all of the sounds of English in initial, medial, and word-final positions (for example, *p*ig, pu*pp*y, cu*p*). Let us review a typical study to see how this information can be used to make a decision about the articulation status of children like Kelly.

Prather and her colleagues (1975) gathered developmental "norms" on seven groups of two- to four-year-old children. The youngest group was approximately twenty-four months old, the next youngest group twenty-eight months old, and so forth to forty-eight months; there were twenty-one children in each group. Figure 7–1 is an adaptation of the articulation data that these researchers obtained. The left end of each horizontal bar in Figure 7–1 indicates the lowest age at which over 50 percent of the children in each group produced the designated sound correctly. The right end of each bar indicates the lowest age at which 90 percent articulated it correctly. Following the work of Sander (1972), Prather and her colleagues suggest that the left end of each sound bar might be viewed as the "age of customary production" for that sound. Also, they suggest that the right end of each sound bar could be called the "outside limit of normalcy" because this is the earliest age at which 90 percent of an age group consistently said the sound correctly. By this definition, children who are not saying a particular sound correctly by the age indicated for the right end of each bar could be considered delayed in the acquisition of that sound. These normative data suggest two generalizations about articulatory development of consonants.[2]

First, speech-sound development is a lengthy process. Articulation proficiency may not be complete until well into the ninth year and even beyond (Sax, 1972). Look at the group of sounds in Figure 7–1 that have arrows on the right side of the bars. Beginning with the

---

[2] We will not discuss vowel development here except to note that children generally acquire all vowels well before they acquire all consonants. Older children who continue to misarticulate vowels generally are severely delayed in speech development.

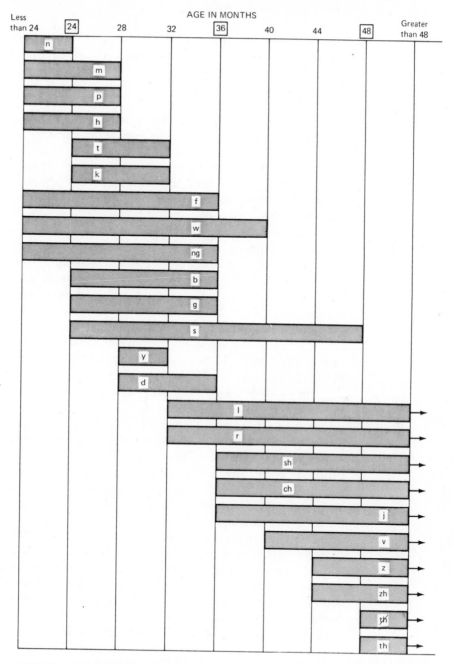

FIGURE 7-1. *Average age estimates (50%) and upper age limits (90%) of customary consonant production. When the percentage correct at 24 months exceeded 70%, the bar extends to "less than 24." When the 90% level was not reached by 48 months, the bar extends to "greater than 48." (After E. Prather, D. Hedrick, and C. Kern, Articulation development in children aged two to four years. Journal of Speech and Hearing Disorders, 40, 179–191, 1975.)*

l sound and on down, notice that even as late as four years of age, ten of the twenty-four consonants remain to be acquired by many children. A second and related point is that some sounds clearly emerge earlier than others. Ninety percent of the twenty-eight-month-old children were making *n, m, p,* and *h* correctly. Contrast this with the group of sounds beginning with *y* down to *th,* none of which were said by 50 percent of an age group *until* the twenty-eight-month-old children.

To return to four-year-old Kelly, how does her articulation proficiency compare to these normative data? A simple way to procede would be to first note the sounds that 90 percent of forty-eight-month-old children say *correctly* (see Figure 7–1). Fourteen consonants meet this criterion: *n, m, p, h, t, k, f, w, ng, b, g, s, y,* and *d.* In fact, the "outside limit" for correct production of half of these sounds occurs well before thirty-six months. Now, looking back to Kelly's error pattern (page 269), we see that she is still making errors (mostly omissions) on each of these fourteen sounds except *h, w,* and *y.* On this basis, we can conclude that Kelly is indeed behind in articulatory development.

Recall that clinicians are also quite interested in the types of errors children make when they misarticulate sounds. Suppose that we show a three-year-old boy a picture of a piece of rope and he says, "That's a *wope.*" Then a year later, when asked to name the same picture he says. "It's a *ɹope*" (that is, a palatalized *r*). His *r* is still incorrect, but relative to a year ago he has made a "better" error. Is this progression, from *w/r* to *ɹ* typical of children on their way to correct production of the *r* sound? Table 7–1 is an adaptation of information of this sort taken from a study of children from Edinburgh, Scotland (Anthony et al., 1971). The procedures were similar to the American studies just discussed. In this study, however, phoneticians transcribed in fine detail each child's response to target phonemes. The reasons for assigning each error to one of the columns scaled on phonetic maturity are based on some technical considerations. What the reader should grasp from Table 7–1 is that acquisition of each speech sound is itself a developmental process, just as is acquisition of the entire inventory of sounds in a language. To reach the adult forms of each of the sounds of a language, children apparently progress through increasingly more mature versions. This is shown in Table 7–1 for the phonemes *v* and *ch* and for the initial cluster *str.*

To summarize, description of the speech sounds that children say as they progress through the early years is called articulatory development. At this time we have agreement on at least the general timetable for children's productive "mastery" of speech sounds. By the age of three to four years, they should be saying all the vowels correctly and articulating enough of the consonants correctly to be quite intelligible to listeners. The nasals (*n, m,* and *ng*) and all the stop-plo-

Table 7–1. PHONETIC DEVELOPMENT OF SPEECH SOUNDS.*

SPEECH SOUND	TEST WORD	ATYPICAL SUBSTITUTIONS	VERY IMMATURE	IMMATURE	ALMOST MATURE	ADULT FORM
v Word-final position	glove	s, p, d	fth, b	(bilabial fricative)	f	v
ch Word-initial position	chimney	k	ş, th, sh, t	tth, ts, ts, ts, ts ts, thtl, thr, stw, stw, stl	t, sh	ch
str Word-initial cluster	string	r, s	t, tw, st, tr, sr, tl	thtl, thr, stw, stw, stl	str, str	str

*See pages 266–268 for an explanation of the phonetic symbols.

After A. Anthony, D. Boyle, T. Ingram, and M. McIsaac, *The Edinburgh Articulation Test.* Edinburgh: Churchill Livingstone, 1971.

sives (*p, b, t, d, k,* and *g*) should be well articulated by this time. There may be substitution or omission errors on some stop-plosives, however, and any type of error on the rest of the consonant sounds. Keep in mind that the normative studies described have yielded group data. They cannot be interpreted to indicate that all children go through the very same sequence of speech development. We have no assurance, for example, that all children must master *l* before they master *r*, or that all children learn all the stop-plosive sounds before they learn all the fricative sounds. An account of the processes underlying the sound-by-sound sequence of emergence in a given child, appears to call for more than descriptive phonetic information. In the next section, we review such information.

Normal Phonological Development

Although to this point we have consistently referred to *articulation* disorders, the title of this chapter uses the term *phonological* disorders for good reason. *Phonology* is the study of how speech sounds function in a language (Hyman, 1975). Just as each language of the world has grammatical rules, it also has rules that pertain to the structure and function of speech sounds. And normal phonological development requires the child to acquire these rules. An example here should be helpful to differentiate the terms *phonological* and *articulatory* when applied to delayed speech.

Suppose a normally developing three-year-old girl says *th* for *s* in words like "*th*ip" (*s*ip) and "*th*oup" (*s*oup), but says *s* for *th* in other words, such as "tee*s*" (tee*th*) and "mou*s*" (mou*th*). That is, she demonstrates that she is able to make both *s* and *th* correctly, but she doesn't say each sound in the right place. Should we claim that this girl makes "articulatory" errors? A more telling description of her errors should account for the fact that she is *consistently* mistaken about when to say *s* versus *th*. To be more formal, we could posit two rules that describe her phonological behavior on these sounds. Her rules are:

> *Rule 1:* If *s* occurs in word-initial position . . . say *th* (*s*ip becomes "*th*ip")
>
> *Rule 2:* If *th* occurs in word-final position . . . say *s* (tee*th* becomes "tee*s*")

In normal speech development, such rule-guided articulatory behavior may last for only a brief period, if at all. However, children who persist in certain types of articulation behaviors are those whom we identify as having a phonological disorder.

A phonological view of speech-sound errors has developed only within the last decade. In fact, many issues remain so controversial that uses for the terms *articulatory* versus *phonological* have not yet been standardized. We prefer to think of phonological as the generic term—all articulatory behavior is ultimately phonological—and hence the choice of title for this chapter.

Before we discuss child phonology, a brief outline of the components of adult phonology is warranted. As in the task of acquiring syntactic and semantic forms, children learn to comprehend and produce the phonological forms of adult language. The phonology of a language is comprised of components and rules in three areas: (1) an inventory of phonemes, (2) distributional rules and sequence rules, and (3) phonetic change rules.

Adult Phonology

Inventory of phonemes: An inventory of phonemes provides the building blocks for a phonological system. Out of all the sounds that he can make, the child learns which sounds occur in adult words. For example, the child who is to speak English must eventually master an inventory of forty-six phonemes, while the Hawaiian child has only thirteen phonemes to learn. Furthermore, sounds that are contrastive within one language may not be contrastive in another. For example, the phonemic system of the Menominee Indians does not have words that depend on a contrast between *p* and *b*. To a Menominee speaker, English words like *p*at and *b*at may sound the same. A Hindi speaker, however, must discriminate among several variants of *p*-like sounds—contrasts that English speakers do not need to learn to discriminate.

Interestingly, sounds that are not frequently used as phonemes in languages of the world are also those that children learn later or tend to misarticulate. Lip sounds such as *p, b, m*, for example, are extremely frequent in languages, whereas *zh* is infrequent. Recall that *p, b*, and *m* are mastered early by English-speaking children while *zh* is mastered later. This parallel between the frequency of usage of a sound in language inventories and its age of mastery in children has led to considerable theorizing. A popular theory is that some sounds are simply *more difficult* than others to discriminate and especially to articulate. As we will discuss later, the "ease of production" theory of speech acquisition has dominated approaches to management programming for children with deviant speech.[3]

Distributional rules and sequence rules: In addition to a sound inventory, each language has rules for the distribution of sounds within words and for permissible sequences of sounds. For example, the *ng* sound cannot occur (that is, is not *distributed*) as the first sound of an English word, nor can the *zh* sound begin an English word or the *h* sound end a word. Moreover, some sequences of phonemes are simply "illegal" in certain positions in words. Consider what happens when there is need to coin a new word, as when a new product requires a catchy name. Which one of the following names for a new wonder deodorant may at least be a candidate ... SHPIP ... GROACH ... ZLART? Among these otherwise worthy candidates, actually only GROACH would be linguistically permissible. English phonology permits beginning a word with *gr*, but it does not allow a word to begin with *shp* or *zl*.

The origin of distributional and sequence rules has to do with historical facts about a language and, to some extent, with certain speech production constraints. The point is that the phonological rules of a language condition our articulatory experience. For example, the sequence *mpst* as in *glimpsed* looks as though it would be difficult to articulate—yet adults have no trouble pronouncing this sequence in word-final position. However, a phonetically simpler but nonpermissible sequence of sounds, such as *tl* or *sr* in word-initial position (for example, *tl*eef, *sr*eep), is vaguely uncomfortable for us to pronounce.

Children are never taught distributional rules or phoneme se-

---

[3] Locke (1972) asked a group of college students to whisper all the English consonants and decide which were "hardest" to say in terms of requiring more muscular effort or tension. Ranking for all sounds was positively correlated with data on percentage of mastery by three-year-olds ($r = .66$). That is, to a certain degree, sounds ranked "hardest" were those least well articulated by three-year-old children—lending some support to an "ease of production" theory. Try this yourself. As you whisper some of the earlier (*p, t, k*) and later (*sh, v, zh*) sounds, do the later sounds seem "harder" to articulate?

quencing rules as, for example, they are taught spelling rules. Yet studies of children and adults indicate that we have knowledge of at least some phonological rules independently of speech. Consider a SCRABBLE player contemplating a tray of letters. Suppose that the only consonants drawn were an R, S, and T. The experienced player might arrange these letters in the tray to visualize permissible consonant combinations for both beginnings and endings of words. What is the only sequence of these letters, R, S, T, that could be used to begin a word? To end a word? STR is the only possible beginning combination, for example, "*str*aw," while RST or RTS are the only permissible final combinations, for example, "bu*rst*," "fli*rts*."

Phonetic change rules: The third component of the adult phonological system that children eventually abstract and acquire is rule-bound phonetic changes in the articulation of phonemes in words. Actually, each phoneme of a language is pronounced slightly differently in words, depending on adjoining sounds, stress patterns, and other factors. These differences too may be described by a set of phonological rules. Some rules cover many individual phonetic situations, while others apply only to a limited number of cases. Here is an illustration of a fairly general rule that changes the duration of vowels—a *vowel-lengthening* rule:

> Say the word *beat* . . . now say the word *bead*. Notice the difference in the length of the vowel in each word? Although the vowel in each word is pronounced as "ee," you should perceive the "ee" in the second word, *bead*, as just a little longer in duration than the "ee" in *beat*. Try the words *mop* . . . and *mob*. Again, the vowel "o" sound should have been just a little longer in the second word, *mob*. What is happening here is that vowel sounds are longer in duration before *voiced* final consonants than when they precede *voiceless* final consonants. Although there is an articulatory basis for understanding this phonetic change rule, vowels do not *have* to function in this way—it's just a regular (rule-bound) characteristic of adult English phonology.

Subtle differences in sound production are not trivial; they are basic to natural-sounding speech. The fact that native speakers of a language "know" such rules becomes evident when we look at second-language learning. The phonetic change rules of a second language are hard to learn, in part because of their complexity, but also because of interference from the rules of the first language. Programming natural-sounding speech for talking computers requires considerable attention to just this type of phonetic detail. The speech of Hal, the fanciful talking computer in the movie classic *2001: A Space Odyssey*, was far more "normal" sounding than what even contemporary speech synthesis programs can generate.

To review, adult phonology consists of (1) an inventory of phonemes, (2) distributional and sequence rules for the occurrence of phonemes in words, and (3) phonetic change rules. The speech of young children sounds childlike because it takes children quite a few years to reach the adult norm in each of these areas. With this background on what children need to acquire, we can proceed to a discussion of child phonology.

Child Phonology

Comprehension: If the infant is to progress to adult phonology, he must first learn to comprehend (discriminate) differences between sounds. Precisely at what age the average child is able to discriminate among all the speech sounds of his language is as yet unknown. Some propose that the child has discriminated all the sounds of a language before he ever begins meaningful speech (Smith, 1973; Stampe, 1973), while others (Olmstead, 1971; Waterson, 1971) assume that such discriminations develop in parallel with speech production. Support for the former position comes from studies that indicate that infants are able to respond differentially to at least some speech sounds (Eimas, 1974). For example, infants of a few weeks can detect the acoustic differences between similar-sounding sounds such as *b* and *g*—as evidenced by a change in their heartrate or sucking response when conditioned to one sound and another is introduced. Many studies indicate, however, that the ability to discriminate behaviorally between like-sounding phonemes in words, for example, "dea*f*" versus "dea*th*," improves with increasing age (Garnica, 1973; Edwards, 1974). Clinically, the child who consistently says "I *f*ink so" instead of "I *th*ink so" may actually fail to discriminate between *f* and *th*, placing the locus of the problem within auditory discrimination, not articulatory production. Such important questions are under study by a number of research groups.

Research is also underway to determine when children comprehend the rules of adult phonology. A few studies indicate that preschool children can choose permissible from nonpermissible words (Messer, 1967; Menyuk, 1968), but more recent evidence disputes earlier claims (Fincham and Mills, 1974). It is hard to construct methodologically "clean" ways to find out what preschool children know about phoneme sequence rules—it's fairly easy with older children and adults (as in our "deodorant" and SCRABBLE illustrations). Over twenty years ago, Whorf (1956) proposed that children know all the phonological rules of a language by six years of age. More contemporary research suggests that, indeed, children *begin* this task quite early, but that some phoneme-sequence and phonetic-change rules may not be acquired until well into grade-school years (Moskowitz, 1973).

Acknowledging that a child learns to comprehend as well as produce the adult phonology has considerable clinical implication. We just mentioned the auditory discrimination question; here is another case example. Suppose that we have a young girl who omits all final stop-consonants. If we ask her to say the words *beat* and *bead,* as in our previous vowel-lengthening rule illustration, her responses to each word will be similar—she says *bee* for both words. However, if we listen very closely, we may observe that she prolongs the "ee" sound in her attempt to say *bead* slightly longer than her "ee" in her attempt at *beat.* Such behavior indicates that this child "knows" the vowel-lengthening rule involved. In linguistic terms, she *marks* the voicing feature of the final consonant *d,* although she does not actually articulate either *d* or *t* in word-final position. The clinician can use these production data to make inferences about a child's comprehension of adult phonology. In fact, just these sorts of appraisal procedures are becoming of interest to clinicians (Bernthal and Weiner, 1976; Page and Lauffer, 1977). The goal is to develop individualized management strategies for a child, based on comprehension development as well as production development.

Production: Earlier we gave examples of the omission, substitution, and distortion errors that occur in normal speech development and persist in some children. For example, we said that a young child might say "He'da pwetty witto goggie" for *He's a pretty little doggie.* A list of articulation errors for this sentence would include *w/r* (*w* for *r* substitution), and *g/d* among others. We now inspect such errors from a different perspective.

Many clinicians have begun to view children's articulation errors as the reflection of phonological tendencies called *natural processes.* Essentially, *natural processes* act to simplify the speech of children learning any language (Oller, 1973). Some developmental psycholinguists propose that we can explain "articulation" errors in child phonology by understanding how natural processes act on adult phonology to simplify speech. A detailed look at theoretical issues underlying this view is beyond our scope. However, let us use the "goggie" example above to illustrate one natural process in child phonology.

A child's utterance of "goggie" for *doggie* is viewed as an instance of an *assimilation process*—in this case, an assimilation involving the consonants *d* and *g.* The assumption is that at an early stage of normal phonological development, children cannot say two different consonants (or vowels) in a word correctly. To say each correctly would tax their phonological system beyond its competence. What happens in this situation is that an assimilation process operates on the two consonants. That is, the child will make one of the consonants either exactly like the other one (for example, "*doddie,*" "*goggie*") or will make one resemble the other in some way (for example, "*dottie,*" "tokkie"). This assimilation of sounds is viewed as *natural* in the sense that the articulatory results follow phonetic logic. Such strategies allow the child to communicate in the face of difficult articulatory demands. *Why* some children persist in such behavior (that is, why they are delayed phonologically) is discussed shortly. The point is that the concept of natural processes promises to become a powerful analytic tool for describing both normal and delayed speech (Shriberg and Kwiatkowski, 1977, 1978, 1979).

Table 7–2 is a list of some natural processes that are well attested in children. The processes are divided into three types, according to the way in which each operates to simplify a child's speech output. The first type reduces the complexity of syllables within a word—by either deleting the final consonant, deleting an unstressed syllable, or deleting a particular sound in a consonant cluster (Branigan, 1976). A second type simplifies by assimilation, as in our "goggie" for *doggie* example. The third group includes many types of phonemic substitutions, wherein presumedly easier sounds to articulate or perceive replace more difficult ones. Just as an approximate developmental schedule for the emergence of speech sounds has been determined (see Figure 7–1), a normal timetable for natural processes such as those listed in Table 7–2 might be possible to assemble.

Recall the list of articulation errors that we presented for Kelly on page 269. Such information is a beginning step to describe her speech. But this list leaves out a substantial amount of error data,

Table 7–2. SOME NATURAL PROCESSES IN NORMAL PHONOLOGICAL DEVELOPMENT.

Natural Phonological Processes	Examples	
	ADULT WORD	*CHILD WORD*
SYLLABLE-SIMPLIFICATION PROCESSES		
Deletion of the final consonant	ba*ll*	"ba___"
Deletion of the unstressed syllable	*a*way	"___way"
Cluster reduction	*st*op	"___top"
ASSIMILATION PROCESSES		
Regressive (backward) assimilation	*doggie*	"goggie"
Progressive (forward) assimilation	tele*vis*ion	"tele*viv*on"
SUBSTITUTION PROCESSES		
Stopping—fricatives are replaced by stop-plosives	*sh*oes	"*t*ood"
Fronting—palatal and velar sounds are replaced by alveolar sounds	ba*k*e	"ba*t*e"

Portions of this table are based on materials discussed in D. Ingram, Phonological disability in children. In D. Crystal and J. Cooper (Eds.), *Studies in Language Disability and Remediation*, Vol. 2. London: Edward Arnold Ltd., 1976.

such as what sound replaced the target sound *in a particular syllable structure* and so forth. The assumption is that Kelly's articulation errors are not random, but rather, that they follow certain universal simplification strategies (natural processes). The speech-language pathologist attempts to analyze delayed speech with the goal of producing a set of descriptive statements (rules) that summarize a child's phonological system. Specifically, a natural-process analysis will seek to answer three questions: (1) Which natural processes are normal for the child's age? (2) Which natural processes are typical of a younger child? (3) Are there any idiosyncratic processes—phonological rules that are not typical of even younger children?

To understand and formulate a management approach for children with delayed phonology requires an assessment of both their comprehension of adult phonology and the simplification strategies that underlie their "articulation" errors. However, such analyses, no matter how linguistically sophisticated, serve only to describe speech behavior. They do not explain *why* some children persist in such behavior. Next, we look at factors that have been causally associated with developmental phonological disorders.

Factors Associated with Delayed Phonological Development

Why do most children learn to articulate clearly, while some children fall markedly behind in speech development or persist in misarticulating one or two sounds? To begin with, normal speech acquisition depends upon two factors: adequate biological development and healthy psychosocial interactions. From infancy on through the preschool years, adequate perceptual-motor development is necessary for a child to attend to and comprehend the structure of speech. This effort is maintained by social consequences; children are motivated to learn to talk clearly because it brings personal satisfaction.

It is useful to restate that the speech errors of children with developmental phonological disorders cannot be traced to major perceptual-motor or psychosocial deficits. But if no major deficit is apparent, what then *is* the cause of developmental speech errors? The array of factors that has been studied as possible causes is impressive. Table 7–3 is a summary of selected findings from over forty years of research. We cannot comment in depth on each of these and other factors that have been studied, but we can underscore some points of information.

Perceptual-Motor Factors. Any neurological deficit during the developmental period can retard speech development. Children who are as severely delayed in intellectual and perceptual-motor development as

Table 7–3. SUMMARY OF RESEARCH ON SELECTED PERCEPTUAL-MOTOR AND PSYCHOSOCIAL FACTORS AND ARTICULATORY PROFICIENCY.

CAUSAL FACTORS	RELATIONSHIP TO ARTICULATORY PROFICIENCY
PERCEPTUAL-MOTOR FACTORS	
Development and physical health	No relationship between such variables as height, weight, age of crawling or walking, childhood diseases, and articulation.
Intelligence	Within the normal range of intelligence, a slight positive relationship between intelligence and articulation.
Auditory discrimination	Considerable evidence that speech defective children score below nondefective children on tests of speech sound discrimination.
General motor skills	No relationship between such variables as speed or accuracy of eye-hand coordination, balance or rhythm, and articulation.
Oral Area	
Oral structures	No difference between superior and inferior (adult) speakers on size or shape of lips, tongue, and hard palate.
Dentition	No sound-specific relationships between dental irregularities and articulation errors (excepting certain types of lisps).
Oral sensation	Some evidence that poor articulators score lower than normals on oral-form recognition tasks.
Oral motor	Some evidence that children with very poor articulation score lower than normals on tests of rapid speech movements.
PSYCHOSOCIAL FACTORS	
Socioeconomic level	Some evidence that proportionally more children from low socioeconomic homes (as indexed by parent occupation) have poor articulation.
Sex and sibling status	Some evidence that girls, first borns, and children with increased spacing between siblings have better articulation at some ages.
Personality and adjustment	Some evidence that children with severe articulation errors have a greater proportion of adjustment and behavioral problems than nondeviant children.

Based in part on materials reviewed in H. Winitz, *Articulatory Acquisition and Behavior*, Chapter 3. Englewood Cliffs, N.J.: Prentice-Hall, Inc., 1969.

to warrant special education services have a high probability of having a phonological disorder. Provided that a child is within the normal range on the developmental milestones, however—such as age of crawling and walking—such factors do not predict rate of speech development or eventual outcome. The same is true of individual differences in intelligence and physique that are within the normal range. These findings should allay the concerns of parents whose child seems somewhat slower than other children in early intellectual or physical performance, or who has frequent childhood illnesses. To a certain extent, speech development appears to be independent of development in other areas. In fact, we find children with developmental speech errors among the healthiest, brightest children in a classroom.

Deficits in speech-sound discrimination abilities have frequently been cited as the cause of speech errors. One task facing the child is to discriminate the sounds used as phonemes in adult phonology. We said earlier that a child who says "I *f*ink so," for example, may not actually discriminate *f* versus *th* in word-initial position. A number of literature reviews indicate that articulatory-deviant children score lower than nondeviant children on conventional tests of auditory discrimination[4] (Winitz, 1969; Powers, 1971). For a tidy causal explanation, we would expect children to have difficulty discriminating the very sounds that they misarticulate. Clinically, however this is not always the case. In fact, conventional tests of auditory discrimination have been criticized on a number of methodological grounds (Beving and Eblen, 1973; Schwartz and Goldman, 1974; Wensman and Scott, 1977); the effects of factors such as attention, motivation, memory, and other cognitive and linguistic variables are difficult to remove from the test results.

Research indicates that the absolute size and shape of the tongue, lips, hard palate, and other structures are not critical factors in developmental speech disorders. For example, having a tongue that is too large or too small relative to the oral cavity may require adjustments for a child in order to achieve good fricative production. But, the adage "speech is in your ears" is pertinent here. Once a child comprehends the sounds of adult phonology, he should be able to find some way of matching his production of a sound to his auditory percept of the sound. Good ventriloquists are able to make radical adjustments within the oral cavity in order to simulate normal-sounding articulation. If you try talking with a pen clenched between your teeth, thus inhibiting jaw movement, you are able to accommodate quite rapidly and produce clearly intelligible speech.

Dentition is another well-studied variable in developmental speech disorders (Shelton et al., 1975). Even children with badly misaligned teeth seem to learn to articulate without distortion. With the exception of certain types of lisps associated with open-bites, deviant dentition does not seem to lead to specific types of articulation errors. Of course, missing those "two front teeth" does cause temporary speech problems for the first-grade age child. Normally, though, children accommodate to the novel space within a few weeks and return to good *s* sounds even before their new incisors are fully in place (see Figure 7–2). A person with a new set of dentures usually requires a

---

[4] Conventional tests of auditory discrimination ask a child to indicate whether two words sound "the same" (for example, *ship-ship*) or "different" (for example, *wed-red, deaf-death*). This format has been used to obtain one total score that reflects the number of correct discriminations across a large number of items (for example, Templin, 1943; Wepman, 1958).

FIGURE 7–2. *A six-year-old girl whose "two front teeth" have fallen out just in time for her school picture. Her s sounds may be distorted for a few weeks.*

similar period of adjustment. Here too, one's ear will guide the tongue in finding a position for good *s* production.

Research on the role of motor and oro-sensory requisites in speech production has found some differences between normal and deviant speakers. There is some evidence that children who are severely delayed in speech development have reduced ability to make rapid speech movements and reduced ability to make oro-sensory judgments. Tests for speech mobility ask a child to perform speech movements rapidly, such as "Say *pa-ta-ka* as fast as you can for five seconds." Oral sensation is tested by asking children to identify and discriminate small geometric shapes placed in the mouth. For this latter task, the information needed to identify the differences among the shapes is assumedly conveyed by touch-pressure receptors located along the surface of the tongue and other structures in the oral cavity.

In summary of the research on perceptual-motor factors, we can only make a probability statement. The average performance of a group of children with *severely* delayed speech is likely to be lower than the average performance of normal children on conventional tests of auditory discrimination, tongue and lip mobility, and oral sensation.

Psychosocial Factors. Several psychosocial variables also have been associated with delayed speech, as summarized in Table 7–3. Studies of the socioeconomic backgrounds of speech-delayed children (controlled for dialectical differences) indicate that proportionally more misarticulating children come from lower socioeconomic backgrounds (Shriberg, 1975b). Fine-grained analyses of the learning environments of children from different socioeconomic strata are needed to interpret such findings. Explanations typically focus on the nature of affec-

283

tive and linguistic stimulation and reinforcement for speech performance. Other studies indicate that first-borns and more widely spaced siblings have better speech. The factor proposed to explain these data is that parents spend more time talking and interacting with children in less dense sibling structures.

The author has proposed a social-learning theory of delayed phonological development that attempts to account for the effects of family structure on the acquisition of specific types of articulatory errors (Shriberg, 1975b). Briefly, our research indicates that if a child with *s*- errors is from a two-child family, the child is far more likely to be the first-born. Children with *r*- errors, however, are far more likely to be later-born children from large families. Observational data will be needed to understand how parent-child and child-child processes might lead to such sound-specific effects.

In summary, there are no certain answers to the question, What causes a developmental phonological disorder? We have seen that normal speech development requires the child to comprehend adult phonology and eventually, to master the articulatory movements that underlie speech production. Several perceptual-motor factors have been associated with severely delayed speech; however, we have only a few clues as to why some children and adults have residual misarticulations on only one or two sounds, such as *s* or *r*. Clinicians continue to refer to people in both these groups as having "articulation" disorders because so much past research and clinical experience are tied to the articulatory level of description. Currently, our best view of developmental phonological disorders is that they result from some disturbance in the learning process. The clinician working with children and adults must look for possible factors associated with this disturbance on an individual basis. The next section considers this assessment process.

ASSESSMENT OF DELAYED PHONOLOGY

Referral for Speech Testing

There are four situations, roughly corresponding to increasing age, when people are referred for speech assessment. The earliest occurs sometime during the preschool period, when a child from two-and-one-half through four years has become of concern to his parents. Before approximately two-and-one-half years, the toddler is stockpiling sounds and words and parents are generally happy with just about anything and everything their child produces. But some preschool children begin to worry their parents because they simply cannot be understood without greater effort—parents find that they must ask the child to repeat and rephrase his utterances. Or perhaps the child's failure to "make himself understood" occasions a passing remark from the pediatrician, a grandparent, or from a well-meaning neighbor. Here are comments mothers have made on our clinic intake form:

> Erica's speech is very difficult to understand. It can be impossible unless the listener has some knowledge of what Erica's trying to get across.

> My husband and I thought maybe Brian has some speech problem. I had a problem with the letter *r* and my husband with the letter *p*. We are bringing Brian to the clinic to have another and maybe more professional opinion.

> This child is intelligent, healthy, normal in all respects except that she is lacking in certain sounds. She substitutes sounds for those she's unable to pronounce. We feel that not being able to be understood, combined with her natural shyness would be a distinct disadvantage to her.

Parents who have children such as those described in these referral comments are well advised to seek an appraisal by a speech-language pathologist. By four years of age, as previously reviewed, children should be saying all the vowels correctly and their remaining consonant errors should not be so severe as to markedly interfere with intelligibility. Because severe delays in speech could be associated with deficits in perceptual-motor or psychosocial factors, scheduling an early appraisal of speech, hearing, and language for a child who is not easy to understand is a wise course of action.

A second point when children may be seen for appraisal is from pre-kindergarten to first-grade age. Most public schools have a screening program for assessing the speech, hearing, and language of all children who are new to the school. In fact, many school districts have extensive "preschool round-up" programs wherein children who are to enter kindergarten are screened at four years of age and even earlier. The goal of such programs is to identify children with special educational needs in order to begin special services as early as possible. If a child has multiple articulation errors or is not readily intelligible when screened at this time, intervention may begin immediately. In cases in which a child has only a few sounds in error, the clinician may decide to defer any management decision until a reappraisal, to be held when a child reaches third or fourth grade.

The third point for assessment, which occurs in the third or possibly fourth grade, involves only certain children. In the early-grade screening the clinician made note of those children who had articulation errors; now the follow-up. Recall that if the outside limits for normal speech acquisition are placed at seven to eight years, third- to fourth-grade children who are to correct on their own all have done so by now. Although there is both clinical and acoustic evidence that comprehension and production development normally continue even beyond this age (Roe and Milisen, 1942; Kent, 1976), most clinicians schedule a routine check to see which children have corrected by this time. Thus, for some children, those with residual errors on only one or two sounds, speech management does not begin until third or fourth grade.

Finally, a fourth point for speech assessment occurs when the person is self-referred or is referred by someone else. In some school systems, for example, there is no routine screening done by clinicians. Teachers are given training to recognize different speech disorders and referrals for speech assessment come from teachers right up through high-school grades (Neal, 1976). Or a child or adult of any age may drop by the school clinician's office, call up the local clinic for an appointment, or simply walk in off the street to discuss his or her speech.

> Emerick and Hatten (1974) describe Bill, a high-school senior, who came to the speech clinician on his own accord for help with what he called "my damn lisp."

> Rita was a college senior who came to our clinic on the recommendation of an internship supervisor. She had been refused an internship in Elementary Education, in part because of her speech. Rita felt that she "talks too fast and piles up on her words." Speech testing indicated that she lateralized *s, z,* and *sh* sounds. Although she demonstrated that she could produce these sounds correctly, she was unable to discriminate between correct and incorrect production.

Rita's experience is not uncommon. At the college level, many teacher training programs require that students "pass" a speech screening. The assumption is that future teachers are expected to present good speech models for students, especially if they plan to teach in elementary grades. In our experience, university students who are informed during a screening that they have clinically notable articulation errors seldom follow through with appraisal appointments at the university speech clinic. Possible reasons for their reluctance to obtain speech services (which are usually provided without cost) are introduced later in a discussion of handicap.

Clinical Assessment of Phonology

Assessment of the child or adult referred for speech testing may take less than an hour, several hours, or several sessions — depending on the needs of the client, the clinical setting, and the theoretical orientation of the clinician. A minimal assessment would include (1) a developmental and social history review, (2) a speech mechanism examination, (3) a hearing screening, (4) a language assessment, and (5) an assessment of phonology by means of one or more test procedures. Additionally, the clinician may administer perceptual-motor tests, such as auditory and oro-sensory discrimination tests. In many clinical settings, other professionals would be available also for intellectual and psychological testing and for testing other extralinguistic areas. Our emphasis here is limited to phonological assessment. The purpose of all testing is *to help make some type of decision;* for phonological assessment, the clinician may test (1) *to compare,* (2) *to predict,* or (3) *to monitor.*

Testing to Compare. The most common purpose for assessing a child's articulation is to compare his or her performance to the performance of children the same age. The question to be answered is, Does this child's phonological development fall within the normal (age-adjusted) range of performance? Normative data that describe when children *comprehend* adult phonology (distributional rules, sequence rules, and so forth) are expected to emerge in the near future. Current clinical procedures, however, are pretty much limited to testing speech *production.* Testing to compare a person's speech production to expected performance for his or her age takes one of three general forms.

First, for initial comparison, the clinician may conduct a *screening* appraisal. For a quick screening, clinicians often have a person say a few words that contain the consonant sounds most often articulated incorrectly: specifically, *s, z, sh, zh, ch, j, v, th,* and *th* (Winitz, 1969). The clinician might ask a child to count to ten to yield productions of *r* (th*r*ee), *f* and *v* (*f*i*v*e), and *s* (*s*ix), among other sounds. Or the clinician might ask a child to name colors, for example, b*l*ue, o*r*ange, and so forth. Using simple words, reading phrases, and a brief sample of spontaneous speech, the competent clinician can usually tell in less than one minute whether a child or adult in fact does have articulation errors that bear a closer look.

The second procedure for comparison testing is undertaken for persons who demonstrate errors in the screening examination. One of several commercially available comparison "tests" is administered, although some clinicians prefer to use their own materials. We have put quotes around the word *tests* because these materials are simply an arrangement of pictures chosen to evoke all the English vowels, diphthongs, and consonants. They are not truly standardized measures. The typical test procedure is to ask a child to say the names of each picture and to score his articulation of the target sounds in each word

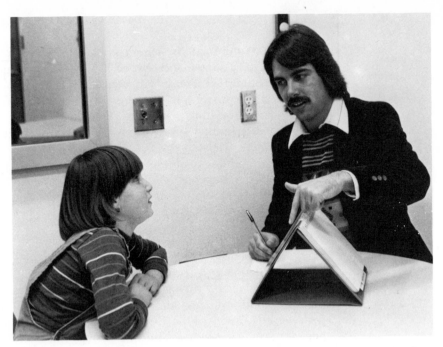

FIGURE 7–3. *A speech-language pathologist administering a comparison phonology test.*

as correct or incorrect[5] (see Figure 7–3). If a child does not seem to know the name of each picture spontaneously, the clinician may need to provide a model of the word. The model of the sound may be sufficient to evoke a correct production, whereas spontaneous picture naming would have yielded an error production. Using such procedures, the clinician can usually obtain a complete inventory of the number of sounds in error in approximately fifteen minutes. The discussion of Kelly's articulation test results (page 269) illustrates how comparison testing is used to determine if articulation is age-appropriate.

The third form of comparison testing includes a variety of analytic procedures that go beyond the routine testing just described (McReynolds and Engmann, 1975; Ingram, 1976; Faircloth and Dickerson, 1977; Shriberg and Kwiatkowski, 1980). The goal is to describe precisely how the person's phonological performance differs from normal. For this purpose, the clinician might obtain a tape recording of the person talking under natural conditions. Although audio and video tapes each have their technical limitations (Shriberg and Kent, in preparation), tapes can be analyzed in several ways. For children with multiple misarticulations, a description of the natural processes that

---

[5] As in all articulation testing, the judgment of correct versus incorrect articulation of a phoneme relies solely on the perceptual standards of the examiner. Teaching clinicians to do this job requires a considerable training effort. This author's students spend "many" hours in a listening-viewing laboratory to gain competence in scoring the tape-recorded articulatory responses of disordered children.

simplify speech output will be useful. Or for a child who has a problem only with the *r* sound, for example, the clinician can determine whether he ever says a correct *r*—and if so, how frequently and in what types of phonetic environments. Detailed analyses provide important data for choosing appropriate management approaches.

Testing to Predict. Prediction of a child's course of articulatory development is a second purpose for testing. Parents want to know if their child will need the services of a clinician, and if services are needed, how long it will take until a child is "corrected." Excellent efforts have been made to develop reliable procedures for predicting articulation improvement (Van Riper and Erickson, 1969; McDonald and McDonald, 1974). Predictive testing has centered on obtaining information of two sorts.

First, the severity of a child's articulatory errors provides predictive information. For example, a *five-year-old* girl who is saying all the vowels correctly but only a few consonants correctly will not acquire the full consonant system for several years. The concept of consistency of error is related here. For example, if an *eight-year-old* boy says *s* correctly 80 percent of the time, the clinician would probably not recommend speech management. The prediction is that this child will go on to self-correct completely. If, however, his *s* is correct only 20 percent of the time in a free-speech sample, the clinician may place the child in a management program on the assumption that the child will not correct without help. In short, the more severe and consistent the problem, the poorer the prognosis for rapid self-correction.

The second predictive consideration is whether a child is *stimulable* on a sound. Even if a child consistently produces a sound incorrectly, he may be able to say it correctly if the clinician provides him with intensive auditory, visual, and tactile stimulation. To test if a child is stimulable on *s*, for example, the clinician might say, "Dave . . . *watch* my mouth closely . . . close your teeth *lightly* together . . . *listen* carefully, . . . now say . . . *ssss*." After several trials of this type of modeling and stimulation, some children will be able to say a correct *s*. If so, the clinician may make the judgment that the child will acquire a correct *s* without management. This latter procedure is very commonly used by school clinicians in early-grade screening.

Unfortunately, neither of these procedures—consistency/severity of error and stimulability—are wholly reliable for predicting which children will and which will not self-correct. Evidently there are other factors related to spontaneous correction. Clinical experience suggests that the more problems the child has in other areas of motor, cognitive, or social development, the higher the probability that the child will not self-correct developmental articulation errors.

Testing to Monitor. Testing to monitor speech progress is done for both the child put on a waiting list for possible management and for the child already on a management program. In each case, the clinician wants to gauge the extent to which articulation is improving from one assessment period to the next. Depending upon the particular phonological behaviors of interest—a particular sound, a class of sounds, a particular speech situation—a clinician may develop individual monitoring tasks to track progress over time. For tracking purposes, administration of an entire comparison test would be inefficient. A child or adult may require monitoring for many months to insure that speech gains are maintained after dismissal from a management program.

To summarize, clinicians have different purposes for assessing phonological behaviors. The most common purpose is to compare a person's articulatory behaviors to "normal" performance. Also, clinicians need to predict what changes in articulatory behavior may occur with and without management, and to monitor progress over time. Future developments in phonological testing will undoubtedly include more formalized analysis procedures for assessing what the child "knows" about adult phonology as well as for more telling analysis of what the child produces. We anticipate increased use of mini-computors housed within the clinical setting to accomplish these complex and time-consuming analyses.

Prevalence of Delayed Phonology

The prevalence of children who may be called "speech handicapped" because of developmental errors has been surveyed periodically for over sixty years (Blanton, 1916). The most recent large-scale study was undertaken in the late 1960s (Hull et al., 1971). Hull and his colleagues sent a fleet of specially equipped buses to carefully selected cities across the nation. Trained examiners used two procedures to evaluate articulation in school-age children: a picture-naming task, for testing a child's articulation of each sound; and a rating on a brief speech sample. For the latter task, adult General-American speech was used as the reference standard for ratings of "acceptable articulation," "moderately deviant," or "extremely deviant." The study found that 2 *percent* of the children in the United States may be considered to have "extremely deviant" articulation.

This latest figure compares well with past findings. Approximately twenty to thirty children out of every thousand children in the elementary school have delayed phonological development. Moreover, we know that there is another group of children who may misarticulate only one or two sounds (residual speech errors) up to and beyond third grade. Are *they* handicapped too? After a discussion of management approaches, we will be in a good position to return to this question.

MANAGEMENT OF DELAYED PHONOLOGY

Children with Delayed Speech

Choice of Management Approach. Children with severely delayed speech are first seen by a clinician in preschool years or early elementary school. Assessment might indicate that the speech delay is associated with significant deficits in other areas of functioning—deficits that require special educational services. Alternately, in the absence of associated problems, the child may be classified as having a *developmental* phonological disorder. We will sketch a picture of what lies ahead for the latter child. For both the child with delayed speech and the child or adult with only residual speech errors, the recommended management approach will depend on many factors.

One frequent management recommendation, particularly for the very young child who has had limited opportunities to be with other children, is for the child to attend a normal preschool program. We have seen children with mild to moderately delayed speech make remarkable gains in speech development in such environments. Sensitive preschool teachers provide socialization and communication experiences that encourage children to listen carefully and talk comfortably. For some children, this experience may be entirely sufficient.

A second management possibility—more suited for the young child with severely delayed speech—is enrollment in a special preschool program, one that emphasizes oral language development (Shriberg and Kwiatkowski, 1977). Programs that are staffed by child development and communication disorders specialists are becoming increasingly more prevalent in clinics and schools across the United States. Many programs emphasize parental involvement, wherein parents are full participants in the speech and language stimulation activities.

A third possibility is for the preschool or school-age child to participate in group or individual work that is directly focused on modification of phonological behaviors. This management approach is most often provided by an itinerant speech-language pathologist, a person who travels among schools providing individual or group management on a weekly schedule.

The quality and frequency of service available to children with phonological problems depends on philosophical and administrative issues. Some children will be able to receive intensive daily help; for others, only limited services will be available within the school system. Furthermore, some clinicians will limit their management activities to the confines of "the speech room," while others will reach out more into the classroom, the home, and the community. The clinician must assess each child's needs, determine what resources are available to meet those needs, and choose a course of management. Regardless of the content of a management program, the sequence of objectives can be divided into two successive stages of learning: (1) *response development,* and (2) *transfer of training.*

Response Development.   The response development stage of management focuses on teaching the child new phonological behaviors. By definition, the child with delayed speech will have errors on a number of sounds. If we view a child as having "articulatory" problems with each error sound—that is, the child needs to learn "how to say" sounds—programming will concentrate on speech production. If, however, these errors are seen as the output of phonological rules that differ from adult phonology, then programming will focus on teaching "when to say" each sound. Let us look briefly at each of these alternative approaches to response development.

The clinician who takes an essentially articulatory view of a child's errors starts with a list of errors. For example, Joanne, a four-year, eight-month-old child seen at our clinic, had the following articulation responses to a three-position, picture-naming task:

	INITIAL POSITION	MEDIAL POSITION	FINAL POSITION
CORRECT PRODUCTIONS	p, b, m, t, d, n, h	m, b, h	m
INCORRECT PRODUCTIONS			
Omissions	w, y, r, l	p, t, d, k, g, f, th, s, z, sh, zh, ch, j, w, y, r, n, ng	p, b, t, d, k, g, t, v, th, s, z, sh, zh, ch, j, r, l, n, ng
Substitutions	t/k, b/g, t/f, t/th, t/sh, t/ch, b/v, d/th, d/j	w/l	(none)
Distortions	z	(none)	(none)

At first sight, this list of errors is overwhelming. Of the twenty-five English consonants, Joanne misarticulated twenty (plus many vowel sounds). Where should the clinician begin with this severely involved child? Consider the following eight possible rationales for choosing a management sequence; each rationale suggests a specific sequence, as listed to the right:

RATIONALE	SEQUENCE OF RESPONSE DEVELOPMENT FOR JOANNE'S ERRORS
FOLLOW THE NORMAL DEVELOPMENTAL SCHEDULE	
(1) Teach individual sounds in the order that they normally emerge.	n, m, p, b, t, k, f, etc.
(2) Teach sound classes in the order that they normally emerge: nasals, stop-plosives, fricatives, affricates, glides.	n, m, ng; p, t, k, b, d, g; etc.
OBTAIN EARLY PERSONAL SUCCESS	
(3) Teach sound most important to child or parents first, for example, sound in child's first or last name, etc.	j ("Joanne"), etc.
(4) Teach most visible sounds first; they are easiest to learn because child can see how they are made.	m, p, f, w (all lip sounds), etc.
(5) Teach error sound that child produces correctly most often first; child will progress faster on such sounds.	For Joanne, this would be one of the nasals or stop-plosives.
CONSIDER THE IMPACT ON INTELLIGIBILITY AND PERCEIVED DEVIANCE	
(6) Correct omissions first, then substitutions, then distortions; this follows order of intelligibility and social impact.	Progress *across* Joanne's errors by *rows;* all her omission errors. then all her substitution errors, etc.
(7) Correct all initial position errors first, then medial and final; this follows order of impact.	Progress *down* Joanne's errors by *columns;* all her initial position errors, then all her medial position errors, etc.
(8) Correct sounds that occur most frequently in children's speech first; they have more significant impact than less frequent sounds.	n, r, t, s, d, etc. (n is the most frequent consonant, then t, etc. Based on Carterette and Jones (1974)

Each of these eight approaches has something to recommend it and has its advocates among clinicians. Although some combination of these considerations is usually adopted, the most common approach is to teach the normal development schedule (1 and 2). The assumption that sounds like *p, b,* and *m* are "easier" to produce than sounds like *s, r,* or *l* has strong intuitive appeal. Furthermore, for a child as young as Joanne (four years, eight months), she may still acquire the late-emerging sounds on her own. If speech-sound development is simply a reflection of increasing fine-motor control, such a view is certainly defensible; earlier we presented alternative views.

Whatever sequence is chosen for correcting the misarticulations of children like Joanne, the procedures used for response development will include some common components. The clinician will focus on teaching the child the tactile, auditory, and visual cues for production of each sound. In some cases, the clinician may deem it necessary to begin by familiarizing the child with the "speech helpers"—the movements of the tongue and lips as they are used to make speech sounds. Discrimination activities, in an attractive format suited to the age of the child, are created to help the child to differentiate correct from incorrect speech behaviors. The clinician will use combinations of instructions and models of correct behavior to bring the child to the point where target sounds are consistently produced correctly in syllables or words. Each sound is individually taken through a course of response development until ready for transfer of training procedures. Following is the response development procedure written in our clinic for Joanne:

JOANNE: 4 YEARS, 8 MONTHS

Teaching Objective: To increase speech intelligibility through development of the fricative sound class: *sh* was chosen as the target sound because it was the only fricative on which Joanne was stimulable for correct production. (Note the combination of considerations that led to choosing the *sh* sound to work with first.)

Goal: For Joanne to produce *sh* correctly in consonant-vowel and vowel-consonant syllables 80 percent of the time following a clinician model.

Procedure: The consonant and the vowel portions of each syllable (as listed) were prolonged and attempts were made to bring the two sounds together. Blocks or hand movements were paired with sounds to illustrate the combining process. Stimuli were presented twice. Each correct production was rewarded with a check on a chart. After six checks were accumulated Joanne received a sticker to paste on a card to take home.

There are a rich variety of response development approaches for children with delayed speech. In particular, production approaches emphasizing sound features (frication, voicing) have become of interest to clinicians (Costello and Onstine, 1976; Rosenwinkel, Paden, and Hodson, 1976; Weiner and Bankson, 1978).

An alternative approach to response development, as indicated previously, looks beyond the sounds or features that are in error. The clinician attempts to understand the common phonological processes that underlie the child's production errors. Once these processes are understood, the clinician begins systematic teaching to change the child's phonological system.

The following excerpt from a clinical report describes one procedure used for a child with final consonant deletions. Note that the emphasis is on the concept (rule) of ending words with the correct sound, as opposed to focusing on the articulatory components of the individual sounds in error:

BRETT: 4 YEARS, 5 MONTHS

Teaching Objective: To teach Brett consistent use of *m, n, p, t, s,* and *z* at the ends of words. (Brett had articulated each of these sounds correctly at least three times during the articulation assessment although they were also used to replace other sounds.)

Procedure: Word and phrase drills were used. Pictures of the following words were obtained: ca*t*, ca*p*, ca*n;* mo*m*, mo*p;* no*te*, no*se;* comb, coa*t,* co*ne* (additional sets were included later). Teaching steps for these minimal-contrast words included playing a matching game. Brett was given two or three cards to match (for example, coa*t*, co*mb*, and co*ne*); to do so, he had to say each word correctly, which meant inserting the final sound:

(a) at the word level
(b) in the phrase "Give me _____ ."
(c) in the expanded phrase "I want the _____ now."

Token reinforcement was given during each articulation setting (Brett went on to become 90 to 95 percent successful at all three levels of this task.)

Phonological approaches such as above stress "when to say" sounds. They help the child with delayed speech to reorganize his phonological system. Their potential for helping a child to make rapid improvement in speech development is exciting (for example, see Hodson, 1977).

A clear division between the two approaches to response development that we have presented — the articulatory approach and the phonological approach — is not always apparent. Some children seem to require intensive work on sound production, while others appear to "have" most of the sounds, but need to discriminate when to use them. Most children require some work in both areas.

Transfer of Training. Systematic programming for transferring newly developed phonological behaviors to more complex *linguistic* and *psychosocial* environments is required in the transfer of training for the child with delayed speech. Linguistically, the clinician will have the child progress from using the phonological behavior in words, then in phrases, then in sentences, and finally in normal spontaneous speech. Considerations in arranging for this progression take into account the type of phonetic and phonological information about adult phonology that we have discussed. The more the sequence of practice materials is in accord with phonetic principles and knowledge of normal phonological development, the more likely the child will progress rapidly and successfully. For example, consider a child who has just learned to say each final consonant correctly in a list of twenty monosyllabic words. We would not expect the child to perform as well if each word was now to be said in a different sentence. A better intermediate step would be to have the child say the words in a simple repetitive carrier phrase, such as *give me the* book, *give me the* bat, *give me the* map, etc. This technique was illustrated previously in the program for Brett.

Psychosocial programming attempts to transfer the target phonological behavior to normal communication environments outside of the clinic. Once the child has transferred phonological learning to more complex linguistic stimuli, we can expect some generalization to outside settings. To ensure that the child does "carry-over" the correct behaviors, however, clinicians will provide the child with extensive experience in self-monitoring his behavior in the classroom, on the playground, at the supper table, and so forth. And when the child is ready for it the clinician may set up simulations of stressful situations, such as reading aloud in front of a small audience.

Finally, we know that with the best of clinical programming and child motivation, regressions do occur. The responsible clinician will also try to program for a gradual weaning of the child from the clinical situation, while still monitoring to be sure that gains are maintained. The schedule of management sessions will gradually be decreased until a child is on his own. Particularly for this latter phase of transfer of training as well as for the earlier transfer phase, recruitment of parents, teachers, and others for maintenance monitoring is efficient and effective. The clinician may drop by the child's class or check with the teacher periodically.

Children with Residual Speech Errors

Choice of Management Approach. The child with residual errors on only one or two sounds is not likely to have been referred to a speech-language pathologist during preschool years. Children with distortion errors on *s* or *r* or perhaps on a few other sounds may have been identified by the school clinician in an early screening. As discussed earlier, services for such children may be deferred until third or fourth grade if provided at all.

During the past decade, significant advances have been made in management programs for people with residual speech errors. In comparison with the problems presented by the younger child with delayed speech, the management task for this group can be focused directly on articulation change. Accordingly, procedures that maximize practice of articulatory behaviors are usually warranted. In the clinical sense, however, the individual abilities and interests of each child or adult still figure prominently in the selection and day-to-day implementation of articulation management programs. People of all ages require differing measures of psychological support as they proceed through an intensive program of learning tasks. Gerber (1977), in a review of just these issues, notes:

> Though certain aspects of articulation therapy may be improved through the use of some preconstructed program material and trained paraprofessionals, the knowledge, skill, and sensitivity of the professional clinician remain as the indispensable core of the process of articulation modification.

Response Development. For people who cannot articulate the target phoneme correctly, even with intensive stimulation, the clinician needs to find ways to develop the correct articulatory behavior. Simply modeling the correct sound may not be sufficient to evoke a close approximation to the target sound. Moreover, it is difficult to describe how sounds such as *s* and *r* are made (the tongue postures are not visible) or to actually assist a child in positioning his tongue correctly for these sounds. Effective programming to develop the child's perception of movements underlying correct production requires thorough knowledge of the phonetics of speech and programming principles.

One example of a program that has been used successfully for teaching the *er* sound[6] to children who have not been able to learn how to produce it by other means is presented in Table 7–4. In a series of steps, the child is taken through the several pre-skills that are necessary for success at the final step. To produce *er*, a child needs to know where his tongue tip is and to be able to lift it to the alveolar ridge (Steps 1 to 4 in Table 7–4). He needs to be able to sustain phonation for five seconds while moving the tongue tip independently of the jaw (Steps 5 to 7). The last step (Step 8) is to have the child sustain phonation and drag his tongue along the roof of his mouth. If the instructions have been followed correctly, a good *er* is usually evoked by this program in less than six minutes. Notice that the clinician has never modeled the *er* sound. In fact, we suspect that as soon as the child thinks he is trying to say *er*, he connects with his old habitual error pattern — so the program tries to bypass this potential interference. Notice too, that all along the way, the child has been rewarded for behaviors that he "can-do" — a fundamental programming principle. If the child cannot easily meet criteria on any of the steps, the clinician's job is to develop *branching* steps. Branching steps are smaller instructional modules that teach the child to master individual perceptual-motor steps within the eight-step program. Once an *er* sound is evoked consistently, clinicians can use a variety of procedures to teach the use of the sound in syllables and proceed with some transfer activities.

If a child *can* say an error sound correctly in at least one word, how-

[6] The International Phonetic Alphabet symbol for the *er* sound (as in b*ir*d) is [ɝ].

Table 7-4 A PROGRAM FOR TEACHING PRODUCTION OF THE ER /ɝ/ SOUND.

GOAL (PHASE)	STEP	INSTRUCTION (ANTECEDENT EVENT)	RESPONSE DEFINITION	REINFORCEMENT (SUBSEQUENT EVENT)	TERMINATION CRITERIA	DATA (✔ 0) TRIALS 1	2	3	4	5
I. PART NAMES AND BASIC MOBILITY	1.	"Stick your tongue out." (Model)	Tongue extended beyond lips.	"Good" — "Put it back in" — "Again" or "Not quite" — and reinstruct.	3 consecutive times					
	2.	"Stick your tongue out and touch the tip with your finger." (Model)	Touches very tip of tongue with index finger.	Same as above.	3 consecutive times					
	3.	"Put your finger on the bumpy place right behind your top teeth." (Model)	Finger placed on alveolar ridge at midline. Have child lower jaw while retaining finger contact so clinician can confirm.	"Good" — "Again" or "Not quite" and reinstruct.	3 consecutive times					
	4.	"Now, put the tip of your tongue 'lightly' on that bumpy place." (Model)	Very tip of tongue placed lightly on alveolar ridge at midline. Have child raise and lower jaw while retaining tongue contact to confirm position.	Same as above.	3 consecutive times					
II. TONGUE CONTROL AND SUSTAINED PHONATION	5.	"Now, put your tongue tip there again, and say /l/." (2 second model)	Produces /l/ for 2 seconds. Make sure he does not say [ʌl]	"Good" — "Again" or "Not quite" and reinstruct. "Make sure your tongue is there before you turn on your voice box."	3 consecutive times					

		Produces /l/ (not [ʌl]) for 2 seconds.	"Good" and hold up finger for next response or reinstruct	3 consecutive times
6.	"Say /l/ each time I hold up my finger." (clinician holds up finger)	Produces /l/ (not [ʌl]) for 2 seconds.	"Good" and hold up finger for next response or reinstruct	3 consecutive times
7.	"Now say /l/ for as long as I hold my finger up, like this: (hold up finger and model for 5 seconds) Ready, – go." (hold up finger for 5 seconds)	Produces a 5 second /l/ with no phonation breaks and minimum tongue movements.	Same as above.	5 consecutive times
III. EVOKE /ɝ/				
8a.	"Say a long /l/ but this time as you're saying it, drag the tip of your tongue slowly back along the roof of your mouth – so far back that you have to drop it." Accompany instructions with hand gesture of moving fingertips back slowly, palm up.	Tongue tip is dragged back slowly sustaining phonation until tip has to drop and a good /ɝ/ is heard. Jaw should not drop during this movement.	"Good, that's the sound I want – exactly like that again." or "Not quite" and reinstruct. If criterion is not met because child is not moving tongue back correctly, go to Step 8b.	5 consecutive times
8b. B R A N C H	"Let's practice pulling the tip of your tongue back across the roof of your mouth. Pretend you are licking whipped cream off the roof of your mouth. Do it without making any sound."	Child's report is only available response.	"Did you drag the tip of your tongue slowly back along the top of your mouth? – pressed lightly? – touching until you have to drop it?" "Like this." Use hand cues demonstrating each of the above.	Return to Step 8a when child indicates he has it.

From L. Shriberg. A response evocation program for /ɝ/. *Journal of Speech and Hearing Disorders, 40*, 92–105, 1975.

ever, the clinician does not need to teach the child how to say the sound as above. Many response development approaches have been developed that utilize a "keyword" (Janzen and Shriberg, 1977). One procedure, called the paired stimuli technique (Irwin and Weston, 1975), *pairs* a word in which a sound *is* said correctly with a succession of words in which the child *does not* say the target sound correctly. For example, if the child can say a good *s* in the word "mouse" reliably, the paired stimuli technique capitalizes on this by pairing "mou*s*e" with other *s*-words; a sample training session might progress as follows:

CLINICIAN:	(pointing to picture of a mouse)	"Say this"
CHILD:		"mou*s*e"
CLINICIAN:	(judges the *s* to be socially acceptable)	"Good" (or the clinician presents a token or some sort of reinforcer)
	(quickly points to a picture of a nurse)	"Say this"
CHILD:		"nur*th*"
CLINICIAN:	(judges *s* unacceptable)	(says nothing)
	(points to picture of mouse again)	"Say this"
CHILD:		"mou*s*e"
CLINICIAN:	(judges the *s* to be socially acceptable)	"Good"
	(quickly points to picture of a goose)	"Say this"
CHILD:		"goo*s*e"
CLINICIAN:	(judges *s* acceptable)	"Good"

This type of training would go on until the child learns to say a correct *s* in a set of *training* words. In practice, children learn to go through the pictures without the clinician's prompts. It is quite intriguing to watch a child gradually "get it" in terms of learning to use the same articulatory behaviors (the *correct s*) in both words.

Transfer of Training. The procedures here are the same in principle as those discussed for multiple articulation errors. However, because there may be only one or two corrected sounds to habituate in conversational speech, the entire management process is generally shorter. Again, parents and teachers are usually recruited to help a child monitor his speech under differing conditions. Determining how long monitoring sessions should last each day is a critical consideration in programming. Asking too much of a child too soon can kill progress. Management outcomes are determined in great part by motivational components. The clinician who is insensitive to individual differences in this area may find that his clients simply fail to maintain the newly learned "good speech."

Prognosis

What happens to children with articulation errors who do *not* receive speech management? And for those who do receive speech services, what percentage are corrected and how long does it usually take? These are questions asked by parents, teachers, potential clients, and of course, by state and federal agencies as they deliberate the allocation of funds for speech services. Let us first consider children who do not receive speech services.

The child with truly *developmental* phonological errors does have a fairly good chance of eventually self-correcting without therapy services (Sax, 1972; Huskey et al., 1973; Bralley and Stoudt, 1977). However, research has simply failed to produce a predictive instrument that can tell parents and clinicians what the prognosis is for a *given* child. The most general prognostic statement we can make for the untreated child with severely delayed articulation is that he will take longer than his peers to acquire all the sounds. On this issue, we fully support some principles developed by Johnson (1967) in his cogent discussion of the "clinical point of view in education." Johnson suggests that the prognosis for children with deviant articulation is heavily influenced by the nature of early classroom experiences. The enriched speech environments provided in favorable surroundings, as opposed to unhappy early education, promote the desire for good speech. It is not simply because a child "gets older" that he self-corrects articulation errors; rather, the *desire* to communicate and *rewarded performance* appear to be the basic keys to self-improved speech.

The prognosis for children who *are* provided with speech therapy is again favorable. Beyond this generalization, however, we can only reiterate that variance in child, clinician, and setting currently defies straight-forward prognostic power. Despite the best efforts of qualified clinicians, some children just cannot seem to learn to articulate a sound correctly—or they cannot learn to transfer a corrected sound to everyday speech.

Do people with residual speech errors have an educational, social, or vocational handicap? Should schools provide speech services to a child with, for example, a slight lisp? As we stated at the outset of this chapter, such questions have become of serious concern. We will inspect the issues carefully and conclude with our point of view.

Educational Considerations. To begin with, *handicap* refers to a condition in which there is a "limitation" in functioning. Viewed this way, the young child whose speech is difficult to understand is readily defined as handicapped. During preschool years, parents may find many ways to support the child and provide for normal development and socialization. But when the child moves out of the protective family orbit and into the wider social world of the street, playground, and classroom, the handicap of delayed speech becomes more costly. Although the evidence is not certain, delayed phonological development may underlie difficulties in learning to read and other cognitive tasks (Winitz, 1969; Kavanagh and Mattingly, 1972; Locke and Kutz, 1975). For the child with severely delayed speech there is little debate. Because delayed speech handicaps the child in academic areas and in social development, speech services should be provided. Indeed, under the guidelines of Public Law 94–142, the Education of All Handicapped Children Act, schools are obligated to provide services for such children.

Social Acceptance Considerations. The debate begins when we shift from the obvious needs of the child with delayed speech development to consider children and adults with only one or two sounds in error. Is such behavior handicapping? In fact, examples of social and personal penalties because of misarticulations can be drawn from many sources.

Personally, we have heard our clients' speech described by others as "babyish," "mushy," "sloppy," "lazy," and "ridiculous." Keep in mind that such perceptions were in reaction to residual articulation errors on only a few sounds. In fact, Kleffner (1952) found that fourth-grade children react unfavorably to children who have an articulation error on only one frequently occurring speech sound. Emerick and Hatten (1974) cite the example of Glen, a fifth grader who distorted only the *l* and *r* sounds. When asked if anyone had ever mentioned his speech to him, he replied that some children had called him "Elmer Fudd." This example is particularly revealing because it touches on the issue of unfavorable speech stereotypes in the media. Elmer Fudd's *w/r* errors were associated with his rather ineffective personality. And, Sylvester the Cat and Daffy Duck, both of whom were drawn to be likable "bad guys," had pronounced *s* distortions.

Gill (1974) interviewed a group of elementary-school children with articulation disorders of varying degrees of severity to get some firsthand impressions of how young children with articulation errors experience their early academic and social world. The following edited transcript illustrates one girl's responses to some of Gill's questions:

MELANIE: GRADE 4

INTERVIEWER: Does your speech bother your mom and dad?

CHILD: No.

INTERVIEWER: No—do they ever say anything to you about it?

CHILD: They correct me.

INTERVIEWER: Does anyone ever call you names because you've got an r that's not quite right?

CHILD: No.

INTERVIEWER: If your r is not quite right, is it OK with you?

CHILD: Sometimes I get mad.

INTERVIEWER: Do you—at yourself—because you can't say it?

CHILD: Uhuh.

INTERVIEWER: Does it [the r error] make any difference to you?

CHILD: Um—not when I'm playing.

INTERVIEWER: When does it make the *most* difference to you?

CHILD: When I'm reading aloud.

Nearly all children in this study, many of whom had only one or two sounds in error, could recount negative experiences in speech situations. Most of these children expressed a marked dislike for reading aloud in front of the class (see Figure 7–4). One child with a defective r said: "I see the r, especially in the middle of the word, and get afraid." Virtually all children in this study said that their parents try to help them with their speech sounds. In the words of one child, "sometimes that's good and sometimes that's bad!"

Vocational Considerations.   Acceptance of articulation differences depends upon the communication setting. Colloquial speech situations tolerate a certain imprecision that may be unacceptable in vocational situations. People whose work requires extensive public speaking may find that minor articulation errors can affect intelligibility or detract from the speaker's message. Some vocations, such as dispatchers and air-traffic controllers, call for precise articulation. In most settings, though, it is more the impressions that articulation errors create in the minds of others that is critical.

The results of two studies are pertinent here. Mowrer (1974) investigated whether the presence of slight and pronounced lisps in adult male speakers would affect businessmen's ratings of these speakers. Mowrer found that even the presence of a slight dentalized lisp (s) in adult males was associated with lowered ratings on estimates of the speaker's intelligence, speaking ability, education, masculinity, and social appeal. Silverman (1976) reports similar effects for a female speaker. Listeners who heard tapes of the speaker simulating a moderate lateral lisp (s) rated her more negatively on thirty-seven out of

FIGURE 7-4. *Some children have an early and persistent fear of speaking in front of a group. Young children with articulation errors may avoid "show and tell" presentations. Later, they may fear reading out loud in front of the class. (Courtesy of Dick Swift, Foto.)*

forty-nine personality attributes than when speaking without the lisp. Importantly, business administration students rated her as "nonhandicapped" in the no-lisp condition and as "handicapped" in the lisp condition.

Consistent with the definition of handicap presented on page 302, however, the degree of handicap posed by articulation errors is relative to a person's assets. We can cite examples of celebrities, political figures, and even well-known television newspersons who have slight and even pronounced articulation errors. Evidently, such errors have not "stood in the way of success." In fact, some well-known people are best characterized by a speech trademark—recall Humphrey Bogart's exquisite *s* distortion, "Play it again, Sam."

A Point of View.   Let us now deal directly with the issue: Is it ethically and financially defensible for school systems to provide speech therapy services for all elementary school children who misarticulate only one or two speech sounds? Clinicians disagree among themselves on the correct answer to this question—we believe that provision of services to these children is quite justifiable.

Our position is based on two assumptions. First, we assume that

304

a developmental articulation error is no less "handicapping" in and of itself than a similar error due to structural or motor deficits. That is, classificatory labels such as "cleft palate" and "dysarthria" tell us little about either the severity of the speech disability or the extent to which the disability is a handicap. In fact, acceptance of a speaker's mis-articulations may even slightly favor the person who presents some obvious physical "reason" for the misarticulation.

Second, we assume that the basic problem is one of technology and economics. If rapid and effective programs for correction of even minor articulation differences were available in the schools, parents would surely want their children to receive those services. Because of the new federal laws, public-school clinicians have found themselves under pressure to provide services for severely involved children— children who were not previously seen in the schools. And in contrast to the needs of these multiply handicapped children, the child with a distorted *r* or *s* just seems to be less of a priority. But, we can't define away a problem simply by realigning caseload priorities.

The need, then, is for effective and efficient articulation manage-ment programs—programs that can be administered by well-trained paraprofessionals (Galloway and Blue, 1975; Scalero and Eskenazi, 1976), a child's parents (Costello and Bosler, 1976), and even other school children (Evans, 1974; Groher, 1976). As in other areas of health-care services, the use of paraprofessionals for a variety of tasks in com-munication disorders appears to be quite successful. But we do have one final comment on who should work with children with articulation er-rors and at what age children should be scheduled for therapy.

Although there is a need for predictive instruments that can identify those children who will outgrow their errors by third or fourth grade, *most* children *do* self-correct. Considering also that chil-dren may progress faster in a management program begun in third grade than one started earlier (Diedrich, 1975), we think that children with errors on only a few sounds should not be given services until that age. A critical proviso for this point of view, however, is that chil-dren should have a competent screening in early grades. If a kinder-garten or first-grade child feels handicapped *in any way* by speech er-rors, management services should begin then rather than later. It may be that the management program for such a child stresses inter-personal growth as much or more than articulation modification. Fur-thermore, we submit that speech-language pathologists, not para-professionals, are best equipped to conduct such early screenings for just this reason. That is, we should screen to detect children with "communication" problems, not articulation problems. As we look at our clients as individuals, as people rather than as "artic" cases, we find strong commitment to this point of view.

REFERENCES ANTHONY, A., BOYLE, D., INGRAM, T., and McISSAC, M., *The Edinburgh Articulation Test.* Edinburgh: Churchill Livingstone (1971).

ARLT, P., and GOODBAN, M., A comparative study of articulation acquisition as based on a study of 240 normals, aged three to six. *Language, Speech and Hearing Services in Schools,* 7, 173–180 (1976).

BERNTHAL, J., and WEINER, F., A reexamination of the sound omission: Preliminary considerations. *Journal of Childhood Communication Disorders,* 1, 132–138 (1976).

BEVING, B., and EBLEN, R., "Same" and "different" concepts and children's performance on speech sound discrimination. *Journal of Speech and Hearing Research,* 16, 513–517 (1973).

BLANTON, S., A survey of speech defects. *Journal of Educational Psychology,* 7, 591–592 (1916).

BRALLEY, R., and STOUDT, R., A five-year longitudinal study of development of articulation proficiency in elementary school children. *Language, Speech and Hearing Services in Schools,* 8, 176–180 (1977).

BRANIGAN, G., Syllabic structure and the acquisition of consonants: The great conspiracy in word formation. *Journal of Psycholinguistic Research,* 5, 117–133 (1976).

CARTERETTE, E., and JONES, M., *Informal Speech: Alphabetic and Phonemic Texts with Statistical Analyses and Tables.* Berkeley: University of California Press (1974).

COSTELLO, J., and BOSLER, S., Generalization and articulation instruction. *Journal of Speech and Hearing Disorders,* 41, 359–373 (1976).

COSTELLO, J., and ONSTINE, J., The modification of multiple articulation errors based on distinctive feature theory. *Journal of Speech and Hearing Disorders,* 41, 199–215 (1976).

DIEDRICH, W., Some factors which differentiate articulation learning. Paper presented to the Annual Convention of the American Speech and Hearing Association, Washington, D.C. (1975).

EDWARDS, M., Perception and production in child phonology: The testing of four hypotheses. *Journal of Child Language,* 1, 205–219 (1974).

EIMAS, P., Linguistic processing of speech by young infants. In R. Schiefelbusch and L. Lloyd (Eds.), *Language Perspectives—Acquisition, Retardation, and Intervention.* Baltimore: University Park Press (1974).

EMERICK, L., and HATTEN, J., *Diagnosis and Evaluation in Speech Pathology.* Englewood Cliffs, N.J.: Prentice-Hall (1974).

EVANS, C., The effectiveness of the S-PACK when administered by 6th-grade children to primary-grade children. *Language, Speech and Hearing Services in Schools,* 5, 85–90 (1974).

FAIRCLOTH, M., and DICKERSON, M., Conversational speech analysis. Short Course presented to the Annual Convention of the American Speech and Hearing Association, Chicago (1977).

FINCHAM, S., and MILLS, J., Implicit phonological rules in children: An examination of Messer's and Menyuk's work. *The Journal of Psychology,* 88, 175–189 (1974).

GALLOWAY, H., and BLUE, C., Paraprofessional personnel in articulation therapy. *Language, Speech and Hearing Services in Schools,* 6, 125–130 (1975).

GARNICA, O., The development of phonemic speech perception. In T. Moore (Ed.), *Cognitive Development and the Acquisition of Language.* New York: Academic Press (1973).

306

GERBER, A., Programming for articulation modification. *Journal of Speech and Hearing Disorders,* 42, 29–43 (1977).

GILL, M., Functional articulation disorder: Its relationship to the phenomenon of handicap. Unpublished paper, University of Wisconsin (1974).

GROHER, M., The experimental use of cross-age relationships in public school speech remediation. *Language, Speech and Hearing Services in Schools,* 7, 250–258 (1976).

HODSON, B., A heirarchy for phonological therapy. Paper presented to the Annual Convention of the American Speech and Hearing Association, Chicago (1977).

HULL, F., MIELKE, P., TIMMONS, R., and WILLEFORD, J., The national speech and hearing survey: Preliminary results. *Asha,* 13, 501–509 (1971).

HUSKEY, R., KNIGHT, N., OLTMAN, S., and IRWIN, J., A longitudinal study of spontaneous remission of articulatory defects of 1665 school children in grades 1, 2, 3. *Acta Symbolica,* 4, 73–80 (1973).

HYMAN, L., *Phonology: Theory and Analysis.* New York: Holt, Rinehart and Winston (1975).

INGRAM, D., Phonological disability in children. In D. Crystal and J. Cooper (Eds.). *Studies in Language Disability and Remediation,* Volume 2. New York: Elsevier-North Holland Publishing Co. (1976).

IRWIN, J., and WESTON, A., The paired stimuli monograph. *Acta Symbolica,* 6, 1–76 (1975).

JANZEN, K., and SHRIBERG, L., *How to Evoke and Generalize "R": A Compendium of 36 Evocation and Phonetic Context Procedures.* Madison, Wisconsin: The University Book Store (1977).

JOHNSON, W., The clinical point of view in education. In W. Johnson, S. Brown, J. Curtis, C. Edney, and J. Keaster (Eds.), *Speech Handicapped School Children,* (3rd. Ed.). New York: Harper & Row (1967).

KAVANAGH, J., and MATTINGLY, I., *Language By Ear and By Eye: The Relationships Between Speech and Reading.* Cambridge, Mass.: MIT Press (1972).

KENT, R., Anatomical and neuromuscular maturation of the speech mechanism: Evidence from acoustic studies. *Journal of Speech and Hearing Research,* 19, 421–447 (1976).

KLEFFNER, F., A comparison of the reactions of a group of fourth-grade children to recorded examples of defective and non-defective articulation. Unpublished doctoral dissertation, University of Wisconsin (1952).

LOCKE, J., Ease of articulation. *Journal of Speech and Hearing Research,* 15, 194–200 (1972).

LOCKE, J., and KUTZ, K., Memory for speech and speech for memory. *Journal of Speech and Hearing Research,* 18, 176–191 (1975).

McDONALD, E., and McDONALD, J., Norms for the Screening Deep Test of Articulation. Unpublished monograph. ESEA Title III Grant Number 73024 (1974).

McREYNOLDS, L., and ENGMANN, D., *Distinctive Feature Analysis of Misarticulations.* Baltimore: University Park Press (1975).

MENYUK, P., Children's learning and reproduction of grammatical and nongrammatical phonological sequences. *Child Development,* 39, 849–859 (1968).

MESSER, S., Implicit phonology in children. *Journal of Verbal Learning and Verbal Behavior,* 6, 609–613 (1967).

MOSKOWITZ, A., On the status of vowel shift in the acquisition of English phonology. In T. Moore (Ed.), *Cognitive Development and the Acquisition of Language.* New York: Academic Press (1973).

MOWRER, D., Social consequences of lisping in the speech of adult males. Paper presented to the Annual Convention of the American Speech and Hearing Association, Las Vegas (1974).

NEAL, W., Speech pathology services in the secondary schools. *Language, Speech and Hearing Services in Schools,* 7, 6–16 (1976).

OLLER, D., Simplification in child phonology. Paper presented to the Third Western Conference of Linguistics, Victoria, British Columbia (1973).

OLMSTEAD, D., *Out of the Mouth of Babes.* The Hague: Mouton (1971).

PAGE, J., and LAUFFER, M., Vowel duration in the presence of final consonant deletion. Paper presented to the Annual Convention of the American Speech and Hearing Association, Chicago (1977).

POOLE, I., Genetic development of articulation of consonant sounds in speech. *Elementary English Review,* 11, 159–161 (1934).

POWERS, M., Clinical and educational procedures in functional disorders of articulation. In L. Travis (Ed.), *Handbook of Speech Pathology and Audiology.* New York: Appleton-Century-Crofts (1971).

PRATHER, E., HEDRICK, D., and KERN, C., Articulation development in children aged two to four years. *Journal of Speech and Hearing Disorders,* 40, 179–191 (1975).

ROSENWINKEL, P., PADEN, E., and HODSON, B., Phonologically-based therapy for children with multiple misarticulations. Paper presented to the Annual Convention of the American Speech and Hearing Association, Houston (1976).

ROE, V., and MILISEN, R., The effect of maturation upon speech defective children in elementary grades. *Journal of Speech and Hearing Disorders,* 7, 37–45 (1942).

SANDER, E., When are speech sounds learned? *Journal of Speech and Hearing Disorders,* 37, 55–63 (1972).

SAX, M., A longitudinal study of articulation change. *Language, Speech and Hearing Services in Schools,* 3, 41–48 (1972).

SCALERO, A., and ESKENAZI, C., Use of supportive personnel in a public school speech and language program. *Language, Speech and Hearing Services in Schools,* 7, 150–158 (1976).

SCHWARTZ, A., and GOLDMAN, R., Variables influencing performance on speech sound discrimination tests. *Journal of Speech and Hearing Research,* 17, 25–33 (1974).

SHELTON, R., FURR, M., JOHNSON, A., and ARNDT, W., Cephalometric and intraoral variables as they relate to articulation improvement with training. *American Journal of Orthodontics,* 67, 423–431 (1975).

SHRIBERG, L., A response evocation program for /ɝ/. *Journal of Speech and Hearing Disorders,* 40, 92–105 (1975a).

SHRIBERG, L., Preliminaries to a social learning theory of deviant child phonology. Paper presented to the Annual Convention of the American Speech and Hearing Association, Washington, D.C. (1975b).

SHRIBERG, L., and KENT, R., *Clinical Phonetics.* (In preparation).

SHRIBERG, L., and KWIATKOWSKI, J., Natural process analyses for children with severely delayed speech. Paper presented to the Annual Convention of the American Speech and Hearing Association, San Francisco (1978).

SHRIBERG, L., and KWIATKOWSKI, J., *Natural Process Analyses (NPA): A Procedure for Phonological Analyses of Continuous Speech Samples.* (Baltimore: University Park Press (1980).

SHRIBERG, L., and KWIATKOWSKI, J., Phonological programming for unintelligible children in early childhood projects. Paper presented to the Annual Convention of the American Speech and Hearing Association, Chicago (1977).

SILVERMAN, E., Listeners impressions of speakers with lateral lisps. *Journal of Speech and Hearing Disorders,* 41, 547–552 (1976).

SMITH, N., *The Acquisition of Phonology: A Case Study.* Cambridge, England: Cambridge University Press (1973).

STAMPE, D., A dissertation on natural phonology. Unpublished doctoral dissertation, University of Chicago (1973).

TEMPLIN, M., A study of sound discrimination ability of elementary school pupils. *Journal of Speech and Hearing Disorders,* 8, 127–132 (1943).

TEMPLIN, M., *Certain Language Skills in Children.* Minneapolis: University of Minnesota Press (1957).

VAN RIPER, C., and ERICKSON, R., A predictive screening test of articulation. *Journal of Speech and Hearing Disorders,* 34, 214–219 (1969).

WATERSON, N., Child phonology—A prosodic view. *Journal of Linguistics,* 7, 179–211 (1971).

WEINER, F., and BANKSON, N., Teaching features. *Language, Speech and Hearing Services in Schools,* 9, 29–34 (1978).

WELLMAN, B., CASE, I., MENGERT, I., and BRADBURY, D., Speech sounds of young children. *University of Iowa Studies in Child Welfare,* 5, 1–82 (1931).

WENSMAN, D., and SCOTT, D., A comparison of four tests of auditory discrimination. Paper presented to the Annual Convention of the American Speech and Hearing Association, Chicago (1977).

WEPMAN, J., *Auditory Discrimination Test.* Chicago: Language Research Associates (1958).

WHORF, B., *Language, Thought and Reality.* New York: Wiley (1956).

WINITZ, H., *Articulatory Acquisition and Behavior.* New York: Appleton-Century-Crofts (1969).

signpost   Among the most common of all speech disorders are those having to do with the voice. Voice disorders come in many forms and exist as problems of function in either the larynx or the passageways above it (that is, the throat, mouth, and nose). Chapter 8 provides descriptions of the wide variety of voice disorders and considers their causes. The territory is partitioned to cover disorders that result from abuse and misuse of the larynx, disease of the larynx, psychological disturbance, and faulty use or disease of the throat, mouth, or nose. Methods for evaluating the disordered voice and for screening for voice disorders in school-age children are considered as are methods for managing the various forms of disorders. For the latter, treatments range from something as simple as voice rest at one extreme to surgical amputation of the larynx at the other. An exciting development in the voice disorders area has come over the management horizon and is considered in Chapter 8. This development pertains to the perplexing disorder called spastic dysphonia, previously believed to be most likely of psychological origin. Seemingly impossible to remediate by conventional voice therapy, this disorder is now treated by a surgical procedure that severs one of the nerves supplying the larynx. Study of Chapter 8 is important not only for itself, but because it provides an important base of knowledge for understanding subsequent chapters in the book where voice disorders are discussed together with other problems (for example, orofacial disorders and dysarthria).

Daniel R. Boone

voice
disorders

INTRODUCTION

We hear disordered voices around us every day in friends, relatives, politicians, television stars, teachers, auctioneers—just about anybody in any walk of life. This chapter is concerned with what causes voice disorders, and what can be done about them. Because a disordered voice is a relative thing, existing as both a problem of production by the speaker with perception by the listener, it is important that our first business be to define what we mean by voice disorders. Following this, we will consider the prevalence of voice disorders. We proceed from there to detailed descriptions of various disorders and at the same time consider information specific to causative factors associated with each. Our next topic is the procedures commonly used by the speech-language pathologist for the evaluation and diagnosis of voice disorders. Finally, discussion is offered about clinical management steps and therapy procedures that are often used to remediate disorders of voice.

ON DEFINING VOICE DISORDERS

The emphasis in this chapter is on disorders of phonation. Lesser attention is given to disorders of resonance, their being discussed also in Chapter 9. Voice disorders labeled as "hoarseness, breathiness, harshness" are examples of *dysphonia*, which means a disorder of phonation. Undoubtedly, you have heard voices to which you would apply such labels. The hoarse voice of the tired politician at the end of a strenuous oral campaign is an example of dysphonia. Another example is the overly breathy voice of the "sexy" actress. Many dysphonias are the result of faulty use of the voice (for example, too loud, too high a pitch) with the patient having no demonstrable disease or structural disorder. Other dysphonias are the result of organic problems that prohibit the larynx from functioning normally. Still others may be related to psychological problems. If the patient has no voice at all, whatever the cause of the problem, the disorder is called *aphonia.*

While disorders of phonation have their bases in dysfunction within the larynx, *disorders of resonance* are usually the result of dysfunction in the upper airway. Such disorders may be the result of faulty usage of the upper airway (for example, tongue, pharynx, velum) or of organic problems of different parts of the upper airway. An example of a resonance disorder is the voice that sounds excessively nasal or what the layman might characterize as "talking through the nose."

PREVALENCE OF VOICE DISORDERS

It is difficult to provide information concerning the prevalence of voice disorders in the United States. One problem is that most available data are concerned with dysphonias only and disregard voice disorders that are resonance-based. A second problem is that most studies have been confined to the school-age child, with little attention given to other groups. A further problem is that prevalence data depend upon factors affecting the populations studied and upon the nature of the criteria used to designate voice abnormality. For example, a young primary-school population in certain areas of the country will demonstrate a high incidence of slight dysphonia and too little nasal resonance during the winter months when head colds are at their peak. And, what one observer might believe is a mild dysphonia might be judged by another observer not to be a clinically significant problem. With these problems of interpretation in mind, the uncertainty of specifying "the" prevalence of voice disorders is apparent. Nevertheless, we can get some idea of prevalence by considering several reports. Milisen (1971) places the national prevalence of phonation disorders for the general population at about 1 percent. Senturia and Wilson (1968) report a 6 percent figure for a large school-aged population. Hull et al. (1976) found that 3 percent of the school-age population demonstrated disorders of phonation. These figures and our own dealings with various populations prompt us to estimate that, on the average, *prevalence is probably in the neighborhood of 3 percent. If resonance-based voice disorders are included, then we would expect that a reasonable figure might be a percentage point or two higher.*

VOICE DISORDERS:
DESCRIPTIONS AND CAUSATIVE FACTORS

Voice disorders manifest themselves in different ways and from various causes. Here we consider these ways and causes. Voice problems related to functional misuse or abuse of the vocal mechanism are described in our first subsection on phonation disorders related to vocal hyperfunction. Other phonation disorders are caused by organic disturbances of the laryngeal mechanism. These are the focus of a second major subsection. Next, much rarer voice disorders are described in a subsection dealing with dysphonias related to psychogenic problems. Finally, we discuss resonance-based voice disorders.

Phonation Disorders Related to Vocal Hyperfunction

Most dysphonias are related to misuse or abuse of the laryngeal mechanism. Misuse involves using the voice inappropriately while singing or speaking. Forms of *vocal misuse* include phonating at high intensity levels, phonating at abnormally low or high frequency levels, and initiating voice with hard glottal attack, such as in sudden explosive phonation onsets (Dunn, 1961). *Vocal abuse* involves using the laryngeal mechanism excessively for vegetative or affective phonation. Abusive vegetative vocal behaviors include excessive throat clearing and coughing. Affective excesses are heard in yelling, crying, or laughing. Phonation disorders related to various misuses and abuses are often categorized as *hyperfunctional voice disorders* (Froeschels, 1943; Boone, 1977).

Vocal hyperfunction can lead to various dysphonias. Some of these are related simply to using the vocal folds in a less than optimal manner. It is just that because of faulty habits of vocal performance, the patient produces a voice that is judged to be abnormal. Any good mimic or imitator can demonstrate such dysphonias. Some patients do not show adverse laryngeal consequences from vocal hyperfunction. Others, however, eventually show clinically significant changes in the membraneous tissue of the larynx. Thus, less than optimal use of the voice may actually damage important laryngeal tissues, particularly along the glottal margin.

In this section, we consider some of the most common phonation disorders related to vocal hyperfunction. The cause of each disorder is presented, followed by a brief mention of overall management strategy. Later in the chapter, the voice therapy part of management is presented in detail. Table 8-1 provides a listing of the disorders covered.

Table 8–1. PHONATION DISORDERS RELATED TO VOCAL HYPERFUNCTION TOGETHER WITH CAUSE AND TYPE OF MANAGEMENT REQUIRED.

DISORDER	CAUSE	MANAGEMENT
Functional dysphonia	Faulty vocal fold approximation and vocal hyperfunction	Voice therapy
Traumatic laryngitis	Excessive vocal abuse	Voice rest
Vocal fold thickening	Vocal hyperfunction	Voice therapy
Vocal nodule(s)	Vocal hyperfunction	Small nodule(s): Voice therapy Large nodule(s): Surgery and voice therapy
Vocal polyp(s)	Vocal hyperfunction	Small polyp(s): Voice therapy Large polyp(s): Surgery and voice therapy
Contact ulcers	Excessively low frequency and/or hard glottal attacks	Voice therapy
Spastic dysphonia	Faulty vocal fold approximation and/or possible central-nervous-system lesion	Voice therapy and surgery
Phonation breaks	Vocal hyperfunction	Voice therapy
Pitch breaks	Inappropriate frequency level	Voice therapy

Functional Dysphonia. Problems of hoarseness, harshness, raspiness, stridency, breathiness, etc., may exist in the patient independent of any organic pathology. In such cases, the patient exhibits dysphonia because of *faulty vocal fold approximation and vocal hyperfunction.* For example, a young woman who wants to produce what to her is a sexy voice might speak deliberately with a breathy voice. To do this, she must bring her vocal folds together laxly, perhaps leaving a posterior glottal opening. This produces the voice she wants and a voice that others perceive as excessively breathy. Any form of dysphonia related to faulty vocal fold approximation is classified as *functional dysphonia.* In addition, only if all organic disease is ruled out medically would a dysphonia be classified as a functional dysphonia. Hoarseness and other manifestations of dysphonia are often the initial symptoms of serious laryngeal disease. Therefore, it is important that the patient with dysphonia for more than 10 days, unless he or she has a severe cold or allergy, have the benefit of *indirect laryngoscopy* (a mirror viewing of the vocal folds) by a physician to determine the cause of the problem. *It cannot be stressed strongly enough that any persistent dysphonia should be evaluated medically.* Voice therapy is the treatment of choice for patients with functional dysphonia.

Traumatic Laryngitis.   Many of us have experienced temporary dysphonia after prolonged cheering and yelling at a sporting event. It is difficult to hear our own voices above the loud noise of the crowd and often we are unaware of the high frequency and high intensity levels we are using. Many children, of course, yell like this every day. Anyone who *abuses the vocal mechanism extensively* may experience an increase in the mass of the structures along the glottal margins of the vocal folds. Under the trauma of intense phonations, the glottal membranes become swollen, irritated, and reddened. The thickening that occurs produces a temporary laryngitis. The voice sounds hoarse and breathy. The cure is voice rest. After the sporting event, most of us enjoy a night of rest, not using the voice, and by morning much of the laryngitis has disappeared. Severe traumatic laryngitis, however, may require several days of voice rest. It is best for the patient not even to whisper, because whispering may add light phonation and put the vocal folds back into contact again.

Vocal Fold Thickening.   *Continuous vocal misuse and abuse may cause irritation along the glottal membrane in the vicinity of the anterior-middle-third juncture of the vocal folds* (Luchsinger and Arnold, 1965). This site corresponds to the midpoint of the membranous-bound segment of the glottis where the amplitude of vocal fold excursions and the impact collision forces of the two folds are the greatest. In the case of *vocal fold thickening,* a soft additive tissue initially appears at the site of irritation. This tissue continues to accumulate until layers of callous-like epithelium begin to cover the membrane in the irritated area. To protect itself from erosion and loss of tissue, the membrane begins to thicken appreciably and takes on the status of a lesion. Normal adduction of the vocal folds is prevented and the voice turns out to be breathy and variously dysphonic. Thickenings are early warnings of vocal hyperfunction and they can be eradicated by significantly reducing or eliminating abusive vocalizations. Thus, a voice therapy program is the preferred method of management. In cases where vocal fold thickening remains untreated, continued abusive behaviors may lead to the development of vocal nodules or vocal polyps.

Vocal Nodule(s).   *If vocal fold thickening is focal in nature, a clearly recognized callous-like nodule will develop.* Usually such a nodule develops on one vocal fold at its anterior-middle-third juncture. Its presence then irritates the corresponding site on the other fold (see Figure 8–1). The result is the development of *bilateral nodules.* If untreated, the nodules will progress to larger and larger sizes. It is difficult for someone with nodules to sing or to act or to use the voice for anything beyond simple normal day-to-day phonation. Vocal nodules, by their additive mass, generally result in a lowering of fundamental frequency. Because vocal fold approximation is impaired, there is also a leakage of air which produces what we hear as breathiness and hoarseness. Some individuals may require surgical removal of masses, followed by voice therapy. Most vocal nodules, however, can be eradicated or significantly reduced by voice therapy that is designed to decrease vocal hyperfunction. The condition shown in Figure 8–1 was eliminated after six weeks of twice-weekly voice therapy.

Vocal Polyp(s). *The same kind of abuse that can produce a vocal nodule can also produce a vocal polyp* (Brodnitz, 1967). Just like nodules, polyps usually develop at the anterior-middle-third junction of the vocal folds. They are generally more vascular and softer in texture than nodules and do not offend the corresponding site on the other vocal fold. This means that *polyps are usually found only unilaterally.* Polyps produce the same kinds of dysphonias we hear for nodules. Although early polyps are responsive to voice therapy that reduces vocal hyperfunction, advanced polyps generally require surgical removal followed

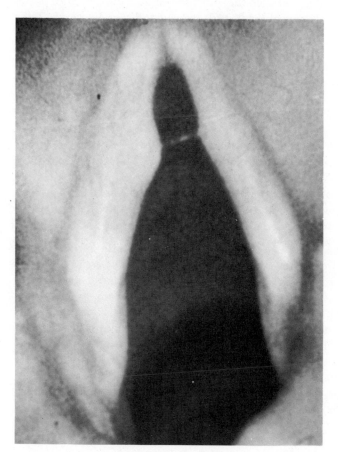

FIGURE 8–1. *A well developed nodule on the right vocal fold (left in the picture because it is a mirror-laryngoscopic view). Note the slight thickening at the corresponding site on the left vocal fold. A mucous spittle thread is seen to be crossing the glottis between the right nodule and the left thickening. (From D. Boone,* The Voice and Voice Therapy, *2nd Ed. Englewood Cliffs, N.J.: Prentice-Hall, 1977.)*

by voice therapy. Vocal polyps are much more common in adults than in children and can often be traced to a rather specific period of vocal abuse. For example:

> A thirty-four-year-old man had experienced a normal voice all of his adult life until appearing in a local community theater. During the last week of strenuous voice rehearsals, he began to experience a feeling that "my voice was going to pop out of my neck." By the time the play opened, the patient was severely dysphonic. He continued in the part for a three-week run, experiencing loss of voice each evening after the performance. Following the completion of the play, he was seen by a laryngologist and found to have a large unilateral polyp. Surgery and voice therapy were required.

Contact Ulcers. Some people speak with such a slamming together of the arytenoid cartilages that they develop *contact ulcers* (open sores) on the glottal membranes along the cartilages (Cherry and Margulies, 1968). Contact ulcers occur at the juncture of the middle and posterior one-thirds of the vocal folds and are most always bilateral. They are often *found in patients who speak near the bottom of their frequency range and who speak with hard glottal attacks.* Hard glottal attacks may produce irritations of the mucosal coverings of the arytenoid cartilages and eventually bring about ulcerations of the membranes. Patients with contact ulcers generally complain of pain in the neck area (sometimes they have "referred pain" to an ear), but do not generally experience dysphonia. They also often complain of general laryngeal-area fatigue, with such symptoms as throat dryness or a "burning" throat following prolonged speaking or singing. There are no typical voice symptoms. Most problems of contact ulcer resolve quickly once the patient is involved in a voice therapy program where he learns to use his voice at higher frequency levels and to eradicate his tendencies for hard glottal attacks.

Spastic Dysphonia. No voice problem is more puzzling than *spastic dysphonia.* In this disorder, the *vocal folds are brought together so tightly that the patient is scarcely able to phonate.* Phonation, is characterized by a "choked vocal attack and a tense, squeezed voice, accompanied by extreme tension of the entire phonatory system" (Luchsinger and Arnold, 1965). The typical patient experiences a normal voice some of the time. At other times, however, the patient experiences a "strangling in the throat" with hardly any voice at all. The contrast between normal phonation and marked interruption of phonation is similar to that seen in some stutterers. The cause of spastic dysphonia is uncertain. Aronson (1973) classifies the problem as a conversion-type psychiatric disorder. Speech-language pathologists report only marginal success in working with the disorder on a voice therapy basis. Some (Robe, Brumlik, and Moore, 1960) believe that the disorder has an organic basis in the central nervous system. Recently, an otolaryngologist (Dedo, 1976) reported good treatment success by cutting the recurrent laryngeal nerve on one side, producing in the patient a paralysis of one vocal fold. This procedure is followed by voice therapy in many cases.

Phonation Breaks. Some patients experience involuntary intermittent cessations of phonation as they are speaking. This problem, termed *phonation breaks,* usually occurs *after the patient has experienced an extended period of vocal hyperfunction.* The patient's laryngeal mechanism appears to become fatigued. The larynx will be voicing normally when suddenly the vocal folds abduct spontaneously to widen the glottis and preclude phonation. One such patient was a disc jockey on a hard-rock radio station. He maintained an elevated frequency level and spoke in an overall "hyper" manner. On the half-hour, he would read the news for five minutes and during this time he experienced phonation breaks in which his voice suddenly and intermittently "cut out" on him. People all over the area were having their radios checked for malfunctions. The man was warned by his employer to either get over the phonation breaks or lose his job. He was seen for voice therapy. Decreasing his hyperfunctional vocal behaviors (high frequency, high intensity, hard glottal attack) resolved his problem and prevented further difficulties.

Pitch Breaks. The pitch breaks experienced by adolescent boys as they pass through puberty are a normal phenomenon. Breaks may appear over a period of about six months and then disappear as the laryngeal mechanism fully matures. *If they occur in adults well beyond puberty and have no organic cause, pitch breaks are an abnormality.* There are two types of breaks: upward (the more common) and downward. Breaks usually come without warning and often produce embarrassment. They are almost invariably related to speaking at an inappropriate pitch level. If the speaker is operating at the bottom of his pitch range, his voice will break upward. Downward pitch breaks are generally observed in people who are speaking at inappropriately high pitch levels. A slight change of pitch level, no more than one full musical tone higher or lower (depending on whether the breaks are upward or downward), will usually eliminate the problem.

Phonation Disorders Related to Organic Problems

There are some phonation disorders related strictly to organic disease or structural problems. Here we consider the most common of these, their causes, and the primary management strategies involved. Table 8–2 provides a listing of these disorders.

Infectious Laryngitis.   Some individuals suffer from laryngitis when they have a cold or upper respiratory infection. These infections may cause other symptoms such as fever and malaise. People with severe allergies may also suffer from laryngitis. The *vocal folds become swollen and reddened from infection or allergy,* resulting in difficulty producing firm vocal fold approximation. The resulting dysphonia is often described as a "wet" hoarseness. It can be treated by reducing or eliminating the cause of the irritation, usually by some type of systemic medication. As long as the patient exhibits laryngitis, he should be placed on strict voice rest. *Infectious laryngitis* is a medical problem, not a problem for the speech-language pathologist.

Papilloma.   Juvenile papilloma is the most common and severe of all childhood diseases of the larynx. Papillomas are *wart-like growths* that occur anywhere in the airway. They are believed to be viral in origin (Singelton and Adkins, 1972; Urabec, 1975), and like other viruses are difficult to treat. Papillomas growing on the vocal folds not only cause dysphonia, but because of their rapid growth, they represent a

Table 8–2. PHONATION DISORDERS RELATED TO ORGANIC PROBLEMS TOGETHER WITH CAUSE AND TYPE OF MANAGEMENT REQUIRED.

DISORDER	CAUSE	MANAGEMENT
Infectious laryngitis	Viral, bacterial infection	Systemic or topical treatment of infection; voice rest
Papilloma	Virus	Close medical-surgical management; no voice therapy
Leukoplakia and hyperkeratosis	Irritants, such as tobacco	Cessation of irritant; close medical-surgical management; no voice therapy
Granuloma and hemangioma	Trauma to glottal membranes	Cessation of trauma; surgery; search with patient for best voice after surgery
Endocrine changes	Hormonal change or lack of hormonal change	Control of endocrinal problem; voice therapy
Laryngeal webbing	Trauma to glottal margin by disease or mechanical insult	Surgery; keel implant; voice therapy
Laryngeal trauma	Direct blow to larynx	Reconstructive laryngeal surgery as required; voice therapy
Vocal fold paralysis	Trauma to innervating nerve(s); cerebro-vascular accident	Medical treatment; surgery sometimes; voice therapy
Carcinoma	Irritants; virus; trauma	Medical-surgical; voice therapy
Laryngectomy	Extensive carcinoma requiring total removal of larynx	Medical-surgical; artificial larynx; esophageal speech

serious threat to the maintenance of an open airway. Papillomas require close medical-surgical monitoring. When they become big enough to interfere with either voice or breathing, they must be reduced surgically. Each child with papillomas has his own set of voice and respiratory symptoms, depending on the site and the extent of the papillomas. Fortunately, most childhood papillomas disappear about the time of puberty. There are times, however, when papillomas continue into young adulthood or when young adults will acquire papillomas for the first time. These two occurrences are rare but are considered to be more serious threats to health than the papillomas found in younger children. Papilloma patients are not candidates for voice therapy. They require medical management.

Leukoplakia and Hyperkeratosis. Adult patients sometimes experience lesions called *leukoplakia*. These are whitish patches that may occur on the tongue, along the inner cheek, in the pharynx, and in the larynx. Leukoplakia is generally the *result of a continuous and chronic irritation, such as tobacco smoke*. When leukoplakia occurs in the larynx, it may produce chronic dysphonia and a marked lowering of frequency. Once identified, leukoplakia requires close medical-surgical management and is not responsive to voice therapy per se. Some patients who have leukoplakia removed profit from voice therapy, learning to use their scarred laryngeal mechanisms as optimally as possible.

    Hyperkeratosis is a brown crusty lesion that may appear in the larynx, particularly along the vocal fold margins. These *lesions are potentially malignant* and must be watched closely by the physician. If voice symptoms are present, they usually involve low pitch, harshness, and hoarseness. Voice therapy is not indicated for hyperkeratosis of the larynx.

Granuloma and Hemangioma. Sometimes the *glottal membrane is traumatized in an accident or during intubation.* Possible outcomes of this trauma are enlarging tumors called *granulomas* or *hemangiomas*. Intubation granuloma may result from a surgical procedure in which a breathing tube is forced through the glottis and the membranous surfaces of the vocal folds are bruised or lacerated. Patients who have experienced intubation during surgery, often as part of an anesthesiology procedure, should be examined closely for the possible presence of either a granuloma or hemangioma. A large tumor of either type can have devastating effects on phonation, including no voice at all, particularly if the tumor body obstructs the airway and prevents the vocal folds from approximating. Both granulomas and hemangiomas require surgical removal. Voice therapy is sometimes required postoperatively to help the patient reinstate normal phonation.

Endocrine Changes.   Some post-pubescent adolescents and adults experience voice frequency levels inappropriate for their age and sex. Many times these inappropriate levels are purely the result of functional misplacement of frequency. On rare occasions, the problem is related to some type of *endocrine dysfunction.* For example, some women have developed low-pitched voices from taking virilizing drugs, such as some of the early contraceptive pills (Damste, 1967). The vocal folds thicken as part of the overall virilization and they tend to vibrate at a lower frequency. Such thickening is not reversible and the low-pitched voice remains a persistent characteristic. Only with voice therapy and deliberate effort to elevate frequency can the patient achieve a frequency level more compatible with her age and sex.

High-pitched voices in young men are rarely the result of delayed puberty and in most cases represent a learned way of phonating. In those rare cases of incomplete puberty, the endocrinologist can often facilitate pubertal change, including the lowering of voice frequency, with relatively simple treatment by male hormone. Voice therapy may be indicated to aid the patient in developing optimal vocal skills that are compatible with his "new" adult larynx.

Laryngeal Webbing.   Trauma to the vocal folds, either by injury or by severe infection, can sometimes permit a membranous webbing called *synechia* to grow between the two folds. This webbing comes about when the *injured membranes of the two folds grow together.* Depending on the size and extent of the web, it can have serious consequences on the airway and on the voice. The voice is often high-pitched, hoarse, and lacking adequate loudness. As the web grows posteriorly and begins to cover the airway opening, the patient may experience symptoms of shortness of breath. Webs must be removed surgically. Later, the patient becomes a candidate for voice therapy.

Laryngeal Trauma.   A direct blow to the larynx from a hard object may *fracture the laryngeal cartilages and/or displace them from their proper alignment* with one another. Such *trauma* may require that the larynx be reconstructed surgically. Reconstruction usually has as its primary goal, the preservation of the airway. Preservation of the voice is a secondary goal. As the patient progresses with his newly reconstructed larynx, attention should be given to the sound of his voice. The typical post-trauma voice is low-pitched, breathy, and dysphonic. Cases have been observed where, from a direct frontal blow, the thyroid cartilage was driven backward toward the arytenoid cartilages. The result is a markedly shortened overall length of the glottis and floppy vocal folds in which the tissue hangs limply in the glottal space. After the larynx has been reconstructed surgically, voice therapy is usually required.

Vocal Fold Paralysis.   *If one or more of the laryngeal nerves is cut or damaged, the patient may experience vocal fold paralysis.* Paralysis may be *unilateral* or *bilateral* and of two types: *adductor paralysis* (an inability to bring the folds together) and *abductor paralysis* (an inability to separate the folds). The type of paralysis is determined by the specific nerve that is impaired and the position that the vocal folds were in when the "power was cut." The most common form of vocal fold paralysis is the unilateral adductor variety. Here the patient has one vocal fold paralyzed in an out or paramedian position and cannot bring it into the midline for normal phonation. Figure 8–2 portrays this condition for a right recurrent laryngeal-nerve paralysis. Patients with unilateral adductor paralysis experience an extremely breathy voice. Because the glottis is open at all times, there is no problem with breathing. After damage, the recurrent laryngeal nerve may slowly regain function and voice may return to near normal. However, in some individuals the paralysis is permanent. Certain medical procedures may help patients who exhibit the problem permanently. Voice therapy is also called for with such patients.

Other kinds of vocal fold paralyses, unilateral and bilateral abductor, or bilateral adductor, present serious threats to the airway. The patient either suffers from an insufficient opening of the airway to maintain normal respiration (the effect of abductor paralysis) or from excessive airway opening which can cause aspiration or strangling (the effect of bilateral adductor paralysis). Preservation of the airway is the primary goal; therefore, the problem must be managed by the physician. Voice therapy is only indicated after respiratory adequacy has been restored.

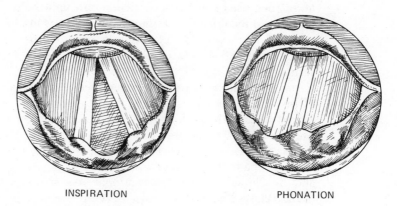

INSPIRATION   PHONATION

FIGURE 8–2.   *An artist's conception of laryngoscopic views of the vocal folds in a patient with right recurrent laryngeal-nerve paralysis (adductor type). The left panel shows the configuration during inspiration, while the right panel shows a compensated attempt to close the glottis for phonation.*

Carcinoma. *Carcinoma* or *cancer* of the larynx is frequently character- ized in its early stages by hoarseness (International Association of Lar- yngectomees, 1964). Laryngeal malignancies can often be treated suc- cessfully by radiation, limited surgery, or both. Following successful medical therapy, the patient may profit from a voice therapy program designed to teach optimal use of the larynx. The kind of voice ther- apy provided depends, of course, on the presenting vocal symptoms. These are directly related to the site and the extent of the carcinoma and its medical treatment. Extensive carcinomas may require removal of the larynx, a procedure known as laryngectomy.

Laryngectomy. If radiation and limited surgery fail, a *partial laryngec- tomy* (removal of one vocal fold), called *laryngofissure,* can be per- formed. With a partial laryngectomy the patient can compensate and continue to be capable of important laryngeal functions. Phonation will be impaired, however, with a severe breathy dysphonia. Surgical reconstruction may be needed to provide a laryngeal structure to which the normal vocal fold can approximate. Only by having some kind of laryngeal valving capability can the patient slow airflow through the larynx and build up sufficient subglottal air pressure to enable a usable voice. Partial laryngectomy generally requires min- imal assistance from the speech-language pathologist. The task is to work on the best phonation the patient can produce with his severely altered larynx.

A *total laryngectomy* involves *complete removal of the larynx* and the creation of a permanent tracheostoma (hole in the front of the neck) (see Figure 8–3). All pulmonary air goes in and out of the trachea through this opening and the oral, nasal, and pharyngeal cavities are cut off from the lungs. Laryngectomy patients, known as *laryngec- tomees,* because of this lack of airflow through the nose and mouth, ex- perience difficulties in smelling and tasting. They must also take care to avoid the aspiration of water through the tracheostoma. Perhaps the greatest problem faced post-operatively is the lack of voice and its serious affects on the ability to communicate. The psychological trauma that the patient may experience from the surgical amputation of his larynx and the loss of normal speech and voice may be min- imized in part through the help of other laryngectomees. Clubs have been formed by laryngectomees to help new laryngectomees and spouses adjust to the emotional, psychological, and vocational prob- lems the patient may face after surgery. These clubs are organized and developed by the International Association of Laryngectomees (IAL, 1964). The patient must develop a new substitute voice, either by using an artificial larynx or esophageal voice.

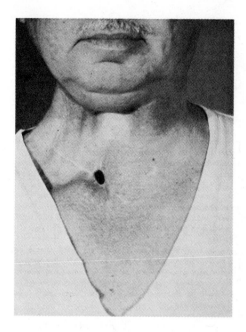

FIGURE 8–3. *A photograph of a patient who has undergone laryngectomy and who presents a tracheostoma. All pulmonary air moves in and out through this opening in the patient's neck. (From E. Lauder,* Self-Help for the Laryngectomee. *San Antonio, Texas: Edmund Lauder, 1977.)*

Phonation Disorders Related to Psychogenic Problems

Disorders with a *psychogenic basis* are sometimes referred to as *conversion, hysterical,* or *functional disorders* (used to mean no organic cause). Classically, a conversion psychiatric disorder is characterized by the patient using a symptom as a substitute for adjusting or coping with a problem. For example, a middle-aged professor received a series of promotions requiring increasing responsibility. Coincidental with his inability to keep up, which resulted in his providing poor leadership, he developed severe stomach-intestinal cramps. No organic cause was found for his condition, which forced him to resign several important responsibilities. A subsequent diagnosis by his psychiatrist speculated that his physical discomforts were "conversion symptoms." Developed conversion symptoms may be far removed from the psychological stress or possible neurotic needs of a given patient. *Some patients develop voice problems as their symptom substitute.*

The most frequently occurring psychogenic voice problem is aphonia. Here the patient exhibits a lack of voice during speech attempts, despite the fact that the larynx is normal by all medical criteria. A diagnosis of psychogenic voice disorder is made when the patient demonstrates normal vegetative function of the larynx (such as is observed in throat clearing or coughing) under indirect laryngoscopy, but is unable to use the larynx to phonate voluntarily. Aronson (1973) describes such patients as also demonstrating elevated and rigid posturings of the larynx. The patient with psychogenic aphonia usually refers himself to a physician or a speech-language pathologist. He is embarrassed and penalized by his lack of voice. As hard as he wishes to speak, he cannot "find" his voice.

> A thirty-nine-year-old computer programmer experienced functional aphonia for a period of five months. No matter how he tried, he could only whisper when he attempted to phonate. For four months, he received psychiatric therapy and it was the feeling of his psychiatrist that his "voice symptoms might be conversion symptoms reactive to his guilt feelings surrounding the break-up of his marriage." Despite psychotherapy, his aphonia continued. Symptomatic voice therapy was initiated and the patient was able to produce voice during the first therapy session. After three therapy sessions, he developed normal voice which he has maintained for the past ten years.

As soon as indirect laryngoscopy confirms the patient's laryngeal normality, voice therapy may begin. Generally, the prognosis is excellent.

Some patients present psychogenically based voice disorders that are some form of dysphonia rather than aphonia. For these patients, their dysphonic voices may serve them in their life adjustment just as an aphonic voice does another patient. The patient with a psychogenically based dysphonia is not as symptomatically obvious as the aphonic patient. The dysphonias exhibited are of a variety and are perceived as being similar to those related to vocal hyperfunction or organic problems. A trial period of voice therapy is usually indicated and will usually produce some voice improvement.

Resonance-Based Voice Disorders

Resonance-based voice disorders are the result of either faulty use of the upper airway or of organic problems of various segments of the upper airway. Here we consider such disorders under four headings: functional nasal-resonance problems, organic nasal-resonance problems, functional oral-resonance problems, and organic oral-resonance problems.

Functional Nasal-Resonance Problems. Functional nasal-resonance problems are of two types: *hypernasality,* in which the listener perceives an excessive nasal sounding quality to the voice, and *hyponasality* or *denasality,* in which the listener perceives an inadequate degree of nasal quality to the voice. In both of these types, *the patient simply elects to regulate the nasalization of his speech in an atypical manner.* In hypernasality, the problem is one of permitting too much acoustic energy and air to flow through the nasal chambers, while in denasality, the problem is one of too little nasal acoustic energy and airflow. Hypernasality is usually associated with voiced consonants and vowels while denasality is usually restricted to the nasal consonants, *m, n,* and *ng.* Certain speakers exhibit excessive nasal resonance for the vowels adjacent to the three nasal consonants. All other voice production is characterized by normal resonance. These patients appear to open the velopharyngeal port too soon (before the preceding vowel) and leave it open too long (continue the opening for the vowel after the nasal consonant). This disorder is designated as *assimilative hypernasality.*

Sometimes different forms of hypernasality are simply characteristic of a particular region of the country (for example, certain residents of Missouri or Eastern New England), or they are a family vocal trait. In these cases, the patterns represent differences rather than disorders and should be considered for therapy only if the individual who has the characteristic strongly wants to change it. The desire to change is sometimes coupled with a move to a different part of the country where the individual's speech suddenly is perceived as "strange." Functional nasal-resonance problems are responsive to symptomatic voice therapy.

Organic Nasal-Resonance Problems. Resonance problems are also related to organic factors in some patients. Such disorders are the consequence of the patient's difficulty regulating the velopharyngeal port. Hypernasality can be the result of structural defects of the velopharyngeal mechanism, such as in clefts of the palate, congenitally short palate, trauma to the palate, etc. Hypernasal voice quality can also be related to various neurological disturbances where the velopharyngeal mechanism is weakened or paralyzed (Darley, Aronson, and Brown, 1969). And, it is not uncommon to find hypernasality in the voices of patients with significant hearing impairments that preclude them from being able to adequately monitor voice production. The problem of assimilative hypernasality, when it is of organic origin, is sometimes an early symptom of a serious neurological disease. Patients who have never previously exhibited the problem should be examined closely once assimilative hypernasality is first perceived. Following appropriate medical intervention for the organic cause of hypernasality problems, symptomatic voice therapy is the treatment of choice.

Organically based denasality is typically found to be the result of excessive velopharyngeal port closure under circumstances where the patient wants relatively free egress of acoustic energy and airflow from the nasal chambers. It is often related to the "stuffy nose" sounding voice of patients with enlarged tonsils and adenoids, severe allergies, nasal infections, or excessive surgical correction of a previously existing velopharyngeal inadequacy. Correction of the nasopharyngeal blockage is the management goal. Voice therapy is rarely needed.

Functional Oral-Resonance Problems. Oral-resonance problems that are related solely to faulty adjustments of the upper airway are not very prevalent. One such disorder, however, is seen with sufficient frequency that it warrants consideration here. That disorder is the "thin," baby-type voice that persists in certain adult patients (Fisher, 1966). This voice is the result of excessively anterior and high carriage of the tongue body. The voice pattern is also often accompanied by distortion of sibilants (such as in frontal lisps). Baby-type voice is often a self-referral problem in which the patient strongly wants to change his voice. Symptomatic voice therapy is the treatment of choice and involves the use of approaches for altering tongue position.

Organic Oral-Resonance Problems. Oral-resonance problems that are organically based can have their genesis in a variety of causes. Two of these are particularly apparent in the clinical population seen by most speech-language pathologists: oral-resonance problems of the hearing impaired and oral-resonance problems of the neurologically impaired.

Most speakers with significant hearing impairment exhibit some problem in oral resonance. The problem for such speakers is a voice quality that is perceived as "coming from the throat." The quality is not unlike that that many normal speakers produce when trying to phonate on inspiration. Pharyngeal resonance in the hearing-impaired speaker appears to be the product of a tongue carriage that is too far posterior. Positioning of the tongue in this fashion results in shifts in the locations of the major resonances of the vocal tract, thus giving rise to the listener's perception of a distinct voice quality that is characteristic of "the deaf."

Oral-resonance defects are prominent in speakers with dysarthria (see Chapter 10). The range of deviations heard in dysarthric speech is great, primarily because the range of motor-speech control problems is great. The principal problems have to do with combined jaw-tongue positionings. It is not uncommon to hear problems related to excessive pharyngeal sizes and excessive jaw lowerings in the neurally impaired patient. Symptomatic voice therapy is the principle management strategy for use with such patients. In some patients with nervous system disease, no improvement or only minimal improvement may be possible.

EVALUATION OF VOICE DISORDERS

Some patients with voice disorders are discovered through routine school-screening programs. Other persons are referred to the clinician by other professional persons such as laryngologists, general medical practitioners, neurologists, etc. Sometimes the patient is eager to come to the speech-language pathologist for help and sometimes he comes only because he was told to do so. Another group of patients is self-referred. They come for help because they find their voice to be penalizing. They may never have the right voice, they may be embarrassed, their voice may wear out, or they may face unemployment or some kind of vocational penalty because of their faulty voice. In general, the patient who possesses the self-motivation to seek therapy and who strongly wants to improve his voice presents a favorable prognosis.

In the first subdivision of this section, we present a typical voice-screening procedure used in the schools by speech-language pathologists. A second subdivision considers the various components of a comprehensive voice evaluation such as would be administered to those children picked up in screening as well as others, both children and adults, who come from various referral sources.

Voice Screening

Most children with voice disorders are identified by the clinician via school-screening programs. A typical form for use in such a screening is shown in Figure 8–4. This form is completed after the clinician listens to the child talk conversationally and read one of a number of available standard passages appropriate for his reading level. Any specification of "1" (poor) or "2" (fair) on any aspect of the form is taken to indicate a problem that requires the child to receive a full voice evaluation at a later date. Various descriptors of deviation, such as "breathy" or "harsh," are added to the remarks section of the checklist if "1" or "2" are specified. Children with "3" (average) or "4" (good) ratings require no further attention by the speech-language pathologist. A "3" rating is given to those children who sound like their peers of the same age and sex. A "4" rating is reserved for the child who appears better than average on a specific aspect of voice. Some children will receive a "0" (cannot determine) specification, possibly because they were too frightened or apprehensive to speak, or perhaps they could not be validly screened because of a severe infection or allergy. Children with a "0" rating would be rescheduled for screening in a week or two. For those children displaying a voice quality disorder or a

```
VOICE-SCREENING CHECKLIST FORM
```

	Cannot Determine	Poor	Fair	Average	Good
Voice quality*	0	1	2	3	4
Pitch					
Level	0	1	2	3	4
Variability	0	1	2	3	4
Loudness					
Level	0	1	2	3	4
Variability	0	1	2	3	4
Resonance*	0	1	2	3	4

*If 1 or 2 are circled, provide descriptors of deviations (for example, voice quality is breathy, harsh; resonance is hypernasal, etc.).

Remarks:

FIGURE 8–4. *A typical checklist form for use in a school voice-screening program. For details see text.*

resonance problem, a referral would be made for an evaluation by a physician. Pitch and loudness problems would be explored further by the speech-language pathologist before making such a referral because they sometimes vary from week to week or are situation-specific (for example, the child is quiet in the office and noisy on the playground).

As medical reports come back to the speech-language pathologist, the findings may include such statements as "Normal larynx," or "This child has bilateral vocal nodules," or "Multiple papillomas were observed at various sites within the larynx." The clinician uses this information in planning remediation strategies. Using the examples just cited, a voice therapy program would be aimed at vocal hyperfunction for both the child with the normal larynx and the child with nodules. The child with multiple papillomas would not be scheduled for voice therapy.

Except for those identified in screening programs, most voice patients are either self-referred or referred by physicians to the speech-language pathologist. *All patients who are selected for voice therapy should receive a medical evaluation of their problem as part of the total voice evaluation, prior to receiving voice remediation.* Here we consider the voice evaluation with regard to the case history, respiratory observations and measurements, phonatory observations and measurements, and other considerations.

Case History. It is important that a detailed case history be taken. Patients can often provide history information specific to the problems they have been experiencing in voice. Young children, of course, often shrug their shoulders with professed lack of concern and any information must come from parents and teachers. At the other extreme is the neurotic adult who gives excessively detailed information about specific dysphonic symptoms.

Case histories often begin by determining when the disorder began. In general, the longer the duration of the problem, the poorer the prognosis. Long-term acceptance of the dysphonia by the patient often indicates poor self-motivation to improve.

Variability of the problem gives important prognostic information. Patients who start out the day with relatively normal voices, only to suffer voice deterioration after prolonged voice usage, are generally those who are experiencing vocal hyperfunction. By contrast, patients with allergies and infections often begin their vocal day with marked dysphonia, only to experience a clearing of voice with usage. Knowledge of situational variation is also important in understanding the problem. Some patients report a sudden deterioration of voice in certain situations, such as talking to an authority figure, a parent, or to a member of the other sex.

The daily voice use of the patient may give clues to the problem. Typical problem conditions include the salesman who talks all day, the classroom teacher who uses voice all day, the actor who performs in a large theater with poor acoustics and no amplification, the administrator who spends his days on the telephone arguing his point of view, and the auctioneer. All of these conditions present heavy vocal demands in an atmosphere of tension.

General tension is often an important component of a tense sounding voice. We have all experienced the tension symptoms of tightness in the throat with an accompanying change in the quality of our voices. What are the patient's feelings about himself, about his work setting, his love life, his long-term goals, his financial status? These are all potentially important pieces of information. Emotional problems that are disturbing the patient might well contribute to his dysphonia (Murphy, 1964; Aronson, 1973).

Other case history inquiries should consider the possible effects on the voice of excessive smoking, of drinking alcohol, of the use of drugs and hormones, and of the influence of past illnesses and surgical procedures.

Respiratory Observations and Measurements. Any clinical evaluation of dysphonia should include information on the patient's respiratory performance. Four types of information are especially pertinent: (1) driving pressure, (2) flow through the glottis, (3) lung volume changes, and (4) motions of the body wall (Hixon, 1972).

Pressure: One of the best methods available for perceiving the effects of air pressure on voice is to *listen carefully to voice loudness.* A voice that sounds loud has higher driving pressure than a voice that is perceived as soft. Useful observations for evaluating the patient's ability to regulate respiratory pressure might include determining whether his average loudness level is appropriate, determining how well he can change loudness, considering whether his loudness variations in conversational speech are normal, etc. Important information is provided through observations of how well the patient can maintain a relatively constant loudness throughout phrases. Relatively constant loudness suggests relatively good pressure control.

Several devices are available for measuring the respiratory driving pressure directly during speech. The simplest way to estimate this pressure is to measure the pressure in the mouth during speech sounds where the lips are closed and the larynx is open, such as during the production of *p.* For these sounds the peak pressure in the mouth and the lung pressure are equal, thus permitting the determination of the average lung pressure by measuring oral pressure (Netsell, 1969). Inexpensive pressure measuring gauges and manometers can be used to quantify the pressure the patient can produce when blowing into them through a mouthpiece. According to Netsell and Hixon (1978), if a patient can generate 5–10 cm H_2O of pressure over a period of five seconds in a blowing task where there is a small air leak, he probably has sufficient respiratory drive to produce voice that is adequate for most voicing demands.

Flow: Airflow through the glottis is an important indicator with regard to the functional state of the larynx. The production of a vowel usually averages in the neighborhood of 100 cc per second of airflow through the glottis. If a larynx is operating in a hyperfunctional manner, as with a disorder like spastic dysphonia, flow will be much lower than normal. At the other extreme might be the flow in a patient with a breathy voice in which there would be a characteristic elevation in flow. The clinician can make some reasonable inferences concerning whether flow might be deviating from normal values just by listening closely to the patient's voice and making some judgments with respect to whether the voice being produced seems to be coming from a relatively constricted or wide open glottis.

There are a number of ways to measure flow through the larynx during voice production. The most popular is the pneumotachometer, a device held at the patient's mouth to sense the flow. During vowel productions, the flow from the mouth is the same as that through the larynx, providing the patient does not have a velopharyngeal leak (his nose can be held closed if he does). One of the advantages of flow measurements is that they enable the clinician to determine something about the state of the glottis without inserting instruments down into the larynx. If the clinician knows the lung volume of the patient (see next section), he can also gain a crude estimate of flow by simply timing the expirations associated with different utterances. A typical task of this nature might be to see how long the patient can sustain vowels.

Lung volume: As the patient provides history information to the clinician, his overall respiratory performance can be observed. Does he appear short of breath as he breathes quietly? Are there noticeable deviant breathing patterns, such as shoulder elevation on each inspiration? Does the patient run out of breath before he finishes what he wants to say? Does he expire air wastefully before beginning phonation? Many such difficulties are manifested in evaluations of lung volume. The normal speaker operates above his resting level and initiates speech from about twice as deep a breath as he takes for normal breathing (Hixon, Goldman, and Mead, 1973). It is important to determine if the patient is operating in this optimum midrange or whether he is working harder than normal by talking at larger or smaller volumes than these. Although some judgment can be made about volume adequacy by simply observing the patient change lung volume while speaking, it is preferable to directly measure such volume changes during breathing and speech activities. The most commonly used volume measuring instrument is the spirometer. Important measurements to be made on patients with the spirometer include the *vital capacity* and *tidal volume* (Hixon, 1973). Vital capacity is the maximum amount of air that can be expelled from the lungs after a maximum inspiration. The tidal volume is the amount of air inspired or expired during a normal breathing cycle.

Motions of the torso: The respiratory pump is made of different parts, each of which is capable of movement. An important part of the respiratory evaluation includes making observations relative to the different coordinations among the system's different parts. Clinical devices have been developed (Hixon, Mead, and Goldman, 1976) that can track fast movements of the respiratory system and display them. One such device measures changes in the anteroposterior diameters of these structures. Perhaps what is most important is information obtained specific to the synchrony of movements of the rib cage and abdomen during speech breathing. Some clinical problems, like voice disorders related to cerebral palsy or other nervous-system disorders, often show severe problems in the synchrony of respiratory parts. The patient cannot develop a good functional voice because of severe aberrations in the control of his rib cage and abdomen. Information of this nature is critical to planning an effective management strategy.

Phonatory Observations and Measurements. As the patient discusses his voice problem with the clinician, the latter will be making direct judgments concerning the disordered voice. These judgments will include considerations of loudness, pitch, and quality, all of which will be judged normal or abnormal on the basis of the clinician's perceptual impressions. Thus, an important part of the phonatory observation process lies in the ear of the clinician. One word of caution is that the voice heard in the clinical office may not always be the voice the patient uses in his "real world." For example, the five-year-old who comes in for a speech examination is often frightened of the setting and of the unknown examiner, exhibiting his fright with a voice that is barely audible. In attempting to get to know the phonatory habits of voice patients, we may have to observe the rock singer straining for high notes as she sings above a band blazing away at maximum intensity level, the preacher yelling at his congregation about the evils of liquor, the auctioneer yelling his bids back to four hundred farmers assembled in a large barn, etc. The speech-language pathologist must make major efforts to observe the patient in his natural vocal setting. In the next four subsections, we consider the most important observations and measurements to be made in the phonatory evaluation—those dealing with loudness-sound pressure level, pitch-frequency, quality-spectrum, and glottal attack.

Loudness and sound pressure level: We hear different loudness levels in normal voices. These levels are in part determined by the speaking environment. For example, voice is loud on the playground but quiet in the hospital room. Level is also highly influenced by the role the speaker is playing. That is, the preacher may use loud voice at some places in his sermon but use soft voice while talking to congregation members after the church service. Not only do we change our average loudness from time to time during speech, we also put a great deal of loudness variation in our voices to make them interesting to listen to and to convey information to the listener. The voice heard in the clinic should be judged specifically with regard to the adequacy of its average loudness and variations in loudness. An initial question is Does the patient talk with the same loudness and variation as his normal speaking peers?

Loudness cannot be measured directly but is tied closely to sound pressure level of the voice. One method of assessing average level and its variations is to have the subject speak into a microphone attached to a device such as a VU meter or a sound level meter. Sound level meters may be arranged to provide a dial reading of sound pressure level or they can be coupled to devices where a permanent read-out of voice level is made on paper. Figure 8–5 shows a sound level meter with a dial for determining sound pressure level. Using a device such as this, the clinician would measure the average sound pressure level of the voice during various speech activities. For example, during conversational speech the patient would be compared

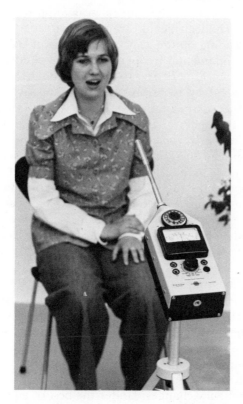

FIGURE 8–5. *A typical sound level meter for use in assessing the patient's control of voice sound pressure level. (Courtesy of Bruel and Kjaer Instruments, Inc., Cleveland, Ohio.)*

against the level typical of normal speakers positioned 1 meter from the microphone, 65 dB. Comparison would also be made against the maximum range of normal individuals for sustained vowels, about 30–40 dB. Loudness-sound pressure level information would be compared by the clinician and related to such factors as the respiratory drive and how open the patient's mouth is during activities.

Pitch and fundamental frequency: Judgments must be made as to whether or not the pitch level of the patient's voice is appropriate for his age and sex. Similarly, pitch variability must be assessed. An example where the two might be deviant in the same patient is the characteristic voice of the deaf speaker.

Our perception of pitch depends heavily on the fundamental frequency of the voice. Measurement of the latter is important in any evaluation. Most adult males have a fundamental frequency somewhere between B_3 and D_3 on the musical scale or 120–140 Hz. Frequency values below or above these values would likely show noticeably in the speaker's voice and be judged as "too low or too high," respectively. The fundamental frequency for adult females usually falls between G_3 and A_4 on the musical scale, approximately 190–215 Hz. Prepubescent children demonstrate a great range of fundamental frequencies, depending on their age and the size of their vocal mechanism; however, fundamental frequency values of children are typically found to range from F_3 (170 Hz) to above G_4 (400 Hz). Frequency is generally determined by recording the spontaneous conversation of the patient and then extracting six or seven vowels out of this sample for analysis by a frequency analyzer or by comparison against a piano or pitch pipe. The *modal fundamental frequency,* or the frequency that occurs most often, is then recorded.

The frequency range of the patient is determined by finding the lowest frequency and the highest frequency he can produce. The typical normal frequency range is about one and a half octaves. On occasion, there are patients who simply cannot produce different frequencies even when attempting to model the clinician. With such a patient, the vocal response to the request to sing "Happy Birthday" generally verifies a severe monotone disability.

After the total frequency range is calculated, the optimum frequency can be determined. It lies about one-fourth from the bottom of the total range, including falsetto. When falsetto is excluded, the total range can be divided by three and the frequency one-third from the bottom is the optimum frequency. When the patient operates at his optimum frequency he can vary his fundamental frequency contour so that with relative ease he can produce downward and upward fundamental frequency changes. Under the best of all possible circumstances the patient's modal fundamental frequency and his optimum frequency will exist at about the same level.

Quality and spectrum: The perceptual judgments we make about dysphonic voices we hear are often very private. That is, we sometimes have a hard time agreeing with one another on what to call a voice quality disorder. Of the three parameters that can be defective in dysphonia (loudness-pitch-quality), quality is, perhaps, the most difficult to pin down in subjective clinical listening. We may "know" that a voice is inferior in quality when we compare it with the voices of other people, but we lack the terminology and even suitable technical procedures to document quality disturbances. Thus, the clinician must attempt to describe verbally what the quality disturbance is that he hears. It is helpful in studying quality to make a voice recording of the patient as part of his evaluation. This recording should include a conversational and reading sample, as well as prolonged vowel utterances. A recording provides the speech-language pathologist with a means for careful repeated listening to the patient's voice. Voice recordings also permit comparison of the patient's voice at the time of evaluation with subsequent recordings, such as a post-therapy recording made at the termination of management.

Instruments that can provide the clinician with spectrum information on which his quality judgments are based include the sound spectrograph. It provides a visual "voice print" of patients' utterances. Using such a display, the clinician can compare the patient's voice with those of normal speakers. Figure 8–6 shows voice prints for utterances judged to have the perceptual qualities of normal voice, nasal voice, breathy voice, harsh voice, and hoarse voice.

Glottal attack: Evaluation should also include a close listening to determine whether or not the patient has a breathy glottal attack, normal phonation onset, or hard glottal attack. A breathy attack is usually characteristic of the patient who habitually speaks with a breathy voice quality. A hard glottal attack, the abrupt onset of phonation, is a common vocal abuse heard in patients who have hyperfunction. Besides listening for attack differences, it is possible to quantify glottal attack through the use of flow measurement techniques and spectrum measurement techniques. For example, measurements on patients with breathy glottal attacks reveal large flow magnitudes at the onset of phonation. These reflect the wastage of air accompanying such onsets.

Other Considerations.   As part of the voice evaluation, the patient should be examined by the clinician relative to the adequacy of structure and function of the various parts of the speech mechanism. Facial muscles, teeth, hard and soft palates, tongue, and pharynx should

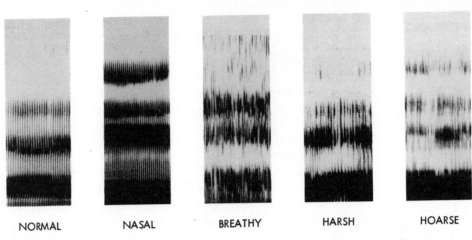

FIGURE 8–6. *Voice prints illustrating the acoustical correlates of different voice qualities judged perceptually. (From W. Zemlin,* Speech and Hearing Science. *Englewood Cliffs, N.J.: Prentice-Hall, 1968.)*

all be examined. For phonatory defects, the clinician should be alert for possible beginnings of nervous system diseases because many problems reflect their beginnings through subtle variations of voice. If there are suspicions of possible nervous system involvement, the speech-language clinician should make an appropriate referral to a neurologist. Problems of infection or allergy, which may be contributing to a dysphonia, may be observed as a reddened pharynx, enlarged tonsils, or inability to breathe through the nose. Again, the clinician should make appropriate referrals. Patients with resonance problems may be observed to have fistulae (small openings) in the palatal area, submucous clefts, obvious velopharyngeal inadequacy, or enlarged lymphoid tissue. Any problems identified would require further investigation and probably medical referral.

MANAGEMENT OF VOICE DISORDERS

After voice disorders are identified and evaluated, they require some type of management. This section highlights the management strategies involved for the four disorder types discussed earlier.

Voice Therapy for Vocal Hyperfunction

The majority of voice problems are due to vocal hyperfunction. People with such problems misuse and abuse their laryngeal mechanism. If vocal excesses are chronic, some of these people develop vocal pathologies such as vocal fold thickening, vocal nodules, vocal polyps, and contact ulcers. Medical-surgical intervention is sometimes required. The decision of whether or not to perform surgery requires that the physician evaluate the size of the lesion, its location, its possible interference with breathing, etc. Generally, voice therapy is the preferred method of treating hyperfunctional voice problems, whether additive lesions have developed or not. The need for voice therapy is illustrated by the following case:

> A man was seen for voice therapy who had previously experienced recurring vocal nodules. He would develop bilateral nodules, have them removed surgically, and within several months of their removal they would reappear. Such recurrence had taken place on four occasions. After the last surgical removal, he was finally referred for voice therapy. Successful attempts at reducing his continuous throat-clearing habit and his continued yelling on the job prevented any further recurrence of his nodules.

Voice therapy, for both children and adults, is usually carried out in the following sequence for vocal hyperfunction problems:

1. Identifying vocal misuses and abuses.
2. Reducing vocal misuses and abuses.
3. Searching with the patient for the best voice he can produce.
4. Employing various approaches to maintain the optimum voice.

Identifying Vocal Misuses and Abuses. A good deal of time must be spent in attempting to isolate the type of vocal behaviors that may be hurting the patient's vocal mechanism. Misuses must be considered, such as whether the patient is habitually using too high a fundamental frequency, too high an intensity level, etc. Excessive crying and yelling are two of the behaviors that are often identified in the abusive repertoires of preschoolers with voice problems. For school-age children, direct observation of the child at play is often the best way to isolate abusive vocal behaviors. In addition, talking directly with the child, his peers, his teachers, and his parents will often reveal a particular habitual vocal behavior that might be abusive. In adults, abuses may cover a wide range, from excessive yelling to constant throat clearing. Sometimes vocal misuses and abuses in adults can only be identified by direct observation of the patient in a particular work setting. The identification of vocal misuses and abuses is an extremely important first step in a voice therapy program. Consequently, the clinician must go "all out" in the search.

Reducing Vocal Misuses and Abuses.   Once vocal misuses and abuses are identified, steps must be taken to significantly reduce them, or, if possible, to eliminate them. Direct counseling of the child and his parents is usually necessary, and it alone often results in substantial reductions in misuses and abuses. The extremely hyperactive child and his parents may require the professional counseling of a child psychologist or psychiatrist. Usually, however, the speech-language pathologist can play the central role in reducing or eliminating the child's vocal misuses and abuses. School-age children, sometimes placed together in a small voice therapy group, can be counseled and instructed as to the need to curb vocal excesses. In fact, a peer "buddy" can be used successfully to monitor each child's vocal behaviors (Deal, McClain, and Sudderth, 1976). An excellent method for making the child aware of the frequency of his vocal abuses, and an aid to reducing them, is to ask the child, perhaps with the help of a peer, to keep track of the number of times he finds himself yelling each day. In doing this, he might keep a tally card, marking down each time he catches himself yelling or is caught yelling. He then marks down the total number of yells on a graph at the end of each day and graphs his behavior from day to day. By plotting his daily yell totals over a period of, perhaps, two weeks, it soon becomes apparent whether his abusive behaviors are decreasing.

For the adult patient, direct counseling is usually a sufficient method of calling various misuses and abuses to attention and of getting on the road to their reduction. Usually, the more obvious abuses are an easy task for the patient to self-eradicate. For example, it is easy to bring to awareness such abuses as excessive smoking and excessive yelling on the job. Subtle, cumulative abuses require more attentive self-watchdogging by the patient. Throat clearing is a subtle but major offender. Frequent throat clearing is a behavior that, by its scraping action, greatly irritates the mucosal membranes of the vocal folds. Irritated membranes tend to exude more mucous as a protection and the patient once again feels the need to clear his throat. The cycle is set. The patient may be counseled to use a "silent cough" (Zwitman and Calcaterra, 1973), to sniff forcefully through the glottis periodically, and to swallow offending mucous. When the cumulative importance of repeated throat clearing is pointed out to the patient, he will usually make deliberate efforts to curb the behavior, efforts that usually are successful.

Searching for the Best Voice.   Generally, the best voice for the patient is a voice that is similar in loudness, pitch, and quality to other persons of the same age and sex. A substantial portion of the therapy process is spent by the clinician and patient searching for this "best voice." The search is a continuous part of the therapy process even as voice changes are progressing. This is because the voice's best performance may be heavily influenced by a particular pathology. For example, the best voice of a seven-year-old girl may be a significant improvement over what she is using at the start of therapy, but still be inappropriately low-pitched because of large vocal nodules on the margins of both vocal folds. As the nodules begin to reduce in size, the possibilities for finding additional "best voices" increase. Searches for the best voice can be done by ear alone, but it is a good idea to conduct them with the aid of some type of a loop-tape recording device. Then, once the best voice is found, and a model is available that needs to be kept, this model can be maintained as long as is desired. The major role of the speech-language pathologist in the continuous searching process is to help the patient produce the best possible voice by introducing him to various facilitating approaches (Wilson, 1972; Boone, 1977; Perkins, 1977). Some approaches that have proven especially useful are working on a new pitch level, a new loudness pattern, a larger mouth opening, and learning to use more sweeping vocal inflections. The search for the best voice is by no means random. It is based on a reasoned approach in which the clinician skillfully moves the patient along a number of avenues of change until the appropriate combination of changes is found (Boone, 1974; Drudge and Philips, 1976).

Some patients may require specific respiratory training in efforts to find their best voices. For example, the patient can learn to extend his expiratory breath through such activities as counting further and further on one expiration, extending the time of his expirations, and increasing the loudness of his voice. Normal speakers have a tendency to match their expirations with the verbal passage they wish to say (Otis and Clark, 1968); therefore, extending by one-word increments the length of a verbal passage on each expiration is a good way of developing better expiratory control.

Once an optimal way of phonating is identified, the patient needs extensive drill and practice using the approaches that produce such improvement. The best voice for the individual is often the easiest one to produce. It is good therapy, therefore, to contrast the old pattern of voicing with the new, letting the patient experience the difference between the two types of productions.

Maintaining the Optimum Voice. Once the patient has produced a target voice model through searching with his clinician, practice is then given to help maintain the new, desired voice. Ear training, using the best voice as the model, plays an important part in voice therapy. It is important to know if the patient can discriminate between his old, faulty voice and the new one he is able to produce as the outcome of the "search." A discussion is given in which the old and new voices are contrasted. This might include differences in how the two voices sound, how they "feel" to the patient, how they might "look" different in a mirror, etc. As therapy goes on, various types of feedback are provided for the patient to help him understand what he is doing with his voice and to aid him in changing various aspects of his phonation. Examples include audio information from a loop-tape recorder, mirror images of mouth opening, flow data relevant to the nature of glottal attack, meter readings of voice intensity level, etc. With all uses of such feedback, it is important that the clinician demonstrate to the patient that he can favorably alter his voice productions by doing particular things. In most cases of vocal hyperfunction, the new voice, once learned, is easier to use than the old forced way of talking.

Negative practice, deliberately using the old way of production, is a good way to let the patient experience again the effort he expends in talking incorrectly. The clinician explains to the patient in language the patient can understand why he must do the various things he does in voice therapy. Imagery is often used to produce particular vocal effects. For example, telling the patient, "Bring your voice up from your throat and place it right behind your nose" is pure imagery with no physiologic correlate. Such an instruction, however, might well make a noticeable difference in the quality of the patient's voice. While the clinician must know the acoustics and physiology of voice, his application of such knowledge to the actual patient must be tempered by the patient's ability to understand instructions and to apply them in modifying his voice. Successful voice clinicians must use words and concepts their patients understand.

We close this section on vocal hyperfunction by attending to some special considerations of management for one vocal hyperfunction disorder in particular—spastic dysphonia. Earlier we mentioned the recent success in treating this disorder through surgical sectioning of the recurrent laryngeal nerve on one side. This success has focused attention away from common beliefs of a psychogenic basis for the disorder and instead suggests that the problem may be neurologically based. Indeed, it may be that we should be considering the treatment of spastic dysphonia under our heading for organic disorders. Be that as it may, the procedure of Dedo (1976), wherein one nerve is cut, appears to be successful because when the patient goes to speak following surgery, he cannot seal off the airway in his old hyperfunctional manner, one vocal fold being fixed in an out (abducted) position. Thus, the patient is left with a slightly breathy dysphonia but with no further struggle to phonate. Additional surgeons are now doing the "Dedo procedure," generally with gratifying results, but it is still too early to evaluate the merits of the procedure for all patients with spastic dysphonia. Voice therapy is sometimes called for after surgery to teach the patient optimum use of the "new" voice.

Voice Therapy for Organically Based Voice Disorders

Most organic voice disorders are produced by structural changes of the larynx or other parts of the vocal tract. These pathological changes, as described earlier, are generally the result of disease or injury. While the management of such disorders is primarily medical-surgical, voice therapy is often an important part of the needed overall rehabilitation strategy. In this section, we briefly consider the medical-surgical part of the management process and give a moderate elaboration of the actual voice therapy procedures that might be used. The order of our discussion roughly parallels that used earlier in Table 8–2.

As we mentioned earlier, the organic problem of infectious laryngitis does not require the services of the speech-language pathologist. This problem is one of an active disease process, usually viral or bacterial in origin, and so it requires systemic treatment by the physician. The only prescription of the speech-language pathologist to the patient is strict voice rest until the infection subsides. This prescription is made to prevent any undue damage to the structures of the larynx.

Problems of papilloma are the most serious of vocal tract diseases of children. The speech-language pathologist's most important role in this type of disorder is to be an important part of the early identification process. The primary treatment for papilloma is medical-surgical. Papillomas grow rapidly and pose a serious threat to the airway, so that they require close and often long-term supervision by the physician. Although voice therapy is not called for pre-operatively, it sometimes may be indicated after surgery, if the larynx or pharynx are severely scarred (Cooper, 1971).

Diseases like leukoplakia, hyperkeratosis, and carcinoma are additive lesions to the larynx or other sites of the vocal tract and are serious conditions requiring close medical-surgical treatment by the physician. No voice therapy is indicated prior to this medical intervention. In some cases, the services of the speech-language pathologist might be called for after the disease processes are totally controlled.

Trauma to the larynx, particularly that which causes changes along the glottal margin, sometimes results in such conditions as granuloma, hemangioma, laryngeal web, or destruction of muscles and/or cartilages. These traumatically-induced problems and their resulting severe dysphonias require surgical intervention. Granulomas, heman-giomas, and webs must be surgically removed. If extensive laryngeal trauma is involved, laryngeal reconstruction may be required. After such surgical treatment has restored an adequate airway and relatively functional vocal fold approximation, voice therapy is usually needed. The speech-language pathologist searches with the patient for the best voice that can be produced, manipulating parameters of loudness, pitch, and quality, similarly to what is done with hyperfunctional voice disorders. Voice therapy following laryngeal trauma and its surgical repair is highly individualized, depending on the site and the extent of the damage, as well as the success of the repair.

Obviously, voice problems resulting from endocrinal or hormo-nal problems require primary intervention of the physician. The basic physical problem, such as the markedly delayed onset of puberty in a male, must be corrected medically as soon as possible. Patients with hormonal problems generally exhibit pitch problems, voices too low or too high in frequency for their age and sex. Speech-language patholo-gists have had good success in helping such patients develop funda-mental frequency levels that are more compatible with those of their normal peers.

Turning to vocal fold paralysis, we are faced with a variety of conditions. The most frequently occurring is paralysis of the unilateral adductor type, which we will consider here. The patient cannot bring his paralyzed fold into the midline, resulting in a breathy, severely hoarse voice. Unless the patient is experiencing some airway prob-lems, such as occasional aspiration of liquids, the physician usually does not recommend any kind of surgical repair. Occasionally, after long-term paralysis (beyond nine months), the surgeon may inject tef-lon in the paralyzed fold to enlarge it and permit better vocal fold adduction (Kirchner and Toledo, 1966). More often, voice therapy is the preferred method of treatment for unilateral adductor paralysis. The therapy may develop forceful glottal attack or use the pushing approach (Brodnitz, 1967), which by combining arm pushing with phonation often enables the normal fold to cross over beyond the midline to approximate the paralyzed fold. Prolonged use of the pushing technique often results in a more normal sounding voice. Other forms of vocal fold paralysis (unilateral or bilateral abductor, or bilateral adductor) require various other combinations of surgery and voice therapy.

The post-laryngectomy patient must develop a new voice source. Diedrich and Youngstrom (1966) have called this new voice "alaryn-geal speech." Post-operatively, the patient is often introduced to an ar-tificial larynx, a vibrating-type instrument which introduces sound into the oral cavity. The patient articulates "on top" of this alaryngeal sound to produce speech. There are two general types of sound vibrators used, an electronic type which produces a buzzing sound not too unlike the sound of an electric shaver and a reed type which sets up a vibration pattern as air from the tracheostoma passes through it. Two electronic-type instruments are shown in Figure 8–7. Interesting comparisons have been made of the intelligibility of the patient's speech using artificial larynges. The reed-type instrument, particularly an inexpensive model known as the Tokyo Artificial Larynx (Bennett and Weinberg, 1973; Weinberg and Riekena, 1973), is often judged by listeners to produce the most intelligible speech. To use the artificial larynx, the patient merely whispers what he wants to say. Whispering includes the articulations necessary to produce speech while the "voice sound" comes from the artificial larynx.

Many laryngectomees learn *esophageal speech.* Here the patient learns to trap air in his esophagus and bring it up voluntarily, producing a belchlike voice. By articulating this belchlike sound, the person produces another form of alaryngeal speech. Most laryngectomees appear to favor the esophageal speech form of communication over using an artificial larynx. Both forms of voicing are used by many laryngectomees. Esophageal speech is taught by any one of three methods: injection, inhalation, and swallow. In the injection method, as the patient articulates stop-plosive sounds, he traps intraoral air with his tongue. He compresses the air within his mouth, making its

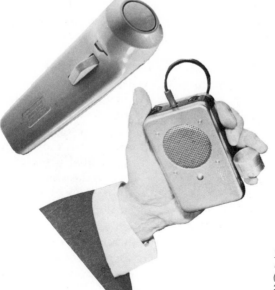

FIGURE 8–7. *Two electronic-type artificial larynges. At the top is a Western-Electric artificial larynx and at the bottom is a Cooper-Rand model. (From D. Boone,* The Voice and Voice Therapy, *2nd. Ed. Englewood Cliffs, N.J.: Prentice-Hall, 1977.)*

pressure higher and driving it out the mouth and down the esophagus. The air trapped below the esophageal opening (the cricopharyn-
geal sphincter) then is driven outward, producing a sound, like we do
when we belch or burp, as it passes through the compressed esophageal sphincter. In the inhalation method, the patient takes an exaggerated breath. This increases the size of the esophagus and lowers
the pressure within it. If the patient combines a sniff with the exaggerated inhalation, this opens the esophagus. Intraoral air is then
sucked into the esophagus. The air becomes trapped and can then be
driven out of the esophagus to produce a sound as it passes through
the opening-exit of the esophagus. In the swallow method, the patient
actively attempts to swallow air directly into the esophagus. During
swallowing the tongue rides high and presses against the palate, creating a high intraoral air pressure, as in the injection method. The
esophagus is open as part of the swallow and air moves into it. Of the
three methods of esophageal speech, the injection method is the
easiest for most patients to learn.

Laryngectomees are one group of patients seen by the speech-
language pathologist who have their own rehabilitation club. The
International Association of Laryngectomees (IAL) was founded over
thirty years ago and is a vital program of the American Cancer Society
(IAL, 1964). The primary focus of the IAL is to aid the new laryngectomee in making the transition from having no voice to having functional communication once again.

Voice Therapy for Psychogenically Based Voice Disorders

Direct symptom modification of a dysphonic or aphonic voice must
not ignore the individual with the disorder. Tense individuals, for example, may exhibit voices that sound tense. The patient may need
psychotherapy or counseling more than he needs voice therapy.
There are occasional voice problems where the voice disorder seems
to have a psychogenic basis and where the disorder serves the patient
in some way. Not long ago it was commonly believed that many voice
symptoms had a conversion cause and that to remove the voice symptom was only to encourage the transfer of the symptom to some other
body site. Consequently, psychotherapy was often done with voice patients instead of direct voice remediation. Gradually this psychological
emphasis has begun to change and direct modification of voice symptoms has become more common. Less concern is now being given to
possible symptom transfer. Stevens (1968) reports no transfer of conversion symptoms in three hundred patients with conversion hysteria

after sodium amytal interviews that successfully reduced the patient's conversion symptom. The speech-language pathologist should provide psychological support as needed, but generally work on direct symptom modification of the voice. If a trial period of voice therapy produces no voice improvement and the patient seems to "hold on" to his voice symptom, the patient at that point might be referred to a psychologist, counselor, or psychiatrist.

The most common psychogenic voice disorder is aphonia. Here the patient has no voice at all and communicates by gesture and whisper. The causes of aphonia are often difficult to identify. Voice therapy for aphonia searches with the patient to establish vegetative phonation (coughing, throat clearing, humming) on a volitional basis. These vegetative phonations are then extended into prolonged vowels. From there, monosyllabic words are introduced and soon the patient is able to speak consistently with some voice. In fact, it is not unusual for an aphonic patient to experience some restoration of voice during the first voice therapy session. It generally requires several sessions, however, for the patient to develop a normal voice. Once an aphonic patient recovers his normal voice, he rarely reverts back to aphonia. Symptomatic voice therapy, searching for phonation and extending it into the speaking situation, is the preferred method of treating aphonia.

Before we leave the topic of aphonia, we should mention that one of the dangers of prolonged voice rest as a treatment for a vocal disorder is that phonation sometimes cannot be resumed after the voice rest restriction has been lifted.

> A five-year-old child with vocal nodules was placed on a five-month period of voice rest by his physician. After completing what must be judged as an unusually excessive period of voice rest, the child was told to "go ahead and talk." The child persisted with his whispered, aphonic voicing pattern, despite all pleas from family and the embarrassed physician. It took eight sessions of voice therapy, searching with the child for vegetative phonations, before he was able to use voice. The boy did all he could to cooperate, perhaps trying too hard. The prolonged voice rest had produced an aphonia which appeared almost as if the boy had forgotten "how to voice." Once normal voicing was experienced, the child did not experience aphonia again.

Patients who develop psychogenic dysphonias have a normal larynx. In voice therapy with such patients, they can usually produce normal phonation under certain conditions. Often by asking the patient to use a different pitch level, or intentionally produce a louder voice, he can produce a voice free of dysphonia. Some patients will revert back to their dysphonic productions as soon as the target voice model "approaches" what the patient apparently feels is his normal voice. Many of the same facilitating approaches used with vocal hyperfunction, such as opening the mouth more or changing glottal attack, will aid these patients to develop a voice relatively free of dysphonia. Such an approach was used with a forty-seven-year-old woman who worked as an elementary school receptionist.

> Her severely dysphonic voice made phone work almost impossible. Direct attempts to modify her voice produced good results initially after only several sessions of voice therapy. However, subsequent to this therapy, she encountered some severe psychological stresses in her personal life and she soon developed another dysphonia. She received psychological counseling as well as voice therapy. Once again, her voice was restored.

This patient illustrates that patients with psychogenic voice disorders often benefit from a dual therapy approach: Counseling and psychotherapy may be provided by the psychologist or the psychiatrist concurrent with voice therapy provided by the speech-language pathologist.

Voice Therapy for Resonance-Based Voice Disorders

The speaker with excessive nasalization or inadequate nasalization may have a physical or structural cause for his problem. As described in Chapter 9, the speech-language pathologist must give priority to assessing the oral and nasal structures that contribute to nasalization. While some resonance-based disorders are functional in nature, the vast majority of nasalization disorders are the result of some structural abnormality, such as cleft palate, palatal insufficiency, hypertrophied adenoids, and so forth. The primary task in management is to first determine if structural adequacy and normal function can be produced by the surgeon, the prosthodontist, the otolaryngologist, or the orthodontist. Specific attempts at voice therapy for resonance-based disorders should be deferred until the physical aspects of the problem have been identified and an overall plan for management has been initiated. Specific therapy approaches for problems of nasalization are provided for the reader in Chapter 9 and will not be repeated here.

Voice therapy is sometimes helpful for correcting problems in oral resonance. The voice may sound better when the patient increases his mouth opening. Similar to the teacher of the singing voice, the voice clinician knows that many good voices sound "muffled" because of lack of optimal oral resonance. Lack of mouth opening can often be directly modified by such therapy approaches as exaggerated chewing, using a yawn-sigh, and working to develop an open-mouth posture. Increased mouth opening usually results in a noticeable improvement in overall voice quality and resonance.

Some patients demonstrate the voice qualities described earlier in the chapter related to excessive anterior or posterior carriage of the tongue. Anterior focus, producing the "thin" voice, can be minimized by having the patient practice rapid productions of back consonants and back vowels for extended drill periods. Posterior resonance-focus can be minimized by having the patient produce a series of whispered front consonants and vowels; rapid drill must be practiced over extended periods of time (Boone, 1966). As the patient practices different tongue carriage, he should be asked to note the different feelings and sounds between the old and new productions.

REFERENCES

ARONSON, A., *Psychogenic Voice Disorders.* Philadelphia: Saunders (1973).

BENNETT, S., and WEINBERG, B., Acceptability ratings of normal, esophageal, and artificial larynx speech. *Journal of Speech and Hearing Research,* 16, 608–615 (1973).

BOONE, D., Dismissal criteria in voice therapy. *Journal of Speech and Hearing Disorders,* 39, 133–139 (1974).

BOONE, D., Modification of the voices of deaf children. *Volta Review,* 68, 686–692 (1966).

BOONE, D., *The Voice and Voice Therapy,* (2nd Ed.). Englewood Cliffs, N.J.: Prentice-Hall (1977).

BRODNITZ, F., *Vocal Rehabilitation.* Rochester, Minn.: Whiting Press (1967).

CHERRY, J., and MARGULIES, S., Contact ulcer of the larynx. *Laryngoscope,* 78, 1937–1940 (1968).

COOPER, M., Papillomata of the vocal folds: A review. *Journal of Speech and Hearing Disorders,* 36, 51–60 (1971).

DAMSTE, P., Voice change in adult women caused by virilizing agents. *Journal of Speech and Hearing Disorders,* 32, 126–132 (1967).

DARLEY, F., ARONSON, A., and BROWN, J., Clusters of deviant speech dimensions in the dysarthrias. *Journal of Speech and Hearing Research,* 12, 462–496 (1969).

DEAL, R., McCLAIN, B., and SUDDERTH, J., Identification, evaluation, therapy, and follow-up for children with vocal nodules in a public school setting. *Journal of Speech and Hearing Disorders,* 41, 390–397 (1976).

DEDO, H., Recurrent laryngeal nerve section for spastic dysphonia. *Annals of Otology, Rhinology, and Laryngology,* 85, 451–459 (1976).

DIEDRICH, W., and YOUNGSTROM, K., *Alaryngeal Speech.* Springfield, Ill.: Charles C Thomas (1966).

DRUDGE, M., and PHILIPS, B., Shaping behavior in voice therapy. *Journal of Speech and Hearing Disorders,* 41, 398–411 (1976).

DUNN, H., Methods of measuring vowel formant bandwidths. *Journal of the Acoustical Society of America,* 33, 1737–1746 (1961).

FISHER, H., *Improving Voice and Articulation.* Boston: Houghton Mifflin (1966).

FROESCHELS, E., Hygiene of the voice. *Archives of Otolaryngology,* 37, 122–130 (1943).

HIXON, T., Respiratory function in speech. In F. Minifie, T. Hixon, and F. Williams (Eds.), *Normal Aspects of Speech, Hearing, and Language.* Englewood Cliffs, N.J.: Prentice-Hall (1973).

HIXON, T., Some new techniques for measuring the biomechanical events of speech production: One laboratory's experiences. *American Speech and Hearing Association, Report No. 7,* 68–103 (1972).

HIXON, T., GOLDMAN, M., and MEAD, J., Kinematics of the chest wall during speech production: Volume displacements of the rib cage, abdomen, and lung. *Journal of Speech and Hearing Research,* 16, 78–115 (1973).

HIXON, T., MEAD, J., and GOLDMAN, M., Dynamics of the chest wall during speech production: Function of the thorax, rib cage, diaphragm, and abdomen. *Journal of Speech and Hearing Research,* 19, 297–356 (1976).

HULL, F., MIELKE, P., WILLEFORD, J., and TIMMONS, R., *National Speech and Hearing Survey.* Fort Collins: Colorado State University (OE Project 50978, Bureau of Education for the Handicapped, Office of Education, HEW) (1976).

International Association of Laryngectomees, *Helping Words for the Laryngectomee.* New York: International Association for Laryngectomees (1964).

KIRCHNER, F., and TOLEDO, P., Vocal cord injection. *Journal of the Kansas Medical Society,* 67, 125–129 (1966).

LUCHSINGER, R., and ARNOLD, G., *Voice-Speech-Language, Clinical Communicology: Its Physiology and Pathology.* Belmont, Calif.: Wadsworth (1965).

MILISEN, R., Methods of evaluation and diagnosis of speech disorders. In L. Travis (Ed.), *Handbook of Speech Pathology.* New York: Appleton-Century-Crofts (1971).

MURPHY, A., *Functional Voice Disorders.* Englewood Cliffs, N.J.: Prentice-Hall (1964).

NETSELL, R., Subglottal and intraoral air pressures during the intervocalic contrast of /t/ and /d/. *Phonetica,* 20, 68–73 (1969).

NETSELL, R., and HIXON, T., A noninvasive method for clinically estimating subglottal air pressure. *Journal of Speech and Hearing Disorders,* 43, 326–330 (1978).

OTIS, A., and CLARK, R., Ventilatory implications of ventilation. In A. Bouhuys (Ed.), *Sound Production in Man.* New York: New York Academy of Sciences, 155 (1968).

PERKINS, W., *Speech Pathology: An Applied Behavioral Science.* St. Louis: C. V. Mosby (1977).

ROBE, E., BRUMLIK, J., and MOORE, P., A study of spastic dysphonia. *Laryngoscope,* 70, 219–245 (1960).

SENTURIA, B., and WILSON, F., Otorhinolaryngic findings in children with voice deviations. *Annals of Otology, Rhinology, and Laryngology,* 72, 1027–1042 (1968).

SINGLETON, G., and ADKINS, W., Cryosurgical treatment of juvenile laryngeal papillomatosis. *Annals of Otology, Rhinology, and Laryngology,* 81, 784–789 (1972).

STEVENS, H., Conversion hysteria: A neurologic emergency. *Mayo Clinic Procedures,* 43, 54–64 (1968).

URABEC, D., The inverted Schneiderian papilloma. *Laryngoscope,* 85, 186–220 (1975).

WEINBERG, B., and RIEKENA, A., Speech produced with the Tokyo artificial larynx. *Journal of Speech and Hearing Disorders,* 38, 383–389 (1973).

WILSON, D., *Voice Problems of Children.* Baltimore: Williams and Wilkins (1972).

ZWITMAN, D., and CALCATERRA, T., The "silent cough" method for vocal hyperfunction. *Journal of Speech and Hearing Disorders,* 38, 119–125 (1973).

signpost   The orofacial region is subject to a wide range of congenital and acquired structural disorders. Many of these disorders cause or are associated with communication disorders. Chapter 9 is concerned with those orofacial disorders that most commonly affect human communication. Included are the relatively minor problems that affect communication, such as enlarged adenoids, and the devastating affects associated with congenital orofacial syndromes and surgical removal of the tongue. Major emphasis is placed on the condition of orofacial clefting, the most common cause of speech disorders in individuals with structural problems of the orofacial complex. Speech, voice, hearing, and language disorders that accompany orofacial disorders are described and attention is given to methods for the evaluation and management of the communication disorders encountered in individuals with orofacial problems. The management of communication problems in persons with major orofacial disorders is one of the biggest professional challenges to be faced by the speech-language pathologist. It also represents the area where the person trained in communication disorders is most likely to be found heading an interdisciplinary team of allied professionals such as the plastic surgeon, otolaryngologist, prosthodontist, dentist, genetic counselor, psychological counselor, audiologist, and vocational rehabilitation counselor.

9

Stanley J. Ewanowski & John H. Saxman

orofacial
disorders

Mr. Murphy knew before his surgery that there was a chance the cancerous growth discovered beneath his tongue the week previous was not the only cancer site. What he did not really appreciate was how extensive the tissue removal was to be. Because a secondary site had been discovered on the floor of his nose, portions of the hard palate and the velum, as well as his entire mandible on the left side of his face and a large portion of his tongue were removed. The shock of discovering that half his lower face was missing, was alleviated somewhat when the reconstruction possibilities were explained to him. It would be a long time, however, before he would be able to regain functional speech. William Murphy was fortunate that his "cure" was not considered complete with the removal of the cancerous tissues. His road back to a good quality of life was difficult and full of struggles. Only through the cooperative efforts of a rehabilitation team and the constant support of his family and friends was he able to eventually return to his job as a shop foreman. At fifty-four years of age his life started somewhat anew.

A variety of conditions can affect the structures of the pharyngeal-oral-nasal complex. Some are present at birth while others are acquired later in life. Those present at birth are generally the result of faulty development during the embryological stage or the result of hereditary traits that bring about less than optimal orofacial features. Acquired orofacial disorders, by contrast, may be the result of disease processes or traumas, such as automobile or industrial accidents or surgical removal of tissues. The effects of congenital and acquired orofacial disorders on speech production are highly variable, depending on such factors as the extent of deviation from normal and the capabilities of the individual to compensate for deviation. All aspects of communication can be affected. Disorders of speech, voice, hearing, or language are possibilities; for some individuals all aspects may be disordered to some degree.

In this chapter we divide orofacial disorders into two broad categories: (1) orofacial clefts and (2) other orofacial disorders. This division allows us to allot the major portion of several subsections to problems faced by the individual born with a cleft of the lip and/or palate. More is known about such types of orofacial disorders than about any other — you are more likely to encounter a child or an adult who has an orofacial cleft than any other orofacial disorder of comparable severity. It is useful to begin our discussion with a brief account of orofacial embryology. We will then discuss the types and causes of orofacial disorders, followed by a discussion of the communication disorders associated with orofacial problems. The last two sections of the chapter deal with some of the important principles and procedures involved with the evaluation and management of communication disorders associated with orofacial problems.

OROFACIAL EMBRYOLOGY

Because many orofacial disorders have their beginnings during the first months of intrauterine life, the materials in this first section provide an essential background for later discussion. Following conventional divisions used by developmental biologists, we describe normal developmental features with regard to the *external face* and the *internal face*.

Development of the External Face

Up to the fourth week of embryological development, the mass of evolving tissue hardly looks like the human beings we know. At best, it is difficult to identify which part of an embryo will become the nose, or the lips, or the maxilla, or the mandible. However, from the fourth to the eighth week of intrauterine development, a clearly recognizable human face will emerge. Stages of this development are seen clearly in the series of drawings shown in Figure 9–1 and warrant our attention.

Beginnings of a mouth are visible at about four weeks (Figure 9–1a) when the *oral plate* ruptures and the pharynx is placed in communication with the space outside the embryo's head. First signs of the nose appear at approximately five weeks (b), soon after which the *nasal pits*

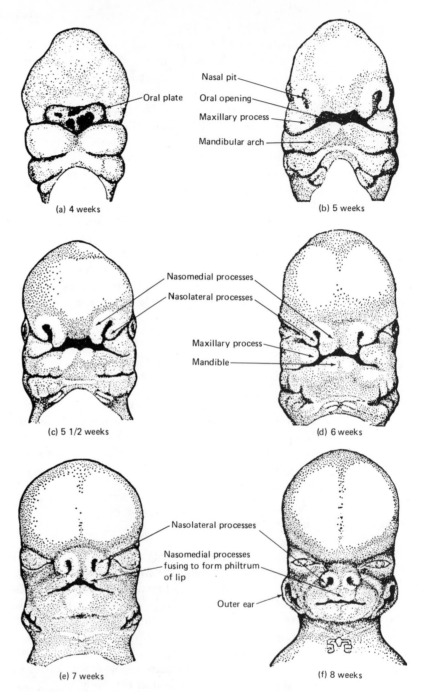

FIGURE 9–1. *Some of the important stages in the formation of the external face in the human embryo. See text for discussion. (Modified from B. Patten,* Foundations of Embryology, *2nd Ed. New York: McGraw-Hill, 1964.)*

or indentations begin to migrate toward the midline of the face. At about this same time, the *mandible* is nearly developed except for a prominent notch in the middle of its upper surface. The *maxilla* (colloquially called the upper jaw), at about five weeks, can be seen as two processes moving from the side of the head toward the center of what will ultimately be the face.

Between the fifth and sixth weeks (c), the tissue surrounding the nasal pits begins to grow rapidly to form the *nasolateral* and *nasomedial* processes. When development is complete, the nasolateral processes will form the *alae* (lateral wings of the nostrils). The nasomedial processes will contribute to the formation of several structures: the mid-portion of the nose, the mid-portion of the upper lip, the mid-portion of the maxilla, and the entire frontmost portion of the hard palate, called the *primary palate*.

Near the sixth week (d), a deepening of the nasal pits, further growth of the nasolateral and nasomedial processes, and nearly final development of the mandible take place. Clearly defined grooves separate the three processes (nasolateral, nasomedial, and maxillary) from each other during this stage. Later in this chapter, we will inspect this normal embryological development from the perspective of orofacial disorders. The point here is that these grooves should not continue to be present much beyond the sixth week of intrauterine life.

Sculpting of the external face is well along the way by the seventh week (e). The nasal pits have deepened so that a *nasal cavity* has been formed. Of crucial importance is the joining of the nasolateral and nasomedial processes to complete the formation of the external nose. Also notice in Figure 9–1e that the lower nasomedial processes and the maxillary processes have joined to a degree that nearly completes the formation of the *upper lip*.

By the eighth week (f), the external face has clearly arrived. The eyes, which up to this time have been located on the sides of the head, now are at the front of the face. The ears, which have been developing along the side of the neck, now are on the lower sides of the head. Fusion of the upper lip is complete and upper lip features such as the central *Cupid's Bow* (upper-margin curve) and *philtrum* (center dimple) are present. From this point on, the external face grows in size until birth. Thus, in just sixty days the structures of the external face take on their essential form.

Even more directly associated with later speech production skills is the growth and development of the tongue and the hard and soft palates. While the external face is developing, these and other structures of the internal face have simultaneously begun to evolve. We will now discuss this interdependent development of the key parts of the internal face.

Development of the Internal Face

The first indications of tongue development appear as swellings along the inside front and side borders of the mandible. These *lingual swellings*, as they are called, increase in size from their first appearance at approximately four weeks of intrauterine life until they merge and create the shape of the tongue as we know it. Except for further growth in size, the tongue is almost completely developed by the tenth week.

Above the tongue, at about the eighth week, changes are underway in the space behind the former nasal pits. This space, becoming the *nasal chambers*, develops *conchae* (shell-like structures) along its side walls which will become entryways to the *sinuses*. During the sixth to tenth week of embryological development the foundation for the hard palate and the floor of the nasal cavities, the *palatine shelves*, begin their migration toward the midline of the internal face. This movement toward midline coincides with the lowering of the tongue mass which had previously rested within the developing nasal chambers. Prior to the time that the palatine shelves become joined to form the main mass of the hard palate, the *primary palate* (see Figure 9–2), at the very front of the roof of the mouth, has developed. The primary palate includes that portion of the upper airway that will develop into the lip, the alveolar ridge, and the hard palate segment extending back to the *incisive foramen* (a hole behind the alveolar ridge through which passes nerve and blood supply to the palate). As depicted in Figure 9–2, the primary palate and the *secondary palate* (that portion formed by the joining of the palatine shelves behind the incisive foramen) coordinate their growth to form a single structure: the *bony* or *hard palate*. At approximately the seventh week, the side margins of a part of the primary palate begin to join with the margins of the frontmost part of the horizontally-oriented palatine shelves. Once fusion has taken place in the front portion of the roof of the mouth, it progresses backward, rather like the closing of a zipper, until the entire length of the palatal shelves is united by the end of the tenth or eleventh week. Failure of the shelves to unite with the primary palate or with each other will result in a cleft of the hard palate.

During the tenth to twelfth week of orofacial development, the soft palate tissue fuses. Tissue that will form the soft palate's muscles begins to migrate toward the midline from both sides of the back of the mouth during the fifth to sixth week. By the tenth week this tissue

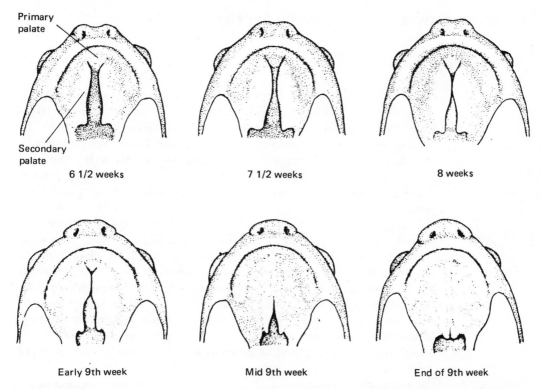

Primary palate

Secondary palate

6 1/2 weeks 7 1/2 weeks 8 weeks

Early 9th week Mid 9th week End of 9th week

FIGURE 9–2. *A schematic illustration of joining of the primary and secondary palates to form the bony portion of the roof of the mouth. Notice how the closure of the opening between the two halves of the bony palate proceeds from front to back, somewhat akin to the closing of a zipper. See text for further discussion. (Modified from B. Patten, Embryology of the palate and the maxillofacial region. In W. Grabb, S. Rosenstein, and K. Bzoch, Eds.,* Cleft Lip and Palate: Surgical, Dental, and Speech Aspects. *Boston: Little, Brown, 1971.)*

has grown and moved into a horizontal orientation along with the palatine shelves. As soon as the rearmost portion of the palatine shelves has fused, the soft palate tissue begins to fuse in a front-to-back progression, further closing the developmental zipper. Failure of this tissue to join, as with failure of the palatine bones to join, results in several clinical conditions that we will discuss later.

What should be appreciated from this brief review is that embryological development of the orofacial complex is exquisitely timed. Each structure of the face develops on schedule and at prearranged times the structures fuse and continue to grow as one. The direction and timing of this growth and development is uncompromising: Even a slight deviation from schedule can result in a profound orofacial disorder.

TYPES AND CAUSES OF OROFACIAL DISORDERS

Orofacial Clefts

Historical accounts tell of orofacial clefts in Egyptian mummies (Lufkin, 1938), in early Romans (Mettler, 1947), in ancient Chinese (Boo-Chai, 1966), and in pre-Columbian Peruvians (Weinberger, 1948). To the present, many thousands of children are born every year with orofacial clefts—in all races and all cultures of the world. For the most part, these clefts are confined to the lip and or hard and soft palates, although rarer clefts do occur at other sites within the orofacial complex.

Figure 9–3 is a photograph of a newborn human with a congenital cleft lip and cleft hard and soft palates. The view shows the orofacial clefts prior to their surgical closure so that the magnitude of the problem can be appreciated. For a moment, try to imagine yourself as a parent of this child when told shortly after his birth that your baby has a cleft of the lip and palate. Surely this would be a most anxious time, laden with emotion. After the initial impact of hearing and/or seeing that your baby is not the physical perfection that was hoped for and anticipated, a flood of questions and concerns might

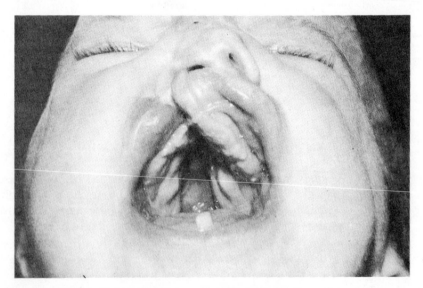

FIGURE 9–3. *A newborn human with a congenital cleft lip and cleft hard and soft palates. Notice that the cleft of the lip is to one side and that the nasal cavity can be seen directly through the unfused roof of the mouth.* (From W. Perkins, Speech Pathology, *2nd Ed. St. Louis, 1977. The C. V. Mosby Co.; courtesy of John Goin, M.D., Los Angeles.)

occur to you such as: Will my baby be okay? What will happen to my baby? How serious is the problem? Can I cope with this situation? How will my family and friends react? Why did this happen to us? What went wrong? What can be done to help my baby be normal? How many other people have babies like mine? It is important that these questions and the many more that arise are answered to the satisfaction of the parents. In this chapter, we try to answer some of these questions to the satisfaction of the reader; a reasonable place to start is to consider just what are orofacial clefts.

As the name implies, a *cleft* is a *separation or space between parts that are normally joined,* thus interrupting the continuity of the structure. Recall in our review of embryological development, that a key feature of normal orofacial development is the normal joining of structures. We saw (Figure 9–1) that one of the important steps in the formation of the external face is the joining of several processes: the nasolateral, nasomedial, and maxillary processes. We also saw (Figure 9–2) that internal face formation is likewise dependent upon the joining of structures; the primary palate develops at the front of the mouth to fuse with the secondary palate which itself develops from the joining of the two palatine shelves. Although orofacial clefts can be acquired through various traumas, the vast majority of those of the lip and/or hard and soft palates are due to congenital failures of these structures to join. Of the many ways to classify types of congenital clefting (Berlin, 1971), a division into two general types is convenient: (1) clefts of the lip and/or alveolar process (gum ridge), the embryological primary palate, and (2) clefts of the hard and/or soft palates, the embryological secondary palate.

Clefts of the Lip and/or Alveolar Process: Primary Palate Disorders. Clefts of the primary palate may involve the upper lip, the alveolar process back to the incisive foramen, or both the upper lip and alveolar process. Figure 9–4 illustrates three types of clefts of the lip. The lip can be affected on one or the other side (unilateral), or both sides (bilateral), and clefts on each side may vary in extent. One convention for describing the extent of a cleft is to partition it into thirds, with 3/3 representing a complete cleft of a structure. The clefts depicted in Figure 9–4 are (a) a complete unilateral cleft, (b) a bilateral cleft complete on one side and incomplete on the other, and (c) a bilateral cleft complete on both sides. The clefts portrayed serve only as examples. A wide variety of combinations of lip site and cleft extent conditions may be found.

A comment needs to be made here about a term that students often bring with them to an introductory course in communication disorders. In the course of teaching about orofacial disorders we are

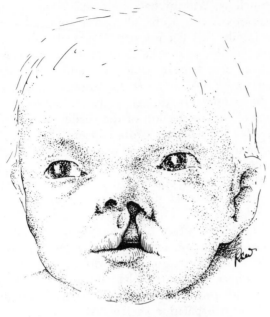

(a) Left unilateral
    lip cleft   3/3

(b) Bilateral lip cleft
    Right 3/3
    Left   1/3

(c) Bilateral lip cleft
    Right 3/3
    Left   3/3

FIGURE 9–4. *Three examples of the variety of possible congenital clefts of the upper lip. See text for discussion. (Modified from C. Wells,* Cleft Palate and Its Associated Speech Disorders. *New York: McGraw-Hill, 1971.)*

often asked about the term "harelip." Is this an accepted professional term? Most assuredly it is not. The term is never used by persons engaged professionally with children and adults with cleft lips and/or palates. As with many colloquial expressions for disordered physical or mental conditions, harelip (split down the center as a rabbit's lip) is poor for accuracy and poor for promoting values of human dignity.

    When there is a complete cleft of the lip, an accompanying cleft of the alveolar process immediately behind the lip should be suspected, although it is not obligatory. Like clefts of the lip, clefts of the alveolar process can be unilateral or bilateral and either complete or incomplete. In addition to their occurring in association with clefts of the lip, clefts of the alveolar process may also occur in isolation. Figure 9–5 portrays several of the possible types of clefts of the alveolar process with and without associated clefts of the lip. Shown are (a) unilateral and (b) bilateral complete clefts of the alveolar process alone, and (c) unilateral and (d) bilateral complete clefts of the alveolar process and lip together.

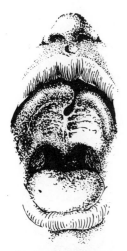

(a) Left unilateral
   alveolar cleft   3/3

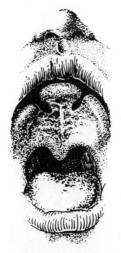

(b) Bilateral alveolar cleft
   Right 3/3
   Left 3/3

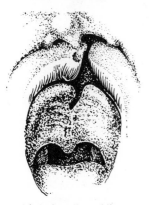

(c) Left unilateral lip
   and alveolar cleft

   Lip 3/3
   alveolar process   3/3

(d) Bilateral lip and
   alveolar clefts

   Lip 3/3, right and left
   alveolar process   3/3,
   right and left

FIGURE 9–5. *Four examples of the variety of possible congenital clefts of the alveolar process with and without associated clefts of the lip. See text for discussion. (Modified from C. Wells,* Cleft Palate and Its Associated Speech Disorders. *New York: McGraw-Hill, 1971.)*

Clefts of the Hard and/or Soft Palates: Secondary Palate Disorders. Figure 9–6 illustrates six of the possible types of clefts of the secondary palate arranged in order of progression from the back of the velum (uvula and soft palate) forward. This array includes several types of associated problems that warrant comment. For convenience

(a) Soft palate cleft   1/3
   with bifid uvula

(b) Soft palate cleft   1/3
   with bifid uvula and
   short soft palate

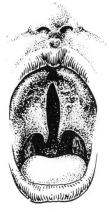

(c) Soft palate cleft   3/3
   and hard palate cleft   3/3

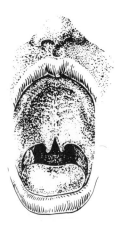

(d) Soft palate cleft   3/3
   and submucous hard
   palate cleft   3/3

(e) Left unilateral complete cleft,
   lip and palate

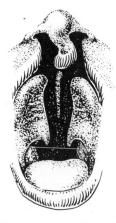

(f) Bilateral complete cleft,
   lip and palate

FIGURE 9–6. *Six examples of the variety of possible congenital clefts of the hard and soft palates with and without associated clefts of the lip and alveolar process. See text for discussion. (Modified from C. Wells,* Cleft Palate and Its Associated Speech Disorders. *New York: McGraw-Hill, 1971.)*

of discussion, letter designations only will be used to refer to the six panels.

Panels (a) and (b) depict 1/3 clefts of the soft palate with accompanying clefts of the uvula. In panel (b) the soft palate is also congenitally short, a problem to be discussed later. Panel (c) shows a complete cleft of the soft and hard palates, while panel (d) depicts a similar situation but with the unjoined hard palate shelves being hidden by mucosal tissue across them. This latter condition, referred to as a *sub-mucous cleft,* is sometimes not immediately obvious to the observer and requires special care by the clinician for its detection, as we discuss later when dealing with evaluation. Continuing with Figure 9–6, panel (e) depicts a cleft of the soft and hard palates that extends into the alveolar process and lip on the left side. Finally, panel (f) shows a bilateral complete cleft of the palate and lip. Note that the midline partition of the nasal cavity can be seen through the cleft.

It is important to notice in Figure 9–6 that these unrepaired clefts vary in several dimensions in addition to place of cleft. Such factors as the width of the cleft, displacement of structures from their usual positions, and amount of tissue in the various structures adjacent to the cleft are important considerations when selecting among alternative ways to repair the cleft.

Causes and Incidence of Clefts of the Lip and/or Palate. The search for the causes of orofacial clefting involves many disciplines, such as developmental biology, genetics, and physical anthropology. As with all congenital disorders, parents of children with clefts want to know why it happened. They usually ask: What went wrong? At present, physicians and genetic counselors would probably point to four possibilities: (1) genetic inheritance, (2) intrauterine environmental factors known to damage the embryo, (3) chromosomal aberrations, and (4) mutant genes (Fraser, 1971).

These four causal possibilities have been implicated differentially across the variety of types of orofacial clefts that we have just discussed. Hereditary factors are important to both lip and palate clefts, though evidence suggests that hereditary factors are more pervasive in clefts of the lip alone. Cleft lip with or without a cleft palate is probably best explained by a multifactored threshold inheritance model. Basically, it involves multiple genes for clefting "threshold" before the trait is expressed (Falconer, 1965). Also important in a multifactored model is the interaction of genetic factors with the intrauterine environment. A small percentage of cleft lip births can be related to chromosomal abnormalities; however, these infants usually do not survive the first year of life. Cleft palate only is more difficult to account for causatively and appears to involve a more direct inheritance model where genetic factors can be demonstrated.

The most frequently cited incidence figure for orofacial clefts in the United States is 1 in 700–770 live births (Slaughter and Phair, 1952; Gilmore and Hoffman, 1966). Clefts of the lip, with or without cleft palate, are more common than clefts of the palate only. Males have more clefts of the lip with or without cleft palate than females, whereas females have more clefts of the palate only than males. These and other incidence differences across nationalities and races are considered by developmental biologists, physical anthropologists, and other research specialists as they continue their attempts to understand the causes of orofacial clefting. We are far from having all the answers.

Other Orofacial Disorders

For convenience, we will divide our discussion of other orofacial disorders into those involving the tongue, the velopharyngeal mechanism and the nose, and the facial skeleton. As mentioned earlier, less is known about these disorders than about orofacial clefts.

Disorders of the Tongue. Embryological development of the tongue occurs as the lingual swellings increase in size and fuse to become an almost fully developed tongue by about the tenth intrauterine week of life. The tongue is not as prone to embryological disorders as are other orofacial structures; however, some types of congenital disorders and several types of acquired disorders of the tongue occur.

Absence of the tongue is called *aglossia*. Congenital aglossia or *hypoplasia* (abnormally small tongue) is very rare and newborns with such a disorder usually present multiple-handicapping orofacial problems.

Acquired aglossia and partial loss of the tongue, unfortunately, is not rare today. In earlier times, removal of the tongue happened for reasons other than medical and was accomplished by persons not trained in medical sciences. Who can forget the chill of horror when the evil Duke told his henchmen to *"Rip out his tongue,"* if their captive didn't tell when the rendezvous was planned. Or, "If you breathe so much as a word of what you just heard, I'll have your tongue cut out." Whether fact or fancy, the expectation was that the victim would never talk again.

Nowadays, surgical removal of all or a portion of the tongue (*glossectomy*) is an accepted treatment for oral cancer, which is diagnosed in approximately 15,000 persons in the United States in a given year according to estimates of the American Cancer Society (1978). Cancers in the mouth, some involving the tongue, constitute around 5–9 percent of all cancers (American Cancer Society, 1978). Treatment for many of these cancers will involve radical surgery resulting in total or partial glossectomy.

Disorders of the Velopharyngeal Mechanism (Excluding Clefting) and the Nose. In addition to palatal clefts, a number of other structural deviations of the velopharyngeal mechanism and nose may exist. Some of these are congenital and others are acquired.

Congenital disorders are highly varied, involving either excesses or insufficiencies of pharyngeal-nasal tissues. They may also include abnormalities in shape and fabric. The most often observed are disorders related to the structure of the pharyngeal walls, length of the velum, and blockages of the nasal pathway. Genetically determined growth factors underlie most of these congenital disorders. Common among this type are velopharyngeal dysfunctions caused by a velum that is too short to make contact with the back wall of the pharynx (review Figure 9–6b) or a pharyngeal space that is enlarged to the extent that the velum, even if of normal length, cannot reach the pharyngeal wall (Spriestersbach, 1965). The principle consequence of either condition is an inability on the part of the child to achieve adequate velopharyngeal closure. Also observed congenitally are disorders of velar structure, including inappropriate muscle insertion locations on the velum that preclude a velum of adequate length from being able to rise to an appropriate level for pharyngeal contact. As a result of certain types of surgical reconstruction of the congenitally malformed velopharynx, there may be a restricted mobility of the mechanism during function. Finally, nasal pathway blockages come in several forms congenitally and include deviated septa (mid-line partitions), collapsed alae (nasal wings), and abnormal shaping of the tortuous nasal chambers. Such disorders result in problems with usual nasal breathing and in the normal passage of sounds through the nose.

Acquired disorders of the velopharyngeal mechanism and nose occur in both children and adults. These disorders are the result of disease processes, traumas, and the surgical removal of tissues. Most prominent in children are disorders related to the blockage of the pharyngeal-nasal airway by enlarged adenoids or deviated septa resulting from accidental blows to the face. Such disorders prevent the passage of air and acoustic energy through the nose and sometimes give the speaker the type of voice quality we have all experienced when we have a cold. We can all remember times when we tried to say "I got a cold in my nose" only to hear it come out as "I got a cold id by doze." We speak *hyponasally* or *denasally* under such circumstances.

Oftentimes, surgical removal of excessive adenoid tissue leads to a contrasting problem in children; that is, the "cure" for a blockage gives them another problem of the velopharynx. In a certain percentage of children *adenoidectomy* leads to velopharyngeal incompetency (Wallner et al., 1968; Neiman and Simpson, 1975). This is because the location of the adenoids in the back of the upper throat is such for some speakers that the mass of tissue actually assists in filling the velopharyngeal space for closure of the airway into the nose. In some children surgical removal of this tissue leaves the space too large so that the velum and sidewalls of the pharynx cannot form an airtight seal. Air now flows easily into the nose but so does acoustic energy and the child may now sound *hypernasal* in voice quality, as the following case history illustrates:

> Josie, six years old, had undergone an adenotonsillectomy one year prior to being seen in the speech clinic. Her surgery was reportedly done to relieve the chronic conditions of middle-ear infection and recurring sore throat. Josie's speech and voice characteristics were entirely within normal limits prior to her surgery. In the period immediately following surgery, her utterances were hypernasal due to the adenoid removal. This hypernasal quality persisted (usually readjustment to the changed spatial relationships within the velopharynx occurs within three months) with no improvement toward her previous normal-sounding voice. Lateral head x-ray studies revealed that Josie's velum could not make contact with the posterior wall of her pharynx. The surgical removal of her excessive adenoid tissue had opened up an abnormally deep nasopharyngeal cavity (upper throat). Although her middle-ear condition and sore throat problem improved as a result of her surgery, the unfortunate side-effect for her was a voice disorder in need of clinical management.

Acquired velopharyngeal disorders in adults are usually the result of disease processes that require surgical intervention and/or involve space occupying growths, or they are a consequence of injuries to the orofacial complex. As illustrated in the introductory paragraph to this chapter, Mr. Murphy's need for surgical removal of tissue from the velum and nose is a typical example encountered by the speech-language pathologist working in an orofacial clinic. If the velum is left without sufficient bulk to fill the velopharyngeal space, adequate velopharyngeal closure for speech cannot be obtained. Fortunately, for Mr. Murphy and for others whose velopharyngeal or nasal mechanisms are altered for some reason, several management procedures are available.

Disorders of the Facial Skeleton. Congenital and acquired disorders of the facial skeleton often contribute to disorders of communication. We will consider congenital disorders here because of their prevalence and because they often are expressed in clusters of symptoms (*syndromes*) that together have major impacts on communication. Peterson (1973), in her review of the literature of speech disorders associated with craniofacial (head and face) syndromes, lists twelve different syndromes for which there is some mention of speech. We will highlight only a few of these syndromes.

One major category of craniofacial disorders is that of *premature craniofacial synostosis.* This lengthy term refers to the early ossification (closure) of the bones along the suture lines of the developing skull. Early closure prevents the normal growth of the skull, the upper part of which needs to increase severalfold in volume during the period from infancy to adulthood. The two most notable syndromes associated with premature craniofacial synostosis are *Apert's syndrome* and *Crouzon's syndrome.* Each involves the arrested growth of several sutures of the skull and midface with resulting characteristic appearance features and disorders of function. Of the two, Apert's is more rare and generally more severe in its expression. Figure 9–7 is a photograph of a child with Crouzon's syndrome. Note the bulging eyes, along with an underdeveloped midfacial region. Common features of such children often include a small pharynx, malocclusion and dental deviations, outer-ear deformities, and cleft palate. Frequently observed, as in the boy in Figure 9–7, is an excessively high-arched palatal vault that is filled with excessive soft tissue. An opened-mouth posture is also characteristic of the disorder. Obviously, children with such extensive orofacial complications will very likely have communication disorders (Peterson, 1973).

We conclude our discussion of disorders of the facial skeleton by illustrating the extremely wide range of structural variations that may

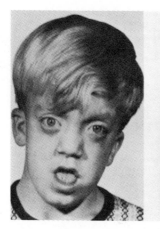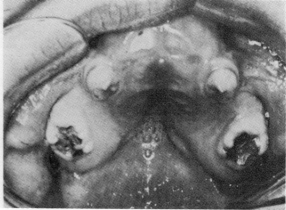

FIGURE 9–7. *Photographs of (a) a child with Crouzon's syndrome and (b) the roof of his mouth. Note the usual opened-mouth posture at rest and the excessive soft tissue that fills the palatal vault. Bulging eyes and an underdeveloped midfacial region are also apparent. (From S. Peterson, Speech pathology in craniofacial malformations other than cleft lip and palate. In Proceedings of the Conference — Orofacial Anomalies: Clinical and Research Implications, American Speech and Hearing Association, Report No. 8, 111–131, 1973.)*

be observed in orofacial disorders and that may contribute to communication disorders. Figure 9–8 shows six individuals with various facial skeleton abnormalities. Important features include underdevelopment of one half of the face, (a) and (b); underdevelopment of the midface, (c); widely spaced eyes, (d) and (e); developmental abnormality of the nose, (d); and developmental abnormality of the outer ear, (f). Most of the skeletal disorders discussed here have been traced to mutant

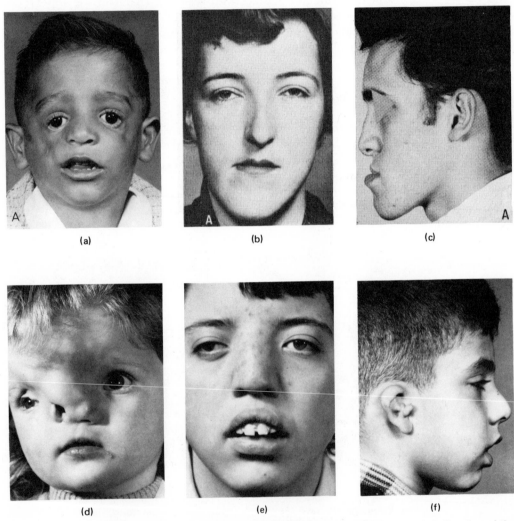

(a)   (b)   (c)

(d)   (e)   (f)

FIGURE 9–8. *Photographs of six persons with a variety of congenital disorders of the facial skeleton. See text for description of the disordered features of each individual. (From J. Longacre, Ed.,* Craniofacial Anomalies: Pathogenesis and Repair. *Philadelphia: Lippincott, 1968, and from J. M. Converse, Ed.,* Reconstructive Plastic Surgery. *Philadelphia: Saunders, 1964.)*

genes and chromosomal aberrations. Speech-language pathologists and audiologists can play a major role in helping many of these individuals overcome certain of their physical and psychosocial handicaps.

COMMUNICATION DISORDERS ASSOCIATED WITH OROFACIAL DISORDERS

Orofacial Clefts

Speech and Voice.   Most of us learned to talk using an upper airway system that contained all the necessary working parts. For the child born with a major orofacial cleft, especially of the secondary palate, learning to talk may become one of the major challenges in life. It is easy to appreciate why. As we discuss later, the cleft structures may be surgically joined within the first few months of a child's life. These early, or *primary,* surgical repairs provide the child with a functional mechanism for feeding—their essential purpose is to normalize the upper airway for basic life functions.

For approximately 70 percent of children with clefts of the lip and palate, or palate alone, primary surgical repair will also enable normal speech development. The remaining 30 percent, however, will possess a velopharyngeal mechanism that is not adequate for the purpose of speech (Moll, 1968). Tissue deficiency or inadequate movement following surgery are the primary factors in continuing velopharyngeal incompetency in some children. This incompetency is the main cause of several speech and voice disorders. Here we describe three important characteristics of the speech and voice of persons with repaired clefts of the lip and palate or palate only: (1) misarticulation of speech sounds, (2) hypernasal voice quality, and (3) reduced loudness. We will avoid the use of the term "cleft-palate speech" in describing the speech characteristics of persons with orofacial clefts. This unfortunate verbal stereotype focuses attention on the individual's disorder and thereby masks the individual uniqueness of each person with a repaired cleft.

Misarticulation of speech sounds: The primary communication disorder of persons with orofacial clefts as a group, is decreased intelligibility of speech because of misarticulation of speech sounds. Considerable data are available on the articulatory skills of individuals with clefts of the lip and/or palate. Individuals with clefts of the lip alone seldom have articulatory disorders, although surgical repair of the lip may result in an upper lip that is somewhat taut from the standpoint of usage for speech (Spriestersbach, Moll, and Morris, 1961). Those with palatal clefts of various natures are most likely to show articulatory disorders especially if they have not had adequate palatal repair as a result of primary surgery. Thus, the articulatory skills observed in groups of individuals with repaired cleft palates can be expected to vary considerably in accordance with the success of the repair to the velopharyngeal mechanism. Here we shall characterize speakers with clefts as a group, including children who have various degrees of velopharyngeal incompetence and children who may have such developmental delays in articulatory skills as noncleft children sometimes have (see Chapter 7).

The first general research finding is that most children with repaired palatal clefts are delayed in articulation development relative to children without clefts (Bzoch, 1956; Counihan, 1960). Children without clefts obtain articulatory skills rapidly at the beginning of speech sound development and then taper off in speed of acquisition. Children with clefts, by contrast, are relatively slow in skill acquisition at first and then accelerate in speech sound development as more time goes by (Saxman and Bless, 1973). As a group, however, their eventual performance remains below the performance of children without clefts. A variety of structural, physiological, psychological, and hearing loss factors can be pointed to as possible contributors to the delays and different rates of acquisition in children with clefts in comparison to those without clefts (Spriestersbach, 1965).

The second general finding is that individuals with clefts tend to have certain types of articulation errors more often than other individuals. For example, stop-plosives, fricatives, and affricates tend to be misarticulated more often than nasals and semivowels. And voiceless consonants tend to be distorted more often than their voiced cognates (Moll, 1968). These characteristics are readily explained by the fact that an incompetent velopharyngeal mechanism precludes the speaker from appropriately managing the speech airstream to generate speech sounds requiring the development and maintenance of high oral air pressures. Pressure is partially spent through air leakage out the nose. You can experience the difficulty in building up oral pressure for speech in the face of a leak by trying to say *pah* repeatedly with a large bore tube between your lips. You will find it is extremely difficult to compensate for the leak the tube imposes and that your speech production abilities instantly deteriorate for the high-pressure *p* sound.

Related to the leakage of air through the nose because of velopharyngeal incompetence is the problem of *audible nasal emissions*. These are turbulently produced sounds generated within the nooks and crannies of the nose as air intended for oral impoundment is diverted through the open velopharynx. Try letting air through your nose as you produce each stop-plosive, fricative, and affricate in the sentence "Please pass the ketchup." If you let air come out freely, you should have noticed that you were making nasals in the place of stop-plosives, and perhaps nasalizing all vowels as well. Certainly speech produced in such a manner is distracting to the listener and may interfere with communication.

The third general research finding on the articulatory skills of individuals with clefts of the palate is that they use some non-English sounds as substitutions for English phonemes. For example, for the six English stop-plosives /p, t, k, b, d, g/, a person with velopharyngeal incompetence might use a *glottal stop* utterance (Bzoch, 1956). Recall from Chapter 2 that glottal stops are made by closing the glottis, building up pressure within the trachea, and then suddenly reopening the glottis to release a transient puff of air. The usefulness of adopting such a compensatory type of sound production for stop-plosives is obvious. A plosive sound produced at the larynx involves the development of pressure in the speech mechanism before the velopharyngeal mechanism is encountered. There is nowhere for the air to leak out if the sound is generated at the larynx. Substituting a glottal stop for the normal stop-plosive production of English is somewhat of a tribute to the compensatory capabilities of the human speech mechanism. Notice that for the usual voiceless stop-plosives of speech that the glottal stop maintains their same manner of production (stop-plosive), the same voicing feature (voiceless), and simply changes the place of production posteriorly to an articulator (the larynx) which is relatively unaffected by velopharyngeal incompetence.

Yet another compensatory substitution pattern found in certain individuals with repaired clefts of the palate is the use of *glottal* and *pharyngeal fricatives* in place of the conventional fricative consonants of English (Bzoch, 1971; Trost, 1978). In Chapter 2 we learned that glottal fricatives are produced by constricting the airway at the level of the larynx and driving airflow through the constriction to produce a turbulent sound. Pharyngeal fricatives are similarly produced but the constriction is formed by positioning the tongue close to the back wall of the throat or by decreasing the side-to-side diameter of the throat by moving the side walls of the pharynx inward. Air is then forced through the constricted pharyngeal airway to produce a turbulent sound. Note that the compensatory behavior involves the generation of sound upstream of the location where air leakage from the mechanism occurs. In all cases where these non-English speech sound substitutions are used, they involve the same manner of production—fricative—as the phonemes for which they are substituted.

Hypernasal voice quality: Ask a beginning student of speech-language pathology to characterize the speech of someone with velopharyngeal incompetence and the answer will most likely be something like: "He sounds like he's talking through his nose." This impression comes about largely in response to the *hypernasal* voice quality of many speakers with velopharyngeal incompetence. Hypernasality refers to a listener's subjective judgment of the degree to which the sound energy of speech is partitioned for transmission through the mouth versus the nose (Moll, 1964). Only voiced consonants, vowels, and diphthongs are candidates to be perceived as hypernasal because the voiced acoustic energy must be available for the nose to filter in some way. Try for yourself to sound hypernasal on *s* . . . then on *z*. You will find that you can be hypernasal only on *z* because, of the two sounds, only *z* includes voicing.

A number of factors affect the degree of perceived hypernasality of voiced sounds. One important factor is the position of the tongue within the oral cavity. If the tongue is positioned such that it makes it harder for acoustic energy to flow out of the mouth, a greater proportion of voiced sound energy will travel through the nose. The principle is simple: The path taken by the sound energy will depend on the relative resistance to energy flow between the oral and nasal pathways. The flow of sound energy through the nose, then, is determined not only by the relative competence of the velopharyngeal mechanism itself. But it is also related to how open the oral airway is and how much of the generated sound is permitted to pass along the oral route.

Other factors associated with perceived hypernasality include a speaker's relative intelligibility and vocal pitch. Those whose speech is rated severely defective or whose intelligibility is rated very low are more likely to have a greater degree of hypernasality in their voice (Subtelny and Subtelny, 1961). Furthermore, Moll (1968) states that the hypernasality found in individuals with cleft palates decreases slightly when these individuals are instructed to raise their usual pitch levels. These and other factors deserve careful consideration when making clinical evaluations of hypernasality.

Reduced loudness: People coming in contact for the first time with a child or adult who has a repaired cleft of the palate often remark that the person speaks too softly. Sometimes these people mistakenly assume that this soft voice reflects psychosocial factors, such as reduced self-confidence or self-consciousness. Although these factors may be contributory, aeromechanical and acoustical bases for the reduced loudness are foremost contributors.

For vowels, diphthongs, and many voiced consonants, the problem is that an incompetent velopharyngeal mechanism allows sound produced at the larynx to pass through the nasal segment of the upper airway. Sound does not travel as freely through the nose as through the mouth. The many nooks and crannies of the nose give it a very large surface area that absorbs acoustic energy and acts as a sound damper (Curtis, 1968). Because of this absorption, nasalized voiced sounds are produced at overall energy levels that are lower than normal and cause the voice to be perceived as softer than normal. Alternately sustain the sounds *m* and *ee* and notice how the loudness of these two differ; the first is passed through the nose and the second through the mouth.

For many consonant sounds of speech, an incompetent velopharyngeal mechanism precludes the adequate buildup of oral air pressure that is required behind airway occlusions and obstructions to generate normal speech sounds (Subtelny, Worth, and Sakuda, 1966). This means that sounds like voiceless stop-plosives, fricatives, and affricates, in particular, will fail to have their normal "crispness" when produced; consequently they are perceived as being too soft. Trying to generate sounds orally in the face of velopharyngeal incompetence is like trying to blow up a tire that has a leak in it.

Before we move on to other communication disorders associated with orofacial disorders, we conclude this section with a case history relevant to some of the speech and voice characteristics we have been discussing:

Brad was born with a unilateral cleft lip and a complete cleft of the hard and soft palates. He was the second child born to Mr. and Mrs. Martin. Although Brad's cleft lip had been surgically repaired before he left the hospital, his cleft palate was not surgically closed until he was almost two years old. During that formative twenty-two-month period, Brad was not without vocalization; to the contrary, he was just as "talkative" as his older sister Mary had been at that age. There was a difference, however, between Mary's early speech sounds and those of Brad. Mary's early speech, although far from perfect, was easily identified by both parents as intending some object or action and seemed to contain a reasonable sampling of appropriate consonant sounds. Brad's speech, however, seemed to be mostly vowel-like utterances with associated grunts and snorts and nasal sounds. Actually, he was producing most vowel sounds appropriately except for nasalization, and omitting most consonants but substituting sounds produced by articulatory constrictions at the back of his pharynx and at his larynx. Even following surgical repair of the cleft, young Brad's speech intelligibility was poor and improved slowly, so much so that his parents were quite anxious about his starting school in the fall. Evaluation at a local university speech clinic led to the discovery that Brad as yet had velopharyngeal incompetency and would probably require additional surgical procedures or other physical management of his velopharyngeal mechanism followed by intensive speech therapy.

Brad's story is not unusual, it is typical of the 30 percent of children who require more than a single primary repair of a cleft of their palates. Fortunately, as we will see, considerable help is available for such children.

Hearing. Disorders of hearing are very prevalent among individuals with orofacial clefts. These disorders most often are the result of middle-ear dysfunction, involve both ears, and fluctuate in degree of severity over time (Hayes, 1965; Paradise, 1975).

Disorders of the middle ear exist in nearly all infants under the age of two with unrepaired clefts of the palate (Stool and Randall, 1967; Bluestone, 1971) and in 70 to 80 percent of older children with repaired cleft palates (Skolnick, 1958). This incredible prevalence of middle-ear disorders is primarily attributable to a disease called *otitis media.* As we will discuss in Chapter 12, otitis media involves an inflammation and/or infection of the middle-ear system that is accompanied by the presence of liquid in the middle-ear cavity. Agreement is fairly universal that the root of the otitis media problem in individuals with palatal clefts is a malfunctioning of the *Eustachian tube* (see Chapters 3, 12, and 13), a conduit that interconnects the back of the nasal chamber on each side to the middle-ear space on the corresponding side. Normal Eustachian tube function includes frequent opening of this conduit to allow the pressure within the middle-ear space to equalize with that outside the body and to allow any possible liquid accumulations within the middle-ear space to drain into the nasal portion of the pharynx. In many individuals with palatal clefts, the muscles that normally serve to open and close the nasal end of the Eustachian tube are cleft and do not function normally (Prather and Kos, 1968). The consequence: The tube remains closed, pressure and liquid build up in the middle-ear cavity, inflammation and infection occur, the middle-ear sound transmission system is impaired, and a conductive-type hearing loss occurs (see Chapter 12 for details).

Hearing losses that accompany cleft palate disorders are obviously present during the critical early period of communication skill learning (Prather and Kos, 1968). Consequently, they can and do have an adverse effect on some aspects of communication development. In some individuals, hearing losses have also been found to interfere with certain aspects of intellectual and social development (Smith and McWilliams, 1966; McWilliams, 1971). Although the hearing losses resulting from middle-ear pathology in many individuals with cleft palates are not profound, they nevertheless are an important contributor to the overall communication problem and must be followed closely by the speech-language pathologist and audiologist. Because fluctuations can be expected in the middle-ear disease process, they can also be expected in the hearing capability of the person with a cleft. We might expect fluctuating and disordered hearing to contribute to problems of development in speech and voice skills. A question of paramount interest to parents and educators is whether hearing loss also affects language development in the child with a cleft palate. From what you've read, especially in Chapters 1 and 4, do you think individuals with cleft palates are likely to have language problems? Why?

Language. If you said "yes," you are at least partially right. The answers lie in a series of studies that allow several hypotheses about "why" language may be affected in individuals with clefts.

Until about 1970, most studies of children with palatal clefts indicated that they have delayed language development. These children say their first words later than physically normal children (Bzoch, 1956), use shorter and less complex sentences (Spriestersbach, Darley, and Morris, 1958), and overall have significant delays in language comprehension and usage (Philips and Harrison, 1969). But as we learned in Chapter 1, language development research has undergone major changes in the last decade.

Essentially, studies in the 1970s suggest that the magnitude of the problem is less than previously thought or that there is no language problem at all. Buescher and Paynter (1973), who assessed a variety of language abilities of children with repaired clefts, concluded that these children performed within the normal range. Depressed expressive language skills manifested primarily in length and complexity of utterances were noted by Whitcomb, Ochsner, and Wayte (1976); however, Horn (1972) found that the syntactic structures of four-to-six-year-old children with palatal clefts were immature but not significantly delayed when compared to children without clefts of the same age. Still more evidence: no differences in the written language skills of cleft versus physically normal children were found by Ebert, McWilliams, and Woolf (1974); no differences from normal in the language skills of children with clefts who have intelligible speech (Bland, 1974). Finally, Pannbacker (1975) found that adults with clefts produce utterances that are shorter and less variable than adults without clefts but that they do not differ from normal adults in either syntax or vocabulary.

How should we interpret these data? They seem to suggest that there may be some lag in language acquisition during the early years of development for many children with orofacial clefts, but as the individual gets older the gap closes. By adulthood, no significant language differences remain. Exactly why this lag occurs is of great interest; consider three hypotheses:

HYPOTHESIS 1: DISRUPTION IN EARLY EXPERIENCE

The thrust of this hypothesis is that disruption in oral touch-pressure sensation, oral cavity exploration, perceptual-motor deprivation, prolonged hospitalization during the formative language period, etc., contribute to language delay in children with cleft palates (Smith and McWilliams, 1968; Nation, 1970). A variant of this hypothesis would include reduced hearing sensitivity, as discussed in the previous section, during the first two years of life (Nation, 1970; Paradise, McWilliams, and Bluestone, 1972; Saxman and Bless, 1973).

HYPOTHESIS 2: INSUFFICIENT LANGUAGE STIMULATION

The central position advanced by this hypothesis is that the child with a cleft palate will need additional stimulation to promote normal language development because of his greater difficulty with oral-verbal development (Philips and Harrison, 1969). Delay results when the child does not receive adequate stimulation from his parents, perhaps because of their low expectations for verbal responsiveness given the child's physical problems. (This hypothesis should be easily appreciated from our studies of Chapters 1 and 4.)

HYPOTHESIS 3: NEGATIVE REACTIONS OF LISTENERS

This hypothesis could also be termed the social-penalty hypothesis. Basically, the hypothesis is that negative reactions, or at least non-reinforcing reactions by listeners, cause the child to limit the frequency and elaboration of speech-language attempts (Spriestersbach et al., 1958; Morris, 1962).

Notice the important implications that each of these hypotheses has for habilitation of language function in children with cleft palates. Further study is needed to determine which hypothesis might lead to the most useful language acquisition programs. The hearing status of these infants should be of primary concern to parents, speech-language pathologists, audiologists, and physicians. Early language intervention approaches, reduction in the length of time children are hospitalized for orofacial surgery, parent counseling programs—these and other services can markedly decrease the likelihood of language and speech delays in children born with palatal clefts.

Other Orofacial Disorders

The speech, voice, hearing, and language characteristics of individuals with orofacial disorders other than clefts have not been extensively studied. Thus, we will make only brief mention of a few characteristics that cross all the orofacial disorders other than orofacial clefts.

Speech and Voice. If a particular orofacial disorder involves the tongue, misarticulations are predictable. *Congenital* or *acquired aglossia* is the extreme example. Children born without a tongue will need to perform language through alternative modes of communication than speech. Adults who have had all or part of their tongues removed will have difficulty with sounds that normally require the tongue as a sound generator and sound shaper through filtering. The amount of tissue removed from the tongue has a direct relationship to the residual intelligibility of the patient's speech. Generally, greater tissue loss is associated with greater loss in intelligibility (Kalfuss, 1968; Skelly et al., 1971). Partial glossectomy patients make extensive use of the residual tongue stump in movement patterns approximating those of normal speakers. By contrast, total glossectomy patients use compensatory gestures involving such remaining structures as the lips, cheeks, floor of the mouth, velum, pharyngeal walls, and vertical positioning of the larynx. The lips are especially active compensators of the upper airway when major segments or the total tongue are removed surgically; for example, *take* becomes *pape, no* becomes *mow,* and so forth. Peterson (1973) describes a fifteen-year-old boy who had to find compensatory movements-positions for several upper airway structures because of severe midfacial underdevelopment including a maxilla that was much smaller than the mandible. One of the most interesting features about this boy's speech was his ability to compensate by producing /f/ as a lingualabial (tongue-lips), /r/ as a bilabial fricative (two lips, like a Bronx cheer), and /t/ and /d/ with the front part of the tongue held against the lower teeth. Peterson indicated that none of these four phonemes was defective when heard; only when watching the boy speak did the observer consider the sounds defective.

Congenital or acquired orofacial problems that affect the interrelated adjustments of the tongue, mandible, maxilla, lips, and so on may all contribute to disordered speech skills. The challenge to the speech-language pathologist is to accurately determine which components of orofacial problems do and which do not preclude the development of adequate speech skills. Because of the remarkable compensatory flexibility of the upper airway mechanism, it is no easy task to provide an accurate prognosis for speech skill development. One need only see a patient or two with major oral deformity and who without professional help has made successful speech compensations to realize that the speaker can come a long way back. With professional help the road is usually even more rapidly traveled.

Voice disorders are found in many orofacial disorders other than those involving orofacial clefts. The most often reported of such disorders are problems of hypernasal voice quality, which have been documented in Pierre Robin syndrome (Bloomer, 1971), in mandibulofacial dysostosis (Peterson-Falzone and Pruzansky, 1976), in hemifacial microsomia (Peterson, 1973) and in orofacial-digital syndromes (Peterson, 1973), to mention a few. An extremely high, arched hard palate and limited movement of the velum are typical of the physical findings believed to contribute to hypernasal voice deviations. Abnormal tongue carriage within the upper airway coupled with these abnormalities of the palate could understandably affect the filter characteristics of the speech mechanism. Hyponasality and some other oral resonance deviancies generally associated with blockage of the nasal pathway have also been observed in orofacial disorders other than clefts of the palate (Bloomer, 1971; Peterson, 1973). We have already alluded to the nature of such problems acoustically in our discussion of the problems of adenoidectomy.

Hearing. Loss of hearing has been reported in orofacial disorders in which palatal clefts have not necessarily been an associated problem. As with speech, voice, and language problems, the reporting has been sparse. Bilateral conductive hearing losses (see Chapter 12) have been reported in cases of hemifacial microsomia (Massengill et al., 1971). These losses are in addition to the abnormalities resulting from such middle-ear pathologies as otitis media. Varying degrees of hearing loss have been reported in Apert's syndrome (Peterson, 1973). Now that procedures for the routine testing of newborns are becoming well-established (see Chapter 12), the hearing abilities of all children born with orofacial disorders should become better understood and more adequately documented.

Language. The language characteristics of children and adults with orofacial disorders other than clefts are virtually unknown. For the less severe forms of structural involvement, such as nasal obstructions or tissue removal, there is no direct reason why the affected individual should have any language disorders. On the other end of the continuum, children born with devastating orofacial disorders may experience just those factors that have been associated with language delay in children with orofacial clefts—perceptual-motor deprivation, hearing losses, low expectations for verbal responsiveness from parents, and social penalties that limit frequency and elaboration of speech attempts. These and other factors would certainly mitigate against the child with orofacial disorders acquiring language normally. But we must emphasize that they only are *potential* problems. Individual differences in language acquisition are dependent on a complex of factors that are completely independent of a person's orofacial structure. Where mental retardation has been associated with orofacial disorders, as is frequently the case in such syndromes as Apert's (Massengill et al., 1971), Crouzon's (Peterson, 1973), and Cornilia de Lange's (Moore, 1970), some degree of language retardation is expected and usually observed (see Chapter 4). As we consistently point out, group trends should never blind us to the richness of individual differences among and unique capabilities of those who may bear a particular medical diagnostic label.

EVALUATION OF OROFACIAL DISORDERS IN RELATION TO COMMUNICATION

To this point we have examined the normal development of the orofacial complex, the types and causes of orofacial disorders, and how such disorders are related to communication disorders. We will now focus on the evaluation of communication behavior in persons with orofacial disorders. We will concentrate our evaluation on speech and voice. Language and hearing evaluation are dealt with at length in Chapters 4 and 12, and the principles outlined there apply here. While speech and voice have also been considered in Chapters 7 and 8, certain aspects deserve special comment in their relation to orofacial disorders. We will begin our discussion with a general examination of the orofacial complex, followed by the perceptual evaluation of certain speech and voice characteristics, and the means available for physiologically analyzing upper airway problems.

General Examination of the Orofacial Complex

An important part of any evaluation of the communication capabilities of a person with an orofacial disorder is a comprehensive examination of the orofacial complex, including the external and internal face. Mainly this examination provides information about the possible contribution of deviant orofacial components to speech and voice performance (Bloomer, 1971).

Examination of the external face calls for a systematic evaluation of the symmetry of the left and right halves, appropriate proportioning among the different parts of the face, and attention to facial expression, coloration, and skin conditions. Evaluation should be done in both full-face and profile because departures from normal facial configurations are often observed in patients with communication disorders related to orofacial problems. A review of Figure 9–8 will reveal some of the more common clinical observations. Often one side of the face may be underdeveloped, or the midface may be underdeveloped and appear "sunken." The eyes may be wide-spaced. Excess or insufficient tissue may be apparent for different structures. Outer-ear structures such as the pinna and external ear canal may be deformed or the ears may be mispositioned on the side of the head. Mandibular size may be inappropriate for the size of the skull or various aspects of the facial skeleton may be distorted and out of proportion. The nose may be deviant in either its wings (alae) or the tip. The lip may be deformed, possibly unrepaired surgically, or if repaired perhaps with inadequate results that may leave prominent notch deformity of the upper lip. These and many other aspects are often observed in clusters and in various combinations.

Examination of the internal face involves a thorough inspection of the pharyngeal-oral-nasal or upper airway portion of the speech mechanism. Usually the biting relationship between the upper and lower teeth and the interrelationship between the maxilla and the mandible is determined first. In the normal individual, the maxilla is slightly larger than the mandible and fits directly over it so as to slightly overhang it around all three sides. Frequently, in patients with cleft palates, the upper dental arch is collapsed inward such that the tooth-bearing portion of the arch does not align properly with the teeth carried by the lower arch. Proceeding through the examination of the internal face, the teeth in both arches are counted, missing, extra, or misaligned teeth noted, and any other dental abnormality that might affect speech production recorded. Generally, the more severe the dental problems, the more likely they are to contribute to the patient's speech difficulties.

After examining the dental structures, attention is directed to the space between the upper lip and the gum ridge. In cases of alveolar ridge clefts, *fistulae* (holes) can sometimes be found that connect this space with the front part of the nasal cavity and may require repair to eliminate the passage of liquids from the oral to nasal cavities.

Then, with the patient's mouth opened about three-quarters and his head tilted back slightly, the examiner must inspect the structures inside the oral and pharyngeal cavities. The hard palate is first examined for its height and width, scar tissue, malformations, misplaced teeth, clefts, fistulae, etc. An examination for submucous cleft of the hard palate is made by feeling the central portion of the back of the palate with a rubber-finger cot. Direct light on the palate will also sometimes reveal a submucous cleft by different colorations of the normally bony palate and a portion that is not joined by other than mucuosa. A blue tint suggests a submucous cleft. The soft palate is then examined for its length, scar tissue, clefts, symmetry, etc. The uvula is inspected especially for the possibility of its being bifid (split into halves). A bifid uvula is a strong clinical sign of possible submucous clefting. Movement patterns of the soft palate should be observed when the patient says *ah* several times. Frequently, individuals who have what appear to be well-repaired palatal clefts have little movement upward and backward of the velum.

Next the back portion of the oral cavity and the pharynx are examined. Special instruments are used to see above the bottom edge of the velum or below the surface of the tongue. At the entryway to the pharynx, it is important to examine the *faucial pillars* (muscle bands running from the soft palate to the tongue and pharynx) and the tonsils that lie between them on each side. As mentioned earlier, some patients may have enlarged tonsils that may contribute to their speech production problems. Even more important, in cases where the soft palate is short, the presence or absence of adenoid tissue could mean the difference between the velopharynx closing or not closing during speech. Unless a special mirror is used, the adenoids cannot usually be seen when viewing the pharynx directly by eye. The mobility of the lateral walls of the pharynx at the level of the soft palate should also be determined. This is best done by observing these walls during *ah* productions.

Finally, to the extent possible, the speech-language pathologist should examine the nasal cavity for alar deformities, deviated septa, various blockages, swellings, etc., and whether or not the patient has difficulty breathing quietly through the nose. This type of thorough inspection usually requires the services of a physician, most likely the otolaryngologist who is specially trained to make such examinations.

Perceptual Evaluation of Speech and Voice Disorders

Procedures for the evaluation of speech and voice disorders in persons with some type of orofacial disorder are basically the same as those used for any other individual. (These procedures are discussed most notably in Chapters 7, 8, and 10.) There are, however, certain features of the speech and voice problems of individuals with orofacial disorders that deserve special mention in the present context: making judgments concerning (1) misarticulations and (2) hypernasal voice quality.

There are some peculiar types of misarticulations found in persons with various orofacial disorders, especially those with incompetent velopharyngeal mechanisms as found in many individuals with clefts of the palate. In addition to more common types of misarticulations, such as omissions, substitutions, and distortions, sound productions that include glottal stops, glottal and pharyngeal fricatives, nasal emissions, nasal snorts, and other forms of abnormal utterances predominately reflect difficulties in generating and modifying speech sounds because of air leakage into the nasal cavities (Bzoch, 1971). These types of misarticulations are of diagnostic significance to the speech-language pathologist and the occurrence of such utterances should be taken into account when scoring articulation evaluations of patients with orofacial disorders. To determine the possible presence of these peculiar types of misarticulations, a special subtest may be used which samples phonemes whose production relies heavily on adequate velopharyngeal function. That is, the sounds that are most likely to be influenced by velopharyngeal leakage of air are those requiring the development of high oral pressures — stop-plosives, fricatives, affricates. One such subtest is the *Iowa Pressure Articulation Test* (Morris, Spriestersbach, and Darley, 1961), a group of items from the *Templin-Darley Tests of Articulation* (1960) containing phonemes that require high oral pressures for their generation and are most often misarticulated by persons with velopharyngeal incompetence related to palatal clefting.

Using standard articulation testing methods (Chapter 7) and those designed specifically to evaluate certain unique aspects of articulation in orofacial disorders, the speech-language pathologist must try to determine which part of a speaker's problem with articulation reflects the physical adequacy of the speech mechanism and which reflects the level of phonological development. Especially important in this regard is the degree to which the speaker is able to modify his articulation. The speech-language pathologist would try to get the patient to produce correctly, or as nearly so as possible, each of the sounds determined to be in error during testing. This is done first in isolation, then in syllables, next in words, and finally in phrases and sentences. The rationale for testing modifiability is to determine the best type of treatment. For example, if the patient can correctly produce his error phonemes when first stimulated auditorily by the clinician, it often means that he may have the physical potential to produce normal speech but needs speech therapy to change his usual behavior. By contrast, if the patient can not change his articulatory behavior despite intensive stimulation by the clinician, it may well mean that he has a faulty speech mechanism and needs additional surgery or prosthetic management before speech therapy techniques are employed. The skillful use of articulation testing in patients with orofacial disorders can provide substantial insight into the physiological problems these patients may be working under.

In turning from articulation to voice, recall that the principal voice quality deviation observed in patients with orofacial disorders is hypernasality. Because hypernasality is a percept, its extent can only be specified through perceptual judgments. That is, no device but the human listener can measure hypernasality. Although so-called objective techniques have been proposed to assess the degree of nasal cavity participation in speech (Counihan, 1971; Fletcher, 1976), none can replace the ear of the listener. The final arbitor in all decisions about the extent to which a given speaker is hypernasal is you — the listener (Moll, 1964). Faced with this reality, it becomes apparent that judgments of the extent to which a voice sounds hypernasal are important. Speech-language pathologists arrive at these in several ways; most widely used are various forms of rating scales. A simple rating procedure might include only having to decide the presence (+) or the absence (−) of hypernasality in a patient. More desirable usually is a system that assigns descriptors to the degree of hypernasality. For example, it might be designated as mild, or moderate, or severe, and so forth. Speech-language pathologists frequently use an equal appearing interval scale. The listener might be asked to judge a given speech sample from a patient along a continuum of perhaps 5–7 intervals corresponding to degrees of hypernasality ranging from normal voice quality to severely hypernasal voice quality. Figure 9–9 depicts one such scale. Try to simulate the degrees of hypernasality you think might correspond to the intervals along the scale by making your own voice vary in degree of hypernasality.

Physiological Analysis of Upper Airway Problems

Many of the events of speech production are hidden from our view and occur so rapidly that we cannot possibly follow them without the aid of modern instruments designed for such purposes. In this section, we highlight how physiological measurement procedures enable the speech-language pathologist to more accurately specify the capabilities of the patient with an orofacial disorder. Limited space requires that we be selective and so we will deal only with the problem of evaluating velopharyngeal function—by far the most studied aspect of the upper airway because of its prevalent dysfunction in persons with orofacial disorders. There are several methods available for evaluating the adequacy of velopharyngeal closure during speech. Aerodynamic, radiographic, and optical probe methods are the most often used and will receive attention here.

Aerodynamic procedures include the measurement of air pressures inside the mouth and airflows from the nose (Hardy, 1965; Warren

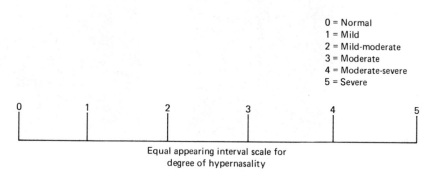

0 = Normal
1 = Mild
2 = Mild-moderate
3 = Moderate
4 = Moderate-severe
5 = Severe

Equal appearing interval scale for
degree of hypernasality

FIGURE 9–9. *An equal appearing interval scale for degree of hypernasality. Range selected is 0–5, occupying five intervals of degree of deviancy in voice quality from normal to severe. Normal represents a voice quality lacking in perceived hypernasality and severe represents the most significantly deviant hypernasality that the listener would encounter in patients.*

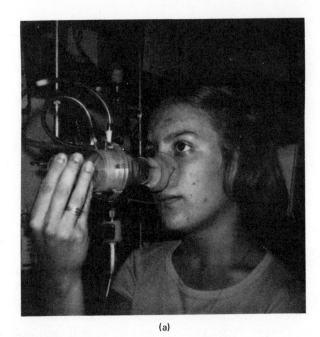

(a)

Before surgery

After surgery

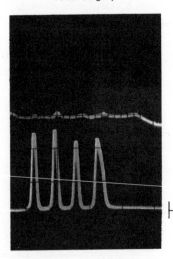

Nasal airflow

Oral air presssure

1 second

(b)

FIGURE 9–10. *Subject fitted for aerodynamic recordings of nasal airflow and oral air pressure (a) and recordings from a patient who demonstrated velopharyngeal incompetence (before) and then underwent successful surgical repair for her problem (after) (b). Note that for puh repetitions before surgery the nasal airflow is relatively high and the oral air pressure is relatively low. After surgery, however, the nasal airflow is nil and the oral air pressure is relatively high.*

and Ryon, 1967). These procedures enable the clinician to determine first if there is a leakage through the nose when the velopharynx should be closed for speech and second the extent of this leakage. Figure 9–10a shows a subject with air pressure and airflow instrumentation in place for making aerodynamic recordings. Figure 9–10b shows recordings for a patient who initially demonstrated velopharyngeal incompetence and then underwent surgical repair for his problem. Note in the "before" recording that during repeated *puh* utterances the flow out of the nose is relatively high and the pressure in the mouth is relatively low. In the "after" recording (following surgery), flow is nil and pressure in the mouth is higher. Clearly, this patient's incompetent velopharynx has been appropriately repaired such that she no longer leaks air from the nose and is able to build up normal pressures for consonant production. Using various aerodynamic procedures, it is possible to determine many aspects of the adequacy of velopharyngeal function for speech, including the amount of resistance offered to airflow through the nose (Isshiki, Honjow, and Morimoto, 1968) and the area of the opening through the velopharynx into the nasal cavity (Warren and DuBois, 1964). Aerodynamic procedures also enable the speech-language pathologist to evaluate the timing of velopharyngeal closure events during speech in relation to the actions of other parts of the speech mechanism. For example, it is possible to tell whether the patient can close the velopharynx but fails to do so at the proper time within the stream of speech.

Radiographic studies of velopharyngeal function during speech involve x-ray "pictures" of the head in various angles that permit viewing of the velopharynx from the side, front, and base (Bjork, 1961; Moll, 1965; Skolnick et al., 1975). These observations enable the speech-language pathologist to gain such information as the length of the velum, the distance between the velum and the back wall of the pharynx, the presence or absence of excessive adenoid tissue—all critical in evaluating the competency of the velopharynx. When such x-rays are in the form of motion pictures or continuous motion videotape records, they enable the evaluation of the adequacy of motion of such tissues as the velum and pharyngeal walls. Thus, while aerodynamic procedures enable a determination of the presence of a leak through the velopharynx and the size of that leak, x-ray procedures add the dimensions of knowing which structures are inadequately doing their jobs for velopharyngeal function and how they are functioning. Figure 9–11 helps us appreciate the general usefulness of radiographic procedures in evaluating problems of the orofacial region. There we see a side-view of the head during xeroradiographic x-ray exposures. Panel (a) shows the patient at rest and panel (b) shows the same patient producing the consonant phoneme /s/. As can be seen in panel (c) the patient is achieving closure of the velopharynx by raising

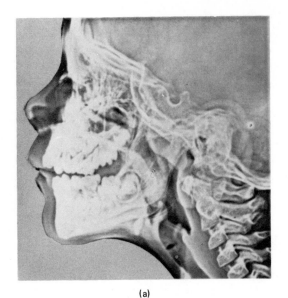

(a)

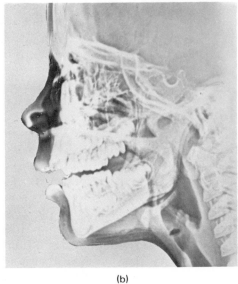

(b)

Eustachian tube
orifice

Adenoid
tissue

Hard palate

Velum during rest

Velum during
/s/ production

Posterior
pharyngeal wall

Cervical
vertebrae

(c)

FIGURE 9–11. *Xeroradiographic exposures of the head of a patient who is at rest (a) and who is sustaining the consonant phoneme /s/ (b). The schematic overlay in panel (c) traces the outline of the velum for the two exposures and shows that the patient achieves closure of the velopharynx by raising the velum against an enlarged pad of adenoid tissue.*

the velum against an enlarged pad of adenoid tissue. Obviously, x-ray procedures provide far more than just information about the function of the velopharynx. Notice in Figure 9–11 that such things as the shape and position of the tongue and lips can also be observed for analysis.

Optical probe methods for velopharyngeal evaluation come in several forms. These all provide for direct viewing of the velopharyngeal mechanism, either from above or below the velopharyngeal opening between the mouth and nose. Typically, optical probes amount to some form of tube that carries a light source for illuminating the velopharynx and an optical viewing system connected to an eyepiece through which the clinician can see the velopharynx. Some probes are passed through the nose so that the velopharynx can be viewed from above (Miyazaki, Matsuya, and Yamaoka, 1975), while others are passed through the mouth to provide a view of the velopharynx from below (Zwitman, Gyepes, and Ward, 1976). The use of the nasally inserted probe allows the clinician to sample an unlimited variety of speech, although the procedure is sometimes uncomfortable for the patient. Orally inserted probes, by contrast, are more comfortable, except for occasional gagging; however, they limit the types of speech that the clinician can sample because the tube containing the probe restricts normal motions of the tongue and lips.

Using the types of observations we have discussed for evaluating communication disorders of patients with orofacial problems, the speech-language pathologist would be working to determine what could be done to assist in the improvement of such patients' communication disorders. These determinations would then lead to the management of the patients' problems, as we now discuss.

MANAGEMENT OF OROFACIAL DISORDERS IN RELATION TO COMMUNICATION

The Team Approach

An outstanding feature of the recent history of habilitation for individuals with clefts of the lip and/or palate has been the successful application of team management to the complex of problems that often result. The discussion to follow will be in the context of the rehabilitation-habilitation team, though in practice formal teams are not involved with the treatment of all the disorders included in this chapter. There has been a strong movement, particularly within the American Cleft Palate Association, to extend the concept of the team management approach to the other orofacial disorders. One might consider the "cleft-palate team" as an excellent model for an orofacial-disorders team in which the coordinated expertise from many professional disciplines would be applied to serve the needs of those with congenital and acquired orofacial problems.

Why is a team of professionals desirable? Consider for a moment the case of cleft lip and palate and the myriad of possible problems that confront the child and his parents, each of which could involve a different professional discipline in its resolution. Initially there are the health problems of the infant and surgical management that could involve the pediatrician and plastic surgeon. Even after surgical closure of the cleft, a cosmetic defect, dental problems, and speech, language, and hearing disorders often remain. Depending upon the severity of the individual's problems, the child could require direct services from a pedodontist (children's dentist), an orthodontist (professional who aligns teeth and dental arches), an otolaryngologist (ear, nose, and throat physician), a plastic surgeon, a speech-language pathologist, an audiologist, and a psychologist. The complexity of the treatment plan and the interdependence of management procedures requires a high level of coordination and cooperation among these professionals. In examining the major concerns involved in the management of individuals with orofacial disorders, we partition the following discussion into subsections dealing with surgical, dental, communication disorders, and other aspects of management. Our discussion focuses mostly on management of orofacial cleft problems; however, management of other orofacial disorders is also presented.

Surgical Management

Those individuals who are born with clefts of the lip will require and undergo surgery very early in their lives. The primary reason for early repair of a cleft lip is to permit as near normal feeding as possible. Another reason is to improve the appearance of the child for social acceptance. Some surgeons advocate lip repair within the first forty-eight hours after birth (Cannon, 1967); others advocate a delay of from two to twelve weeks (Bauer, Trusler, and Tondra, 1971). Still others follow a general rule-of-thumb known as the "10-10-10" rule. This rule says repair the lip when the child is 10 weeks old, weighs 10 pounds and has 10 grams per 100 milliters of hemoglobin (a blood constituent) (Dibbell, 1978).

Unilateral clefts of the lip can almost always be adequately repaired in a single surgical procedure. Bilateral lip clefts, however, usually take two or more operations to repair them adequately. Figure 9–12 shows photographs of children who have undergone unilateral and bilateral cleft lip repair. Note some of the post-surgical residuals

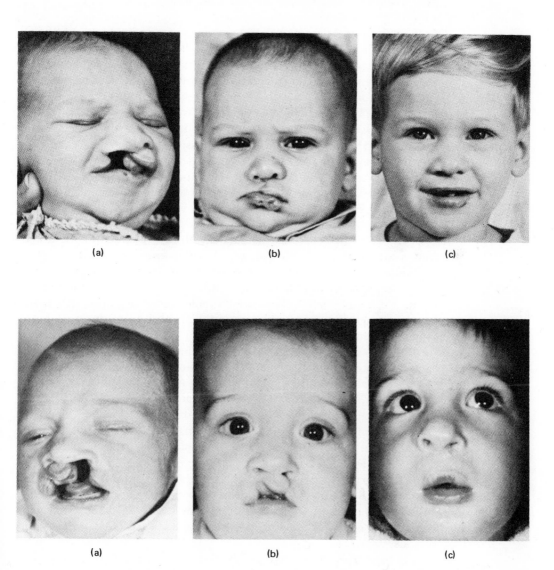

FIGURE 9–12. *Two children who have undergone surgical repair for clefts of the lip. Uppermost panels reveal a wide complete unilateral cleft of the lip with mucous pits of the lower lip (a), the status of the lip two months after primary surgery (b), and the status of the lip at four years of age after maxillary bone grafting and minor lip and nasal revisions (c). The mucous pits of the lower lip have been excised. (From D. Millard, Rotation-advancement in the repair of unilateral cleft lip. In W. Grabb, S. Rosenstein, and K. Bzoch, Eds.,* Cleft Lip and Palate: Surgical, Dental, and Speech Aspects. *Boston: Little, Brown, 1971.) Lowermost panels reveal a bilateral cleft of the lip (a), the status of the lip following left-side adhesion (b), and the status of the lip following definitive bilateral surgical lip repair (c). Note the post-surgical residuals in the area of the lip and the nose. (From P. Randall and W. Graham, Lip adhesion in the repair of bilateral cleft lip. In W. Grabb, S. Rosenstein, and K. Bzoch, Eds.,* Cleft Lip and Palate: Surgical, Dental, and Speech Aspects. *Boston: Little, Brown, 1971.)*

in the child with bilateral cleft repair. For some individuals, additional surgery for cosmetic reasons may have to be done at later times.

Whereas surgical repair of lip clefts is done early in life, clefts of the palate typically are repaired much later. The majority of surgeons do the initial repair of the palate between one and two years of age, with eighteen months being the frequently chosen age (Grabb, 1971). The reasons for closing the palatal cleft are to provide a mechanism for normal speech production, to decrease otological disease, to promote normalized dental occlusion, and to allow separation of the nasal and oral cavities. Note that the communication aspects—speech and hearing—are given top priority. This is a very common notion among plastic surgeons involved with the repair of palatal clefts (Dibbell, 1978).

In the majority of cases the palatal cleft can be closed in one procedure with either one or two stages. A wide variety of specific surgical techniques are used to close the hard and soft palates when they are cleft. The scope of this chapter does not lend itself to discussion of the details of any of them. The reader should know, however, that tissue from around the cleft is used in making the repair. The occasional use of bone grafts in the hard palate and alveolar process necessitates getting tissue from outside the oral cavity. Most importantly, nearly all palatal surgical procedures strive to both close the cleft and insure that adequate soft palate length is made available (see Grabb, Rosenstein, and Bzoch, 1971, for a thorough review of available palatal surgery procedures). Not all individuals with lip and/or palatal clefts will be fortunate enough to only undergo a single surgical procedure. For many there will be additional or "secondary" procedures at various times in their lives. For the lip there may be need to (1) lengthen, shorten, add, or take away tissue, (2) correct a mismatch of adjacent parts of the prominent upper lip margin, (3) fill in a residual notch, (4) create a space between the lip and the gum ridge, or (5) eliminate prominent scars. Most secondary lip surgery is done to improve function, although some is solely for cosmetic reasons.

Secondary surgery may also be required on the hard and/or soft palates. Again, a need to improve function usually dictates the timing and the techniques involved. Secondary palatal surgery may be performed to (1) eliminate velopharyngeal incompetency resulting from a short or immobile soft palate, (2) close unwanted or abnormal openings (fistulae) in the palate, and (3) move all or part of the hard palate either forward or backward in order to properly align the dental arches. The most widely used secondary surgical procedure for establishing velopharyngeal competence is the *pharyngeal flap* procedure (Yules and Chase, 1971). This procedure creates a tissue blockage between the nasal and oral cavities that effectively reduces escape of air and sound energy through the nasal cavity. In simple terms, this procedure involves a suturing of a strip of tissue fabric from the back wall of the throat to the soft palate to create a barrier across the velopharyngeal airway.

For individuals with orofacial disorders other than orofacial clefts, surgical management is frequently used. For example, for a person with an underdeveloped maxilla or overdeveloped mandible, the bones of these structures may be cut, parts may be moved in relationship to one another, or pieces of bone may be added or taken out. Figure 9–13 illustrates one type of *osteotomy* (bone cutting) procedure. A protruding mandible is set back into alignment with the maxilla by removal of a portion of the body of the mandible and a repositioning of its front segment. While speech improvement may not always be the primary goal in such operations, it should be apparent that in some instances it would likely be one of the end results. When more of the orofacial complex has developed abnormally or become deformed, more extensive surgical procedures may be needed. Other facial

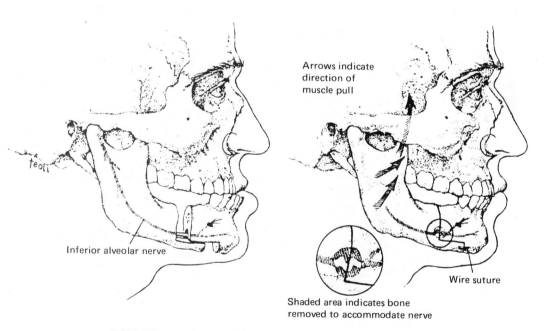

FIGURE 9–13. *One form of osteotomy on a protruding mandible in a patient with many missing lower teeth. A portion of the mandible is removed surgically and the front of the mandible is repositioned to align with the maxilla. (From R. Dingman and T. Dodenhoff, Surgical correction of mandibular deformities. In W. Grabb, S. Rosenstein, and K. Bzoch, Eds.,* Cleft Lip and Palate: Surgical, Dental, and Speech Aspects. *Boston: Little, Brown, 1971.)*

bones may need alterations, repositionings, and so forth to bring the orofacial structures to more normal relationships. Improved function is again the primary goal with cosmetic improvement also a major consideration.

Dental Management

The need for dental management, beyond maintaining good oral hygiene and repairing teeth with cavities, is much higher in individuals with orofacial disorders than it is among the general population. Typically, these individuals require dental treatment for such problems as (1) teeth erupting in the wrong place, (2) teeth growing crooked, (3) poor spacing due to extra or missing teeth, (4) segments of the dental arch being out of line with other segments, and (5) abnormal bite relationships. Although not considered dental problems per se, persistent velopharyngeal incompetency and palatal fistulae may also require dental prostheses, as we will describe shortly. This is usually the case when surgical management is not appropriate or when it has been unsuccessful.

Very young children with dental problems associated with an orofacial disorder should ideally be treated by a pedodontist, a specialist in child dentistry (Olsen, 1971). The pedodontist will want to do restorative work (cavity filling) as early as possible in order to insure that all the teeth possible are maintained in the mouth. This promotes good eating, facilitates alveolar process growth, prevents the spread of dental disease, and assists in the development of speech. Sometimes early treatment of occlusion problems or dental alignment deviations is also carried out. Timing of dental therapy must be coordinated with that of surgery in order to insure proper sequencing and prevent interference of one treatment program with another.

As the individual with an orofacial disorder grows older, dental problems may change as will treatment approaches. Straightening and aligning teeth in proper relationship one to the other is an important consideration for optimal speech development. Dental misalignment can contribute to distortion-type articulation errors. Various types of braces or appliances are used to straighten and align teeth. Figure 9–14 illustrates how braces are used for a child whose lower teeth have overgrown his upper teeth. Contrast of appearance before and after treatment is marked in this child and illustrates the extent to which dental intervention can improve orofacial structural relationships.

A problem often observed in individuals with clefts that extend through the alveolar process as well as the hard palate is referred to as *buccal segment collapse*. In these cases, because the alveolar process is in two pieces, the portion that is directly under the cheek (buccal segment) is forced inward. The result is an abnormal narrowing of the front part of the upper jaw. The consequence for speech is that this collapsing makes it difficult for the patient to position the tongue properly for sounds like *t, d, n,* and *l.* Distortions or substitutions for these sounds may result. Expansion of the maxillary dental arch is the orthodontic treatment approach used to correct this problem. To prevent speech problems from developing because of this type of alveolar process collapse, expansion should ideally be done at as early an age as possible; this frequently turns out to be in the vicinity of eleven to twelve years of age.

The final area of dental treatment to be discussed is that of prosthetics. There are a number of different types of dental prostheses used to treat problems related to orofacial disorders. These include plastic palates, called *obturators,* that cover holes in the hard palate, devices to build up or push out underdeveloped portions of the front part of the maxilla, and temporary or fixed bridges to fill in spaces where teeth are missing. To illustrate this general area of treatment, we will briefly consider the *speech bulb prosthesis.*

Some individuals with repaired cleft palates will continue to be velopharyngeally incompetent. If, for any reason, secondary surgical correction cannot be made or is not considered to be the best management approach for a particular individual, then a special dental pros-

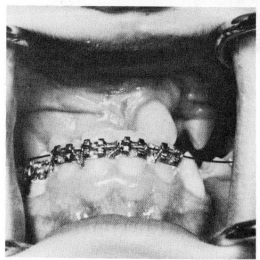 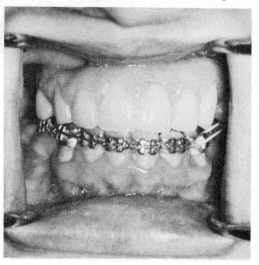

(a)   (b)

FIGURE 9–14. *An example ofovereruption of the mandibular anterior teeth (a) and its successful management through orthodontic bracing (b). (From W. Olin, Orthodontics. In W. Grabb, S. Rosenstein, and K. Bzoch, Eds.,* Cleft Lip and Palate: Surgical, Dental, and Speech Aspects. *Boston: Little, Brown, 1971.)*

thesis can be constructed. One such prosthesis is shown in Figure 9–15. An acrylic plastic device, called a bulb or obturator, is attached to a fitting molded to the shape of the hard palate (see Figure 9–15a, b, and c). When placed in the mouth, the bulb portion fits up behind the soft palate within the pharynx. The rest of the appliance is against the hard palate and around the teeth (see Figure 9–15d). If the lateral walls of the pharynx move sufficiently, they will come in contact with the sides of the bulb and cause closure of the velopharyngeal airway. Nasal emissions and hypernasality can thus be reduced or eliminated.

Communication Disorders Management

As discussed earlier, many individuals with orofacial disorders have problems of communication and will require help to eliminate these problems. Conservative estimates state that between 20–45 percent of individuals who have had cleft palates and have undergone full surgical management will still require speech remediation (Moll, 1968); 30 percent is the most often quoted statistic in this regard. We have no comparable data for individuals with palatal clefts who are treated with prostheses or for those with other types of orofacial disorders. However, we would estimate that the need for communication therapy is equally high in these two groups.

Because we all agree that it is very important to correct abnormal characteristics of communication in individuals with orofacial disorders at some time in their lives, it is crucial to do so before "the scars of rejection or the feeling of abnormality and difference are formed in their developing personalities" (Bzoch, 1971). This means that management of the various communication problems should begin as early as possible. For some children, this may be before one year of age, while for others it may be when they are two or three. Each individual's unique needs must be taken into account in determining exactly when to begin an intervention program.

The earliest form of communication therapy recommended is speech and language stimulation by the parents (Hahn, 1971; Philips, 1971). Parents, as well as other family members, provide the models of speech and language that the growing child eventually acquires. They demonstrate, through their own talking, how speech that is free of misarticulations and nasalization problems is produced. They also provide a full range of oral language experiences. Although the child may not be able to produce speech without deviancies, he or she is encouraged by the model to talk as much as possible. The more practice the child gets in speaking, the more likely that favorable changes in speech-language skills will take place and that new skills will be learned. In addition to providing a model for "good" speech and lan-

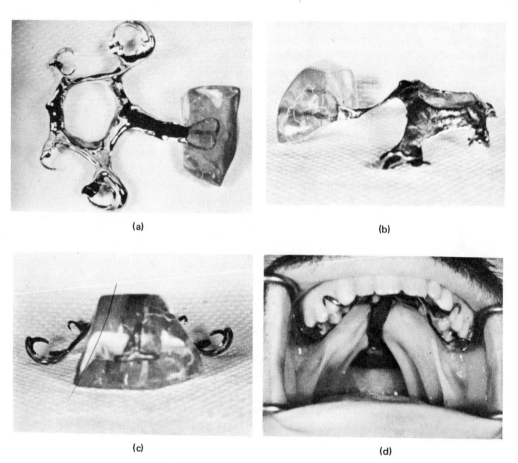

(a)

(b)

(c)

(d)

FIGURE 9–15. *A speech bulb prosthetic appliance for use in blocking the velopharyngeal airway: (a) shows top, (b) right-side, and (c) back views. Panel (d) is a view of the appliance in position within the patient's oral cavity. (From I. Adisman,* Cleft palate prosthetics. *In W. Grabb, S. Rosenstein, and K. Bzoch, Eds.,* Cleft Lip and Palate: Surgical, Dental, and Speech Aspects. *Boston: Little, Brown, 1971.)*

guage during this early time in the child's life, parents are encouraged to accept and reinforce all the child's communication attempts—to make communication a pleasant, enjoyable experience.

Hopefully with good parental modeling and reinforcement for speech attempts, major speech, voice, and language problems can be prevented. In other cases, however, direct or formal therapy procedures may be needed, including learning articulation patterns that have not developed or relearning those patterns that were learned incorrectly, eliminating or reducing hypernasality, increasing loudness, and expanding oral language skills.

Therapy for articulation problems in those individuals whose orofacial structure and function are not significantly abnormal to begin with or are made nearly normal through physical restoration is very much like that used with persons having developmental articulation problems as presented in Chapter 7. Where structural and functional problems still exist, special procedures are needed (Wells, 1971). For example, when the maxilla is underdeveloped, the tongue tip may be carried too far forward and may be positioned improperly for the production of such sounds as *t* or *d* or *l*. The individual with such a problem would need to be taught how to most effectively position the tongue tip behind the upper, front teeth in order to have the correct place of articulation for these sounds. When there is velopharyngeal incompetence and nasal emission present during the production of sounds such as *s* or *sh*, the back of the tongue may be positioned near the back wall of the throat and a pharyngeal fricative may be produced. A person who does this needs to be taught to (1) distinguish between front and back sounds, (2) position the tongue forward in the mouth, and (3) practice having air flow gently over the tongue in this new position and between lightly closed teeth. Auditory and visual cues are used to supplement the direct teaching of tongue placement.

In cases where voice quality is deviant, that is either hypernasality or hyponasality exists, a trial period of voice therapy will determine if these characteristics can be behaviorally modified. If changes can be brought about, then a voice therapy program is in order. For example, a patient whose mouth opening is small and whose tongue is carried high in the mouth, will have accentuated hypernasality. Such an individual would be taught to observe the differences in voice quality during production of the vowel *ah* versus the vowel *ee*. Production of *ah* insures the largest mouth opening and the lowest tongue position. Practice material is then devised which uses low vowels and consonants that keep the oral airway as large as possible. Sometimes hypernasality is more perceptible when the individual speaks very quietly or with reduced vocal effort. In such cases, therapy may be aimed at increasing vocal effort in order to insure maximum closure of the velopharyngeal airway. Care must be taken, however, not to induce a laryngeal sound quality problem as a result of excessively loud talking (see Chapter 8). Hyponasality can sometimes be found in cases where secondary palatal surgery, using a pharyngeal flap, was done to correct velopharyngeal incompetency. This lack of nasalization is due to poor functioning of the revised velopharyngeal mechanism. Therapy would be directed at (1) improving nonspeech nasal breathing, (2) learning to sustain isolated *m* and *n* sounds and have them be directed through the nasal passages, (3) practicing vowels in combination with nasal consonants, and (4) producing words and sentences containing numerous nasal sounds.

A number of different therapy techniques have been proposed to deal with velopharyngeal incompetence itself. These include (1) blowing (Kantner, 1948), (2) blowing and whistling (Shprintzen, McCall, and Skolnick, 1975), (3) direct electrical stimulation of the palate (Peterson, 1974), (4) use of a palatal exerciser (Lubit and Larsen, 1969), and (5) use of various types of biofeedback procedures to increase control of palatal and pharyngeal wall movement (Moller et al., 1973; Shelton et al., 1975). Shelton, Hahn, and Morris (1968) question the use of nonspeech exercises alone as a viable method for improving velopharyngeal function. When used in conjunction with speech, however, a number of the more recent procedures may have some value for some individuals.

Other Areas of Management

Otological and Audiological. Early management of the otological problems presented by individuals with orofacial disorders is crucial (Paradise, 1975; Yules, 1975). In preceding sections of this chapter, we discussed both the causes and consequences of otological and audiological deficits. These are dealt with in even more detail in Chapters 12 and 13. Here we will examine just a few of the ways in which these problems are handled.

Middle-ear disorder, the most common otological problem, can be treated by both surgical and medical techniques (Fahey, 1965; Yules, 1975). Decongestants and antibiotics are used to combat infections. Removal of liquid from the middle-ear cavity and the placement of ventilating tubes in the eardrums often bring about normalization of the middle-ear cavity (see Chapter 13). Surgical repair of the soft palate often establishes improved Eustachian tube function which in turn permits the middle ear to function better.

For some individuals, removal of diseased tonsils and adenoids is indicated. Infection in these tissues can contribute to middle-ear problems. However, caution must be exercised in performing adenoidectomies on those individuals who have normal but borderline velopharyngeal competency. As illustrated by our earlier case history of Josie, certain children may be using adenoid tissue as a base against which the soft palate can abutt to achieve velopharyngeal closure. Removal of this base may result in severe velopharyngeal incompetence.

For hearing loss that is not medically treatable, audiological management may be indicated (see Chapter 13). Possibilities might include (1) fitting with a hearing aid, (2) auditory training, (3) speechreading (lipreading), (4) preferential seating in classrooms, and (5) special education placement.

Psychological. Research to date has not revealed the presence of any particular personality types among individuals with orofacial disorders (Goodstein, 1968; Clifford, 1973). Rather, there is a normal crosssection of personality types in this population. Nor has research been able to point out that the families of individuals with orofacial disorders are any different psychosocially than are families of those without such disorders. However, there will be individuals and families in which orofacial disorders exist who have psychosocial problems and may require help to resolve them.

Some of the specific areas in which an individual with an orofacial disorder may need help are: (1) self-acceptance of being different, (2) social competence, (3) anxiety over repeated surgeries, (4) concern about future education and/or employment, and (5) uncertainty about marriage and offspring.

Families having one or more of their members with an orofacial disorder have their own areas of concern for which help may be needed. Parents may be faced with feelings of guilt, remorse, anger, hostility, frustration, and the like over having a child with a physical deformity. They may be anxious about the possibility of having the disorder occur in children they may have in the future. Worry over the financial burdens the child will create may be substantial. Their ability to provide the best possible care for their child is an ever-present concern.

How does having some type of orofacial disorder affect the older child or adolescent? Even though a cleft lip and palate may be surgically or prosthetically repaired, defective articulation and hypernasality can still interfere with communication functioning. Abnormal dental growth and development, frequently found in association with orofacial clefts, can contribute to feeding difficulties, speech disorders, and undesirable appearance, among other things. Numerous surgical procedures, requiring frequent hospitalizations, can have an adverse affect on the psychosocial development of some children with orofacial disorders. The adolescent may not feel he or she is part of the "in group" because the nose that is still deformed or the upper lip that is scarred or the ear that is very low set calls attention as a physical difference. Nonsocializing or withdrawal may result.

Surely by the time a person who was born with an orofacial disorder reaches adulthood few, if any, problems or obstacles should remain. For most adults, this is the case. There are some, however, who are still faced with problems directly or indirectly associated with their orofacial disorders. Despite surgical management, dental treatment, and speech therapy, speech may still be poor. Surgery may not have been able to eliminate all of the external signs of the original disorder. The face they have may not be the face they want. Getting and holding a job if one sounds and looks "different" may not be easy. Finding a mate, getting married, possibly having a family, may all be frought with problems.

For those with congenital or acquired orofacial disorders, the road to recovery may be long and will require great individual courage. As with all other disorders described in this text, it is the individual, not the disorder itself, who ultimately determines the uniqueness of management goals and outcomes.

REFERENCES

American Cancer Society, *Cancer Facts and Figures.* New York: American Cancer Society Publications (1978).

BAUER, T., TRUSLER, H., and TONDRA, J., Bauer, Trusler, and Tondra's method of cheilorrhaphy in bilateral cleft lip. In W. Grabb, S. Rosenstein, and K. Bzoch (Eds.), *Cleft Lip and Palate: Surgical, Dental, and Speech Aspects.* Boston: Little, Brown (1971).

BERLIN, A., Classification of cleft lip and palate. In W. Grabb, S. Rosenstein, and K. Bzoch (Eds.), *Cleft Lip and Palate: Surgical, Dental, and Speech Aspects.* Boston: Little, Brown (1971).

BJORK, L., Velopharyngeal function in connected speech. *Acta Radiologica Supplement,* 202 (1961).

BLAND, J., A language comparison of intelligible preschool children with cleft palate and non-cleft palate preschool children. Unpublished master's thesis, University of North Carolina, Chapel Hill (1974).

BLOOMER, H., Speech defects associated with dental malocclusion and related abnormalities. In L. Travis (Ed.), *Handbook of Speech Pathology and Audiology.* New York: Appleton-Century-Crofts (1971).

BLUESTONE, C., Eustachian-tube obstruction in the infant with cleft palate. *Annals of Otology, Supplement 2* (1971).

BOO-CHAI, K., An ancient Chinese text on the cleft lip. *Plastic and Reconstructive Surgery,* 38, 89–91 (1966).

BUESCHER, N., and PAYNTER, E., Linguistic abilities of children with palatal clefts. Paper presented to the Annual Meeting of the American Cleft Palate Association, Oklahoma City (1973).

BZOCH, K., An investigation of the speech of preschool cleft palate children. Unpublished doctoral dissertation, Northwestern University, Evanston, Illinois (1956).

BZOCH, K., Categorical aspects of cleft palate speech. In W. Grabb, S. Rosenstein, and K. Bzoch (Eds.), *Cleft Lip and Palate: Surgical, Dental, and Speech Aspects.* Boston: Little, Brown (1971).

CANNON, B., Unilateral cleft lip. *New England Journal of Medicine,* 277, 583–585 (1967).

CLIFFORD, E., Psychosocial aspects of orofacial anomalies: Speculations in search of data. In Proceedings of the Conference—Orofacial Anomalies: Clinical and Research Implications. *American Speech and Hearing Association, Report No. 8*, 2–29 (1973).

COUNIHAN, D., Articulation skills of adolescents and adults with cleft palates. *Journal of Speech and Hearing Disorders*, 25, 181–187 (1960).

COUNIHAN, D., Oral and nasal sound pressure measures. In W. Grabb, S. Rosenstein, and K. Bzoch (Eds.), *Cleft Lip and Palate: Surgical, Dental, and Speech Aspects.* Boston: Little, Brown (1971).

CURTIS, J., Acoustics of speech production and nasalization. In D. Spriestersbach and D. Sherman (Eds.), *Cleft Palate and Communication.* New York: Academic Press (1968).

DIBBELL, D., Personal communication (1978).

EBERT, P., McWILLIAMS, B., and WOOLF, G., A comparison of the written language ability of cleft palate and normal children. *Cleft Palate Journal*, 11, 17–20 (1974).

FAHEY, D., Otologic care of cleft palate cases. *Laryngoscope*, 75, 570–587 (1965).

FALCONER, D., The inheritance of liability to certain diseases, estimated from the incidence among relatives. *Annals of Human Genetics*, 29, 51–71 (1965).

FLETCHER, S., Nasalance versus listener judgments of nasality. *Cleft Palate Journal*, 13, 31–41 (1976).

FRASER, F., Etiology of cleft lip and palate. In W. Grabb, S. Rosenstein, and K. Bzoch (Eds.), *Cleft Lip and Palate: Surgical, Dental, and Speech Aspects.* Boston: Little, Brown (1971).

GILMORE, S., and HOFFMAN, S., Clefts in Wisconsin: Incidence and related factors. *Cleft Palate Journal*, 3, 186–199 (1966).

GOODSTEIN, L., Psychosocial aspects of cleft palate. In D. Spriestersbach and D. Sherman (Eds.), *Cleft Palate and Communication.* New York: Academic Press (1968).

GRABB, W., General aspects of cleft palate surgery. In W. Grabb, S. Rosenstein, and K. Bzoch (Eds.), *Cleft Lip and Palate: Surgical, Dental, and Speech Aspects.* Boston: Little, Brown (1971).

GRABB, W., ROSENSTEIN, S., and BZOCH, K., (Eds.), *Cleft Lip and Palate: Surgical, Dental, and Speech Aspects.* Boston: Little, Brown (1971).

HAHN, E., Directed home training problems for cleft palate infants. In W. Grabb, S. Rosenstein, and K. Bzoch (Eds.), *Cleft Lip and Palate: Surgical, Dental, and Speech Aspects.* Boston: Little, Brown (1971).

HARDY, J., Airflow and air pressure studies. In Proceedings of the Conference—Communicative Problems in Cleft Palate. *American Speech and Hearing Association, Report No. 1*, 141–152 (1965).

HAYES, C., Audiological problems associated with cleft palate. In Proceedings of the Conference—Communicative Problems in Cleft Palate. *American Speech and Hearing Association, Report No. 1*, 83–90 (1965).

HORN, L., Language development of the cleft palate child. *Journal of the South African Speech and Hearing Association*, 19, 17–29 (1972).

ISSHIKI, N., HONJOW, I., and MORIMOTO, M., Effects of velopharyngeal incompetence upon speech. *Cleft Palate Journal*, 5, 292–310 (1968).

KALFUSS, A., Analysis of the speech of the glossectomee. Unpublished doctoral dissertation, Wayne State University, Detroit (1968).

KANTNER, C., Diagnosis and prognosis in cleft palate speech. *Journal of Speech and Hearing Disorders*, 13, 211–222 (1948).

LUBIT, E., and LARSEN, R., The Lubit palatal exerciser: A preliminary report. *Cleft Palate Journal,* 6, 120–133 (1969).

LUFKIN, A., *A History of Dentistry.* Philadelphia: Lea and Febiger (1938).

MASSENGILL, R., WILLIS, V., GERTNER, L., and FETTEROLF, J., Documentation of syndactyly and Treacher-Collins syndrome for possible concomitant speech disorders. *British Journal of Disorders of Communication,* 6, 45–51 (1971).

McWILLIAMS, B., Psychosocial development and modification. In Proceedings of the Conference—Patterns of Orofacial Growth and Development. *American Speech and Hearing Association, Report No. 6,* 165–187 (1971).

METTLER, C., *History of Medicine.* Philadelphia: Blakiston Co. (1947).

MIYAZAKI, T., MATSUYA, T., and YAMAOKA, M., Fiberscopic methods for assessment of velopharyngeal closure during various activities. *Cleft Palate Journal,* 12, 107–114 (1975).

MOLL, K., Objective measures of nasality. *Cleft Palate Journal,* 1, 371–373 (1964).

MOLL, K., Photographic and radiographic procedures in speech research. In Proceedings of the Conference—Communicative Problems in Cleft Palate, *American Speech and Hearing Association, Report No. 1,* 129–140 (1965).

MOLL, K., Speech characteristics of individuals with cleft lip and palate. In D. Spriestersbach and D. Sherman (Eds.), *Cleft Palate and Communication.* New York: Academic Press (1968).

MOLLER, K., PATH, M., WERTH, L., and CHRISTIANSEN, R., The modification of velar movement. *Journal of Speech and Hearing Disorders,* 38, 323–334 (1973).

MOORE, M., Speech language, and hearing in de Lange syndrome. *Journal of Speech and Hearing Disorders,* 35, 66–69 (1970).

MORRIS, H., Communication skills of children with cleft lips and palates. *Journal of Speech and Hearing Research,* 5, 79–90 (1962).

MORRIS, H., SPRIESTERSBACH, D., and DARLEY, F., An articulation test for assessing competency of velopharyngeal closure. *Journal of Speech and Hearing Research,* 4, 48–55 (1961).

NATION, J., Determinants of vocabulary development of preschool cleft palate children. *Cleft Palate Journal,* 7, 645–651 (1970).

NEIMAN, G., and SIMPSON, R., A roentgencephalometric investigation of the effect of adenoid removal upon selected measures of velopharyngeal function. *Cleft Palate Journal,* 12, 377–389 (1975).

OLSEN, N., Pediatric dentistry. In W. Grabb, S. Rosenstein, and K. Bzoch (Eds.), *Cleft Lip and Palate: Surgical, Dental, and Speech Aspects,* Boston: Little, Brown (1971).

PANNBACKER, M., Oral language skills of adult cleft palate speakers. *Cleft Palate Journal,* 12, 95–106 (1975).

PARADISE, J., Middle ear problems associated with cleft palate. *Cleft Palate Journal,* 12, 17–22 (1975).

PARADISE, J., McWILLIAMS, B., and BLUESTONE, C., Associations in cleft palate children between early otologic management and later mental, speech, and language development. Paper presented to the Meeting of the American Cleft Palate Association, Phoenix (1972).

PETERSON, S., Electrical stimulation of the soft palate. *Cleft Palate Journal,* 11, 72–86 (1974).

PETERSON, S., Speech pathology in craniofacial malformations other than cleft lip and palate. In Proceedings of the Conference—Orofacial Anomalies: Clinical and Research Implications, *American Speech and Hearing Association, Report No. 8,* 111–131 (1973).

PETERSON-FALZONE, S., and PRUZANSKY, S., Cleft palate and congenital velopharyngeal incompetency in mandibulofacial dysostosis: Frequency and problems in treatment. *Cleft Palate Journal,* 13, 354–360 (1976).

PHILIPS, B., Stimulating language and speech development in cleft palate infants. In W. Grabb, S. Rosenstein, and K. Bzoch (Eds.), *Cleft Lip and Palate: Surgical, Dental, and Speech Aspects.* Boston: Little, Brown (1971).

PHILIPS, B., and HARRISON, R., Language skills of preschool cleft palate children. *Cleft Palate Journal,* 6, 108–119 (1969).

PRATHER, W., and KOS, C., Audiological and otological considerations. In D. Spriestersbach and D. Sherman (Eds.), *Cleft Palate and Communication.* New York: Academic Press (1968).

SAXMAN, J., and BLESS, D., Patterns of language development in cleft palate children aged 3 to 8 years. Paper presented to the Annual Meeting of the American Cleft Palate Association, Oklahoma City (1973).

SHELTON, R., HAHN, E., and MORRIS H., Diagnosis and therapy. In D. Spriestersbach and D. Sherman (Eds.), *Cleft Palate and Communication.* New York: Academic Press (1968).

SHELTON, R., PAESANI, A., McCLELLAND, K., and BRADFIELD, S., Panendoscopic feedback in the study of voluntary velopharyngeal movements. *Journal of Speech and Hearing Research,* 40, 232–244 (1975).

SHPRINTZEN, J., McCALL, G., and SKOLNICK, M., A new therapeutic technique for the treatment of velopharyngeal incompetence. *Journal of Speech and Hearing Disorders,* 40, 69–83 (1975).

SKELLY, M., SPECTOR, D., DONALDSON, R., BRODEUR, A., and PALETTA, F., Compensatory physiologic phonetics for the glossectomee. *Journal of Speech and Hearing Disorders,* 36, 101–114 (1971).

SKOLNICK, M., Otologic evaluation in cleft palate patients. *Laryngoscope,* 68, 1908–1949 (1958).

SKOLNICK, M., SHPRINTZEN, J., McCALL, G., and ROKOFF, S., Patterns of velopharyngeal closure in subjects with repaired cleft palates and normal speech: A multi-view videofluoroscopic analysis. *Cleft Palate Journal,* 12, 369–376 (1975).

SLAUGHTER, W., and PHAIR, G., A complete cleft-palate program. *Journal of Speech and Hearing Disorders,* 17, 123–128 (1952).

SMITH, R., and McWILLIAMS, B., Creative thinking abilities of cleft palate children. *Cleft Palate Journal,* 3, 225–283 (1966).

SMITH, R., and McWILLIAMS, B., Psycholinguistic abilities of children with clefts. *Cleft Palate Journal,* 5, 238–249 (1968).

SPRIESTERSBACH, D., The effects of orofacial anomalies on the speech process. In Proceedings of the Conference—Communicative Problems in Cleft Palate. *American Speech and Hearing Association, Report No. 1,* 111–127 (1965).

SPRIESTERSBACH, D., DARLEY, F., and MORRIS, H., Language skills in children with cleft palates. *Journal of Speech and Hearing Research,* 1, 279–285 (1958).

SPRIESTERSBACH, D., MOLL, K., and MORRIS, H., Subject classification and articulation of speakers with cleft palates. *Journal of Speech and Hearing Research,* 4, 362–372 (1961).

STOOL, S., and RANDALL, P., Unexpected ear disease in infants with cleft palate. *Cleft Palate Journal,* 4, 99–103 (1967).

SUBTELNY, J., and SUBTELNY, J., Intelligibility and associated physiological factors of cleft palate speakers. *Journal of Speech and Hearing Research,* 2, 353–360 (1961).

SUBTELNY, J., WORTH, J., and SAKUDA, M., Intraoral pressure and rate of flow during speech. *Journal of Speech and Hearing Research,* 9, 498–518 (1966).

TEMPLIN, M., and DARLEY, F., *The Templin-Darley Tests of Articulation.* Iowa City, Iowa: Bureau of Education Research and Service (1960).

TROST, J., Articulatory addition to the classical cleft palate speech: The pharyngeal stop, the mid-dorsum palatal stop, and the posterior nasal fricative. Paper presented to the Annual Meeting of the American Cleft Palate Association, Atlanta (1978).

WALLNER, L., HILL, B., WALDROP, W., and MONROE, C., Voice changes following adenotonsillectomy. *Laryngoscope,* 78, 1410–1418 (1968).

WARREN, D., and DuBOIS, A., A pressure-flow technique for measuring velopharyngeal orifice area during continuous speech. *Cleft Palate Journal,* 1, 52–71 (1964).

WARREN, D., and RYON, W., Oral port constriction, nasal resistance, and respiratory aspects of cleft palate speech: An analog study. *Cleft Palate Journal,* 4, 38–46 (1967).

WEINBERGER, B., *An Introduction to the History of Dentistry.* St. Louis: C. V. Mosby (1948).

WELLS, C., *Cleft Palate and Its Associated Speech Disorders.* New York: McGraw-Hill (1971).

WHITCOMB, L., OCHSNER, G., and WAYTE, R., A comparison of expressive language skills of cleft palate and non-cleft palate children. *Journal of the Oklahoma Speech and Hearing Association,* 3, 25–28 (1976).

YULES, R., Current concepts of treatment of ear disease in cleft palate children and adults. *Cleft Palate Journal,* 12, 315–322 (1975).

YULES, R., and CHASE, R., Secondary techniques for correction of palatopharyngeal incompetence. In W. Grabb, S. Rosenstein, and K. Bzoch (Eds.), *Cleft Lip and Palate: Surgical, Dental, and Speech Aspects.* Boston: Little, Brown (1971).

ZWITMAN, D., GYEPES, M., and WARD, P., Assessment of velar and lateral wall movement by oral telescope and radiographic examination in patients with velopharyngeal inadequacy and in normal subjects. *Journal of Speech and*

signpost   A heterogeneous group of speech disorders exists as the result of various disturbances in voluntary control over the speech musculature. These disturbances are consequences of different forms of damage or maldevelopment of the nervous or muscle systems and are called *dysarthria*. Chapter 10 considers the wide variety of causes of these disturbances and shows how the overall portion of the territory having to do with dysarthria can be divided to encompass six major types of disturbances. Methods for the evaluation of such disturbances are discussed and attention is devoted to what the symptoms of dysarthria may reveal about the nature of the disease process. Methods for management of dysarthria are given prominent coverage, including the new promises of biofeedback procedures and some things that can be done for individuals whose speech is rendered essentially useless by their control problem. Dysarthria is one of the most difficult to remediate of all the disorders of human communication, and it is a disorder that will be faced more and more as the average life expectancy eases upward and the neurological diseases of the aged become more common. Few, if any, communication disorders are more widely seen by health-related personnel who deal daily with individuals suffering from neurological diseases. And, few, if any, communication disorders are more challenging to the speech-language pathologist who is charged with the task of helping the dysarthric patient attain usable speech or an alternate mode of communication.

10

Arnold E. Aronson

dysarthria

INTRODUCTION

Movement, sensation, thought, memory, language, and speech are ephemeral qualities, difficult to reconcile with the fact that they owe their existence to nerve cells and nerve impulses. Nonetheless, Sir Charles Sherrington, father of modern neurophysiology, has said, "the brain is the organ of the mind." Injure or destroy it and conscious existence will change.

To what extent can neurological disease affect life? Mild: A temporary reduction in sensation or movement of the fingers due to an injured nerve in the arm. Worse: A paralyzed arm or leg, partial loss of vision or hearing, a disturbance in control over the speech musculature. Worse still: Loss of ability to formulate vocabulary and syntax, to comprehend what is heard or read, to calculate, to write. The worst?

Perhaps you read about him in the *Tribune,* clergyman, forty-eight, bright, energetic, penetrating eyes, an ingenuous personality, before his illness. It began with a tour of New Guinea, flying by small missionary plane from town to town—Karmiu, Gorka, Okapa—shaking hands with many natives, some ill with eye, respiratory, and skin diseases. He contracts a sore throat, cough, and fever which persist until his return to the United States. An ordinarily articulate man and accomplished extemporaneous speaker, he becomes concerned, while addressing a church convention, over the necessity of hunting for the "right words." He begins to lose his train of thought during his conversational speech and has trouble with memory for recent events. He is put in a hospital where a search begins for the cause of these disturbing signs. While there, he begins to have trouble in translating his thoughts into words. He relates well to others and can explain things, though with hesitation.

On testing, nonetheless, he cannot retain numbers, and although he comprehends commands, he is slow when asked to distinguish right from left. He can barely remember what he has read. He pauses and searches for words when asked to name objects. His right arm becomes tremorous to a small degree and his gait unsteady. A brain-wave test shows an abnormality, a "slowing in the left frontal region," though other laboratory tests are normal. His condition begins to deteriorate. His speech worsens. He becomes less and less verbal. Within a week he cannot name a thing, and he repeats responses to previous questions. No longer can he spell or define words. His writing becomes almost illegible. He cannot write spontaneously nor transcribe what is said to him. He has lost all ability to calculate. Then, there comes a jerking of his right arm, and his already unsteady gait worsens. He comprehends nothing, and cannot count aloud. He sits and looks around as if he could respond but is mute. He cannot walk without support and his extremities are rigid. The jerking of his arm gets worse. Alertness is diminished. He becomes incontinent. Arm jerking becomes bilateral and constant. He smiles and recognizes relatives, occasionally. Only liquids or pureed foods can be swallowed. His extremities become even more rigid and go into constant purposeless movement. His loyal wife and sister-in-law attend to him as often as they can, never giving up hope, but, he dies. Neurologists believed that he had contracted a virus of the central nervous system called Jakob-Cruetzfeldt disease, related to the equally lethal Kuru, indigenous to New Guinea.

From this melancholy case history, we see how movement, sensation, thought, memory, language, and speech can be destroyed one by one from expanding neurological disease. We also get some notion of how many specialists might be involved in assisting patients with neurological disease. Neurologists attempted to diagnose and treat the patient. Nurses cared for him around the clock. Psychologists examined his intellectual functions. Speech-language pathologists evaluated his communication abilities. Physical therapists attempted to rehabilitate his gait disorder. Occupational therapists stood by awaiting the possibility of a reversal or arrest of his neurological disease.

Among the barrage of symptoms this patient showed was dysarthria, a disorder in control over the speech musculature. Dysarthria is one of the multitude of symptoms of neurological disease that can occur by itself or in combination with others. This chapter is concerned with dysarthria and how it interferes with oral communication. We begin with a definition of dysarthria and then move on to a discussion of reasons for its study. From there we turn to the causes of dysarthria. These considerations are followed by a discussion of the various types of dysarthria. Then we deal with the evaluation of patients with dysarthria, followed by a final section concerned with their management.

ON DEFINING DYSARTHRIA

Dysarthria is the technical term that designates *a disturbance in voluntary control over the speech musculature.* The term encompasses a group of speech disorders that result from various forms of damage to components of the central and/or peripheral nervous systems. The control problems themselves are the result of paralysis, weakness, or incoordination of the speech muscles. The patient is simply unable to speak with normal muscular speed, strength, precision, or timing. We can hear the effects of these muscular aberrations; problems of phonation because of interference with the laryngeal and respiratory musculature, of resonation because of interference with the muscles of the soft palate and pharynx, and of articulation because of interference with the lip, tongue, and jaw musculature. Prosody, the melody, stress, and rhythm patterns of contextual speech is disordered because of the cumulative problems of these different motor-speech systems.

In some people, dysarthria is so mild that it escapes all but the experienced clinician. In others, however, muscular weakness and incoordination are so severe that speech is unintelligible and practically useless. Many would say that the most serious and incapacitating disorders of speech are found within the dysarthria group. The term *anarthria* is often used to denote nearly unintelligible dysarthric speech or the complete absence of speech for reasons related to dysarthria.

Dysarthria and anarthria are no respectors of age. They are found in various forms throughout the life span of man. Some are the result of congenital or early damage to the nervous system and others are acquired during later stages of life.

REASONS FOR STUDYING DYSARTHRIA

If we listened to the speech of individuals with severe dysarthria or anarthria, we would agree that their speech was worthless as a means of communication. We could predict serious psychological and economical consequences for people with such speech and we would clearly appreciate the urgent demands by patients, families, and physicians for speech rehabilitation. At the risk of introducing undue pessimism, it must be stated that the speech-language pathologist's ability to help most individuals with severe dysarthria is limited. Confronting speech clinicians and speech scientists today is an imperative to *develop better methods with which to help dysarthric patients acquire more intelligible speech.* Fortunately, some inroads are being made toward this goal.

Another purpose in becoming knowledgeable about dysarthria is that the ability to isolate and differentiate one type from another can *aid the physician in the diagnosis of neurological disease.* There is a cause and effect relationship between the location of damage within the nervous system and the type of dysarthria that results. Each of the different anatomical and functional components of the nervous system serves a specific purpose in the initiation and coordination of movements of structures comprising the speech mechanism. Should a particular motor component of the nervous system be damaged, its special function will be impaired. That impairment will reveal itself by means of a specific kind of movement abnormality which will produce similarly specific dysarthric speech changes that can be identified by the skilled clinician.

One of the main objectives of the neurologist is to locate the tissue damage causing abnormal sensation or movement. Any clinical or laboratory information that can help him in his search is vital. *Many neurological diseases reveal themselves first, and often only, by way of peripheral speech mechanism malfunction.* As Grewel (1957) has pointed out, dysarthria is discernible at an early stage in neurological disorders, sometimes even suggesting a tentative diagnosis to the trained ear, when neurological examination still shows no convincing signs or symptoms. It has happened time and time again that the presence of dysarthria, so mild as to be misconstrued by some as a variation of normal function or as a psychogenic problem, was identified by a sensitive clinician whose alertness led the way to the diagnosis of a neurological disease. These experiences have taught us to appreciate that aberrant motor-speech behavior can be like a fingerprint or laboratory test warning of the presence and location of tissue damage in the nervous system.

CAUSES OF DYSARTHRIA

Signs and symptoms of neurological disease depend upon where the disease strikes the nervous system and not upon the type of disease itself. For example, severe damage to a nerve by a tumor, inflamation, or laceration would result in the same problem, a paralysis of the muscles served by that nerve. This is not to say that the time-course of the evolving symptoms is not dependent upon the type of disease, because it is. Contrasting the consequences of the breaking of a blood vessel in the brain and of a tumor growing in the same region should make this apparent. The breaking of the blood vessel is a sudden event and produces a sudden paralysis, say of an arm and a leg. The growing tumor will also produce a paralysis of the same arm and leg but it would be a paralysis of gradual rather than abrupt onset.

Although there are many injurious agents within the realm of neurological disease, they all have one factor in common—they interfere with or completely destroy the functioning of the nerve cell. Any abnormality of tissue, whatever its cause, is referred to as a *lesion*. Conditions that produce lesions of neural tissue and thus are capable of causing dysarthria can be classified under the following headings: (1) vascular diseases, (2) infectious diseases, (3) metabolic diseases, (4) tumors, (5) trauma, (6) degenerative diseases, (7) toxins, and (8) cerebral palsy.

Vascular Diseases

Vascular means blood vessels—arteries and veins. Interference with the blood supply to neurons can decrease their efficiency or kill them. A disease of blood vessels that occurs abruptly and causes rapidly developing neurological signs is called a *cerebrovascular accident (CVA) or stroke*. There are different types of CVAs. If a blood vessel breaks and bleeds into the brain, it is called *intracerebral hemorrhage*. If it becomes clogged by clotted blood, by scar tissue from blood vessel walls, or by inflammation, neurons fail to receive a normal blood supply in a condition called *thrombosis*. If it becomes clogged by a fragment of blood, fat, air, or bacteria traveling from some other location, and cells are deprived of blood, the condition is designated as an *embolism*.

> While shaving one morning, a fifty-five-year-old right-handed insurance salesman became dizzy and complained of a headache. He called out to his wife and the next moment dropped his razor into the sink and slumped to the floor. Shortly thereafter he regained consciousness, but his right arm and right leg and right lower half of his face were paralyzed. When he tried to speak, he could only produce grunting noises. An x-ray of the blood vessels of the brain revealed an occlusion of a branch of one of the arteries supplying the motor areas of the left frontal lobe.

Infectious Diseases

Blood vessels and coverings of the brain can be invaded by *infectious microorganisms*. These can enter the brain either directly from skull fracture or they may travel to the brain from other parts of the body via the blood vessels. Meningitis from meningococcus, pneumococcus, streptococcus and influenzal organisms, abscess, and fungal, viral and neurosyphilitic conditions are some examples of central nervous system infections that may result in neurological disorders.

Metabolic Diseases

Many metabolic diseases have neurological complications. Some of these include blood diseases such as polycythemia, sickle-cell anemia, and leukemia. Two other metabolic conditions that may result in neurological symptoms are disorders of amino acid metabolism and disorders of carbohydrate metabolism. Neuroendocrine problems are most often manifested as a result of disease of the pituitary, adrenal, and thyroid glands.

Tumors

Another name for tumor is *neoplasm*. Here we are concerned primarily with *intracranial tumors,* those that occur within the cranial cavity, although tumors of the spinal cord and cranial and spinal nerves also cause dysarthria. Tumors encroach on normal nerve tissue and blood vessels, destroying nerve cells in the vicinity. The most common intracranial tumors are called *gliomas* of which there are several: astrocytoma, ependymoma, medulloblastoma, and ogligodendroglioma. *Meningiomas* are tumors of the meninges and not of the brain per se, but they press into the brain having effects similar to brain tumors.

Trauma

Common in modern society because of motor vehicle accidents, falls, and assaults, are closed-head injuries and depressed-skull fractures. These have effects on the brain in the form of concussion, edema, and contusion or laceration. Because of the massive traumatic effects of such injuries the consequences can be disastrous.

A twenty-five-year-old factory worker riding to work on his motorcycle was forced off the road by a passing car and skidded into a telephone pole. Even though he was wearing a helmet, he suffered a severe concussion. He remained comatose for two months and then passed into a state of apparent alertness but unresponsiveness to any questions or commands. Several weeks later he began to make sounds, but his attempts to articulate were unintelligible. He was later transferred to a rehabilitation unit for treatment of quadriparesis and dysarthria. He was also found to be suffering from severe intellectual deficit.

Degenerative Diseases

Despite his protestations, a fifty-seven-year-old attorney and advertising company executive was brought to the clinic by his wife. Four months prior to his examination he began to show changes in his behavior that

413

disturbed his family and business associates. Always a spirited conversationalist with an excellent mind and vocabulary, he began to grow less verbal until he would no longer volunteer conversation, speaking only when asked a direct question. His work declined in quality and his handwriting became almost illegible. His wife decided to bring him for an examination after she found him wandering up and down the sidewalk apparently confused as to the location of his house. On examination, his sensation, gait, muscle strength, and coordination were normal. However, he had considerable difficulty naming simple objects. His recent memory was poor. Laughing frequently and inappropriately, he could not understand what all the fuss was about as he thought nothing was the matter with him.

This is not an unusual story for a degenerative central nervous system disease. There are several types, some diffuse, involving large portions of the brain, others affecting only certain nerve cell groups. A common diffuse category is exemplified by the case study above, *pre-senile dementia*, in which there is widespread loss of neurons affecting most of the outer layers of the cerebral cortex. These diseases are spontaneous and of unknown cause, often beginning in the late forties or fifties. Other more focal degenerative diseases are one form of Parkinson's syndrome, chorea, cerebellar degenerative disease, and amyotrophic lateral sclerosis. Each of these produces a different type of dysarthria.

Toxins

Three kinds of toxic agents can interfere with nervous system functioning: (1) toxic metabolic products of diphtheria, tetanus, and botulism; (2) inorganic metals, typically arsenic, bismuth, lead, manganese, and mercury; and (3) organic substances such as methyl alcohol, barbiturates, and carbon monoxide.

A seventy-six-year-old owner of a large farm had been experiencing muscular weakness and loss of tactile sensation for approximately one year. On examination, his speech was dysarthric and his tongue, jaw and palatal musculature weak. Laboratory studies revealed large amounts of arsenic in the clippings of his hair and fingernails. Further investigation revealed that his wife had for several years been showing paranoid behavior, and his daughter, when she visited her father's farm, discovered arsenic in the table sugar.

"Cerebral Palsy"

Cerebral palsy is not a specific disease. The term refers to a group of motor and sensory neurological conditions that result from damage or failure of embryonic development of the central and/or peripheral nervous systems. The neurological impairment may occur in utero, at birth, or early in life. The latter is arbitrarily defined to include the first three to five years. Agenesis of the nervous system, trauma, anoxia, infections and toxic products are typical agents that can result in neurological damage. Neurological signs and symptoms are the result of damage to the cortico-spinal and cortico-bulbar tracts, basal ganglia and cerebellum, resulting in spasticity, athetosis, and ataxia, respectively. Visual and auditory disturbances, sensory deficits, and intellectual impairment are common. Many other diseases contribute to dysarthric symptoms in children, but they are beyond the scope of this chapter.

TYPES OF DYSARTHRIA

In this section, we present the characteristics of dysarthria in relation to the location of nervous system disease. Our discussion is subdivided to handle the six major types of dysarthria: flaccid, spastic, ataxic, hypokinetic, hyperkinetic, and mixed.

Flaccid Dysarthria

Dysarthria resulting from lesions of the peripheral nervous system, or lower motor neuron system, is called *flaccid dysarthria*. It is named for the type of paresis or paralysis that results. *Paresis means a pathological muscular weakness with some residual strength of muscular contraction. Paralysis means complete inability to contract muscles because of pathological weakness.* Flaccid conditions result when there is a lesion at any point along the motor unit. The flaccid (meaning flabby) label implies *weakness, lack of normal muscle tone, and reduced or absent reflexes.* Depending upon the site of the lesion along the lower motor neuron, a number of other signs may be present. Damage to the cell body or the axon will produce *fasciculations,* small, spontaneous twitches of muscle. Damage to the cell body, axon, or muscle will produce muscle *atrophy* in which the muscle gets smaller in size. Failure of neuromuscular transmission at the myoneural junction will result in *progressive weakening* with repetitive or sustained muscular activities, with recovery of strength after rest.

Any one or any combination of peripheral nerves may be impaired and a wide variety of flaccid symptoms may be present. There may be selective impairment of certain speech mechanism structures or impairment that influences nearly all aspects of motor speech behavior, and severity can range from mild weakness to complete paralysis. Finally, all types of movements may be impaired—volitional, automatic, and reflexive—and it is more likely that individual muscles will be involved as opposed to the disorganization of entire movement patterns. Next, we highlight the influences of isolated cranial and spinal nerve lesions, followed by a consideration of multiple lesions.

Isolated Cranial and Spinal Nerve Lesions. The nerves of primary importance to motor speech production are cranial nerves XII, X, VII, and V, and the spinal nerves associated with respiration. All of these can be damaged either *unilaterally or bilaterally.* Most unilateral lesions result from damage to the nerve somewhere between where it emerges from the skull and its junction with the muscle it serves, for outside the skull the nerves of a pair are widely separated and less likely to be vulnerable to the same lesion. By contrast, lesions within the skull usually result in bilateral involvement of muscles because the nuclei of the neurons lie close to one another and are vulnerable to the same lesion.

Cranial nerve XII—Hypoglossal: Unilateral damage to the hypoglossal nerve results in flaccid paresis or paralysis of the half of the tongue on the same side as the damage. Weakness and lack of tone are apparent on the involved side along with a wasting of muscle, wrinkling and furrowing of the tongue surface, and fasciculations. Upon protrusion, the tongue will deviate toward the involved side (see Figure 10–1). Elevation of different parts of the tongue may be possible, but there is less strength and precision of tongue contact with other structures within the oral cavity. Unilateral damage has a relatively mild influence on speech because the patient is able to compensate for the disturbance. Usually the problem is confined to imprecise tongue adjustments that lead to slight articulatory distortions.

Bilateral lesions of the hypoglossal nerve have more serious consequences than unilateral lesions. Both sides of the tongue show signs of flaccid involvement and the range of motion of the tongue may be severely limited. The patient may demonstrate difficulty in protruding the tongue, in depressing it, in placing it against the cheek, in lateralizing it and in elevating its different parts. Intelligibility of speech is usually severely impaired. Consonants relying heavily on tongue movements are either grossly distorted or absent. Vowels, although abnormal, usually retain their identity. Contextual speech often sounds like a succession of vowel utterances.

Cranial nerve X—Vagus: Damage to the vagus nerve may result in flaccid impairment of any one or a combination of the larynx, pharynx, and soft palate.

Unilateral lesions involving the larynx most often implicate the

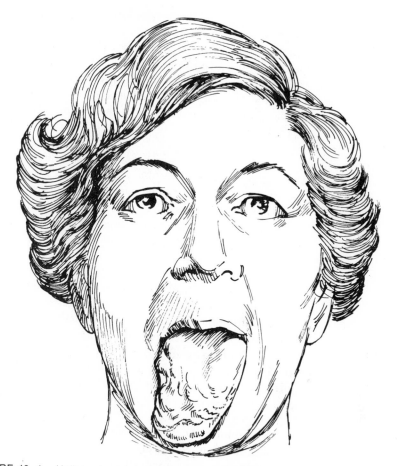

FIGURE 10–1. *Unilateral weakness of the tongue resulting from a lesion to the hypoglossal nerve (right side). Unilateral atrophy of the tongue has occurred. Note that the tongue is wrinkled and furrowed on the right side and curves toward the paralyzed side.*

recurrent laryngeal branch of the vagus, and more often the left than the right because the course of the left branch is longer and more exposed. The consequence of unilateral damage is impairment of the muscles controlling the adductor-abductor functions of the vocal fold on the corresponding side. Usually the involved vocal fold is immobile and fixed in a position slightly lateral to the midline (see Chapter 8). If asked to cough, the patient may do so weakly and with less than normal sharpness. The major dysarthric deficit is flaccid dysphonia in which the voice may be breathy, harsh, hoarse, weak, and unchanging in loudness or pitch. Occasionally two pitch levels (*diplophonia*) are perceived because the normal and paralyzed vocal folds vibrate at dif-

417

ferent frequencies. Conversational speech may be characterized by short phrases because the air supply is rapidly depleted during breathy voicing and inspiratory sounds may be heard because the patient cannot move the involved vocal fold "out of the way."

If damage impairs the innervation to both vocal folds, the muscular and speech effects will be far more serious than in the case of unilateral involvement. Most of the dysphonic characteristics of unilateral involvement are seen in greater severity in bilateral damage, except for diplophonia.

Damage to the vagus nerve on one side can also cause flaccid paresis or paralysis of the pharyngeal constrictors and soft palate. With regard to the latter, involvement is manifested by the affected side of the palate being suspended at a lower level than the normal side during rest and phonation (see Figure 10–2a). The patient with unilateral velopharyngeal involvement will usually demonstrate only a mild problem of hypernasality in speech.

Bilateral damage to the vagus nerve may cause a weakness or paralysis to both sides of the pharynx and soft palate. In this condition, both sides of the palate are suspended at a lower than normal level for rest and phonation (see Figure 10–2b and 10–2c). Motion of the soft palate is restricted or absent. The consequences for speech of bilateral velopharyngeal problems are major. Marked hypernasality may result and be accompanied by audible emission of air through the nose. Articulation of consonants requiring high intraoral air pressure may be distorted because of air leakage through the impaired velopharyngeal port.

Combined flaccid disturbance of the larynx and velopharyngeal mechanism from vagus damage may result in sufficient air wastage during speech that conversational utterance is marked by a reduction in the number of syllables per expiration. There may also be an increase in the volume of air expired per syllable and an increase in the frequency of breathing for speech.

Cranial nerve VII—Facial: Unilateral damage to the facial nerve leads to flaccid involvement of the corresponding side of the face. The affected side takes on a "sagging" appearance in which it lies lower than the normal side. The mouth is drawn toward the unaffected side, especially during an activity like smiling. Lip function will be impaired on the flaccid side of the face and the patient may experience difficulty compressing the lips, opening them, and shaping them. Unilateral damage has a relatively unimportant influence on speech production. Consonants involving the lips may be slightly deviant but little effect on vowels is noted except for those requiring extreme lip postures.

Bilateral facial nerve damage results in weakness or paralysis of

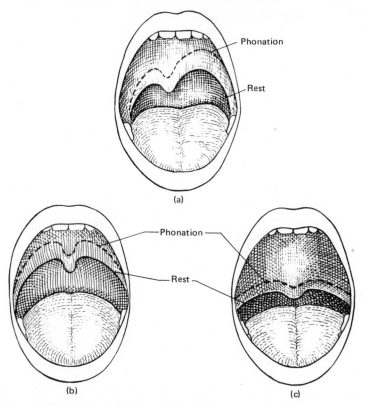

FIGURE 10–2. *An artist's drawing of three conditions of soft palate function: (a) Right unilateral soft palate paresis resulting from a lesion to the vagus nerve. Note that the right side of the soft palate hangs lower than the left side during rest and phonation. (b) Normal appearance of the soft palate at rest and upon elevation during phonation. (c) Bilateral soft palate paresis. Note that the soft palate hangs lower than in (b) and that its curvature is flatter during both rest and phonation. (From F. Darley, A. Aronson, and J. Brown,* Motor Speech Disorders. *Philadelphia: Saunders, 1975.)*

the entire face. The entire lower lip sags and the range of motion and compression capabilities of the lips are markedly impaired. It may be impossible for the patient to round and protrude the lips. With severe involvement, he may be unable to touch his teeth with his lips. The smile of the patient is typically horizontal, instead of the corners of the mouth pulling upward. Bilateral facial nerve damage can have serious consequences on speech production. Defective articulation is the hallmark of the disorder, particularly of bilabial and labiodental sounds. Much of the problem has to do with the patient's inability to develop oral pressure in the presence of a weak lip seal, especially for stop-plosive sounds. Vowels also are often distorted because of difficulty with lip posturing.

Cranial nerve V – Trigeminal: Unilateral lesions to the motor division of the trigeminal nerve result in flaccid weakness of the jaw muscles on one side. The jaw will deviate toward the paretic or paralyzed side. Patients with unilateral damage usually can elevate the jaw to occlude the teeth through action of the muscles on the intact side of the jaw. Thus, unilateral lesions, although they produce asymmetrical movements of the jaw, do not usually seriously impair speech.

In bilateral damage, the jaw hangs down as if in open-mouthed astonishment. Bilateral damage causes serious difficulty in elevating the jaw or otherwise controlling it purposefully. Patients with such involvement show highly unintelligible speech because the jaw cannot be positioned properly in order for articulatory movements to be made by the tongue and lower lip. Bilabial, labiodental, and lingual consonants are produced deviantly, as are many vowels. The seriousness of bilateral paralysis can be appreciated by attempting to speak normally while keeping the mouth wide open.

Spinal nerves: Lesions to the spinal cord and/or peripheral spinal nerves may result in flaccid paresis or paralysis of various muscles of the respiratory system. A variety of combinations of impairment among the rib cage wall muscles, the diaphragm, and the abdominal wall muscles may be observed, depending upon the site of lesion. Disabilities often include shallow breathing, a reduction in vital capacity, a reduction in inspiratory reserve volume, and a reduction in expiratory reserve volume. The patient may not be able to inspire rapidly between speech phrases. He may demonstrate reduced loudness of voice because of inadequate expiratory force and may show problems in maintaining loudness over long stretches because of expiratory force control problems. Some patients will speak in short phrases because expiratory muscle weakness prevents them from moving the respiratory system through normal lung volumes. A frequently observed symptom is various dyssynchronies in function of the different parts of the respiratory system. Considerable compensation for weakness often occurs in patients so that rather diffuse damage may be required to seriously impair respiratory function for speech (Hixon, 1970).

Multiple Cranial and Spinal Nerve Lesions. Multiple nerve lesions may result in a combination of involvements of different speech structures and varying degrees of muscular weakness. The flaccid dysarthria that results depends upon the combined effects of isolated nerve lesions, and the speech symptoms vary greatly from patient to patient. In a study including thirty patients with multiple cranial nerve lesions of various causes and combinations, Darley, Aronson, and Brown (1969a, b) found the following audible characteristics: hypernasality, imprecise consonant productions, breathiness of voice, monopitch, nasal emission, audible inspiration, harsh voice quality, short phrases, and monoloudness. From this list, it is apparent that most of the acoustic characteristics related to isolated cranial nerve lesions are in constellation when multiple-nerve flaccid dysarthria is manifested.

Many neurological diseases can cause a generalized flaccid dysarthria. Among them are failures of embryonic development of several cranial nerve nuclei, various types of muscular dystrophy, and myotonic dystrophy. Perhaps the most widely recognized neurological syndrome affecting multiple cranial and spinal nerves is myasthenia gravis. In this myoneural-junction disease, muscles become progressively weaker with sustained use. Flaccid dysarthria is manifested in increasing dysphonia, deteriorating articulation, and increasing hypernasality. After rest, the patient may speak normally again, but if he continues, muscle fatigue will return. Figure 10–3 shows a patient with bilateral facial weakness as a part of generalized flaccid weakness due to myasthenia gravis.

Spastic Dysarthria

Dysarthria that results from lesions to the closely intertwined pyramidal and extrapyramidal systems is called *spastic dysarthria*. This form of dysarthria derives its names from the spastic paresis or paralysis that gives rise to the disordered speech symptoms. Symptoms include *muscular weakness, greater than normal muscular tone, slow movements, limited range of motion, and hyperactive reflexes.* The patient's voluntary control is

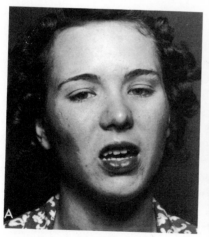 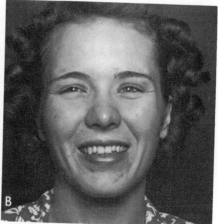

FIGURE 10–3. *Bilateral facial weakness in a patient with generalized flaccid involvement due to myasthenia gravis. (a) The patient is attempting to smile. (b) After drug treatment a normal smile is possible. (From F. Darley, A. Aronson, and J. Brown,* Motor Speech Disorders. *Philadelphia: Saunders, 1975.)*

greatly impaired and entire skilled movement patterns may be disordered.

Unilateral damage to the direct and indirect components of the upper motor neuron system results in a condition known as *spastic hemiplegia*. Only muscles on the side of the body opposite the lesion are affected. With respect to speech musculature, unilateral damage usually has significant consequences only for the lips, lower face, and tongue. These structures are impaired because they are the only ones that do not have major proportions of fibers distributed to lower motor neurons on the same side of the body as the lesion. In spastic hemiplegia, the patient's mouth may sag on the side having muscle involvement and his tongue may deviate toward this weaker side. Unilateral spastic dysarthria is usually not severe. Typically, only articulation is impaired. Impairment may be in the form of mild to moderate articulatory difficulty in the production of consonants and vowels that require major lip gestures or that require intricate maneuvers of the tongue. Often unilateral spastic dysarthria will improve within several days of the occurrence of the lesion because the patient learns to compensate for the muscular weakness.

Bilateral lesions of the direct and indirect components of the upper motor neuron system result in a markedly different and more severe disorder than is found in unilateral lesions. Muscles on both sides of the body are functionally impaired. All components of the speech mechanism may show deviancies. Respiratory problems may be manifested in reduced lung volumes, inability to maintain air pressure, difficulty in producing sustained, steady expiratory movements during speech, and inability to rapidly change the pressure and flow needed for conversational speech. Problems at the laryngeal level are often in the form of hyperadduction of the vocal folds producing a constricted glottal aperture. The velopharyngeal mechanism typically manifests limited and slow movement, and the articulatory mechanism shows a variety of spastic difficulties in the tongue, lips, and jaw. The major audible characteristics of bilateral spastic dysarthria were determined for thirty patients by Darley et al., (1969a, b) and include the following: imprecise consonants, monopitch, reduced stress, harsh voice quality, monoloudness, low pitch, slow rate, hypernasality, strained-strangled voice quality, short phrases, distorted vowels, pitch breaks, breathy voice quality, and excess and equal syllable stress.

Ataxic Dysarthria

Damage to the cerebellum may result in a neurological control problem referred to as ataxia and characterized by patient *difficulties in regulating force, speed, range, timing, and direction of volitional movements.*

Ataxia is also manifested in *lower than normal tone in the muscular system, essentially normal reflexes, and tremor during voluntary efforts.* Cerebellar damage may influence various functions, including gait, balance, limb coordination, and speech. Difficulty with the latter is designated as *ataxic dysarthria* and most often is the result of bilateral damage to the cerebellum.

Patients with ataxic dysarthria may show involvement of the respiratory, laryngeal, and articulatory systems to various degrees. Interference with the velopharyngeal mechanism is relatively rare. The most often deviant speech dimensions in ataxic dysarthria include the following (Darley et al., 1969a, b): imprecise consonants, excess and equal syllable stress, irregular articulatory breakdown, distorted vowels, harsh voice quality, prolonged phonemes, prolonged intervals between phonemes, monopitch, monoloudness, and slow rate. In mild cases of ataxic dysarthria, only the control of articulation may be significantly impaired. In severe ataxic dysarthria, the social, emotional, and occupational impact may be major because speech is highly unintelligible. Severe ataxic dysarthria typically involves a major respiratory control problem and sudden changes in pitch and loudness may be apparent. Ataxic dysarthria usually rivets the attention of listeners because the speech produced gives the impression that the speaker is "drunk." Persons with ataxic dysarthria are often mistakenly accused of being inebriated, and they find themselves having to explain the nature of their speech problem to their business associates, friends, and others.

Hypokinetic Dysarthria

Damage to the paired substantia nigra may prevent the manufacture of the neural transmitter dopamine and impair its transfer in sufficient amounts to the striatum. The result is an extrapyramidal-system movement disorder termed *hypokinesia.* Manifestations of hypokinesia include *slow movements, movements limited in extent, abnormal posturings, loss of automatic movements, increased tone of muscles, and rhythmic resting tremor* in different structures. Patients with hypokinesia often exhibit *difficulties in starting and stopping their movements and seem to make movements rigidly. Reflexes are usually normal or slightly hyperactive.*

All of the manifestations just mentioned are characteristic of Parkinsonism, the foremost syndrome involving hypokinesia. The main general symptoms of the patient with advanced Parkinson's disease are his slow, shuffling walk, his rather masklike immobile facial appearance, and his overall lack of muscular vigor. The patient with Parkinsonism is often forced into a life that is limited in work and socialization. Many patients, however, manage to struggle relatively successfully against the debilitating effects of the disease.

The *hypokinetic dysarthria* of Parkinsonism may encompass the entire peripheral speech musculature. The respiratory system may show restricted volume excursions in tidal breathing or other voluntary efforts at changing lung volume. Short phrases may be all that the patient can muster, and loudness may be markedly reduced because of insufficient expiratory force capability for speech. The laryngeal mechanism often demonstrates restricted actions of both its intrinsic and extrinsic musculature. Pitch, loudness, and quality of voice may all be affected by hypokinesia. The efficiency of phonation is greatly reduced in many patients and a seeming inflexibility of laryngeal behavior is a common characteristic. Articulatory function is usually impaired because of the reduced range of motion involving the lips, tongue, and jaw. Disturbance may range from mildly imprecise articulatory performance to almost total unintelligibility. In advanced stages of the disease, the patient may be forced into almost complete silence. In a study of thirty-two patients with Parkinsonism (Darley et al., 1969a, b) found the following speech characteristics: monopitch, reduced stress, monoloudness, imprecise consonants, inappropriate silences, short rushes of speech, harsh voice quality, continuously breathy voice, reduced pitch level, and variable rate.

Hyperkinetic Dysarthria

The term *hyperkinesia* refers to a group of abnormal involuntary movement disorders resulting mainly from various lesions of the extrapyramidal system. Hyperkinesias exist along a continuum of rapidity from very slow to very fast, each form being difficult or impossible to inhibit. It is not within the scope of this chapter to discuss the effects on speech of all the possible involuntary movement disorders. The important commonality among these disorders is that each of them interferes with whatever speech events happen to be taking place at the moment. This interference can occur in all parts of the speech mechanism and in different combinations in different patients. To highlight the problems involved, we will consider the features of hyperkinetic dysarthria in four disorders: myoclonus, chorea, dystonia, and essential tremor.

Palato-Pharyngo-Laryngo-Diaphragmatic Myoclonus. The imposing name of this disorder identifies the gamut of muscular systems that can be involved. Patients vary from one another, however, and not every patient shows evidence of myoclonic movements in all of the structures mentioned. Myoclonic movements are sudden, jerking, shocklike, unsustained, contractions large enough to move a body part. Symptoms can be either unilateral or bilateral. The soft palate is most commonly abnormal. On inspection, it shows rhythmic upward and downward movements at a rate of about one to four beats per second. Myoclonic movements may be seen in the larynx through its varying adductor movements and through oscillations of the skin surface of the neck. Myoclonic action in the pharynx may be seen to occur at the same rate as in the soft palate and larynx. In the case of the diaphragm, its myoclonic action can be noted by small displacements of the abdominal wall. Intermittent nasalization problems may occur in the patient with myoclonus, but the main symptom of disordered speech is found in phonation. Momentary interruptions of phonation may occur as a result of involuntary movements in the larynx and/or diaphragm. Most often, these are not of sufficient magnitude to significantly interfere with the intelligibility of contextual speech, but they are readily apparent on vowel prolongations.

Chorea. There are two forms of chorea, a childhood form known as Syndenham's chorea (sometimes called St. Vitus Dance) and an adult form called Huntington's chorea. The childhood form is believed to be inflammatory or infectious in origin and recovery from it is usual. The adult form is an inherited, degenerative disease for which the prognosis is poor. Symptoms usually appear in the patient's forties or later. Movements of chorea last less than a second and result in unpredictable actions of the body parts affected. Figure 10–4 illustrates adjacent frames from a motion picture film of a patient with Huntington's chorea showing unusual and unpredictable changes in facial movements. Abnormal movements are not the only problems of patients with Huntington's chorea. Intellectual deterioration and personality changes often accompany the disease. These are not only socially and occupationally incapacitating, but often require institutionalization during later stages of a patient's illness. Motor speech may be normal for several seconds until involuntary movements intervene. These may throw such structures as the lips, tongue, jaw, larynx, and respiratory system out of their normal positions for the production of sounds. There is no consistent pattern to this form of hyperkinetic dysarthria, no repeatable phenomenon; the speech effects are as random as the disordered movements that produce them. All basic motor processes of the speech act can be impaired, and the listener gets the impression that the patient is producing speech in fits and starts. As the patient proceeds with speech, he seems to be on guard against speech breakdowns and he is constantly trying to make compensations for them. In a study of thirty patients with the adult form of chorea, the following speech characteristics were identified (Darley et al., 1969a, b): imprecise consonants, prolonged intervals, variable rate, monopitch, harsh voice quality, inappropriate silences, distorted vowels, excess loudness varia-

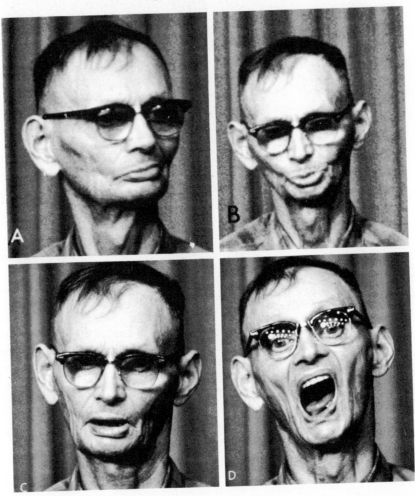

FIGURE 10–4. *Photographs of a patient with chorea, illustrating quick involuntary movements of the head, face, lips, and mouth. Intervals between photographs are only a few seconds. (From F. Darley, A. Aronson, and J. Brown,* Motor Speech Disorders. *Philadelphia: Saunders, 1975.)*

tion, prolonged phonemes, monoloudness, short phrases, irregular articulatory breakdown, excess and equal stress, hypernasality, reduced stress, strained-strangled voice quality.

Dystonia. Dystonia is the slowest of all the hyperkinesias. Its abnormal involuntary movements result from gradually building muscular contractions that prominently distort posture and then slowly subside.

These movements interfere significantly with voluntary movements and cause them to be slow in reaching their target excursions. The consequence is movement inaccuracies. Dystonic symptoms may appear in all parts of the speech mechanism. Puckering and retraction of the lips are commonly observed along with tongue protrusion, retraction, twisting, and elevation. The jaw may be depressed extensively or go through involuntary lateral movements, or the teeth may involuntarily clench. The neck and larynx may demonstrate spasms that unpredictably displace the head and shift the position of the vocal folds and larynx proper. And, the respiratory musculature may take on unusual postures that preclude normal respiratory function. Some patients learn to temporarily extricate themselves from dystonic movements or positions by pressing or touching a particular region of their anatomy, say the cheek, the mandible, or the back of the head. When dystonia involves structures of the speech mechanism, there is distortion of speech through the waxing and waning of bizarre postures of the different parts of the system. Patients become very self-conscious about their extraneous movements.

> Perhaps the most courageous patient I ever met was a forty-four-year-old elementary school principle who had gradually developed dystonia. His disease had progressed to a point whereby laryngeal spasm choked off the phonated airstream, and his tongue protruded from his mouth so much of the time that he had to articulate while the tongue was protruded. Lip pursing and spreading, and movements of the jaw occurred continuously. The sum of the involuntary movement patterns resulted in virtually unintelligible speech. The appearance of this man, with his tongue gyrating out of his mouth and his head crooked and twisted around to one side was, as anyone could imagine, distracting to the point of being almost unbearable. Yet, he continued to work in his office conducting his affairs despite his disability, smiled to the extent that he could control a smile, retained his intellect, and tried to maintain his sanity as he awaited some discovery that would ameliorate his disorder.

In thirty patients with dystonia, the following speech characteristics were identified (Darley et al., 1969a, b): imprecise consonants, distorted vowels, harsh voice quality, irregular articulatory breakdown, strained-strangled voice quality, monopitch, monoloudness, inappropriate silences, short phrases, prolonged intervals, prolonged phonemes, excess loudness variation, reduced stress, voice stoppages, reduced rate of utterance.

Organic Voice Tremor. Organic voice tremor is a laryngeal manifestation of essential tremor. It is also known as heredo-familial tremor. Although organic voice tremor can occur at any age, it is typically a

disorder that affects individuals beyond the age of fifty. If it first occurs beyond this age, it is referred to as *senile tremor*. Tremor rate typically ranges between four and eight cycles per second (Brown and
Simonson, 1963) and is manifested in the voice by variations in pitch
and loudness. Tremor may occur in the larynx alone or it may also
occur in the head, mandible, or hands. The quavering of the voice is
quite regular and is best observed when the patient prolongs vowels.
Tremor can be heard in contextual speech as well, but it is far less obvious than under the condition of vowel phonation. Sometimes the
tremor is so severe that each cycle of the tremor contains an arrest of
the voice. This is caused by complete, momentary adduction of the
vocal folds, and some patients with this symptom have been mistaken
for those who have spastic dysphonia (see Chapter 8). In some patients, the respiratory musculature will also show signs of tremor.
These can be observed and heard as rhythmic interruptions of the ex-
haled airstream and they contribute to variations in voice intensity
(Hixon and Minifie, 1972).

Mixed Dysarthria

Being no respector of neuroanatomical geography, neurological disease can damage any or all components of both the central and peripheral nervous systems at the same time. When this occurs, more
than one form of dysarthria may be exhibited in the same patient. A
confounding symptomatology results in which there is a *mixed dysarthria* and where one form of dysarthria may be more prominent than
others. Mixed dysarthria is usually a consequence of diffuse neurological disease. The more widespread the damage the greater the
number of motor speech components involved. Here we consider
three of the various neurological disorders that manifest mixed dysarthria: amyotrophic lateral sclerosis, multiple sclerosis, and Wilson's
disease.

Amyotrophic Lateral Sclerosis.   Amyotrophic lateral sclerosis is a degenerative disease affecting cell bodies of both the upper and lower motor neuron systems. It is of unknown cause and presents motor symptoms that are a mixture of *flaccid and spastic* paresis or paralysis. This
mixture may not be equal, with the signs of either flaccidity or spasticity predominating at any time. The disease impairs all components of
the speech mechanism and the prognosis for patients with the disease
is poor. Course of the disease is without remission and in later stages
there may be intellectual and personality deterioration. Patients with
amyotrophic lateral sclerosis have severe problems with speech intelligibility in the later stages of their disease. Thirty such patients

studied at Mayo Clinic (Darley et al., 1969a, b) showed the following speech characteristics: imprecise consonants, hypernasality, harsh voice quality, slow rate, monopitch, short phrases, distorted vowels, low pitch, monoloudness, excess and equal stress, prolonged silent intervals, reduced stress, prolonged phonemes, strained-strangled voice quality, breathiness, audible inspiration, inappropriate silences, and nasal emission. The length of this list is evidence of the devastating effect the disease has on speech motor control. Tragically, the typical figure given for survival from the time of appearance of initial symptoms of the disease is three years, although patients have been known to live for as long as fifteen years from the time of onset.

Multiple Sclerosis. Multiple sclerosis is a disease resulting in a loss of the fatty myelin sheath covering the axon of the neuron. It is a disease of young adults; the majority experiencing it have onset between the ages of twenty and forty. Because demyelinization is diffuse, the symptoms of the disease are highly variable. Onset is characterized by sensations of numbness or tingling, double vision, and impairment of vision. Motor signs consist of both *spastic and ataxic* involvement. Intellectual and personality changes may be in evidence. The disease may fluctuate in severity, becoming worse or better, but the ultimate course is one of worsening. Not all patients with multiple sclerosis manifest dysarthria. In a group of 168 patients studied by Darley, Brown, and Goldstein (1972), the following speech characteristics were observed to be deviant in the following rank order: impaired loudness control, harsh voice quality, defective articulation, impaired emphasis, impaired pitch control, hypernasality, inappropriate pitch level, breathiness, and sudden articulatory breakdowns.

Wilson's Disease. Wilson's disease is a heredo-familial disease in which excess amounts of copper are deposited in tissues of the brain, liver, and cornea of the eye. Onset is most common between the ages of eleven and twenty-five and, unless treated, the disease is fatal. A variety of neurological signs and symptoms are found in Wilson's disease. These include mainly *spasticity, ataxia, and hypokinesia.* Any of the three elements in the mixture may predominate in certain patients. Accordingly, the speech behaviors of patients with Wilson's disease may show a variety of spastic-ataxic-hypokinetic dysarthria characteristics in various combinations and various severities. In a study of twenty patients with Wilson's disease, Berry et al. (1974a, b) noted the following characteristics: monopitch, monoloudness, reduced stress, imprecise consonants, slow rate, excess and equal stress, prolonged intervals, inappropriate silences, harsh voice quality, prolonged phonemes, short phrases, hypernasality, low pitch, strained-strangled voice quality, and irregular articulatory breakdown.

EVALUATION OF DYSARTHRIA

Our ability to detect the presence of dysarthria, to identify its neuro-logical type, and to evaluate it is dependent upon three kinds of ex-amination procedures: (1) speech analysis through listening; (2) in-spection of the peripheral speech mechanism; and (3) physiological and acoustical analyses of speech.

Speech Analysis through Listening

The speech-language pathologist's auditory perception of abnormal speech is extremely important for identifying and differentiating among the different types of dysarthria. There are two common ways of listening to speech in the evaluation. One is to listen for specific elements within prescribed speech tasks in an attempt to isolate which structures or subsets of structures are impaired. The basis for this procedure is that certain structures are mainly responsible for certain aspects of production in different sounds. An example of this way of listening is the evaluation of laryngeal function by requesting prolon-gation of a vowel as long, steadily, and clearly as is possible. The eval-uator listens for abnormalities of voice quality, pitch, loudness, dura-tion, and steadiness. To effectively use isolated speech structure analysis in this way, the speech-language pathologist must have a thor-ough understanding of normal speech physiology.

Another common way of listening to dysarthric speech requires a connected discourse speech sample. The speech-language pathologist attends to the totality or "Gestalt" of the patient's speech and attempts to make judgments about the function of speech output parameters and their different interactions. The respiratory system might be sus-pected of dysfunction via a patient's low voice loudness, mono-loudness, or uncontrollable alterations of loudness. The laryngeal mechanism might be suspected of control problems if a patient exhib-its excessively low or high voice pitch, or sudden unexpected changes in pitch or voice tremor, or a voice that is perceived as monopitched. Laryngeal control problems might also be revealed through running speech manifestations of voice quality disorders, such as breathiness or harshness. Resonance problems with the voice, such as hyper-nasality or hyponasality, are usually demonstrated in the perceptual totality of the patient's speech and would suggest possible velopharyn-geal inadequacy and nasopharyngeal obstruction, respectively. And fi-nally, motor disorders of the articulatory musculature are revealed by a generalized lack of precision in the production of consonants, such perceptually noticeable events as shortening of sound durations, abnormally slow or rapid speech rates, progressive increases in rate during running speech, alternations in rate from slow to fast, and intermittent breakdowns in the accuracy of articulation. The clinician's ear is an important clinical device. It is in fact the final arbitor with regard to the overall impact that the dysarthria has on the listener.

Tape recordings of the patient's speech are indispensable to speech analysis through listening. They enable multiple listenings to the same segments of speech so that both types of observations mentioned above can be made. Repeated recordings during treatment also provide the clinician with an acoustical documentation of progress or lack thereof.

Inspection of the Peripheral Speech Mechanism

A general inspection of the peripheral speech mechanism is an important part of any examination for dysarthria. Such an inspection can take advantage of information obtained through vision, touch, and testing of muscular strength and speed. While mechanism inspection for dysarthria involves many of the same aspects as would be considered for other organically-based disorders (see Chapters 8 and 9), it is especially important that the major emphasis be given to neurological components of the motor speech problem.

The respiratory system must be examined with regard to the range of motions its different parts can accomplish, the speed with which different adjustments can be made, the synchrony of motion between the rib cage and abdomen, and the general steadiness of control that the patient can exert. Difficulties in respiratory control can often be foreseen through examination of the patient's torso musculature. Patients with weak or paralyzed abdominal musculature, for example, will often have flabby, protruding abdominal walls. Those with muscular involvement of the rib cage, may demonstrate an inward sucking of the spaces between the ribs when the pressure inside the lungs is lowered during inspiration (Hixon, 1970). And, patients with involvement of the diaphragm, may show limited outward movements of the abdominal wall during attempts to contract their diaphragms. Shallow breathing may be noted, or involuntary motions of the respiratory muscles may be seen, or tremor may be observed in certain muscles of the torso. In some patients, palpation of different segments of the respiratory mechanism may reveal extreme stiffness because of musculature being under excessive tone. In general, the speech-language pathologist will put the patient through a series of moderate respiratory "gymnastics" to determine the locations of muscular involvement. Certain patients will appear to have no respiratory difficulties during quiet respiration, only to show problems of greater magnitude once they are required to intentionally perform outside their tidal breathing volumes and pressures.

Adequate evaluation of the laryngeal musculature via visual inspection can only be accomplished through either indirect or direct laryngological examination by a physician. This is an important step that must be taken to determine if there is any unilateral or bilateral weakness of the vocal folds. If the speech-language pathologist has evidence that respiratory function for speech is adequate, he will be able to make some reasonable inferences concerning laryngeal involvement by observing whether or not the patient can significantly change loudness and pitch of the voice. Or, the clinician may note that the patient shows inspiratory stridor (breathing noise) between speech attempts because of an abductor weakness of the vocal fold(s). The clinician's suspicion of a bilateral adductor weakness of the vocal folds might also be aroused by the observation that there is a reduced strength or sharpness to the patient's cough. Further, the patient might demonstrate difficulty impounding pressure within his lungs if he manifests an adductor laryngeal weakness and cannot adequately seal the lower from upper airways.

Testing of the velopharyngeal mechanism is done mainly through determining the presence and extent of the gag reflex by stroking the posterior pharyngeal wall with a probe. Hyperactive or hypoactive reflexes may indicate spastic or flaccid paralysis, respectively. Symmetry of the soft palate is also important. Although some individuals have assymmetrical soft palates, that is, one side hangs down lower than the other, because of tonsillectomy, most have assymmetrical soft palates because of unilateral upper or lower motor neuron lesions. The soft palate should also be tested for voluntary movement as, for example, during the production of a sustained vowel. Often, in dysarthria, this will reveal an absence of movement or markedly reduced movement on the paralyzed side and retraction toward the nonparalyzed side.

Inspection of the tongue would be carried out along the following lines. With the tongue at rest on the floor of the mouth, or very slightly protruded to overlap the lower incisor teeth, the examiner would look to determine if the tongue was of normal size and bulk. He would further assess whether it was shrunken, furrowed, and had fasciculations, suggesting a unilateral or bilateral lower motor neuron lesion. It would then be determined whether or not the patient could voluntarily protrude the tongue. Note would be made as to whether protrusion is straight or deviates abnormally to one side or the other, whether the tongue can be lateralized to touch the angle of the mouth, and whether it can resist the examiner's pressure applied against protrusion with a tongue depressor.

Intactness of the jaw musculature can be examined by noting if the resting jaw hangs normally or lower than normal, indicating possible muscular weakness or paralysis. Restriction in the ability to protrude, retract, lateralize, depress, or elevate the jaw would be taken as an important indicator of muscular weakness during voluntary movements. Strength of the musculature can also be tested by providing a resistive force against the jaw digitally and having the patient attempt to raise and lower the jaw against this force.

Examination of the facial musculature at rest is important in order to determine if the angles of the mouth are symmetrical or whether there is paresis on one or both sides. By having the patient attempt to retract the angles of the mouth, as in smiling, the examiner can judge whether both sides of the mouth elevate equally or whether one does so to a lesser extent, indicating weakness on that side. Spreading, protrusion, and rounding activities of the lips are also good ways to test the functional integrity of the lip musculature. In addition, it is useful to determine the force with which the lips can be compressed, as for example, when the patient attempts to resist the examiner's pulling of a tongue depressor from between the patient's lips.

Physiological and Acoustical Analyses of Speech

Increasingly, clinical centers and hospitals are including physiological and acoustical analyses of dysarthria. Chapters 8 and 9 discuss these physiological and acoustical procedures as they apply to voice and orofacial disorders. These same procedures are applicable to the evaluation of dysarthria. Here we will highlight some of the uses made of three techniques that are highly valuable in evaluations of dysarthria: electromyographic evaluation, cinefluorographic evaluation, and spectrographic evaluation.

Electromyographic Evaluation. Electromyography is a technique for monitoring the electrical activity associated with muscle contraction. Through its use, it is possible to reach reasonable conclusions concerning the function of individual muscles or groups of muscles (Leanderson, Meyerson, and Persson, 1971, 1972; Marquardt, 1973; Netsell, Daniel, and Celesia, 1975). Most often electrical activity is recorded through electrodes positioned on the surface of the body over the muscles of interest. Electromyography is especially telling of dysarthria because it provides information about the strength of muscle contractions, the speed of muscle events, and the coordination of muscles events. Figure 10–5 shows contrasting electromyographic recordings taken from the upper lip of a normal individual and the upper lip of a person with Parkinson's disease. The patient with Par-

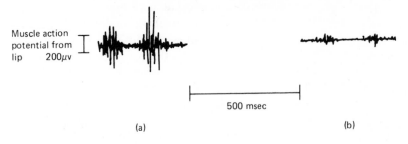

Muscle action
potential from
lip   200μv

500 msec

(a)   (b)

FIGURE 10–5. *Electromyographic recordings from the upper lip: (a) of a neuro-logically-normal individual, and (b) of a patient with Parkinson's disease. Each speaker is saying the word "pop". Note that the patient's recording shows muscle action potentials that are shorter in duration and lower in amplitude than normal. (Adapted from R. Net-sell, B. Daniel, and G. Celesia, Acceleration and weakness in Parkinsonian dysarthria.* Journal of Speech and Hearing Disorders, *40, 170–178, 1975.)*

kinson's disease shows muscle action potentials that are shorter in duration and lower in amplitude than those for the normal speaker. A reasonable interpretation of this patient's recording is that it shows a weakness in the neuromuscular control signals governing the behavior of the upper lip. By skillfully using electromyographic recordings, the clinician can clearly document the neuromuscular conditions that exist as a result of a disease process. It may then be possible to provide a more rational plan of rehabilitation. Given the severe physical involvements of many dysarthric patients, it is often necessary to study them at only a few muscle sites. Lip study is especially appealing because it does not involve the insertion of measurement devices inside the speech mechanism.

Cinefluorographic Evaluation. Cinefluorographic (x-ray motion picture) observations are highly useful in evaluating dysarthric speech behavior (Hardy 1967; Netsell, 1969; Logemann et al., 1973; Kent, Netsell, and Bauer, 1975). More than any other technique, cinefluorography enables the clinician to determine the range of movement, extent of incoordination, speed of movement, and so forth that exist within and between parts of the upper airway. Assessment can be made with regard to the general motions of structures on playback of x-ray movies, or in frame-by-frame analyses in which the motions and positions of structures can be traced in fine detail (Kent et al., 1975). Cineflurographic procedures handle one of the major problems in analyzing the speech of the dysarthric patient, namely, that most of the critical speech structures are unobservable from outside the patient. It must be realized, however, that such procedures are not without attendant radiation risks. It is because of this that clinical researchers are in the process of developing less hazardous procedures that will provide some of the same information (Hixon, 1972; Abbs and Gilbert, 1973).

434

Spectrographic Evaluation. Certain aspects of dysfunction are subject to quantification through spectrographic (voice print) analyses of dysarthric speech (Lehiste, 1965; Kent and Netsell, 1975). Abnormal motions of the speech mechanism give rise to corresponding abnormal acoustic events. Thus, when speech of the dysarthric patient is analyzed by electronic devices that display its acoustic patterns, the clinician is able to use such displays to determine certain features of the patient's problem. Figure 10–6 shows an example of how such an

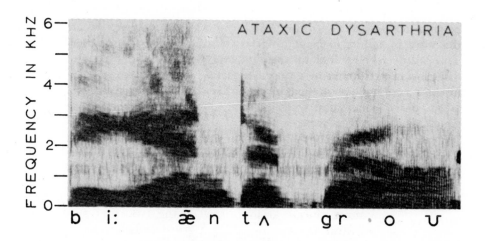

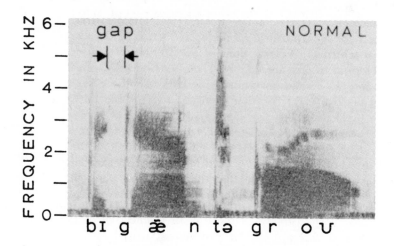

FIGURE 10–6. *Sound spectrograms (voice prints) for productions of the phrase "began to grow": (a) for a speaker with ataxic dysarthria, and (b) for a neurologically-normal speaker. Note that the dysarthric speaker's utterance is significantly longer than normal and that a stop gap does not exist for the /g/ in the word "began". (From R. Kent and R. Netsell, A case study of an ataxic dysarthric: Cineradiographic and spectrographic observations. Journal of Speech and Hearing Disorders, 40, 115–124, 1975.)*

analysis is of value in interpreting mechanism (Kent and Netsell, 1975). There the acoustic pattern for an utterance of an ataxic dysarthric patient and a normal speaker are available for contrast. From the displays, it can be seen that the dysarthric patient's speech is significantly "stretched out" in time and that she failed to produce a stop gap for the g in the word "began." Careful evaluation of the two contrasting voice prints reveals other abnormalities that the skillful clinician would detect. Often the clinician can gain important information from spectrographic analyses for use in planning certain aspects of speech rehabilitation. Although the use of spectrographic analysis requires a considerable amount of phonetic sophistication on the part of the speech-language pathologist, such an analysis often pays off handsomely.

MANAGEMENT OF DYSARTHRIA

Successful therapy with a dysarthric patient depends upon many factors. Some dysarthrias are more resistent to treatment than others because of their type, severity, or course. In addition, the respiratory, laryngeal, and upper airway systems differ from one another with respect to their responsiveness to therapy of various types. Probably the most critical variable of all is the type of disease causing the dysarthria. Diseases that are progressive, as for example, amyotrophic lateral sclerosis and multiple sclerosis, are formidable therapeutic adversaries. Certain other diseases remain static, and although the nervous system does not regenerate, at least the speech-language pathologist and the patient are not fighting a deteriorating situation. Still other diseases, through surgery or drug therapy, actually improve, and along with the improvement, the capacities of the neuromuscular system improve.

The management of most neurological diseases requires the services of many specialists. If the disease is treatable by drugs, the neurologist will prescribe and regulate the needed medications. If there is a muscular disability of the upper and lower extremities, the skills of the physiatrist and/or physical therapist may be required. If the disability interferes with the use of the patient's upper extremities for manual skills, the occupational therapist may have an important responsibility. If there is an intellectual or emotional disorder, the psychologist and/or psychiatrist would be included in plans for the patient's care. And the list goes on and on as the needs of different patients are determined.

Management goals for the patient's dysarthria must be realistic. Although we would prefer to obtain normal speech, we must often be satisfied with a small to moderate amount of improvement that can make the difference between unusable speech and speech that can fulfill the patient's needs. The speech-language pathologist must aim for the best the patient can possibly achieve, but with full awareness that no amount of desire or work can overcome certain problems of neurological control.

Although speech is the management focus of the present chapter, we must not lose sight of the fact that the diseases which cause the patient's motor speech disorder also threaten him psychologically and economically. Onetime active, intelligent, socially well-integrated people who gradually or suddenly lose their power to express their thoughts and emotions clearly and persuasively, often suffer a precipitous depression following the onset of motor system disease. Thus, the speech-language pathologist often must include a psychotherapeutic purpose to the management process, lending to the patient encouragement, support, and friendship as well as technical competence. Even in patients whose speech is rapidly disintegrating because of a degenerative neurological disease, epitomized by amyotrophic lateral sclerosis, there is value in working against the overwhelming odds. This is the least we can do until medical science and its allied specialties find more definitive treatments for neurological diseases.

In the subsections that follow — medical-surgical intervention, mechanical intervention, neurological facilitation approaches, learning-relearning therapies, and aids and alternate modes of communication — we highlight some of the major management techniques for motor-speech disorders.

Medical-Surgical Intervention

Although medical-surgical options are limited, certain of them may considerably improve function. Some therapies pertain to specific structures or subsystems of the speech mechanism while others have an influence on all portions of the mechanism. Examples of altering specific speech structures are provided by the following two cases.

A fifty-three-year-old lawyer, and candidate for district judge, underwent surgery for the removal of a tumor in his neck. Unavoidable surgical damage to the left recurrent laryngeal nerve resulted in an extremely breathy voice quality with a harsh edge to it and a considerable reduction in loudness. In spite of rigorous voice therapy attempting to force the normal vocal fold to make contact with the paralyzed one, the size of the glottal opening remained too large. The patient was becoming increasingly concerned over his inability to make effective campaign speeches. Under general anesthesia, a plastic, Teflon, was injected into the paralyzed vocal fold, thereby increasing its bulk and filling some of the glottic space (Kirchner and Toledo, 1966). This mass-increasing procedure enabled the intact vocal fold to meet the enlarged paralyzed vocal fold and good adduction and glottal area control resulted. A considerable improvement in the loudness and quality of the patient's voice occurred which enabled him to participate fully in his campaign for public office.

Todd, a five-year-old boy with cerebral palsy, had speech that was characterized by hypernasality, a breathy voice, and imprecise consonant productions. Evaluation revealed that part of his problem was the result of weak musculature of the soft palate which precluded his achieving adequate velopharyngeal closure (Hardy, 1967). Inadequate closure accounted for the hypernasal quality of his voice, and because of his difficulty in impounding oral pressure, it accounted for a major part of his articulatory difficulties. Surgery was performed to create a pharyngeal flap (a suturing of a strip of tissue fabric from the back wall of his throat to his soft palate). This flap enabled Todd to achieve a much improved seal between the oral and nasal cavities. His hypernasality problem reduced to a point where it did not require clinical attention and the intelligibility of his speech made measurable gains, although not dramatic. A speech-therapy program was initiated to help him maximally profit from his "altered" mechanical system. Further gains in speech intelligibility were achieved by working on a program of slowing his articulation and concentrating on the precision of his consonant productions.

Attention to specific structures, such as the two just illustrated, requires that the physician and the speech-language pathologist work together closely. Although the final decision on medical-surgical procedures rests with the physician, this decision is often greatly influenced by the speech-language pathologist's judgment as to whether or not a given procedure will change the patient's speech to an extent that justifies the procedure.

Drug therapies are sometimes successful in altering the dysarthric patient's capabilities for producing speech. The consequences are usually more general than are those for most currently used surgical intervention procedures. Three examples of disease that are often successfully treated through drug therapies are Parkinsonism, myasthenia gravis, and Wilson's disease.

Drug treatment for Parkinsonism is, perhaps, the most popularly known of these three. This disease is now successfully treated in a high percentage of cases through administration of a biochemical substance known as Levodopa or L-Dopa. This substance substitutes for the chemical dopamine, the neural transmitter substance that is in insufficient supply within the central nervous system of patients with Parkinson's disease. Treatment with L-Dopa results in marked improvement in the patient's general hypokinesia and with it often comes a corresponding improvement in speech. Not all patients treated with L-Dopa show significant improvement in motor-speech skills, but those who do sometimes show rather marked improvement.

Myasthenia gravis responds dramatically to biochemical treatment. Treatment with the substance Prostigmine restores functional neurotransmission at the myoneural junction and improves general muscular strength throughout the body. After treatment, the patient is able to perform muscular activities without showing the marked signs of fatigue that typically characterize the disease. The beneficial effects on motor-speech performance are so contrastive with those of the nontreated condition of the patient that it is hard to believe that the speech produced is coming from the same individual in both cases.

As a last example of drug treatment success, we note the influence of Pennicillamine on patients with Wilson's disease (Goldstein et al., 1969). Tests of the effects of Pennicillamine on patients have shown improvement, not only in their overall neurological status, but also in their speech. When administered in proper dosages, Pennicillamine combines with free copper in the blood. This copper is then excreted from the system rather than being deposited in and doing damage to nerve cells. In a study by Berry et al. (1974a, b), practically all of the defective speech characteristics observed in patients prior to the administration of the drug diminished in severity after the beginning of drug therapy.

> One of the first patients of Goldstein et al. (1969) was a woman of twenty-six with a family history of Wilson's disease. She experienced onset of the disease at age fourteen when she noticed a decrease in the size of her handwriting. By age twenty-one she was bedridden and thrashing around with flailing of her extremities. Her speech at that time was almost totally unintelligible. Articulation was slow and laborious and constantly distorted by involuntary tongue movements. She was unable to sustain a vowel and her voice was then described as "a series of spurts of sound with complete loss of melody." Within a year of being placed on Pennicillamine, she began walking, dressing herself, printing words, then writing. Her walking was ataxic. She began feeding herself and, in general, improved steadily. Four years from the time of initiation of drug therapy her articulation had improved to the point of near normalcy, although her rate remained slow and her voice monopitched. She had tremor on prolongation of vowels and her rate of repeating syllables was slow. Currently, her motor-speech disorder is almost undetectable.

Certainly this case history has a far more encouraging ending than the one with which we started this chapter.

Mechanical Intervention

Mechanical devices often enable the dysarthric patient to obtain more usable speech. The following case example illustrates how a mechanical device improved the speech of a patient who suffered a cervical spinal cord injury that left him with flaccid paresis of the expiratory muscles.

> Larry, a young infantryman, returned to his home after a tour of combat duty in Vietnam. Two weeks after his homecoming, he was at a party with friends, left while inebriated, and drove his car over an embankment. He was thrown from the car and suffered a broken neck and an injury to his spinal cord which left him quadriplegic and with weakness of the muscles of his rib cage wall and abdominal wall. His speech was markedly reduced in loudness and characterized by inordinately long inspiratory pauses (Hixon, 1970). When he talked, his weak rib cage wall muscles would raise the pressure inside his lungs and force his diaphragm downward and his belly outward. To counteract this abnormal action, Larry was fitted with a snug corset from his pelvis to the bottom of his rib cage. This provided a firm mechanical base for his rib cage muscles to develop pressure against and resulted in an immediate improvement in the loudness of his speech. The corset also forced his abdominal wall inward and his diaphragm upward. This made it so that he could inspire far more rapidly during pauses in his speech.

Mechanical devices, like specific medical-surgical therapies, have their greatest potential for application with specific structures or subsystems of the speech mechanism. The velopharyngeal mechanism is probably the part of the speech mechanism that is most often mechanically managed in dysarthric speakers. In cases where velopharyngeal inadequacy results from palatal weakness or paralysis, the problem is often approached through the use of a palatal-lift prosthesis (see Figure 10–7). This is a removable dental device that is fixed to the teeth and contains a plate that elevates the impaired soft palate and holds it in a fixed position. The prosthesis enables closure of the velopharyngeal port and thus helps to eliminate problems of hypernasality and low intraoral air pressure on consonant sounds. The following case is an example of a favorable outcome achieved through use of a palatal lift prosthesis. This case is doubly interesting because it involves a combined drug and mechanical approach.

> A seventeen-year-old high school student had severe flaccid dysarthria consisting of breathiness, hypernasality, nasal emission, and articulatory imprecision. After a diagnosis of myasthenia gravis was made she was placed on the drug *pyridostigmin bromide* (Mestinon). Nevertheless, her soft palate remained weak and she was fitted with a palatal-lift prosthesis which successfully reduced her velopharyngeal insufficiency for speech. One month later she wrote, "I'm eating fairly well . . . have had steak . . . a little difficulty but am trying . . . the prosthesis is working

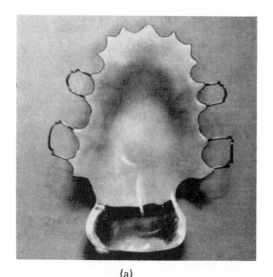
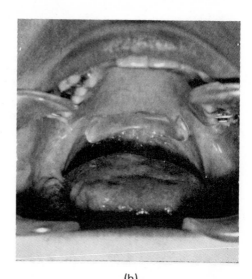

(a)   (b)

FIGURE 10–7. *Photographs of a palatal-lift prosthesis: (a) outside the mouth, and (b) in position inside the mouth of a patient with a structurally normal but paralyzed soft palate. (From J. Gonzalez and A. Aronson, Palatal lift prosthesis for treatment of anatomic and neurologic palatopharyngeal insufficiency.* Cleft Palate Journal, 7, 91–104, 1970.)

out fine, I find it much easier to talk with it in . . . was a little hesitant at first but now I'm glad I have it . . . friends at school kid me about sounding like I have a cold . . . with the prosthesis one can hardly tell I have any problem with speech at all . . . it is amazing how much this has helped me . . . lately I'm only wearing the prosthesis when I go out to meet new people . . . hardly ever have to wear it at home . . . my palate is still weak when I say certain sounds, but my speech is getting better without it. It really makes me feel a little more at ease with people." As her medication became more effective, her need for the prosthesis diminished.

Other mechanical assists are of value in managing patients with dysarthric speech. Some that have been used beneficially include devices to posture the torso, devices to posture the head and neck, devices to fix a weak jaw in the closed position, devices to position weak lips, etc.

Neurological Facilitation Approaches

Clinicians use a variety of therapy approaches that we can classify under the heading of neurological facilitation. We will mention two of these approaches in our introductory concern for management.

Certain patients with dysarthria, particularly those children with cerebral palsy, sometimes benefit from physical management programs that purposefully place the patient in particular body positions.

This is done to preclude various reflexive behaviors from interferring with the desired function of the musculature. These reflex inhibiting postures, or RIPs, as they are called, may facilitate greater control by the patient over different portions of his speech mechanism (Bobath and Bobath, 1952). What the clinician does is to use manual applications to different parts of the patient's body to force the patient out of any retained infantile reflex patterns (Mysak, 1968). One such manipulation, for example, might involve the clinician working to reduce extensor spasm of the neck as the patient inspires and flexor spasm of the neck as he expires. Discussion of the variety of reflex inhibiting postures is beyond the scope of our concern. Use of the procedures requires a thorough knowledge of the basic reflex patterns of posture and movement throughout the body, neck, and head (Mecham, Berko, and Berko, 1960; Mysak, 1968).

A second approach, biofeedback therapy, is fulfilling its early promise as a useful neurological facilitator. Such therapy takes different forms but basically involves the presentation of some type of biological signal to the patient for him to use as an additional information source relative to the ongoing regulation of his behavior. The approach is exemplified in electromyographic biofeedback procedures that have been used in attempts to control spasticity or excesses of movement (Cleeland, 1971; Harrison and Connolly, 1971). The patient is supplied either with a visual portrayal of the electrical activity of his contracting muscles or with some form of analog tone that bears relationship to the state of contraction of his muscles. Dramatic success with such procedures is becoming more and more common (Netsell and Cleeland, 1973; Daniel and Guitar, 1978), as is illustrated in the following case example based on the observations of Netsell and Cleeland (1973).

> A sixty-four-year-old woman with a fifteen-year history of Parkinsonism underwent bilateral thalamic surgery for relief of her symptoms. As a consequence of her surgery, she developed a complete bilateral retraction of her upper lip (such as one sees in attempts at bearing the upper teeth). Retraction was so severe that her upper gum was exposed and she could not make lip closures for speech. The electrical activity associated with the patient's upper lip contractions was processed and made available for her to hear through a loudspeaker. After several therapy sessions, she had made considerable progress toward removing the undesirable lip retraction. She demonstrated complete control of the lip in nonspeech activities and showed instances of normal lip function while repeating structured speech material. Much of her conversational speech still showed some degree of lip retraction.

This case illustrates that it is possible to gain control over neuromuscular function that one might otherwise "write-off" as being unmodifiable. Such an observation is a bright spot on the treatment horizon.

Another example of the successful use of biofeedback with dysarthrics involves the use of pressure-indicating devices, such as a water manometer, as system output targets for use in strengthening weak respiratory muscles (Netsell and Hixon, 1978). Patients are shown visual indications of the magnitude of pressure they are developing with their respiratory muscles and then placed on behavior modification programs aimed at reinforcing more and more stringent pressure control requirements. The use of biofeedback in this context often enables the patient to increase the strength of his weak rib cage wall and abdominal wall muscles and, correspondingly, the loudness of his speech.

Learning-Relearning Therapies

The principle behind learning or relearning to produce speech sounds more intelligibly in the face of neurological damage is *compensation.* Even when the speech mechanism is severely impaired, the patient usually has some capability of calling up a reserve of strength and coordination to partially overcome his dysarthria. An example is the patient whose articulation is impaired by paralysis or incoordination of the lip and tongue musculature and who can often articulate more intelligibly by doing so at a *slower rate* where the parts of his involved mechanism have more time to move to needed positions and contacts. Patients with ataxic dysarthria are responsive to therapy that teaches *emphasis on all syllables* of speech in order to counteract the tendency to distort vowel sounds. Some patients, such as those with Parkinsonism, need to be reminded to phonate more loudly and to articulate with greater excursions of the lips, mandible, and tongue. The central notion surrounding compensation of the speech mechanism is that speech can be produced in a variety of ways and the end product will still be acceptable perceptually. This can be appreciated by producing speech segments as one normally would and then producing the same segments with a pencil clenched between the teeth. This normal reorganization of motor behavior is analogous to that which dysarthric speakers must go through in their compensations.

Learning-relearning therapies are instituted after all attempts have been made to make the patient's mechanism as "whole as possible" through medical-surgical, mechanical, and neurological facilitation techniques. That is, everything possible has been done for the patient except behavioral therapy involving speech production itself. Thus, relearning therapies are an attempt by the patient and speech-language pathologist to systematically go through the patient's speech problem and institute therapies that maximize the patient's use of his respiratory system, laryngeal system, resonance system, and articulatory system. Often plans first involve working on one subsystem at a time. For example, the patient who needs to strengthen his respiratory muscles to provide sufficient pressure for speech would concentrate on that aspect of management first. To do otherwise, would be wasteful because no degree of articulatory training would be of value without an adequate airstream to valve for speech purposes.

Elsewhere in this book, we have discussed the procedures available for managing deviances in the different subsystems of the speech mechanism (see Chapters 7, 8, and 9). These same procedures apply to the management of dysarthria, except that, perhaps more than for any other disorder, the speech-language pathologist must be concerned with the management of a number of subsystem problems simultaneously.

Other Aids and Modes of Communication

It is common, tragically, that neurological impairment in some patients is so profound that speech is unintelligible and irremediable. No amount or type of therapy can ever realistically be expected to improve the patient's speech enough for it to be useful. We must simply face this fact and seek other ways to help the patient. Some of these include electronic amplification systems, manual communication, and communication boards of different forms.

Loudness is a particular problem for certain dysarthric patients, those with Parkinsonism being a prime example. Often paradoxically able to produce louder, more articulate speech on demand, patients with Parkinsonism seem to have inordinate difficulty maintaining such improved function when they are not under the direct authority of a clinician. Certain patients who have severe symptoms and whose speech is almost inaudible have been known to benefit from electrical amplification systems they can carry with them or that they can use in restricted surroundings, such as in an office.

Manual communication, such as the sign language and finger spelling schemes used by some deaf individuals, may be a profitable alternate mode of communication for some dysarthric patients. Potential success depends, of course, on the intactness of the language, intellect, and upper extremities of the patient. Patients with severe speech musculature involvements do not always have equally severe involvements of the arms and hands, and some forms of manual communication can often be profitably instituted.

The principle alternate mode of communication for the profoundly neurologically involved dysarthric patient is the communication board (McDonald and Schultz, 1973). Two such boards are shown in Figure 10–8. Communication boards are devices at which

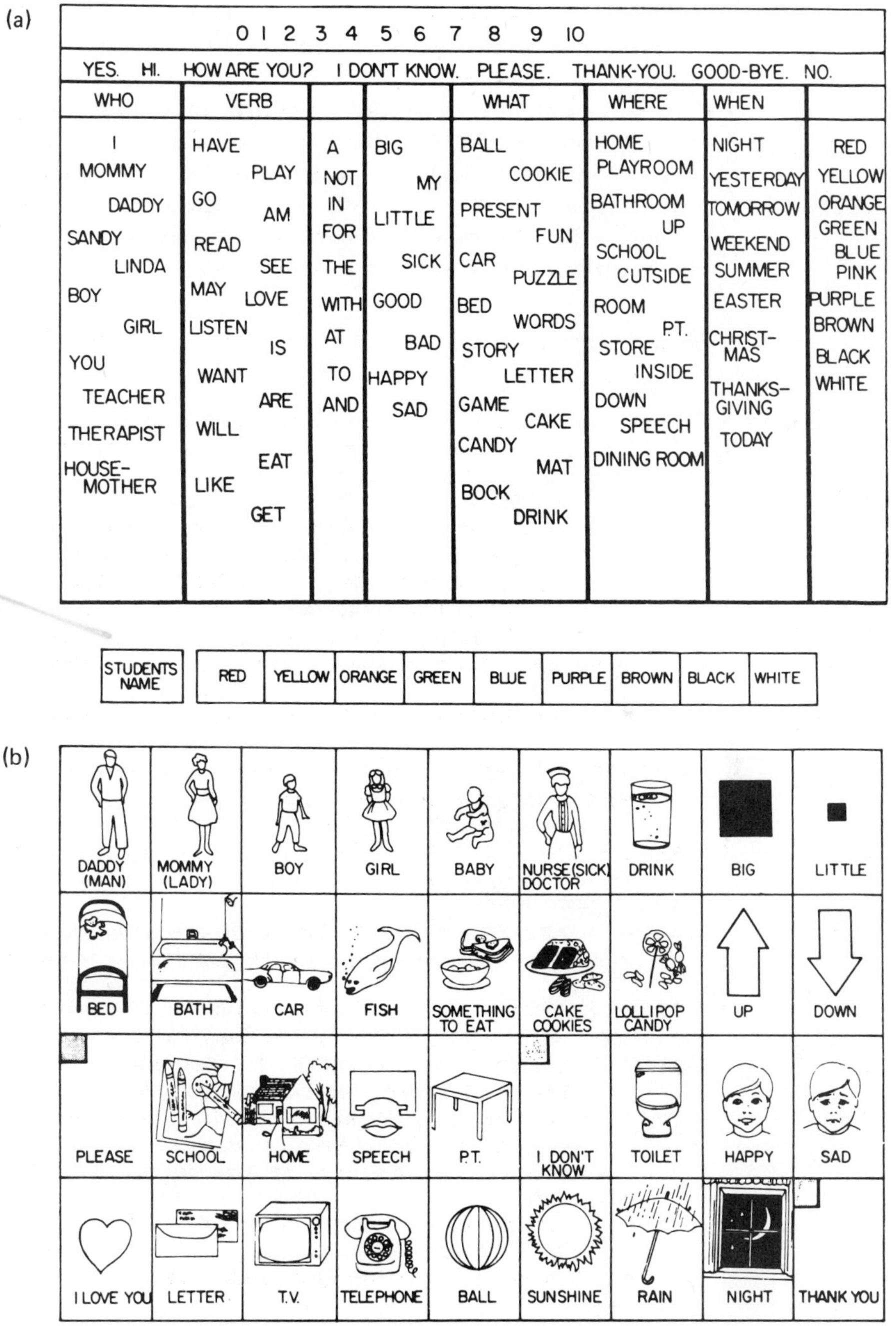
(a)
0 1 2 3 4 5 6 7 8 9 10
YES. HI. HOW ARE YOU? I DON'T KNOW. PLEASE. THANK-YOU. GOOD-BYE. NO.
WHO
VERB
WHAT
WHERE
WHEN
I
MOMMY
DADDY
SANDY
LINDA
BOY
GIRL
YOU
TEACHER
THERAPIST
HOUSE-MOTHER
HAVE
PLAY
GO
AM
READ
SEE
MAY
LOVE
LISTEN
IS
WANT
ARE
WILL
EAT
LIKE
GET
A
NOT
IN
FOR
THE
WITH
AT
TO
AND
BIG
MY
LITTLE
SICK
GOOD
BAD
HAPPY
SAD
BALL
COOKIE
PRESENT
FUN
CAR
PUZZLE
BED
WORDS
STORY
LETTER
GAME
CAKE
CANDY
MAT
BOOK
DRINK
HOME
PLAYROOM
BATHROOM
UP
SCHOOL
OUTSIDE
ROOM
P.T.
STORE
INSIDE
DOWN
SPEECH
DINING ROOM
NIGHT
YESTERDAY
TOMORROW
WEEKEND
SUMMER
EASTER
CHRIST-MAS
THANKS-GIVING
TODAY
RED
YELLOW
ORANGE
GREEN
BLUE
PINK
PURPLE
BROWN
BLACK
WHITE
STUDENTS NAME
RED
YELLOW
ORANGE
GREEN
BLUE
PURPLE
BROWN
BLACK
WHITE
(b)
DADDY (MAN)
MOMMY (LADY)
BOY
GIRL
BABY
NURSE (SICK) DOCTOR
DRINK
BIG
LITTLE
BED
BATH
CAR
FISH
SOMETHING TO EAT
CAKE COOKIES
LOLLIPOP CANDY
UP
DOWN
PLEASE
SCHOOL
HOME
SPEECH
P.T.
I DON'T KNOW
TOILET
HAPPY
SAD
I LOVE YOU
LETTER
T.V.
TELEPHONE
BALL
SUNSHINE
RAIN
NIGHT
THANK YOU

FIGURE 10–8. *Communication boards for use as alternate modes of communication for profoundly neurologically impaired patients: (a) sentence construction board, and (b) picture communication board. (From E. McDonald and A. Schultz, Communication boards for cerebral-palsied children.* Journal of Speech and Hearing Disorders, *38, 73–88, 1973.)*

the patient is seated or that he can carry with him on which are printed the letters of the alphabet, frequently used words, key phrases, pictures, etc. The patient communicates on the expressive side by pointing to items on the board, or in more sophisticated systems by pushing buttons that illuminate various items. Devices of this nature, including a new generation of portable electronic voice synthesizers, are a form of speech for the speechless dysarthric patient — a means for the otherwise communicatively incapacitated patient to be in verbal contact with his surroundings.

REFERENCES   ABBS, J., and GILBERT, B., A strain gage transduction system for lip and jaw motion in two dimensions: Design criteria and calibration data. *Journal of Speech and Hearing Research,* 16, 248–256 (1973).

BERRY, W., ARONSON, A., DARLEY, F., and GOLDSTEIN, N., Effects of Penicillamine therapy and low-copper diet on dysarthria in Wilson's disease (hepatolenticular degeneration), *Mayo Clinic Proceedings,* 49, 405–408 (1974a).

BERRY, W., DARLEY, F., ARONSON, A., and GOLDSTEIN, N., Dysarthria in Wilson's disease. *Journal of Speech and Hearing Research,* 17, 169–183 (1974b).

BOBATH, K., and BOBATH, B., A treatment of cerebral palsy based on the analysis of the patient's motor behavior. *British Journal of Physical Medicine,* 15, 107–117 (1952).

BROWN, J., and SIMONSON, J., Organic voice tremor. *Neurology,* 13, 520–525 (1963).

CLEELAND, C., Conditioning and the dystonias. Paper presented to the Symposium on New Applications of Conditioning to Medical Practice, University of Wisconsin, Madison (1971).

DANIEL, B., and GUITAR, B., EMG feedback and recovery of facial and speech gestures following neural anastomosis. *Journal of Speech and Hearing Disorders,* 43, 9–20 (1978).

DARLEY, F., ARONSON, A., and BROWN, J., Clusters of deviant speech dimensions in the dysarthrias. *Journal of Speech and Hearing Research,* 12, 462–496 (1969a).

DARLEY, F., ARONSON, A., and BROWN, J., Differential diagnostic patterns of dysarthria. *Journal of Speech and Hearing Research,* 12, 246–269 (1969b).

DARLEY, F., BROWN, J., and GOLDSTEIN, N., Dysarthria in multiple sclerosis. *Journal of Speech and Hearing Research,* 15, 229–245 (1972).

GOLDSTEIN, N., TAUXE, W., McCALL, J., GROSS, J., and RANDALL, R., Treatment of Wilson's disease (hepatolenticular degeneration) with Penicillamine and low-copper diet. *Transactions of the American Neurological Association,* 94, 34–35 (1969).

GREWEL, F., Classification of dysarthrias. *Acta Psychiatrica et Neurologica Scandinavica,* 32, 225–237 (1957).

HARDY, J., Suggestions for physiological research in dysarthria. *Cortex,* 3, 128–136 (1967).

HARRISON, A., and CONNOLLY, K., The conscious control of fine levels of neuromuscular firing in spastic and normal subjects. *Developmental Medicine and Child Neurology,* 13, 762–771 (1971).

HIXON, T., Clinical implications of recent advances in speech breathing mechanics. Paper presented to the Convention of the American Speech and Hearing Association, New York (1970).

HIXON, T., Some new techniques for measuring the biomechanical events of speech production: One laboratory's experiences. *American Speech and Hearing Association, Report No. 7,* 68–103 (1972).

HIXON, T., and MINIFIE, F., Influence of forced transglottal pressure changes on vocal sound pressure level. Paper presented to the Convention of the American Speech and Hearing Association, San Francisco (1972).

KENT, R., and NETSELL, R., A case study of an ataxic dysarthric: Cineradiographic and spectrographic observations. *Journal of Speech and Hearing Disorders,* 40, 115–134 (1975).

KENT, R., NETSELL, R., and BAUER, L., Cineradiographic assessment of articulatory mobility in the dysarthrias. *Journal of Speech and Hearing Disorders,* 40, 467–480 (1975).

KIRCHNER, F., and TOLEDO, P., Vocal cord injection. *Journal of Kansas Medical Society,* 67, 125–129 (1966).

LEANDERSON, R., MEYERSON, B., and PERSSON, A., The effect of L-dopa on speech in Parkinsonism: An EMG study of labial articulatory function. *Journal of Neurology, Neurosurgery, and Psychiatry,* 34, 679–681 (1971).

LEANDERSON, R., MEYERSON, B., and PERSSON, A., Lip muscle function in Parkinsonian dysarthria. *Acta Otolaryngologica,* 74, 271–278 (1972).

LEHISTE, I., *Some Acoustic Characteristics of Dysarthric Speech: Bibliotheca Phonetica.* Basel, Switzerland: Karger (1965).

LOGEMANN, J., BLONSKY, E., FISHER, H., and BOSHES, B., A cineradiographic study of lingual function in Parkinson's disease. Paper presented to the Annual Convention of the American Speech and Hearing Association, Detroit (1973).

McDONALD, E., and SCHULTZ, A., Communication boards for cerebral-palsied children. *Journal of Speech and Hearing Disorders,* 38, 73–88 (1973).

MARQUARDT, T., Characteristics of speech production in Parkinson's disease: Electromyographic, structural movement, and aerodynamic measurements. Unpublished doctoral dissertation, University of Washington (1973).

MECHAM, M., BERKO, M., and BERKO, F., *Speech Therapy in Cerebral Palsy.* Springfield, Ill.: Charles C Thomas (1960).

MYSAK, E., *Neuroevolutional Approach to Cerebral Palsy and Speech.* New York: Teachers College Press (1968).

NETSELL, R., Evaluation of velopharyngeal function in dysarthria. *Journal of Speech and Hearing Disorders,* 34, 113–122 (1969).

NETSELL, R., and CLEELAND, C., Modification of lip hypertonia in dysarthria using EMG feedback. *Journal of Speech and Hearing Disorders,* 38, 131–140 (1973).

NETSELL, R., DANIEL, B., and CELESIA, G., Acceleration and weakness in Parkinsonian dysarthria. *Journal of Speech and Hearing Disorders,* 40, 170–178 (1975).

NETSELL, R., and HIXON, T., A noninvasive method for clinically estimating subglottal air pressure. *Journal of Speech and Hearing Disorders,* 43, 323–330 (1978).

signpost   Disorders of the timing aspect or flow of speech are documented as far back as the beginning of recorded history. They have, from then to the present, continued to be an unsolved human-behavior puzzlement that taunts and frustrates those who inquire. Chapter 11 discusses these disorders of flow with regard to their manifestations of abnormal fluency, rate, and rhythm of speech. This discussion is organized around the two major types of flow disorders: stuttering and cluttering. The obligatory features of these two disorders are, respectively, abnormal timing of speech-sound initiation and excessive speech rate. Various other features of these two disorders are dealt with in Chapter 11, together with discussions of their origins, ways to evaluate their status, and implications for helping persons who have problems with either of them. The more frequently occurring of these two disorders, stuttering, has recently become the object of a rekindling in research interest and clinical thought. A number of persons have suggested that the origins of stuttering are vested in poor coordination skills, especially as such skills pertain to control of the larynx in cooperation with other parts of the speech mechanism. Chapter 11 considers different sides of this possible solution to the riddle of the cause of stuttering and gives the student evidence to weigh relative to this currently popular notion about the age-old problem of stuttering.

William H. Perkins

disorders of
speech flow

INTRODUCTION

Whatever the nature of stuttering, it is universal in time and place. It is mentioned in clay tablets from Mesopotamia written centuries before Christ. A 2500-year-old Chinese poem speaks of it. Demosthenes was presumably cured of it. Not only is it documented back to the beginning of recorded history, it is apparently found in all cultures, regardless of how primitive or refined. From Moses to Darwin, from Virgil to Marilyn Monroe, the problem has existed. Van Riper (1971) lists forty-one languages from around the world that have a name for it. Further, it is found without respect to status or intelligence. Anyone with the capacity to speak can stutter, whether he be a pauper or prince. The solution to this perplexing disorder has not yet been found. But when it is, it will likely have to describe some condition so universal in man as to explain why stuttering may be inherent in the ability to speak.[1]

This chapter is about disorders that primarily involve the temporal aspects or the "flow" of speech. Of these, the most prevalent and perhaps the most dramatic is stuttering. This is the problem we know the most about and it is the one to which we will give greatest attention. But stuttering is not the only disorder involving the temporal aspects of speech. Cluttering is a second type of flow disorder that will be discussed later in this chapter. To understand each of these disorders, stuttering and cluttering, we must first understand three dimensions that underlie the flow of speech: fluency, rate, and rhythm.

---

[1] American speech-language pathologists do not generally distinguish between the term "stuttering" and the term "stammering." Those who do make a distinction generally use "stuttering" to refer to repetitions and "stammering" to identify speech stoppages (both of these behaviors will be described later in this chapter). We will follow the convention in the United States and use "stuttering" to include "stammering."

Fluency is the vital characteristic of how smoothly sounds, syllables, words, and phrases are uttered. Determination of whether or not units of speech "flow along" fluently is a matter of judgment. No absolute criterion exists for saying that a repetition, prolongation, or hesitation is abnormal. That decision can only be made by the individual listener. Society is remarkably tolerant of some forms of disrupted fluency—hence the term *normal disfluency*. Normal disfluency is the professional jargon used to identify mostly hesitations and repetitions that the listener considers typical of everyday speech. Repetitions of words and phrases and hesitations that reflect what speakers do as they assemble ideas occur so frequently in everyone's speech that we usually think of these disfluencies as being normal.

Rate is the speed with which the elements of speech are produced. Generally, rate is measured in syllables or words per minute. Most of us speak at an average rate of between two hundred to three hundred syllables per minute. Although rate can be unusually fast or slow, it rarely is judged to be defective when considered alone. It is when speech becomes so rapid as to blur intelligibility or so slow as to be monotonous that rate is considered abnormal.

Rhythm is the timing of the elements of speech. As listeners, we tend to impose rhythmic structure on any speech we hear (Allen, 1973). When this timing applies to longer elements, it concerns the manner of grouping syllables and words into phrases. This is language rhythm that is not much involved in disorders of speech flow. Timing of the shorter elements, the individual vowel and consonant segments of the syllable, is intimately related to fluency and its abnormalities. This is segmental rhythm, which when disrupted, is perceived as choppy jerky speech.

STUTTERING

Features and Definitions

Nothing plagues the area of stuttering so much as controversy among so-called stuttering "authorities." Controversy persists over causes, nature, treatment, and, not the least, proper definition. One point of agreement, however, is that stuttering is not a "thing" in the mouth of the speaker. Stuttering involves a judgment made by a listener about a speaker's fluency. This judgment can be quite different when it is made by the stutterer listening to himself than when it is made by someone else listening to the stutterer.

Some who consider themselves severely troubled by stuttering may rarely be heard to stutter by anyone else. They apparently respond to private sensations of impending difficulty with speech fluency. These sensations were formalized in Johnson's definition that he intended to apply to all who stutter: "Stuttering is an anticipatory, apprehensive, hypertonic avoidance reaction" (Johnson et al., 1948). This means that stuttering is what a speaker does when he or she in turn expects it to happen, dreads it, tenses in preparation for it, and finally, tries to avoid it. Note, however, that this only defines what the stutterer experiences privately, not what the listener observes publicly.

Johnson's view has dominated research, theory, and therapy of stuttering for several decades. Underlying it is the conviction that those who stutter are not essentially different from those who do not. Stutterers do what normal speakers do when they are disfluent, which can include repeating phrases, words, syllables, and sounds, prolonging sounds, and hesitating before speaking. The only difference between stutterer and nonstutterer in this view is in the stutterer's reaction to the listener's reaction to the stutterer's normal disfluency; stuttering is what the stutterer does when he attempts not to stutter.

A concept competing with Johnson's view has arisen in recent years. This alternative view reaffirms the idea that stuttering behavior differs from normal disfluency. The layman at least thinks he can distinguish stuttering from normal disfluency. Actually, neither layman nor speech-language pathologist can identify some types of "stuttering" with complete certainty. But these difficulties have most to do with where the foothills of stuttering begin. Little doubt exists about the difference between the plains of fluency and the mountains of stuttering.

Consider for yourself whether you would judge the disfluencies in the following interchange as stuttered or normal:

JOE: I know, I uh, well, maybe we, we should do it.
HAL: N, no, we, we, we, we, we, shouldn't.
JOE: Why can't, why not, why not, try it?
MEL: Be, bec_____ause it w, won't work.
HAL: Let, let's sssssee if there's a ch, choice.

You probably would agree that all three speakers are disfluent. Likely you would agree, too, that Hal and Mel stutter. They seem to have trouble starting sounds after they know what they want to say. Joe, on the other hand, seems uncertain of what he is trying to say. Even though he repeats some single syllable words, his disfluencies appear to reflect linguistic uncertainty rather than phonetic difficulty. More specifically, Joe uses interjections ("uh," "well"), word repetitions ("we, we"), phrase repetitions ("why not, why not"), incomplete phrases ("I know, I, uh, well"), and phrase revisions ("why can't, why not"). By contrast, both Hal and Mel repeat sounds ("n, no," "w, won't") and syllables ("we, we, we, we, we," "be, bec____ause"); Hal prolongs sounds ("sssssee"), and Mel breaks a word with a hesitation ("bec____ause"). Joe is disfluent mainly on larger units of speech (phrases, words, and syllables) while Hal and Mel's disfluencies are primarily on smaller units (sounds and syllables). Whereas Joe's disfluencies seem to reflect normal attempts to formulate his ideas, Hal and Mel's disfluencies reflect their struggles to speak words they have already chosen.

Being confirmed stutterers, Hal's and Mel's speech efforts may include all sorts of responses associated with their blockages (Bloodstein, 1975a). Some responses may involve physiological changes in biochemical, neurological, cardiovascular, and respiratory activity (Perkins, 1970). Some may be dramatically observable, such as eye blinks, head jerks, jaw or lip tremors, respiratory gasps, changes in speech rate, changes in vocal quality, changes in intonation, tongue protrusions, or even occasional tongue swallowing. Some may be more subtle, but observable, such as speech rhythm in periods of "sticky" fluency that hovers on the edge of stuttering. And, some may include covert devices for concealing overt indications of stuttering.

Several terms have been used to describe behaviors that stutterers employ in their efforts to appear fluent. To head off anticipations of difficulty, *antiexpectancy measures* may be used. These may involve speaking in a monotone, using a different pitch level, or any other change in speech that the stutterer may be trying in his effort to reduce his dread of becoming stuck (Van Riper, 1963). *Avoidance tactics* of word substitution or circumlocution are designed for evasion of certain "feared" words altogether. *Postponement maneuvers* are strategies to delay initiation of a feared word until chances of saying it normally improve. These maneuvers often take the form of strategic pauses, repetitions of words or phrases, or interjections of stereotyped expressions, such as "you know," or "well you see," over and over until the feared word is finally attempted. *Starting devices,* of which "uh" prefixed to the feared word is typical, are used to help initiate the difficult first sound. Finally, if stuttering does occur, a number of *escape techniques,* ranging from jerking the head to backing up for another "run" at the word, may be used to try to "break" the block.

Thus the ways in which one can stutter are innumerable. The physiological responses may or may not occur; the overt behavior may vary from one stoppage to another; and the concealment strategies may shift from moment to moment if they are used at all. Not only is stuttering different from person to person, it even differs within the same person from moment to moment.

How does one make sense of a problem that comes in such a variety of forms? Has stuttering no common denominator by which we can define its occurrence? The answer is far from unequivocal, but the definition we propose captures what the stutterer does that the listener can observe: *Stuttering is the abnormal timing of speech sound initiation.* The basis for this definition is suggested in Figure 11–1.

Figure 11–1 summarizes judgments of stuttering behavior made in a number of studies (Boehmler, 1958; Williams and Kent, 1958; Johnson et al., 1959; Young, 1961; Huffman and Perkins, 1974). What does the speaker do to evoke a judgment of stuttering? Clearly, the likelihood of labeling behavior stuttering as opposed to normal disfluency goes up as the size of the disfluent speech unit becomes smaller. Only on speech sounds do all types of stuttering disfluency occur. Although repetitions, hesitations, and interjections can involve larger speech units, only speech sounds can be prolonged. Even a syllable cannot be prolonged without increasing the duration of a sound within it. Moreover, all of the concealment devices are aimed at coping with words with difficult sounds. Antiexpectancy measures help "head off" the dread of becoming stuck on sounds; avoidance tactics circumvent the feared words; postponement manuevers delay initiation of the first sound; starting devices aid in the initiation of that sound; and escape techniques are used to get through the blocked sound.

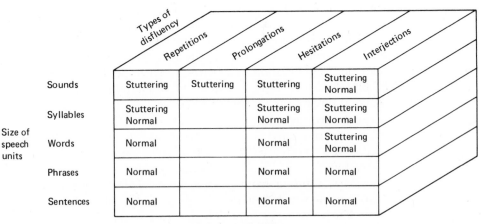

Judgments of disfluency

FIGURE 11–1. *Types of disfluency and size of speech units as determinants of judgments of stuttering. Only with sounds can all types of disfluency occur. The larger the speech unit, the more a disfluency is apt to be judged as normal. (Modified from W. Perkins,* Speech Pathology: An Applied Behavioral Science, *2nd Ed., St. Louis, The C. V. Mosby Co., 1977.)*

Thus, judgments of stuttering need not involve phrase, word, or syllable disfluencies, nor do they necessarily involve concealment tactics, nor physiological responses, nor subtle or dramatic associated struggle behavior. Clearly, what these judgments do require is disfluent production of sounds. They reflect difficulty starting the first sound in words and syllables (Johnson and Brown, 1935). Conceivably, they could also involve difficulty initiating subsequent sounds within a syllable. So whether these production disfluencies occur in initiation of an utterance or in transitions between syllables or sounds, they necessarily involve abnormal timing of speech movements for starting sounds. This is the behavior most likely to be judged as stuttering.

Prevalence

What percentage of the population stutters? The usual estimate is that at any one time somewhere in the neighborhood of 1 percent of the population as a whole stutters (Milisen, 1971). However, this figure must not be taken with certainty. One reason for caution is that researchers vary considerably, in fact, in determining how severe and for how long one has to stutter to be called a stutterer. Without doubt, stuttering develops in childhood and possibly as many as 80 percent of these children will recover (Sheehan and Martyn, 1966). Yet, the prevalence often reported for adults as well as children is 1 percent, which makes one wonder about the number who have actually recovered, or about the accuracy of estimates of the prevalence of children or adults who stutter (Young, 1975). If somewhat less than 1 percent is reasonably accurate, this would mean that about a million and a half people in the United States stutter. Of these, anywhere from two to ten times as many will be males than females.

Development

As with so much else about stuttering, opinions vary as to its onset and development. Differences lie not so much in observations about the course of its beginning as in how to interpret these observations. Without convincing evidence for one view or another, these debates are free to continue. To know with certainty how stuttering actually is acquired, we need to have systematic longitudinal studies of many children. Such research is exceedingly difficult and time consuming, and only a few attempts have been made (Johnson et al., 1959; Bloodstein, 1961; Andrews and Harris, 1964; Van Riper, 1971). Most of these have the basic weakness of having relied on memories of the stutterers or their parents, rather than on direct observation. Nonetheless, they show enough agreement that we can piece together a probable picture of how and when stuttering likely begins.

Course of Development: Observations. Experts agree on at least four features that characterize the acquisition of stuttering:

1. It begins for the majority somewhere between ages two and seven.
2. Onset is marked by fragmentation of syllables and words.
3. It fluctuates in severity so that the course of development is not steady.
4. It changes with time; beginning forms of stuttering differ from advanced forms.

Let us look closer at these four features.

First, although the age of onset ranges from two to seven years for most children, it peaks between three and four. Realistically, stuttering begins when someone, usually a parent, detects and labels it as stuttering. This probably means that the bulk of seriously fragmented speech appears when the child begins to put words together into phrases. That these fragmentations have to occur within the context of a linguistic utterance is clear. About one fourth of prelinguistic vocal play during infancy includes syllable repetitions that rarely seem to be considered stuttering (Winitz, 1961). The fact that the onset of stuttering is sometimes not reported before age seven may indicate that some parents are slow in detecting a difference between normal and abnormal disfluency, which seems possible. It may mean that the disfluency that first appeared with connected speech had to become more severe or different in some way before it was recognized as stuttering, which seems probable (in light of our previous discussion). Or it could mean that stuttering blossomed suddenly after several years of normal speech, but why this would happen would be difficult to understand.

A second feature of stuttering acquisition is that syllable and word fragmentations can, from the outset, take the form of repetitions, prolongations, hard vocal attacks, and forceful articulatory pressures. Though many repetitions are effortless, even the simplest can show signs of tension in the earliest forms of stuttering. That these interruptions tend to be qualitatively different from normal disfluencies is suggested by two types of evidence. First, all children fragment phrases and sentences in their efforts to express themselves grammatically. In fact, normal-speaking children may be even more disfluent in these large units of speech than children who stutter. But those who do stutter differ from those who do not by consistently having more difficulty with small speech units (Johnson et al., 1959) as we discussed. They show more syllable repetitions and sound prolongations. A second type of evidence that stuttering evolves from a different type of disfluency than normal speech was provided by Stromsta (1965). Stromsta found that young children who showed forceful articulatory pressure symptoms of complete blockage when initiating syllables had a high probability of becoming confirmed stutterers.

The third characteristic of the acquisition of stuttering is fluctuations in severity. These are typically greatest when stuttering begins with easy repetitions (Bloodstein, 1975a). Periods of weeks or months may go by with no difficulty only to be followed by a sharp increase in severity. The significance of these fluctuations is that to talk of stutterers as being at stages of development is all but meaningless. A popular notion that still prevails (even though some who promoted it have abandoned it) is that stuttering goes through two main phases, primary and secondary, with possibly a transitional phase in between. The primary stage was thought to involve simple repetitions and prolongations. Struggles to avoid these disfluencies were considered to mark the secondary stage. Appealing as this distinction may seem, it has proven false. Whether a person has stuttered a few months or many years, he frequently shows behavior that could be called primary one week and secondary another. Thus, to label a stutterer according to the stage of stuttering he or she is presumed to be in is to hang a tag on a person that is misleading.

Finally, a fourth characteristic of the acquisition of stuttering is that an overall pattern of development can be discerned. Despite fluctuations in severity, a young child beginning to show signs of stuttering will not continue to be disfluent in the same manner in which he began. He will either get better or worse. If his syllable repetitions and prolongations are effortless, he has a good chance of recovering. On the other hand, if a child begins to struggle with his fragmented syllables and words, chances are he will become worse. The more he struggles, the more complicated his stuttering becomes. While in the beginning it is essentially episodic, as it progresses it becomes chronic. Although severity continues to wax and wane, periods of freedom from stuttering become shorter and eventually disappear (Luper and Mulder, 1964).

How, then, does remission come about? The usual reason given is, "I just outgrew it." Such evidence as is available suggests that about half of the children who stutter generally recover by puberty. As many as four out of five may recover without help before reaching college, although this estimate is probably high (Martyn and Sheehan, 1968; Young, 1975). Of these, the majority seem to recover during early adolescence. Most have had no professional help, and those who have had help generally do not attribute their improvement to therapy. We will return to this issue later; a case example at this point should be instructive. Herb is one of several persons from the author's files whose records will be used in this chapter to illustrate features of stuttering.

> When Herb was approximately four, he was frustrated by the fragmentations that disrupted the flow of his speech. But he did not appear anxious about speaking or about himself as a speaker, so his repetitions were at the same pace as the rest of his speech. As Herb's struggle for fluency mounted, the tempo changed. He now stuttered mainly when he "got excited and talked fast." Frequency of syllable repetitions increased. He began to pull words and syllables apart and plod through them one sound at a time. Instead of the logical repetition "bee, bee, beet" if he were trying to say "beet," he was apt to tackle the first sound "b" separately from the following vowel "ee." As a result, a new vowel sound intruded into his production and what he said was "buh, buh, beet." He prolonged vowels that became marked with tension and sometimes tremors. When he entered school, he began to show concern. He knew he was having trouble with his speech and he was beginning to think of himself as a "stutterer." The disorder was still intermittent, though, so he had occasional relief from the frustration of his struggles. As Herb's trouble advanced, the contortions of stuttering began to appear. Facial grimaces, tongue protrusions, head jerks, and the like seemed to be used as escape devices to get speech blockages unstuck. He began to feel helpless and to fear those words and situations with which he had the most difficulty. And on the heels of fear came avoidance. He developed a large vocabulary of synonyms for feared words. He used circumlocutions. He avoided listeners and situations in which he expected trouble. As an adult, he took a job in a brokerage firm in St. Louis. Unfortunately, he was so much in terror of stuttering that he quoted fictitious prices on which he did not expect to stutter rather than risk blockage on the actual prices that should have been given. His tenure in this position was brief.

Herb's experiences reflect the nature of life for a person who has become confirmed in stuttering. The problem usually starts early enough and the effects are powerful enough that it becomes an integral part of existence. The stutterer's life can literally be built around stuttering.

Course of Development: Interpretations. Why does stuttering generally follow the course of development just described? Here is where opinions vary. The most popular view has been articulated by Bloodstein (1961, 1974). He has argued persuasively for years that stuttering is the struggle that is learned in order to maintain fluency in anticipation of disfluency. Stuttering reflects the stutterer's belief that to achieve a smooth flow of speech is treacherously difficult. Therefore, to speak is to expect disruption in the form of tension and fragmentation of the utterance. As a rule of thumb, tension produces prolongations, fragmentation generates repetitions.

This much of the explanation fits advanced stuttering remarkably well. What seems doubtful is the necessity of stuttering being the culmination of an *anticipatory* struggle reaction. Without doubt, increased expectation of stuttering does, in truth, increase stuttering. And granted, confirmed stutterers can predict many of the words on which they will stutter. Practically none, however, can predict them all, and some have no discernible expectancy, yet stutter severely. Certainly beginning stutterers have little, if any, anticipation of disruption. Their moments of stuttering seem to catch them by surprise. They often feel that something outside of their control has blocked their speech. Once caught, they may be frustrated and struggle to break free. To say, though, that they anticipate difficulty is to impute awareness of impending trouble when that awareness simply may not exist.

What would seem to be a more universal statement is that stuttering is the fragmentation of syllables and words that occurs when the speaker has significant difficulty in coordinating the actions of various portions of the speech mechanism. Anticipation and dread of difficulty heightens the probability of discoordination and fragmentation, but is not essential to it. The tensions of early stuttering are probably not from anticipation but from the reality of being stuck. They mirror the child's annoyance and frustration at being unable to make all of the movements of speech fit together.

With this amendment of the anticipatory view, we can easily understand a case such as Don's that occurred two decades ago.

> Don was a normal healthy young boy of three. His earliest attempts at connected speech appeared with full blown stuttering complete with struggle and prolongations. His father was amazed and puzzled by his son's difficulty. As a speech-language pathologist educated with the cautions of Johnson's diagnosogenic theory, he knew that no one had called attention to Don's early speech attempts, much less punished them. He decided, wisely, to immerse Don in attention, so he took him on a camping trip. Within months, struggle and tension abated and such disfluency as remained has never since been a problem.

Couple the idea of speech mechanism discoordination with Bloodstein's explanation and the full gamut of stuttering is covered, as is illustrated in the following description of Corine.

> Corine, a young mother, quivered and stumbled over practically every syllable of a standard reading passage when she read it aloud. Her eyes blinked, her jaw jerked, she even swallowed her tongue occasionally.

Her beauty in repose was marred by these grotesque distortions. Corine had the complete paraphernalia of chronic stuttering: fears, avoidances, postponement devices, starter devices, and anticipation of struggle with every syllable. However, when we asked her to read the same passage silently with the articulatory movements of normal speech, she could hardly believe what happened. She began the reading with the same dread as before, but to her amazement, nothing became stuck. Gone were the tremors and struggles. Gone for that matter was the feeling of stuttering. Later, observers who analyzed our video tapes with the sound off did not detect from her silent reading that she was anything but a normal speaker.

Some argue that these reductions of stuttering are a consequence of distracting the stutterer's attention with a novel task from his anticipation of difficulty. Another favorite argument is that stuttering is reduced during silent speech because communicative responsibility is reduced if the speaker cannot be heard. Were these arguments valid, then when an electrolarynx is used (as an alternative voice source; see Chapter 8), stuttering should not vary whether speaking aloud or silently. The same novelty is present and the speaker is audible under both conditions; in one the listener hears voice and the electrolarynx, in the other only the electrolarynx is heard. To the contrary, neither communicative responsibility nor distraction affect the outcome. Stuttering is as severe as ever when the usual complex coordinations for speaking aloud are required; when simplified with silent speech, the disorder vanishes immediately. Clearly, the struggles of stuttering involve more than anticipation of difficulty that increases with communicative responsibility.

Origins of Stuttering

Historic Overview. Perhaps the most lawful statement about stuttering that can be made is that it seems to be highly individualized. What appears to cause stuttering for one person does not seem to cause it for another. In fact, one can hardly find a treatment with which someone has claimed success and many others reported failure — from incising a wedge from the tongue to orating with pebbles in the mouth. That no one has yet understood the cause of stuttering well enough to treat it with universal effectiveness is abundantly evident in the multitudes of techniques that litter the therapeutic landscape. Because solid evidence still does not command one explanation as being better than others, freedom to speculate prevails (Sander, 1975). The result is as plentiful a supply of theories of stuttering as we have therapies of stuttering.

To explain such an elusive problem has challenged the clinical imagination back to antiquity. Not surprisingly, theoretical explanations begat treatments. Because stutterers had greater difficulty in familiar surroundings, the Oracle of Delphi banished them. Romans thought stutterers had to be exorcised of evil spirits. During the Middle Ages, evil was driven from the tongue with everything from hot irons to hot wines, cathartics to blood-letting.

Most current views had their roots in the nineteenth century. This includes such ideas as stuttering as a disorder of rhythm, as a laryngeal disorder, as a learned disorder, and as a neurosis (Van Riper, 1970). In this century, two pioneers of speech pathology, Lee Edward Travis and Robert West, offered widely influential views of stuttering as a constitutional problem. Travis, in his *theory of cerebral dominance,* held that the stutterer's dominant hemisphere in the brain does not exert sufficient control of speech organization. He suspected that this hemisphere does not withstand the disintegrating effects of emotional stress. West, in his theory of *dysphemia,* hypothesized an organic predisposition to dysfluency[2] as being basic to much stuttering.

However, by mid-century, Charles Van Riper and Wendell Johnson had led a surge of interest away from the constitutional view. Van Riper argued that stuttering is highly integrated behavior that is learned. Johnson not only denied that stutterers are constitutionally different, but also rebelled against the view that stuttering is a neurosis. Having established that theories of stuttering have an exceptionally lengthy history, we turn to a discussion of the four main theoretical approaches: learning origins, psychodynamic origins, linguistic origins, and biologic origins.

Learning Origins.   Johnson's (1955, 1959) ideas spawned an era of research and theorizing about stuttering that still prevails. As his thinking evolved, he put increasing emphasis on interaction between listener and speaker. He argued that the probability of learning to stutter grows, first, as important adults in a child's world set high standards of fluency and react negatively to disfluency, and second, as the child's speech is filled with disfluencies to which the listener can react. In this form, Johnson's concept is called the *interactional* or *evaluational theory.*

Three features of disfluency have been the focus of research aimed at demonstrating that stuttering is learned behavior. Several decades ago, Johnson and his colleagues discovered that stuttering di-

---

[2] Note the spelling of *dys*fluency in this instance. Because West suspected a pathological basis for stuttering, the prefix "dys" is more appropriate than "dis," which means "opposite of." Thus *dis*fluency implies that departure from fluency is essentially normal and is not a consequence of an organically faulty speech mechanism.

minishes with repeated readings of the same passage. This feature became known as the *adaptation effect*. They also observed that the stuttering that still occurred in later readings was on words in the passage that had been stuttered in earlier readings. They called this feature the *consistency effect*. Later work revealed that several hours after the adaptation effect is demonstrated, stuttering will have increased to its former level. This phenomenon was dubbed with a term from learning theory: *spontaneous recovery effect*.

Those who followed Johnson's leads have taken these three features as fundamental aspects of stuttering behavior. The adaptation effect was seen for some time as resembling the learning process and was thought to be a laboratory model of clinical relapse. Others, who hold different opinions of stuttering, have pointed out that the adaptation effect differs notably from the learning process. Moreover, normal disfluency shows essentially the same adaptation effect as does stuttering (Williams, Silverman, and Kools, 1968). For such reasons, these features have not lived up to the hopes held for them of being clinically valuable measures of stuttering as learned behavior (Wingate, 1966b, c).

The consistency effect is presumed to reflect the apprehension that is learned in expectation of stuttering. What better explanation of why stuttering tends to occur more on some words than others: It is because the stutterer learns to fear difficulty with certain "Jonah" words and sounds. A difficulty has arisen in recent years, however, with this analysis. The consistency effect, like the adaptation effect, is also found in normal disfluency (Williams, Silverman, and Kools, 1969). If apprehension is what separates the abnormal disfluencies of stuttering from those that are normal, then one has trouble explaining how the consistency effect is an indicator of the stutterer's anxiety about speech when this effect is also present in the relaxed normal disfluencies of the nonstutterer.

The concept that stuttering is learned has spread in several directions. Bloodstein (1958, 1975a, b) has elaborated *anticipatory-struggle* aspects of the problem in what he now calls the continuity hypothesis. In this view, what the child who develops stuttering learns are expectations of speaking difficulty and the struggle responses to cope with them. Anticipating difficulty, he becomes so cautious as he approaches and attacks feared words that, like a tense tight-rope walker who falls, any possibility of saying them fluently dwindles. Paraphrasing Bloodstein, stuttering is what a person does who tries to speak not wisely, but too well.

Shames and Sherrick (1965) have explained how stuttering can evolve from normal disfluency by applying operant principles of learning. They have looked at normal disfluencies as operant behavior, that is, as behavior that operates on the environment to produce consequences. When these consequences are favorable, the disfluencies are reinforced and, presumably, can be shaped into stuttering by complex schedules of positive and negative reinforcement.

. Applying principles of learning theory, Brutten and Shoemaker (1967) have proposed that two types of learning are involved in the acquisition of stuttering. First, through classical conditioning, the child becomes apprehensive of speaking conditions that are associated with difficulty. These negative emotional responses are considered to be disruptive of fluency. Then, through instrumental conditioning (a learning theory term for operant conditioning), those strategies that help the child cope with his disfluency struggles are reinforced and so become part of his characteristic manner of stuttering.

Another view, cast in a learning framework and borrowing heavily from counseling and psychotherapeutic concepts, is the conflict theory. Sheehan conceived the theory a quarter century ago as an approach-avoidance struggle to speak and not to speak. More recently, he has extended this basic idea to conflicts with false roles in dealing with feelings of shame, guilt, and concealment (1970). Sheehan sees stuttering to a large extent as a false-role disorder in which concealment tactics predominate; stripped of "tricks, crutches, and other false-role behavior, little stuttering would remain." As evidence for his view, Sheehan points to the ease with which stutterers can insert effortless offhand remarks into the midst of even severe stuttering. For example, one of our adult stutterers blocked on a syllable for a full two minutes. During the struggle to produce a single syllable, he would take a breath, comment fluently on how tough this syllable was to say, and then plunge back into his block. When he *tried* to be fluent he could not; but, when he abandoned this false role he could be fluent.

Psychodynamic Origins. The possibility that stuttering is a symptom of neurosis is a view held by some speech-language pathologists and by many psychiatrists and clinical psychologists. The view stems from psychoanalytic theory, a theory that has grown every which way. Freud tinkered with it. His disciples tinkered with it. About everyone who has used it has tinkered with it. The result is a marvelously intricate assemblage of metaphors more than a unified body of knowledge. But for all its faults, it does have vitality.

Common to all psychodynamic versions is the assumption that any symptom, stuttering included, is a disguised manifestation of repressed needs. The exact nature of these needs, which Travis (1971) calls unspeakable feelings, varies with the psychodynamic theory being considered (Glauber, 1958; Wyatt, 1958; Murphy and Fitzsimmons,

1960; Barbara, 1962; Blanton, 1965; Perkins, 1965). Typically, they include unacceptable feelings of aggression, dependence, and sexuality. The conflicts that ensue over the disavowed earthy pleasures of sucking, eating, biting, chewing, and swallowing are fought for control of the speech apparatus. The id seeks expression of these primitive needs; the superego attempts to thwart their release through speech; and the ego attempts to mediate the psychic battle while using the speech act for logical discourse. The fact that some forms of stuttering resemble biting, sucking, and swallowing provides a bit of evidence to which psychodynamic theorists point for support.

Following is an example of the value of stuttering as a neurotic symptom that serves ego-defensive functions. Everett, a minister, said this during a therapy session:

> I'm afraid to reveal my inner self because people won't think I'm human. When I look at my thoughts inside, they're white and important, but when I speak them they change color to black and they seem so degraded and foolish. It's like I'm constantly painting masterpieces. Of course, I know they aren't real masterpieces, but they feel like it inside. The only way I can protect them is to spoil them so people won't know for sure that they weren't masterpieces. You know, I just realized that that's what I do to my speech and my ideas when I stutter.

Because psychodynamic concepts are all but impossible to test with scientific rigor, their support derives mainly from therapeutic results. These results leave considerable doubt about the validity of the psychoanalytic concept of stuttering. Although stutterers are likely to feel better about themselves and their speech after psychotherapy, most will continue to stutter.

Linguistic Origins. Evidence has been accumulating for several decades that indicates that linguistic factors are involved in stuttering. Stuttering in adults occurs mainly on initial consonants, on relatively long words located near the beginning of a sentence, on nouns, verbs, adverbs, or adjectives, and on infrequently used and unpredictable words (Bloodstein, 1975a). Studies have shown that normal disfluencies also have the same tendencies (Silverman and Williams, 1967).

Why and how linguistic operations are related to disfluency is still as much a matter of speculation as most other things we know about stuttering. For an answer, attention has centered on language encoding processes. For example, both normal disfluency and stuttering tend to occur at points of greatest uncertainty in verbal planning for what one is about to say (Soderberg, 1967). Also along this line, a model has been proposed recently by Bloodstein (1974) that relates the child's early stuttering to uncertainty about the syntactic structure of the statement he is planning. Certainly, these seem fruitful leads to understanding the repetitions of phrases and incomplete parts of phrases that characterize the normal disfluencies of those who stutter as well as of those who do not. These leads, however, do not seem to account too well for the syllable and sound disfluencies that listeners judge as stuttering. They do not explain easily, for example, why more stuttering occurs on initial consonants than on initial vowels.

One linguistic characteristic, the rhythm of speech, has been the focus of several theorists, Wingate (1976) in particular being a recent advocate. Available evidence suggests that the rhythm of speech is related to the abnormal disfluencies of stuttering. Timing of the motor elements of speech production underlies syllable stress. It is mistiming of these motor elements that Van Riper (1971) concludes is the basic nature of stuttering. For instance, the adaptation effect, described previously, will not occur when different words are stressed in each reading. That is, stuttering will not be reduced in successive readings of the same passage if the stutterer is instructed to vary the stress patterns for each reading. Then too, people who stutter are not as "sound minded" as nonstutterers. They have more difficulty deciphering the meaning of "slurvian" speech; an example is "scene owe weevil," which translates as "see no evil." (Wingate, 1966a, 1967).

Beyond such experimental evidence on the effects of rhythm on stuttering are the anecdotal reports of stutterers themselves. Bloodstein (1950) had 204 adult stutterers rate 115 speaking situations for the extent to which their stuttering was reduced or absent. Of the ten situations that were most effective, five involved speaking to a predetermined rhythm. Adherents to anticipatory-struggle theory are inclined to explain such situations as reducing stuttering because communicative responsibility is lessened, thereby reducing apprehension about stuttering. For instance, reduction of stuttering when speaking to animals or children is typically explained as a reduction of communicative responsibility. Another of their favored explanations is that the situation distracts attention from expectancy of stuttering, so in accordance with their theory, the likelihood of stuttering is reduced. Reasoning underlying the distraction effect is that because stuttering is thought to result from anticipation of difficulty, distraction from that anticipation will free the stutterer from his preparations to struggle with a feared word. The evidence, however, is on the side of a rhythm hypothesis. Tests of the distraction effect, and to lesser extent of communicative responsibility, have provided little support and often have opposed these explanations (Beech and Fransella, 1969).

Biologic Origins. About every organic condition that can be thought of has been studied during the last half-century in the search for a cause of stuttering: (1) *genetic origins*—Some researchers have investigated the strong tendency for stuttering to occur in two to ten times as many males as females, and for it to run in families, especially in families with twins; (2) *neurological disabilities*—Researchers have examined laterality, cerebral dominance, various brain-wave rhythms, perseveration, and general and oral motor coordinations for evidence of neurological disability among stutterers; (3) *metabolic disabilities*—Metabolic states evidenced in such conditions as diabetes, epilepsy, allergy, disease, and the effects of various pharmaceuticals have been inspected in relation to stuttering; and (4) *sensory disabilities*—Researchers have looked at many sensory variables, such as those found in deafness and hearing loss, the effects of loud noise on stuttering, tactile and kinesthetic sensitivity and discrimination in oral structures, and delays in auditory feedback of one's own speech.

The conclusion reached several years ago from the results of this massive work is that stutterers cannot be differentiated biologically as a group from normal speakers. Granted, individual stutterers who deviate sharply from the norm can be found, but the same is true of normal speakers. Likewise, common characteristics can be seen among stutterers, but similar characteristics are common to nonstutterers (Perkins, 1970). The inability of those who assumed the burden of proving a biological difference to muster convincing evidence was generally taken as confirmation that stuttering is learned behavior. After all, if stuttering isn't due to an organic flaw, then how else could it be acquired except by learning? However, one biological explanation of stuttering that has emerged in several forms in the last few years, the *laryngeal origin* of stuttering, warrants particular consideration here. Glimmerings of a possible laryngeal key to stuttering have been apparent in both clinical and research experience.

Clinicians have suspected for at least a century that the larynx is involved in stuttering. With the recent advent of clinical techniques for establishing fluency, this suspicion has grown. Use of a loud noise reduces stuttering considerably for many. Why it works is a mystery, but some think it is because the sound of the voice is obscured. One technique that has gained considerably more favor for clinical use is to impose an artificial rhythm with an electronic metronome. The most widely used technique for modifying stuttering involves delayed auditory feedback (DAF). If one attempts to speak at a normal rate when he hears his speech delayed, like an echo, the flow of words is usually disrupted. Goldiamond (1965) discovered that when stutterers prolong their syllables sufficiently to prevent DAF from disrupting speech, their stuttering is all but eliminated. Because the same results are achieved by speaking with prolonged syllables without DAF, the crucial condition for fluency appears to be a retarded articulatory rate. A slow rate may aid fluency by facilitating the immensely complex coordinations of phonation with articulation and respiration (Perkins, 1973a).

Recent experimentation has further implicated laryngeal activity in stuttering. Stuttering is reduced by reducing the number of vocal cord adductions and abductions for voiced and voiceless sounds (Adams and Reis, 1971). Greater reduction has also been found when laryngeal coordinations are rehearsed in repeated adaptation readings (Brenner, Perkins, and Soderberg, 1972). Some of the observations are not new; they have been known for years, but they have taken on new significance. The folklore of stuttering has long included such activities as whispering, singing, choral speaking, and rhythm as powerful means of reducing stuttering. Wingate (1969) concluded that these activities improve fluency because the stutterer is induced, one way or another, to do something with his voice that he does not ordinarily do. The search continues for what this something might be.

Increasingly, the answer that is appearing is that fluency is dependent on smooth coordination of phonation with respiration and articulation. When coordinations are simplified by whispering instead of using a normal voice, stuttering is reduced sharply. When coordinations are further simplified by mouthing words silently without voice or by substituting an electrolarynx for the voice, any stuttering that remains is all but eliminated. Even more importantly, this result opens the door to lawful statements about stuttering: It has held true with hardly an exception for more than a hundred stutterers who have participated in various forms of this experiment (Perkins et al., 1976).

Learned versus Biologic Origin. That laryngeal discoordination with articulation and respiration plays a central role in stuttering seems as certain as anything we know about this disorder. A basic question that remains is reflected in the two spellings: "disfluency" and "dysfluency." As discussed in a previous footnote, whereas *dis*fluency implies normalcy, *dys*fluency implies abnormalcy. Proponents of Bloodstein's anticipatory-struggle theory frequently explain stuttered disfluencies as the disintegration of smoothly timed speech caused by apprehension of stuttering. Hence, these disruptions are *not* viewed as a consequence of some organic pathology—rather, they are viewed as learned behavior. One trouble with this explanation is that many instances of stuttering are not preceded by expectancy and anxiety. Another difficulty is that even after a stutterer's apprehension has been desensitized, his stuttering is still likely to persist (Ingham and Andrews, 1971b; Gray and England, 1972). These objections aside, if one grants that stuttering develops from normal disfluency, then the underlying discoordinations must be learned (Brutten and Shoemaker, 1967). But as Wingate (1966c) demonstrated, although principles of learning can account for how disfluencies change once they occur, these principles do not explain how they happen in the first place.

Still another troublesome feature of the case for stuttering being learned is that the normal disfluency, from which it presumably arises, is qualitatively different from the abnormal disfluency of stuttering. Normal disfluency is characterized by repetitions of large units of speech, such as phrases or parts of phrases. These disfluencies seem to be a consequence of linguistic uncertainty. Abnormal disfluency, on the other hand, involves small units of speech: syllables and sounds. These are the motor-speech units that are disrupted when phonatory, articulatory and respiratory synergies are mistimed (Adams, 1974). They are seen considerably more frequently in the speech of persons who stutter than of those who do not. Not only is this true for older children and adults who are confirmed stutterers, it is also apparently true for preschool children who are judged by their parents to have just begun to stutter (Floyd and Perkins, 1974).

Thus, the prospect that West (1958) contemplated years ago has arisen again; namely, that stuttering has its origin in children whose speech coordination skills are marginal. Obviously, this implies that children who develop stuttering may be born with a deficient biologic mechanism for coordinating speech. That such a mechanism could be inherited is not too surprising. The strong tendency for stuttering to run in families and for it to occur in males more than females points to a genetic origin (Andrews and Harris, 1964). The tide of professional interest swung away from constitutional explanations several decades ago. During this period, the preferred explanation for a problem was that it had been learned. The tide is shifting again. Research interest in a genetic difference has been rekindled. Whether conclusive evidence will be found that such a difference exists remains to be seen.

Even if a genetic difference is found, we need not invoke the stigma of pathology. Instead of saying that children who stutter are abnormal, we can account for their difficulties with an explanation Van Riper (1971) offered that is probably the most sensible; People vary in any skill. As long as they are within the limits of a normal distribution of abilities for a particular skill, they are considered normal. Certainly one of the most complex skills of all is coordinating, at extraordinarily rapid rates, the one hundred or more muscles used for speech. People undoubtedly vary in this ability. Some people are able to time all the movements of speech easily, while some have difficulty. The possibility that young children who are not adept at this ability are the ones who have the greatest chance of developing stuttering seems entirely credible. The intricacies of speech being what they are, the wonder is that only one in a hundred people stutter.

What is a clinician attempting to accomplish when examining a person who stutters? In brief, he or she is trying to describe the problem accurately, determine conditions that produced and maintain it, and plan how best to treat it. The way to proceed is to gather information for two purposes: *description* and *assessment* (Perkins, 1977).

Description. Description is the fundamental task of fact-finding. Obviously, we can measure existing conditions more accurately than we can past history, so we can have greater confidence in behavior that can be observed directly than in case history recollections of what happened when. Still, stuttering has a history, and it can reveal information of importance to the assessment. To this end, Johnson and his colleagues (1963) have suggestions for ways of conducting interviews and for types of questions to ask to obtain a useful case history.

Generally, though, testing and observing will yield the most valuable description of the problems of the person who stutters. But the guiding questions for the clinician during the examination are, "Why do I need this information," and "What will I do with it?" The answers to these self-imposed questions determine which tests to administer and which questions to ask the client. Were we physicians concerned primarily with a diagnosis, for instance, we would want to know the etiology of a person's stuttering. We could then treat the cause rather than the symptom. Not only are most of us not physicians, but even if we were, no pathology is known to cause stuttering, so no medical treatment is available. Thus, the purpose of an examination is to accomplish a behavioral assessment, not a medical diagnosis.

Assessment. The information needed by the speech-language pathologist will be used to answer the primary questions of an assessment:

1. What is the nature and severity of the problem?
2. What is the prognosis for improvement?
3. What is an appropriate treatment?

Let us consider how these questions can be answered. We should note at the outset that although many tests about stuttering have been developed, few have been standardized. This leaves clinicians largely to their own devices to obtain their answers.

Several determinations must be made to decide about the nature and severity of stuttering. Some clinicians proceed by using Johnson's (1961) index of disfluency. With it, frequency of occurrence of all types of disfluency can be described. The decision, however, as to when a disfluency is to be judged as normal as distinguished from stuttered (with the implication that it is abnormal) is based on much more than a frequency count of disfluencies. For one thing, only syllable and sound disfluencies have a high probability of being considered as stuttering. But normal speakers hesitate and repeat syllables and sounds, so other factors such as duration and amount of struggle with the disfluency also contribute to a judgment of stuttering. Then, too, the speaker's reputation for fluency must be considered. If he is suspected of stuttering, even the slightest bobble in his flow of speech may be taken as confirmation of the suspicion.

As we discussed earlier, a determination of whether or not stuttering has occurred is an exceedingly complex judgment—one that does not lend itself readily to use of a standardized measure. Equally complex is the judgment of severity, about which we have precious little research evidence. Whose stuttering is more severe, the preschool child or the adult who struggles and strains to speak? Or, consider the person who repeats 10 percent of his syllables effortlessly—is his stuttering more severe than the attractive woman whose rare disfluencies severely distort her face? Lacking evidence, one opinion is as good as another.

Taking a different tack, some clinicians in recent years have circumvented the tough judgment of which syllable disfluencies are normal and which are abnormal. These clinicians have assumed that disfluencies are the nuclei of stuttering; hence, any type of disfluency holds the potential for stuttering. Those who work from this premise for the most part use behavior modification procedures for which reliable measurement of syllable disfluency is important. Accordingly, they have constructed equipment for counting and timing normal and disfluent speech. An example of equipment for counting syllables and keeping track of elapsed speaking time is shown in Figure 11–2.

Difficult as it is to judge stuttering, the judgment of who is a stutterer is even more troublesome. Some people who are never heard to stutter by others are deeply troubled by what they themselves are firmly convinced is stuttering. They can be as much concerned with fear that their techniques for avoiding stuttering will fail as others are with their overt disfluencies. Thus, another aspect of stuttering to be assessed is the speaker's attitude toward himself and his problem. Several scales have been developed for this purpose such as the Iowa Scale of Attitude Toward Stuttering, the Stutterer's Rating Scale of Speech Situations, the Rating Scale of Severity of Stuttering Reactions, and more recently, the Erickson Communication Inventory (Johnson, Darley, and Spriestersbach, 1963; Erickson, 1969).

So far our discussion has revolved entirely around assessment of the nature and severity of stuttering, about which a fair amount of

FIGURE 11–2. *Clinical equipment for counting syllables, disfluencies, and measuring cumulative speaking time.*

work has been done. When we turn to assessment of the prognosis for improvement we find ourselves for the most part in unexplored territory. Fortunately, we have the information reviewed earlier in this chapter on spontaneous recovery. It tells us that the prognosis is poor for those who have complete blockages rather than syllable repetitions at onset, for those who stutter severely, and for those who hold a self-concept of being a stutterer.

When we turn to assessment for the purposes of determining appropriate treatment, we again face the problem of inadequate evidence. A popular view prevails that stuttering has been resistant to lawful description because so many different factors can cause it. If this view were accurate, then presumably we should have different treatments for different types of stuttering. Without doubt, we have an abundance of therapies, literally dozens. But in fact, no one has presented any evidence that one works better with one type of stuttering than another. In reality, selection of type of treatment generally has more to do with the theoretical persuasion of the clinician than with the results of assessment of the individual who stutters.

Much as we may deplore our ignorance, hope is in sight. More than a fourth of the scientific research that has been done on stuttering has been done in this decade. How soon we will have definitive evidence on which to base our assessments is difficult to predict. That we are rapidly improving the foundation of knowledge on which to base our clinical decisions is a current reality. The day may be near when we can reliably predict who will profit most from which type of therapy.

Implications for Help: Children

What considerations do clinicians bear in mind when preparing to help children who stutter? Those who are persuaded that stuttering is a learned disorder that grows out of normal disfluency have written prolifically about prevention of the problem (Johnson, 1949; Murphy, 1962; Luper and Mulder, 1964; Johnson et al., 1967; Bloodstein, 1975b). Their major recommendation is to listen to the child. Care for what he is saying; it is important to him. Try not to call attention to his disfluencies as being undesirable. Above all, avoid labeling his hesitations as stuttering or him as a stutterer. All children are normally disfluent, so treat him as being normal, not as being different. Nothing is gained by calling his disfluencies stuttering, nor by labeling him as a stutterer. Worse, much can be lost. He can become aware that he speaks abnormally and begin to struggle for fluency. When he learns to hesitate, he will then display the characteristics of stuttering. Until then, he is a normal-speaking child whose perception of himself as being normal can be preserved by the important listeners in his life treating him as being normal. Viewed this way, stuttering develops more in the "ear" of the listener than in the "mouth" of the speaker.

Without doubt, the recommendation to listen attentively with genuine interest is fundamental. But it can be distorted, as some operant theorists suspect it is when a child's stuttered speech commands more attention than his moments of fluency. These theorists hold that if stuttering is learned, then one way or another it must produce reinforcing consequences. Jerry's dialogue with his mother is suggestive of how a five-year-old may learn to value his disfluency. Jerry was playing with his Tinker Toys and his mother was in the kitchen when this interchange began:

> "Mommy, where does this go?" No reply. "Mommy, I can't make this work." No reply. "It won't fit!" Jerry's frustration mounted and his mother remained preoccupied. "M,m,mommy! Come here!" She came. "M_____ommy, I can't make it fit." She kneeled beside him and gave him her full attention. Intentionally or not, Jerry's mother responded selectively to his stuttering.

The caution to attend mainly during fluency and less during stuttering is controversial, and on the face of it, seems hard-hearted.

The fact is, though, that an aspect of stuttering that can be learned is its capacity to rivet attention. Who is so calloused as to turn away or interrupt a stutterer in the midst of a block? This can be powerfully reinforcing for a child, or adult for that matter, who otherwise makes little impact on his listener. No matter that the reaction may be negative. Any form of attention is apt to be better than none at all.

This recommendation is intended to head off learning a need for stuttering. The idea is not to punish the child for stuttering, nor to call undue attention to disruptive disfluencies, nor to label them stuttering and him or her a stutterer. Rather, the point is to avoid reinforcing stuttering by paying special attention to it. Instead of listening attentively mainly when the child stutters, turn the reaction around. Listen most when he speaks easily and least when he does not. If he is disfluent so frequently that you would have little fluent speech to reinforce, then of course, this recommendation would be inappropriate. Better that he be heard than that his message be lost because he stuttered too much.

A related recommendation is to foster the child's security. Insecurity is the breeding ground for reinforcement of stuttering. A secure child receives enough attention that he has a good chance of not needing stuttering to obtain it. The child who hungers to be heard at any price is the one who may discover the power of stuttering to meet his need.

There are also the theorists who suspect that those children whose speech coordination capacity is tenuous are the children most likely to develop stuttering. They offer the following recommendations for facilitating coordinations.

1. *Be an exemplary model.* This includes slowing down, calming down, and developing a better more secure attitude. Demonstrated as living examples by parents and teachers, these are powerful therapeutic tools. They are not admonitions to be laid on the child in the time honored tradition of "do as I say, not as I do." In this form they would do far more damage than good. They would call the child's attention to his trouble and put him under pressure to conform. The injunctions "Slow down!", "Calm down!", "Feel secure!" translate into speed up, tense up, and be on guard.

Instead, speak softly, smoothly, and slowly. Prosody is the first feature of speech that the child imitates. Provide a fast jerky model and the child will follow with his attempt at fast jerky speech. If he is prone to disfluency, both speed and jerkiness imperil his ability to time all the parts smoothly. The probable result will be fast jerky disfluency that paves the road to stuttering.

2. *Reduce communicative pressure.* The child's ability to coordinate

speech may be marginal. If competition to get a word in edgewise is great, disruption of these coordinations is likely. Many other less explicit conditions also contribute to communicative pressure, such as in the following experience. Terry had spent the day painting a clay rabbit he had made in nursery school. His father came home that evening, tired as usual, opened a beer and buried himself in his paper. Terry came over and started telling his father about the rabbit he had made for him as a gift. No response. Terry continued intermittently in rapid spurts with little success at gaining attention. He stuttered a bit during this monologue. His father finally looked up, accepted the rabbit with perfunctory thanks, and went back to his paper. Terry retired to his room. No overt pressure here, but what a profound lesson in how not to make speech effortlessly enjoyable.

3. *Keep the child rested and healthy.* Fragile coordinations are all the more fragile when the child is tired or sick.

Finally, what we know about acquisition of stuttering leads to this major recommendation. *Recognize the danger signs of early stuttering that warn of its becoming permanent.* These include: (1) severe stuttering; (2) blockages and prolongations rather than easy repetitions at onset; (3) a self-concept of being a stutterer; and (4) late onset of recovery from stuttering. The old pediatric admonition to concerned mothers, "Leave him alone and he'll outgrow it," will prove to be true for the majority of children who show incipient stuttering. The grave risk with this admonition, however, is that predicting who will and who won't recover spontaneously is an uncertain business at best. If periods of normal fluency are growing shorter, if struggle and frustration are increasing, then a parent should seek professional advice from a speech-language pathologist.

Implications for Help: Adults

Adult stuttering could be defined facetiously as a disorder for which each clinician has his own treatment. The fact that no therapy yet described works far better than any other leaves everyone free to experiment. Nonetheless, the majority of these therapeutic efforts are built around one of three views of how to relieve confirmed stuttering: (1) relieve the symptom of stuttering by resolving the underlying neurosis with psychotherapy; (2) relieve fear of stuttering and teach "fluent stuttering"; (3) relieve fear of stuttering by replacing it with normal speech.

Psychotherapy. More than cursory observations about psychotherapy as the major method of treatment of stuttering are beyond the scope of our discussion. This would be true even if psychotherapy were a phenomenally successful means of improving stuttered speech, which it is not. Because stuttering is seen as a surface expression of underlying unresolved neurotic conflict, what must be resolved, presumably, are basic personality problems. Concern is not so much with stuttering as with the person who stutters. Jeff's situation points up the scope of a patient's life in which a clinician becomes involved by working from a psychodynamic framework.

> When Jeff was first seen for treatment, he was a quiet subdued thirty-year-old longshoreman. He started therapy with a fairly severe problem of stuttering about which he complained bitterly and on which he blamed everything. At the same time, he was working for a college degree. He had received excellent grades and had spent seemingly endless hours worrying and studying for his courses. As his stuttering began to disappear, he became openly belligerent, particularly toward those teachers and students who complimented him on his grades. In effect, he shifted his attitude toward speech to his school work. He no longer stuttered nor was concerned about speaking, instead he became increasingly fearful that he would fail in his last semester before graduation, especially in those subjects in which he had done well. When confronted with the excellence of his earlier work, he discounted it as not proving anything because he always performed his achievements secretly. By maintaining anonymity no one would expect anything of him or know about him in the event that he did fail. He distrusted the value of his past performance so much that he said, "I don't dare give up worrying and stewing about these exams, even though I know they're easy and I know the material, because if I went in and just did the best I could I know it wouldn't be enough. I just can't run the risk of finding out for sure that everything I've done is really a big fake."

Although Jeff's speech improved during two years of psychotherapy, some stuttering remained. Why his stuttering did not disappear completely is as perplexing as why it decreased in severity at all.

The aim of psychotherapy, whether with children or adults, is to reshape the stutterer's life into new and more effective designs. The investments and risks are awesome. Years may be required to give treatment a fair trial. The clinician's responsibility for personality changes that accompany success can weigh heavily. Equally heavy is his responsibility for failure when the stuttering, which was the original complaint, persists. So far, no effective method of predicting who will succeed and who will not has been reported.

Still, psychotherapy can be an essential tool to use in conjunction with other methods of treatment, as is considered later in this chapter. The limit placed on our discussion is for the use of psychotherapy in reshaping personality and resolving neurosis. For purposes that are this sweeping, the psychotherapeutic process requires extensive training and should be reserved for use by those whose preparation and competence have been demonstrated.

Fear Reduction and Fluent Stuttering. The traditional therapy of today began as a reaction against the traditional therapy of a half century ago. Used then were "techniques" like speaking in time with arm swinging or toe tapping, tricks that provided instant fluency. But such therapy was criticized sharply for two reasons. First, critics argued that relapse was almost certain to follow this cheaply purchased fluency. And second, they argued that the relapsed stutterer would be in worse condition than he was before. He would be more certain than ever that any form of speaking was better than stuttering, and that he was helpless to prevent disruption of his speech. Doubts about justification of these criticisms have been raised recently by Wingate (1976). In any event, the alternative view that was developed by Bryngelson, Johnson, and Van Riper at the University of Iowa was that stuttering is not to be dreaded or avoided. They said, in effect, "you may be a stutterer all of your life, so learn to stutter effortlessly and openly, and try to live with it gracefully."

From this origin has come today's traditional therapy of stuttering as an anticipatory-struggle disorder (Brutten and Shoemaker, 1967; Sheehan, 1970; Gregory, 1973; Van Riper, 1973). The central idea has remained intact, although techniques of implementing it have been refined. Basic to the recommendations of these theorists is the conviction that the root of stuttering is in the struggle to be fluent. They pursue two major objectives. One is to help the stutterer improve his attitude about his speech and himself. The other is to help him stutter effortlessly and fluently.

Several approaches are taken to change a stutterer's attitudes. He is encouraged to observe what he does and how he feels in situations in which he stutters. He also observes listener's reactions to see for himself if they are as devastating as he expects them to be. He is urged to stutter openly and frequently, partly to increase opportunities for his own observation of his speech, and partly to desensitize his dread of stuttering. To this end, striving for fluency is deplored. This means that he must try not to hide his blocks with all of his devices for avoiding them; to hide leads to deception, guilt, and shame. Too, this approach means that family, friends, and teachers can help in several ways: They should encourage talking, make talking enjoyable, not interrupt, tease, or mock. Others should praise a stutterer's easy fluent stuttering, but not false fluency purchased at the price of suppressed stuttering. The stuttering individual should be encouraged to try to understand others as well as himself. The greater the stutterer's self-esteem, the more realistically he can appraise himself and his problems.

As the stutterer becomes more aware that he can master his own behavior, that he is not helpless to let blocks happen to him, that he can control them rather than them controlling him, that he need not avoid or postpone feared words and situations, he then learns ways to stutter effortlessly, if not fluently. To accomplish this, many clinicians use Van Riper's (1973) three procedures: pull-outs, preparatory sets, and cancellations.

Pull-outs are what the stutterer does to extricate himself from a block. Instead of using gasping, jerking pull-outs, he learns to ease himself out of difficulty with smooth controlled prolongations. *Preparatory sets* are the preparations made to stutter. In the old stuttering, they include the anticipatory rehearsals of the expected difficulty. Stuttering, then, is the fulfillment of this expectation that has been rehearsed. What is learned as the new preparatory set is to initiate speech movements from a state of rest rather than from a tense "frozen" position of the speech mechanism. *Cancellation,* Van Riper's third procedure for fluent stuttering, is what the stutterer does as soon as an instance of stuttering stops. He pauses, then stutters again, but this time uses a modified version of his stuttering that is simpler. These modifications include his new pull-outs and preparatory sets. He cancels the old stuttering pattern by substituting a more effortless one.

Each of the above procedures was used in an effort to reduce Melinda's fear of speaking and to help her speak easily:

> Melinda, a college student, was so afraid of stuttering that she was all but speechless. She would sit with her clinician by the hour with tears streaming down her face, adamant in her refusal to say a word lest she stutter. The heroic measure of setting a deadline for termination from the clinic if she was not going to speak was required to obtain rudimentary cooperation. After months of patient coaxing and goading, she finally permitted herself to stutter openly, but reluctantly. Once she was willing to stutter, efforts were begun to simplify her struggles. Instead of holding her breath and protruding her tongue when she blocked, she learned after hours of self-observation to hold her tongue behind her teeth lightly and prolong the syllable on which she was stuck until she could glide smoothly to the next syllable. During clinic sessions she practiced cancelling old stuttering patterns by repeating each blockage with her new pull-out technique. Eventually, she was able to use essentially the same technique as she approached a feared word. She practiced initiating phrases easily on which she expected difficulty. Whereas before she tensed her tongue and jaw in preparation for forcing her way through a feared word, she now used expectancy of stuttering as a signal to pause, relax her speech mechanism, and begin speech on an easy exhalation.

Whether Melinda ever mastered these procedures well enough to retain control of her stuttering is uncertain. During her second year of therapy, she moved to another state.

Replacement of Stuttering with Normal Speech. Early in the 1960s, work began on what has come to be known as "behavior modification" of stuttering. As a distinctive name, this term is somewhat misleading in that the traditional approach is equally behavioral and equally concerned with modification of speech. Still, the term does identify a treatment approach based largely on operant conditioning principles that is used with a wide range of behavior disorders, of which stuttering is one. In bare outline, this approach entails use of techniques for quickly shaping fluent speech that, with the use of operant principles, can be stabilized and transferred to daily life.

Considerable skepticism about the efficacy of these procedures has been voiced by advocates of traditional therapy of stuttering. They remind us that currently used shaping techniques, such as rhythm-paced speech, slow speech, and variations in phrasing were what currently traditional therapies were a rebellion against half a century ago. The objection then, and the concern now, is that these "quick cure" procedures buy immediate relief from stuttering, but at a high price on two counts. One is that the speech produced is slow and monotonous. The other is that the fluency is temporary and wears away as the novelty fades.

Those who use behavior shaping procedures have recognized that fluency is easy to establish but difficult to maintain if it is not incorporated in normally expressive speech. Indeed, when fluent speech sounds unnatural, many stutterers view this "cure" as worse than their "disease." They would rather stutter expressively than be fluent monotonously. Accordingly, fluency at any price has long since ceased to be the goal of treatment of many of these behavior modification systems.

What behavior modification clinicians offer instead are elaborately systematized programs for shaping an approximation of normally fluent speech (Brady, 1968; Ryan, 1971; Andrews and Ingham, 1972; Perkins, 1973b; Webster, 1974). Generally, they do an analysis of skills required for normal speech. They then use a technique, such as rate control or rhythm to help elicit these skills. By means of operant procedures, speech is shaped into an approximation of normalcy. It is then transferred to daily life and stabilized for permanence. Behavior modification clinicians proceed on the assumption that normal speech skills are abandoned temporarily when stuttering occurs. Thus, as long as normal skills are preserved, stuttering is precluded.

Despite the sound and fury, the objectives of traditionalists and behavior shapers are not that different. Both attempt to make speaking

FIGURE 11–3. *Moments of stuttering in a young man.*

easier and to improve the stutterer's attitude about himself and his speech. Traditionalists start by helping the stutterer accept his stuttering. Along the way, they will aid him in stuttering more effortlessly and inconspicuously (see Figure 11–3). They hold the reasonably well-founded belief that as his attitude improves, so will his speech. Behaviorists come at the same objective from the opposite direction. Proceeding on the assumption that nothing succeeds like success, they strive to establish normal speech as the starting point and let change in attitude follow.

Interestingly, what the behavior shapers seem to have devised is a procedure that goes a step beyond the traditional clinician's efforts to establish fluent stuttering. Instead of beginning with modification of the stuttering block and then moving forward to modification of the preparatory set for stuttering, the behavior shapers move even farther forward. They seek to prevent preparatory sets for stuttering from even occurring in the first place by preserving the skills of normal fluency. They do not attempt to suppress stuttering; they seek to head it off before it begins. Whether severe or mild or any of the myriad other characteristics of stuttering, they see these characteristics as dropping out with the establishment of fluency. No matter, for them, the infinitely different forms in which speech can go wrong. Instead, they focus attention on how to install the common elements of speech when it is right.

As for the criticism that replacement of stuttering with normal

FIGURE 11–4. *Client using a delayed-auditory-feedback instrument to shape fluency.*

speech offers only temporary relief, efforts have been made to find out if this is true. Some who devised such approaches have assumed the burden of proof for their departure from tradition. They have gone to considerable lengths to measure, test, and report the outcomes of their therapeutic procedures (Ingham and Andrews, 1971a; Andrews and Ingham, 1972; Brady and Brady, 1972; Perkins et al., 1974; Webster, 1974). What these and other workers have demonstrated is that the major objections are not justified in the majority of cases treated with behavior modification procedures. Upwards of 90 percent show long-term improvement, and about half of these improve enough to sound like normal speakers. Lacking equivalent evidence, we must rely mainly on rating scale data and the clinical observations of traditional clinicians for a comparison. The impressions of the latter suggest lasting improvement in from 30 to 50 percent of their clients (Gray and England, 1969; Prins, 1970; Gregory, 1972).

Permanence is a universal problem for all management procedures, including the behavior modification approaches as well as traditional techniques. Perhaps one of the chief values of the fluency shaping approaches is that they can be used to psychotherapeutic advantage. Because stuttering can be replaced with normal speech relatively quickly, this type of approach provides a powerful tool for confronting the stutterer with the reality of what he wants (see Figure 11–4). By giving the stutterer the relief from speech disruption he says he seeks, he can see for himself whether or not fulfillment of his wish for fluency is the blessing he anticipated. Many discover that stuttering is not that devastating a problem after all. At this point psychotherapy may be needed to resolve issues that are of concern.

For those who do seek to maintain their new speaking skills, permanence of their success depends in large measure on their reception at home, school, and work. We usually make two firm recommendations to relatives, teachers, and others who will be interacting with a newly fluent client:

1. *Attend carefully to his new speech.* Like any new skill, it is easily disrupted. Keep communicative pressure low. The necessity to speak loudly or rapidly is sure to produce a breakdown. His return to familiar places invites return to old habits, which include stuttering. Ease his transition into daily life with his new speech. This is the toughest step of all for him. He needs encouragement and support at this time more than ever.

2. *Avoid teasing, mocking, or disapproval of the new speech.* It will be tender. If it is cultivated, chances of its growing into sturdy normal speech are good. But it is just as easily tromped to extinction. The reception it receives will do much to determine its fate.

Three brief examples are to the point:

Darth was in his mid-fifties. His new wife was in her twenties. He hated stuttering and demonstrated his ability to maintain normal speech regularly during treatment. She, in turn, detested the sound of his new fluency. She encouraged him to forget about his speech and just stutter. Needless to say, she won. Darth abandoned the fluency he had achieved as soon as treatment ended.

Joe, a twenty-two-year-old, brought his mother to his group to display the progress of which he was proud. Her opening remark before the group was, "God, Joe, you sound like an idiot." In truth, he had progressed from severe stuttering to such normal speech that students who met him in the lobby didn't know he had a speech problem. Within a month after therapy, his stuttering was as bad as ever.

By contrast, Miriana's husband thought her new speech sounded "sexy." He observed that most other men thought so, too, which did much for Miriana's confidence, and his jealousy. By the end of intensive treatment in 1973, she had gone from severe stuttering to completely fluent speech a bit on the slow side of normal. Her rate has picked up as time has passed, and she has become more expressive. What she has carefully preserved though, in addition to fluency, is a "sexy" voice.

Despite mountains of research and voluminous ponderings, the age-old problem of stuttering is still with us. Is it so baffling that no lawful statement can be made about it? Is it true that once a stutterer always a stutterer? Certainly no responsible claim has been made that stuttering can be "cured." But hope is on the horizon. New research directions are opening that may lead to the permanent establishment of normal speaking skills in many who are now sorely troubled by stuttering.

CLUTTERING

For whatever reason, stuttering is a problem that has intrigued many of the best minds in speech-language pathology for decades. Why the equally puzzling problem of cluttering has not attracted similar attention is this country is difficult to explain. It seems to have captured the interest of European phoniatrists as much as has stuttering. In fact, most of what we know about cluttering comes from clinical practice. This type of research does not permit conclusions that one can hold with confidence. Thus, you may detect an aura of uncertainty hovering over our discussion of cluttering.

Definitions

Definitions of cluttering are notoriously vague. For example, Luchsinger and Arnold (1965) define cluttering as "a disability to formulate language, resulting in confused, hurried, and slurred diction on the basis of a congenital, inheritable, and constitutional limitation of the total psychosomatic personality structure." Or, consider Weiss' (1964) description (paraphrased here) of cluttering: Cluttering is the verbal manifestation of *central language imbalance* that involves dysfunction of the highest level of cerebral integration that governs all channels of communication such as speaking, reading, writing, rhythm, and musicality. As you can see, because these are hardly precise definitions, an estimate of the prevalence of cluttering would be all but meaningless. Nonetheless, the term is useful for identifying speech flow problems chiefly of rate and rhythm.

Features of Cluttering

Cluttering is an umbrella term that covers a wide array of what are presumed to be neurologic conditions that can affect fluency, rhythm, and rate. Furthermore, the behavior it denotes, when peeled to bare essential, is difficult to separate from stuttering. A case in point is ten-year-old Bobby, who showed more evidence of the central language imbalance that Weiss (1964) believes is characteristic of cluttering than did most incipient stutterers.

Bobby's speech was delayed in development, and when it began, it literally tumbled out in a rapid, dysfluent, and grammatically disorganized flow with many articulatory errors. He talked in torrents. Strings of syllables and words were repeated, but rarely were prolongations heard. He seemed to be searching for words. He also seemed not to listen to himself, which may account for his appearing to be unconcerned about the hurried mess he made of communication.

This review of Bobby's speech is a better description of cluttering than of stuttering in its early stages. However, Bobby was eventually classified as a stutterer because he finally began to show signs of avoidance and fear, especially of situations that gave him trouble. He also called himself a stutterer. Unlike stutterers, the clutterer's characteristic attitude about his speech problem is indifference. Obviously, this could account for why so few clutterers are seen for treatment and why the disorder seems so rare. When urged to seek help, the clutterer's typical response is, "Why? Nothing's wrong with me."

Of more than two dozen features of cluttering that are purportedly symptomatic of this disorder, actually only a few are obligatory: lack of awareness of the disorder (as illustrated above), excessive rate, and erratic rhythm leading to slurred garbled speech that can be unintelligible. Other features, such as grammatical deficiency, impaired reading, bizarre handwriting, poor musical ability, and bodily incoordinations are often but not necessarily present (Luchsinger and Arnold, 1965). Let us look closer at some of the characteristics of cluttered speech often reported.

The obligatory feature of excessive rate appears to be related to word and phrase length. Acceleration seems proportional to the number of syllables spoken. Thus, the longer the word or phrase, the more apparent cluttering becomes. Not surprisingly, clutterers tend to speak in short explosive bursts. The resulting speech is jerky and dysrhythmic. Although generally deficient in musical abilities, too, those clutterers who can manage to sing show improved intelligibility.

Closely related are faulty patterns of respiration, phonation, and articulation. Clutterers tend to ignore phrasing patterns used by normal speakers for expression of a logical sentence. Instead, they jump in irregular spurts from one gasping breath to the next. Along with peculiar respiration goes peculiar vocal characteristics. Their voices tend to be poorly produced, and often "break" on stressed vowels. Too, they typically are monotonous. Perhaps the most apparent feature of cluttered speech is the distorted articulation. Sounds and syllables may be omitted, substituted, transposed, and repeated. Unstressed syllables may be skipped entirely, and major word elements may be replaced with "uh." The net result approaches unintelligibility.

Presumably, as part of the central language disability, grammatic accuracy is often affected in writing as well as in speech. Infantile errors persist in such forms as wrong verb tense, wrong prepositions, and wrong pronouns. Difficulties in reading and writing are also frequently found in the clutterer. The clutterer reverses and omits letters, reads and writes in opposite directions from normal, carelessly misspells, and shows jumbled handwriting that is as disintegrated as his speech.

Features of Clutterers

Cluttering is thought to be a pervasive problem affecting the whole person. Clutterers are reported to show such traits as hyperactivity, distractibility, impulsiveness, forgetfulness, untidiness, and emotional instability. Lack of intelligence is in no way implied by cluttering, however. Clutterers purportedly show the same range of intelligence as is found in the normal population. But that intelligence is said to be skewed toward exact reasoning. They often are thought to be outstanding in mathematical and quantitative areas. They also may show striking ability to memorize even poetry and prose, but apparently this does not aid oral expression. Despite excellent general memory, they seem to show a short auditory memory span, which could contribute to their poor auditory attention and inferior musical ability. Their choice of occupations tends to reflect their areas of strength. They favor precise, concrete occupations, and they particularly avoid the talking and performing professions (Weiss, 1964; Luchsinger and Arnold, 1965).

Origins of Cluttering

Most of the work done on cluttering has been medical research done in Europe. The problem has been linked with left-handedness and mixed laterality, and specifically appears to involve deficits in high level auditory functioning. Two lines of inquiry into causes have been pursued (Weiss, 1964). Genetic investigations have been prompted by the basic tenet of cluttering theory that central language imbalance is hereditary. Evidence for this consists mainly of clinical impressions that it runs in families. Hereditary factors, of some as yet unknown types, are considered to be the etiology of true cluttering. Symptomatic cluttering, the other line of inquiry pursued, is viewed as symptomatic of neurological involvement. Electroencephalographic studies have consistently shown more irregularities in brain waves of clutterers than stutterers. Although the origins of cluttering are open to dispute, this problem with all of its accompanying language disabilities is probably a more profound disorder than stuttering.

Implications for Help

Goals for management of cluttering simply follow the deficits that we have described: reduce excessive rate, correct articulatory errors, improve vocabulary, improve writing, compensate for grammatical insecurity, and improve concentration in details of linguistic formulation and expression (Weiss, 1960). Procedures for accomplishing these goals have been described elsewhere (Bradford, 1963). As with stuttering, so too with cluttering, more is accomplished by demonstrating than by dictating. When a clutterer speaks slowly and carefully, he does fairly well. Yet telling him to speak slowly and carefully is to tell the wind to stop blowing. He can do so for brief periods, but he can't seem to maintain it. Perhaps the short attention span he is thought to have interferes.

Beyond these specific therapeutic aims is global concern for the clutterer's ability to integrate with society. Because he is so unaware of his cluttered communication, he tends to be oblivious of conventions of self-expression. Thus, his habilitation is about as much dependent on improvement of attitudes as of speech.

We recommend that parents, teachers, and others try to control the tempo around a clutterer, rather than trying to control his tempo directly. Remove the need for haste. Provide a model of slow unhurried speech in a leisurely-paced home with plenty of time to listen. Because he is so unaware of his pell-mell incoherent tumblings, he seems surprised when he is not understood. Tell him that you can't understand his swift speech. A caution, though. Carried too far, pressures for intelligibility mount, frustrations rise, and the possibility of compounding the problem with fears and avoidances looms. Cluttering is a difficult problem with which to cope. As with stutterers, a clutterer's attitudes toward himself and communicative situations play a key role in acquiring and maintaining fluent speech. In our roles as parents, teachers, or just casual listeners, we *can* help.

REFERENCES   ADAMS, M., A physiologic and aerodynamic interpretation of fluent and stuttered speech. *Journal of Fluency Disorders,* 1, 35–47 (1974).

ADAMS, M., and REIS, R., The influence of the onset of phonation on the frequency of stuttering. *Journal of Speech and Hearing Research,* 14, 639–644 (1971).

ALLEN, G., Section from Netsell, R., Speech physiology. In F. Minifie, T. Hixon, and F. Williams (Eds.), *Normal Aspects of Speech, Hearing, and Language.* Englewood Cliffs, N.J.: Prentice-Hall (1973).

ANDREWS, G., and HARRIS, M., *The Syndrome of Stuttering.* London: Heinemann (1964).

ANDREWS, G., and INGHAM, R., An approach to the evaluation of stuttering therapy. *Journal of Speech and Hearing Research,* 15, 296–302 (1972).

BARBARA, D., *The Psychotherapy of Stuttering.* Springfield, Ill.: Charles C Thomas (1962).

BEECH, H., and FRANSELLA, F., Explanations of the "rhythm effect" in stuttering. In B. Gray and G. England (Eds.), *Stuttering and the Conditioning Therapies.* Monterey, Calif.: Monterey Institute for Speech and Hearing (1969).

BLANTON, S., Stuttering. In D. Barbara (Ed.), *New Directions in Stuttering.* Springfield, Ill.: Charles C Thomas (1965).

BLOODSTEIN, O., *A Handbook on Stuttering.* Chicago: National Easter Seal Society for Crippled Children and Adults (1975a).

BLOODSTEIN, O., A rating scale study of conditions under which stuttering is reduced or absent. *Journal of Speech and Hearing Disorders,* 15, 29–36 (1950).

BLOODSTEIN, O., Stuttering as an anticipatory struggle reaction. In J. Eisenson (Ed.), *Stuttering: A Symposium.* New York: Harper & Row (1958).

BLOODSTEIN, O., Stuttering as tension and fragmentation. In J. Eisenson (Ed.), *Stuttering: A Second Symposium.* New York: Harper & Row (1975b).

BLOODSTEIN, O., The development of stuttering: III. Theoretical and clinical implications. *Journal of Speech and Hearing Disorders,* 26, 67–82 (1961).

BLOODSTEIN, O., The rules of early stuttering, *Journal of Speech and Hearing Disorders,* 39, 379–394 (1974).

BOEHMLER, R., Listener responses to non-fluencies. *Journal of Speech and Hearing Research,* 1, 132–141 (1958).

BRADFORD, D., Studies in tachyphemia, VII: A framework of therapeusis. *Logos,* 6 59 (1963).

BRADY, J., A behavioral approach to treatment of stuttering. *American Journal of Psychiatry,* 125, 843–848 (1968).

BRADY, J., and BRADY, C., Behavior therapy of stuttering. *Folia Phoniatrica,* 24, 335–359 (1972).

BRENNER, N., PERKINS, W., and SODERBERG, G., The effect of rehearsal on frequency of stuttering. *Journal of Speech and Hearing Research,* 15, 483–486 (1972).

BRUTTEN, R., and SHOEMAKER, D., *The Modification of Stuttering.* Englewood Cliffs, N.J.: Prentice-Hall (1967).

ERICKSON, R., Assessing communication attitudes among stutterers. *Journal of Speech and Hearing Research,* 12, 711–724 (1969).

FLOYD, S., and PERKINS, W., Early syllable dysfluency in stutterers and nonstutterers: A preliminary report. *Journal of Communication Disorders,* 7, 279–282 (1974).

GLAUBER, P., The psychoanalysis of stuttering. In J. Eisenson (Ed.), *Stuttering: A Symposium.* New York: Harper & Row (1958).

GOLDIAMOND, I., Stuttering and fluency as manipulable operant response classes. In L. Krasner and L. Ullman (Eds.), *Research in Behavior Modification.* New York: Holt, Rinehart and Winston (1965).

GRAY, B., and ENGLAND, G., Some effects of anxiety deconditioning upon stuttering frequency. *Journal of Speech and Hearing Research,* 15, 114–122 (1972).

GRAY, B., and ENGLAND, G., *Stuttering and the Conditioning Therapies.* Monterey, Calif.: Monterey Institute for Speech and Hearing (1969).

GREGORY, H., An assessment of the results of stuttering therapy. *Journal of Communication Disorders,* 5, 320–334 (1972).

GREGORY, H., *Stuttering: Differential Evaluation and Therapy.* New York: Bobbs-Merrill (1973).

HUFFMAN, E., and PERKINS, W., Dysfluency characteristics identified by listeners as "stuttering" and "stutterer." *Journal of Communication Disorders,* 7, 89–96 (1974).

INGHAM, R., and ANDREWS, G., Stuttering: The quality of fluency after treatment. *Journal of Communication Disorders,* 4, 279–288 (1971a).

INGHAM, R., and ANDREWS, G., The relation between anxiety reduction and treatment. *Journal of Communication Disorders,* 4, 289–301 (1971b).

JOHNSON, W., An open letter to the mother of a stuttering child. *Journal of Speech Disorders,* 14, 3–8 (1949).

JOHNSON, W., Measurements of oral reading and speaking rate and disfluency of adult male and female stutterers and nonstutterers. *Journal of Speech and Hearing Disorders, Monograph Supplement 7,* 1–20 (1961).

JOHNSON, W. (Ed.), *Stuttering in Children and Adults.* Minneapolis: University of Minnesota Press (1955).

JOHNSON, W., and Associates, *The Onset of Stuttering.* Minneapolis: University of Minnesota Press (1959).

JOHNSON, W., and BROWN, S., Stuttering in relation to various speech sounds. *Quarterly Journal of Speech,* 21, 481–496 (1935).

JOHNSON, W., BROWN, S., CURTIS, J., EDNEY, C., and KEASTER, J., *Speech Handicapped School Children.* New York: Harper & Row (1948).

JOHNSON, W., BROWN, S., CURTIS, J., EDNEY, C., and KEASTER, J., *Speech Handicapped School Children.* New York: Harper & Row (1967).

JOHNSON, W., DARLEY, F., and SPRIESTERSBACH, D., *Diagnostic Methods in Speech Pathology.* New York: Harper & Row (1963).

LUCHSINGER, R., and ARNOLD, G., *Voice-Speech-Language.* Belmont, Calif.: Wadsworth (1965).

LUPER, H., and MULDER, R., *Stuttering: Therapy For Children.* Englewood Cliffs, N.J.: Prentice-Hall (1964).

MARTYN, M., and SHEEHAN, J., Onset of stuttering and recovery. *Behavior Research and Therapy,* 6, 295–307 (1968).

MILISEN, R., The incidence of speech disorders. In L. Travis (Ed.), *Handbook of Speech Pathology and Audiology.* New York: Appleton-Century-Crofts (1971).

MURPHY, A. (Ed.), *Stuttering: Its Prevention.* Memphis: Speech Foundation of America (1962).

MURPHY, A., and FITZSIMMONS, R., *Stuttering and Personality Dynamics.* New York: Ronald (1960).

PERKINS, W., Physiological studies. In J. Sheehan (Ed.), *Stuttering: Research and Therapy.* New York: Harper & Row (1970).

PERKINS, W., Replacement of stuttering with normal speech: I. Rationale. *Journal of Speech and Hearing Research,* 38, 283–294 (1973a).

PERKINS, W., Replacement of stuttering with normal speech: II. Clinical procedures. *Journal of Speech and Hearing Research,* 38, 295–303 (1973b).

PERKINS, W., *Speech Pathology: An Applied Behavioral Science.* St. Louis: C.V. Mosby (1977).

PERKINS, W., Stuttering: Some common denominators. In D. Barbara (Ed.), *New Directions in Stuttering.* Springfield, Ill.: Charles C Thomas (1965).

PERKINS, W., RUDAS, J., JOHNSON, L., and BELL, J., Stuttering: Discoordination of phonation with articulation and respiration. *Journal of Speech and Hearing Research,* 19, 509–522 (1976).

PERKINS, W., RUDAS, J., JOHNSON, L., MICHAEL, W., and CURLEE, R., Replacement of stuttering with normal speech: III. Clinical effectiveness. *Journal of Speech and Hearing Research,* 39, 416–428 (1974).

PRINS, D., Improvement and regression in stutterers following short-term intensive therapy. *Journal of Speech and Hearing Disorders,* 35, 123–135 (1970).

RYAN, B., Operant procedures applied to stuttering therapy for children. *Journal of Speech and Hearing Disorders,* 36, 264–280 (1971).

SANDER, E., Untangling stuttering: A tour through the theory thicket. *American Speech and Hearing Association,* 17, 256–262 (1975).

SHAMES, G., and SHERRICK, C., A discussion of nonfluency and stuttering as operant behavior. In D. Barbara (Ed.), *New Directions in Stuttering.* Springfield, Ill.: Charles C Thomas (1965).

SHEEHAN, J.,*Stuttering: Research and Therapy.* New York: Harper & Row (1970).

SHEEHAN, J., and MARTYN, M., Spontaneous recovery from stuttering. *Journal of Speech and Hearing Research,* 9, 121–135 (1966).

SILVERMAN, F., and WILLIAMS, D., Loci of disfluencies in the speech of nonstutterers during oral reading. *Journal of Speech and Hearing Research,* 10, 790–794 (1967).

SODERBERG, G., Linguistic factors in stuttering. *Journal of Speech and Hearing Research,* 10, 801–810 (1967).

STROMSTA, C., A spectrographic study of dysfluencies labeled as stuttering by parents. *De Therapia Vocis et Loquelae, Volume 1. Societatis Internationalis Logopaediae et Phoniatriae XIII Congressus Vindobonae Anno MCMLXV, Acta.* August (1965).

TRAVIS, L., The unspeakable feelings of people with special reference to stuttering. In L. Travis (Ed.), *Handbook of Speech Pathology and Audiology.* New York: Appleton-Century-Crofts (1971).

VAN RIPER, C., Historical approaches. In J. Sheehan (Ed.), *Stuttering: Research and Therapy.* New York: Harper & Row (1970).

VAN RIPER, C., *Speech Correction: Principles and Methods.* Englewood Cliffs, N.J.: Prentice-Hall (1963).

VAN RIPER, C., *The Nature of Stuttering.* Englewood Cliffs, N.J.: Prentice-Hall (1971).

VAN RIPER, C., *The Treatment of Stuttering.* Englewood Cliffs, N.J.: Prentice-Hall (1973).

WEBSTER, R., A behavioral analysis of stuttering: Treatment and theory. In K. Calhoun, H. Adams, and K. Mitchell (Eds.), *Innovative Treatment Methods in Psychopathology.* New York: Wiley (1974).

WEISS, D., *Cluttering.* Englewood Cliffs, N.J.: Prentice-Hall (1964).

WEISS, D., Theory of cluttering. *Folia Phoniatrica,* 12, 216–223 (1960).

WEST, R., An agnostic's speculations about stuttering. In J. Eisenson (Ed.), *Stuttering: A Symposium.* New York: Harper & Row (1958).

WILLIAMS, D., and KENT, L., Listener evaluations of speech interruptions. *Journal of Speech and Hearing Research,* 1, 124–131 (1958).

WILLIAMS, D., SILVERMAN, F., and KOOLS, J., Disfluency behavior of elementary school stutterers and nonstutterers: The adaptation effect. *Journal of Speech and Hearing Research,* 11, 622–630 (1968).

WILLIAMS, D., SILVERMAN, F., and KOOLS, J., Disfluency behavior of elementary school stutterers and nonstutterers: The consistency effect. *Journal of Speech and Hearing Research,* 12, 301–307 (1969).

WINGATE, M., Prosody in stuttering adaptation. *Journal of Speech and Hearing Research,* 9, 550–556 (1966a).

WINGATE, M., Slurvian skill of stutterers. *Journal of Speech and Hearing Research,* 10, 844–848 (1967).

WINGATE, M., Sound and pattern in "artificial" fluency. *Journal of Speech and Hearing Research,* 12, 677–686 (1969).

WINGATE, M., Stuttering adaptation and learning: I. The relevance of adaptation studies to stuttering as "learned behavior." *Journal of Speech and Hearing Disorders,* 31, 148–156 (1966b).

WINGATE, M., Stuttering adaptation and learning: II. The adequacy of learning principles in the interpretation of stuttering. *Journal of Speech and Hearing Disorders,* 31, 211–218 (1966c).

WINGATE, M., *Stuttering: Theory and Treatment.* New York: Irvington Publishers (1976).

WINITZ, H., Repetitions in the vocalizations and speech of children in the first two years of life. *Journal of Speech and Hearing Disorders, Monograph Supplement 7,* 55–62 (1961).

WYATT, G., A development crisis theory of stuttering. *Language and Speech,* 1, 250–264 (1958).

YOUNG, M., Onset, prevalence, and recovery from stuttering. *Journal of Speech and Hearing Disorders,* 40, 49–58 (1975).

YOUNG, M., Predicting ratings of severity of stuttering. *Journal of Speech and Hearing Disorders, Monograph Supplement 7,* 31–54 (1961).

signpost   Hearing disorders come in several forms, exist over a wide range of severities, and affect people of all ages. Often, they have adverse educational, social, and economic impacts on those who have them, impacts that can be handicapping. Chapter 12 is the first of the book's two chapters devoted to hearing disorders. A part of the chapter focuses on descriptions of the three classifications of disorder types: those in which sound transmission is interrupted or blocked along its normal route to the sensory organ of the ear; those in which the sensory organ and/or nervous system are functioning abnormally; and, those in which a combination of these first two is operating. Another part of the chapter considers the more common causes of hearing losses. These include, among others, such factors as impacted earwax, liquid in the middle-ear cavity, toxic drugs, loud noises, birth disorders, and just plain growing older. The means for detecting and quantifying hearing losses have come a long way in the past quarter of a century and are continuing to become more exacting and sophisticated. Two sections of Chapter 12 deal with these means of detection and quantification: One section considers them as they currently exist in the form of routine tests in hearing clinics; the other section considers those means available in the form of highly specialized tests designed to serve well-defined purposes within the hearing-test battery. Hearing loss is perhaps the highest ranking of all causes of human communication disorders. Thus, the material of Chapter 12 is of double-edged importance to the reader: First, because of the large portion of the communication disorders territory that hearing loss influences; and, second, because hearing loss stands a good chance of affecting each of us personally sometime during our lifetime.

12

Terry L. Wiley

hearing disorders
and audiometry

INTRODUCTION

In many respects, we are what we hear. Much of our early learning takes place through hearing channels. What a child sees and hears early in life largely determines how the child will interact and communicate with other people. Accordingly, one of the first questions we should ask when confronted with a person having educational or communication problems is: Can this person hear? The ways in which we go about answering this question and the variety of possible answers form the bases of this chapter.

Our coverage is divided into four areas: hearing measurement, types of hearing loss, causes of hearing loss, and special auditory tests. The reader should gain an appreciation of the diagnostic process involved in hearing measurement and the implications of test findings for the person with a hearing impairment. This material provides the framework for Chapter 13, which discusses habilitation and rehabilitation options for people who have hearing problems.

HEARING MEASUREMENT

Purposes of Hearing Measurement

The clinical measurement of hearing is done primarily for one of two purposes. One purpose is to identify hearing problems that may be caused by ear disease or damage to auditory structures. In early childhood, for example, a hearing loss may indicate a medical problem, such as an ear infection. Because medical treatment of ear diseases is successful more often in early stages of the disease process, it is critical that such problems be detected and treated as soon as possible. A second purpose for hearing measurement is for educational and habilitation/rehabilitation planning. In those cases of hearing loss for which medical treatment is not an appropriate alternative, it is important that nonmedical treatment measures be instituted as early as possible. Information obtained from the hearing evaluation is required to make decisions about personal amplification (such as a hearing aid), school placement, vocational guidance, and the need for language and speech services.

Often it is difficult to differentiate children with hearing losses from children with other developmental disabilities. If a child presents a significant delay in the development of speech and language skills, it may be due to hearing loss or to another developmental disability. It is particularly critical that children with developmental disabilities receive hearing tests to determine whether a hearing loss accounts for or is contributing to their developmental disorder. It would be unfortunate, for example, if a child were placed educationally in a facility for the mentally retarded when the underlying problem was hearing loss.

Hearing loss is sometimes called the *hidden handicap* because it usually has no obvious physical manifestation. Unlike other disorders, such as blindness or physical problems, hearing loss may not be easily recognized. Indeed, it is often only *after* parents are informed that hearing-test results indicate their child has a hearing loss that they consider that a hearing problem may be the reason for other difficulties the child is having at school or at home. These problems point to the need for hearing assessment of *all* children early in life, particularly at the time of entry into school programs. Before we begin our treatment of hearing measurement and hearing disorders, a brief sketch of the people who train for a career in audiology is warranted.

Audiology and the Audiologist

Audiology is the science or study of hearing and its disorders. An *audiologist* is a person trained in the evaluation and treatment of hearing problems. The audiologist's role in the treatment of hearing disorders is nonmedical. That is, the orientation of the audiologist is toward the habilitation/rehabilitation needs of people with a hearing loss that are not correctable by medical or surgical means. The audiologist is concerned with whether a person needs a hearing aid, the special educational needs of persons with a hearing loss, and with other habilitation/rehabilitation services such as lipreading (speechreading) and auditory training.

The medical evaluation and treatment (both surgical and non-surgical) of the ear is the province of the *otolaryngologist.* The oto-laryngologist is a physician — usually the audiologist is not. Although audiology and otolaryngology are independent professions, they often overlap in terms of case management. It is important, for example, that the audiologist refer patients with a hearing loss to an oto-laryngologist. The otolaryngologist determines, with the aid of the in-formation provided by the audiologist, whether or not the hearing loss is the result of an ear pathology that can be treated by medical or surgical means. This decision must be made before other nonmedical treatment methods are considered by the audiologist. The specific lo-cation of a pathology within the auditory system is often determined using results from both otologic *and* audiologic examinations. Cross-referral of patients between audiologists and otolaryngologists is nec-essary, therefore, for complete patient management.

The American Speech-Language-Hearing Association recommends standards of training and ethical practice for the profession of au-diology. If member clinicians satisfy these requirements they may receive the Association's Certificate of Clinical Competence in Audi-ology (CCC-A). Requirements include: (1) a Master's degree or equiva-lent in the field; (2) evidence of a prescribed amount of supervised clinical practicum during graduate training; (3) evidence of at least one year of supervised work in the area following completion of the Master's degree; and (4) successful performance on a national ex-amination. The audiologist, then, is a highly trained professional committed to the habilitation/rehabilitation needs of people with hear-ing disorders.

Audiometry

Audiometry is the measurement of hearing. The term generally is quali-fied according to the type of signal used for testing, such as *pure-tone* audiometry or *speech* audiometry, and by the medium employed for the transmission of sound (*air-conduction* or *bone-conduction*). The con-cept of *threshold,* discussed in Chapter 3, underlies most tests of hear-ing sensitivity. A pure-tone threshold is the level at which a person can just detect the presence of a tone. The concept applies also to speech thresholds, except the speech threshold is the level at which the listener is just able to follow or identify speech stimuli (usually words). This latter measure is called the *Speech Reception Threshold* (SRT). Regardless of the test signal used, a tone or speech, the thresh-old measure is statistical in nature. That is, it is a level at which a lis-tener responds appropriately to a percentage of the signals presented.

In audiometry, threshold is usually defined as the signal level at which the listener just detects (tones) or identifies (speech) 50 percent of the signals presented.

Audiometric thresholds are influenced by a number of variables, including the instructions to the subject, the positioning of the earphone (or other transducer) on the head, and the psychophysical threshold measurement technique used. In addition, clinical subjects show individual threshold variability that may be related to factors such as motivation, the nature of the ear problem, the patient's ability to comply with the test situation, and ongoing physiological changes inherent to the auditory system. These are just some of the problems encountered in hearing testing; they underscore the statistical and variable nature of threshold measurements. The goal in hearing testing is to control for those variables that can be eliminated or reduced (such as earphone placement and patient compliance) and to be aware of those uncontrollable variables that may influence test results.

Clinical audiometry includes two basic types of *relative* measurements. The measurements are relative because a given patient's responses are compared to the responses of a control group of subjects with normal auditory function. *Hearing sensitivity* measurements require a listener to judge whether a sound is present or absent (detection). For example, the minimum sound pressure level normal listeners require for audibility at each frequency (Chapter 3, Figure 3–17) is a measurement of hearing sensitivity. *Auditory discrimination* or *acuity* measurements are estimates of an individual's ability to perceptually segment or differentiate acoustic events. As we discuss shortly, tests of speech identification or speech intelligibility measure auditory discrimination skills.

Audiometers

A critical requisite for hearing testing is an acoustic system that enables control of the signals presented to the listener. In this section we discuss some of the common instruments used for hearing testing and describe how these units work.

An *audiometer* is an electronic instrument used to measure hearing. It allows the audiologist to present controlled acoustic signals to a listener in order to test auditory function. The aspect of control is concerned with the intensity, frequency or spectrum, and temporal characteristics of signals used to test some component of hearing.

Audiometers are of two broad types, dependent on the signal being generated: *pure-tone audiometers* and *speech audiometers*. Audiometers may also be subtyped by the range of frequencies and output levels available (wide-range versus limited-range audiometers) and by their physical size (console versus portable audiometers). Most audiometers used in diagnostic facilities are console units equipped to function both as a pure-tone audiometer and as a speech audiometer. Figure 12–1 shows examples of a portable and a console audiometer. More sophisticated audiometers may provide for automatic control of signal frequency, signal level, and the recording of test results. Some units even provide the capability of interfacing the audiometer with a digital computer for controlling various test parameters and for automated analysis of test results.

Certain control features are common to most audiometers:

FREQUENCY SELECTOR

This control enables the tester to select test signals from a set of fixed-frequency tones ranging usually from 125 to 8000 Hz in octave steps. Wide-range units may also provide some interval frequencies (for example, 750, 1500, and 3000 Hz).

INTERRUPTER SWITCH

A switching network is provided that enables the tester to turn the test signal on or off when desired. The switching circuit is designed to turn the signal on or off without audible clicks that may interfere with perception of the intended signal. Some units provide for automatic switching of signals according to prescribed temporal characteristics of the test signal.

HEARING LEVEL [HL] SELECTOR

The HL dial controls the intensity of the signal being presented to the listener. This control usually is graduated in steps of 5 dB (and sometimes smaller) and usually is adjustable over a range of at least 110 dB. The HL dial and the frequency selector are designed to operate synchronously with the *compensation network* of the audiometer. This network provides for the required sound pressure level (SPL) at each frequency that corresponds to audiometric zero. At a given HL setting, then, the absolute SPL output varies across frequency according to the normal threshold-of-audibility curve (see Figure 3–17 in Chapter 3). When the HL dial is set to 0-dB, for example, the absolute SPL will be 7.5 dB at 1000 Hz, but it will be 25.5 dB at 250 Hz. Both of these SPL values correspond to 0-dB HL for the respective frequencies. (More is said about audiometric zero in the section of this chapter entitled "The Audiogram.")

OUTPUT [MODE] SELECTOR

The output or mode selector on an audiometer enables the tester to route the test signal to various receivers used to present the acoustic signals to a listener. The *receiver* or *transducer* converts electrical signals to

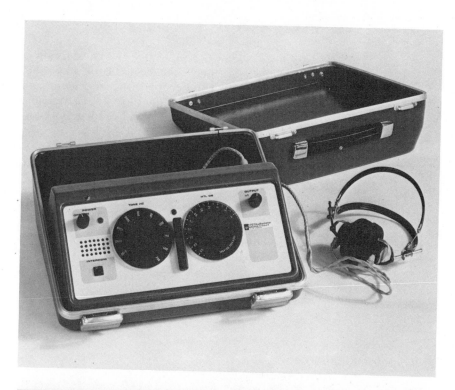

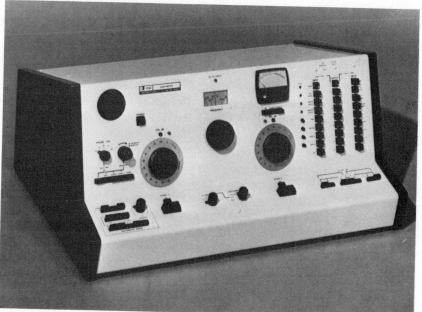

FIGURE 12–1. *A portable audiometer (above) and a console audiometer (below). The basic features of audiometers are described in the text. (Pictures courtesy of Grason-Stadler Company, Concord, Mass.)*

acoustic signals for test presentation. The two most common receivers available on commercial audiometers are a set of *earphones* and a *bone-conduction vibrator*. Earphones provide for airborne acoustic signals; a bone-conduction vibrator is used to transmit vibratory energy through the skull to the cochlea (from its application point on the mastoid portion of the temporal bone or on the forehead).

An alternative mode that is available on many audiometers is a *masking circuit*. This provides for routing a masking signal (usually a noise) to the nontest ear during audiometric testing. The masking circuit is provided with a variable attenuator used to adjust the level of the noise, and some audiometers offer a variety of masking noises. This type of circuit is necessary for bone-conduction audiometry and for cases of moderate-to-severe unilateral hearing loss where the test signal may be intense enough to be heard in the nontest ear. To rule out this possibility, a noise is introduced in the nontest ear. The noise elevates the threshold in that ear (masks it) and eliminates it from the test situation. This insures that subject responses are only for the test ear.

Audiometric Standards

To make valid and reliable comparisons of patients' auditory thresholds (or other measures) with normative data, it is necessary to establish standard procedures and conditions under which such measurements are obtained. In addition, before we can compare findings from one clinic with those of other clinics, we must insure that the measures were obtained under similar conditions. These types of audiometric requirements have led to the establishment of national standards for audiometers and for test conditions under which hearing tests are conducted. Such standards have been issued by the *American National Standards Institute* (ANSI), an independent agency formed to draft and maintain standards for many types of scientific measurements, including audiometry. ANSI provides standards for the type of signal to be used in audiometry, including specifications for output levels, earphone types, distortion limits, and other aspects of the signal that are critical to audiometry. Other standards specify such things as permissible background noise in the test room, acoustics terminology, preferred frequencies for acoustic measurements, and standards for bone-conduction measurements. ANSI standards are reviewed on a periodic basis to account for new research findings and to incorporate technological advances. It is essential that the audiologist be familiar with the appropriate standards and that all audiometric equipment be calibrated in accordance with the most recent ANSI specifications.

Audiometer Calibration

Audiometer *calibration* insures that an audiometer is producing the signal indicated by its settings. By means of calibration, the audiologist determines whether or not a test signal is actually at the desired level, at the desired frequency, in the correct transducer, and free of unwanted noise or distortion. This is what we meant earlier when we said that an audiometer allows the audiologist to present *controlled* acoustic signals. The audiometer standards mentioned earlier specify the procedures to be used. In addition to specified physical checks on the electrical and acoustical characteristics of the audiometer, there are a number of procedures that can be used to check the performance of the instrument that do not require electronic gear. For example, the output level of the audiometer across frequency should be checked indirectly by monitoring the audiologist's or tester's hearing levels on a daily basis. Other gross checks can be made by physical inspection of the unit and by listening to the output signal as it is varied in frequency, level, and output mode. The audiometer should be checked daily for any gross problems; a complete electroacoustic calibration should be conducted every two to three months depending on audiometer usage. The current calibration date should be indicated by some notation affixed to the audiometer. Anyone using an audiometer should adopt the view that it is out of calibration until proven otherwise.

The need for routine calibration of the audiometer cannot be overstated. An invalid audiogram due to lack of proper calibration can potentially have adverse consequences for both the patient and the audiologist. If the output of the audiometer is too high (intense), persons with a hearing loss might appear to have normal hearing. A substantial hearing problem could go untreated, with potentially severe consequences for the patient. By contrast, if the output of the audiometer is too low, persons with normal hearing will test out as having a hearing loss. This could lead to misdiagnosis. It could result in incorrect labeling and wholly inappropriate educational programming for the individual.

Pure-Tone Audiometry

Pure-tone audiometry has two primary diagnostic forms, *screening* and *threshold*. In screening audiometry, the audiometer is set at a *fixed* Hearing Level (usually 10–20 dB HL). Then, with the earphones in place on the listener, the tester sweeps across the available signal frequencies checking for a response to the air-conducted tones at each frequency setting. Screening audiometry is used for situations in which a large number of subjects need to be tested in a short period of time. The results of screening are used primarily to "pass" those subjects who present hearing sensitivity within normal limits. Those who fail the screening then receive a threshold test. Threshold audiometry is the determination of *detection* thresholds for each of several frequencies from 125 through 8000 Hz. Table 12–1 is a basic outline of procedures for pure-tone threshold audiometry. These procedures should be undertaken only by qualified personnel.

Table 12–1. GUIDELINES FOR THRESHOLD DETERMINATION IN MANUAL PURE-TONE AUDIOMETRY.

DETERMINATION OF THRESHOLD

The basic procedure for threshold determination consists of (1) familiarization with signal and (2) threshold measurement. The procedure is the same regardless of frequency, output transducer, or ear under test.

FAMILIARIZATION.   The listener should be familiarized with the task prior to threshold determination by presenting a signal of sufficient intensity to evoke a sharp and clear response. The step of familiarization assures the examiner that the listener understands and can perform the response task. The following two methods of familiarization are commonly used:

1. Beginning with the tone continuously on but completely attenuated, gradually increase the sound pressure level of the tone until a response occurs.
2. Present the tone at a Hearing Level of 30 dB. If a clear response occurs, begin threshold measurement. If no response occurs, present the tone at 50 dB HL and at successive additional increments of 10 dB until a response is obtained.

THRESHOLD MEASUREMENT.   The method described is recommended as a standard procedure for manual pure-tone threshold audiometry.

1. *Tone Duration.* Threshold exploration is carried out by presenting continuous tones of 1–2 sec in duration.
2. *Interval Between Tones.* The interval between tone presentations shall be varied but not shorter than the test tone.
3. *Level of First Presentation.* The level of the first presentation of tone for threshold measurement is 10 dB below the level of the listener's response to the familiarization presentation.
4. *Levels of Succeeding Presentations.* The tone level of succeeding presentations is determined by the preceding response. After each failure to respond to a signal, the level is increased in 5-dB steps until the first response occurs. After the response, the intensity is decreased 10 dB and another ascending series is begun.
5. *Threshold of Hearing.* Threshold is defined arbitrarily as the lowest level at which responses occur in at least half of a series of ascending trials with a minimum of three responses required at a single level.

Excerpted from Determination of Threshold from *Guidelines for Manual Pure-Tone Threshold Audiometry*, recommended by the American Speech and Hearing Association, *Asha*, 20, 297–301, 1978.

Bone-conduction audiometry is conducted like air-conduction audiometry as described in Table 12–1. In bone-conduction testing, however, a vibrator is used to transmit the signal through the bones of the skull to the cochlea. The vibrator is placed on the forehead or the mastoid portion of the temporal bone (behind the pinna) and thresholds are measured for the desired audiometric frequencies. Figure 12–2 shows a boy undergoing pure-tone air- and bone-conduction audiometry.

Persons with normal outer- and middle-ear systems will have similar thresholds for air- and bone-conducted signals. For persons with obstructions or diseases of the outer or middle ear, however, hearing sensitivity will be *better* by bone conduction because this mode of sound transmission essentially bypasses the affected structures. When a person's bone-conduction thresholds are better than his or her air-conduction thresholds, the difference between these thresholds at each test frequency is termed an *air-bone gap*. An air-bone gap is characteristic of conductive hearing loss, as we discuss later.

The Audiogram

The description of the Hearing Level selector on an audiometer (page 496) explains briefly how Hearing Level relates to the normal

 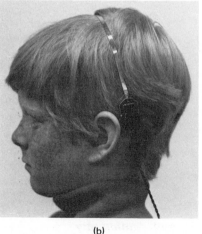

(a)   (b)

FIGURE 12–2. *A child undergoing audiometric testing. Panel (a) shows the headphones in position for air-conduction testing. Panel (b) shows mastoid placement of the vibrator for bone-conduction testing. During bone-conduction testing, an earphone would normally be placed over the ear opposite the vibrator for masking purposes.*

hearing sensitivity curve introduced in Chapter 3 (see Figure 3–17). At this point, it is important to expand that explanation. The standard plotting of the hearing sensitivity curve facilitates comparison of human hearing with other sounds, including the average intensity of speech (Davis, 1978a). Were we to consider the hearing sensitivities of those with hearing losses against the normal hearing sensitivity curve, we would have to deal conceptually with two inconveniences: (1) our normal reference is a curved line of nearly constantly changing slope and (2) less sensitive than normal hearing ("hearing loss") is plotted upward graphically—a counterintuitive convention for something that is getting "poorer." To handle these two inconveniences, another graphic representation of hearing sensitivity across frequency is used conventionally. This representation, called an *audiogram*, portrays the reference zero by a straight horizontal line near the top of the graph, while hearing loss (that is, sensitivity less than normal) is plotted downward. One way to think of what the calibration of the audiometer and the labeling of its intensity dial as "hearing loss" does for us graphically is that it takes our familiar hearing sensitivity curve in Figure 3–17, straightens it out, turns it over, and lets us conveniently see at a glance the extent to which each comparison subject deviates from normal. In this section, we will detail the exact format of the audiogram and typical symbols used to record audiometric data. A sample audiogram is shown as Figure 12–3. Hearing Level (dB) is plotted on the linear vertical axis and signal frequency (Hz) is indicated on the logarithmic horizontal axis. The format of the audiogram is such that one octave along the frequency axis corresponds in dimensional scale to 20 dB on the Hearing Level axis. It is customary to indicate the specific calibration standard used for Hearing Level designations. The ANSI-1969 designation in Figure 12–3, for example, means the Hearing Level calibration is in accord with the ANSI-1969 standard for audiometers. Recommended symbols for audiologists to use are also included. Pure-tone symbols on the audiogram may be color coded, with red indicating threshold measurements for the right ear and blue indicating results for the left ear. Notice in Figure 12–3 that separate symbols are used to note bone-conduction thresholds and measurements made with a masking noise in the nontest ear (masked thresholds). We will refer to these symbols and concepts of an audiogram again later.

Speech Audiometry

The results of pure-tone tests often are not sufficient to predict the perceptual or communication problems a person may experience in everyday listening situations. What is also important to quantify is how well a person understands speech. Although speech signals are more

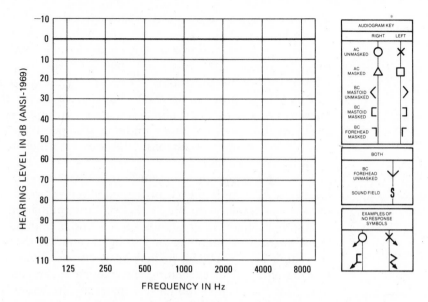

FIGURE 12-3. *Sample audiogram for recording audiometric test results. The key to the right of the audiogram contains the symbols recommended by the American Speech and Hearing Association (1974) for various tests. Right-ear results (thresholds) are usually coded in red and left-ear results in blue.*

difficult to control, audiologists have developed a number of procedures that use some form of speech as the test signal.

Two basic measurements are taken during routine speech audiometry: (1) the *lowest level* at which a subject can just identify speech; and (2) *how well* a person understands speech. The first measure, called the *Speech Reception Threshold* (SRT), uses familiar two-syllable words (such as baseball, railroad, etc.) as test signals. The test words are called *spondees* because they are spoken with equal stress on both syllables. The method for SRT measurements is similar to that used to obtain pure-tone thresholds. The words are presented to the listener and the intensity level of the words is varied up and down until a level is achieved where the listener identifies 50 percent of the words correctly. This 50 percent level is the SRT. The SRT is actually a test for the threshold of intelligibility because the test requires correct identification of words rather than a simple detection of the presence or absence of the speech signal. The latter task would constitute a *Speech Detection Threshold.*

Recall that the audiometric frequencies most critical for hearing and understanding speech range from approximately 250 to 4000 Hz. The audiometric frequency region from 500 to 2000 Hz is often termed the *speech range*, and the frequencies 500, 1000, and 2000 Hz are designated as the *speech frequencies*. Accordingly, for each ear, the SRT is found to be approximately equal to the lowest (best) thresholds for pure tones of 500, 1000, and 2000 Hz. This crosscheck on the validity of pure-tone thresholds is one of the clinical uses of the SRT. The major purpose of the SRT, however, is to set the baseline for measures of speech discrimination abilities. In other words, before we can assess how well a listener understands speech that is comfortably loud, it is necessary to establish the level at which he just begins to identify spoken material.

Speech discrimination measures are obtained to estimate how well a listener understands speech presented at a level well above the threshold of intelligibility (or SRT). Speech discrimination scores indicate how well a person understands speech under optimal listening conditions. Such information is used to determine the extent of a person's communication problem, in making decisions about the benefits of a hearing aid, and in evaluating the habilitation/rehabilitation needs of the individual. Conventional test materials are monosyllabic (one-syllable) word lists. The words in each list contain phonemes with approximately the same frequency of occurrence as exists in any long-term sample of everyday speech. Words are presented to the listener at a comfortable listening level (above the SRT); test results are expressed in terms of the percentage of words per list the subject identifies correctly. The word lists may be presented in one ear or the other using earphones, or they may be presented through loudspeakers in the test room. The latter procedure, called *sound-field* testing, is useful in testing persons (such as young children) who will not tolerate earphones. Sound-field testing is also used to evaluate speech-discrimination performance while the person wears a hearing aid.

TYPES OF HEARING LOSS

Having considered the basic ways that audiologists test hearing, we now are prepared to look at the many forms of hearing loss. Within each of the three major types of hearing loss—*conductive, sensorineural,* and *mixed*—we focus on three questions: What anatomical structures are affected? What audiometric findings are typically present? What effects do each type of loss have on everyday communication?

Conductive Hearing Loss

Conductive hearing losses are almost always due to abnormalities of the outer or middle ear. The term conductive is descriptive: It is an interruption or blockage of sound conduction to the cochlea that accounts for the hearing loss. Wax in the ear canal or interruptions in the ossicular chain (middle-ear bones) are examples of conditions that restrict the flow of sound energy from the outer ear and middle ear to the inner ear.

The primary audiometric sign of a conductive hearing loss is an air-bone gap. As discussed earlier, an air-bone gap is present when hearing sensitivity by bone conduction is significantly better than by air conduction. An air-bone gap can occur because the path of sound transmission for bone conduction is primarily through the bones of the skull directly to the inner ear. In bone-conduction audiometry, the pure-tone signals bypass the affected outer- and middle-ear structures. A sample audiogram showing conductive hearing loss is shown as Figure 12–4a. Note that although the air-conduction thresholds are depressed by 50–60 dB, bone-conduction thresholds are within normal limits (0–dB HL).

The primary effect of a conductive lesion is to reduce the level of the sound reaching the inner ear. The impairment is primarily a loss in hearing sensitivity, not in speech discrimination. If the blockage can be overcome, hearing will be basically normal. Or, if the sound level can be increased by using an amplification device, the person will again be able to hear and understand speech. Fortunately, the alternative of a hearing aid is often unneeded due to excellent medical and surgical procedures for conductive lesions. These procedures are discussed in Chapter 13.

Sensorineural Hearing Loss

Hearing loss resulting from damage or disease to any portion of the inner ear or neural auditory pathways is classified as *sensorineural*. Because the problem lies in the inner ear or neural pathways (or both), the hearing loss for air- and bone-conducted signals *will be similar.* An audiogram for a patient with a sensorineural hearing loss is shown as Figure 12–4b. Notice that the bone-conduction thresholds are the same as the air-conduction thresholds—there is *no* air-bone gap. The finding that bone-conduction thresholds are worse than normal and that there is no air-bone gap indicates a problem somewhere in the inner ear (cochlea), auditory nerve, and/or neural pathways.

In contrast to conductive hearing loss, sensorineural hearing loss does not involve only a loss in hearing sensitivity; typically, there is a reduced ability to discriminate speech. Thus, the person has trouble understanding speech at a normal level. Even when speech is made louder the person will still have some difficulty in understanding. The situation is analogous to the sound from an inexpensive radio. You

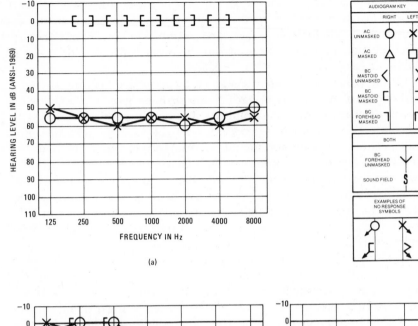

(a)

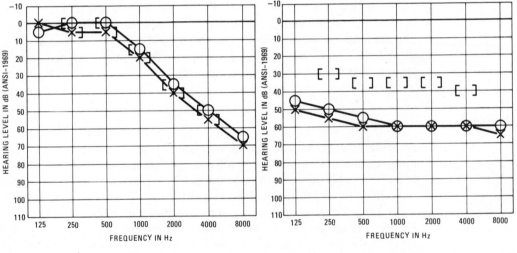

(b)

(c)

FIGURE 12–4. *Audiometric illustrations of three types of hearing loss.* (a) *Audiogram for a conductive hearing loss. This example shows a bilateral (both ears) conductive loss that is flat (approximately equal across test frequencies) in configuration. The conductive typing is indicated by normal bone-conduction thresholds in the presence of a significant hearing loss by air conduction. Bone-conduction thresholds are not presented for 125 and 8000 Hz; for technical and other reasons, commercial audiometers typically do not provide bone-conduction signals at these frequencies.* (b) *Audiogram for a high-frequency sensorineural hearing loss. The example is a bilateral loss. It is sensorineural in type because bone-conduction thresholds are equal to air-conduction thresholds at all frequencies.* (c) *Audiogram for a bilateral mixed hearing loss. A sensorineural loss is suggested by the depression (loss) in bone-conduction thresholds. The conductive component is indicated by the greater loss by air conduction than by bone conduction (air-bone gap).*

can turn the volume up, but it still sounds fuzzy. Because the distortion associated with sensorineural hearing loss is present regardless of how loud the speech is presented, the affected person will not always experience good success with a hearing aid or other amplification device. Available medical and surgical procedures offer little benefit to people with sensorineural hearing loss. Alternative educational and therapeutic approaches to the problems of sensorineural hearing loss are required.

A brief comment on the identification of high-frequency sensorineural hearing loss is appropriate here. In the past, attempts have been made to screen for hearing loss using informal test procedures such as listening for a watch tick, looking for a detection response to a low-frequency tuning fork, and listening to whispered speech. To the extent that such procedures are still in use, they present major weaknesses as tests of human hearing, particularly in the case of high-frequency hearing loss. The person with a high-frequency hearing loss and normal hearing for low frequencies can pass tests that require only detection of a watch tick, a low-frequency tuning fork, or speech because these signals contain adequate low-frequency energy. The primary energy of speech, for example, is contained in the vowels, the energy of which is mainly in the lower frequencies. Thus, we underscore the need for proper audiological understanding whenever hearing is to be tested, even at the screening stage.

Mixed Hearing Loss

A *mixed* hearing loss is a combination of both conductive and sensorineural losses. Figure 12–4c is a sample audiogram for a mixed hearing loss in both ears. Note that air-conduction thresholds are poorer than normal, averaging about 60 dB, and bone-conduction thresholds are also depressed, averaging 35 dB. There is an average air-bone gap of approximately 25 dB suggestive of some conductive hearing loss. In addition, there is a loss by bone conduction, indicating some abnormality of the inner ear and/or auditory nerve. We may think of the air-conduction thresholds as reflecting the total transmission loss occuring at locations anywhere between the outer and inner ear, and the loss in bone conduction as reflecting the disorder located at the inner ear or auditory nerve. In our example, the total 60-dB loss is made up of a 35-dB sensorineural loss and a 25-dB conductive loss.

In addition to testing for conductive and sensorineural loss, then, the audiologist knows that both sensorineural and conductive lesions can exist simultaneously in the same patient. A child with a significant sensorineural hearing loss, for example, can still experience an ear infection or other ear disease that may result in a conductive component (overlay) in addition to the sensorineural loss. By contrast, a person with a substantial conductive loss may also present reduced bone-conduction sensitivity indicating sensorineural involvement.

Classification of Hearing Loss

In addition to knowing whether a person's hearing loss is conductive, sensorineural, or mixed, we also want to know the degree of the hearing loss. Because we are mainly interested in a person's ability to hear everyday speech, the customary procedure for classifying degree of loss involves a computation of the *pure-tone average* (PTA). A person's PTA is his or her average pure-tone thresholds for the speech frequencies: 500, 1000, and 2000 Hz. Table 12–2 indicates various degree classifications based on average pure-tone thresholds in the better ear for these frequencies. For an idea of the prevalence of the five degrees of hearing loss listed, approximately 1.9 percent of the population of the United States will present bilateral hearing losses ranging from *slight* to *extreme* (Schein and Delk, 1974; Davis, 1978b). If the population of the United States is estimated at 220 million, this means that there are more adults in the United States alone with significant hearing loss than the combined populations of Colorado, Nebraska, Nevada, and Utah!

As indicated in the rightmost column of Table 12–2, the ability

Table 12–2. DEGREE CLASSIFICATIONS OF HEARING LOSS (HANDICAP).

AVERAGE HEARING LEVEL (ANSI-1969) FOR 500, 1000, AND 2000 Hz IN THE BETTER EAR	HANDICAP CLASSI- FICATION	ABILITY TO UNDERSTAND SPEECH
< 25 dB	Not significant	No significant difficulty with faint speech
26–40 dB	Slight	Difficulty only with faint speech
41–55 dB	Mild	Frequent difficulty with normal speech
56–70 dB	Marked	Frequent difficulty with loud speech
71–90 dB	Severe	Can understand only shouted or amplified speech
> 90 dB	Extreme	Usually cannot understand even amplified speech

Adapted from H. Davis, Hearing handicap, standards for hearing, and medicolegal rules. In H. Davis and S. Silverman, Eds., *Hearing and Deafness*, 4th Ed. New York: Holt, Rinehart and Winston, 1978b.

to hear and understand speech decreases with increased hearing loss. The validity of this generalization is dependent on a number of factors, however, including the age of the person at the onset of the hearing loss, the type of hearing loss, the type of lesion producing the problem, the configuration of hearing loss across frequencies, and the amount of hearing loss in each ear. In other words, it is difficult to describe the communication problems of a hearing-impaired person with a single number. *Hearing loss and hearing handicap simply do not mean the same thing.* Two people having hearing losses that fall in the same degree category may demonstrate widely different abilities to communicate in everyday life. The classification of hearing loss by degree, then, is useful for keeping statistical records. The terms "mild," "marked," and so forth are classifications that may not be valuable for medical diagnoses, however, or for educational and habilitation/rehabilitation purposes.

CAUSES OF HEARING LOSS

To maintain consistency with the discussion of normal hearing processes in Chapter 3, we consider the various causes for hearing loss according to the anatomical location of specific lesions or disorders. Consistent with the scope of this text, only the more common disorders are considered under each subheading.

Outer Ear

Any condition that results in a mechanical blockage of the ear canal may interfere with sound transmission—the end result could be a conductive hearing loss. The most common of such problems in the ear canal is the accumulation of *cerumen* (earwax). Wax may build up and eventually block the flow of sound to the eardrum. Other possibilities include tumors growing in the ear canal or foreign bodies that have become lodged in the ear canal. A wide variety of items have been removed from people's ear canals including rocks, beans, and safety pins! A point to underscore here is that removal of such objects trapped in the ear canal should be attempted only by trained medical personnel.

A congenital (present at birth) condition of the outer ear that may result in hearing loss is *atresia*. Atresia is a condition in which a baby is born without an ear canal and in which the pinna may be malformed, reduced in size (*microtia*), or absent (*anotia*). When the external canal is missing, leaving no direct path for the flow of sound to the eardrum, the infant will experience a mild to moderate conductive hearing loss in that ear. Children with congenital atresia are pictured in Figure 12–5. Abnormalities of the pinna alone cause little problem in hearing, but they may present a cosmetic problem for the child. In these cases, a plastic surgeon can construct a new pinna. In some cases, it may be necessary to surgically construct a canal, a tympanic membrane, and a middle ear.

In some forms, *external otitis* may lead to a hearing problem. External otitis is a general term for inflammation or infection of the outer ear (pinna and ear canal). Such conditions are more common in warm climates where fungi cause a large portion of the infections. External otitis also may result from irritation or scratching of the ear canal. This can occur as the result of various childhood accidents or as a result of attempts to clean out the ear canal with a hair pin or other sharp object. The mucous lining along the ear canal is extremely delicate. We should heed the advice that otolaryngologists give in the ear clinic — "don't put anything in your ear smaller than your elbow."

External otitis also can occur when contaminated water gets in the ear canal. The condition is often called *swimmer's ear* because it often is initiated from swimming in polluted water. The infection of ex-

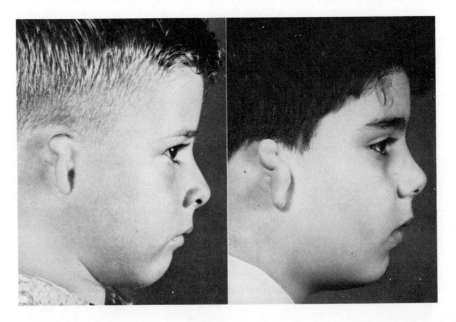

FIGURE 12–5. *Photographs of two children with congenital atresia and microtia of the outer ear. (From J. Longacre,* Craniofacial Anomalies: Pathogenesis and Repair. *Philadelphia: Lippincott, 1968.)*

ternal otitis may be accompanied (in advanced forms) with discharge from the ear canal and inflammation of the eardrum. If the ear canal swells shut or is blocked by accumulated scales of skin, a mild conductive hearing loss may result. Usually, however, the major problem with external otitis is the infection or inflammation and associated discomfort rather than hearing loss. One of the most prominent symptoms of external otitis is when a person feels pain as the external ear is manipulated.

Finally, a condition that may result in an apparent conductive hearing loss is a *collapsing ear canal.* In some patients the ear canal may be quite *flaccid* (floppy) and *stenotic* (narrow). When an earphone is placed over the ear, the canal may close due to the weight of the earphone and cushion. This, in turn, will result in what appears to be a slight to mild hearing loss, usually for high-frequency signals (Chaiklin and McClellan, 1971). The audiologist must be on the alert for such cases. If a collapsing canal is suspect, a piece of plastic tubing can be inserted into the ear canal to maintain an opening for hearing testing.

Middle Ear

The most common disorder of the middle ear that may result in hearing loss is *otitis media.* Otitis media denotes inflammation and/or infection of the middle ear. It is quite common in early childhood and often accompanies upper respiratory infections. Most of us have, at one time or another, experienced *otalgia* (an earache) associated with otitis media.

Otitis media often begins with a head cold, but also may occur as a complication of other childhood diseases such as influenza, scarlet fever, measles, and allergies. The accompanying nasal secretions may infect the Eustachian tube causing it to become inflamed and to swell shut. A similar situation can occur with enlarged tonsils and adenoids; they can push against the tube and eventually cause it to close. When the tube is closed, for any length of time, a subatmospheric pressure develops in the middle ear. This causes retraction of the tympanic membrane (it is forced inward), and is often accompanied by an accumulation of secreted liquid within the middle-ear cavity. The subatmospheric pressure and accumulated liquid restricts the free movement of the ossicular chain, resulting in conductive hearing loss.

Several classifications of otitis media are recognized, depending on the stage of the disease process and the nature of the liquid accumulated in the middle-ear space. In early stages of the disease, there may be little or no hearing loss and the primary symptom may be an inflamed tympanic membrane. The eardrum may be red in color as it is observed through an *otoscope,* an instrument equipped with a light source used to visually examine the ear canal and eardrum. The disease may progress to *serous otitis media* in which a thin, watery liquid accumulates in the middle-ear cavity. Under otoscopic examination, the liquid level can often be seen. If left untreated, the liquid may thicken into a viscous, puslike substance and become infected; this latter stage is termed *suppurative otitis media.* Both serous and suppurative otitis media may be accompanied by inflammation of the tympanic membrane. In the case of suppurative otitis media the liquid may become so thick that it distends the eardrum out of the middle-ear space and the patient may experience appreciable pain. Eventually, the drum may break and the liquid may discharge into the ear canal. In general, the more advanced the disease stage, the thicker the liquid becomes, and consequently, the greater the hearing loss.

A disease that may occur as a complication of otitis media and marginal perforation of the tympanic membrane is *cholesteatoma,* or more properly, *keratoma* (Schuknecht, 1974). This is a cyst within the middle ear. The cyst is created by epithelium (skin) that has grown from the ear canal, through the perforation in the eardrum to form a sac in the middle-ear cavity. Usually, the cyst is located in the region of the pars flaccida of the tympanic membrane. As the epithelium continues to regenerate, the sac becomes larger and larger. A patient with a cholesteatoma often reports a foul-smelling discharge from the ear—the discharge of degenerative substance from the sac. The disease requires immediate attention. With early detection, there may be little or no hearing loss. If left untreated, the cholesteatoma may cause bone erosion leading to destruction of the ossicles. This, of course, would lead to a mild to marked conductive hearing loss. Eventually, erosion can extend into areas adjacent to the temporal bone resulting in intracranial complications.

Otosclerosis is a progressive disease that often causes conductive hearing loss. It is a hereditary disease of the bony capsule surrounding the inner ear. In the early stage of otosclerosis, new spongy bone begins to grow around the footplate of the stapes where it attaches to the oval window. The new bone eventually hardens and may fix the stapes rigidly in the oval window. Fixation interferes with the movement of the stapes in and out of the oval window during sound transmission. The result is a loss in energy transfer of ossicular vibrations to the cochlea and this, in turn, results in conductive hearing loss.

Otosclerosis probably begins at or shortly after birth, but may not manifest itself in hearing loss until adolescence or early adulthood. The disease typically involves both ears, but it can occur unilaterally in some cases. In early stages of the disease, the hearing loss usually will be conductive and will affect only the lower frequencies. As the disease progresses, however, hearing sensitivity will be reduced for higher frequencies. With complete stapes fixation, hearing loss may be as much as 50–60 dB for all audiometric frequencies. At this point, bone conduction sensitivity also is often reduced, particularly in the region of 2000 Hz. This depression of bone-conduction thresholds near 2000 Hz is called *Carhart's notch,* a characteristic audiometric finding in people with otosclerosis. Audiometric findings for a patient with surgically confirmed otosclerosis are shown in Figure 12–6a.

Other disorders of the middle ear that may cause hearing loss include congenital anomalies, tumors, and ossicular discontinuities. Congenital atresia, for example, discussed earlier in relation to the external ear, may often be associated with malformations of the ossicles as well as anomalies of the pinna and ear canal. Other congenital problems may involve malformations of one or more of the ossicles or stapedial fixation. Although tumors of the middle ear are rare, such a condition, when present, may also interfere with the free movement of the ossicles, resulting in hearing loss. Any condition resulting in a disruption or separation of the ossicles will cause a substantial conductive hearing loss. If the ossicles are completely separated, the loss may be as great as 60–70 dB. Although ossicular discontinuities may be present at birth or be associated with middle-ear disease, their most prevalent cause is head trauma (blow to the head). An audiogram for a patient with an ossicular disruption is shown as Figure 12–6b.

Inner Ear

Presbycusis. *Presbycusis,* hearing loss associated with advancing age, is the most common hearing disorder. Although aging may affect all portions of the auditory system, the major effects occur within cochlear structures. The effects of aging on the auditory system probably begin at adolescence, but it is later in life when the progressive hearing loss becomes significant enough to interfere with communication. The hearing loss typical of presbycusis is a bilateral, high-frequency hearing loss. As age increases, the hearing loss actually involves both high and low frequencies, but it is considerably greater for the high-frequency region. Hearing-loss contours as a function of age for men and women are shown in Figure 12–7. The individual contours show the progression of loss for several test frequencies.

Because presbycusic individuals retain some residual hearing for low- and mid-frequency sounds, they usually can hear another person talking and also can understand a good portion of what is being said. However, because the high-frequency loss affects consonant in-

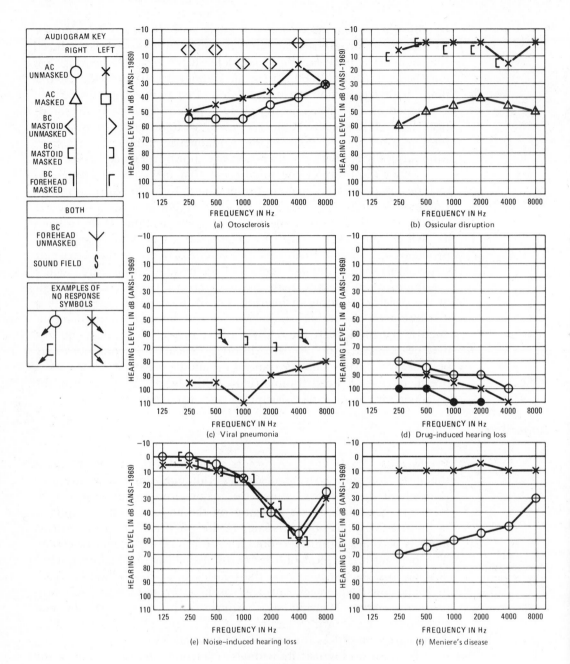

FIGURE 12–6.

FIGURE 12–6. *Sample audiograms for hearing losses resulting from six different causes. Corresponding panels on the facing page present comments pertinent to each audiogram.*

(a) Otosclerosis

Pre-operative audiogram for a 19-year-old man with surgically confirmed otosclerosis. Note that the air-conduction audiogram tilts upward. That is, hearing loss is greater at lower frequencies and gradually lessens with higher frequencies. There is a sizeable air-bone gap, particularly at 250 and 500 Hz, consistent with a conductive hearing loss. "Carhart's notch," typical of otosclerosis, is indicated by the depression in bone-conduction thresholds at 2000 Hz.

(b) Ossicular disruption

Pre-operative audiogram for a 24-year-old man with a surgically confirmed disruption of the ossicular chain in the right ear. Hearing sensitivity is normal in the left ear and the presence of a conductive hearing loss in the right ear is consistent with ossicular disorders. The ossicular disruption was caused by a fracture of both crura (legs) of the stapes.

(c) Viral pneumonia

Audiogram (left ear only) for a man who experienced a severe hearing loss in his left ear during hospitalization for viral pneumonia. The loss reflects cochlear damage due to the viral infection. (After H. Schuknecht, Pathology of the sensorineural system. In D. Tower, Ed., The Nervous System, Vol III: Human Communication and Its Disorders. *New York: Raven Press, 1975.)*

(d) Drug-induced hearing loss

Progressive effects of kanamycin on hearing in a middle-aged woman with chronic renal failure, undergoing dialysis and awaiting transplant surgery. Following treatment with kanamycin on several occasions, she developed sudden severe bilateral sensorineural hearing loss. The loss at sudden onset is indicated by the conventional audiogram symbols (O: right ear, X: left ear). Bone-conduction thresholds are not shown. Despite immediate withdrawal of kanamycin and emergency dialysis, the hearing loss worsened. After one month, the hearing loss in both ears progressed to the levels indicated by the filled circles. The loss was total in both ears after two months. (Adapted from A. Morrison, Ed., Management of Sensorineural Deafness. *Boston: The Butterworth Group, 1975.)*

(e) Noise-induced hearing loss

Audiogram depicting a noise-induced hearing loss. Note the characteristic "notch" in the region of 4000 Hz.

(f) Meniere's disease

Audiogram for a 32-year-old man with a six month history of right-ear Meniere's disease. Bone-conduction thresholds are not shown. (Adapted from A. Morrison, Ed., Management of Sensorineural Deafness. *Boston: The Butterworth Group, 1975.)*

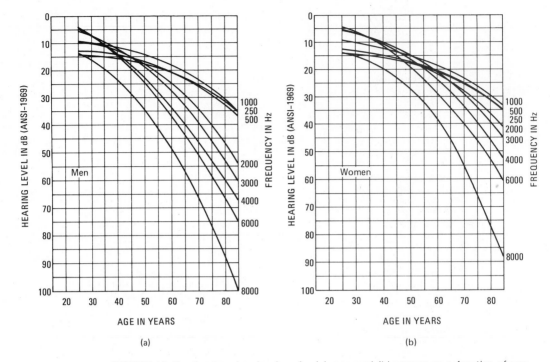

FIGURE 12–7. *Average hearing loss for (a) men and (b) women as a function of age. The greater loss for men is thought to reflect more frequent exposure to industrial and other types of noise. Data are based on the composite curves by Spoor (1967) modified to conform to ANSI-1969 standards. (Adapted from C. Lebo and R. Reddell, The presbycusis component in occupational hearing loss. Laryngoscope, 82, 1399–1409, 1972.)*

telligibility, the person may not hear or may misinterpret words that are critical for understanding the entire message. Misunderstanding may lead to a response that is inappropriate. Even casual communication can be frustrating, not only for the person with the hearing loss, but also for the person attempting to communicate with that individual. The development of rehabilitation options for persons with presbycusis is particularly challenging.

Hereditary and Congenital Factors. Hereditary hearing losses appear in many different forms. Depending on the genetic factors involved, the hearing loss may be conductive or sensorineural and may affect low, middle or high frequencies. Like otosclerosis, not all hereditary disorders affect hearing early in life. The actual age of onset for hearing loss may vary from birth to adulthood depending on the syndrome or disease. The hearing loss is usually one of several abnoralities resulting from the genetic structure of the parents. Effects on the auditory system (in the case of sensorineural hearing loss) are seen as a lack of proper development of the cochlea or as a progressive deterioration of the sensory structures. Both a parent and the child may present hearing loss, or the child may present a hearing loss with no familial history of deafness or hearing loss.

Congenital factors are the most frequent cause for sensorineural hearing loss in children. Congenital disorders of the auditory system may or may not occur as a result of hereditary factors. Congenital problems may involve disorders in embryological development, toxicity or trauma during pregnancy, and/or toxicity or trauma during delivery. Dependent on the structures affected, the resultant hearing loss will be conductive or sensorineural. Examples of congenital problems that may cause hearing loss include: prolonged anoxia (lack of oxygen) in the newborn infant; Rh incompatibility of the parents; toxemia during pregnancy, and intracranial hemorrhage in the newborn. The latter problem is of particular risk-significance in premature babies.

A brief note on the significance of age of onset of hearing loss is appropriate here. It is customary to differentiate hearing losses present at birth (*congenital*) from hearing losses acquired later in life (*adventitious* or *acquired*). As might be expected, the consequences of congenital hearing loss are typically more severe than those associated with adventitious hearing loss. If the child has already acquired speech and language skills before the onset of hearing loss, the effects on communication, although substantial, are less dramatic than in the child with a congenital hearing loss, who is forced to learn speech and language patterns through a distorted system.

Infections. Bacterial infections and viral infections can damage or completely destroy inner-ear structures, resulting in sensorineural hearing loss. Infections may invade the cochlea via the bloodstream and eventually damage fine structures within the inner ear. Maternal *rubella* (German measles), for example, is a major cause of severe to extreme congenital hearing loss. In this disease, a virus passed from the mother to the unborn infant results in cochlear damage in the embryo. Other infectious diseases of childhood that may cause hearing loss or deafness are mumps, meningitis, scarlet fever, and diphtheria. In some cases, the onset of hearing loss due to infection is subtle. In others, the onset is dramatically sudden. For example, Figure 12–6c is an audiogram for a man who suffered a severe unilateral hearing loss during a bout of viral pneumonia. Such case examples point to the need to watch for any signs of hearing loss in persons with infectious diseases. Fortunately, the incidence of many of these problems, particularly as they affect children, has been reduced through immunization and proper medical follow-up.

Drugs. Many prescription and over-the-counter drugs have potentially damaging effects on the inner ear. A brief list includes streptomycin, dihydrostreptomycin, neomycin, kanamycin, quinine, arsenic, lead and common aspirin (when used in large dosages). In addition to hearing loss or deafness, taking certain drugs may cause side effects such as *tinnitus* (ringing or noises in the ear) and dizziness. The potential effects of a drug on hearing will vary with the drug dosage and with the individual. Importantly, the harmful effects of a drug on hearing may not be manifested until well after the drug has been discontinued. Figure 12-6d is an example audiogram that illustrates the immediate and progressive effects on hearing of one drug, kanamycin.

Noise-Induced Hearing Loss. Exposure to sounds of sufficient intensity and duration can result in damage to portions of the auditory system and may cause hearing loss. Many types of industrial and farm equipment and intense rock music are examples of environmental noises that may be harmful to the auditory system. For short-duration noise exposures, the effects of the noise may be only temporary. Perhaps you have experienced temporary hearing loss after a rock concert, after mowing the lawn with a noisy power lawnmower, or after riding a motorcycle or a snowmobile. Repeated exposure to intense noise (as in certain industrial settings), however, may result in a permanent hearing loss. Hearing loss caused by repeated noise exposure is termed *noise-induced hearing loss.* If the hearing loss results from a single exposure to intense noise, which is less common, it is classified as *acoustic trauma.* Intense, impulsive noises such as gunfire and explosions, for example, can be extremely hazardous.

The auditory structures that are primarily affected by noise exposure are within the cochlea. Specifically, it is usually the hair cells and their supporting structures that are damaged or destroyed. The result is a permanent sensorineural hearing loss. The region of greatest hearing loss will be slightly higher in frequency than that of the noise causing the hearing loss or will occur in the region of 4000 Hz. The latter condition, often called a *4000-Hz notch,* is typical of patients with noise-induced hearing loss. A sample audiogram is given in Figure 12–6e. With repeated exposure, losses such as illustrated in Figure 12–6e will become worse, involving more of the high frequencies. The progression of hearing loss associated with continued exposure to high-intensity industrial noise is shown in Figure 12–8. Note that with continued noise exposure the hearing loss increases and spreads into the speech frequencies. People who must be exposed to excessive noise should at least consider wearing ear protectors such as earplugs or ear muffs.

Meniere's Disease. Meniere's disease (*endolymphatic hydrops*), the last inner-ear condition we discuss, is typically characterized by sudden onset of a unilateral hearing loss. The person experiences a feeling of fullness or stuffiness in the ear, and may have attacks of tinnitis, ver-

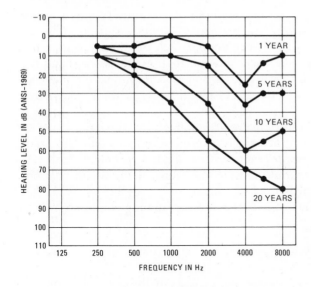

FIGURE 12–8. *Typical progression in hearing loss in relation to years of exposure to high intensity industrial noise. Both ears would be affected similarly. (Hayes A. Newby,* Audiology, *3rd Ed., © 1972, p. 251. Reprinted by permission of Prentice-Hall, Inc., Englewood Cliffs, N.J.)*

tigo (a whirling sensation), nausea, and perhaps, vomiting. The exact cause of Meniere's disease is unknown but it is thought to be a result of excessive liquid pressure within the cochlear duct.

As illustrated in Figure 12–6f, the sensorineural hearing loss associated with Meniere's disease usually is unilateral. The loss generally is flat across audiometric frequencies, but may be slightly worse for lower frequencies. The patient's ability to discriminate speech in the affected ear is usually poor. The hearing loss often fluctuates and may worsen during recurrent episodes of the disease. Because the person has one good ear, everyday communication is not affected to any major extent. Meniere's disease may still be quite handicapping, however, due to the severe and often sudden attacks of vertigo. Such episodes may interfere with many everyday activities, such as driving an automobile. A friend of the author who suffered from Meniere's disease experienced vertigo in two- or three-day episodes during attacks of the disease. During this time he could not work and was virtually bedridden.

Lesions of the Auditory Nerve

Disorders of the auditory nerve (cranial nerve VIII) are less common than disorders of the outer, middle, and inner ears. One type of disorder, *acoustic neuroma,* warrants discussion. An acoustic neuroma is a growth or tumor (neoplasm) on the trunk of the auditory nerve. The tumor imposes pressure on the fibers of the nerve trunk causing abnormal auditory function.

The characteristic auditory symptom of an auditory nerve tumor is a unilateral sensorineural hearing loss of unknown origin. The affected patient often will have very poor speech discrimination, or will demonstrate poorer speech discrimination than might be expected for the specific amount of hearing loss. Speech discrimination may become so poor that the patient cannot identify any of the speech items under test.

Tumors of the auditory nerve are unilateral in the large majority of cases, hence they do not usually present a major communication problem. The lesion does present a major medical problem, however, and suspected patients should receive immediate medical consultation. Because of the close proximity of the tumor to the brain, continued growth of the lesion may constitute a life-threatening condition.

Lesions of the Central Auditory Nervous System

The central auditory nervous system consists of the auditory pathways from the cochlear nucleus to the auditory cortex (see Chapter 3, Figure 3–16). These structures are to be differentiated from the peripheral auditory system—the outer, middle, and inner ear structures up to the entrance to the cochlear nuclei of the auditory pathways. Although a complete discussion of lesions and diseases of the central auditory pathway is beyond our scope, a few concepts should be mentioned.

Lesions of the peripheral structures and the auditory nerve usually result in a loss of hearing sensitivity. They often can be identified with special tests of auditory function. Disorders of the central auditory nervous system, however, are much more difficult to diagnose. Usually there is no loss in hearing sensitivity. In addition, unlike peripheral disorders, a lesion of the central auditory nervous system may show itself in abnormal auditory function on the side (ear) opposite to the site of the disorder. If the person has a lesion of the right side of the brain, for example, auditory function may remain intact if sound is channeled through the right ear, but will be abnormal in the left ear.

The audiometric procedures that have been developed for diagnosis of central auditory disorders are quite varied. These procedures typically involve some degradation of the signal such as filtering (passing only certain frequencies of the signal) or presenting the signal in the presence of a competing message or noise. Other techniques involve *dichotic* (both ears) presentation of different speech samples or signals; comparisons of discrimination scores are made for the two ears. In the Staggered Spondaic Word (SSW) Test (see Brunt, 1972), for example, two different two-syllable words are presented so that they overlap across ears. Whereas normal listeners will identify correctly both words, people with central auditory problems have difficulty interpreting speech when it is mixed across the two ears. At the present time, the effects of various lesions at different locations within the central auditory nervous system are not completely understood.

SPECIAL AUDITORY TESTS

An introductory chapter on hearing measurement would be incomplete without some discussion of the array of special auditory tests currently available to the audiologist. By special we do not mean that the test procedures to be described are administered only rarely. Rather, *special* here refers to specificity of purpose within an audiologic test battery. For example, some lesions within the auditory system manifest themselves in auditory dysfunctions other than a loss in hearing sensitivity. Special audiologic procedures have been devised that are useful not only in predicting the specific site of these lesions but also in describing the overall auditory behavior characteristic of the particular hearing disorder (see Jerger, 1963; Rose, 1971; Katz, 1972; Jerger, 1973; Katz, 1978; Rose, 1978). There also are special behavioral-audiometric techniques for testing infants, mentally retarded children, children and adults with neuromotor problems, and other hard-to-test patients (Fulton and Lloyd, 1969, 1975). Other special tests are used to determine if a person is malingering (feigning a hearing loss). From these many clinical procedures we have selected three for brief description; acoustic-impedance measurements, tests of abnormal loudness function, and electrophysiological procedures.

Acoustic-Impedance Measurements

Acoustic-impedance measurements have gained increased use in a variety of health care settings. Before describing the various types of acoustic-impedance measurements, some comments on their value as a clinical tool are important to consider.

First, it should be understood that a person with normal thresholds for pure tones may *not* have normal, healthy ears. You may recall from our earlier discussion that in early stages of otitis media, for example, there may be little or no hearing loss. Indeed, active ear disease may be present in a large percentage of children who have normal hearing (Eagles, 1972). Here is where acoustic-impedance techniques are particularly valuable: middle-ear disease is often reflected in abnormal acoustic-impedance measurements. Second, acoustic-impedance procedures do not require a behavioral response from the person under test. For an uncooperative or hyperactive patient, measurements can be obtained with the person under mild sedation or even while asleep. In the following discussion we have summarized only a few of the major procedures for acoustic impedance testing, with emphasis on clinical applications. Testing is discussed under two categories, *static* and *dynamic* measures.

Static Acoustic-Impedance Measurements. The term acoustic impedance refers to the total opposition encountered by an acoustic wave. Clinically, measurements of acoustic impedance estimate the opposition encountered at the lateral (outer) surface of the tympanic membrane. Figure 12–9 illustrates a child undergoing acoustic-impedance testing and summarizes the measurement procedure.

Static acoustic-impedance measurements are those taken with the middle-ear muscles relaxed (not contracted) and with air pressure in the ear canal at an ambient (atmospheric) condition. Static measures are best expressed in absolute physical units (such as acoustic ohms) because measurements are compared across subject groups with various pathologies. Two broad categories of middle-ear lesions have static acoustic impedance values that differ from normal values. Lesions that result in a stiffening or damping of the ossicular chain present acoustic-impedance measurements that are *higher* than normal. Such lesions prevent free movement of the ossicles and provide greater than normal opposition to sound transmission. Examples of lesions that stiffen the ossicular chain are serous otitis media and otosclerosis. Disruptions to some portion of the ossicular chain, in contrast, result in static acoustic-impedance measures that are *lower* than normal. With lower values, we are dealing with a loose middle-ear transmission system in which there is little opposition to incoming

FIGURE 12–9. *Illustration of a child undergoing acoustic-impedance testing. Acoustic-impedance measurements (static measures, tympanometry, and others) are made in the ear containing the probe unit. The probe unit has three openings connected to soft plastic tubes. One tube leads to an air pump used for introducing air pressure changes in tympanometry. A second tube is connected to a sound source that enables the audiologist to present a tone into the sealed ear canal. The third tube is connected to a microphone that monitors the sound pressure level of the probe tone. The acoustic impedance at the eardrum is proportional to the level of the probe tone in the canal. Accordingly, indirect estimates of acoustic impedance can be made by monitoring the sound pressure level of the probe tone.*

sound. For an idea of the relative values of static measurements for various lesions, persons with normal middle-ear function have values of 1000 to 2000 acoustic ohms. Static acoustic impedance for persons with serous otitis media, however, may be as high as 10,000 acoustic ohms. Patients with ossicular disruptions may present static values as low as 200 to 600 acoustic ohms.

Dynamic Acoustic-Impedance Measurements. *Dynamic* acoustic-impedance measurements are estimates of the acoustic impedance at the tympanic membrane made under conditions that are known to change the transmission characteristics of a normal middle-ear system. That is, they involve doing something that alters the normal state of the middle ear and observing the associated effects on acoustic-impedance values. We know that in a normal auditory system, the acoustic impedance at the eardrum changes when the air pressure in the external ear canal is increased or decreased relative to ambient pressure and when the middle-ear muscles contract. Of the many dynamic measurements of acoustic impedance, we will limit our discussion to two major types, *tympanometry* and *acoustic-reflex* measurements.

Tympanometry is the measurement of acoustic impedance at the tympanic membrane as the air pressure in the external ear canal is varied both above (positive) and below (negative) ambient or atmospheric pressure. Recall that for static acoustic-impedance measurements, the air pressure in the ear canal was set at ambient. Tympanometry, however, evaluates the influence of air-pressure *changes* in the ear canal on the opposition to the flow of sound at the eardrum. For a normal middle ear, the acoustic impedance at the eardrum will increase if the air pressure in the ear canal is made higher or lower than ambient pressure. The air-pressure changes have a stiffening effect on the normal middle-ear system; this effect is reflected in greater acoustic impedance. In various diseases or abnormalities of the middle ear, however, the effect may be altered. In serous otitis media, for example, the middle-ear transmission system may already be stiffened due to the damping effect of the liquid in the middle-ear cavity. Accordingly, air-pressure changes will have little effect on acoustic-impedance measurements.

Tympanometry is also useful in the assessment of Eustachian tube function. By finding the pressure setting at which acoustic impedance is minimal, we can determine the resting pressure in the middle-ear cavity. A high negative (subatmospheric) resting pressure in the middle ear indicates an obstructed Eustachian tube. This type of procedure is particularly useful in picking up middle-ear disease in early stages when there may be no obvious otoscopic signs. Eustachian-tube obstruction is often a precurser of otitis media. In addition to the pathologies discussed, specific types of tympanometric patterns have been found in other middle-ear lesions, such as ossicular discontinuities, otosclerosis, and eardrum abnormalities. Figure 12–10 is a presentation of tympanometric curves associated with normal ears and with selected middle-ear problems. The test equipment automatically prints out these curves, called *tympanograms.*

Acoustic-reflex measurements, the second type of dynamic acoustic-impedance measure, have considerable potential in middle-ear testing. If an acoustic signal of sufficient intensity and duration is presented to a normal ear, the *stapedius* muscle (see Chapter 3) will

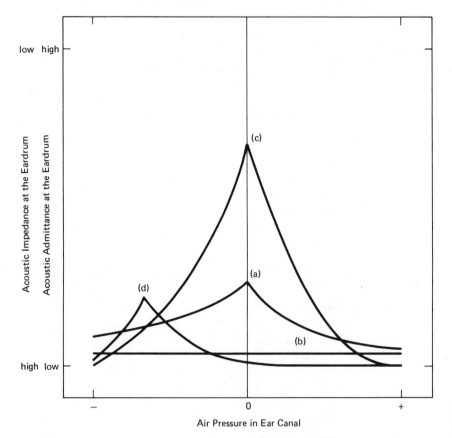

FIGURE 12–10. *Tympanograms for several middle-ear conditions. Two variables are represented on the vertical axis, acoustic admittance and acoustic impedance. Acoustic admittance is the reciprocal of acoustic impedance; as acoustic impedance goes up, acoustic admittance goes down and vice versa. Tympanogram (a) is for a normal ear. Note that acoustic impedance increases with positive or negative pressure in the ear canal. Tympanogram (b) is typical of a liquid-filled middle ear (serous otitis media). Here, there is little or no change in acoustic impedance with changes in air pressure because the eardrum is already stiffened due to the presence of middle-ear liquid. Ossicular disruption is typified by tympanogram (c). Note the abnormally large changes in acoustic impedance with air-pressure changes, indicating a hypermobile middle-ear system. Tympanogram (d) is associated with an obstructed Eustachian tube. Acoustic impedance is lowest at a negative ear-canal pressure, suggesting a negative resting pressure in the middle ear.*

contract. Stapedial contraction causes a stiffening of the ossicular chain and a corresponding increase in the acoustic impedance at the tympanic membrane. This is called an *acoustic reflex*. Certain characteristics of acoustic-reflex measurements have been found to correlate with specific degrees and types of hearing disorders. The acoustic reflex is typically absent in the presence of a significant conductive lesion, for example. Acoustic-reflex measurements also are being used to provide an indirect indicator of loudness recruitment (discussed next), to objectively predict hearing sensitivity in patients that are difficult to test with behavioral procedures, and to differentiate pathologies at different locations within the peripheral auditory system. Good reviews of these and other acoustic-impedance topics are available elsewhere (Jerger, 1975; Feldman and Wilber, 1976; Northern, 1976).

Tests for Abnormal Loudness Function

A second area of specialized tests focuses on cochlear and auditory nerve lesions. As we have just discussed, acoustic-impedance measurements are extremely useful in the diagnosis of middle-ear disorders. Here we take a brief look at how abnormalities in loudness perception can be used to characterize lesions of the inner ear and auditory nerve.

Recruitment of Loudness. *Loudness recruitment* is defined as an abnormal growth in loudness with increased sound intensity. As the intensity of an acoustic signal is increased in an ear exhibiting loudness recruitment, loudness increases at a more rapid rate than would be expected in a normal ear. This abnormal loudness growth is an indicator of cochlear damage or disease. An abnormally slow rate (or reduction) in loudness growth with increased sound intensity (*decruitment of loudness*), by contrast, is often associated with lesions of the auditory nerve.

Audiometric tests for loudness recruitment consist primarily of loudness balance procedures. In cases of unilateral hearing loss, the growth of loudness in the ear with the loss is compared to the loudness growth in the opposite (normal) ear. The patient is asked to judge the loudness of a single tone as it is alternated between the ears. The tone is set at a fixed level in the better ear and presented to the listener. Then it is switched to the poorer ear and the listener judges whether the tone is louder or softer than it was in the better ear. If the tone is louder, the level is turned down; if it is softer, the tone is increased in intensity level. The goal is to find the intensity level of the tone in the poorer ear judged equal in loudness to the tone in the better ear (Hood, 1969). The level of the reference tone (better ear) is varied in graduated steps until a loudness-growth function is demonstrated for the two ears (see Figure 12–11). Various categories or degrees of loudness recruitment may be determined by evaluating the characteristics of this loudness-growth function.

In cases of bilateral sensorineural hearing loss the loudness-balance procedure is carried out separately in each ear (monaural). A patient is asked to balance the loudness of two tones of different frequencies in the same ear. The reference tone is selected from the frequency region where the patient's hearing sensitivity is approximately normal; the comparison tone is selected from the frequency region of hearing loss.

Auditory Adaptation. *Auditory adaptation* is the reduction in loudness of a *sustained* acoustic signal having sufficient duration and intensity. Clinically, auditory adaptation is manifested as a reduction in loudness over time in response to a sustained signal. The phenomenon has

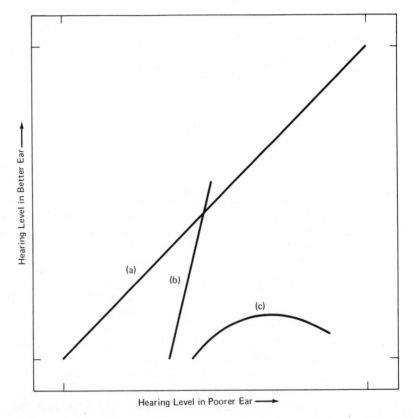

FIGURE 12–11. *The growth of loudness as a function of signal intensity: (a) normal; (b) loudness recruitment (cochlear lesions); (c) decruitment of loudness (lesions of the auditory nerve).*

been termed *tone decay* because a sustained tone presented near threshold will fade to inaudibility for patients experiencing substantial auditory adaptation. Auditory adaptation is common to lesions of both the cochlea and the auditory nerve. The primary difference is that the rate of auditory adaptation is greater for lesions of the nerve. For a given signal duration, then, the amount (dB) of auditory adaptation is generally much greater with lesions of the auditory nerve than with cochlear lesions.

Audiologists use several versions of threshold tone-decay procedures: all involve similar tasks for the subject under test. In the Threshold Tone-Decay Test (Carhart, 1957), for example, the task is to find the intensity level the person requires in order to hear a tone for a full 60 seconds. The listener is presented with a tone at or just above threshold and is instructed to signal (perhaps by raising a hand) for as long as the tone is heard. If the tone fades to inaudibility before the end of 60 seconds, the level of the tone is immediately increased by 5 dB and timing starts over. This process is continued until a level is reached where the person hears the tone for the entire 60 seconds. The results of such procedures are usually expressed in terms of the amount (dB) of intensity change required for the patient to hear the tone over the predefined duration. In general, patients with a normal auditory system show little or no auditory adaptation, patients with cochlear lesions may show as much as 20–30 dB of auditory adaptation, and patients with a lesion of the auditory nerve may show extreme auditory adaptation. Indeed, with some patients who have a nerve lesion, the level of the tone can be increased to the limits of the audiometer without the patient hearing the tone over the entire prescribed duration. Some tone-decay procedures also provide for an evaluation of the time course of the adaptation effects. These latter procedures are the most effective tone-decay tests in terms of differentiating cochlear and auditory nerve lesions.

Electrophysiological Procedures

Electrophysiologic audiometry, the last type of specialized test procedure that we discuss, uses changes in the electrical properties of the person under test as an index of response to sound. Electrophysiological techniques typically monitor one of several autonomic systems or the electrical activity of the central nervous system. Like acoustic-impedance testing, the response system is not under the subjective control of the subject. Consequently, electrophysiological procedures offer distinct advantages for testing young children and other difficult-to-test patients.

Of the several autonomic systems that have been used as physiological indices of auditory function, the functional activities of the heart, lungs, and sweat glands are probably most used clinically. Signal-presentation techniques used in testing are similar to those used in behavioral testing, but the response consists of a change in the ongoing physiological activity of whatever autonomic system is being monitored. For cardiac responses, for example, the variable typically used is heartbeat rate. When the patient hears a signal, changes in ongoing heartbeat rate are observed. Similarly, respiratory changes with signal presentation are observed as time-locked changes in the rate or depth (amplitude) of breathing. For sweat-gland activity, or electrodermal audiometry (EDA), a common approach is to record the skin's electrical resistance using small disc electrodes applied to the fingertips. A response to acoustic stimulation is indicated by a change (such as amplitude or latency shifts) in skin resistance brought about by pairing the test signal with a noxious signal (shock) during pretest conditioning. This *galvanic skin response* (GSR) test procedure has been used primarily with uncooperative patients, particularly those who may be feigning a hearing loss in order to receive financial compensation.

Electroencephalic audiometry (EEA) or *electric response audiometry* (ERA) is a group of techniques that test hearing by monitoring central nervous system functioning (Davis, 1976). Test signals are presented to the subject through earphones and the electrical activity of the brain (brain waves) is monitored by means of small disc electrodes placed on the outside of the skull. Electrical potentials coincident with the signals are sampled to determine if responses are present. Responses consist of systematic changes in electrical activity occurring only when appropriate signals have been presented. Specific procedures have been developed to test the cochlea, auditory nerve, and the central auditory system. Electrophysiological audiometry is particularly valuable for testing children or adults while they are under anesthesia or sedation or merely asleep. As with all the special tests described here, the goal is to characterize the lesion and associated hearing disorder so that proper habilitation/rehabilitation services can be initiated.

REFERENCES   American National Standards Institute, *Specifications for Audiometers,* ANSI S3.6–1969. New York: American National Standards Institute (1970).

American Speech and Hearing Association, Guidelines for audiometric symbols. *Asha,* 16, 260–264 (1974).

American Speech and Hearing Association, Guidelines for manual pure-tone threshold audiometry. *Asha,* 20, 297–301 (1978).

BRUNT, M., The staggered spondaic word (SSW) test. In J. Katz (Ed.), *Handbook of Clinical Audiology.* Baltimore: Williams and Wilkins (1972).

CARHART, R., Clinical determination of abnormal auditory adaptation. *Archives of Otolaryngology,* 65, 32–39 (1957).

CHAIKLIN, J., and McCLELLAN, M., Audiometric management of collapsible ear canals. *Archives of Otolaryngology,* 93, 397–407 (1971).

DAVIS, H., Acoustics and psychoacoustics. In H. Davis and S. Silverman (Eds.), *Hearing and Deafness,* (4th. Ed.). New York: Holt, Rinehart and Winston (1978a).

DAVIS, H., Hearing handicap, standards for hearing, and medicolegal rules. In H. Davis and S. Silverman (Eds.), *Hearing and Deafness,* (4th. Ed.). New York: Holt, Rinehart and Winston (1978b).

DAVIS, H., Principles of electric response audiometry. *Annals of Otology, Rhinology, and Laryngology,* 85, Supplement 28, 1–96 (1976).

EAGLES, E., Selected findings from the Pittsburgh study. *Transactions of the American Academy of Opthamology and Otology,* 76, 343–348 (1972).

FELDMAN, A., and WILBER, L. (Eds.), *Acoustic Impedance and Admittance – The Measurement of Middle Ear Function.* Baltimore: Williams and Wilkins (1976).

FULTON, R., and LLOYD, L. (Eds.), *Audiometry for the Retarded.* Baltimore: Williams and Wilkins (1969).

FULTON, R., and LLOYD, L. (Eds.), *Auditory Assessment of the Difficult-to-Test.* Baltimore: Williams and Wilkins (1975).

HOOD, J., Basic audiological requirements in neuro-otology. *Journal of Laryngology,* 83, 695–711 (1969).

JERGER, J. (Ed.), *Handbook of Clinical Impedance Audiometry.* Dobbs Ferry, New York: American Electromedics Corp. (1975).

JERGER, J. (Ed.), *Modern Developments in Audiology.* New York: Academic Press (1963).

JERGER, J. (Ed.), *Modern Developments in Audiology,* (2nd Ed.). New York: Academic Press (1973).

KATZ, J. (Ed.), *Handbook of Clinical Audiology.* Baltimore: Williams and Wilkins (1972).

KATZ, J. (Ed.), *Handbook of Clinical Audiology,* (2nd Ed.). Baltimore: Williams and Wilkins (1978).

NORTHERN, J. (Ed.), *Selected Readings in Impedance Audiometry.* Dobbs Ferry, New York: American Electromedics Corp. (1976).

ROSE, D. (Ed.), *Audiological Assessment.* Englewood Cliffs, N.J.: Prentice-Hall (1971).

ROSE, D. (Ed.), Audiological Assessment, (2nd Ed.). Englewood Cliffs, N.J.: Prentice-Hall (1978).

SCHEIN, J., and DELK, M., *The Deaf Population of the United States.* Silver Spring, Md.: National Association of the Deaf (1974).

SCHUKNECHT, H., *Pathology of the Ear.* Cambridge, Mass.: Harvard University Press (1974).

signpost   Chapter 13 concludes our introductory journey through the territory of communication disorders. As the second of the book's two chapters concerned with hearing disorders, it describes many things that can be done to help the person with an impaired hearing mechanism. These include medical intervention involving surgery and drugs, sound amplification through the use of a personal hearing aid, enhancement of skills in using auditory, visual, situational, and linguistic cues to improve speech comprehension, and special service programs to meet educational, social, economic, and psychological needs. A major section of the chapter is devoted to the special problems of the child who is born with a significant hearing loss or who acquires such a loss before developing speech and language skills. Consideration is given to the sometimes emotional controversy of whether such children should be taught to speak, to use manual forms of communication such as fingerspelling and sign language, or to use some combination of these modes of communication. At least seven million men, women, and children in the United States have significant hearing losses in both ears. For all these people, and for those with less severe losses, restoration that allows full participation in the hearing world cannot always be achieved. New inroads to management, however, are being made constantly. One of these, the surgically-implanted auditory prosthesis (a sort of "artificial ear"), is discussed in the final section of Chapter 13. It is yet another example of the creative, world-wide research efforts that offer hope to persons with communication disorders.

13

Craig C. Wier

habilitation and
rehabilitation
of the
hearing impaired

INTRODUCTION

Most communication between people is by means of speaking and listening. When hearing sensitivity is sufficiently poor, normal conversational communication becomes difficult, or even impossible. For young children, a significant hearing loss can disrupt the normal process of speech and language acquisition with consequent effects on emotional and educational development. For adults, onset of a significant hearing loss can affect their personal, social, and professional lives. Many different professionals may share the responsibility for helping the hearing-impaired person communicate effectively and live a full life in the hearing world. Audiologists, speech-language pathologists, otolaryngologists, vocational and educational counselors, clinical psychologists, social workers, and special classroom teachers of the hearing impaired all may be called upon to provide services to counteract hearing loss and its effects.

The procedures used to reduce the disabilities resulting from hearing loss are described in this chapter. The chapter's primary focus is on services provided by persons trained in the speech and hearing sciences. Most of these services are intended to directly improve hearing-impaired persons' residual auditory and communicative abilities. However, aid for emotional, social, educational, or vocational problems that arise secondary to a hearing loss is also very important to the success of the remediation program, and services in these areas are described as well, but in less detail.

Services to be discussed fall into two categories: habilitation and rehabilitation. *Habilitation* is the term used to describe programs for children with hearing losses at birth (congenital) or those acquired prelingually (before speech and language develop). *Rehabilitation* is the term used to describe similar programs for persons with hearing losses acquired after speech and language have been well established. As we shall learn, the needs of the hearing-impaired adult with well-established speech and language skills are substantially different from those of the congenitally, or prelingually hearing-impaired child.

In the sections to follow, we begin with a discussion of the semantics of deafness and hearing impairment. This is followed by a consideration of the distribution of hearing loss in the population and of the degree of hearing loss in relation to communication handicap. Next, different modes of remediation for hearing impairment are discussed. From there we turn to the social and psychological effects of acquired hearing loss and then the special problems faced by the hearing-impaired child. At the end of the chapter, we consider what the future might hold for the remediation of hearing losses. Some of the discussion in the chapter is equally applicable to both children and adults while other discussion is not. In many ways rehabilitation is simpler than habilitation and thus provides a more suitable opportunity for the introduction of basic concepts about the management of the hearing-impaired individual. Thus, to the extent feasible, we introduce concepts of remediation of adult hearing loss before or concurrently with those concepts more specifically related to the effects of congenital or prelingual hearing loss.

SEMANTICS OF DEAFNESS AND HEARING IMPAIRMENT

The effect of "labeling" people is well known to sociologists. Labeling persons with ethnic or religious epithets, or with intelligence-test scores is recognized to be a powerful influence on the individual's life style and level of achievement. Labels influence the way persons see themselves and the way others see them. Individual characteristics are often swamped by attributes believed to be common to all members of the group carrying a particular label.

Use of the term *deaf* has such an effect. Ross and Calvert (1973) review the effects of the label *deaf* on behavior of parents, relatives, and teachers of the hearing-impaired child, and ultimately on the child's own behavior. Categorized as deaf, a child is assumed to have certain characteristics associated with the label and is treated accordingly. Ross and Calvert point out that because he is "deaf," he cannot hear; and because he cannot hear, it follows that:

> There is little point in speaking to him.
> He will need a special means of communication.
> He will need to be educated in a special school environment with special means of instruction.

He cannot be expected to use a hearing aid to good effect.

He will not be expected to succeed or excel at intellectual, social, or vocational endeavors.

Equipped with the label *deaf* and treated in the fashion described above, a child with even a moderate hearing loss can become "deaf" by fulfilling the expectations of those around him. These consequences apply equally for the hearing-impaired adult. There is a continuum of hearing loss, and the range of behaviors associated with coping with that loss run the gamut of human behavior. The fact that a person has a hearing loss of a given severity bears no necessary relationship to the entirety of that person's behavior. Recognition of this situation leads us to avoid the use of the cover term *deaf* in this chapter.

DISTRIBUTION OF HEARING LOSS IN THE POPULATION

Accurate and comprehensive data on the prevalence of hearing impairments are not available. From Elliott's (1978) recent review of the data we can assume that slightly more than 3 percent of the total population of the United States has "trouble hearing in . . . both ears." This percentage translates into about seven million persons.

The prevalence of hearing loss is not evenly distributed across the population. The percentage of the total population with significant hearing loss increases with the age of the population sampled. Thus, the number of hearing-impaired adults is much greater than the number of hearing-impaired children (see Table 13–1). In part, these statistics reflect the facts that childhood spans far fewer years than adulthood and that hearing-impaired children grow into hearing-impaired adults. The number of persons with hearing losses acquired after speech and language skills are developed is many times larger than the number of persons with significant congenital and prelingual hearing-impairment. Several population trends suggest that the disparity in prevalence figures between children and adults with hearing impairment will grow.

The increased life expectancy of people living today will swell both the total number of people and the proportion of the total population living into their sixties, and beyond. On this basis, we can predict that the total number of adults with significant hearing losses will increase. At the other end of our life span, the birthrate in the United States and other industrialized nations has been declining. In addition, a combination of genetic counseling, vaccination programs against infectious diseases, and improved medical treatment for infant diseases will further reduce the number of children with prelingual hearing losses. Of course, the same trend toward improved medical care will also result in the survival of infants with severe and often multiple handicaps, including hearing loss, who would previously have died in infancy. Nevertheless, these trends should combine to reduce both the proportion and the total number of children with impaired hearing. The total number of persons with a significant bilateral hearing loss is about seven million, but only about two hundred thousand of these persons lost their hearing prelingually[1] (Elliott, 1978).

Table 13–1 shows the proportion of the population in the United States with "significant bilateral impairment"[2] (Schein and Delk, 1974). The proportion increases steadily from about one-quarter of one percent under age six to over 17 percent for persons aged sixty-five and older. As just discussed, the absolute numbers of persons affected also increases substantially as a function of age.

In addition to the factor of age, there are also differences in the prevalance of hearing loss as a function of sex. The proportion of men with hearing losses is greater than the proportion of women at all ages. Furthermore, the amount of hearing loss present in the total population is greater for men than women, with men's hearing declin-

Table 13–1. PREVALENCE OF SIGNIFICANT BILATERAL (BOTH EARS) HEARING IMPAIRMENT BY AGE IN THE UNITED STATES IN 1971.

AGE	PERCENTAGE OF HEARING-IMPAIRED POPULATION IN AGE GROUP*	NUMBERS IN AGE GROUP BASED ON ESTIMATED 1978 POPULATION OF 220,000,000**
<6	0.26	61,000
6–16	0.85	417,000
17–24	0.86	256,000
25–44	1.36	698,000
45–64	4.48	2,029,000
≧65	17.37	3,668,000

*Data on the percentage of the hearing-impaired population in each age group are from J. Schein and M. Delk, Jr., *The Deaf Population of the United States.* Silver Spring, Md.: National Association of the Deaf, 1974.
**Numbers of individuals falling under each age category are based on an estimated 1978 population for the United States of 220,000,000 and using the Schein and Delk (1974) report on percentages for 1971.

[1] In this instance, prelingual is defined to be the period before acquisition of the principle structures of adult speech and language (nominally during the first three years of life). This use of the term is not intended to convey the impression that significant components of speech and language behavior are not present earlier. Some researchers think language-specific behaviors are present by age six months, or even earlier (see Chapter 1).

[2] Because persons with a hearing loss in only one ear are usually only inconvenienced and not communicatively impaired, all reference to hearing loss in this chapter will be to *bilateral* hearing loss, with hearing levels referred to the *better* ear.

ing more rapidly with increasing age than women's (review Figure 12–8 once again).

All of these factors affecting the distribution of hearing loss—improved medical treatments, better detection procedures, population trends, increasing life span, and sex differences—have important implications for delivery of services to persons with hearing losses. In both total numbers and in terms of the proportion of persons with significant hearing loss, the number of persons needing services will increase. Most of these persons will be elderly. Although there are likely to be fewer congenitally or prelingually hearing-impaired children, those children with hearing impairments will more often have additional, and perhaps more severe, nonauditory handicaps.

DEGREE OF HEARING LOSS AND THE COMMUNICATION HANDICAP

The communication handicap of the hearing-impaired person results from difficulty in comprehending conversational speech. And, comprehension of speech is dependent upon the extent to which an individual can detect the various acoustic characteristics of individual speech sounds. Vowels, for example, which have periodic components in their spectra with most of their energy in the frequencies below 2000 Hz, require adequate hearing of the lower frequencies. Voiceless fricatives, like *s* or *sh* by contrast, are aperiodic, noiselike sounds with most of their energy above 2000 Hz. They require adequate hearing of higher frequencies. Speech sounds also vary in their overall sound pressure level; vowels are generally higher in level than consonants. The English vowel *ah*, for example, is about 30 dB more intense than the consonant *s*. The acoustics of speech sounds is much more complex than we have presented here, but we can generally characterize vowels as relatively intense, relatively low-frequency sounds, while consonants are relatively less intense, relatively high-frequency sounds. Recognizing these general characteristics of speech will help us to understand the problems hearing-impaired persons have in understanding speech.

Figure 13–1 illustrates how reduced sensitivity and the acoustic characteristics of conversational speech can be viewed audiometrically for a single patient. This patient has a noise-induced hearing loss that is primarily high-frequency in nature. Shown in the figure are the patient's audiogram (repeated for the better ear from Figure 12–6e) and a superimposed plot of the frequencies and sound pressure levels typically contained in conversational speech. The superimposed plot represents the same conversational speech area circumscribed in Figure

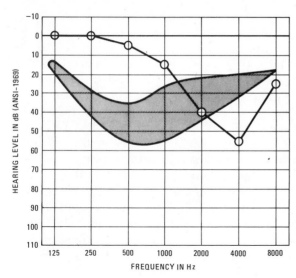

FIGURE 13–1. *Right-ear audiogram for a patient with a noise-induced hearing loss. (Data are repeated from Figure 12–6e, excluding those for bone conduction.) Also shown is the range of frequencies and hearing levels typically contained in conversational speech (the shaded area on the audiogram). The latter speech-area plot is the same as in Figure 3–17, except that the area is drawn on audiogram coordinates here. Note that the patient's hearing level is below the speech-area in the high-frequency region. See text for further discussion.*

3–17 except that in the present case it is plotted on audiogram coordinates. Note in Figure 13–1 that the patient's hearing level is below the circumscribed area for conversational speech in the high-frequency region of his audiogram. Persons with a loss in hearing sensitivity like that shown in Figure 13–1 will hear conversational speech with normal loudness because the most intense portions of the speech spectrum are in their area of normal or near-normal hearing. They will have difficulty understanding speech, however, because they will miss so many of the low-intensity, high-frequency components that carry information about consonants. For example, they might confuse the word pairs dea*th* and dea*f* (*th* vs. *f*), or cla*ss* and cla*sh* (*s* vs. *sh*), which differ primarily in the low-intensity, high-frequency information of their final consonants.

For other configurations of hearing loss, we expect patterns of difficulty in understanding spoken speech that are closely related to the audibility of individual speech sounds and the given audiometric configuration. Most hearing losses slope toward the high frequencies. We know that the spectral content of most consonant sounds is in the higher-frequency region of the spectrum, and that of the vowels is in the lower-frequency region. Consonants are also generally briefer and less intense than vowels. Given these spectral and temporal relations between consonants and vowels, we can easily predict that most people with impaired hearing will misunderstand consonants much more frequently than vowels; and the higher the frequency information characteristic of a particular consonant, the more often it will be missed.

The magnitude of the communication deficit—that is, the

537

amount of difficulty in normal spoken communication—can be roughly gauged by the pure tone averages (PTAs) obtained for the thresholds at 500, 1000, and 2000 Hz. Table 12–2 shows the expected degree of handicap as a function of PTA along with an estimate of the degree of difficulty expected in understanding speech. Some caution must be used in making generalizations between PTAs and communication difficulties. Persons with Meniere's disease, for example, often have much more difficulty understanding speech than would be expected from their PTAs. This suggests that in addition to their loss in sensitivity, patients with hearing loss from Meniere's disease also have a loss in frequency selectivity, or ability to discriminate one sound from another. The generalizations represented in Table 12–2, therefore, are only "rules-of-thumb" for describing the consequences of a loss in sensitivity. Be aware that exceptions to these relations between PTA and degree of handicap may occur.

Descriptions of the degree of handicap associated with losses in pure-tone sensitivity are based on data from hearing-impaired adults. The situation for children with prelingual hearing losses is much more complicated. How much residual hearing is necessary to support the normal acquisition of speech and language skills? At this time, no one knows. Multiple factors are surely involved, including the degree of hearing loss, parent/child relationships, mode of early communication, other handicaps, and so forth. Some of these factors will be discussed in detail in the section on habilitation in children.

MODES OF REMEDIATION

Some hearing losses can be remediated by medical intervention, but many cannot. The following sections describe medical and nonmedical procedures that completely resolve or at least improve the communication capabilities of hearing-impaired persons. Some procedures reduce the hearing loss itself; others improve communication skills in the presence of a continuing reduced hearing sensitivity. Procedures described in the subsections on Medical Remediation, Amplification, and the Basics of Hearing Aids are equally applicable to both children and adults. The remaining subsections are directed toward services for adults, with analogous procedures for children set aside for discussion later in the chapter.

Medical Remediation

Once a hearing loss has been detected and evaluated by an audiologist, the patient must be referred to an otolaryngologist for medical evaluation. As discussed in Chapter 12, otolaryngologists are physicians trained to treat diseases of the ear. Many conductive hearing losses can be entirely eliminated or substantially improved by medical intervention. Most sensorineural hearing losses are irreversible; however, a few do respond to appropriate medical intervention.

Conductive Hearing Losses. Conductive hearing losses result from conditions that impair the impedance-matching properties of the outer- and middle-ear systems to the inner ear. Chapter 12 describes various conditions of both the outer- and middle-ear systems that produce conductive hearing losses.

Conditions that involve blockage of the outer ear can be remediated by their removal. These include excessive earwax, foreign objects, and tumor growths. In most cases, medical remediation will restore hearing to normal or near-normal. Exceptions occur when a tumor has also invaded the middle-ear system. Figure 13–2a shows the audiogram of a forty-year-old man before and after the excision of a tumor in his right ear canal. Prior to surgery he demonstrated a marked hearing loss because the tumor blocked sound transmission through the ear canal. Following surgery, his hearing improved to within normal limits.

Congenital atresia, or the absence of an ear canal (see Chapter 12 and Figure 12–5), if complete, is accompanied by a 50–60 dB conductive hearing loss. In addition to the external malformation, persons with congenital atresia of the outer ear often have associated malformation of the middle ear. Many surgeons will attempt outer-ear reconstruction only if there is an intact middle-ear system. The difficulties of surgical management of these disorders are great and the potential for success of the more elaborate surgery involving both outer- and middle-ear systems are significantly less.

The most common source of conductive hearing loss is inflammation, and/or infection of the middle ear, namely, otitis media. After otitis media has been detected, the medical treatment will depend upon the stage of the disease. If it is in the serous stage (see Chapter 12), antibiotic medication may be prescribed to prevent the growth and accumulation of bacteria which could take the disease to its next stage, suppurative otitis media. In this later stage, the liquid trapped in the middle ear is thickened by bacterial invasion and unless the condition is halted, the eardrum may burst from the pressure. To prevent the eardrum from rupturing, the otolaryngologist will prescribe antibiotics to reduce the inflammation and may perform a *myringotomy*. In this simple surgical procedure, as illustrated in Figure 13–3, an incision made through the eardrum permits the middle-ear cavity to drain and the middle-ear pressure to be released. If the otitis media is chronic, ventilating tubes may be fitted through the eardrum. Ventilating tubes are tiny plastic tubes that perform the Eustachian tube's normal function of aerating the

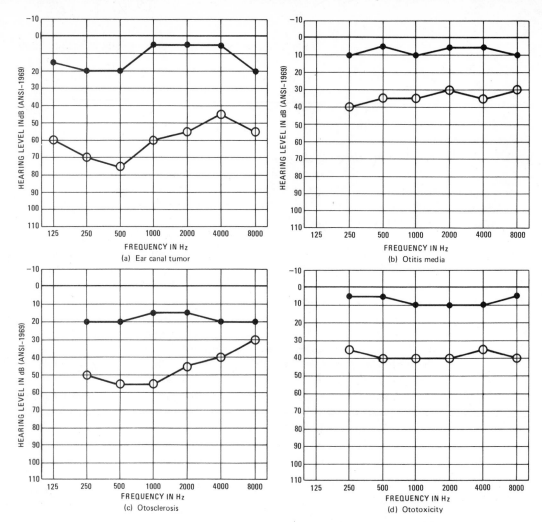

FIGURE 13–2. *Sample audiograms for hearing losses (open circles) of four different causes, ear canal tumor, otitis media, otosclerosis, and ototoxicity, and for the same ears tested following appropriate medical remediation (filled circles). Only the right ear results are shown in each audiogram and bone-conduction results are excluded to avoid cluttering the audiograms. Corresponding panels below present comments pertinent to each audiogram.*

(a) Ear canal tumor

Audiogram for a forty-year-old man before (open circles) and after (filled circles) surgery for the removal of a tumor in his right ear canal. Note that the patient demonstrated a marked hearing loss at all frequencies tested prior to removal of the tumor.

(b) Otitis media

Audiogram for a five-year-old boy before (open circles) and after (filled circles) medical remediation using antibiotic medication for otitis media. In this case the middle-ear problem was successfully managed in the serous stage of otitis media.

(c) Otosclerosis

Audiogram for a fifty-five-year-old woman before (open circles) and after (filled circles) a surgical stapedectomy involving the use of a pistonlike prosthesis to replace the stapes. Notice that for the ear shown the surgery brought the patient's hearing to within normal limits at all frequencies.

(d) Ototoxicity

Audiogram for a twenty-two-year-old woman while salicylate intoxicated from high doses of acetysalicylic acid (common aspirin) (open circles) and twenty-four hours later (filled circles) after discontinuing aspirin use. Notice the marked improvement into the normal-hearing range following discontinuation of the drug.

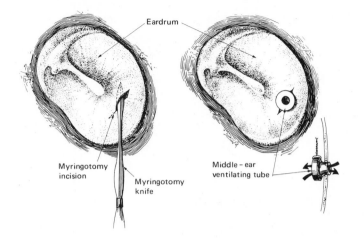

FIGURE 13–3. *Graphic illustration of a myringotomy (left panel). An incision is made through the eardrum to drain the middle-ear cavity and normalize its pressure. Middle-ear ventilating tubes are sometimes inserted through the incision (right panel) to perform the Eustachian tube's normal function. (From D. Joseph, Some medical implications regarding the hearing impaired student. In R. Cozad, Ed., The Speech Clinician and the Hearing-Impaired Child. Springfield, Ill.: Charles C Thomas, 1974.)*

Labels on figure: Eardrum; Myringotomy incision; Myringotomy knife; Middle-ear ventilating tube

(prostheses) that may be used to replace a human stapes are shown in middle ear and keeping it at atmospheric pressure. Figure 13–2b shows the audiogram of a five-year-old child during serous otitis media and after the middle-ear condition has returned to normal following medical treatment with antibiotics.

It is important to note that chronic or sporadic otitis media may result in conductive hearing loss in children who also have sensorineural hearing loss. For a young child with a mild or moderate sensorineural loss of 40–60 dB, the addition of a 25 or 30 dB conductive loss may further impair communicative performance. Hearing-impaired children must be carefully monitored in insure that such situations, if they develop, are quickly treated.

Other conductive losses in the middle ear may result from dislocations of the ossicular chain due to a blow to the head or from a tumor growing in the middle-ear cavity. Surgical reconstruction of a dislocation anywhere along the ossicular chain may restore normal hearing. Removal of a tumor and subsequent reconstruction of the linkage between the tympanic membrane and the oval window may also restore normal or near-normal hearing.

One frequently occurring problem in adults is otosclerosis. As described in Chapter 12, otosclerosis is a condition in which abnormal growth of bony material can lead to a "cementing" of the footplate of the stapes to the oval window. The result is a conductive hearing loss of significant magnitude. Often normal or near-normal hearing can be restored in a procedure called a *stapedectomy*. Figure 13–4 shows the sequence of procedures involved in a typical stapedectomy. Access to the cemented stapes is gained through the ear canal by "peeling back" the tympanic membrane. Normal stapedial function is then restored by inserting an artificial stapes. Some of the variety of artificial stapes

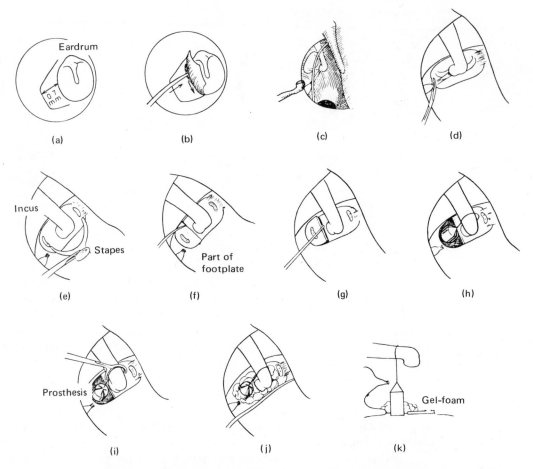

FIGURE 13–4. *Diagrammatic illustration of a typical stapedectomy procedure including gaining access to the middle ear by lifting a flap of skin from the ear canal and retracting the tympanic membrane (a-c), cutting the stapedial tendon (d), breaking and removing the U-shaped portion of the stapes (e), breaking loose and removing a portion of the fixed footplate from the oval window (f, g), fitting a prosthesis to replace the stapes to the incus (h, i), and sealing the open area of the oval window around the prosthesis (j, k). (From A. Morrison, Otosclerosis. In J. Ballantyne and J. Groves, Eds.,* Scott-Brown's Diseases of the Ear, Nose, and Throat, Vol. 2: The Ear, *3rd Ed. Philadelphia: Lippincott, 1971.)*

(prostheses) that may be used to replace a human stapes are shown in Figure 13–5. Figure 13–2c shows the improvement in the hearing of a fifty-five-year-old woman with otosclerosis following a stapedectomy. Prior to surgery she had a hearing loss that produced frequent difficulty in her comprehending normal conversational speech; after surgery her hearing is within the normal range at all frequencies.

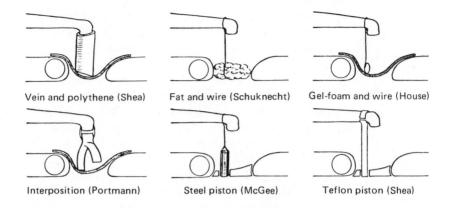

Vein and polythene (Shea)   Fat and wire (Schuknecht)   Gel-foam and wire (House)

Interposition (Portmann)   Steel piston (McGee)   Teflon piston (Shea)

FIGURE 13–5. *Diagrammatic representation of some of the variety of prostheses used to replace the human stapes during stapedectomy. The faucetlike projection in the upper part of each panel is the incus. The oval window is along the bottom of each panel. The different prostheses connect the incus to the oval window. (From A. Morrison, Otosclerosis. In J. Ballantyne and J. Groves, Eds.,* Scott–Brown's Diseases of the Ear, Nose, and Throat, Vol. 2: The Ear, *3rd Ed. Philadelphia: Lippincott, 1971.)*

Sensorineural Hearing Losses. Sensorineural hearing losses are usually permanent and irreversible. A few types of sensorineural loss, however, may be prevented or reversed if the situation is detected early enough. For example, cases presenting the symptoms of Meniere's disease have been demonstrated to be allergic reactions. When the allergens are removed from the patient's diet or environment, hearing returns to normal (Clemis, 1974). Similarly, high doses of quinine or acetylsalicylic acid (common aspirin) can cause temporary threshold shifts of as much as 40–50 dB across the frequency range. When medication is suspended, the hearing returns to normal over time. Figure 13–2d shows a hearing loss resulting from salicylate intoxication and the normal thresholds twenty-four hours after discontinuing aspirin use. Note that the extent and configuration of this sensorineural loss on the audiogram is very similar to that for the case of otitis media shown in Figure 13–2b. However, this is a sensorineural loss whereas otitis media produces a conductive loss. The form of the audiogram does not give us information about the nature of the hearing loss.

Another source of sensorineural hearing loss that may often be partially reversible is an auditory nerve tumor (acoustic neuroma). Such tumors are not malignant and may grow slowly over many years. They produce a hearing loss, mild tinnitus, and vertigo. The location of these tumors at the base of the brain makes their continued growth life-threatening and their surgical removal a serious operation. Depending upon the size of the tumor, how long it has been present, and the surgical procedure used for its excision, sometimes all or a portion of the person's hearing sensitivity returns once the tumor is removed.

Other common sources of sensorineural hearing loss are permanent and irreversible given the present state of knowledge and technology. These include ototoxic responses to the aminoglycoside antibiotics (see Figure 12–6d), noise-induced hearing loss (see Figure 12–6e), and the general decline in auditory function with age, called presbycusis. Schuknecht (1974) has reviewed the pathophysiology of these hearing losses and his text is an excellent source for a more detailed look at diseases of the ear.

Most hearing losses of sensorineural origin within the cochlea, or the auditory pathways to the brain, are not remediable by medical intervention. Permanent congenital or acquired sensorineural hearing losses with their consequences for impairment of oral communication, must be managed through nonmedical remedial services. Individuals with sensorineural losses, then, are those most often served by habilitation and rehabilitation programs.

Amplification

If medical intervention is unable to restore normal or near-normal hearing, alternative methods of assistance must be considered. One obvious tactic is to in some way increase the intensity of sounds before they reach the impaired auditory system. In a sense, this is equivalent to doing a portion of the auditory system's work for it. We might expect to restore normal hearing if we increase the intensity of sounds in a fashion that corresponds to the pattern of hearing loss. For example, if at 250 Hz the impaired ear is 60 dB less sensitive than the normal ear and we increase the intensity of the acoustic signal at 250 Hz by 60 dB, the system would be able to detect a 250-Hz tone at the same level as a normal ear. Similarly, if at 4000 Hz the impaired ear's threshold is poorer than normal by 50 dB, we would want to make the energy around 4000 Hz 50 dB more intense. This process of increasing signal intensity is called *amplification* and amplification is the primary function of the hearing aid.

Unfortunately, the real world is rather more complicated than the idealized situation we described above. Sensorineural hearing losses are characterized by distortions of the signal as well as reductions in sensitivity. Thus, merely restoring "normal" sensitivity by means of a hearing aid will not produce normal sounding speech. Furthermore, if the hearing loss is sufficiently severe, the amount of amplification required in theory to produce "normal" sensitivity would deliver sounds to the auditory system that would be unpleasantly loud, thereby defeating the purpose of the endeavor. Perhaps you have personally experienced some sense of this reality by trying to talk loudly to an elderly person with a sensorineural hearing loss (presbycusis) only to have them say something like "Don't talk so loud! I can hear you; I just can't understand what you are saying!"

Despite these and other problems, the most common form of amplification, the personal hearing aid, remains a powerful tool to improve the hearing-impaired person's communication capabilities. In this section we describe the basic components of hearing aids and procedures used to determine which combination of hearing-aid features provide the most benefit to individual hearing-aid users.

Basics of Hearing Aids. All modern hearing aids have three basic components: a microphone, an amplifier, and a receiver. The microphone and receiver transduce energy from one form to another. Thus the tiny microphone on a hearing aid converts acoustic energy into electrical energy (like a telephone mouthpiece does), while the receiver performs the reverse conversion, transforming the electrical energy back into acoustical energy (like a telephone earpiece does). Between these two components is the amplifier, a device that increases the signal level between the input and output.

Figure 13–6a schematically represents these components and their function. If the signal at the microphone is a sinusoidal pressure wave with a fixed amplitude (see Chapter 3), the acoustic signal is transduced by the microphone into an electrical equivalent. The amplifier then increases the amplitude of the sinusoid; finally, the receiver transduces this signal into an acoustic pressure wave more intense than the signal originally entering the hearing aid. In principle, the hearing aid is rather like a miniature public address system.

Figure 13–6b illustrates some signal levels that might be obtained from a real world hearing aid. With an overall level of 65 dB SPL as an input signal (approximately the level of conversational speech) an amplifier that makes this signal 55 dB more intense will yield an output level of 120 dB SPL. The amount the input signal level is increased by the amplifier (the output level minus the input level) is called the *gain*. Thus, in the situation illustrated in Figure 13–6b, the hearing aid provides 55 dB of gain.

Hearing-Aid Evaluation. Selecting the most appropriate hearing aid for a patient who will benefit from amplification is a difficult task. It is not simply a matter of looking at the data obtained from audiometric testing and then "prescribing" a particular model hearing aid. The amount of gain that will produce the greatest possible improvement in

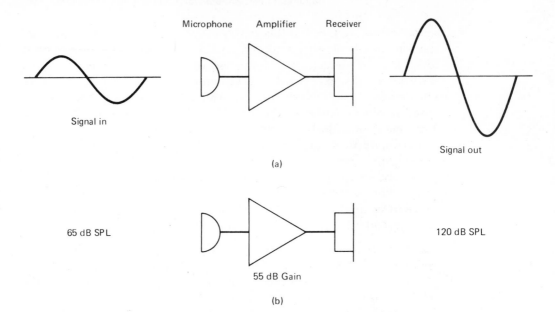

Microphone   Amplifier   Receiver

Signal in

(a)

Signal out

65 dB SPL   120 dB SPL

55 dB Gain

(b)

FIGURE 13–6. *Schematic illustration of the function of a hearing aid. Panel (a) depicts the three components of modern hearing aids: microphone, amplifier, and receiver. Sounds introduced into the microphone are converted into voltages which the amplifier intensifies and the receiver then converts back into sounds. Panel (b) shows some signal levels for a situation in which an aid provides a gain of 55 dB between the input level and output level.*

the patient's communication skills cannot be accurately predicted from the audiogram and routine test findings alone. Let us look carefully at some major considerations.

Routine audiometric evaluation usually provides data on the patient's unaided speech reception threshold (SRT) and speech discrimination scores. Because it provides the baseline for evaluating the patient's aided performance in these areas, this information must be obtained at the time of the hearing-aid evaluation if it is not available from prior testing. Additional data are also required from the patient before attempting to fit a hearing aid. We need to know the patient's *loudness-discomfort level* and his *most-comfortable-loudness level.* These data are obtained by asking the patient to listen through earphones while the clinician speaks to him over a microphone. The clinician slowly increases the signal level until the patient responds that the speech is too loud. The clinician usually will raise the level just a bit more to be sure that the maximum tolerable level has been reached. The decibel value of the level at which the patient responds is then recorded as the loudness-discomfort level. The same type of procedure is followed to obtain the patient's most-comfortable-loudness level. The patient is asked to indicate the intensity level that is most comfortable—the level at which he would not mind listening to speech over a long interval. One other descriptive quantity may be calculated at this time: the *dynamic range* of the patient's residual hearing. This value is simply the difference between the speech reception threshold and the loudness-discomfort level. If the dynamic range is too small, say less than 25 dB, the patient may not be a good candidate for hearing-aid use, or may require a special type of aid that compresses signal information into a narrow intensity range.

Having obtained the additional audiometric data that are required beyond routine testing, the decision can be made as to what type of hearing aid to fit to the patient. Figure 13–7 shows a variety of contemporary hearing aids with their relative sizes preserved. Included is an aid that fits entirely within the outer ear, an aid that fits behind the ear, an aid in a package that can be worn in a shirt pocket

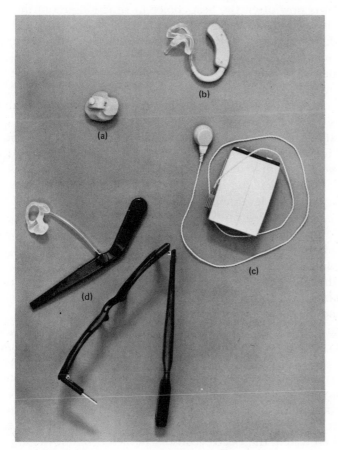

FIGURE 13–7. *A variety of contemporary hearing aids, including one that fits entirely within the outer ear (a), one that fits behind the ear (b), one that can be worn in a shirt pocket or in a body harness (c), and one built into eyeglass frames (d). (Courtesy of Dr. W. Wilson, University of Washington Child Development and Mental Retardation Center.)*

or in a harness strapped to the body, and an aid built into eyeglass frames.

The decision concerning the type of aid is simpler now than it once was. At one time only the larger body aids could provide sufficient gain to serve severely and profoundly hearing-impaired listeners. Now, ear-level aids are capable of providing as much as 60–70 dB of gain, enough even for some types of profound hearing losses. For some individuals, ear-level aids (in-the-ear, behind-the-ear, and eyeglass aids — see Figure 13-7a, b, and d) are adequate and appropriate. Body aids are often still fitted to very young children, however, because they can be firmly attached to the child by means of cloth straps across the chest. Body aids are also frequently used by older persons who have difficulty manipulating the very small controls on an ear-level aid. The type of hearing aid most rapidly gaining in popularity is the "in-the-ear" aid. Recent technical advances have improved the electroacoustic performance of the in-the-ear aid to the extent that it is now often the best choice in situations requiring gain in the vicinity of 35 dB, or less.

In addition to determining the type of aid, the foremost task is to carefully match the electroacoustic characteristics of the aid to the hearing-impaired person's particular hearing loss. Thus, different aids must be considered and tested with regard to how they might improve the communicative performance of the patient. All combinations of desired electroacoustic characteristics are not available in all types of aids. Three electroacoustic characteristics that are usually considered for any aid include its *gain, maximum power output,* and *frequency response.* The first of these, gain, was defined earlier as the amount of amplification the unit provides; that is, the difference between the input signal level and output signal level. The second characteristic, maximum power output, is the greatest signal level the aid is capable of producing. The third characteristic, frequency response, is a standardized expression of the range of frequencies over which the aid amplifies.

With the ideal goal in mind of fitting the patient with the aid that maximizes his communicative performance, the aids selected as the best candidates are tested on the patient one at a time. In each case, the gain is initially turned to a comfortable listening level and the patient's speech reception threshold is measured. This threshold is designated as the patient's *aided* speech reception threshold. Aided speech discrimination performance is then evaluated just as it is in the basic audiological evaluation, using monosyllable word tests. Occasionally, competing noise may be added and speech discrimination re-evaluated under these more difficult listening conditions. After different aids have been tested, the electroacoustic characteristics of the aid that produces the greatest improvement in the patient's test performance are then recommended to him. Typically, the patient then arranges to purchase an aid with these recommended characteristics.

The reader should be cautioned that in clinical practice the fitting of a hearing aid represents an imperfect solution to the problems faced by the patient with a hearing loss who needs amplification. For one thing, the validity of test materials commonly used to evaluate speech communication performance imposes a limitation on the evaluation process. Although everyday speech communication is by no means limited to isolated monosyllabic or spondaic words, these remain the items most often used to test speech reception thresholds and speech discrimination performance, respectively. Recent reports have suggested the superiority of more complex stimulus materials and listening situations (Jerger and Hayes, 1976; Kalikow, Stevens, and Elliott, 1977). Another limitation in traditional procedures is imposed by the methods used to describe the hearing aid's electroacoustic performance. The hearing aid is usually tested in a standardized, but highly artificial, environment that does not accurately represent the aid's performance when worn on a human listener. Selection procedures that assume the performance of aids measured under such standardized test conditions approximates the amplification present at the hearing-impaired listener's eardrum are questionable. (See Pascoe, 1976, for a review of some of the important concerns.)

Perhaps the major problem in providing amplification for patients is obtaining hearing aids with the exact electroacoustic and physical characteristics desired for the range of patient hearing losses encountered. Until recently this problem was made worse due to inadequate quality control in the manufacture of hearing aids and the lack of standards specifying the amount by which individual aids may vary from published specifications. New standards have partially rectified the latter situation (Olsen, 1976; Wilber, 1976; Kasten, 1977) by specifying limits of variability from the manufacturer's published specifications that the individual aid must meet. For example, an individual aid must provide amplification below 2000 Hz within ± 4 dB of its specifications. Improved standards of this type help both those who wear hearing aids and those who serve these users.

The audiologist's job is not done after fitting a person with the best available choice of a hearing aid, and the patient's job is only begun. The patient must be oriented to his aid. The first step in this orientation is to provide the user with an understanding of what his hearing aid can and cannot do for him. He must understand that no available hearing aid can restore his hearing to an unimpaired state. Most hearing-aid candidates have a sensorineural hearing loss and such a loss results in complex changes in the auditory system's function (Evans and Wilson, 1977). Hearing aids can only make sounds louder. If sounds are unclear or distorted when heard without an aid, they are likely to continue to sound unclear or distorted, albeit louder, when listening with a hearing aid. Nevertheless, the proper use of a well-fitted hearing aid can significantly improve communication even under these less than ideal circumstances.

Once the patient understands the limitations of amplification he must then be instructed in how to care for his aid. Fortunately, maintenance of a hearing aid is not complicated. The earmold must be kept clean and the sound tube must be kept free of wax or other potentially occluding debris. And the user or the parents of a young user should keep careful watch on how long batteries last in the aid. Because they usually last only about one to four weeks, spares must be kept available to replace them at the first signs of weakening.

Finally, the audiologist must provide the adult patient with a program to help him adapt to the new world of sounds he will now hear with his aid. The schedule to be followed is essentially similar for all new users. The time span during which successful adaptation takes place, however, varies a great deal. When a hearing aid has just been fitted, the sudden introduction of the nearly continuous barrage of sound associated with everyday living can be extremely disconcerting. The distress created by these amplified sounds can cause the hearing-impaired listener to reject the hearing aid. To avoid this negative response, the new hearing-aid user should be provided with a schedule for becoming accustomed to the aid and proficient in its use.

Initial use of the aid might be restricted to the home. In this relatively quiet situation the user will become adjusted to the sounds of his own voice, the voices of family members, friends, and the many household noises that were previously inaudible to him. The new user should be encouraged to experiment with the gain control of the aid, turning the gain up or down as the situation seems to require. The most satisfied hearing-aid users are usually active ones; that is, persons willing to learn to manipulate the aid to their best advantage. Next, the hearing-aid user's listening environment might be expanded to include situations in which several people are present and talking simultaneously; for example, company for dinner, or a small cocktail party. Still later, the new user can move to outside his home—a walk in the neighborhood, a trip to church or to the bank—gradually becoming reacquainted with the acoustic bustle of the modern world. Only after the new user has become adapted to listening in these relatively controlled situations should he venture into the uncontrollable cacophony of a grocery store or a shopping center. Throughout these latter varied experiences the user should be encouraged to continue to further experiment with the gain control and to turn the aid off in particularly noisy circumstances. Hearing-impaired persons who faithfully follow this simple schedule, allowing perhaps two weeks to two months to reach the final stage, are more likely to become satisfied hearing-aid users than those who do not.

Auditory Training

New hearing-aid users often find that the sounds they now hear again are distorted or different than the way they remember them. For both speech and nonspeech sounds, they may have difficulty recognizing or identifying their source or meaning. The more severe the loss and the longer it existed before the hearing aid was fitted, the more likely the listener will have some difficulty. *Auditory training* is the process of training the hearing-aid user to recognize common environmental sounds, the voices of family and friends, and to discriminate speech sounds with only auditory cues. As just discussed, the activities in the schedule for learning to use a new aid are, in some less formal sense, auditory training.

More formal forms of auditory training may also be used as part of a rehabilitation program. The patient may be asked to identify common environmental sounds from recordings. Training may consist of a face-to-face situation between the aid-user and the clinician. The clinician will speak to the patient with his mouth covered to force reliance on only auditory cues to identify the speech sounds produced. Consonants, particularly sounds with high-frequency components and low intensity, like *f, th, s,* and *sh* are the most difficult speech sounds for many hearing-impaired listeners to hear and to identify. Thus, auditory training provides practice in learning to recognize these speech sounds anew, a few at a time, and in various contexts.

Training Nonauditory Cues

Many nonauditory cues are used by speakers and listeners. Three of the most important are linguistic, situational, and visual cues. Some nonauditory cues are present in all speech communications, while others, for example, visual cues, are present only when the listener is able to see the speaker's face. No matter what their source, nonauditory cues provide supplemental information that can make meaningful a message that is unintelligible on the basis of auditory information alone. Thus, remediation that capitalizes on the hearing-impaired listener's full awareness of available nonauditory cues can significantly improve his communication capabilities.

Linguistic Cues. The structure of human language imposes limitations on what sound elements may occur and how permissible elements can be ordered. Remember from the discussion in Chapter 7 how distributional and sequence rules make certain sound events in a language simply "illegal" (see pages 275–276). Only a limited number of speech sounds are used within a language system. In General American English that number is a little over forty (see Chapter 2). Some of the speech sounds of English are used in other languages as well, and many speech sounds used in non-English languages are not present in English. Furthermore, within English not all of the acceptable speech sounds occur with equal frequency. For example, *t* occurs much more frequently than *d* (Denes, 1963).

This simple fact about language, that all elements do not occur with the same frequency, is true at all levels of linguistic analysis. Consider further that some words occur more frequently than others. The speech sounds *k* and *f* occur with about equal frequency, but the word *call* occurs much more frequently than the word *fall*. Just as all native speakers of a language acquire knowledge of the syntactical structure of their language without necessarily being able to explicitly state its grammatical rules, they also have implicit knowledge about the statistical structure of language.

These seemingly obscure facts are important when the listener is forced to interpret a degraded acoustic or auditory signal, as when listening in noise or through an impaired auditory system. In a sentence, for example, if a portion of a word or a whole word is missed, only certain English speech sounds or words are likely to be the missing element. Only those few sounds or words that make the utterance complete and meaningful need to be considered. For example, what do you think the last word in this sentence should _____ ? In fact, according to research in this area, the single most powerful influence on speech comprehension is that the message be meaningful. Experiments using normal-hearing adults as listeners find that it is more difficult to correctly identify a word in isolation than when the same word occurs in the context of a meaningful sentence (Miller, Heise, and Lichten, 1951). Training the hearing-impaired speaker to make maximum use of these and other linguistic cue factors is basic to successful rehabilitation.

Situational Cues.   Another important source of cues to understand a spoken message is the situation in which the conversation is taking place. Casual conversations are often highly stereotypical: "Hi, how are you doing?" "How's your family?" etc. By recognizing the limited number of likely alternative messages that may occur in such a context the hearing-impaired listener is able to "fill in" the missed portions of the message. Even more obvious examples of situational cues are the circumstances under which the conversation takes place; for example, at a baseball game words like "strike," "double play," and "home run" are more likely to be the content of a conversation than "dunk," "full-court press," or "lay up."

Many hearing-impaired listeners will learn to recognize on their own the value of such situational cues. Some will not. The audiologist, or speech-language pathologist responsible for rehabilitation therapy must teach each patient to make maximum use of the nonauditory sources of information in everyday speech communication.

Visual Cues.   When we speak, the movements of our lips, tongue, and mandible can provide useful visual information about which speech sounds are being produced. The two words *fin* and *thin* sound pretty much alike and when we are forced to rely solely upon auditory information to identify which word we heard (without context cues), a correct identification is difficult. However, when we can see the speaker produce each word the decision about which is *fin* and which *thin* becomes an easy task. The *f* is produced with a lower lip-upper teeth contact, whereas *th* is produced with the tongue slightly between the teeth. A few moments of practice with this example, or those that follow, should quickly convince you that there is a considerable amount of information about speech sounds available when the speaker's face is closely observed. Hearing-impaired persons are able to make use of this information to fill in missing speech sounds just as you can.

Not all speech sounds are equally visible. The movements that accompany the production of many consonants are easier to observe than the movements that accompany the production of most vowels. This is a fortunate situation because as we noted earlier consonants as a group are characterized by relatively high-frequency and low-intensity information. Their physical characteristics make them the speech sounds most often missed by hearing-impaired listeners; however, attention to the visual cues accompanying their production provides an alternative source of information that can greatly aid in the identification of those sounds missed or distorted by impaired auditory systems.

Probably the most visible correlate of consonant speech-sound generation is the place of production (see Chapter 2). Those consonants made toward the front of the mouth such as *p, b, m* (lips) and *t, d, n* (tongue tip) are more easily observed than those produced toward the back of the mouth such as *k, g* (back of tongue), and *h* (larynx). Verify this for yourself with a partner you can observe or by watching your own speech movements in a mirror. While *p, b,* and *m* are easier to observe than *k* and *g,* the "speech reader" still faces the problem of deciding *which* sound within a place of production has been produced. To make this decision the listener must rely on auditory and nonauditory cues such as those described earlier. Although visual cues even in combination with other cues do not guarantee perfect identification of speech sounds, they are extremely useful in reducing the number of alternative speech sounds the listener must consider to make sense of the spoken message.

A portion of every rehabilitation program should include instruction to make the hearing-impaired listener aware of visual cues. Many patients will naturally and quickly become aware of the utility of attending to visual cues, while others will require some instruction and structured drill on identification of isolated speech sounds with and without visual cues. This instruction includes making sure that the speaker looks directly at the listener when talking, and that the available light is directed into or toward the speaker's mouth. Erber (1974) reported a series of experiments that identified the relative importance of such environmental factors. His results show that the utility of visual cues decreases (1) with distance from the speaker, (2) as the viewing angle is shifted from "head on," and (3) as the contrast between the illumination on the speaker's face is decreased relative to the level of background illumination. Clearly, to help the hearing-impaired listener "speech read" you should be relatively close to him, face him directly, and insure that your face is well lighted. In turn, the hearing-impaired person must learn to ask his companions to place themselves so that he has the maximum opportunity to see their faces and articulators.

Unfortunately not all hearing-impaired persons are able to make equal use of visual cues. While many hearing-impaired persons shift to the use of visual cues without formal instruction and others are able to develop some skills with instruction and drill, many never seem to be able to "catch on" to the use of visual cues to supplement their comprehension of speech. There seems to be a talent component to the acquisition of speech-reading skills just like there is in the acquisition of musical performance skills. Just as some persons seem to have a "tin ear" for music, some hearing-impaired persons seem to be unable to derive much information about speech from watching the talker's face and mouth.

SOCIAL AND PSYCHOLOGICAL EFFECTS
OF ACQUIRED HEARING LOSS

A hearing loss sufficiently great to disrupt normal conversational speech can also disrupt a person's social and personal life. If a hearing-impaired person is leading a well-adjusted life before his hearing loss, he is likely to continue to do the same after a period of adjustment to his new circumstances. However, if he were previously having difficulties, the reduced sense of contact with the physical and social worlds that accompanies his hearing loss may further reduce his ability to successfully cope with his life. Those persons who work with the hearing-impaired need to be sensitive to the potential difficulties their patients may encounter as a consequence of their hearing loss. The patient needs to be counseled about the common experiences of persons with significant hearing loss.

Ramsdell (1978) suggests that hearing has two psychological aspects: one, a "primitive awareness," and the other, a more commonly recognized role in social communication. A major hearing impairment will disturb both aspects. Our hearing first of all provides us with an awareness of the world. Without actively attending to what is going on around us, we are kept continuously aware of the ongoing activity by our normally functioning auditory system. We hear birds singing, the wind whistling, traffic sounds, the hiss of a ventilating system—all while attending to a particular task at hand, like reading this book. Consider your response when a ventilating system that has regularly been a source of a constant, low-level, background noise suddenly shuts off. The sudden silence makes you alert, and you carefully evaluate your sensory information to determine just what the change in your environment is and what it means before you return to your reading. The reduced awareness of these background sounds is often noted by persons with a major hearing loss. They comment that they feel cut off and isolated from the physical world.

Another example of a passive function of our hearing is its use as a warning system, a source of information about approaching events in our environment. Consider again that you are sitting, reading this text, and you are so engrossed that you fail to attend to the information reaching your ears. The unnoticed approach of a friend is likely to result in a startle response at his first words as a result of his unexpected appearance. Now imagine that you have a significant hearing loss. The potential number of such occasions is greatly multiplied. The perception of the need to be constantly on the alert can be easily extended to behavior that might be labeled "paranoid."

The second psychological aspect of hearing, its role in social communication, is perhaps more obvious than these primitive aspects of hearing. We have discussed several aspects in earlier portions of this chapter; here we want to consider the potential impact of the communication difficulties that remain after our best efforts at remediation.

The difficulties hearing-impaired persons have in communicating often lead to their withdrawal from attempts to communicate. We all have a tendency to avoid difficult situations or tasks. A person with an acquired hearing loss does not change in this aspect of human nature. Unfortunately, the tendency to avoid communication can have a snowball effect—the hearing-impaired person's sense of physical isolation, noted previously, can be accompanied by a sense of social isolation. For an elderly person, this may lead to a further reduction in an already small circle of friends and activities. For a younger person who lives in the midst of an ongoing family life, withdrawal will affect the whole family unit. A "lack of communication" is frequently cited as the most common source of difficulties within families. The additional strain on communication that may result from one family member having a hearing loss can lead to an escalation of interpersonal problems.

Many of these potential problems can be reduced or eliminated with appropriate counseling of both the patient and his family at the time a hearing loss is first evaluated. Information about the type of difficulties he may expect to encounter and situational and environmental aids to communication are helpful in preventing misunderstandings about the role of a person's hearing loss in his overall pattern of behavior. Appropriate personal and/or family counseling can save a patient's job or marriage when the cumulative effects of a hearing loss have become greater than the patient can adapt to without help.

The audiologist frequently sees a patient over a period of years for periodic re-evaluation of hearing. Through these repeated exposures, and a sensitivity to the common problems of the hearing impaired, the audiologist is conferred a special professional responsibility to monitor the patient's ongoing adjustment to his or her hearing loss. If a patient is having difficulties that might be related to his hearing loss—socially, at home, or on the job—the audiologist will try to assure the patient and the family that the difficulties being faced are not unusual. The audiologist should then be prepared to recommend outside sources of professional services within the community that might be of further help with these problems.

SPECIAL PROBLEMS
OF THE HEARING-IMPAIRED CHILD

The ear is the primary sensory channel through which speech and language skills are normally acquired. Often it is a child's failure to produce his first words at around one year that leads parents to suspect a hearing loss. The close tie between the developing child's hearing and the normal acquisition of speech and language skills leads to a very different and significantly more complex set of problems for the young child with a hearing loss when compared with the problems described above for persons who lose their hearing as adults.

Hearing loss in an infant or young child is associated with a broad range of problems, including: (1) delay, or even an absence, of speech and language development (see Chapter 4); (2) deterioration or failure to develop healthy parent-child relationships due to a failure to obtain expected behavioral responses on the part of both parents and child; (3) psychological and social problems ranging from withdrawal from interpersonal relationships to hyperactivity or "acting out" behaviors; and (4) educational retardation or failure (Gregory, 1976). The goal of the intervention procedures to be described later in the chapter is to eliminate, or at least minimize, these potential problems. A number of topics warrant our consideration: the development of speech and language skills, the importance of early detection of hearing impairment, the process of hearing-aid selection and evaluation in children, different modes of communication available for habilitation, and various programs of habilitation into which the child might be placed as he advances from infancy through school age.

Development of Speech and Language Skills

The primacy of the ear in speech and language acquisition is well illustrated by the simple observation that infants born into all the diverse language milieus of the world learn to speak and communicate in the language used in their environment. The normal-hearing child's exposure to the ongoing speech and language activity that surrounds him appears to be a sufficient trigger to initiate the complicated combination of cognitive and linguistic processes required to support speech and language (see Chapter 1). Witness to this is the fact that well before an age at which any formal instruction occurs in most cultures, children acquire essentially all the basic grammatical structures they will use as adults.

Unfortunately, the situation is very different for the hearing-impaired child. Unless an early and ongoing strategy of explicit speech and language training is initiated, the hearing-impaired child will not acquire the speech and language skills of his hearing peers. Without amplification, a child with a severe hearing loss is just able to *detect* conversational speech spoken at a distance of one meter. There is simply not enough auditory information available in such a degraded signal to elicit appropriate responses from the infant.

Studies of the course of sensory and cognitive development in laboratory animals indicate that there may be a "critical period" for the acquisition of many complex responses. If the animal does not encounter a particular stimulus experience during a brief time interval that may be as short as a few hours or as long as a few weeks, the animal may respond inappropriately or not respond at all to that stimulus when encountered as an adult. This critical period apparently has a physiological basis in the developing animal's central nervous system.

Studies of brain-damaged children suggest that there may be analogous critical periods associated with the acquisition of complex human behaviors including speech and language (Lenneberg, 1967). Assuming there are such critical periods associated with the acquisition of speech and language, and that they extend over only the first couple of years of life, it becomes crucial to provide the hearing-impaired child with intensive speech and language stimulation throughout this time interval. Waiting until the child is old enough to go to school before providing concentrated efforts to teach him or her speech and language is to waste a critical and temporary acquisition capability that the child will not recover.

Early Detection of Hearing Impairment

The crucial first step is to detect the hearing loss as early as possible. The cost of screening all newborn infants for hearing loss has been judged too expensive. Instead, a set of criteria has been developed that profiles infants with a high risk of being hearing impaired (Northern and Downs, 1974). These factors include items like close familial history of hearing impairment and medical problems accompanying the infant's gestation and birth. Only infants designated as "high risk" based on their status on these criteria are routinely screened at birth.

But all hearing losses are not present at birth. Some inherited losses, for example, are *progressive* and this makes their detection particularly difficult. A child with a progressive hearing loss may have normal hearing at birth and be profoundly hearing-impaired by age two. The fact that a child was once clearly receptive to sound and later develops unusual behavior can lead to a delay in considering hearing loss as a potentially causal factor in the child's behavior. In other cases, a child born with normal hearing may lose his hearing due to some disease such as meningitis, or perhaps through an ototoxic response to drugs. This points up an important health care practice: *Throughout infancy, the responsivity of an infant to acoustic stimuli following a serious illness should always be closely monitored.*

The average age at which hearing loss is first suspected in infants later found to be hearing-impaired is between three and six months; the average age at which they are first seen in clinics for audiological evaluation is eighteen to twenty-four months. This time lag covers that interval which many investigators believe is critical for the normal development of both parent-child relationships and the child's speech and language skills (Lenneberg, 1967; Menyuk, 1977). The duration of this delay reflects even concerned and observant parents' distrust of their observations about their infant's responses to sounds. Recognizing hearing loss in an infant is a difficult task. Even sophisticated observers sometimes have trouble associating an infant's behavior with acoustic events. The problem of recognizing a hearing loss is made more difficult by the fact that very young infants' sound productions may sound normal even though they are profoundly hearing-impaired. The babbling of hearing-impaired infants is generally believed indistinguishable from the babbling of normal-hearing infants until about six to eight months of age (Fry, 1966, 1975). The parent's difficulties assessing their infant's hearing and their distrust of their own observations and intuitions is often reinforced by a physician's recommendation that the parents "wait a few more months and then see how the child is doing." Both parents and physicians need to be better informed about the importance of early detection. *If parents suspect their child has a hearing loss, they should arrange immediately for an audiological evaluation.*

Hearing-Aid Selection and Evaluation in Children

If it is determined that the child's hearing cannot be brought within the normal range by medical intervention, the next step is to provide appropriate amplification. As was pointed out above, the hearing capabilities of infants and young children are difficult to assess. They have only a limited response repetoire and are cooperative for only short periods of time. All of these difficulties are again apparent when we try to evaluate a hearing aid on a young child (see Figure 13–8).

Faced with these difficulties, it is generally assumed that the electroacoustic characteristics that most improve the speech discrimination performance of adult hearing-impaired listeners will also best serve the young child's needs in acquiring speech and language. Thus, a hearing aid can be selected on the initial estimate of the child's residual hearing sensitivity. Because our measures of hearing sensitivity in young children are crude, any hearing-aid selection must be considered tentative and the evaluation an ongoing process. To allow both for changes in the child's residual hearing and our ability to estimate that hearing, the aid selected should be one that provides a maximum of flexibility in the adjustment of its electroacoustic characteristics.

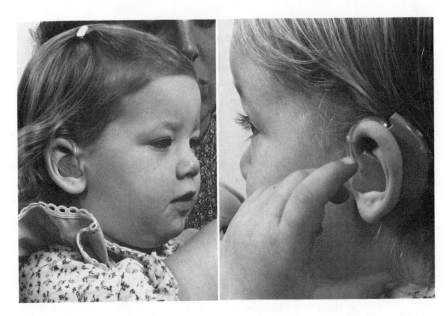

FIGURE 13–8. *A young hearing-impaired child fitted with two behind-the-ear hearing aids. The hearing capabilities of such children are difficult to assess. (Courtesy of Dr. M. Moeller and R. Gutherie, The Boys Town Institute for Communication Disorders in Children, Omaha, Nebraska.)*

Having selected an aid and a range of electroacoustic characteristics, the actual setting of gain and frequency characteristics at the initial evaluation must be made by observing the effects of successive, small adjustments on the child's responsivity to sounds. Does aided conversational speech appear to elicit an alerting response without signs of distress? If the child fails to respond to speech or environmental sounds, the gain can be increased until he does. With these initial adjustments made, the parents should be instructed in how to adjust the pertinent controls and encouraged to try changes in their settings, always carefully observing the child's responses to sounds. The parents must also be instructed in how to care for the aid, how often to change the batteries, and other details. Careful observation of the child's behavior with and without the aid will be necessary both to monitor the functioning of the aid and to keep track of the child's hearing sensitivity.

Following the initial fitting, the parents should return with the child approximately one week later. At that time the audiologist can evaluate the child's adaptation to the aid and monitor the electroacoustic characteristics with which the aid is being operated. In addition, the parents will have an opportunity to ask further questions about the care and use of the aid based on their week of experience. The subsequent follow-up schedule of clinic visits varies with individual clinic programs. A typical schedule would have the parents return with the child for further audiometric and hearing-aid evaluation after one month, with another evaluation at three months, followed by regular re-evaluations at six month intervals thereafter. Of course, the parents are instructed that if they detect any change in the child's behavior, or if there seems to be a problem with the hearing aid, they should arrange for an immediate re-evaluation. The audiologist is concerned too that the child be free of middle-ear infections that could further limit hearing capabilities. Evaluation and re-evaluation schedules such as the above are also part of the parent-infant programs for the hearing-impaired child as described later.

Modes of Communication

With appropriate habilitative services, the overwhelming majority of children with a hearing loss will learn to use the speech and language of their community. The best available estimates indicate that only about 15–20 percent of those children have a loss that is in the severe or profound categories (Watson, 1967). Thus for at least 80 percent of all hearing-impaired children we can expect that with appropriate medical remediation, amplification as required, and some education of the parents concerning their child's special needs, they will acquire normal or near-normal speech and language skills, participate in the regular education system and in the hearing world in general. There seems to be consensus that infants and young children with prelingual hearing losses as severe as about 70 dB can acquire adequate speech and language skills, provided they are enrolled in training programs that emphasize the use of their residual hearing, attention to visual cues in speech perception, and attention to proprioceptive, kinesthetic, and amplified acoustic cues in the development of their own speech production skills.

It is only with children with more severe hearing loss that the centuries-old controversy about the appropriate communication mode arises. That controversy centers around several questions: Should an attempt be made to teach the child to speak and thus acquire language through some combination of the cues described above that help the less severely handicapped child? Or alternatively, should the child be taught a manual communication system that makes no demands on his impaired sensory function? Should he be forced to try to decipher the complexities of speech and language through a severely impaired sensory modality? Or, should he be taught a system that uses an intact sensory modality (vision) and the use of his hands to form "signs"?

The arguments in favor of one or the other of these alternatives are obviously complex. Frequently, they also are tinged with an emotional fervor that impedes their rational analysis. Those who favor an auditory-oral approach point out that it is through speech communication that the normal activities of the hearing world are conducted. If the hearing-impaired child is to participate fully in that world he or she too must be able to speak and comprehend spoken language. In addition, as they may often point out, there is a clear "biological" link between hearing and speech and language. Our auditory and language systems evolved together and the auditory system carries the information that triggers the acquisition of speech and language in the normal-hearing young child's environment. This biological connection between the ear and speech and language acquisition should be exploited to provide the severely hearing-impaired child with these skills. Finally, those in favor of oral-auditory training have for many years pointed to the linguistic inadequacy of signed languages, suggesting, perhaps unjustifiably, that they are impoverished communication systems.

Those on the manual side of the controversy have maintained that while the goals of the advocates of the oral-auditory method are admirable, their success rate is too low; there are too many children that go through years of oral-auditory training *without* acquiring either adequate speech or adequate language skills. They argue that the few successes should not be used as exemplars to rationalize the continued education of all profoundly hearing-impaired children through oral-auditory methods. Those children who do not succeed in oral-auditory programs are portrayed as deprived of adequate communication skills that could be obtained through manual communication. It is also often argued that the attempt to teach profoundly hearing-impaired children by the oral-auditory approach amounts to a sort of cruel-and-unusual punishment that does them further psychological harm by providing them with a model of consistent failure and frustration, all of which could be avoided through manual communication.

While local "hot spots" remain, in recent years there has been a noticeable cooling off in the controversy. The past ten to fifteen years have seen the beginnings of a body of research on the nature of sign language, the cues used by profoundly hearing-impaired children to discriminate speech sounds, the relation between residual auditory capabilities and speech perception and production, and the impact of early use of manual communication on the later acquisition of oral speech. Continued research along these lines should lead to a more empirical basis for the training of young hearing-impaired children in speech and language skills.

At present the principal methods used to provide hearing-impaired children with communication skills are: *fingerspelling, American Sign Language,* various *sign systems based on English syntax, total communication,* and *oral-auditory.* Each of these approaches is briefly characterized below.

Fingerspelling.   Fingerspelling involves the use of a manual alphabet (see Figure 13–9) to spell out each word. It is a frequent component

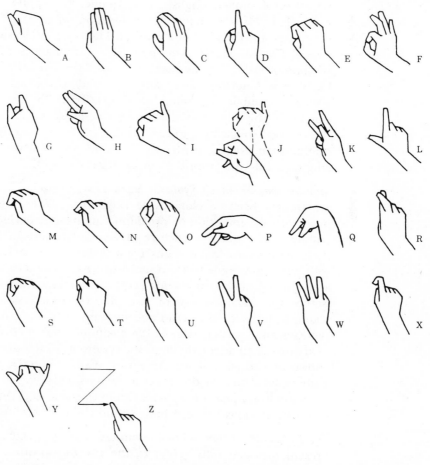

FIGURE 13–9.   *The American manual alphabet as seen by the fingerspeller. All finger positions are static except those for J and Z. (From L. Fant,* Say it With Hands. *Illustrated by Betty G. Miller. Silver Spring, Md.: National Association of the Deaf, 1964.)*

of American Sign Language because there are many English words for which there are no signs. Fingerspelling combined with simultaneous speech is often called the Rochester Method. The simultaneous use of fingerspelling and speech is named after the Rochester School for the Deaf, where it has been used to teach the hearing impaired for nearly 100 years.

American Sign Language. American Sign Language is a system derived from the French sign language brought to this country in the middle of the 19th century by Thomas Gallaudet (after whom the only deaf college in the United States is named). It is a true language with its own syntactical structure, which is quite different from the structure of spoken English. It is frequently supplemented with fingerspelled words in manual conversation when there is no appropriate sign for the object or concept. Figure 13–10 shows the signs for several English words. American Sign Language is the fourth most common non-English language spoken in the United States. You have likely seen American Sign Language used to translate local news on TV or on public television broadcasts. Probably its principal shortcoming in the education of the hearing-impaired child is its lack of "carry over" to learning to read in English. The child fluent in American Sign Language is confronted with the task of learning to read in a language different from the one he regularly uses.

Sign Systems Based on Syntax. Various sign systems based on English syntax have been developed (see Mayberry, 1978). These were developed with the intention of providing language experience that closely parallels the syntactic structure of General American English. All of these systems use many signs from American Sign Language, along with additional signs to represent word endings, verb tenses, prefixes and suffixes. Having the same syntax as spoken American English, it is theorized that the use of one of these sign systems will allow a young child to learn to read and perhaps even learn to speak American English at a later date. In the meantime, the child would have the ready use of an adequate linguistic system in which to make his needs known and to experience the world. Also, it may be that these sign systems, because they do reflect ordinary English syntax, are easier for the parent of a hearing-impaired child to learn, and thus would facilitate conversations between parents and child.

Total Communication. Total communication is a catch-all term at the present that generally refers to the use of various combinations of sign language, sign systems, and fingerspelling simultaneously with spoken language. The notion is that the child will pick out and use

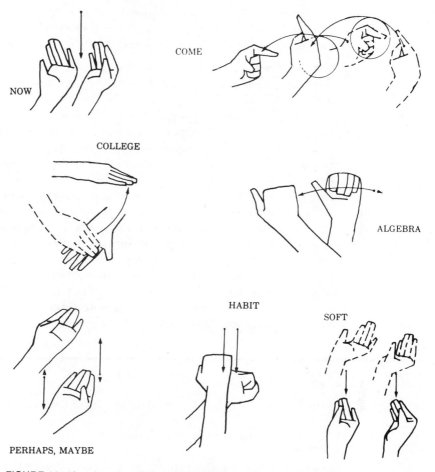

NOW

COME

COLLEGE

ALGEBRA

HABIT

SOFT

PERHAPS, MAYBE

FIGURE 13–10. *American Sign Language signs for several English words. Notice how dependent the signs are on movements of the hands and fingers. Vantage points for the signs shown are those that most clarify their execution, not necessarily as they are seen by the signer or the observer. (From L. Fant,* Say it With Hands. *Illustrated by Betty G. Miller. Silver Spring, Md.: National Association of the Deaf, 1964.)*

those aspects of the presentation that are most accessible. The tremendous range in combination of the different methods and modes of communication as practiced by different teachers makes it extremely difficult to evaluate total communication. There is some evidence, at least in older children, that materials presented simultaneously in more than one sensory modality are learned more slowly than when presented in only one modality. Thus, at present it is not clear whether some form of total communication will become the "best of all possible worlds" with appropriate stimulation for every hearing-impaired child, or "the worst of all possible worlds," providing an unintelligible flurry of activity that the child cannot assimilate.

Oral-Auditory. Oral-auditory methods attempt to develop expressive communication through speech and receptive communication by the use of residual hearing and speech reading. Manual communication of any sort is usually prohibited. Reading and writing are often included as integral components of language training along with speech and speech-reading training. In classroom training there is a great emphasis on drill, and the question of what speech-sound units to use for drill is a basic and unresolved issue. These methods are often criticized for the extent to which repetitious practice is required rather than a creative and active use of the language, which is encouraged in the use of American Sign Language and other sign systems.

An idea of the relative "efficiency" of these diverse systems and methods can be obtained by noting how many elements are required in each system to convey the same information. Figure 13–11 shows such a comparison. The utterance, "I didn't give any Christmas gifts to the teacher," translates into thirty-nine fingerspelled letters in the Rochester Method, but only five American Sign Language signs.

Rochester Method	I D-I-D-N-'T G-I-V-E A-N-Y C-H-R-I-S-T-M-A-S G-I-F-T-S T-O T-H-E T-E-A-C-H-E-R = 39 fingerspelled letters
SEE	I DO+PAST+N'T GIVE AN+Y CHRIST+MAS GIFT+S TO THE TEACH+ER = 15 signs
SEE, LOVE	I DO+PAST+N'T GIVE AN+Y CHRISTMAS GIFT+S TO THE TEACH+ER = 14 signs
Signed English	I DO+PAST NOT GIVE ANY CHRISTMAS GIFT+S TO THE TEACH+ER = 13 signs
Informal Sign System	I D-I-D-N-'T G-I-V-E ANY CHRISTMAS GIFT+S TO T-H-E TEACH+ER = 8 signs + 12 fingerspelled letters
ASL-English Pidgin	ME NOT ANY CHRISTMAS TO-GIVE-A-GIFT T-H-E TEACH+PERSON = 7 signs + 3 fingerspelled letters
ASL	TEACH+PERSON NOT TO-GIVE-A-GIFT CHRISTMAS = 5 signs; *to-give-a-gift* is directional

FIGURE 13–11. *A comparison of the relative "efficiency" of different manual methods of communication. Efficiency, in this comparison, is determined by the number of elements required of each method to convey the same information. (From* Hearing and Deafness, *Fourth Edition, edited by Hallowell Davis and S. Richard Silverman. Copyright © 1978, 1970, 1960, copyright 1947 by Holt, Rinehart and Winston. Reprinted by permission of Holt, Rinehart and Winston.)*

Other manual communication systems require intermediate numbers of manual gestures to translate the message. The effect of the differences in relative efficiency of manual communication apparent in Figure 13–11 on the acquisition of communication skills is unknown.

Parent-Infant Programs

For the hearing-impaired infant and young child, as for normal-hearing children, the primary educator is the parent. Parent-infant programs that attempt to educate the parents about their child's special needs and how to cope with them are the favored habilitation framework for infants and young children. Although specific methods for teaching speech and language may vary, the emphasis is always on helping the parents understand the child's problems and his potentials. Parents are taught to provide their child with optimal stimulation and encouragement. Parenting is a difficult enough task with normal children; the extra demands and strains of parenting a hearing-impaired child are considerable.

Parents themselves usually go through a traumatic period of grieving—shock, denial, anger, and then finally, acceptance—upon confirmation of their child's hearing loss by an audiologist or otolaryngologist. It is important to provide the parents with straightforward information and support while helping them to progress through these stages. Like all of us, parents are individuals who vary in their strengths and weaknesses and providing appropriate support and counseling for the parents is a key factor in the young child's habilitation. Gaining the parents' acceptance of their child's problem and potentials is the first step in securing their commitment to put in the extra time and effort that will be required to provide the child with optimum stimulation.

A parent-infant program may be a clinic-centered program, a home-demonstration program, or some combination of the two. In all programs, trained personnel work with the parents and infant one to five hours per week showing the parents how to stimulate the child in a variety of everyday situations. Special "work times" are also devoted to assessing the child's hearing aid and talking over concerns, problems, etc., that the parents may have about their child or their family situation as it affects the child and vice-versa. The clinician may work with the child and then watch the parent work with the child. The parents and clinician can then talk about what each did. In all cases the parents are seen as active, essential participants in the child's habilitation and the professionals are understood to be resource personnel.

Preschool Programs

Preschool programs can be considered as extensions of parent-infant programs. The parents are still very much involved in stimulating speech and language use in their child, but now they have even more professional help from someone specially trained to teach hearing-impaired children. Preschool programs also play an important role in the social development of hearing-impaired children. Attendance in such programs begins at about two and one-half to three years of age. There is a continued emphasis on speech and language stimulation in addition to the concept-building activities common to most hearing preschool or nursery school programs. Often the parents observe and/or work in the program on a regular basis to maintain contact with their child's developing speech and language skills and their classroom experiences. Whether the program emphasizes oral-auditory methods or manual communication, the child is provided with the opportunity to interact both communicatively and socially with children his or her own age. Often preschool programs will be integrated with normal-hearing children at least part time. This integration provides the hearing-impaired child with more speech and language stimulation than he is likely to receive from his fellow hearing-impaired peers. In addition, it helps prepare him for the experience of attending a regular school classroom. The teacher in a preschool program is able to monitor regularly the progress of each child and should communicate regularly with the parents to maintain continuity between the school and home environments. The continued involvement of the parents through these years cannot be over-emphasized. Again, as in the parent-infant programs, parent groups are frequently maintained in association with preschool programs to provide the parents with support and suggestions for handling the problems associated with parenting a handicapped child.

The School-Aged Hearing-Impaired Child

When the child reaches school age the greatest diversity in educational alternatives is encountered. Some hearing-impaired children will be integrated into normal classrooms, others will spend a portion of their time in normal-hearing classrooms and a portion of their time in classes for the hearing-impaired. Others will attend only special classes for the hearing-impaired, in which the method of communication may be either manual, oral, or total. There is a general goal that most persons involved with the habilitation of the hearing-impaired child ascribe to, that is, to integrate that child into the hearing community to the maximum extent possible. The variety of programs at this level try to meet that goal. Some children with relatively mild losses, and participation from an early age in good parent-infant and preschool programs, will be successfully integrated into normal-hearing classrooms. Others, with more severe losses and/or poor, or inadequate parent-infant and preschool habilitation programs, or perhaps additional handicaps, will not be able to participate in normally-hearing classes at all. Some may require that their continuing education be conducted entirely through manual means of communication, others will be able to communicate with oral-auditory means but would be held back if forced to compete for attention, and try to comprehend the lessons being taught in the noise of a normal classroom environment. At this level there are even fewer easy generalizations than are possible for younger children. Perhaps the best one is that every hearing-impaired child should be treated as an individual in a process of continuing evaluation.

THE FUTURE OF HEARING HABILITATION AND REHABILITATION

There has been an increased emphasis on applied research in all areas of science in recent years. Scientists from many allied fields including electrical engineering, linguistics, and experimental psychology are actively conducting research on problems associated with the effects of hearing loss. As a result, some areas of services to the hearing-impaired can be expected to improve significantly.

We do not have enough space to discuss the different directions in which we expect improvements. One area, however, should be singled out because of the great amount of attention focused on it by the popular press: the *implanted prosthesis.* Many people both within and outside the speech and hearing sciences believe the surgical implantation of a prosthetic device that would "restore" the person's hearing is the ultimate solution to the problem of sensory (cochlear) hearing loss. Such a device would be expected to restore hearing in the same way that prosthetic joints have enabled persons crippled by accident or disease to regain use of their arms, hands, and legs. There is obvious appeal to such an approach. Several dozen persons, in fact, have already been surgically fitted with primitive devices that transduce acoustic signals into electrical activity which is then used to stimulate the auditory nerve (see Figure 13–12). Bilger (1977) has extensively tested fifteen of these persons and described their responses to sounds. He found that the quality of information available to the per-

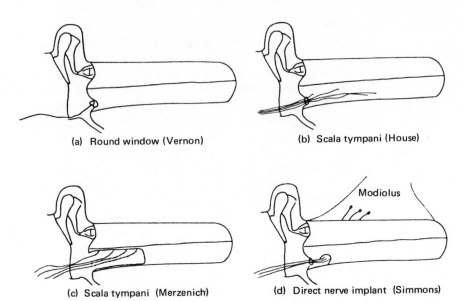

(a) Round window (Vernon)

(b) Scala tympani (House)

(c) Scala tympani (Merzenich)

(d) Direct nerve implant (Simmons)

FIGURE 13–12. *Diagrammatic representation of some of the variety of electrode placements used in prosthetic implants for electrically stimulating the auditory nerve in humans: (a) uses a single wire electrode on the round window. (b) uses small unsupported electrodes placed within the scala tympani. (c) uses several electrodes fitted to a silastic cast within the scala tympani. (d) uses electrodes placed directly into the auditory nerve by passage through the round window and through a perforation made intentionally in the wall of the modiolus. (From T. Glattke, Some implications for research. In W. Hodgson and P. Skinner, Eds.,* Hearing Aid Assessment and Use in Audiologic Habilitation. *Baltimore, Williams and Wilkins, 1977.)*

son listening with an implanted device is very crude and far from a "restored" sense of hearing. The results of these tests have, however, encouraged some researchers to continue to pursue the implanted prosthesis as a potential solution to sensory hearing loss.

To build an effective "artificial ear" of the sort that might more truly "restore" a sense of hearing requires that we know much more about how the normal ear functions in order that we can successfully mimic it. We also need to know much more about the longterm effects of direct electrical stimulation on the central nervous system to be sure that there are no undesireable side-effects. We are, thus, brought full circle, as is so often the case in clinical science. To provide better services to persons with disorders, we must learn more about the normal system's functioning. When the problem is as complex as the amelioration of the effects of hearing loss, we can correctly assume that an enormous amount of basic research, across many disciplines, is necessary to achieve our goal of restoring all hearing-impaired persons to full participation in the hearing world.

REFERENCES   BILGER, R., Evaluation of subjects presently fitted with implanted auditory prostheses. *Annals of Otology, Rhinology, and Laryngology,* 86, Supplement 38
(1977).

CLEMIS, J., Cochleovestibular disorders and allergy. *Otolaryngologic Clinics of North
America,* 7, 757–780 (1974).

DENES, P., On the statistics of spoken English. *Journal of the Acoustical Society of
America,* 35, 892–904 (1963).

ELLIOTT, L., Epidemiology of hearing impairment and other communicative disorders. In B. Schoenberg (Ed.), *Advances in Neurology, Volume 19: Neurological Epidemiology.* New York: Raven Press (1978).

ERBER, N., Effects of angle, distance, and visual illumination on visual reception of
speech by profoundly deaf children. *Journal of Speech and Hearing Research,*
17, 99–112 (1974).

EVANS, E., and WILSON, J., *Psychophysics and Physiology of Hearing.* London: Academic Press (1977).

FRY, D., Phonological aspects of language in the hearing and deaf. In E. Lenneberg
and E. Lenneberg (Eds.), *Foundations of Language Development, Volume 2.*
New York: Academic Press (1975).

FRY, D., The development of the phonological system in the normal and the deaf
child. In F. Smith and G. Miller (Eds.), *The Genesis of Language: A Psycholinguistic Approach.* Cambridge, Mass.: MIT Press (1966).

GREGORY, S., *The Deaf Child and His Family.* New York: Wiley (1976).

JERGER, J., and HAYES, D., Hearing-aid evaluation. *Archives of Otolaryngology,*
102, 214–225 (1976).

KALIKOW, D., STEVENS, K., and ELLIOTT, L., Development of a test of speech intelligibility in noise using sentence materials with controlled word pre-
dictability. *Journal of the Acoustical Society of America,* 61, 1337–1351 (1977).

KASTEN, R., Electroacoustic characteristics. In W. Hodgson and P. Skinner (Eds.),
Hearing Aid Assessment and Use in Audiologic Habilitation. Baltimore: Williams and Wilkins (1977).

LENNEBERG, E., *Biological Foundations of Language.* New York: Wiley (1967).

MAYBERRY, R., Manual communication. In H. Davis and S. Silverman (Eds.), *Hearing and Deafness,* (4th Ed.). New York: Holt, Rinehart and Winston (1978).

MENYUK, P., Language development in deaf children. Paper presented to the Research Conference on Speech-Processing Aids for the Deaf, Gallaudet College, Washington, D.C. (1977).

MILLER, G., HEISE, G., and LICHTEN, W., The intelligibility of speech as a function
of the context of the test materials. *Journal of Experimental Psychology,* 41,
329–335 (1951).

NORTHERN, J., and DOWNS, M., *Hearing in Children.* Baltimore: Williams and Wilkins (1974).

OLSEN, W., Proposed American National Standards Institute standards for specification of hearing aid characteristics. In M. Rubin (Ed.), *Hearing Aids: Current
Developments and Concepts.* Baltimore: University Park Press (1976).

PASCOE, D., Frequency responses of hearing aids and their effects on the speech
perception of hearing-impaired subjects. *Annals of Otology, Rhinology, and
Laryngology,* 84, Supplement 23 (1975).

RAMSDELL, D., The psychology of the hard-of-hearing and deafened adult. In H. Davis and S. Silverman (Eds.), *Hearing and Deafness,* (4th Ed.). New York: Holt, Rinehart and Winston (1978).

ROSS, M., and CALVERT, D., The semantics of deafness. In W. Northcott (Ed.), *The Hearing-Impaired Child in a Regular Classroom.* Washington, D.C.: Alexander Graham Bell Association for the Deaf (1973).

SCHEIN, J., and DELK, M., JR., *The Deaf Population of the United States.* Silver Spring, Md.: National Association of the Deaf (1974).

SCHUKNECHT, H., *Pathology of the Ear.* Cambridge, Mass.: Harvard University Press (1974).

WATSON, T., *The Education of Hearing-Handicapped Children.* Springfield, Ill.: Charles C Thomas (1967).

WILBER, L., Introduction: Electroacoustical standards. In M. Rubin (Ed.), *Hearing Aids: Current Developments and Concepts.* Baltimore: University Park Press (1976).

author index

subject index